Collective Dismissal in the European Union

Collective Dismissal in the European Union

A Comparative Analysis

Edited by

Roberto Cosio
Filippo Curcuruto
Vincenzo Di Cerbo
Giovanni Mammone

Wolters Kluwer

Published by:
Kluwer Law International B.V.
PO Box 316
2400 AH Alphen aan den Rijn
The Netherlands
Website: www.wklawbusiness.com

Sold and distributed in North, Central and South America by:
Wolters Kluwer Legal & Regulatory U.S.
7201 McKinney Circle
Frederick, MD 21704
United States of America
Email: customer.service@wolterskluwer.com

Sold and distributed in all other countries by:
Turpin Distribution Services Ltd
Stratton Business Park
Pegasus Drive, Biggleswade
Bedfordshire SG18 8TQ
United Kingdom
Email: kluwerlaw@turpin-distribution.com

ISBN 978-90-411-5830-7

e-Book: ISBN 978-90-411-5847-5
web-PDF: ISBN 978-90-411-8653-9

Editors

Roberto Cosio is a member of the Italian Bar, and he is qualified to practice before the Supreme Court and the High Courts. He is a practising lawyer, specializing in Labour and Social Security law, and he has filed and discussed cases before the European Court of Justice (ECJ) and the European Court of Human Rights. He is the author of many articles and publications on matters related to European Law, with a focus on the fundamental principles of the European Convention on Human Rights and of the Charter of Fundamental Rights of the European Union. He also writes extensively about Italian Labour Law, with particular regard to the transfer of undertakings and the collective dismissal procedures. He is the President of the Labour Commission of the European Lawyers' Union. He is also a Senior Lecturer at various universities in Italy and abroad.

Filippo Curcuruto became a judge in 1974, and he was first appointed as labour judge to a Court of First Instance. In 1980, he was assigned to a special office within the Italian Ministry of Justice, that drafts legislation. Here he worked for several years dealing with issues, among others, related to European Law. Later on, from 1993 to 1998, he served at the Research Division of the Italian Supreme Court (the *Ufficio del Massimario della Corte di Cassazione*). Afterwards, the Ministry of Justice appointed him the Head of the office dealing with claims brought before the labour Courts by the Ministry employees. In 2002, he was appointed as a Member Judge of the Supreme Court assigned to the Labour chamber and was also nominated as a Member of the Supreme Court's Joint Chambers in civil-law matters, where he worked until 2011. From 2011 to 2015 he served as the President of the Labour Court of Appeal of Rome. From to 2005 to 2009 he was a Senior Lecturer of Labour Law at the Postgraduate School of Law, at the University of Rome 'La Sapienza'. He is the author of several publications in the fields of civil law, civil procedure, labour law and European law. He has also been involved in the initiatives carried out by the Associations of the European labour-law judges (*European Association of Labour Court Judges – EALCJ*, within the European Union (EU), and the *European Labour Court Judges – ELCJ*, within the *International Labour Office*). He retired in 2015.

Vincenzo Di Cerbo became a judge in 1976 and in 1977 was appointed as a first instance judge. From 1993 to 1997 he served in the *'Ufficio del Massimario della Corte di Cassazione'* (the Research Division of the Court). From June 1997 to October 2004 he served as a 'legally qualified member of the Boards of Appeal' at the European Patent Office in Munich and for three years he was appointed the Chairman of the Disciplinary Committee of the Office (2001, 2002, 2003). In 2004, he was appointed as a member of the Italian Supreme Court. From 2010 to 2016, he was also a member of the Supreme Court's Joint Chambers in civil-law matters. Moreover, since 2012 he has been Director of the CED (i.e., IT documentation department of the Supreme Court). From April 2008 to May 2012 he was a member of the Supreme Court Judges Council ('Consiglio Direttivo'). He currently serves as the chairman of a board of the Supreme Court dealing with appeals concerning Labour and Social Welfare. From 2006 to 2016 he was a lecturer at the Post-Graduate School for lawyers, Università della Sapienza, Roma. He is the author of several books and essays in the field of Law (Labour Law, Civil Procedural Law, IP Law).

Giovanni Mammone became a judge in 1977 and in 1998 joined the Research Division of the Italian Supreme Court (*Ufficio del Massimario della Corte di Cassazione).*In 2007 he was appointed as a member of the Italian Supreme Court. From 2002 to 2006 he was elected in the Italian High Council of the Judiciary (*C.S.M.*) representing the adjudicating judges. He currently serves as the President of the Italian Supreme Court on its chamber dealing with Labour and Social Welfare appeals and was also a member of the Court's Joint Chambers in civil law matters. Moreover he has been appointed as the Secretary General to the Supreme Court. As a former member of *C.S.M.* he took part in the activity of the *European Network of the Councils of Justice* (*ENCJ*) and of the *European Judicial Training Network* (*EJTN*). He is actively involved in the initiatives carried out by the Associations of the European labour-law judges (*EALCJ*, within the EU, and the *ELCJ*, within the *International Labour Office*). He has written essays and surveys on civil procedural law, labour law and the judicial system.

Contributors

Miran Blaha was born in 1951 in Ljubljana, Slovenia. After graduating from the University of Ljubljana, Faculty of Law, he was employed for a short time at the Ministry of Justice and at a construction company. From 1984 to 1994 he served a judge at the Labour and Social Court in Ljubljana. From 1994 to 2001 he was a legal adviser at the Constitutional Court of the Republic of Slovenia, and since 2001 he has been a judge of the Supreme Court of the Republic of Slovenia as a member and Deputy Chairman of the Senate for labour and social cases. He is the author of the *Comment of Constitution* of the Republic of Slovenia concerning the section relating to constitutional rights and fundamental freedoms in the field of labour law. He is also the author of a larger number of articles in the field of labour and social law, lecturer at judicial schools for judges as well as at experts' meetings on labour and social issues.

Michel Blatman is holder of a degree from the Faculty of Law and Economics of Paris. Following a career as judge in the provinces, in particular in the jurisdiction of the Court of Appeal of Riom (Auvergne), he has been a judge at the Court of Cassation (Labour Division) for almost eleven years, where he reached the position of senior divisional judge ('Doyen de section'). As editor of articles on labour law doctrine, he has intervened in numerous conferences, the last of which was held during the Franco-Hellenic Days of Thessaloniki in October 2016. Moreover, he also participated in the training sessions of both trade unionists (CGT, CGC, CFDT) and employer syndicates (CGPME), as well as of law professionals (judges, lawyers, employment advisors, labour inspectors, clerks and civil servants, heads of human resources, social security medical advisers). He also gives conferences within various Masters of Social Law in France and abroad and is co-author of a book called *The Health of the Employee – From Health Preservation to Job Protection* ('l'état de santé du salarié – De la préservation de la santé à la protection de l'emploi') at its latest edition in 2014. Mr Blatman, who participated for many years in the works of the European Labour Court Judges (EALCJ), of which he was president for one year, has also been member of the European Labour Court Judges Meeting (ELCJM) sponsored by the International Labour Organisation. He retired as a judge, but is still active as a trainer and is completing a study entrusted to him by the Defender of rights, an independent constitutional institution, on the *Direct Effect of the United Nations Convention on the Rights of the Handicapped People*.

Gerrard Boot works as a professor of Labour Law at Leiden University since 2011. He practised labour law as a lawyer in Amsterdam for more than twenty years working for both employers and employees. In 2009 he became a labour court judge in the District Court of Amsterdam and became judge in the Amsterdam Court of Appeal in 2015.

Merle Erikson is a professor of Labour Law at the Faculty of Law of the University of Tartu. Her main areas of study and teaching are Estonian labour law, international and EU labour law, as well as EU social policy. She is the author of numerous publications in the field of labour law.

Yvonne Erkens works as an associate professor of Labour Law at Leiden University. After she graduated at Leiden Law School, she became an assistant professor of Labour Law at Leiden Law School and Erasmus School of Law of Rotterdam. She practised labour law as a lawyer in The Hague and Leiden, working for an employers' association, and has been behind several collective labour agreements. Since 2004 she has been working full time at Leiden Law School, where she presented her thesis on Labour Law adjudication in 2013. Yvonne Erkens holds various ancillary positions. She is a part-time labour-court judge, acts as a judge in an institute for juvenile delinquents and is a member and vice-chair of the Commission on research integrity of the University of Leiden.

Mario Eylert, Ph.D., is the Chief Justice of the Fourth Senate of the German Federal Labour Court (Bundesarbeitsgericht) – the so-called Tarifsenat or Tariff Senate – since 2012. He was appointed at Germany's highest labour court in 2001 and served until his nomination of Chief Justice in the Court's Second Senate, which deals with dismissal cases ('Kündigungsrecht'). Before joining the German Federal Labour Court, Mario Eylert served at the Berlin Labour Court from 1984 to 1992, and later from 1992 to 2001 as Chief Justice on the Brandenburg Higher Labour Court. He received his Ph.D. in Law from the Free University of Berlin in 1986. At the German Federal Labour Court, Eylert also oversees the relations with foreign courts and judge organizations, and, among others, the European Labour Court judges and the German-Russian Judge Symposium. He is also a member of the Complaints Board of the European School system.

Dr Roland Gerlach studied Law at the University of Vienna from 1981 to 1986. While he was a student, he worked as a research and teaching assistant in the Department of Legal History at the University of Vienna School of Law. After completing his studies with a Ph.D. in law in 1988, he joined the law firm of Dr Georg Griesser. In 1993, he was admitted to the Austrian bar and in 1996, he co-founded the law firm Griesser Gerlach Gahleitner. In 2001, he completed a Postgraduate Program at the London School of Economics (LSE) with an LL.M. in Labour Law. In 2011, Gerlach founded the law firm Gerlach Rechtsanwàlte. This boutique law firm handles the full spectrum of labour and employment issues. It is widely recognized as one of the most highly ranked firms in these fields. He is a member of the Committee of the Vienna Bar Association, as well as a member of the International Bar Association (IBA), the American Bar Association

(ABA) and the Industrial Law Society. He is also the Austrian representative in the board of the European Employment Lawyers Association (EELA). He is a frequent speaker at national and international conferences on all aspects of labour and employment law. He has given talks for the ABA, the IBA, the Cambridge Forum, L&E Global, as well as for private organizations.

Paul Gonzi is a partner at Fenech & Fenech Advocates specializing in Labour Law, Data Protection and ICT Law. After graduating with a Bachelor of Laws, Diploma of Notary Public and Doctor of Laws at the University of Malta in 2006 he earned his Master of Laws (LL.M.) at Queen Mary and Westfield College, University of London. He has nine years of hands-on experience advising clients and as a litigant in various fora, including before the Courts, the Industrial Tribunal, in arbitration and also at Appeal stage in matters of employment, industrial relations, data protection and telecoms. He is also a contributor to various publications and several conferences in his areas of specialization.

Dr Tünde Handó has been the president of the National Office for the Judiciary since 1 January 2012. He is a lawyer, graduated from Eötvös Lóránd University Faculty of Law in 1986. During her studies she was a member of Hungary's first advanced legal studies college called Bibó István College. From 16 April 1986 she worked as a trainee judge at Budapest-Capital Labour Court. After she passed the bar exams in 1990 she was appointed to secretary judge. She started her career as a judge at Budapest-Capital Labour Court on 1 May 1991. Until her appointment as president of the National Office for the Judiciary, she served as the president of the Budapest-Capital Labour Court since 15 April 1999. She became titular regional court judge on 15 July 2003. From 1999 she served as a lecturer at Eötvös Lóránd University Labour Law Department and member of the Bar Exam Committee. In 2008 she became the president of the European Association of Labour Law Judges, and since then she has been a member of the Hungarian Labour Law Association.

Anthony Kerr is a graduate of the Universities of Dublin (TCD) and London (LSE), a sometime Jean Monnet Fellow at the European University Institute and is now an associate professor in the UCD Sutherland School of Law where he is also an Associate Dean for Graduate Studies and Programme Director of the Professional Diploma in Employment Law. He is recognized by the European Commission, for whom he has completed many research projects, as a Level One expert and has been a member of the European Labour Law Network since 2007. He is a member of the Executive Committee of the International Society for Labour Law and Social Security Law and a National Reporter for the International Labour Law Reports. He has extensive experience in carrying out studies, both internationally and domestically, for the purpose of supporting impact assessment, evaluation and monitoring and has wide and extensive knowledge of the implementation of DG EMPL policies, programmes and laws in Ireland.

Mette Klingsten is a Danish Supreme Court Attorney specialized in labour and employment law and works at Mette Klingsten Law Firm based in Copenhagen. She regularly appears before the Danish courts and arbitration tribunals. Mette Klingsten holds several directorships, including in the Royal Danish Theatre, and is the chairman of the board of directors in Copenhagen Phil. She has been an external lecturer on Employment Law at the University of Copenhagen and is author and co-author of several books. Among other books, she has recently published is the second edition of *Employment Law Aspects of the Transfer of Undertakings*.

Pavol Kundrik is a member of the Slovak Bar Association and has been an active attorney-at-law in Slovakia since 2013. He graduated from the Faculty of Law of Comenius University in Bratislava, Slovakia in 2009. His main area of expertise is Civil and Labour Law. Based on his knowledge and experience in this area, he has been promoted to lead the Labour Law Practice Group at PETERKA & PARTNERS, where he has been working as an associate since 2015. The Labour Law Practice Group is the firm's main channel used to serve clients seeking legal advice in Employment- and HR-related legal matters. As the Head of this Practice Group, Pavol leads a team of experienced lawyers from nine PETERKA & PARTNERS offices in the CEE region, and serves its clients worldwide.

Diana Labokaite was born in 1966 in Kaunas, Lithuania. She graduated from the faculty of law at Vilnius university in 1996. From 1996 to 2003 she practiced as a lawyer, since 2003 she was appointed as a judge in Kaunas city district court. She specialized in labour cases. In 2016 she was appointed as a judge of Kaunas regional court and mainly deals with civil cases.

Agata Ludera-Ruszel, Ph.D., is an assistant professor at the Faculty of Law and Administration of the University of Rzeszow and an assistant judge in the Appeal Court in Rzeszow, as well as a member of the Polish Association for Labour Law and Social Security. She has conducted lectures on Labour Law in Spain (Cardenal Herrera-CEU University), Italy (Università degli Studi of Genova), Belgium (Vives University College w Kortrijk) and Latvia (Banku Augstskola School of Business and Finance). She has held scientific internships at the University of Geneva and Humboldt University in Berlin. She is a DAAD fellow and winner of a scholarship by the Ministry of Science and Higher Education in Poland for outstanding young scientists. She is a reviewer of national and international scientific journals; author of several scientific publications on labour law and participant at national and international scientific conferences.

Filipe Marques is a judge at the Labour Section of the Central Instance of the Braga Judicial Court, in Portugal. He graduated in 1999 at the Law School of the University of Coimbra, where in 2003 he obtained an LL.M. in European Law with the thesis *The Principle of Non Discrimination and Direct Taxation in the European Union*. He has been serving as a judge since 2004 – in the Labour field for the past five years. He is the representative of the Portuguese Judges in *MEDEL – Magistrats Européens pour la Démocratie et les Libertés*. Before becoming a judge, he worked as a lawyer in Portugal and Italy (Milano).

Antonio Martin Valverde holds a Law degree from the University of Seville, as well as a PhD in Law from the University of Valencia. He was a professor of Labour Law and

Social Security at the Universities of Salamanca, Cadiz and Seville and Head of the Department of Labor Law and Social Security at the University of Seville (1987–1989).

He served as a judge of the Supreme Court from 1989 until his retirement in September 2013. He was also the president of the Central Electoral Board (Junta Electoral Central) of Spain during the 9th legislature of the Constitution (2008–2012). He has given courses and carried out research at the University of Tübingen (1972), at the Brussels headquarters of the Commission of the European Community (1983), at the University of Göttingen (1993) and at the University of Cologne (1998 and 1999). He has carried out periods of study and jurisdictional exchange in Erfurt, in the Bundesarbeitsgericht (Federal Supreme Labor Court) of Germany (2000), and in Paris, at the Cour de Cassation (Supreme Court) of France (2008).

Dr Valverde represented Spain as Speaker in several national and international conferences and meetings (on Labour Law, European Community Law, Jurisdictional Law and Theory of Law), in Europe and Latin America. He was a member representing Spain, from 2004 to 2014, of the 'European Meeting of Labour Law Judges'. He was a full member and vice-president of the Academia Iberoamericana de Derecho del Trabajo y de la Seguridad Social (Ibero-American Academy of Labour Law and Social Security). He was awarded the Honorary Doctorate of the University of Oviedo (2008), as well as the 'Labour Law Expert of the Year 2015' Award of the Asociación Nacional de Laboralistas (National Association of Labor Experts).

He is the author and co-author of several Works. He is the co-author (with professors Rodríguez-Sañudo and García Murcia) of a Labour Law course - *Editorial Tecnos* (twenty-five editions). He is also the co-author (with Professor García Murcia) of the *Tratado Práctico de Derecho del Trabajo* (Practical Treaty of Labour Law) (Editorial Aranzadi, 2nd edition, 2012, three volumes) and of the *Tratado Práctico de Derecho de la Seguridad Social* (Practical Treaty of Social Security Law) (Editorial Aranzadi, 2nd edition, 2013, two volumes). He is also the author of monographic works of study (ten books and about three hundred publications of studies and essays) on the History of Labour Law, Individual and Collective Labour Law, Labour Procedural Law, Social Security Law and European Social Law.

Tom Moes is the Chairman of the 'Conseil Arbitral de la Sécurité Sociale' (Social Security Arbitration Council), the First Instance Social Security jurisdiction in the Grand-Duchy of Luxembourg, which he joined as a Deputy Judge in January 1995. After his judicial office as Deputy Director of the First Instance Court (Justice de Paix) and as Chairman of the Labour Court in Esch-sur-Alzette (Grand-Duchy of Luxembourg) (1995–2014) he was appointed Chairman of the 'Conseil Arbitral de la Sécurité Sociale' in August 2014. Since July 2012 he has been holding the title of a Honorary Councillor at the Court of Appeal. He is also a Knight of the Grand Ducal Order of the Crown of Oak and an Officer in the Grand Ducal Order of Merit.

Angelika Muller has been serving as a Senior Specialist in Social Dialogue in the Governance and Tripartism Department of the International Labour Office (ILO) in Geneva, Switzerland. She studied law in Belarus and France and has Master degrees in Comparative Labour Law and International Human Resources Management. After ten years of professional experience in the private sector, including in legal departments of several multinational companies, Angelika joined the ILO in 2004. She has been in charge of policy advice and technical assistance on labour law reforms in all regions worldwide. Angelika was also in charge of coordinating the ILO network of the European Labour Court Judges. She has published several comparative studies on social dialogue institutions, labour law and gender equality.

Alan C. Neal is a professor of Law in the University of Warwick. He holds judicial office as an Employment Judge in the London (Central) Employment Tribunal and is Convenor of the European Association of Labour Court Judges.'

Pia Nyblæus is a member of the Swedish Bar Association providing commercial and legal advice to a wide range of industries in M&A and private equity matters, including cross-border issues. She specializes in employment law, comprising human resource services, management contracts, incentive and benefit programs, pension and insurances, collective employment issues, restrictive covenants, trade secrets and termination matters. Pia Nyblæus is a frequently used litigator as well as an arbitrator.

Andriani Papadopoulou holds a Ph.D. in Sociology from York University, Toronto Canada. As a Sociologist/Educator/Researcher and presently a Senior Investigator in the Human Rights Department of the Greek Ombudsman she has acquired extensive expertise on issues that concern immigrants, Roma and, in general, various forms of violations of human rights.

Lubomír Ptáček is holder of a Ph.D. and JuDr. from the Charles University in Prague. Since 2010 he has been a Judge at the Supreme Court of Brno. Prior to that he was President of the Chamber of the Regional Court in Ústí nad Labem, Branch Office Liberec (2003–2010), he was Judge at the Regional Court in Ústí nad Labem, Branch Office Liberec (2001–2003), and was President of Chamber at the District Court of Liberec (1999-2001). Dr Lubomir has been lecturer of the Slovak Judicial Academy for the area of European Private International Law (2009), Member of working group in Child Abduction cases (2007), Czech liaison judge in family law matters (2007, Hague Network Judge) amongst other activities. He is the author of articles in various Law publications.

Paula Roberto is a judge at the Criminal Section of the Court of Appeal of Guimarães, in Portugal.

She graduated in 1988 at the Law School of the University of Coimbra.

She has been serving as a judge since 1993 - in the labour area for the past twelve years.

Before becoming a judge, she worked as a lawyer in Portugal.

Dana Rone is a sworn advocate in Latvia since 2003. She is actively practising in Civil Law cases, including in the field of Employment Law. Ms Rone has graduated from the Faculty of Law of the University of Latvia (LL.M.) in 1998 and from the Riga Graduate School of Law in 2001. She also works in the academic field, as lecturer at the *Turiba* University (Latvia) in the subjects of Public Speech, Civil Procedure Law and Insurance Law. She regularly presents her lectures also in other educational institutions such as the Study Centre of Judges and the Association of Insolvency Administrators. Ms Rone is author of many publications on judicial issues published in Latvia and other countries. She is also a certified mediator since 2014, providing practical assistance to persons involved in disputes to help them resolve their controversies. She has also published various articles on mediation, and is part of the Commission of Certification and attestation of certified mediators as one of the commission members.

Jorma Saloheimo has acted as chairperson at the Finnish Labour Court as from 2001 and President of the Court as from 2010. Before transferring to the judicial career, Saloheimo worked as a labour law researcher and professor in the academic world for twenty years. Saloheimo has published a number of books and articles on various issues of labour law, such as occupational health and safety, equality and collective bargaining. The law of the European Union is well represented in Saloheimo's writings.

Reinhard Schinz, Dr jur. h.c. (Lund), is the Presiding Judge at the Higher Labour Court in Berlin. He works as a lecturer at various universities and is the author of a number of publications on labour law.

Vanja Smokvina graduated in Law in 2006 at the Faculty of Law, University of Rijeka (Croatia). In 2012, he obtained his Ph.D. from the European Law Faculty Nova Gorica (Slovenia), and prepared his thesis on *Free movement of sportspeople and the specificity of labour law status of sportspersons in the EU*. He is an assistant professor at the Chair of Labour and Social Security Law at the Faculty of Law, University of Rijeka (Croatia). He has published four books, more than twenty scientific articles and has presented his works at numerous international scientific conferences (Cambridge, Leeds, Angers, Cologne, Madrid, Roma, Verona, Zagreb, etc.). His main field of interests are labour and social security of specific categories of workers in the sports and marine fields.

Krassimira Sredkova has graduated at the Law Faculty of Sofia University 'St. Kliment Ochridski' and has specializations in Labour Law, Social Security and EC Law from Universities in Austria, Belgium, Germany, Hungary and Russia. She is a professor in Labour Law and Social Security at Sofia University, Ph.D. in Law. She is President of the Bulgarian Association for Labour Law and Social Security and member of the International Association for Legislation. Since 2015, she has been a member of the European Committee of Social Rights in the Council of Europe. Prof. Krassimira Sredkova has more than 250 publications in the fields of Labour Law, Social Security, International Labour Law and the EC-Law.

Nicos Trimikliniotis is an interdisciplinary scholar working in the fields of sociology and law. He heads the team of expert of the Cyprus team for the EU Fundamental Rights Agency. He is also a practicing Barrister. He has carried out research on integration, citizenship, migration, free movement of workers, discrimination and Labour Law. He is the National Expert for Cyprus for the European Labour Law Network. He was the expert for Cyprus of the European networks of experts on Free Movement of Workers (2008–2012) and Labour Law (2010). He has served as a research associate (national expert) with the European University Institute on Citizenship (EUDO, 2009–2010) and on tolerance, pluralism and social cohesion (ACCEPT, 2011). He is also a research associate of the University of Cape Town, South Africa. His latest book is entitled *Mobile*

Commons, Migrant Digitalities and the Right to the City (with D. Parsanoglou and V. Tsianos), Pivot, Palgrave, 2015.

Aurelian Gabriel Uluitu, Ph.D., is an associate professor at 'Nicolae Titulescu' University, Bucharest, Romania, where he teaches Labour and Civil Law since 1999. He was elected as President of the 'Nicolae Titulescu' University in June 2015. He is also a lawyer since 2001, and is a member of the Bucharest Bar. He is the author of over fifty publications in the field of Civil and Labor Law. The latest book he published (as co-author) is *Dictionary of Labour Law,* Universul Juridic, 2015.

Michela Velardo is an Italian qualified lawyer and a member of the Rome and Brussels bar. She specializes in European Social Law and in European Public Law. At present she has pleaded 150 cases before National (Italy and Belgium), European and International Courts. In the past she has been a member of the Legal Service of the European Commission and an official of the Italian Ministry of Justice. She speaks in conferences, lectures in Italian Universities and publishes articles in several prominent law journals.

Summary of Contents

Table of Contents

Foreword

This volume is an important, indeed unique, contribution to the knowledge on the law of collective dismissals in the EU Member States. The texts presented herein, although differently structured, provide an exhaustive picture of the different national systems. This comparative analysis is particularly important in this period where restructuring and redundancies are a major reason of social concern in most European Countries.

A comprehensive knowledge of the legal and collective rules concerning collective dismissals is useful to nurture the academic and policy debate, still controversial, over the appropriate content of the employment protection legislation (EPL).

The overview of the various regulations indicates persistent diversities among the European national systems which are comprehended and allowed under the EU Directive. However, major common trends can also be traced. Indeed the regulation of collective dismissals represents one of the areas of labour law where the European Directives have been most influential in promoting the harmonization of the different national systems.

Harmonization was one of the original purposes of the European community which has been fulfilled only in part, and recently is less and less pursued.

The achievement of promoting common rules is particularly significant in the critical area of collective redundancies, being part of the wider objective of the European social policy oriented towards balancing the requirements of flexibility for employers with the need of security for workers.

As in others areas of social regulation and policies, the European Directive on this matter (one of the first to be approved in 1975), has been pre-empted by some national legislations, for example, *see* the chapter on Germany.

The Directive of 1975, subsequently amended and improved, reproduces the basic requirements present in most national systems, extending them to the rest of the community, including, in particular, countries of Eastern Europe, which adhered to the EU at a later time. In this respect, the Directive cannot be considered simply a ratification of a minimum common denominator, but as a contributor to the evolution of various national legislations.

Moreover, Chapter 29 of this volume appropriately emphasizes that the main rules introduced by the Directive and specified by most national legislators correspond to the international standards set by ILO Convention 158 of 1982, followed also by some Member States which have not ratified the convention. In fact, the European national regulation presents common traits in all the major features of collective dismissals.

First and foremost they share the principle that collective dismissals, when meeting some threshold numbers indicated by the Directive, are subject to procedural requirements whereby the employer must: provide, in good time, the information on the reasons and terms of the terminations to the workers representatives, as well as hold consultations with such representatives on the measures to mitigate the impact on the workers.

Another common indication emerging from the comparative analysis of this volume shows that the information and consultation procedures include an active role of the workers representatives, either local union branches or other representative bodies (works council and the like). These bodies are defined according to the national rules, as the forms of workers representatives are considered to be a matter of national competence by the EU.

The public authorities have always played an important role in the procedure activated by the social parties according to the principle of tripartism, which is promoted by the ILO and followed in many European countries.

Whilst in the past this role included that generally the public employment services had the power to approve the employers' decision on the collective dismissals; today the legislation of most EU countries no longer requires such public authorization (exceptions are represented by some eastern European States and the Netherlands).

The abolition of the administrative approval has left the exclusive competence to control the substantial and procedural legality of the dismissals to the courts (*see* the Spanish case). The administrative authorities remain, however, involved in the collective procedure in many ways: not only must they be notified by the parties during the various steps of the procedure under penalty of nullity or other sanctions, but they may intervene in mediation, also with a specific proposal and may assist the parties in different instances, including in the definition of the measures necessary to prevent dismissals and reduce their impact on the workers concerned.

These measures have developed substantially in the course of time. Most national legislations now commit the employers to consider other options before resorting to collective dismissals. In some countries, like in Italy and Sweden, this matter is regulated by collective agreements (national and decentralized).

The comparative analysis presents a full range of measures finalized to make dismissals an *extrema ratio*. Such measure range from: restriction of hiring, to restriction of overtime and normal hours of work, to internal transfer and mobility, to training and retraining, to early retirement of various kinds, to spreading the workforce reduction over time, or even postponing it.

In countries, such as France, a wide ranging set of measures must be put in place by the employer, particularly in larger firms, and included in an 'employment safeguard plan', to be notified and validated by the administrative authority.

Significant developments are reported by national cases also in the measures finalized to reduce the impact of employers' decisions, in the cases where preventive measures have not succeeded in avoiding or reducing collective dismissals.

The majority of European countries have traditionally defined the criteria to be taken into account in selecting the workers to be discharged; often seniority is one, and in other cases (including Italy) a combination of criteria is considered. The actual definition of the order of priority in collective dismissals is an important and controversial matter of discussion among the employers and the unions (*see* the Swedish and Italian chapters).

Another important measure adopted in many countries through legislation or collective agreements, is to recognize to those workers who have been made redundant, not only a monetary compensation of different amounts, but also a certain priority (for a definite period of time) in the future hiring by the same employer.

More recently, active labour policies have been introduced in quite a few countries in order to facilitate the redeployment or the outplacement of the employees made redundant in other occupations. In this respect, various measures are provided by public and private employment offices, and often directly by the employers, through a 'social plan' usually agreed with the unions. These measures include not only training and retraining, but also personalized assistance in the job search combined with financial support (such as the reemployment bonus recently introduced in Italy), as well as even active assistance to search for a buyer in the case of a planned closure of an establishment (*see* the French case).

Apart from these important common trends, the European national legislations present also some differences, beginning with the concept of dismissal and that of collective dismissal. As mentioned in the introduction, the absence of an explicit statement in the EU Directive concerning this concept, has left wide discretion to the national legislators, and ultimately has emphasized the role of the ECJ in filling the gaps.

The comparative analysis of this volume underlines national differences in two other important matters: the forms and steps of the procedures, as well as the sanctions and remedies in case of violations of the legal and collective rules.

The complexity of procedures has been often denounced (also in Italy) as excessive; and some attempts of simplification have been made, but with uneven results.

The sanction of nullity or invalidity tends to be applied in the most serious cases of violation: such as the lack of notice to the public authorities, and the absolute absence of measures to prevent dismissals (*see* the French and German cases).

Monetary sanctions (damages, fines) are most commonly adopted by national legislators, subject to the requirement of the ECJ that they be effectively 'dissuasive'.

These brief observations, and more extensively the contents of this volume, confirm the progress of European legislations in regulating the socially sensitive area of collective dismissals. A few important aspects need to be further considered with the view to pursue not deregulation but a socially balanced and simplified regulation, in line with the ILO standards and with the principle of the European charter of fundamental social rights.

Tiziano Treu
Emeritus Professor of Labour Law, Catholic University of Milan
President of the International Society for Labour and Social Security Law

Introduction

The main reference point of the EU Member States' national legislations concerning the regulation of dismissals for a workforce reduction is Directive 1998/59/EC of the Council on the approximation of the laws of the Member States relating to collective redundancies (issued on the 20 July 1998, OJ L 225 of 12 August 1998).

In reality, at Community level, the regulation of collective dismissals dates much further back.

On 21 January 1974, the Council of the European Communities issued a resolution for the preparation of a social action plan (in the OJ C 13 of 12 February 1974) which envisaged the issuance of a Directive on such matter. On 17 February 1975 the Council of the European Communities approved Directive 1975/129 concerning the approximation of the laws of the Member States relating to collective dismissals.

The Directive defined the European concept of collective redundancy as 'any dismissal effected by an employer for one or more reasons not related to the individual workers concerned', conditional upon the number of dismissals surpassing a certain numerical threshold.[1] The Directive regulated the terms of fulfilment, envisaging that

1. Article 1 envisaged that: For the purpose of this Directive: (a) 'collective redundancies' means dismissals effected by an employer for one or more reasons not related to the individual workers concerned where, according to the choice of the Member States, the number of redundancies is:

   - for a period of 30 days:
     1. at least 10 in establishments normally employing more than 20 and less than 100 workers,
     2. at least 10% of the number of workers in establishments normally employing at least 100 but less than 300 workers,
     3. at least 30 in establishments normally employing 300 workers or more,
   - or, over a period of 90 days, at least 20, whatever the number of workers normally employed in the establishments in question;
     [...]

   Dismissals, therefore, became collective when, according to the parameters set by the same Article 1, over a short period of time individual dismissals superseded a set number, which varied according to the company size. In such case the consultation and procedural obligations envisaged by the Directive came into force.

in the case of a planned dismissal, the employer had to 'begin consultations with the workers' representatives in good time with a view to reaching an agreement' with the aim to examine all possibilities to avoid or reduce collective redundancies, and mitigate the consequences (Article 2). Upon the outcome of the consultations, in the absence of an agreement, the employer had to notify the competent public authority of any dismissal plan, and provide indications concerning the projected collective redundancies and the consultations carried out, specifying 'particularly the reasons for the redundancies, the number of workers to be made redundant, the number of workers normally employed and the period over which the redundancies are to be effected' (Article 3). The redundancies, according to the Directive, were suspended for at least thirty days, during which the said 'authority' and the employer had to 'seek solutions to the problems raised by the projected collective redundancies' (Article 4).

The philosophy of the Directive was directly inspired by Article 117 of the Treaty, which had the perspective to improve the living and working conditions of the citizens of the (then) European Community. In fact, collective redundancies were not viewed only in terms of the reduction of the workforce due to company downsizing, as envisaged by the inter-confederal agreement, but more generally as a type of withdrawal unrelated to the individual worker, characterized by a plurality of dismissals occurring at the same time.

Directive 1975/129 was supplemented by Directive 1992/56/EEC, which, in application of the principles of the 'Community Charter of the Fundamental Social Rights of Workers' approved on 9 December 1980, classified new types of collective dismissals and increased the information obligations by the employer, basically giving more voice to the unions. As a result, the role and function of the 'workers' representatives' were strengthened, and the information and consultation obligations by the employer were emphasized. Thus, the Directive obliged Member States to ensure that the representatives themselves or the workers had at their disposal 'administrative and/or judicial procedures in order to ensure that the obligations laid down in Directive 75/129/EEC are fulfilled'.

The two Directives of 1975 and 1992 were coordinated and transposed into the already quoted Council Directive n. 59 of 20 July 1998, as a sort of consolidated law. Such Directive repeats the definition of collective dismissals already adopted in the previous Directive 1975/159 and ratifies the key points of the EU legislation which can be summarized in three specific principles: (1) the obligation by the employers to inform and consult the employee representatives in case of a collective dismissal; (2) the setting of the points to be addressed during the consultations as well as the type of information the employers must provide; (3) the indication of the procedure for collective dismissals (written notification of the projected collective dismissal to the competent authority, submittal of the notification to the workers' representatives, the possibility for the workers to interact with the competent authority, the suspension of the dismissals for at least thirty days during which the competent authority assesses the situation in order to propose alternative solutions to the dismissals).

Lastly, Directive 2015/1794 of the European Parliament and the EU Council of 6 October 2015 (OJ 8 October 2016 L 263) concerning the collective dismissals of seafarers, supplements in this regard the directive of 1998. Article 8 of the Directive envisages that the EU Member States adopt the content by 10 October 2017[2].

The above briefly summarizes the Community framework of reference in which the EU Member States national legislations operate. However, the EU legislation being of a general nature allows for a certain degree of flexibility with respect to the national legislations, giving way to frequent uncertainties of application at national level. Many observe, for example, a shortcoming in Directive n. 59 (and of the Directives preceding it) due to the absence of any manifest statement concerning the concept of 'dismissal' (before even that of 'collective dismissals'). Others note the excessive elasticity of the criteria setting the numbers of workers to be dismissed for the reduction of the workforce.

As a result the national legislators, faced with the need to provide practical solutions, have had to fill the gaps of the European legislation, thus leading them to become the major interpreters of the Community Directives. Such situation, which is very common with respect to the relationship between the European and national legislations, has emphasized the role of the Court of Justice, which has frequently been called upon by the judges of the Member States to assess the compatibility of the national legislations with respect to the European Directives as far as collective dismissals are concerned.

A valid example is represented by the still recent sentence of 11 November 2015 (C 422/14, *Pujante Rivera*), which interpreted Directive 1998/59 on two key points: the calculation criteria of the workforce in order to set the company size to be able to apply the collective dismissal procedure, and the concept of 'dismissal' in terms of the limit of the number of workers dismissed, which if superseded is to be considered 'collective'. On the one hand, the Court specified that, in accordance with the Directive, the workers employed through a fixed-term contract or for a specific task must be considered as 'habitually' employed in the establishment of interest. On the other hand, the Court stated that, in order to assess the existence of a collective dismissal in accordance with the Directive, the condition that there must be at least five dismissals[3] that does not apply to contract terminations assimilated to redundancies, but only to dismissals in the narrow sense, that is terminations of an employment contract without the will of the worker, and then adopted without the latter's consent.

2. Article 4 of Directive 1794 envisages: 'Directive 98/59/EC is amended as follows: (1) in Article 1, paragraph 2, letter c) is deleted; (2) in Article 3, paragraph 1, the following subparagraph is inserted after the second subparagraph: "Where the projected collective redundancy concerns members of the crew of a seagoing vessel, the employer shall notify the competent authority of the State of the flag which the vessel flies".'
3. It is to be noted that the second part of Article 1 of Directive 98/59 envisages that 'for the purpose of calculating the number of redundancies provided for in the first subparagraph of point (a), terminations of an employment contract which occur on the employer's initiative for one or more reasons not related to the individual workers concerned shall be assimilated to redundancies, provided that there are at least five redundancies'.

The above-mentioned case clearly highlights some of the flaws of the Directive, bridged by the ruling of the Court of Justice. However, at the same time it demonstrates how national legislations, in their role as regulators of practical solutions, adopt mixed solutions which must be coordinated with the European legislation, at least at the level of interpretation. Thus, as in any matter specifically regulated by one or more Directives, the regulation of collective dismissals in Europe consists of a common basis and, at the same time, of many local legislations, as many as are the countries of the EU.

The knowledge of the European legislation on collective redundancies imposes, therefore, the examination of two basic data: the regulatory Directive and the aggregate of the provisions within the national legislations. Only through the comparison and coordination of these two cornerstones can a real knowledge of the law applicable to collective dismissals within the twenty-eight EU Member States be achieved. The overall data have a projection which, by nature, is purely theoretical, however the knowledge of the different national legislations is essential for the European jurist who intends to face the different implementation experiences in a practical way.

It is in this general context that we are hereby presenting this work. The objective of the editors is to make available to scholars and legal operators, mainly in the professional environment, a useful tool to inform on how articulate the national legislations can be and how much the local legal traditions, as well as the socio-economic situations weigh on the setting of the collective dismissals legislation. At the same time, the book wishes to stimulate a discussion on the different national legislations, so as to understand the common aspects and be able to identify some common lines and the differences between the Member State legislations. The objective therefore, is to describe the fundamentals of the legislations, from the theory to their construction.

The authors of the different national contributions belong to the traditional categories of the legal profession: university professors, forensic workers, judges, public administration executives, all connected by their common profession. The variety of the legal categories of the authors has been coordinated through the editors' underlying approach, with the aim to ensure the consistency of the contribution contents and the synthesis of the topics.

Much space has been given to the individual presentation capabilities, leaving to each the possibility to develop their contribution according to their styling options, in this way providing added value so as to maintain the authenticity of the narration. Therefore, one should not be surprised by the length of some of the texts, which at first glance may appear discordant with respect to other more concise and schematic contributions by other authors.

In conclusion, some considerations of a linguistic nature need to made. Notwithstanding the various contributions have undergone a careful revision from a linguistic point of view, the careful reader will note a certain lexical discordance in some of the texts. This can be explained by the fact that the common use of the English language has deeply affected the structure and terminology of the national languages. The editors feel that this is a further evidence of the book's cultural authenticity, which in no way hinders the fluency of its reading.

Thus, at this stage, we cannot but wish a pleasant reading, with the hope that the commitment of the authors and editors of this book, constitutes a valid support for a better knowledge of the different national laws.

Roberto Cosio
Filippo Curcuruto
Vincenzo Di Cerbo
Giovanni Mammone

CHAPTER 1

Collective Dismissal in Austria

Roland Gerlach

§1.01 THE COLLECTIVE DISMISSAL: THE CASE

[A] Sources of Law

Implementation by Austria of the Collective Dismissal Directive was based on the adaption of the existing provisions of the Labour Market Improvement Act (*Arbeitsmarktförderungsgesetz*) and the Labour Constitution Act (*Arbeitsverfassungsgesetz*). Section 45a of the Labour Market Improvement Act provides for information obligations of the employer towards the local offices of the Labour Market Service (*Arbeitsmarktservice – AMS*). Sections 91, 92, 108 and 109 contain co-determination rights of the works council in a situation of collective dismissal.

[B] Definition

Neither the Labour Constitution Act nor the Labour Market Improvement Act provides a qualitative definition of a collective dismissal. The quantitative definition in section 45a of the Labour Market Promotion Act is based directly on the first alternative set out in Article 1(1)(a) of the Directive, that is, the thirty-day period:

Accordingly, if there is a collective dismissal, then the situation must depend on the number of employees to be made redundant, the size of the company and the intention to dismiss the employees within the thirty-day period. According to section 45a of the Labour Market Improvement Act a situation qualifies as '*collective dismissal*', if a company (with):

- more than 20 and fewer than 100 employees intends to *dismiss* (cf. below on the scope of this term) at least 5 employees;
- more than 100 and fewer than 600 employees intends to dismiss at least 5% of all employees;

- more than 600 employees intends to dismiss at least 30 employees;
- intends to dismiss at least 5 employees older than 50 years.

With regard to the size of an establishment, section 45a of the Labour Market Promotion Act refers to 'employed persons' (*Beschäftigte*). According to an Executive Decree (*Durchführungserlass*) this term includes all '*standard employees*' (*echte Dienstnehmer*) in contrast to independent contractors. As trainees and managing employees are also considered standard employees under Austrian Labour Law they have to be taken into account too.

In accordance with the Directive not all forms of termination of an employment are subject to the information obligations and limits as outlined below. Only terminations induced by the employer have to be taken into account. Therefore, according to the aforementioned Decree, termination of the employment due to the following reasons remains unconsidered:

- notice of termination is given by an employee;
- termination for cause without notice (*Entlassung*);
- expiry of fixed-term contracts;
- termination during the probationary period.

However, the termination of an employment based on a mutual agreement (if initiated by the employer) has to be taken into account.

To assess if the termination of employments requires the notification of the Labour Market Service within the thirty-day period, the day of the announcement of the dismissals is the relevant date, not the actual termination date when the notice period expires (cf. Decision of the Austrian Supreme Court of 27 August 2009, 8 ObA 33/09z).

The announcement of the dismissal is considered to be made when the notice of termination leaves the sphere of the employer, for example when the termination letter is handed over to the employee or the post office/courier (cf. Decision of the Austrian Supreme Court of 13 October 1994, 8 ObA 299/94 following the respective decisions of the European Court of Justice). Not relevant in this regard is the date on which the employee actually receives the notice of termination. In accordance with these principles, in case of a mutual termination agreement the date on which the agreement has been reached is the decisive date (cf. *Olt*, Das Frühwarnsystem bei 'Massenkündigungen' nach § 45a AMFG, ARD 6448/5/2015).

§1.02 THE PROCEDURE

[A] Information Obligations Towards Public Authorities

If a collective dismissal situation occurs, the employer must notify the local employment offices of the Labour Market Service. The Labour Market Service is a state-owned enterprise serving as public employment centre.

The information has to be submitted to the competent regional office at least thirty days prior to giving notice to the first employee.

Accordingly, section 45a Labour Market Improvement Act relies on two thirty-day periods:

- 30-day period. Decisive period to assess if the termination of employments qualifies as collective dismissal in the sense of section 45a Labour Market Improvement Act. This 30-day-period is not bound to certain calendar months but is a moving period.
- 30-day-period between the date of notification of the Labour Market Service on the intended collective dismissal and the announcement of the first notice of termination within the scope of the announced collective dismissal. This 30-day period basically works as a waiting period (*Sperrfrist*) during which a legally effective notice of termination cannot be given. The waiting period starts once the notification has been successfully submitted to the Labour Market Service (cf. Decision of the Austrian Supreme Court of 4 August 2009, 9 ObA 76/09f).

Any failure to observe these rules will render all pertinent dismissals void.

Upon formal request of the employer the Labour Market Service can allow the employer to terminate employment relationships prior to the expiry of the thirty-day waiting period in case the employer can establish that there are important economic reasons. In practice, such an exemption is hardly available, usually the Labour Market Service insists on the full thirty-day period.

The scope of the Labour Market Improvement Act is limited to the obligation of timely and sufficient information. The employer does not have to obtain approval for collective dismissal from any authority or the works council.

[B] Form and Content of the Notification

Employers must send a written notification to the competent regional office of the Labour Market Service at least thirty days prior to the planned first dismissals. A copy of the notification must be forwarded to the works council, which must be informed and consulted on the matter.

The reason for this provision is to give all parties involved (i.e., the employer, the works council and the Labour Market Service) time to explore all possibilities for avoiding the planned dismissals or mitigating the (local) effects of those eventually carried out.

The Labour Market Service provides an official form for the notification, which can be found on http://www.ams.at. The notification has to include information concerning the reasons for the redundancies, the timeframe, number and positions of the employees to be made redundant, their sex, age, qualification and length of employment. Furthermore, the employer must inform about the criteria used in selecting the employees and about any planned (social) measures to prevent negative consequences for the employees to be made redundant. Also, the employer is obliged to provide the Labour Market Service with a copy of the communication to the works council and evidence that the Works Council has been informed according to the relevant provisions of the Labour Constitution Act.

[C] Co-determination Rights of the Works Council in Case of Collective Dismissal

[1] General

Works Councils are responsible for acting as protector and conduit between employers and employees, and for monitoring the compliance of internal social, personal, and business policies. According to section 40 of the Labour Constitution Act, a works council can be established in every plant with at least five regular employees. The number of works council members depends on the number of employees employed in the company. There are separate works councils for blue-collar workers and white-collar workers. By far not all enterprises which meet the requirements of the establishment of a works council actually have a works council because employees are not obliged to exercise their right to elect a works council. A works council serves a term of four years and is elected by all employees of the business who are at least 18 years old. Works councils can be comprised of one member where the business employs between five and nine employees, or can have more than ten members where a business employs more than 100 employees.

The works council supervises the employer's compliance with the laws and collective bargaining agreements (CBAs) relating to employment. In order to fulfil this responsibility, the works council may inspect the business' employment records, especially concerning employee remuneration. Employers are compelled to make routine disclosures of this information to works councils. Furthermore, works councils have a broad entitlement to deliberate on all matters of employee safety and health and may manage in-house trainings, and employee welfare and educational facilities. Once formed, the works council must meet for internal deliberations of pending employment matters at least once per month.

[2] Information and Consultation Obligations Towards the Works Council

In general, the works council is entitled to be informed of all issues concerning the economic situation of the company by the employer. Also financial issues and the general development are covered by these information duties. There is no statutory fixed time frame for giving certain information. However, there are regular meetings between employer and works council, which must take place each calendar quarter or each month upon request.

Sections 108 and 109 of the Labour Constitution Act ('Arbeitsverfassungsgesetz') apply in the situation of collective redundancies. These provisions refer to the definition contained in section 45a of the Labour Market Improvement Act. The works council must be informed immediately or within a timeframe so that it can thoroughly discuss and consult with the employer on the planned collective redundancy. A copy of the notification of the Labour Market Service must be forwarded to the works council.

The employer must notify and consult with the works council before implementing certain business changes, which have an effect on the employees. The employer has to inform the works council about its intention in advance. This is due to the face that, according to the Labour Constitution Act ('Arbeitsverfassungsgesetz', 'ArbVG'), collective dismissals are qualified as a '*major change to the establishment*' entailing serious disadvantages for the entire workforce or a significant number of employees. Therefore, the employer is obliged to supply the works council with relevant information in particular about all social matters concerned.

Sections 108 and 109 of the Austrian Labour Constitution Act state that in case of a planned collective dismissal, the employer must provide the works council with the following information in writing prior to consultation:

- the number, function and qualification of the employees to be made redundant;
- the term of service and the selection criteria;
- the reason for the collective redundancy;
- the number and function of the workforce;
- the timeframe for the planned measures;
- measures to help and avoid any negative economic effects for the employees concerned.

According to its consultation and co-determination rights, the works council is entitled to call in an expert and to present proposals to the employer in order to prevent, eliminate or mitigate unfavourable consequences for the employees. If the planned workforce reduction affects a significant number of all employees, the works council can demand the conclusion of a 'social plan' in form of an 'enforceable' shop agreement. Social plans as shop agreements mainly cover financial arrangements for attending or organizing retraining schemes and special severance payments for employees to be dismissed (*see* in more detail below).

In addition to the collective redundancy notification, employers must notify the works council at least seven days prior to terminating individual employment contracts. The latter also applies if there is no collective dismissal situation. The law does not provide a certain form for this notification of the works council. It is recommended, however, that the works council be notivied in writing.

[3] General Co-determination Rights of the Works Council in Case of Termination of Employments by the Employer

An employer must notify the works council of its intent to terminate the employment of one of its employees at least seven full days prior to giving that employee notice of termination. The works council must respond to the employer's notice within seven days with an official stance regarding the proposed termination of employment. The works council may choose to object, approve, or refrain from issuing a statement regarding the termination. The works council's stance affects the subsequent legal avenues for the employee to challenge the termination for being socially unjust or being based on certain unlawful motives. Employees may also challenge the termination on other grounds, for example, on the basis of anti-discrimination legislation. In this regard the statement of the works council is not relevant.

However, any termination by notice that takes place without the works council being informed is void. All in all, the employee's options for challenging the notice of termination are dependent upon the works council's stance:

- If the works council agrees to the notice of an employee's termination, then they effectively bar the employee from contesting on the grounds that the termination was socially unjust (*see* in more detail below). In this case, the employee may only contest the notice based on a subjective finding of unlawful motive and has the responsibility of filing the challenge.
- If the works council objects to the employer's intent to serve a notice of termination, the works council thereby maintains the right to file a challenge. The only prerequisite to filing the complaint is that the works council has the employee's consent to do so. In this case, the works council would file the appeal against termination with the Labor and Social Court. In the case where the works council files the appeal, the appeal may be based on either unlawful motives, or socially unacceptable circumstances.
  Finally, if the works council refrains from comment, the employee may personally challenge the termination decision. The appeal may be based on either unlawful motives, or socially unacceptable circumstances.

[D] *Excursus*: The Role of Trade Unions

Trade unions do not have any (legal) rights or duties in connection with collective dismissal. However, in such situations the works council members frequently consult with the competent trade unions. Trade unions do not have an active right to initiate negotiation with an employer. However, the works council may invite trade union representatives to the quarterly consultation with the employer if the issue of these meetings concerns a change of the plant or other important matters which substantially affect the employees.

[E] Enterprises Without a Works Council

If a works council has not been established in an enterprise the aforementioned information obligations and co-determination rights do not apply. Austrian legislation does not provide for substitute regulations, for example, in the form of prior information of each individual employee instead of the works council. An important consequence is that employees without works council representation cannot enforce supporting measures such as a social plan. Of course, however, information obligations towards the Labour Market Service apply irrespective of whether a works council exists in a company or not.

Also, according to section 45 paragraph 4 Labour Market Improvement Act, the employer must submit a copy of the information to the Labour Market Service to all employees affected by such measure if no works council has been established (who is usually the recipient of this information).

Even if information obligations do not apply, employees in establishments without works council representation may as well challenge the termination of their employments before the Labour and Social Courts if the requirements set out in the different statutes are met (*see* below).

§1.03 THE SUPPORT MEASURES IN FAVOUR OF EMPLOYEES

[A] 'Social Plan' (*Sozialplan*)

Social plans are legal instruments of collective labour law. They can be agreed on in establishments with at least twenty employees if a restructuring measure leads to vital drawbacks for a substantial part of the workforce. The legal form may either be a collective bargaining agreement or a shop agreement. The purpose of social plans is to prevent, eliminate or mitigate unfavourable consequences for the employees.

One important purpose, it is argued, is to internalize social costs caused through restructurings. Another important purpose is to compensate the employee for otherwise available rights, especially dismissal protection, because restructuring measures typically justify dismissals. The legal requirements for concluding social plans are interpreted through different purposes and the different results are made explicit. Since the introduction of social plans states heavily subsidised them.

If a works agreement is not achieved, both parties (employer and works council) can appeal to the Arbitration Board (*Schlichtungsstelle*), an administrative agency. An Arbitration Board has to be set up upon the request of the works council or the employer. The Arbitration Board's responsibility is to mediate between the parties, propose settlements and procure that an agreement can be reached between the parties. The Arbitration Board must come to a final decision, which usually takes several months. If the notification of the works council did not occur on time, the social plan (shop agreement) will be more expensive for the employer, because the Arbitration Board will take into account these circumstances for the benefit of the employees. In case of collective dismissal, the social plan must take particular account of employees, which are older than 50. Some tax advantages are granted if payments are made pursuant to a social plan. The decision of the Arbitration Board has the legal quality of a shop agreement. It is not subject to legal remedy.

Social Plans usually include one or a combination of the following measures:

- additional voluntary severance payments for redundant employees; the amount of the payments regularly depends on the age of the employee and the length of service as well as on the economic situation of a company;
- rehiring options;
- measures for the vocational qualification for redundant employees;
- relocation of some employees instead of redundancy;
- relocation to another company;
- longer notice periods for employees.

[B] *Excursus*: Pecuniary Claims upon Termination and Voluntary Benefits

In case of (ordinary) termination, the employee is entitled to the following payments:

- Salary/Wage until the termination date (including pro-rata bonus payments).
- Christmas or holiday pay on a pro-rata basis (i.e., 13th and 14th salary).
- Compensation for unconsumed annual leave entitlements.
- Employees whose employment contracts have been concluded after 31 December 2002 are entitled to statutory severance payments (*Abfertigung*) according to the old severance regime (*Abfertigung alt*). The actual amount of this payment which has to be rendered by the employer depends on the length of service and ranges from three monthly remunerations after three years of service to up to twelve monthly remunerations after twenty-five years of service).
- For employees who have entered into their employment contracts on or after 1 January 2003 the new system of severance pay is applicable. These employees (usually) have a severance payment claim against an external fund, not against the employer.

In practice most employers try to enter into mutual agreements on the termination of the employment with the affected employees to minimize the risk of lengthy court proceedings after restructuring. If the economic situation of the company allows to do so, in many cases employers offer certain voluntary benefits such as voluntary severance payments on top of all statutory and contractual claims to reach such agreements even if a social plan has not been concluded. However, such voluntary benefits in general do not enjoy the same favourable tax treatment as payments made pursuant to a social plan.

[C] Protection from Termination of the Employment on the Level of the Individual Employment

In addition to the works council's co-determination rights Austrian Employment Law provides the possibility for employees to take legal action against the termination of their employment. Under Austrian Employment Law in general ordinary termination of an employment relationship does not require any specific reasons such as low performance, misconduct of an employee or operational/economic reasons.

However, for several groups of employees this general principle does not apply – they enjoy a special status subject to different statutes and are protected from termination of the employment (cf. below '*Specially protected group of employees*'). Moreover, the law provides possibilities for employees to challenge the termination of their employment before the Labour and Social Court if either the grounds on which the termination is based are unlawful (e.g., infringe anti-discrimination legislation) or if the termination of their employment is deemed to be 'socially unfair' (cf. '*social unfair dismissal*'). Social unfair dismissal is by far the most frequent reason for legal action against termination of the employment.

[1] Specially Protected Group of Employees

Generally, special protection from termination means that the employer needs to obtain the consent of the Labour and Social Court (or, in case of disabled employees with a formal special status, of a special authority, the '*Sozialministeriumservice*') before notice of termination can be given.

The closure of a plant or other operational reasons may serve as a valid basis for the termination of the employment. However, the mutual termination of the employment is not bound to any authority's consent. Therefore, in practice employers try to find an agreement on the mutual termination of the employment with these groups of employees rather than initiating court/administrative procedures, particularly as notice of termination may not be given before such procedures are concluded and a decision has been submitted to the parties.

[a] Disabled Employees with a Special Status

In Austria, the responsible authority which determines the degree of a disability is the '*Sozialministeriumservice*', which is a special department of the Ministry of Social Affairs. People with a degree of disablement of at least 50% fall within the scope of '*begünstigte Behinderte*' (disabled people with a special status). Employees who have this status are specially protected from termination of their employment - provided these conditions are fulfilled:

- the employment has commenced before 1 January 2011 and the employee has been working for the employer for at least 6 months;
- the employment has commenced after 31 December 2010 and the employee has been working for at least four years for the employer - if the employee already started his employment with this status;
- the employee receives the special status during his/her employment and has been employed for at least six months.

In these cases, an employer must obtain the approval of the '*Sozialministerium-service*' before ordinary notice of termination can be given. However, as outlined above, mutual termination or termination for cause with immediate effect do not require the prior consent of the authority.

In order to obtain the authority's consent, the employer must provide reasons why he/she needs to terminate the employment. § 8 of Disabled Employees Act *(BEinstG)* provides a non-exhaustive list of grounds for termination. The list has been established in consideration of the list provided in section 121 of Labour Constitutional Act which contains the reasons for terminating the employment of a works council (cf. below).

With regard to collective redundancies the following reason is particularly important: consent may be obtained if the employee's area of activity is eliminated and there is no possibility to provide further employment at another workplace without causing significant damage to the enterprise (lit a).

Moreover, the law states that an employee's incapacity to work serves as a valid basis for the termination if the employer can show that there is no possibility to provide further employment at another workplace without causing significant damage to the enterprise (lit b).

The protective legislation mainly focuses on employees with this special status. However, the Disabled Employees Act *('Behinderteneinstellungsgesetz – BEinstG')* also provides anti-discrimination legislation which also protects disabled employees with lower degrees of a disability from discrimination due to their disability.

[b] Works Council

The members to the works council enjoy the strongest protection against termination of their employment. The special protection commences after the election and lasts until three months after the expiry/termination of their mandate (so-called 'cooling off period'). However, there is no cooling off period if the works council's mandate ends due to the shutdown of the entire plant. Section 120 paragraph 4 of the Labour Constitution Act extends the scope of application of these rules to substitute members (*Ersatzmitglieder*) if they have replaced a member of the works council at least for two weeks.

As a rule, as outlined above, the employer may only terminate a works council's employment if the approval of the Labour and Social Court has been obtained. Section 121 of the Labour Constitution Act provides an exhaustive list of reasons for termination. Aside from incapacity to work or persistent breach of work duties, the Labour Constitution Act provides the possibility to terminate an employment for certain, very restricted economic reasons.

In case of a permanent shutdown or reduction of a plant or the shutdown of single entities of an enterprise the court has to consent if the employer can show that there is no possibility to provide further employment at another workplace (at another enterprise of the company) without causing significant damage to the enterprise (section 121 fig 1 Labour Constitution Act). According to case law (*see* decision of the

Regional Higher Court Vienna, 10 Ra 366/96h) to a certain extent the works council has to accept an alternative employment even if the working conditions change for the worse. Also, the employer is only obliged to offer such an alternative workplace if the works council member explicitly asks for this possibility. To obtain the courts consent it is necessary that the implementation of these measures has already begun and the project has left the planning stage.

As soon as the entire plant (not only a part of it) is shutdown, the employer is not bound to the court's consent anymore, because the shutdown of the enterprise automatically terminates the mandate of the works council.

[c] Parents

The scope of protection covers pregnant employees or employees who have been giving birth recently, employees on parental leave (*Karenz)* and employees working parental part time (*Elternteilzeit*). Special protection from termination starts with the pregnancy of an employee and ends four months after the birth of the child. In case the employee (mother or father) takes parental leave, protection from termination of the employment is given until four weeks after this termination. When employees work parental part time, they are also protected from termination of their employment starting from the announcement of their request to work parental part time (however, four months before the start at the earliest) and lasts until four weeks after the fourth birthday of the child. During these protection periods an employer has to obtain the court's consent before he may terminate the employment. Special rules apply in case of the closure of a plant: after a permanent shutdown of a plant (after completion of the shutdown) the Labour and Social Court's approval does not have to be obtained.

[d] Other Groups

Aside from the groups mentioned above, apprentices and employees during military/civil service enjoy special protection from termination as well.

[D] General Protection from Termination of the Employment: Most Important: Socially Unfair Dismissal

If there are five or more employees employed by the company (so basically if there are enough employees to establish a works council even if the workforce did not exercise its right to do so), employees may challenge the termination for being socially unfair and claim reinstatement of their employment.

While appeal on the grounds of unlawful motives is based on the employer's sphere, the effects on the employees' individual situation are decisive in cases of socially unfair dismissals. In a first step the employee has to establish that his/her substantial interests are impaired by the termination. The employee's substantial interests are impaired if the termination causes a considerable impairment of the economic situation (as a general principle, it is required that the employee will have to face income losses of more than 10% in a new employment) or if a longer period of unemployment can be expected. For older employees, the fact of long service with the employer as well as the difficulties which can be anticipated in finding a new employment because of their age have also to be taken into account. Particularly if the terminated employees are older than 40 years and earn a good salary, it is likely that the employee will be able to establish that his/her financial situation is jeopardized. The courts do not assess this question on their own, usually an expert in the field of employment appointed by the court reviews this question and issues an expert statement which is the basis for the court's decision in this aspect.

If the Court finds that the employee's substantial interests are impaired by the termination, the employer may nonetheless justify the termination if:

- the termination is a consequence of an employee's personal capability which impaired the employer's interests (e.g., frequent absences due to illness, lack of capability to perform contractual duties); or
- there are economic reasons which prevent the employer from continuing the employment (e.g., reduction of workforce, shutdown of an entire plant or part of a plant).

Usually, in case of collective dismissal the employer relies on economic reasons in such lawsuits. The court does not assess the economic decision itself (so the court does not assess if, for example, the business decision to close a certain plant is a necessary or effective measure from an economic/financial point of view) but reviews the associated requirement of the termination. Hence the employer has to examine alternatives to keep the employee, for example by offering other job positions suitable for him or her within the establishment or the company.

§1.04 JUDICIAL CONTROL AND SANCTIONS

As outlined above, employers' obligations in case of collective dismissals are limited to information and consultation obligations towards authorities and the works council. Moreover, additional information obligations apply arising from the regulations in the Labour Constitution regarding general protection of employees against the termination of their employment. Noncompliance may have severe consequences and high financial risks.

Collective dismissals are deemed as null and void if the Labour Market Service has not been notified about dismissals qualifying as collective dismissals. The same applies if notice of termination is issued prior to the expiry of the thirty-day waiting period after notifying the regional office of the employment service (if the Labour Market Service did not formally approve the reduction of this period).

Also, if an employer fails to comply with the notification requirements towards the works council pursuant to section 105 of the Labour Constitution Act (which contains general rules on protection from termination of the employment) notice of termination is also considered to be legally ineffective.

In both cases, affected employees may file a complaint with the competent Labour and Social Court (targeted on the reinstatement of the employment). Legislation does not provide for specific time-limits for this kind of legal action. However, according to a decision of the Austrian Supreme Court the employee has the obligation to take such action '*without undue delay*' (Decision of the Austrian Supreme Court of 1 January 2000, 9 ObA 322/99i). The maximum length of this period needs to be assessed on a case-by-case basis. Usually, six months are considered the maximum time-frame for the employee to declare his interests.

Austria has a specific court system for labour and social security matters. Within this system, each Regional Court has a specialized chamber for labour and social welfare matters that acts as the Court of First Instance for labour issues (with the exception of Vienna, which has its own, freestanding Labour and Social Court). These labour courts have jurisdiction over disputes concerning employment-like contractual relationships, unfair dismissal, and the settlement of disputes between employers and employee representative bodies. Labour Courts rule in panels consisting of a professional judge as chairman and two lay judges. The lay judges are appointed upon recommendation of statutory representative bodies of employees and employers.

Noncompliance with information or consultation obligations of the works council regarding collective dismissal have to be taken into account by the arbitration board, if the works council enforces a social plan via the decision of this body.

In addition, infringements of the information obligations in the situation of collective dismissal constitute administrative offences in accordance with section 160 Labour Constitution Act. However, the penalties provided are rather low (currently EUR 2,180) and usually do not constitute a major threat to employers.

CHAPTER 2

Collective Dismissal in Belgium

Michela Velardo

§2.01 INTRODUCTION

The objectives of this chapter are to explain the functioning and application of the collective dismissal procedure in Belgium. This chapter describes the economic elements that characterise the Kingdom of Belgium and the known cases of collective dismissal (section §2.02), followed by an analysis of the procedure of collective dismissal (section §2.03) and concludes addressing the possible remedies and appeals (section §2.04) that can be used by workers to challenge the mentioned procedure.

§2.02 SECTION I

[A] Belgian Economy

Belgium is a small country, located in the heart of Europe, between main western European countries, and its active and important 'European' role inevitably reflects on its economy. Certainly, since the European Coal and Steel community was created in 1951, Belgium has opened its doors to the international context. Due to its international heritage acquired over the years, Belgium has quickly become a key state in fostering international contacts and agreements. More than a thousand public and private international organisations have their headquarters or permanent secretary. This has favoured the development of the tertiary sector (wholesale and retail trade; HORECA, restaurants and Cafés; Banks and insurances; real estate and business services; other private services; transport and communication; health and care; culture, sport and leisure; public and international administration; education). In fact, nearly 90%[1] of the

1. According to the 'SPF Économie, Direction Générale Statistique' study, in 2014 the tertiary sector is formed by 41% women and 44.2% men.

workforce is employed in the service sector. The tertiary sector is followed by the secondary sector, explicitly industries that produce engineering and metallurgy products, chemical products, metals, textiles, glass, petrochemical products and by automobile assembly industries. In 2013, the secondary sector represented 15.1%[2] of the Gross Domestic Product (GDP), while the 68.6%[3] was represented by the tertiary sector. It is the agriculture sector that suffered the most losses. In 2013, agriculture, forestry and fishing constituted only 7% of the GDP.

The global economic and financial crisis that exploded in 2008 did not spare Belgian's labour market, even though Belgium responded better than other European States.

Nevertheless, the crisis of 2008 crossed La Louvière, a Belgium municipality located in the Walloon Region in the province of Hainaut, touching the steel company 'Duferco' that, in 2013, was forced to shut down and layoff more than 800 workers.

From January to September 2014, several restructuring plans were announced. In January 2014, the retail chain Makro Cash & Carry Belgium announced more than 300 redundancies while, in February, Interior Home Store Market announced 222 enforced collective redundancies. In the same month, the Heinz factory in Turnhout was closed threatening 157 employment contracts. In February we can also witness a wave of layoffs in the glass industry with more than 500 workers fired in AGC Glass Europe and in Saint-Gobain Glass. In June, Hewlett-Packard announced 310 layoffs but, most importantly and above all, the Delhaize group announced the collective dismissal of 2,500 workers. In July, it is the brand Cora that announced 447 redundancies in several of its stores and, in September, Doosan Infracore Europe SA, active in the field of metal processing, announced 313 job losses.

[B] Historical Background

The collective dismissal procedure, in Belgium, is known as the 'Renault Procedure'.

Unfortunately, it is regularly mentioned in the press when related to struggling businesses. To be more specific, following the turmoil caused by the closure of the Renault-Vilvoorde factory in 1997, the Government requested the National Labour Council (Conseil National du Travail – CNT) to render an opinion on the effectiveness of information and consultation procedures. Although the council gave a positive opinion, the CNT proposed to establish a link between the employer's obligation of information and consultation to the staff and the individual redundancy occurring when a collective dismissal is being implemented.

The CNT's opinion led to the legislative Act adopted on 23 February 1998, commonly known as 'Renault Act', introducing important legal provisions in favour of employment. This Act, combined with the Royal Decree adopted on 24 May 1976

2. According to the 'SPF Économie, Direction Générale Statistique' study published in 2014, industrial activities have suffered a 0.4% reduction in 2013. Consequently, the industrial sector in the calculation of GDP has passed from 15.4% in 2012 to 15.1% in 2013.
3. According to the 'SPF Économie, Direction Générale Statistique', the tertiary sector in the GDP has increased from 68.2% in 2012 to 68.6% in 2013.

concerning collective redundancies and with the Collective Labour Agreement No. 24 of 2 October 1975 (Convention Collective de Travail No. 24) concerning the procedure of information and consultation with worker representatives in the case of collective redundancies, forms a triptych describing the procedure applicable in collective dismissals.

In the first place, these legal texts establish the definition and objective of collective dismissal. Second, they describe the information and consultation procedure to be followed and establish suitable compensations.

§2.03 SECTION II

[A] Collective Dismissal Procedure

[1] Definition of the Collective Dismissal Procedure

In the broad sense of the term, the word 'dismissal' expresses the unilateral will of the employer to terminate a working relationship with one or more workers. Unlike an individual termination of employment caused, for example, by a serious misconduct of the worker, collective dismissal[4] are all dismissals due to one or more reasons that are not attributed to the workers as individuals if, within a sixty-day period, they affect the following numbers of workers:

Collective Dismissal	
in enterprises with an average of more than 20 and less than 100 employees during the calendar year preceding the dismissal	10
in enterprises employing an average of at least 100 and less than 300 employees during the calendar year preceding the dismissal	10% of the workers
in enterprises employing an average of at least 300 employees during the calendar year preceding the dismissal	30

The rules relevant to individual dismissal continue to apply in the case of collective dismissals; however, specific provisions must also be taken into account.

A collective dismissal is characterized by:

- special procedures of information and consultation;[5]
- an additional ad hoc compensation.

4. Article 1, No. 3 of the Royal Decree on collective dismissal adopted on 24 May 1976.
5. This provision in provided in the Collective Labour Agreement No. 24 of 2 October 1975 on the procedure for information and consultation with representatives of workers with regards to collective redundancies. Article 5 of the same Convention excludes its application to certain categories of workers, such as workers with a fixed-term employment contract or with a project employment contract, unless the collective dismissal occurs before the expiry of the contract or before the conclusion of the project; and fisherman or sailors deployed on a merchant navy.

[2] *Information and Consultation Phase*

In brief, the employer's information and consultation obligations, in case of collective dismissal, take place in the following chronological order:

(1) First, the employer expresses the intention to proceed with a collective dismissal and must provide workers' representatives (works council or, in absence of, the union delegation or, in absence of both, the committee for the prevention and the protection at work, or the workers directly) all relevant information. In any case, the worker must inform workers' representatives in writing about the following:
   - the motivation for the planned dismissal;
   - number and categories of employees involved;
   - number and categories of employees normally employed;
   - time period of the dismissals;
   - proposed criteria used for the selection of employers taken in consideration for dismissal;
   - calculating plan for possible compensation not due in accordance with the law or with a collective labour agreement.

(2) The employer must also send a written copy to the Director of the sub-regional public employment service where the company's headquarters are established (VDAB/FOREM or ACTIRIS) and to the Chairman of the Executive Committee of the SPF Employment, Labour & Social Dialogue.

(3) In an ad hoc meeting, the employer illustrates the above-mentioned documents to workers' representatives (works council / union delegation / CPPT / workers) allowing them to raise comments and suggestions. This will initiate a negotiation phase between the employer and the representatives. Indeed, the employer must consult workers' representatives (works council / union delegation / workers) on the possibility to avoid or reduce the collective redundancies and to mitigate the consequences (social measures for the re-employment or retraining of the dismissed employees).

(4) A dialogue phase begins where representatives may make suggestions and ask questions to the employer. It should be highlighted that the legislation regarding collective dismissals does not provide for a mandatory agreement between the employer and workers' representatives nor for the existence of a social plan or for a further settlement of conditions.

(5) Should the employer continue the dismissal action, the collective dismissal strategy must be notified, by registered mail, to the Director of the sub-regional public employment service where the company's headquarters are established (VDAB/FOREM or ACTIRIS) and to the Chairman of the Executive Committee of the FPS Employment, Labour & Social Dialogue.
   The notification must contain:
   - the company's administrative data (name, address and business nature of the company, the joint administration where the firm is located);

- the number of workers regularly employed;
- the reasons for the planned dismissal;
- the number of workers involved (by gender, age group, occupational category and division);
- the period during which their employment contracts shall expire.

The notification must also contain confirmation and the demonstration that the employer has fulfilled the following four conditions:

- a written report, containing the employer's intention to proceed with a collective dismissal, was presented to workers' representatives;
- the employer has met with the workers' representatives to discuss the intended collective dismissal;
- workers' representatives have had the opportunity to raise questions regarding the intended collective dismissal and formulate arguments or make counterproposals;
- all questions, arguments and counterproposals presented have been evaluated by the employer who has thoroughly replied to all concerns.

On the day the notification is sent, the employer must also:

- display a written copy of the notification in the company;
- provide a copy to workers' representatives (works council or, in absence of, union delegation or, in absence of both, to the committee for the prevention and the protection of work or, in absence of, to the union organizations represented in the relevant joint administration) who may send any comments to the Director of the sub-regional public employment service;
- send a copy (by registered mail) to all workers who are dismissed in accordance with the collective dismissal and whose contracts have already expired on the day the notification was displayed in the company.

(6) Within thirty days of the notification, workers' representatives who have been previously informed and consulted can formulate objections in relation to the non-compliance with the procedure. During this period, the employer cannot dismiss workers involved in the project of collective dismissal, however this does not apply in the case of a company closure resulting from a court decision (e.g., in the context of bankruptcy). This notice period begins from the date of the above-mentioned notification (the date of the post stamp). Its objective is to give the public employment service(s) concerned, the time needed to find a solution to the consequences of the preannounced dismissal.

The Director of the sub-regional public employment service may reduce the thirty-day period if:

- the intended collective dismissal following a company's closure does not result from a court decision;

- the intended collective dismissal takes place in companies that employ workers on docks, ship repairers or manufacturing companies, where the joint committees concerned have adopted a collective agreement that provides a procedure of consultation equivalent to that of the Collective Labour Agreement No. 24.

Except for the two above-mentioned cases, the Director may extend this period up to sixty days beginning from the notification date. The Director, therefore, must inform the employer, at least a week before the expiry of the initial thirty-day period, about the extension and its motifs. The employer may appeal the Director's decision to the sub-regional public employment service committee, which shall render a final decision within thirty days. The appeal, however, does not suspend the Director's decision.

(7) Following the thirty-day period (possibly reduced or extended), the employer can dismiss the workers involved, except when legitimate objections were raised to the employer by the workers' representatives consulted. In this case, the employer shall re-formulate the notification to fulfil the four conditions so that the procedure can be followed and shall forward the new notification to the Director of the sub-regional public employment office. Consequently, a new thirty-day period begins (which may, be reduced or extended accordingly).

The dismissal occurs:

- at the end of the thirty-day period;
- at the end of the reduced period;
- at the end of the extended period (maximum sixty days);
- at the end of the period set by the management committee.

During the thirty days following the dismissal, the dismissed worker can challenge (by registered mail addressed to the employer) the due process (the four phases) unless workers' representatives did not raise objections concerning the procedure, during the thirty-day period after notification.

[3] Ad hoc Compensations in Case of Collective Dismissal

In case of collective dismissal, the employer is required to pay an ad hoc compensation to all the employees involved. Therefore, this compensation is added to the unemployment benefits to which the employees are entitled. The amount of this compensation is equivalent to half of the difference between the net reference salary and the unemployment benefits.

The purpose of this compensation is to alleviate the consequences of the collective dismissal. The guidelines determining the compensation are provided for in the Collective Labour Agreement No. 10, adopted on 8 May 1973 concluded within the CNT on collective dismissals.

In principle, all workers[6] are entitled to compensation in case of collective dismissals. Nonetheless, the agreement above-mentioned does establish categories of workers not entitled to compensation.[7]

The compensation, granted for a four-month period, begins the day after the termination of the employment contract or the day after the expiry of the period covered by compensation in lieu of notice. If the notice period or if the compensation in lieu of notice is longer than three months, then the established period of four months shall only cover the final month after the expiry of the three months.

The only other compensation granted to the dismissed worker are the unemployment benefits. The compensation provided in the Collective Labour Agreement No. 10, adopted on 8 May 1973, does not apply when other collective conventions or agreements provide for compensations equivalent or higher than those established by the Collective Labour Agreement.

[4] Reinstatement Measures

The Economic Recovery Act adopted on 27 March 2009 and its Royal Decree adopted on 22 April 2009 amended the collective dismissal procedure. The new procedure applies only to those dismissals announced as of 7 April 2009 and establishes: (1) an employment unit; (2) reclassification compensation; (3) outplacement.

Restructuring companies with more than twenty workers employed are required to set up an employment unit with the task to guarantee the reinstatement of workers in the labour market. Registration to this unit is compulsory for all workers bound by a permanent employment contract and optional for those with a fixed-term employment contract or for temporary workers.

All workers aged 45 and older must be registered to the employment unit for six months. During this period, they receive a reclassification compensation that is

6. The workers include:

- unemployed workers who are entitled to unemployment benefits;
- unemployed workers who, for no reason of their fault, are not entitled to unemployment benefits;
- workers who have found another employment but are entitled to a lower allowance than that at their previous employment;
- workers who follow a professional formation course and, therefore, are entitled to a compensation that however is lower than their pervious allowance.

7. This category of workers include:

- temporary workers;
- workers employed with a fixed-term employment contract or who have been employed to execute a specific task;
- workers employed in the construction industry;
- workers employed in the steel and coal industry;
- seasonal and canneries workers (fruits, vegetables, jams);
- workers in the fishing industry or those who work in maritime sectors;
- workers entitled to compensation due to the company's closure;
- workers entitled to special compensation accorded to protected categories of workers.

equivalent to the current gross remuneration. This reclassification compensation replaces all or part of the severance pay. In addition, the employment unit should at least make an outplacement offer to each worker who has been dismissed within the restructuring project and registered at the employment unit.

§2.04 SECTION III

[A] Appeals

What if the employer does not respect the 'Renault procedure'? To challenge compliance with the information and consultation procedure, two different appeals are provided: a collective one and an individual one:

[1] Collective Appeal

Workers' representatives (the work council or in absence of, the union delegation or in absence of, the workers) can notify the employer their objections in relation to the non-compliance of the procedure. They must do so within thirty days after the date of posting of the copy of the collective dismissal plan sent to the Director of the sub-regional public employment service. The employer, during this period, may not notify any dismissal to those workers involved in the information and consultation procedure. This allows the employer to be informed about any irregularities before actually proceeding with the dismissal. After this period of thirty days, the employer is deemed to have complied with the information and consultation procedure. In this case, workers can no longer individually challenge the procedure. This system aims to provide legal certainty to the employer who has fully complied with the information and consultation procedure. In the absence of observations from the workers' representatives, the employer can proceed with collective dismissals without the risk of being accused of non-compliance.

[2] Individual Appeal

In addition to the collective complaints procedure, the worker may, under certain conditions, individually challenge the dismissal. If, within the thirty-day period, the workers' representatives have raised no observations, the dismissed worker can no longer challenge the compliance with the information and consultation procedure. However, if objections were made within the thirty-day period, in this case either the employer shall take all appropriate measures to proceed to the dismissal in compliance with the law or the employer believes to have properly fulfilled the obligations and therefore proceeds with the dismissals after the expiry of the thirty-day limit (time during dismiss cannot be made). Within thirty days from the dismissal date or from the date on which the dismissals acquired the character of collective dismissal, the worker can individually challenge the compliance with the information and consultation procedure. Still, if the employee is dismissed within thirty days after the written copy of dismissal was displayed in the company, dismissal is illegal for failure to meet legal deadlines. In this case, the worker can challenge compliance with the information and consultation procedure.

[3] *Civil Sanctions in the Case of Non-compliance with the Information and Consultation Procedure*

Very often, individual dismissals take place within the framework of a collective dismissal. In this case, however, the employer cannot fire an individual worker until the information and consultation procedure has been fully concluded. The law provides for civil sanctions with the objective of neutralising the consequences arising from the dismissal of workers when the information and consultation procedure has not been respected. An individual dismissal may take place with or without a prior notification and with compensation. Two circumstances must be distinguished according to whether the worker who contests the dismissal has been dismissed through prior notification or at the expiry of the employment contract.

(1) When a worker has been dismissed with a prior notification and contests the compliance with the information and consultation procedure, the prior notification, whether already in course or still has to begin, is suspended from the third working day after the worker has informed the employer, through registered mail, that the dismissal procedure has been challenged. This provision obviously applies only if the contestation is legally founded (in case of litigation, the Labour Court shall render a verdict on the legitimacy of the worker's contestation).
Until the employer does demonstrate that all four phases of the information and consultation procedure have been correctly followed, and that the established project of collective dismissal has correctly been notified to the Director of the sub-regional public employment service, the notification remains suspended.
This suspension ends after a sixty-day delay, beginning on the date of the notification of the collective dismissal to the Director of the sub-regional public employment service, in compliance with the legal procedure. These sixty days correspond to the maximum delay (thirty days with an extension of further thirty days) that the employer has to respect before any dismissal. This suspension applies only to the prior notification and does not affect in any way the execution of the employment contract. Consequently, the contract continuous to apply normally, the employer is obliged to provide the agreed work and pay the according allowance. During the suspension of the notice period, the worker is entitled to terminate the employment contract without prior communication nor compensation starting from the notification date that would have expired if the suspension had not intervened. If the employer terminates the employment contract during the suspended period, the employer must reintegrate the worker.

(2) When a worker, whose contract has been terminated with compensation, challenges the compliance with the information and consultation procedure, an explicit demand of reinstatement in the work place must be made to the employer through registered mail. If the contestation is legitimate, the employer must reinstate the worker within thirty days following the third business day after receiving the registered mail. Furthermore, the employer is obliged to pay the worker the lost allowance from the day the contract was terminated. On the other hand, the worker has to return the compensations received after the dismissal. If the employer does not reinstate the worker within thirty days, the employer is obliged to pay the worker, in addition to the compensation for contract termination, a complementary compensation equivalent to the current allowance (in compliance with Article 39 of the law concerning employment contracts adopted on 3 July 1978) covering the period beginning from the day the employment contract was terminated and ending sixty days after the notification to the Director of the sub-regional public employment service. If the employment contract was concluded for a fixed-term or for a specific type of job, the period of compensation shall end, at the latest, on the date of termination indicated on the employment contract.

Bibliography

Books

France Pennings, Yvonne Konijn and Albertine Veldman, SOCIAL RESPONSIBILITY IN LABOUR RELATIONS: EUROPEAN AND COMPARATIVE PERSPECTIVE (2008 Wolter Kluwer).
Hans Arnold, REDUNDANCY LAW IN EUROPE (2008 Wolter Kluwer).
Henrik Hott Larsen and Wolfgang Mayrhofer, MANAGING HUMAN RESOURCES IN EUROPE: A THEMATIC APPROACH (2006 Routledge Taylor & Francis group).
Oliver Wéry, LE DROIT DU LICENCIEMENT COLLECTIF EN BELGIQUE (2010 Wolter Kluwer).
Roger Blanpain, LABOUR LAW IN BELGIUM (2010 Wolter Kluwer).

Articles

Donald Storne, COLLECTIVE DISMISSALS IN BELGIUM, FRANCE, GERMANY AND THE UK: SOME LEGAL, INSTITUTIONAL AND POLICY PERSPECTIVES (2007 MIRE and Institute for Management of Innovation and Technology).

Conventions and Jurisprudence

AFFAIRE RENAULT VILVOORDE-SCHWEITZER (1997-1998).
CONVENTION COLLECTIVE DE TRAVAIL NO 10 DU 8 MAI 1973.
CONVENTION COLLECTIVE DE TRAVAIL NO 24 DU 2 OCTOBRE 1975.
CONVENTION COLLECTIVE DE TRAVAIL NO 5 DU 24 MAI 1971.
COUR DE CASSATION BELGIQUE, ARRÊT N. S000179 N, 04/02/2002.

CHAPTER 3
Collective Dismissals in Bulgaria

Krassimira Sredkova

§3.01 INTRODUCTION

The procedures related to the collective dismissals in Bulgaria are a relatively new legal phenomenon. Their legal regulation is mainly a result of the EU law requirements, since Bulgaria became a Member State on 1 January 2007. This regulation takes into account the requirements of both the EU law and the international legal regulation set forth in the ILO Convention No. 158 of 1982 concerning Termination of Employment at the Initiative of the Employer (even though not ratified by Bulgaria) and Recommendations No. 119 of 1963 and No. 166 of 1982. The law concerning the collective dismissal was promulgated in 1997 with the Unemployment Protection and Employment Promotion Act (later repealed). The case law on these matters is still not extensive. However, collective dismissals are relevant to the Bulgarian society in the situation of profound economic and social changes that started in the 1990s.

§3.02 LEGAL REGULATION OF COLLECTIVE DISMISSALS

The legal regulation of collective dismissals in Bulgarian legislation is provided for in Article 130a and § 1, item 9 of the Supplementary Provisions (SP) of the Labour Code (LC) and in Articles 24-25 of the Employment Promotion Act (EPA).

§3.03 THE COLLECTIVE DISMISSAL: THE CASE

The legal definition of the term 'collective dismissal' is provided in § 1, point 9 SP LC. Under this provision:

'collective dismissal' shall mean the dismissals effected at the employer's initiative for one or more reasons not related to the individual employee concerned, where the number of dismissal is:

(a) at least 10 in enterprises normally employing more than 20 and less than 100 employees during the month preceding the collective redundancies and the redundancies are carried out over a period of 30 days;
(b) at least 10 percent of the number of employees in enterprises normally employing at least 100 but less than 300 employees during the month preceding the collective redundancies and the redundancies are carried out over a period of 30 days;
(c) at least 30 in enterprises normally employing 300 employees or more during the month preceding the collective redundancies and the redundancies are carried out over a period of 30 days;
(d) in case that the employer has dismissed at least five employees within the periods under Litterae (a) to (c), each succeeding termination of an employment relationship which is effected at the employer's initiative for other reasons not related to the individual employee shall be assimilated to the total number of redundancies for the purpose of calculating the number of redundancies under Litterae (a) to (c).

What follows from this definition is that for the term 'collective dismissals', the cumulative presence of four requirements is necessary. They are related to:

(a) *The number of the employees in the enterprise* where the redundancies are effected. It should be not less than twenty employees (arg. § 1, item 9, (a) SP LC). In smaller enterprises the regulation is not applied.
(b) *The grounds for dismissal.* They have two characteristics:
First, the dismissal is effected *'at the employer's initiative'*. This means that it is about a dismissal in the proper sense of this concept – when the termination of the employment relationship is a subjective transformative entitlement of the employer to terminate the employment relationship by a unilateral act. Such grounds are provided for in Article 328 (1) LC. It does not include the grounds on which the employer is obliged to terminate the employment relationship (Article 330 (2) LC) – for example dismissal for breach of discipline.
Second, they are affected *on grounds not related to the conduct of the employee.*
Bulgarian labour legislation establishes explicitly and in a comprehensive manner the grounds for unilateral termination of the employment relationship by the employer (Article 328 and Article 330 LC).[1] Grounds for dismissal, not related to the conduct of the employee are those that are not related with the personality or the conduct of the employee. In the Western European legislations such ground for dismissal are defined as 'economic reasons',

1. *See* Средкова, Кр. *Трудово право. Специална част. Дял I. Индивидуално трудово право.* (Sredkova, Krassimira, *Labour Law. Special Part. I. Individual Labour Law*, 435-462 (University Publishing House 'St. Kliment Ochridski', 2011); Мръчков, В. *Трудово право.* 9. изд. (Mrachkov, Vassil, *Labour Law*, 609-659 (9th ed., Sibi, 2015).

provided for in Article 1 (a) of Directive 98/59/EC. Under the Bulgarian law, the relevant provisions are: closure of the enterprise (Article 328 (1), item 1 LC); closure of part of the enterprise (Article 328 (1), item 2 LC); downsizing of personnel (Article 328 (1), item 2 LC); reduction in the volume of work (Article 328 (1), item 3 LC); upon idling for more than fifteen working days (Article 328 (1), item 4 LC); whereby the position occupied by the employee must be vacated for reinstatement of a wrongfully dismissed employee, who previously occupied the same position (Article 328 (1), item 8 LC); upon change of the requirements for execution of the position, if the employee does not satisfy the said requirements (Article 328 (1), item 11 LC); when performance of the employment contract is objectively impossible (Article 328 (1), item 12 LC).

Dismissal on these grounds shall be done with a notice.

(c) *Number of dismissed employees*. It depends on the size of the enterprise and is determined based on *the number of employees in the month preceding the collective redundancies*. This number shall be: at least ten in enterprises normally employing more than twenty and less than 100 employees; at least 10% of the number of employees in enterprises normally employing at least 100 but less than 300 employees; at least thirty in enterprises normally employing 300 employees or more. The idea is that the redundancies have to affect bigger number of employees.

(d) *The period of redundancies*. It should be relatively short. The law sets it as thirty days. In order to calculate the number of redundancies in this period, the dismissal of any employee shall be added to the total number of redundancies, provided that there were at least five prior redundancies.[2]

§3.04 THE PROCEDURE

[A] Nature

Collective redundancies shall be effected while observing the procedure provided for in the law. It consists of several legal actions that should be implemented prior to effecting the redundancies. Two legal subjects have obligations for implementing the dismissals – the employer and the National Employment Agency (NEA).

2. More about collective redundancies under Bulgarian legislation in **Мръчков, В.** ***Промените в Кодекса на труда и сближаването на българското трудово законодателство с международните норми*** (Mrachkov, Vassil, *The Amendments to the Labour Code and Coordination of Bulgarian Labour Legislation with the International Norms*, **Юридически свят**, issue 2, 147-149 (2004)); **Мръчков, В.** ***Масовото уволнение*** (Mrachkov, Vassil, *The Mass Redundancy*, **Труд и право**, issue 2, Appendix (2009)); **Мръчков, В. Трудово право** (Mrachkov, Vassil, *Labour Law*, 640-644); **Средкова, Кр. Трудово право** (Sredkova, Krassimira, *Labour Law*, 453-455).

[1] Employer's Obligations[3]

[a] Provision of Information

In case of collective redundancies the employer shall be obliged to provide certain information (Article 130a, paragraphs 2-5 LC).

The subject matter of the due information is defined in Article 130a (2) LC. It includes the reasons for the intended redundancies; the number of employees to be dismissed; the number of employees employed in the principal economic activities, groups of occupations and positions at the enterprise; the specific indicators for application of the criteria for the selection of the employees to be dismissed; the period over which the redundancies are to be effected; the compensations due in connection with the redundancies.

The due information should be addressed to:

(a) '*Trade union organisations*'. It indicates all the trade union organisations in the enterprise irrespective of their representativeness.
(b) '*The employees' representatives under Article 7 (2) LC*'. It indicates the persons elected by a General Meeting of the employees, their representatives who represent their interests on issues of employment relationships before the employers.

The representatives of the employees and of the trade union organisations are obliged to make the employees aware of the received information, so that they would be acquainted with the future development of the employment relationships.

[b] Conducting Consultations

Prior to effecting the collective redundancies the employer shall be obligated to also conduct consultations (Article 130a, paragraph 1 and 6 LC).

Subject matter of the said consultations is the measures to prevent or avoid the adverse effects of the dismissal (*see* below §3.04[C]).

Addressee of the obligation for conducting consultations are *the trade union organisations* and *the employees' representatives* under Article 7 (2) LC. They should express the opinion of the employees.

The consultations should be carried out with two categories of representatives – of the trade union organisations and of the employees. Consulting with only one of the categories of representatives is wrongful (Judgement (Judg.) of 19.06.13 on civil case

3. *See* more in Александров, Андр. *Някои практически проблеми в процедурите по информиране и консултиране в случаите на масово уволнение според българското трудово законодателство* (Alexandrov, Andrey, *Some Practical Problems in the Procedures of Information and Consultation in Cases of Mass Dismissal under Bulgarian Labour Legislation*, 363-388 (Jubilee book for Prof. Vassil Mrachkov, ed. Krassimira Sredkova, Trud I pravo, 2015).

(c.c.) No. 163/2013 of Silistra District Court). The case law recognizes that, lacking their trade union organizations and the representatives of the employees, the employer should convene a General Meeting of the employees (Judg. No. 653/2013 on administrative criminal case (a.c.c.) 1152/2013 of Ruse District Court; Judg. of 28.10.13 on a.c.c. of cassation No. 187/2013 of Silistra Administrative Court, etc.).

Consultations are performed in the form of meetings, discussions and search for commonly acceptable solutions to limit the collective redundancies and reduce their effects. Unlike the provision of information where the active role is only for the employer, in consultation both parties have an active role. The procedure and manner of the consultation shall be determined by the parties thereof.

In order to achieve their purpose, consultations should be conducted until a certain deadline prior to the launch of the collective redundancies, which is minimum forty-five days.

[2] Notification of the NEA

The employer should notify the NEA prior to the collective redundancies (Article 130a, paragraph 3 and 7 LC). Addressee of the notification is the local division of the Agency where there is the employer's registered office. The aim is to create a team that should look for means to prevent the redundancies and reduce their adverse effects (*see* below - §3.04[C]).

The employer is obliged to provide a copy of the notification to the representatives of employees and of trade union organisations within three days of its submission to the NEA (Article 24 (4) EPA).

The Support measures in favour of workers.

Pursuant to Articles 24-25 EPA upon receiving a notification for collective redundancies at the local division of the NEA – the Labour Office – forms teams to take the necessary measures to overcome the effects of these redundancies. These teams are the social partnership bodies in the management of labour relations. They involve representatives of the employer, of the municipal administration, of the NEA and of the local division of the National Social Security Institute. The aim is to make joint effort to face the collective redundancies and support the employees concerned, in finding new job placements, vocational training and retraining, etc.

The teams such formed shall conduct negotiations to elaborate draft measures for job-broking in the search for new jobs, for involving employees subject to dismissal into forms of vocational training and retraining, into forms for starting their own business, etc. These measures shall be approved by the Employment Committee and, pursuant to its decision, financing of the said measures shall be provided (Article 25 EPA).

§3.05 JUDICIAL CONTROL AND SANCTIONS

[A] Legal Protection of Wrongfully Dismissed Employee

The termination of employment relationships in Bulgaria is subject to general judicial review. Labour disputes on termination of individual employment relationships fall under the individual labour disputes (Article 357 (1) LC), and individual labour disputes are subject to legal proceedings (Article 360 (1) LC). This refers also to the disputes on collective redundancies.[4]

Each employee, who believes that the termination of his/her employment relationship is wrongful, may request legal protection of his/her right to work. Competent to rule is the District Court of the place of residence, or the location of the registered office of the employer (Article 103 in conjunction with Article 105 of Civil Procedural Code (CPC) or the habitual place where employee works (Article 103 in conjunction with Article 114 CPC). The competent Tribunals in Bulgaria for Labour disputes are the general civil courts.

The employee who believe that his/her dismissal is wrongful would have at his/her disposal four legal actions:

(a) *Legal action for revoking the wrongful dismissal* (Article 344 (1) item 1 LC). The subject matter of the legal action for revoking the wrongful dismissal consists of two cumulatively interrelated claims – for the dismissal to be pronounced wrongful and be revoked. The burden of proof thereof shall rest with the employer since the employer has exercised his right of unilateral termination of the employment relationship (dismissal). Therefore, he should prove the presence of the preconditions for exercising this right and the observance of the relevant procedure (Judg. No. 421/2003 of III civil division (c.d.), No. 1548/2004 of III c.d., No. 76/2005 of III c.d., etc., Supreme Court of Cassation (SCC). Any evidence is admissible – documents, depositions, reports written by technical consultants, etc.
The upholding of this legal action shall have important legal effects:
   (1) The termination of the employment relationship shall be annulled retroactively.
   (2) The period of time between the dismissal and the enactment of the ruling for its revoking shall be considered as the length of the employment service (Article 354 (1), item 1 LC) and social insurance length of service (Article 9 (3), item 2 of the Social Insurance Code – SIC).
   (3) The annulment of the dismissal shall be entered in the workbook of the employee (Article 346 LC). The entry in the workbook is an obligation

4. *See* Средкова, Кр. Трудово право (Sredkova, Krassimira, *Labour Law*, 487-499); Мрълков, В. – В: Мрълков, В., Кр. Средкова, Ат. Василев. *Коментар на Кодекса на труда* (Mrachkov, Vassil, Krassimira Sredkova & Atanas Vassilev, *Commentary to the Labour Code*, 1071-1089 (12th ed., Sibi, 2016).

for the employer and, in case of refusal by the employer to do so, it shall be effected by the Labour Inspectorate.

(4) The employment relationship shall be terminated in case the dismissal is pronounced wrongful (Article 325 (1), item 2 LC).

(b) *Legal action for reinstating to the previous work* (Article 344 (1), item 2 LC)

The subject matter of the proceeding for reinstating the employee consists of three interrelated claims: pronouncing the dismissal wrongful; revoking of the wrongful dismissal; reinstating to work. The burden of proof, such as in the case of annulment for wrongful dismissal, rests with the employer (Judg. No. 981/2004 of III c.d. SCC).

When the judgment is final, the following legal effects occur:

(1) The termination of the employment relationship shall be annulled retroactively.

(2) The period between the dismissal and the entry into force of the judgement for revoking the dismissal, shall be considered as length of employment service (Article 354 (1), item 1 LC) and social insurance length of service (Article 9 (3), item 2 SIC).

(3) The annulment of the dismissal shall be entered in the workbook of the employee (Article 346 LC).

(4) The employment relationship shall be reinstated in the same form that had prior to its wrongful termination. The employee shall be reinstated to the job, he/she used to perform prior to the termination and under the terms and conditions valid at the time of the termination. To that end it is necessary and sufficient for the person reinstated to show up at the workplace within a fourteen-day period from the entry into force of the judgement and declare his/her willingness to continue to perform the job he/she was wrongfully dismissed from (Article 345 (1) LC).

(5) The employment relationship of the employee who has occupied the position after the wrongful termination shall be terminated with a notice (Article 328 (1) item 8 LC).

(6) The reinstated wrongfully dismissed employee is entitled to terminate without notice the employment relationship he/she has taken after his/her dismissal (Article 327 (1), item 8 LC).

The legislation contains important legal guarantees for exercising the right to be restored to the previous position after the wrongful dismissal:

(1) The entitlement to compensation (Article 225 (3) LC). It is due by the employer for a wrongful act performed by him/her (non-admission of the employee to the work he/she was reinstated to), which inflicted a damage to the employee (loss of labour remuneration). The amount of the compensation shall be equal to the damage actually incurred – the gross labour remuneration for the period between the day in which the employee declared his/her willingness to work again to the day of its actual admission to work.

(2) Disciplinary liability. It is imposed on the officials blameworthy for non-admission to work (Article 186 LC). The sanction may be reprimand, warning of dismissal or dismissal for breach of discipline (Article 188 LC).

(3) Administrative penalty liability (Article 413 (2) LC). A culpable failure to enforce a judgement for reinstatement to work is considered an administrative violation of the labour legislation, and in particular of Article 345 (1) LC. The liability shall be imposed to the employer and to the blameworthy officials, unless subject to a severer sanction – for a crime pursuant to Article 172 (2) of the Penal Code (PC) and it takes the form of a fine.

(4) Criminal liability (Article 172 (2) PC). Culpable failure to execute final judgement related to the reinstatement to work has been raised to crime against the citizens' rights and the employer and the blameful officials are criminally liable.

(c) *Legal action for compensation* (Article 344 (1) item 3 in conjunction with Art. 225, paragraphs 1-2 LC).

The subject matter of the legal action for compensation is the actual compensation of the damage suffered by the employee as a result of his/her wrongful dismissal. These damages are expressed in loss of labour remuneration or reduction of the labour remuneration, if the employee has worked in a lower paid job. As ruled by the SCC in Judg. No. 448/1995 of III c.d. the compensation pursuant to Article 225 (1) LC:

> in its natures aims to compensate the damages suffered by the non-defaulting party as a result of the wrongful actions of the other party.

The burden of proof for this compensation rests with the employee. He/she should prove that he/she has remained jobless as a result of the wrongful termination of the employment relationship (Judg. No. 332/2001 of III c.d., No. 298/2002 of III c.d., No. 1323/2003 of III c.d., etc. SCC).

The amount of compensation shall be determined based on two criteria:

(1) Gross labour remuneration of the employee. This is the gross labour remuneration received for the month preceding the month of termination of the employment relationship (Article 228 (1) LC). When the employee has started a different job after the wrongful dismissal, the basis for calculating the compensation is the difference between the two gross labour remunerations – prior to the dismissal and after starting the new job.

(2) The period of suffering the damage. This, as a rule, is the period in which the employee remains jobless or is working at a lower paid job. However, the law sets a maximum limit for this period. It depends on the timing of the wrongfully terminated employment relationship: for an employment relationship of an indefinite duration, the compensation is

due for not more than six months, and for a fixed-term one – until its expiration.

(d) *Legal action for correcting the grounds for the dismissal* (Article 344 (1), item 4 LC).

The legal action for correcting the grounds for the dismissal contests the correspondence between the entries in the documents of the dismissed employee and the actual grounds for terminating the employment relationship – e.g., the cause for dismissal is downsizing of personnel (Article 328 (1), item 2 LC), however the entry says 'reduction in the volume of work' (Article 328 (1), item 3 LC). This is relevant first for the work honour of the employee, but, second, it could have an important legal relevance – for the unemployment benefit, for staring a new job, etc.

The burden of proof for this legal action rests with the employer who has exercised his/her certifying role under the employment relationship.

The legal effect of exercising the legal action is the obligation of the employer to enter what has been established by the Court and change the wording in the workbook of the employee (Article 346 LC). If the employer refuses to do so, this entry is made by the Labour Inspectorate.

It should be emphasized that the Court deals with the legal actions for protection against wrongful dismissal, including in the case of collective redundancies, under the procedure for dealing individual labour disputes. It shall rule on each legal action individually – as a specific case of dismissal irrespective whether collective or individual. Noncompliance with the procedure for information, consultation, etc., in itself does not make the dismissal wrongful.

Examples of the relevant case law of the Bulgarian courts regarding the actions for recognition of a dismissal as wrongful, due to non-observance of some of the elements of the procedure for collective redundancies are Judg. No. 1896/2012 on c.c. 1512/2012 Ruse District Court (Ruse DC), Judg. of 09.06.12 on c.c. No. 12928/2011 Sofia City Court, Judg. of 14.05.14 on c.c. No. 331/2014 Gorna Oriahovitsa District Court. The Courts ruled that the violations of Article 130a LC and Articles 24-25 EPA constitute grounds for administrative penalty liability of the employer, however not for the annulment of the dismissal of the individual employee. As stated by the Sofia District Court in Judg. of 13.06.11 on c.c. No. 39544/2010:

> the obligation of the employer pursuant to Art. 130a of LC to inform and consult employees in case of collective redundancies has no direct relevance for the legality of a particular dismissal and shall not be part of the procedure for individual dismissal (Arg. of § 1, item 9 of SP of LC – collective redundancies are 'not related to the individual employee concerned'). The regulation set forth in the LC and in the Employment Promotion Act procedure in case of collective redundancies has an informative, consultative and supporting (via searching for new jobs) nature with respect to the employees affected by collective redundancies.

[B] Sanctions for Violating the Legal Regulation of Collective Redundancies

The control over the observance of the labour legislation in Bulgaria, included the case of collective redundancies, is exercised by the General Labour Inspectorate (Article 399 LC).[5] The wrongful non-observance of the rules concerning the procedure of collective redundancies is a violation of the labour legislation pursuant to Article 414 LC – violations of labour legislation other than the rules for provision of health and safety at work. For such a violation an administrative sanction shall be imposed – fine for the natural persons, and pecuniary penalty for legal entities and sole traders. This has been persistently recognised in the case law. Judgements No. 1896 of 2012 on c.c. No. 1512/2012 of Ruse DC, Judg. of 09.06.12 on c.c. No. 12928/2011 of Sofia City Court, Judg. of 14.05.14 on c.c. No. 331/2014 of Gorna Oriahovitsa DC, etc., indicate that the violation of the rules for informing and consulting employees pursuant to Article 130a LC, constitute grounds for imposing administrative penalty liability. The same could be said about the violation of Article 83 EPA – non-observance of the obligation to notify the Labour Inspectorate or to undertake collective redundancies prior to the expiration of the thirty-day period following the notification (Judg. No. 377/2013 on a.c. No. 652/2013 of Vratsa DC; Judg. of 14.05.14 on c.c. No. 331/2014 of Gorna Oriahovitsa DC, etc.).

§3.06 CONCLUSION

As indicated in the beginning of this survey, Bulgaria has a short and not very extensive experience in the procedure of collective dismissals. This phenomenon, however, does exist and will continue to exist in the Bulgarian society with its current economic problems. For the Bulgarian scholars, lawmakers and law enforcement authorities it will be very useful to get acquainted with the legal procedures of the other European countries, which have more extensive experience on this matter.

5. *See* Мръчков, В. – В: *Коментар* (Mrachkov, Vassil, *Commentary*, 1150-1152); Мръчков, В. Трудово право (Mrachkov, Vassil, *Labour law*, 947-970).

CHAPTER 4
Collective Dismissal in Croatia

*Vanja Smokvina**

§4.01 INTRODUCTION

The Republic of Croatia became the twenty-eighth European Union Member State on 1 July 2013. This followed a more than ten years of preparation and negotiation process started officially on 21 February 2003 with an application for European Union membership. In these ten years the Croatian legal system was significantly influenced by the European Union acquis (previously acquis communautaire).[1]

The labour law system in Croatia[2] is governed by the Labour Act[3] (LA) which came into force on 7 August 2014.[4] According to Article 2 of the LA, the Act directly transposes the Council Directive 98/59/EC (further: Directive)[5] into the Croatian legal order. However, it will be shown further in the text, the LA lacks some of the Directive's aims. The Directive regulates the minimum standard for collective redundancies, and together with the ILO termination of employment Convention no 158

* This work has been fully supported by Croatian Science Foundation under the project '*Flexicurity and New Forms of Employment (Challenges Regarding Modernization of Croatian Labour Law (UIP-2014-09-9377)*'.

1. *See* Ivana Grgurev, *Croatian Labour Law at EU Accession*, ELLN Working Paper 2/2013, http://www.labourlawnetwork.eu/frontend/file.php?id=495&dl=1 (accessed 10 June 2015).
2. For a complete picture about Croatian labour law system *see* Ivana Grgurev, *Labour Law in Croatia*, Kluwer Law International, 2013.
3. Labour Act, Official Gazette of the Republic of Croatia (further: OG) No. 93/2014 of 30 July 2014.
4. In Croatian the LA since 1995 has been subject to two revisions. Labour Act (1996), OG No. 38/1995, 54/1995, 65/1995, 102/1998, 17/2001, 82/2001, 114/2003, 142/2003, 123/2003, 30/2004, 68/2005, 94/2009; Labour Act (2010) OG No. 149/2009, 61/2011, 82/2012, 73/2013 and Labour Act (2014) OG No. 93/2014.
5. Council Directive 98/59/EC of 20 July 1998 on the approximation of the laws of the Member States relating to collective redundancies, OJ L225/16, of 12.8.1998.

(1982)[6] prescribes just the preconditions for dismissals, which are of procedural nature.[7]

§4.02 THE COLLECTIVE DISMISSAL: THE CASE

The termination of the employment relationship (individual or collective) is always a very important legal, social, psychical and emotional issue especially in a period of economic crisis. In Croatia, in particular a lot of attention is given to redundancies and a big issue is collective redundancies.

The legislative provisions, governing 'collective redundancies' as meaning dismissals, are contained in LA Articles 127 and 128. As in other European Union countries, in Croatia the procedure is very formal (although not completely as prescribed by the Directive). First because the main aim of the special procedure for collective redundancies is to postpone or prevent collective redundancies, taking into consideration employers economic freedom, workers interest for the safety of labour relationship along with the interest of the community in general.[8] In comparison to the previous Labour Acts, the LA actually in force, as it will be shown later on in this paper, has simplified and accelerated the process of collective dismissal, mainly because the employer has no obligation to prepare a redundancy social security plan anymore.[9] With the redundancy social security plan the legal regulations governing collective dismissals were very complex, and this is why the employers tended to avoid this procedure, opting instead for the termination of employment contracts by mutual agreement and severance pay.[10] The redundancy social security plan has not provided to be very useful indeed, but was very complicated and needed a lot of time without a proper positive feedback.[11] In this regard we may say that this is a form of a more flexible approach, but still a bit complex.

Collective dismissal in the Croatian labour law system is defined as follows. The employer who in the period of ninety days might have at least twenty redundancies, out of which at least five employment contracts would be terminated[12] due to business reasons,[13] shall be obliged to begin consultations with the works council in good

6. ILO Termination of Employment Convention No. 158 (1982), Geneva, 68th ILC session (22 June 1982). It is interesting to note that Croatia is the only former Yugoslav country that has not ratified the ILO Convention No. 158. Slovenia, Bosnia and Herzegovina, Montenegro, Serbia and Former Yugoslav Republic of Macedonia have ratified the convention.
7. Sandra Laleta, *Prestanak ugovora o radu*, PhD thesis, Faculty of Law University of Zagreb, 2011, 236.
8. *Ibid.*, 235.
9. LA 2010, Article 121. In this regard *see* Željko Potočnjak, *Najznačajnije novine koje donosi novi Zakon o radu*, 14 HPR 9, 23-24 (2014).
10. Grgurev, *supra* n. 2, at 77.
11. Krešimir Rožman (ed.), *Detaljan Komentar Novog Zakona o radu*, Radno pravo, 2014, 484.
12. In the LA 2010 it was stated 'The employer who intends to have at least 20 redundancies... whose contract would be terminated'. LA 2010, Article 120, paragraph 1.
13. LA, Article 115, paragraphs 2 and 3: When making a decision about a business conditioned cancellation, the employer shall take into account the worker's tenure, age and his maintenance obligations, but this provision shall not apply to employers employing less than 20 workers. It is important to note that this criteria was introduced by the LA 2010.

time[14] and in the manner laid down by the LA, with a view to reaching an agreement aimed at avoiding redundancies or reducing the number of workers affected.[15] These redundancies referred to include the workers whose employment contract is to be terminated due to business reasons and by means of an agreement between the employer and the worker, as proposed by the employer.[16] This means, in line with the Directive provisions, that reasons for such dismissals are not on the workers side (not related to the individual worker)[17] and are not based on a regular notice of employment contract termination (on dismissal on personal grounds, dismissal due to the worker's misconduct or dismissal due to incompetence during probationary period)[18] or by extraordinary notice of the employment contract termination. These two criteria (the number of workers in a ninety-day period and at least five employment contract that would terminate due business reasons) are cumulative.[19] All previously said means that Croatia opted for the second option offered by the Directive[20,21] Just to be clear, if

14. LA, Article 150, paragraph 4.
15. LA, Article 127, paragraph 1.
16. LA, Article 127, paragraph 2. *See also*, LA, Article 151 (Co-decision making):

> '(1) The employer's decisions that may be rendered only with a prior consent of the works council shall include the decisions on:
> 1) dismissing a member of the works council,
> 2) dismissing a candidate for the works council who was not elected, for a period of three months following the establishment of the election results,
> 3) dismissing a worker with reduced capacity for work due to an injury at work or occupational disease and dismissing a disabled person,
> 4) dismissing a worker over 60 years of age,
> 5) dismissing a workers' representative in an employer's body,
> 6) including persons referred to in Art. 34, para. 1 of LA (pregnant woman and person exercising rights during pregnancy, maternity, parental or adoption leave, periods of part-time work, periods of short-time work due to intensified childcare etc.) in collective redundancy, except in cases when the employer has initiated or is conducting liquidation proceedings in accordance with specific provisions.'

17. Laleta, *supra* n. 7, at 239.
18. LA, Article 115, paragraph 1:

> 'The employer shall be allowed to terminate the employment contract for legitimate reasons by giving either the statutory notice or the notice stated in the contract of employment (regular notice of dismissal), in the following cases:
> 1) where the need to perform certain work ceases due to economic, technological or organisational reasons (business conditioned cancellation),
> 2) where the worker is not able to fulfil his obligations from the employment relationship due to his specific permanent characteristics or capacities (dismissal on personal grounds), or
> 3) the worker violates his obligations from the employment relationship (dismissal due to the worker's misconduct), or
> 4) the workers did not satisfy during probationary period (dismissal due to incompetence during probationary period).'

19. Željko Potočnjak, Ivana Vukorepa, *Kritička promišljanja o novom Zakonu o radu*, 10 HPR 1, 15 (2010).
20. Directive, Art. 1(a)(ii)
21. *See also* AG Tizzano Opinion in Case C-52/02, *Commission v. Portugal*, [2004] ECR-I-9387, paragraph 42. Laleta, *supra* n. 7, at 241.

the employer gets into the bankruptcy procedure, the collective redundancies provisions would not apply. Instead, the Bankruptcy Act[22] would be applied.

The criteria of the employer's level (sectoral) organisation for determining the number of workers affected by collective redundancies is not completely clear, even from the Croatian Supreme Court case law. In one decision the Supreme Court said that the number of workers should be determined on the level of every dislocated subsidiary,[23] while in the other decision which concerned the collective dismissal in a district branch school,[24] the Supreme Court said that the number of workers should be determined on the level of the complete school, not just of the district branch school. The author is of the opinion that the Court of Justice of the European Union (furthermore: CJEU) case law reasoning should be taken into consideration in giving an answer to those questions.[25]

To determine that such employment contracts termination was proposed by the employer, as an important criterion, is subject to the hearing of evidence procedure, unless it is stipulated in the notice of dismissal or in the agreement between the worker and the employer.[26] Furthermore, as Laleta rightly points out, it is important to determine the employer's initiative to terminate the contract for collective redundancies procedure and to consider that such dismissals are also constructive dismissals in which the worker terminates the contract because he/she was persuaded by the employer by, for example, saying to the worker that he/she will be transferred to another company or expressly saying to him/her that he/she is planning to make him redundant.[27]

§4.03 THE PROCEDURE

The main feature of the procedural part of the collective redundancies will be elaborated on in this part of the paper, although something has been already said before.

Previously we stressed that the employer, in a case of collective redundancies, is obliged to consult the workers' representatives about such an important decision. The consultation should not be just formal, but a real one with a clear intention while the final outcome of the consultation procedure could be the agreement between the works

22. Bankruptcy Act (Stečajni zakon), OG No. NN 44/1996, 29/1999, 129/2000, 123/2003, 82/2006, 116/2010, 25/2012, 133/2012, 45/2013. *See* particularly Articles 120 and 121.
23. Supreme Court of the Republic of Croatia Judgment No. Revr.18/05 of 9 March 2005 and No. Revr. 667/03 of 11 February 2004.
24. Supreme Court of the Republic of Croatia Judgment No. Revr. 611/04 of 9 Mar. 2005.
25. *See* CJEU case law, C-186/83 *Arie Botzen and others v. Rotterdamsche Droogdok Maatschappij BV.* [1985] ECR-519; C-449/93 *Rockfon A/S v. Specialarbejderforbundet and Danmark* [1995] ECR I-4291; C-270/05 Athinaïki Chartopoiïa AE gegen L. Panagiotidis u. a. [2007] ECR-I-1499; C-182/13 Valerie Lyttle and Others v Bluebird UK Bidco 2 Limited [2015] ECR-I-000; C-392/13 Andrés Rabal Cañas v Nexea Gestión Documental SA, Fondo de Garantía Salarial, [2015] ECR-I-000, C-80/14 *Union of Shop, Distributive and Allied Workers (USDAW) and B. Wilson v. WW Realisation 1 Ltd and Others* [2015] ECR I-000.
26. Rožman, *supra* n. 11, at 485.
27. Laleta, *supra* n. 7, at 247.

council and the employer or a collective agreement.[28] Other important criterion is that the consultation with the works council should begin in good time. The Directive does not determine precisely the time when the consultation should begin, but the CJEU determined in the *Junk Case* that 'the obligations to consult and to notify arise prior to any decision by the employer to terminate the contract of employment'.[29] So, it is in the 'planning phase' that the employer should start the consultation procedure,[30] while the needed 'information can be provided during the consultations, and not necessarily at the time when they start' as the CJEU determined in the *Akavan Case*.[31] As previously said, the Croatian LA, Article 127(1) just says that is to be made *in good time*, while Article 150(4), which deals with the duty to consult the works council in general, says that the complete information related to the proposed decision must be delivered to the works council *in good time*, so as to enable the works council to put forward comments and proposals stemming from the discussion that could have substantial effect on decision making process. To conclude, although the LA does not determine precisely what *in good time* means we should take as relevant the CJEU case law reasoning in the *Junk*[32] *and Akavan Cases*, and consequently define *in good time* in the same way.

In cases in which there is no works council established by workers with their employer, for the consultation procedure the employer shall be obliged to begin consultations with the trade union commissioner,[33] since if no works council has been established with an employer, all the rights and obligations pertaining to works councils under the LA shall be exercised by a trade union's representative.[34] It is from the LA 2003 novelty that the trade union has the right to assume the rights/obligations of the work council in the workers representation procedure.[35] In comparison to the Directive which defines workers representatives as 'workers' representatives provided for by the laws or practices of the Member States'[36] Potočnjak is of the opinion that in such cases, where there is no works council nor trade union, the employer should

28. Željko Potočnjak, *Prestanak ugovora o radu*, 473, (Editor Željko Potočnjak, Radni odnosi u Republici Hrvatskoj, Organizator, Pravni fakultet, 2007).
29. CJEU, C-188/03, *Irmtraud Junk v. Wolfgang Kühnel*, [2005] ECR I-885, paragraph 37.
30. Laleta, *supra* n.7, at 251.
31. CJEU, C-44/08, Akavan Erityisalojen Keskusliitto AEK and Others, [2009] ECR-I-8163, paragraph 52.
32. Laleta is of the opinion that a good option for determining 'in good time' which should be considered and implemented in Croatian law is the British Trade Union and Labour Relations Act (1992), Article 188(7A) which says that the invitation to any of the affected employees to elect employee representatives is important to be issued long enough before the time when the consultation is required by subsection (1A)(a) or (b) to begin to allow them to elect representatives by that time, while the employer shall be treated as complying with the requirements of this section in relation to those employees if he complies with those requirements as soon as is reasonably practicable after the election of the representatives. *See ibid.*, 252-253.
33. Supreme Court of the Republic of Croatia Judgment No. Revr. 141/06 of 12 July 2006. *See also* Supreme Court of the Republic of Croatia Judgment Revr. 805/07 of 28 February 2008, Revr 2032/01 of 22 January 2002 in Rožman, *supra* n. 11, at 498-499.
34. LA, Article 153, paragraph 3.
35. Potočnjak, *supra* n. 27, at 436.
36. Directive, Article 1, paragraph 1.

inform the workers within the 'workers' meeting',[37] where there should be elected workers' representatives who should be consulted in the process of collective redundancies.[38] This is the only open issue left when talking about the implementation of the Directive in the Croatian labour law system. In the past, problematic areas were[39] the Article 2, paragraph 1 of the Directive stating that 'the consultations are to begin with... a view to reaching an agreement',[40] Article 2, paragraph 3(v) 'to notify in writing...the criteria proposed for the selection of the workers to be made redundant...',[41] Article 2, paragraph 3(vi) 'to notify in writing...the method for calculating any redundancy payments'.[42] Taking into consideration that a lot has been done to fully implement the Directive, we could be satisfied in a certain way. More concretely we should be satisfied with the consultation procedure provisions since as Potočnjak points out, those provisions in the LA in force, are in the Directive legal framework.[43] The author agrees but is of the opinion that we just need a few little amendments to completely and properly implement the Directive and to have no ambiguities and misunderstanding, as it was elaborated in the paper.

In order to fulfil the obligation of consultations with the works council, the employer shall be obliged to supply the works council with all relevant information and notify them in writing of the reasons for the projected redundancies, the number of workers normally employed, the number[44] and categories of workers to be made

37. LA, Article 163 'Workers meeting':

> '(1) In order to ensure full scale reporting and discussions on employer's status and development and on activities of the works council, meetings of workers employed with an employer shall be held twice a year, in about equal time intervals.
> (2) If the size of the employer or other particularities require so, meetings referred to in para. 1 of this Article may be held by divisions or other organisational units.
> (3) Workers' meetings referred to in para. 1 of this Article shall be convened by the works council, with prior consultations with the employer, taking into account that the time and place of a workers' meeting do not harm employer's business activities.
> (4) If there is no works council established with an employer, the workers' meetings referred to in paragraph 1 of this Act shall be convened by the employer.
> (5) Not interfering with the right of the works council to convene workers' meetings referred to in paragraph 1 of this Article, the employer may, if he believes it to be necessary, convene a workers' meeting, taking into account that works council's authorities determined by this Act are not restricted.
> (6) The employer shall consult with the works council in regard to convening a meeting referred to in paragraph 5 of this Article.'

38. Potočnjak, *supra* n. 28, at 473.
39. *Ibid.*, 473-474.
40. The obligation to have the consultations with a view of reaching an agreement was introduced with the latest LA from 2014, and was not part of previous provisions. *See* LA, Article 127, paragraph 1.
41. This obligation was introduced by the LA 2010. *See* LA 2010, Article 120, paragraph 2.
42. This obligation was also introduced by the LA 2010. *See* LA 2010, Article 120, paragraph 2.
43. Potočnjak, *supra* n. 9, at 29.
44. 'Just stating the number of workers to be made redundant is not enough to comply with the employers obligation in the consultation procedure, but should be accompanied by other elements and criteria.' Supreme Court of the Republic of Croatia Judgment No. Revr. 240/08 of 17 December 2008.

redundant,[45] the criteria proposed for the selection of the workers to be made redundant,[46] the amount and method for calculating any redundancy payments[47] and other pays to the workers, and the measures designed to alleviate the consequences of redundancy for workers.[48] The author should stress that it is the employers right to internally organize its business, but he has to take into consideration the previously mentioned criteria and methods.[49]

Since in the LA Article 127 no term is expressly established for the works council's feedback, there is an opinion that the works council shall provide the employer with a feedback concerning the proposed decision within eight days.[50] It is the general term, unless otherwise provided by an agreement between the employer and the works council, for a feedback from the works council to the employer when the employer has the duty to consult before rendering an important decision. In case of an extraordinary dismissals the deadline shall be five days.[51] If the works council does not provide its feedback on the proposed decision within those deadline it shall be presumed that it has no comments or proposals.[52]

During the consultations with the works council, the employer shall consider ways and means of avoiding the projected collective redundancies,[53] and this is a new provision compared to the 'old' LA by which the legislator has given a stronger position

45. 'It is the Court opinion that is irrelevant the number of workers employed before the hotel renovation, but relevant is the number of workers present at the time when the preconditions for the termination of employment contracts are met and when the employer has made his decision that is going to make those workers redundant.' Supreme Court of the Republic of Croatia Judgment No. Revr. 545/06 of 4 December 2007.
46. Orešić is of the opinion that 'the criteria proposed for the selection of workers to be made redundant' are the same as the one in the LA Article 115, paragraph 2: 'the worker's tenure, age and his maintenance obligations' and that the employer also may add some additional criteria (such as performance success) which should not be of prevailing importance. Hrvoje Orešić, *Razlika u kriterijima koji se uzimaju u obzir prilikom poslovno uvjetovanog otkaza i otkaza u slučaju kolektivnog zbrinjavanja viška radnika*, Radno pravo 24, 28 (2015). Even the Supreme Court deliberated that 'it is up to the employer to determine other criteria if the employer wants to and it is the employer's autonomous right to determine which criteria would be taken into consideration for collective redundancies and which criteria would be taken more in consideration'. Supreme Court of the Republic of Croatia Judgement No. Revr. 312/07-2 of 22 May 2007, Revr. 23/08 of 9 April 2008 and Revr. 1197/11 of 9 November 2011. Furthermore, those criteria may be determined in a special employer's decision, *see* Supreme Court of the Republic of Croatia Judgment No. (VI/07) Su Ivg, of 11 June 2007.
47. When the employer dismisses the worker following a two-year tenure, and unless dismissal is given due to the worker's misconduct, the worker shall be entitled to redundancy pay in an amount determined on the basis of the worker's tenure with that employer (LA, Article 126, paragraph 1). The redundancy payment could be regulated by the collective agreement or by the agreement between the works council and the employer in a higher amount that the one regulated by the LA (Article 126, paragraph 3: 'Unless otherwise provided for by the law, collective agreement, working regulations or employment contract, may not exceed six average monthly salaries earned by the worker in a period of three months preceding the termination of the employment contract').
48. LA, Article 127, paragraph 3.
49. Supreme Court of the Republic of Croatia Judgment No. Revr. 534/06 of 10 January 2007.
50. Darko Milković, *Prestanak ugovora o radu*, 253 (Editor Hašim Bahtijari, Zakon o radu s komentarima i tumačenjima, TIM press, 2014).
51. LA, Article 150, paragraph 5.
52. LA, Article 150, paragraph 6.
53. LA, Article 127, paragraph 4.

to the work council because there is no employer's obligation to prepare a redundancy social security plan anymore.[54] On the other hand the LA in force has a new provision determining that the employer shall be obliged to supply the works council with the 'measures designed to alleviate the consequences of redundancy for workers'[55] and those measures are a form of substitution for the redundancy social security plan which is not contained in the LA anymore.[56]

Regarding the way of how to count the dates it is important to determine when to start counting the ninety-days' period. According to Croatian doctrine it should be counted from the day of the delivery of notice or the date when the agreement between the worker and the employer determining the termination of the employment contract was stipulated.[57]

Besides the works council, as workers' representative body (or some other body like the trade union, see *supra*), one other very important subject takes its place in the collective redundancies procedure. The employer shall be obliged to notify the competent public authority responsible for employment[58] of the consultations with the works council. The notification shall contain the information on the duration of consultations with the works council, outcomes and conclusions resulting from them, with a statement of the works council attached thereto, should they receive it.[59] The works council may send any comments and suggestions they may have to the competent public authority responsible for employment and to the employer, with regards to the employer's notification,[60] which is also a new provision from 2014 and means that the employer has the obligation to inform the works council about the notification, even though it is not explicitly proscribed.[61] The employer shall be obliged to carry out the consultations with the works council irrespective of whether the decision on collective redundancies is being taken by an undertaking controlling the employer,[62] in accordance with specific provisions.[63]

54. LA 2010, Article 121.
55. Those measures may be determined also by collective agreement. *See* Supreme Court of the Republic of Croatia Judgment No. Revr. 194/09, 3 June 2009. For example, Orešić is of the opinion that one of measure is that the employer cannot place the worker in alternative employment, Orešić, *supra* n. 46, at 29.
56. Rožman, *supra* n. 11, at 487. The Government of the Republic of Croatia in its LA 2014 Draft stated that: 'Giving employer any administrative obligation such as making the redundancy social security plan, since the employer has not have the possibility to decline the termination of employment contracts, does make impossible to the employer to faster the new organisation process in the employer's organisational scheme'. Draft of the LA 2014, RZ.E. No. 606, Croatian Parliament, 7.
57. Rožman, *supra* n. 11, at 485.
58. Croatian Employment Service (*Hrvatski zavod za zapošljavanje*), official site: http://www.hzz.hr (accessed 13 July 2015).
59. LA, Article 127, paragraph 5.
60. LA, Article 127, paragraph 6.
61. Milković, *supra* n. 50, at 253.
62. *See* in this regard Companies Act (*Zakon o trgovačkim društvima*), OG No. 111/1993, 34/1999, 121/1999, 52/2000, 118/2003, 107/2007, 146/2008, 137/2009, 111/2012, 125/2011, 68/2013, Article 475.
63. LA, Article 127, paragraph 7.

Before rendering a decision that is relevant for the position of workers, the employer must consult the works council about the proposed decision and must communicate to the works council the information important for rendering a decision and understanding its impact on the position of workers.[64] The employer shall be obliged to enable the works council to organise meetings, upon their request, and before their final response about the employer's intended decision, in order to obtain additional answers and explanations related to their statement.[65] If the employer does not enable the works council to have such a meeting about the employer's intended decision that would affect the legality of the whole procedure which would then be null and void,[66] *see infra*. It is important to note that the decision about collective redundancies is deemed as an important decision relevant for the position of workers.[67]

Projected collective redundancies notified by the employer to the competent public authority responsible for employment shall take effect not earlier than thirty days after the notification made by the employer to the competent public authority.[68] This means that the employment contracts should not be terminated before the thirtieth day counted from the notification. Workers could be delivered the notice of dismissal before but the termination of the employment contract should be after the thirtieth day.

The competent public authority responsible for employment may, until the last day of the previously stated time limit, at the latest, request the employer to postpone either collective or individual redundancies for a maximum of thirty days,[69] if this can ensure the continuation of employment for the workers during this extended period. Thus, the competent public authority responsible for employment may postpone redundancies only once[70] and for a maximum of sixty days in total. The competent public authority should motivate its reasons to postpone the redundancies (even though it is not explicitly prescribed in the LA) and it should be done in a form of administrative act. It is important to have such reasons be written in a form of administrative act since it in a significant way affects employers constitutional rights (free enterprise rights and freedom to work) which should have an option of judicial protection and control.[71] On the other hand there are also opinions that the employer has no possibility to oppose or take an action against such decision if he thinks the decision is unfounded or without grounds, since, from their point of view, the reasoning should not be written in a form of administrative act, because there is no

64. LA, Article 150, paragraph 1.
65. LA, Article 150, paragraph 2.
66. Željko Potočnjak, *Glavne značajke novog Zakona o radu*, 30 (Editor Marijan Ruždjak, Ogledi o novom Zakonu o radu, Narodne novine, 2010).
67. LA, Article 150, paragraph 3.
68. LA, Article 128, paragraph 1.
69. In the LA 2010 it was stated 'for a period not longer than 3 months'; LA 2010, Article 122, paragraph 5.
70. Opinion of the Ministry of Work and Social Security of the Republic of Croatia, of 12 Mar. 1997, in Potočnjak, *supra* n. 28, at 455. *See also*, Milković, *supra* n. 50, at. 254.
71. Potočnjak, *supra* n. 28, at 455. *See* Constitution of the Republic of Croatia (*Ustav Republike Hrvatske*), OG No. 56/1990, 135/1997, 113/2000, 28/2001, 76/2010, 5/2014, Articles 49 and 55.

such provision determining that.[72] To conclude, it is important to note that the competent public authority has just the right to postpone the redundancies not to change the employer's decision.[73]

§4.04 THE SUPPORT MEASURES IN FAVOUR OF WORKERS

There are few measures designed to support workers in the case of redundancies. Further, some of the most important are described, such as the need for consultations with the works council for a singular dismiss in the collective redundancies procedure, the notice period and severance pay, the right to re-employment for the dismissed worker in the six months' period and the reinstatement for the worker following an unfair dismissal

It is important to note, that irrespective of the outcome of the consultation procedure with the works council, when there was the redundancy social security plan, including cases where the works council gave its support and approved what the employer has decided, the employer was obliged to consult the works council for every single employment contract termination scheduled in the redundancy social security plan. The redundancy social security plan and the decision of dismissal were two different decisions made by the employer, for which the employer needed the consultation with the works council.[74] So, it is a second consultation with the works council, but this time for an individual worker's labour status. Although there is no more redundancy social security plan prescribed by the LA in force, the author is of the opinion that for an individual dismissal made upon the whole collective redundancy procedure prescribed by the LA in its Articles 127 and 128, there should be a second consultation for a singular termination or a contract of employment, this time for every single worker made redundant. It would be useful to suggest, maybe, that since there is no obligation to expressly name the workers who are going to be made redundant, but just the number of workers, the number of categories of workers, criteria and measures, if the employer during the consultation procedure gives the works council and the public authority responsible for employment the list with names of affected worker and when such a list does not get changed after on, the employer has fulfilled its obligation for consultation with the works council for decisions important for the workers.[75] The actual state of LA provisions does not make Croatian labour law system flexible, and for a *de lege frenda* suggestion it would be useful to more precisely elaborate the provisions in this case. But on the other hand this is also a provision which is in favour of workers (*in favorem laboratoris*).

Furthermore, when talking about dismissals, the very important measures to alleviate the period of unemployment and period of new job seek are the notice period and the severance pay. It should be highlighted that the notice period helps the worker

72. Rožman, *supra* n. 11, at 501.
73. Supreme Court of the Republic of Croatia Judgment No. Revr. 263/07 of 5 June 2007. *See also* Grgurev, *supra* n. 2, at 79.
74. *See* County Court in Bjelovar Decision, No. Gž-922/14-2, of 15 May 2014.
75. *See* Supreme Court of the Republic of Croatia Judgment No. Revr. 2032/01-2 of 22 January 2002.

to find a new job after he/she received the decision on the termination of the employment contract. The notice period duration varies depending of the duration of the employment relationship (from two weeks for the worker with less than one year of tenure with the same employer to four months for the worker with twenty years of tenure with the same employer and if the worker reached 55 years of age).[76] Furthermore, the employer shall be obliged to pay compensation and recognise all other rights to the worker released from the obligation to work during the notice period, as if he had worked until the expiry of notice period. During the notice period the worker shall be entitled to be absent from work for at least four hours a week, for the purpose of seeking for new employment.[77]

On the other hand, regarding the severance pay, when the employer dismisses the worker following a two-year tenure, and unless dismissal is given due to the worker's misconduct, the worker shall be entitled to severance pay in an amount determined on the basis of the worker's tenure with that employer. Severance pay for each year of tenure must not be agreed upon or determined in an amount lower than one-third of the average monthly salary earned by the worker in a period of three months prior to the termination of the employment contract. Unless otherwise provided for by the law, collective agreement, working regulations or employment contract, the aggregate amount of severance pay may not exceed six average monthly salaries earned by the worker in a period of three months preceding the termination of the employment contract.[78]

One other kind of protection is the right to re-employment for the dismissed worker. The employer who has dismissed the worker due to business reasons shall not employ another worker at the same post in the period of six months following the date of giving notice of dismissal. Should within such period a need for employment for the same work arise, the employer shall be obliged to offer an employment contract to the worker he has dismissed due to business reasons.[79]

The last measure is the reinstatement of the worker following an unfair dismissal. Where the court establishes that a dismissal was not permissible and that employment was not terminated, it shall order the employer to reinstate the worker. The worker who has challenged the permissibility of dismissal may move the court to issue an interim measure ordering his reinstatement pending a final judicial decision on the merits.[80]

§4.05 JUDICIAL CONTROL AND SANCTIONS

As previously stated, the decision about collective redundancies is deemed as an important decision relevant for the position of workers.[81] It is important to note that a

76. LA, Article 122, paragraphs 1-2.
77. LA, Article 122, paragraphs 4-5.
78. LA, Article 126.
79. LA, Article 115, paragraphs 5-6.
80. LA, Article 124.
81. LA, Article 150, paragraph 3.

decision rendered by the employer contrary to the provisions of the LA governing consultations with the works council shall be null and void,[82] and that according to the Supreme Court of the Republic of Croatia case law those provisions are of *ius cogens* nature.[83] The Croatian doctrine is even of the opinion that the subsequent works council consent could not made such a decision on dismissals valid.[84] So, since such a decision is null and void, the effect of such a decision upon the labour relationship is of the *ex tunc* effect. It means that upon workers demand in the civil law procedure, where the court establishes that a dismissal was not permissible and that the employment relationship was not terminated, it shall order the employer to reinstate the worker.[85]

On the other hand, even if an employer does not consult the works council in the case of collective redundancies (Article 127) which is not per se prescribed as an offence, it is indeed a serious offence. According to Article 228[86] for breaching the Article 150, paragraph 3, a fine shall be imposed on the employer who is a legal person, or on the employer who is a natural person together with the responsible person in the employer who is a legal person, because failing to consult the works council about the issues that he is obliged to consult about in a manner stipulated by Article 150. It is obvious as previously elaborated, that consultation with the works council in the case of collective redundancies is such an obligation.

§4.06 CONCLUSION

In its twenty-five years of independence Croatia has made a lot of progress when talking about the harmonisation with the European Union *acquis*, especially in the labour law system where quite all major amendments of the Labour Act in the last more than ten years due to the harmonisation. Still, there are a few things which could be changed in a better way, mainly to have more clear and unambiguous provisions.

Collective redundancies are one of the most important aspects when talking about the evolution of the Croatian labour law system. In this paper it was demonstrated that, as in other European Union Member States, the procedure for collective redundancies is mostly in line with the Directive. There are still few open issues which are highly imprecise and may open questions of interpretation, and should therefore be

82. LA, Article 150, paragraph 12. *See also* Supreme Court of the Republic of Croatia Judgment No. Revr. 736/04, 29 September 2004.
83. Supreme Court of the Republic of Croatia Judgment No. Revr. 326/04, 27 October 2004 in Potočnjak, *supra* n. 28, at 438.
84. Potočnjak, *supra* n. 28, at 438.
85. LA, Article 124, paragraph 1.
86. LA, Article 228:

> '(1) 1) A fine in an amount ranging from HRK 31,000.00 to 60,000.00 [€ 4,134,00 to € 8,000.00] shall be imposed on the employer who is a legal person for:...
> 23) failing to consult the works council about the issues that he is obliged to consult about in a manner stipulated by this Act (Art. 150),
> (2) An employer who is a natural person and the responsible person in the employer who is a legal person shall be fined in an amount ranging from HRK 4,000.00 to 6,000.00 [€ 533.00 to € 800.00] for an offence referred to in paragraph 1 of this Article.'

made clearer. On the other hand, a clear norm is of extreme importance for the legal certainty, but the economic growth will not be obtained just with impeccable norms. What is needed is a mixture of numerous factors and the labour law rules are one of them.

To conclude, we should always bear in mind that the worker is the weaker party in a labour relationship with an employer and that the norm should protect the worker in a reasonable framework but not in a way to encumber the employer with a lot of administrative duties which do not have a proper reasonable aim but just to postpone something which is a near future. The main aim of the collective redundancies procedure is to find ways and means of avoiding the projected collective redundancies if possible. The author is of the opinion, that the European Union law system and of course the Croatian labour law system should take that road.

References

Draft of the Labour Act 2014, RZ.E. No. 606, Croatian Parliament, 7.

Bankruptcy Act (Stečajni zakon), OG No. NN 44/1996, 29/1999, 129/2000, 123/2003, 82/2006, 116/2010, 25/2012, 133/2012, 45/2013.

CJEU, AG Tizzano Opinion in Case C-52/02, *Commission v. Portugal*, [2004] ECR-I-9387.

CJEU, C-188/03, *Irmtraud Junk v. Wolfgang Kühnel*, [2005] ECR I-885.

CJEU, C-186/83, *Arie Botzen and others v. Rotterdamsche Droogdok Maatschappij BV.*, [1985] ECR-519.

CJEU, C-449/93, *Rockfon A/S v. Specialarbejderforbundet and Danmark* [1995] ECR I-4291.

CJEU, C-270/05, Athinaïki Chartopoiïa AE gegen L. Panagiotidis u. a., [2007] ECR-I-1499.

CJEU, C-44/08, Akavan Erityisalojen Keskusliitto AEK and Others, [2009] ECR-I-8163.

CJEU, C-182/13, *Valerie Lyttle and Others v. Bluebird UK Bidco 2 Limited*, [2015] ECR-I-000.

CJEU, C-392/13, *Andrés Rabal Cañas v. Nexea Gestión Documental SA, Fondo de Garantía Salarial*, [2015] ECR-I-000.

CJEU, C-80/14, *Union of Shop, Distributive and Allied Workers (USDAW) and B. Wilson v WW Realisation 1 Ltd and Others*, [2015] ECR I-000.

Companies Act (*Zakon o trgovačkim društvima*), OG No. 111/1993, 34/1999, 121/1999, 52/2000, 118/2003, 107/2007, 146/2008, 137/2009, 111/2012, 125/2011, 68/2013.

Constitution of the Republic of Croatia (*Ustav Republike Hrvatske*), OG No. 56/1990, 135/1997, 113/2000, 28/2001, 76/2010, 5/2014.

Council Directive 98/59/EC of 20 July 1998 on the approximation of the laws of the Member States relating to collective redundancies, OJ L225/16, of 12 August 1998.

County Court in Bjelovar Decision, No. Gž-922/14-2, of 15 May 2014.

Grgurev Ivana, *Croatian Labour Law at EU Accession*, ELLN Working Paper 2/2013, http://www.labourlawnetwork.eu/frontend/file.php?id=495&dl=1 (accessed 10 June 2015).

Grgurev Ivana, *Labour Law in Croatia*, Kluwer Law International, 2013.

ILO Termination of Employment Convention No. 158 (1982), Geneva, 68th ILC session (22 June 1982).

Labour Act (Zakon o radu 1996), OG No. 38/1995, 54/1995, 65/1995, 102/1998, 17/2001, 82/2001, 114/2003, 142/2003, 123/2003, 30/2004, 68/2005, 94/2009.

Labour Act (Zakon o radu 2010), OG No. 149/2009, 61/2011, 82/2012, 73/2013.

Labour Act (Zakon o radu 2014), OG No. 93/2014.

Laleta Sandra, *Prestanak ugovora o radu*, PhD thesis, Faculty of Law University of Zagreb, 2011.

Milković Darko, *Prestanak ugovora o radu* (Editor Haši Bahtijari, Zakon o radu s komentarima i tumačenjima, TIM press, 2014).

Orešić Hrvoje, Razlika u kriterijima koji se uzimaju u obzir prilikom poslovno uvjetovanog otkaza i otkaza u slučaju kolektivnog zbrinjavanja viška radnika, Radno pravo 24 (2015).

Potočnjak Željko, *Prestanak ugovora o radu* (Editor Željko Potočnjak, Radni odnosi u Republici Hrvatskoj, Organizator, Pravni fakultet, 2007).

Potočnjak Željko, *Glavne značajke novog Zakona o radu* (Editor Marijan Ruždjak, Ogledi o novom Zakonu o radu, Narodne novine, 2010).

Potočnjak Željko, Najznačajnije novine koje donosi novi Zakon o radu, 14 HPR 9, (2014).

Potočnjak Željko, Vukorepa Ivana, *Kritička promišljanja o novom Zakonu o radu*, 10 HPR 1, (2010).

Rožman Krešimir (ed.), *Detaljan Komentar Novog Zakona o radu*, Radno pravo, 2014.

Supreme Court of the Republic of Croatia Judgment No. Revr. 2032/01 of 22 January 2002.

Supreme Court of the Republic of Croatia Judgment No. Revr. 667/03 of 11 February 2004.

Supreme Court of the Republic of Croatia Judgment No. Revr. 736/04, 29 September 2004.

Supreme Court of the Republic of Croatia Judgment No. Revr. 326/04, 27 October 2004.

Supreme Court of the Republic of Croatia Judgment No. Revr. 18/05 of 9 March 2005.

Supreme Court of the Republic of Croatia Judgment No. Revr. 611/04 of 9 March 2005.

Supreme Court of the Republic of Croatia Judgment No. Revr. 141/06 of 12 July 2006.

Supreme Court of the Republic of Croatia Judgment No. Revr. 534/06 of 10 January 2007.

Supreme Court of the Republic of Croatia Judgment No. Revr. 312/07-2 of 22 May 2007.

Supreme Court of the Republic of Croatia Judgment No. Revr. 263/07 of 5 June 2007.

Supreme Court of the Republic of Croatia Judgment No. (VI/07) Su Ivg, of 11 June 2007.

Supreme Court of the Republic of Croatia Judgment No. Revr. 545/06 of 4 December 2007.

Supreme Court of the Republic of Croatia Judgment No. Revr. 805/07 of 28 February 2008.
Supreme Court of the Republic of Croatia Judgment No. Revr. 23/08 of 9 April 2008.
Supreme Court of the Republic of Croatia Judgment No. Revr. 240/08 of 17 December 2008.
Supreme Court of the Republic of Croatia Judgment No. Revr. 194/09, 3 June 2009.
Supreme Court of the Republic of Croatia Judgment No. Revr. 1197/11 of 9 November 2011.

CHAPTER 5

Collective Dismissal in Cyprus

Nicos Trimikliniotis

§5.01 INTRODUCTION

The Republic of Cyprus regulates collective dismissals through a combination of the general law on Termination of Employment and the Cypriot law providing for mass dismissals, N. 28(I)/2001 (herein referred to as the 'Collective Redundancies Law'), enacted prior to accession the of Cyprus to the EU on 1 May 2004 in force since 9 March 2001. As enterprises tend to be small in Cyprus, the possibility of meeting the specifications in dismissing the number of employees required to fall within the definition of *collective dismissals* is rather slim.

Cypriot Labour law derives originally from common law contract principles. It was first developed as a defined area of law with statutory interventions under British colonialism but took its present form with Cypriot independence in 1960 with various statutory provisions that define a distinct area of law, labour or employment law.[1] In the private sector, the competent Court to try unfair dismissals is the Industrial Disputes Court, which consists of a President, appointed by the Supreme Court from a

1. Two new texts have appeared in 2016 which attempt to fill the gap on Cypriot Labour law: Polyviou (2016) and Yiannakopoulou. Until 2016 there was no comprehensive legal textbook on labour law in Cyprus; there are however a number of texts with elements relating to aspects of employment law, particularly in the area of termination of employment. In Greek the basic texts are Antoniou, 2000; Argyropoulou, 2014 and some general or introductory labour law in English. There is a limited body of literature consisting of relevant texts dealing with particular aspects of Labour law and employment, such as Christofi 2000; Ktenas 2010; Trimikliniotis 2012. For aspects related to the employment relationship *see* Trimikliniotis and Demetriou, 2017; new forms of employment *see* Trimikliniotis and Demetriou 2016, Cypriot law of discrimination *see* Demetriou 2015 and free movement of Labour *see* Trimikliniotis 2013. There is some introductory material and resources such as an updated version that summarises the basic provisions in simple, non-technical term is contained in the project funded by the EU Social Fund for Employers Association: ***Τερματισμός της απασχόλησης***, at http://slr.com.cy/wp-content/uploads/2014/05/SLR-Termatismos-tis-Apasxolisis.pdf, *see* OEB 2014a, b, c, d, e, f, g, h.

list of lawyers with at least five years' experience, and two lay members drawn from the employers' associations and the trade unions respectively, both appointed by the President of the Court from a list of names submitted to the Minister of Labour. This Court is not bound by usual rules of evidence and its' decisions may be appealed against at the Supreme Court on a point of law, whilst the Industrial Disputes Court remains the sole arbiter of fact on all cases before it. In the public sector, the labour disputes involving civil servants are dealt with by the Administrative Court.

§5.02 COLLECTIVE DISMISSALS

The legislative provisions governing 'collective redundancies' are contained in the Cypriot law N. 28(I)/2001 was part of the process of the approximation of the laws of the Republic of Cyprus, prior to the accession of the country to the EU in 2004.[2] The issue of collective redundancies and dismissals must be placed in the context of the broader termination of Cypriot Employment Law that sets out the broader framework for legitimate dismissals.

The Termination of Employment Law (Article 22) casts a duty upon an employer who, following a redundancy, wishes to increase again his workforce within eight months from the redundancy to hire back as a matter of priority the employees dismissed upon the redundancy. This duty however is subject to 'the operational needs of the undertaking'.

[A] Redundancies and Dismissal in the Context of Termination of Employment

The Termination of Employment Law N. 24/1967, as amended, defines an employee as any person who works for another under a contract of service or of apprenticeship or under circumstances from which an employment relationship may be inferred. The Court may find that a person falls within the Law's definition of an employee even in the absence of such a contract, if it construes that a relation of employer and employee exists. 'Employer' is to be defined accordingly and includes the government of Cyprus.[3]

In order for an employee to qualify for termination of employment compensation, s/he must be less than 65 years of age[4] and must have been continuously employed by the employer for not less than twenty-six weeks, unless there is a written agreement extending the qualifying period of continuous employment to 104 weeks. The employment relationship is governed by contracts, private or collective, and thus Contract law

2. Most laws, including Labour, were swiftly enacted prior to accession without proper debate or little scrutiny leading up to the eve of accession to the EU.
3. Article 2, Law on Termination of Employment N. 24 of 1967 as amended.
4. An Equality Body decision has criticized this legislative provision and has asked for its revision but no action was taken for its revision by the Attorney General's office yet.

principles apply,[5] which are however supplemented by statutory rights and obligations, primarily to be found in the Termination of Employment Law. This law covers redundancy and arbitrary dismissal of all employees including public employees and was enacted in an effort to transpose Recommendation 119 of June 1963 of the ILO.

In unionized industries, collective agreements have been the norm. Where the employer seeks to terminate a collective agreement, then all three actors of the tripartite system will inevitably be involved: the union(s), the employer and/or the employers' union, and the Ministry of Labour. In the case of private contracts, where an employer seeks to terminate an employee's contract, there is no involvement from any governmental authority. In such a case, the employee is ordinarily left alone to resolve the problem and pursue his/her rights, usually with the assistance of a privately paid lawyer. If the employee is a member of a union, then s/he may request the union's assistance, however there is little that the union can do under these circumstances beyond basic advice to the employee and lobbying the employer. In many services sectors however as well as others such as the agricultural sector, house cleaning and caring as well other services in hotel and catering sector etc., mostly employing migrant workers from third countries[6] and some EU nationals, the basic tools used are private contracts, mostly standard contracts.

The basic rule of termination of employment is that a dismissal is unlawful and therefore gives rise to compensation, if the employer terminates the employment for any reason other than the six legitimate reasons stipulated in Law; one of the legitimate reasons being redundancy.[7] In procedures for termination of employment before the Industrial Disputes Court, there is a presumption that the dismissal was not carried out for any of the legitimate reasons above and the burden of proof is on the employer to prove that the dismissal falls within the above provisions and thus does not give rise to compensation.[8] The law lists a number of specific circumstances which shall *not be*

5. Cypriot employment law consists of Common law (i.e., Court decisions), original derived from general Contract principles, and statutes. Courts only have the power to interpret the law and not rule contrary to any existing statute or create new legislation. 29(1)(c) of the Termination of Employment Law N. 24 of 1967, explicitly notes that the aforementioned statute does repeal or restrict the provisions of the law on Contracts, under Cap. 149 or the principles of Common Law.
6. *See* Trimikliniotis 2010; Trimikliniotis and Demetriou 2011; 2014; 2015.
7. Article 5, Part II of Law on Termination of Employment N. 24 of 1967 as amended. The reasons include: (1) The employee fails to carry out his/her work in a reasonable efficient manner. (2) The employee becomes redundant within the meaning of Part IV of the Termination of Employment Law. (3) The termination is due to an act of God, war rebellion, tempest, destruction of installations by fire not caused by the employer's wilful act or negligence. (4) The contract is for a fixed term and has expired or the employee has reached retirement age as this is fixed by law, custom or contract. In the case of termination because an allegedly fixed contract has expired, the Court may decide that a certain employment relationship is by its nature of indefinite duration in which case termination cannot be justified under this provision. (5) The employee renders himself liable to dismissal without notice. However the employer loses the right to dismiss an employee under this provision when s/he does not exercise this right within a reasonable amount of time from the occurrence of the event giving rise to dismissal. (6) The conduct of the employee is such that it is clear that the employer-employee relationship cannot reasonably be expected to continue (when the employee is guilty of gross misconduct; commits a criminal offence in the course of his duties without the employer's consent; is guilty of immoral behaviour in the course of his duties; repeatedly disregards work rules).
8. Article 6(1), Law on Termination of Employment N. 24 of 1967 as amended.

deemed as falling within the legitimate reasons for dismissal.[9] The length of notice that an employer must give to an employee depends on the employee's length of continuous service:[10]

- one week for a worker employed continuously for 26-52 weeks;
- two weeks for a worker employed continuously for 52-104 weeks;
- four weeks for a worker employed continuously for 104-150 weeks;
- five weeks for a worker employed continuously for 105-208 weeks;
- six weeks for a worker employed continuously for 208-259 weeks;
- seven weeks for a worker employed continuously for 260-311 weeks;
- eight weeks for a worker employed continuously for 312 or more weeks.

Notice time is paid by the employer who may require the employee to accept payment in lieu of notice. No notice (or payment in lieu of notice) needs to be given for employees under probation. Probation should not exceed twenty-six weeks, unless there is a written agreement concluded at the time of the commencement of the employment extending probation to a maximum of 104 weeks. Dismissal for redundancy is justified only on the following grounds:[11]

- The employer has ceased or intends to cease to operate the business where the employee is employed.
- Modernization or other change in the method of production or organization that necessitates a reduction in the number of employees.
- Change in the products, the method of production or the expertise required by the employees;
- Abolition of a specific department.
- Difficulties in placing products on the market or credit difficulties.
- Lack of orders or lack of raw materials.
- Shortages in the means of production.
- Contraction in the volume of work of the business.

ILO Convention No. 158 is also relevant. Article 13 of the ILO Convention No. 158 provides for the obligation of the employer intending to dismiss personnel for economic, technological, structural or other reasons, to provide the necessary information and opportunity to the workers' representatives for consultation on measures to limit the unfavourable impact of the dismissal, including the search for alternative employment. This provision has been repeatedly invoked by the Courts in order to justify their decisions declaring a number of redundancies unlawful, by reason of the employer not having consulted with the trade unions in order to find a milder solution. Interestingly,

9. As per Article 6(1), Law on Termination of Employment N. 24 of 1967. These include membership in a trade union or in a committee for safety at work; acting as a workers' representative or seeking to acquire such an office; bona fide submission of a complaint against the employer alleging violation of civil or criminal legislation; race, colour, gender, family status, religion, political belief, ethnic origin, social descent; pregnancy or motherhood; taking parental leave or leave for reasons of force majeure,
10. Article 9(1), Law on Termination of Employment N. 24 of 1967 as amended.
11. Article 18, Law on Termination of Employment N. 24 of 1967 as amended.

some of the Court cases in question concerned the dismissal of one employee and not collective dismissals or dismissals affecting a certain percentage of the personnel, as provided by Article 13.2 of the Convention. Prior to accession to the EU, in two 1994 cases, the dismissals of two journalists from a newspaper on the ground of redundancy were deemed unlawful because there was no consultation with the trade unions.[12] During the same year the redundancy of another journalist was deemed unlawful because the same employer did not prove the reasons for redundancy, but the Court referred to Article 13 of the ILO Convention No. 158, pointing out that its provisions had not been complied with by the employer.[13] Also, when one of the two largest confederations of trade unions ('SEK') dismissed its chief accountant on the ground of redundancy after fourteen years of service without prior consultation with his representatives, which was the Trade Union of Private Employees, the Court found the dismissal unlawful for this reason, stating that the very reason of existence of SEK required strict compliance with Article 13 of the ILO Convention.[14]

There is a practice that establishing the principle of 'last in first out' in the case of redundancies. Also, section 22 of the Termination of Employment Law casts a duty upon an employer who, following a redundancy, wishes to increase again his workforce within eight months from the redundancy to hire back as a matter of priority the employees dismissed upon the redundancy. This duty however is subject to 'the operational needs of the undertaking'. There is no provision in national law for 'social selection'. To the extent that it is relevant, Article 28(2) of the Constitution guarantees the enjoyment of economic, social and cultural rights by all persons without any discrimination on the grounds of, inter alia, social descent, birth, wealth or social class, therefore discrimination on these grounds is prohibited.

Under Article 7 of the ILO Convention No. 158 and in accordance with case law, an employee has the right to be heard before dismissal on the ground of misconduct or as a result of complaints filed against him. Failure on the part of the employer to grant to the dismissed employee the right to be heard may result on declaring the dismissal unlawful.[15] Under the principles governing redundancies in Cyprus, dismissals aiming at reducing the workforce are allowed but it is for the employer to prove that the preconditions for redundancy are met; if the preconditions are not met, then the dismissals are unlawful and give rise to compensation. A redundant employee loses the right to compensation if s/he declined an offer from the employer for suitable alternative employment.

12. *Dinos Theodorou et al v. Telegraphos Publishing company and Redundancy Fund*, 404/94 and 501/94.
13. *Antonis Michaelides v. Telegraphos Publishing company* 159/94.
14. *Polykarpos Aspromallis v. SEK* 274/94.
15. *Demetris Toumazou v. Andreas Prokopiou Ltd* 880/97; *Michalis Constantinou v. Panart Ltd* 415/95; *Panayiotis Panayiotou v. Kings Head Development Co. Ltd* 719/93.

[B] Collective Dismissal in the Context of 75/129/EEC

In 2001 in the run up to accession, significant changes were introduced to regulate collective redundancies with the legislative provisions contained in the Collective Redundancies Law 28(I)/2001. However, the specific law does not state that it purports to transpose Directive 98/59/EC for harmonizing legislation enacted prior to Cyprus' accession to the EU.[16] The Cypriot law on Collective Redundancies the Collective Redundancies Directive by verbatim copying the working of the directive in the relevant law. It must be noted that overall, there has been no debate on the subject, despite the fact that there has been one important Supreme Court decision in 2003, which will be discussed further on in this chapter.[17]

Article 2 of the *Collective Redundancies Law* 'competent authority' means the Minister of Labour and Social Insurance; 'representatives of the employees' means the representatives of any employees provided for by legislation or practice and 'workers' representatives' means the workers' representatives provided for by legislation or practice. The law defines Article 2 of the *Collective Redundancies Law* defines 'collective dismissals' as dismissals for one or more reasons unrelated to the employees in person where the number of employees dismissed within a thirty-day period is as follows:[18]

- at least ten employees where the organization employs usually more than twenty but fewer than 100 employees, provided that for the purpose of calculating the number of redundancies referred to above, all individual

16. Ο Περί Ομαδικών Απολύσεων Νόμος του2001 (28(I)/2001). There is an unofficial translation of the law provided by the Ministry of Labour and social Insurance at http://www.mlsi.gov.cy/mlsi/dlr/dlr.nsf/All/6956D7065BF32400C2257A800021165A/$file/Law%2028(I)2001%20-%20Collective%20Redundancies.pdf?OpenElement.
17. *UNITED HOTELS (LORDOS) LTD* v. *ΑΝΔΡΟΥΛΑΣ ΣΤΑΥΡΟΥ ΚΑΙ ΑΛΛΩΝ* (Case No. 301 and others) and *LORDOS HOTELS (HOLDINGS) LTD. v. ΓΙΩΡΓΟΥ ΓΟΥΑΣΕΦ ΚΑΙ ΑΛΛΩΝ*, (Case No. 301 274 and others), Appeal civil Case No. 11234, (2003) 1 Α.Α.Δ. 515, 21 April 2003, available at http://www.cylaw.org/cgi-bin/open.pl?file=apofaseis/aad/meros_1/2003/rep/2003_1_0515.htm&qstring=%28%EF%EC%E1%E4%2A%20and%20%E1%F0%EF%EB%F5%F3%2A%29%20and%20%28Lordos%29
18. The Greek text reads as follows: '«ομαδικές απολύσεις» σημαίνει απολύσεις που γίνονται από τον εργοδότη για έναν ή περισσότερους λόγους, οι οποίοι δεν έχουν σχέση με το πρόσωπο των εργοδοτουμένων, εφόσον ο αριθμός των απολύσεων ανέρχεται μέσα σε χρονικό διάστημα 30 ημερών- (α) Τουλάχιστο σε 10, σε επιχειρήσεις που απασχολούν συνήθως περισσότερους από 20 και λιγότερους από 100 εργοδοτουμένους: Νοείται ότι για τον υπολογισμό του αριθμού των απολύσεων που προβλέπονται ανωτέρω, προς τις απολύσεις εξομοιώνονται όλοι οι τερματισμοί της σύμβασης εργασίας οι οποίοι επισυμβαίνουν στους κατ' ιδίαν εργοδοτουμένους τους οποίους αφορούν, υπό την προϋπόθεση ότι οι απολύσεις είναι τουλάχιστο πέντε, (β) τουλάχιστο σε δέκα τοις εκατόν (10%) του αριθμού των εργοδοτουμένων, σε επιχειρήσεις που απασχολούν συνήθως τουλάχιστον 100 και λιγότερους από 300 εργοδοτουμένους, και (γ) τουλάχιστο σε 30, σε επιχειρήσεις που απασχολούν συνήθως τουλάχιστο 300 εργοδοτουμένους.

contracts of employment which terminate by reason of simple expiry shall be included, if the number of actual redundancies is at least five;
- at least 10% of the number of employees in undertakings which normally employ at least 100 and fewer than 300 employees; and
- at least 30, in undertakings, which normally employ at least 300 employees.

However there are a number of exclusions and exceptions to the application of the law. Article 5 of the Law explicitly stipulates that this Law shall not apply:

(a) to any collective redundancies effected in relation to contracts of employment made for a specific period of time or for a specific task, unless such redundancies are made prior to the expiry or prior to completion of these contracts;
(b) in relation to persons employed by the government, by semi-governmental organizations, by local authorities and by legal entities governed by public law; and
(c) In relation to crews of sea-going vessels.

No case has ever been reported as regards the implementation of the collective redundancies since accession to the EU. Overall, there has been no debate on the subject and no case has gone before the court as regards any of the provisions of this law. Enterprises tend to be smaller and family-run in Cypriot context; with the exception of publically owned corporations and the governmental in general few are larger, mainly in the field of banking, education and services and light industry sector. In general, trade unions report an overall lack of mechanism to oversee implementation as is the case with most of the labour law directives.

In the wake of accession to the EU, the Supreme Court dealt with the subject of redundancies in the leading case of *Lordos Holdings*,[19] which was decided unanimously. The case involved an appeal by two hotel owning companies against a decision of the Employment Disputes Court. In 1999 the management of the two companies (the employer) dismissed fifty employees, mainly maids and cleaners on the grounds of redundancy, as Article 9(1) και 18(c) Law on Termination of Employment (24/67). The employees were notified in writing in the same month of the intention to dismiss them on the grounds of redundancy, deemed necessary in the context of modernization of the firm as well as due to changes in the organizational method, production and operation of the business. In the letter to employees, the employer referred to the following changes:

19. *UNITED HOTELS (LORDOS) LTD* v. *ΑΝΔΡΟΥΛΑΣ ΣΤΑΥΡΟΥ ΚΑΙ ΑΛΛΩΝ* (Case No. 301 and others) and LORDOS HOTELS (HOLDINGS) LTD., v. ΓΙΩΡΓΟΥ ΓΟΥΑΣΕΦ ΚΑΙ ΑΛΛΩΝ , (Case No. 301 274 and others), Appeal civil Case No. 11234, (2003) 1 Α.Α.Δ. 515, 21 April 2003, available at http://www.cylaw.org/cgi-bin/open.pl?file=apofaseis/aad/meros_1/2003/rep/2003_1_0515.htm&qstring=%28%EF%EC%E1%E4%2A%20and%20%E1%F0%EF%EB%F5%F3%2A%29%20and%20%28Lordos%29 The unanimous judgement was delivered by judge Nikitas.

(a) The operation of housekeeping, the cleaning of the kitchen and public space would be subcontracted to professionals.
(b) The Health Club would be sublet.
(c) The confectionary section would be closed down and the goods would be bought from outside.
(d) Certain posts would be abolished.

The dismissal resulted in strike action. The dismissed employees sought legal remedy in the Labour Disputes Court (LDC) for unlawful termination of employment. At first instance the LDC awarded damages in lieu of dismissal for failure to give proper notice. It is noted by the Supreme Court that the dismissal for the same reasons had started from 1993.

The appellant employer argued that the Court misconstrued Articles 14 and 15 of the Convention 158 concerning Termination of Employment at the Initiative of the Employer,[20] which regulates the behaviour of the employer in relation to consultation with workers' representatives when the possibility of dismissal and notice of intent of a competent authority. The Supreme Court considered that the essence of Article 14 of the Convention is that it requires the employer to lay off staff, for reasons of technological or structural, two obligations: (1) to give promptly to the workers' representatives the relevant information, which is again determined; and (2) provide in accordance with national legislation and practice timely opportunity for representatives for consultation in relation to the measures to be taken. The stated purpose is to limit the consequences of such a measure. Article 14 imposes similar obligations on an employer who intends to proceed with layoffs for the same reasons, in accordance with national law and practice. The first instance court found that the employer did not comply with the above procedures, explaining how and why. Despite the fact that at the time there was no national legislation governing the subject of negotiation, the LDC stressed that the importance established practice, which was also laid out by the Industrial Relations Code apply (herein referred to as 'the Code'). The Court specifically mentioned Part III of the Code, which regulates the practice of intended dismissal of employees.[21] The Supreme Court approved the approach taken by the LDC which emphasized that the failure to respect of Articles 13 and 14 of the Convention, as well as those of the Code does not automatically mean that the dismissals were unlawful. The Supreme Court quotes the LDC:

> However, such non-compliance, showing prima facie, that the redundancies were not justified regardless of any statutory requirements and whether it is a procedural matter. See *Williams v. Compare Maxam Ltd.* [1982] 1 R.L.R. 83), which is mentioned in the book *Redundancy Law & Practice* [1983] Colin Boum p. 214.

20. Ratified by Law no. 45 του 1985, **Ο περί της Συμβάσεως περί του Τερματισμού της Απασχολήσεως (Κυρωτικός) Νόμος του** 1985. *Cyprus Gazette*, no. 2053 31 May 1985.
21. According to paragraph 1 (a), the employer is under obligation to notify the intention to proceed with layoffs two months before the implementation of the intent. Especially when mass layoffs are desirable to provide greater notice period is to be made, depending on the circumstances specified. The Code refers to the same provision in ILO Recommendation 119 and relevant European Union Directive.

At first instance, the court concluded based on the facts that the employer with the attitude showed that he did not want to negotiate; in reality the notification of the trade unions took place simultaneously with the performance of redundancy notices. It also found that when deciding to abolish the relevant departments the fate of the workers was never considered in the least. As for the operational needs in the housekeeping department, these did not decrease but remained unchanged. Neither did cleaning needs, nor methods change. It was apparent to the Court that the appellants sought to reduce labour costs, in order to satisfy shareholder demands for higher profits. The Supreme Court rejected that the argument by the appellants that the case *Williams v. Compare Maxam Ltd.* is irrelevant. Also it rejected the complaint that the first instance court used the phrase 'collective redundancies' adopted before the enactment of Collective Redundancies Law. The Supreme Court reasoned that the objective consideration of the question whether there is dismissal due to redundancy is not limited to the mere finding that an existing part of the business has ceased. The employer's actions cannot be separated from the surrounding circumstances as this was a single event. The Supreme Court cited the English case of *Hindle v. Percival Boats Ltd.* [1969] 1 All E.R. 836 as an authority for the purposes of the reorganization. Redundancy *does not depend* on how the employer himself describes his act. In *Hindle*, the court observed that the question was

> purely objective in the sense that the test to be applied concerns the actual requirements of the business and not the opinion of employers or anyone else on that point', Bourn Redundancy Law and Practice, (1983) p. 136.

The Supreme Court approved the LDC construction that Articles 13 and 14 of the Convention as well as the relevant elements in the Code of Industrial Relations, which likewise only corroborated the court's broader reading on redundancy. The case of Williams, as quoted in the excerpt of the text *Labour Law Text & Materials*:[22]

> In considering whether the decision of an industrial tribunal is perverse in a legal sense, there is one feature which does not occur in other jurisdictions where there is a right of appeal only on a point of law. The industrial tribunal is an industrial jury which brings to its task a knowledge of industrial relations both from the view point of the employer and the employee. Matters of good industrial relations practice are not proved before an industrial tribunal as they would be proved before an ordinary court: the lay members are taken to know them. The lay members of the industrial tribunal bring to their task their expertise in a field where conventions and practices are of the greatest importance. Therefore in considering whether the decision of an industrial tribunal is perverse, it is not safe to rely solely on the common sense and knowledge of those who have no experience in the field of industrial relations. A course of conduct which to those who have no practical experience with industrial relations might appear unfair or unreasonable, to those with specialist knowledge and experience might appear both fair and reasonable: and vice versa.

A number of other cases have gone before the Labour Dispute Courts, which have followed the *Lordos* decision above.

22. Paul Davies & Mark Freedland (eds.), *Labour Law Text & Materials* (2nd edition 1984).

§5.03 THE PROCEDURE

The procedure stipulated broadly follows the procedure outlined in the Directive.

[A] The Right to Consultation and Information

Article 4 of the Collective Redundancy Law imposes an obligation on any employer who intends to make any collective redundancies 'to consult in good time with the workers' representatives with a view to reaching an agreement'. This is an obligation to notify and engage in consultations with employee representatives as soon as possible and in good faith in order to reach a settlement agreement.[23] The content of the consultation is defined, as stipulated by the Directive:

> (2) These consultations shall, at least, cover the following matters -
> (a) Possible measures to prevent any collective redundancies or to reduce the number of the employees who would be affected; and
> (b) Ways and means for easing the adverse consequences arising from such collective redundancies, through social measures, for example the re-employment or re-training of dismissed employees.

The employer must also give notice to the minister of labour and social insurance of any proposed redundancies at least one month before the intended date of termination. Notice to employee representatives and the minister of labour and social insurance must be given on a standard form and include:

- the reasons for any proposed collective dismissal;
- the number and description of the employees to be made redundant;
- the total number of employees and the description of employees normally employed at the establishment;
- the period during which the proposed redundancies will take place;
- the criteria for selecting employees for dismissal; and
- the calculation method for any redundancy payment other than payments provided by law that govern the termination of employment.

Notice must be given to employee representatives as soon as possible in order to reach a settlement agreement. Notice to the minister of labour and social insurance must be given at least one month before the intended date of termination. When an employer contemplates collective redundancies, she is obliged to consult with employee representatives with a view to reaching an agreement within a reasonable timeframe. Consultations must at least cover the following:

- possible ways of avoiding collective redundancies or reducing the number of affected employees; and
- ways of mitigating the consequences of redundancies using social measures that involve redeploying or retraining redundant employees.

23. *See* CJEU Case C-188/03, *Irmtraud Junk v. Wolfgang Kühnel*.

Further, collective redundancy law provides that there must be a minimum of thirty days from the date that the employer gives notice before the redundancy can legally take effect.

Article 5(1) provides that 'in order that the workers' representatives may put forward any constructive proposals', the employer 'in good time' is obliged, during such consultations:

(a) give to the workers' representatives all useful information; and
(b) notify them in writing of:
   (i) the reasons for the intended redundancies;
   (ii) the number and categories of employees to be made redundant;
   (iii) the number and category of employees normally employed by the employer;
   (iv) the period over which such redundancies will be made;
   (v) the criteria he intends to use for selecting any employees to be made redundant, which are determined as a responsibility of the employer by legislation or practice; and
   (vi) the method for calculating any possible payment as a result of any redundancies, other than payments payable under the Termination of Employment Laws of 1967-1994.

Also, Article 5(2) stipulates that an employer shall furnish the competent authority with a copy of the particulars referred to in subparagraphs (i)-(v) of paragraph (b) of subsection (1) above.

There is an obligation on the employer to notify the Competent Authority in writing of any intended collective redundancies the soonest possible, under Article 6(1). With the proviso that 'in the case of any intended collective redundancies caused by the interruption of the activity of the undertaking as a result of a judicial decision, the employer shall be required to notify the Competent Authority in writing only if the Competent Authority so requests.' It is stipulates that the notification shall contain every relevant information in relation to the intended collective redundancies and the consultations with the workers' representatives, as per Article 6(1). The obligation that specific information is provided. In particular, the reasons for the intended collective redundancies the number of employees to be made redundant, the number of employees normally employed and the period over which the redundancies will be made. Also Article 6(3) provides that the employer shall forward to the workers' representatives a copy of any notifications he/she gives under subsection (1) above, and those representatives may submit their observations to the Competent Authority.

It is stipulated in Article 7.1 that the obligations referred to in sections 4, 5 and 6 of this Law shall apply whether a decision for collective redundancies is taken by the employer himself or by another undertaking which controls the employer. Failure by the undertaking which decided that collective redundancies to make the requisite information to the employer concerned is explicitly no defence to an employer, in any investigation into any alleged contravention of the obligations relating to the provision of information, consultations and notifications (Article 7.2).

The Thirty-day Period

There must be a minimum of thirty days from the date on which the employer provides information to employee representatives and the Ministry of Labour and Social Insurance about the redundancies and the date of intended termination. Article 8.1 provides that any intended collective redundancies which have been notified to the competent authority in accordance shall be put into effect after the expiration of the period of thirty days commencing on the day of providing such notification. This subject to the provisions governing the rights of any employees as to the length of notice required to be given for the termination of their employment. The competent authority, i.e. the Ministry of Labour, is called upon to utilize use the thirty-day period in order to seek solutions to the problems which may arise from any intended collective redundancies (Article 9). Excluded from the above provisions are any collective redundancies caused by the interruption of the activity of the undertaking concerned as a result of a judicial decision (Article 10).

§5.04 SUPPORT MEASURES IN FAVOUR OF WORKERS

To date, Cyprus has no system in place for support measures in favour of workers, other than the general provisions for redundancy.

§5.05 JUDICIAL CONTROL AND SANCTIONS

The Collective Redundancies Law, Article 11 provides for sanctions and for judicial control. It is stipulated that any information disclosed in order to comply with the provisions of this Law shall be regarded as confidential (Article 11.1) and any person not complying with the confidentiality rule, shall be guilty of an offence and shall be liable, on conviction, to a fine not exceeding CYP 1,000, that is, EUR 1,700 (Article 11.2). It is stipulated in the Law the rights of employees to compensation in accordance with the provisions of the Termination of Employment Laws Nothing was not prejudiced by the operation of the Collective Redundancies Law.

There are also criminal sanctions provided. An employer who contravenes any of the provisions of section 4, 5 or 6 in relation to information, consultation and notification, shall be guilty of an offence and shall be liable, on conviction, to a fine not exceeding one thousand pounds. Also when collective redundancies are made before the expiration of the period of thirty days referred to in section 8, the employer shall be guilty of an offence and shall be liable, on conviction, to a fine not exceeding CYP 2,000, that is, EUR 3,417.

§5.06 CONCLUSIONS

Cyprus is facing the results of the economic crisis, which combines, global, EU and national aspects. It is a country in heavy private and public debt and a banking system in crisis. Despite some signs of stabilization as macroeconomic figures indicate, this cannot be said to be the case when it comes to the social indicators. The construction industry is at a standstill, the banking system is shaky; there is still mass unemployment, emigration abroad and thousands of workers have been laid off. In this context, it is essential that the law on redundancy and dismissal operate effectively and smoothly to protect worker rights. Research shows that employment rights have suffered from systemic, policy and legal failures as result of the employers exploiting the weak position of trade unions and the vulnerability of individual workers.[24] The courts seem unable to cope with the sheer numbers of cases before them; the vast majority never reach the court. Oddly enough few Court cases have been decided specifically on mass redundancies. Unfortunately, little public debate has taken place to discuss the failures of the system and how to improve it to address possible abuse of redundancies in Cyprus.

Bibliography

Antoniou, M. (2000) Το *Δίκαιο Τερματισμού της Απασχόλησης στην Κύπρο* [The Law Relating to the Termination of Employment in Cyprus], Ομοσπονδία Εργοδοτών και Βιομηχάνων (ΟΕΒ), Industrial Relations and Labour Law Department.

Argyropoulou, V. (2014) 'Εργατικό Δίκαιο', in Sinodinou, T. E. (ed.) *Κυπριακό Ιδιωτικό Δίκαιο - Κατ άρθρο ερμηνεία – Νομολογία*, Sakoulas, Athens, pp. 551-679.

Christofi, C. (2000) 'Employment', Campbell, (ed.) *Introduction to Cyprus Law*, Neocleous & co., Limassol, at http://www.neocleous.biz/en/download/ebook/neobook.pdf.

Demetriou, C. (2015a) *Report on measures to combat discrimination directives 2000/43/EC and 2000/78/EC, Cyprus Country report 2015, State of affairs up to 1st January 2015, drafted for the European Network of Legal Experts in the Non-discrimination field on the grounds of Race or Ethnic Origin, Age, Disability, Religion or Belief and Sexual Orientation*, to be published.

Demetriou, C. (2015b) *The impact of the crisis on fundamental rights across Member States of the EU - Country Report on Cyprus*, project led by Milieu, commissioned by the LIBE Committee of the European Parliament. Available at http://www.europarl.europa.eu/RegData/etudes/STUD/2015/510017/IPOL_STU(2015)510017_EN.pdf.

Ktenas, N. (2010) 'Employment', Campbell, (ed.) *Introduction to Cyprus Law*, Neocleous & co., Limassol, pp. 991-1015.

OEB (2014a) Εγχειρίδιο Λειτουργού Εργασιακών Σχέσεων: ΒΑΣΙΚΗ ΕΡΓΑΤΙΚΗ ΝΟΜΟΘΕΣΙΑ, funded by the EU Social Fund for Employers Association: Τερματισμός της απασχόλησης, at http://slr.com.cy/wp-content/uploads/2014/05/SLR-Termatismos-tis-Apasxolisis.pdf.

OEB (2014b) Εγχειρίδιο Λειτουργού Εργασιακών Σχέσεων: ΤΕΡΜΑΤΙΣΜΟΣ ΤΗΣ ΑΠΑΣΧΟΛΗΣΗΣ, Εγχειρίδιο για τις πρόνοιες του περί Τερματισμού της Απασχόλησης Νόμου του 1967 στο οποίο συμπεριλαμβάνεται και σχετική

24. *See* Demetriou 2015b; Trimikliniotis, N. and Demetriou, C. (2016).

νομολογία, funded by the EU Social Fund for Employers Association: Τερματισμός της απασχόλησης, at http://slr.com.cy/wp-content/uploads/2014/05/SLR-Termatismos-tis-Apasxolisis.pdf.

OEB (2014c) Εγχειρίδιο Λειτουργού Εργασιακών Σχέσεων: ΕΠΙΛΥΣΗ ΕΡΓΑΤΙΚΩΝ ΔΙΑΦΟΡΩΝ – ΚΩΔΙΚΑΣ ΒΙΟΜΗΧΑΝΙΚΩΝ ΣΧΕΣΕΩΝ, ΟΥΣΙΩΔΕΙΣ ΥΠΗΡΕΣΙΕΣ, ΔΙΑΙΤΗΣΙΑ, funded by the EU Social Fund for Employers Association: Τερματισμός της απασχόλησης, at http://slr.com.cy/wp-content/uploads/2014/05/SLR-Termatismos-tis-Apasxolisis.pdf.

OEB (2014d) Εγχειρίδιο Λειτουργού Εργασιακών Σχέσεων: ΚΟΙΝΩΝΙΚΗ ΑΣΦΑΛΙΣΗ, funded by the EU Social Fund for Employers Association: Τερματισμός της απασχόλησης, at http://slr.com.cy/wp-content/uploads/2014/05/SLR-Termatismos-tis-Apasxolisis.pdf.

OEB (2014e) Εγχειρίδιο Λειτουργού Εργασιακών Σχέσεων: ΑΣΦΑΛΕΙΑ ΚΑΙ ΥΓΕΙΑ ΣΤΟΥΣ ΧΩΡΟΥΣ ΕΡΓΑΣΙΑΣ, funded by the EU Social Fund for Employers Association: Τερματισμός της απασχόλησης, at http://slr.com.cy/wp-content/uploads/2014/05/SLR-Termatismos-tis-Apasxolisis.pdf.

OEB (2014g) Εγχειρίδιο Λειτουργού Εργασιακών Σχέσεων: ΙΣΟΤΗΤΑ ΣΤΗΝ ΑΠΑΣΧΟΛΗΣΗ ΚΑΙ ΚΑΤΑΠΟΛΕΜΗΣΗ ΤΗΣ ΣΕΞΟΥΑΛΙΚΗΣ ΠΑΡΕΝΟΧΛΗΣΗΣ ΣΤΟ ΧΩΡΟ ΕΡΓΑΣΙΑΣ, funded by the EU Social Fund for Employers Association: Τερματισμός της απασχόλησης, at http://slr.com.cy/wp-content/uploads/2014/05/SLR-Termatismos-tis-Apasxolisis.pdf.

OEB (2014h) Εγχειρίδιο Λειτουργού Εργασιακών Σχέσεων: ΕΡΓΑΤΙΚΕΣ ΠΟΛΙΤΙΚΕΣ ΚΑΙ ΚΑΛΕΣ ΠΡΑΚΤΙΚΕΣ, funded by the EU Social Fund for Employers Association: Τερματισμός της απασχόλησης, at http://slr.com.cy/wp-content/uploads/2014/05/SLR-Termatismos-tis-Apasxolisis.pdf.

Polyviou, P. (2016) Η Σύμβαση Εργασίας, Chysafinis & Polyviou, Nicosia.

Trimikliniotis, N. (2013) *Report on the Free Movement of Workers in Cyprus in 2012-2013, National Expert Report for the European Network on Free Movement of Workers within the European Union coordinated by the University of Nijmegen's Centre for Migration Law under the European Commission's supervision*, available at http://works.bepress.com/nicos_trimikliniotis/41/.

Trimikliniotis, N. (2012) *Social and employment situation in Cyprus*, Briefing Note requested by the European Parliament's Committee on Employment and Social Affairs (IP/A/EMPL/NT/2012-001 July 2012 PE 492.43) http://www.europarl.europa.eu/committees/fr/studiesdownload.html?languageDocument=EN&file=75691.

Trimikliniotis, N. and Demetriou, C. (2016) 'New Forms of Employment in Cyprus', Bernd Waas (ed.) *New Forms of Employment in the EU*, Wolters Kluwer International publications.

Trimikliniotis, N. and Demetriou, C. (2017) 'The Employee Concept in Cyprus', Bernd Waas and Marta Otto (ed.) *Restatement of Labour Law in Europe New Forms of Employment in the EU*, Kluwer publications (co-authored with C. Demetriou).

Yiannakopoulou, S (2016) *Κυπριακό Εργατικό Δίĩκαιο*, Nomiki Bibliothiki, Athens.

CHAPTER 6

Collective Dismissal in the Republics of Czech

Lubomír Ptáček

§6.01 LEGAL REGULATION AT THE EU LEVEL

Collective redundancies are regulated at the EU level by the Council Directive 98/59/EC of 20 July 1998 on the approximation of the laws of the Member States relating to collective redundancies (the 'Collective Redundancies Directive' or the 'Directive'). The Collective Redundancies Directive codified previous Council Directive 75/129/EEC of 17 February 1975 on the approximation of the laws of the Member States relating to collective redundancies and related legislation.

The Collective Redundancies Directive aims to improve protection for workers in the case of collective redundancies. It requires employers to consult staff representatives, and it specifies the points which these consultations must cover. The Directive establishes the procedure for collective redundancies, including the obligation of the employer to notify the competent public authority, stipulates when the collective redundancy takes effect, etc.

§6.02 CASE LAW OF THE COURT OF JUSTICE OF THE EU

The Court of Justice ('the Court') has interpreted the Collective Redundancies Directive on numerous occasions. Recently, in judgment of 9 July 2015, Case C-229/14 *Ender Balkaya v. Kiesel Abbruch – und Recycling Technik GmbH*, the Court interpreted the term 'employer' used in the Directive. The Court also lately dealt with the meaning of 'establishment' (judgment of 30 April 2015, Case C-80/14 Union of Shop, Distributive and Allied Workers (USDAW), *see also* judgment of 13 May 2015, Case C-182/13 *Valerie Lyttle and others v. Bluebird UK Bidco 2 Limited*). In addition, the Court examined, for instance, whether the Collective Redundancies Directive had any application to the closure of US military bases (judgment of 18 October 2012, Case C-583/10 *United States of America v. Christine Nolan*); it interpreted the provisions on the obligation of employers to consult staff representatives (judgment of 3 March 2011, Joined Cases C-235/10 - 239/10, *David Claes and others v. Landsbanki Luxembourg SA*; judgment of 10 September 2009, Case C-44/08 *Akavan Erityisalojen Keskusliitto AEK ry and others v. Fujitsu Siemens Computers Oy*; judgment of 16 July 2009, Case C-12/08 *Mono Cas Styling SA, in liquidation, v. Dervis Odemis and others*), or the concept of 'redundancy' and the time at which the redundancy takes effect (judgment of 27 January 2005, Case C-188/03 *Irmtraud Junk v. Wolfgang Kūhnel*).

§6.03 REFLECTION OF THE REGULATION OF COLLECTIVE REDUNDANCIES AT EU LEVEL IN THE CASE LAW OF THE SUPREME COURT OF THE CZECH REPUBLIC

The provisions of the Collective Redundancies Directive have been implemented in the Czech legal order in Articles 62-64 of the Labour Code (Act No 262/2006, Coll.).

The case law of the Supreme Court on collective redundancies deals only marginally with the Directive. In most cases, the appellants dispute in their extraordinary appeal the lower courts' interpretation of relevant terms in the (old) Labour Code (Act No 65/1965 Coll., where the collective redundancies were laid down in Article 52), and at the same time refers to the purpose and wording of the Collective Redundancies Directive. For instance, the judgments of the Supreme Court of 15 April 2010, No 21 Cdo 2243/2009, and of 15 July 2008, No 21 Cdo 3013/2007, concerned the interpretation of term 'competent labour office' in Article 52 (3), 52 (4) and 52 (6) of the old Labour Code. In both cases, the appellant disagreed with the legal opinion of lower courts, according to which the competent labour office may be any labour office, and claimed that it follows from the Directive that the competent labour office should be determined according to the plaintiff's place of residence or place of work. The decision of the Supreme Court of 14 October 2009, No 21 Cdo 3558/2008, and related decision of the Constitutional Court of 25 February 2010, No III. ÚS 1535/08, dealt with the same legal issue. In the latter decision, the Supreme Court found that the employer may notify in writing of projected collective redundancies and forward a copy of written communication with the workers' representatives to any labour office.

Likewise, the Supreme Court interpreted the national implementing provisions in judgments of 18 October 2006, No 21 Cdo 2985/2005, and of 8 November 2007, No 21 Cdo 189/2007. More specifically, it dealt with the provision governing the continuation of the employment relationship after notifying the competent labour office about the collective redundancies (Article 52 (4) of the old Labour Code, which had its origin in Article 4 (2) of the Directive). In interpreting this provision, the Supreme Court took into account the purpose of the rule in question, which is to provide the responsible state authorities with certain amount of time to find appropriate solutions to problems arising from collective redundancies and to protect the affected employees.

CHAPTER 7

Collective Dismissal in Denmark

Mette Klingsten

§7.01 THE COLLECTIVE DISMISSAL

[A] The Danish Collective Dismissals Act

Denmark became a member of the European Union in 1973 and the original Directive 75/129/EEC was based on a Commission proposal put forward by the Commission of the European Communities immediately prior to the UK, Ireland and Denmark acceding to the European Economic Community. As a result of the Council's discussions about the proposal for a council directive, which took place after Denmark had become a member of the European Economic Community, the actual requirements stipulated in the Directive were significantly reduced compared to the original proposal.[1]

As is generally known, the Directive contains three main principles governing collective dismissals. These have remained unchanged since 1975 and which remains the essence of the EU legislation on this topic:

(i) Private companies which employ more than twenty workers ('employees') and which contemplate dismissing a significant number of their employees within a short period of time for reasons not related to the individual(s) concerned are required to start a consultation process with the employees or their representatives with a view to reaching an agreement and with the aim of avoiding or limiting the contemplated dismissals.

1. The Economic and Social Committee made a statement (doc 323/72), cf. the Official Journal of the European Communities C100/73, page 11, which contained comprehensive comments on the proposal for the directive. The European Parliament delivered a statement which was published in the Official Journal of the European Communities C19/73, page 10.

(ii) A competent national authority must be informed of the situation and of the progress and outcome of these negotiations (the consultation process).
(iii) The planned collective dismissals can be effective thirty days, at the earliest, after having notified the competent authority.

The Directive contains two alternative thresholds as regards the number of contemplated dismissals. When Denmark implemented the directive in 1977,[2] one of these alternative thresholds was chosen, and the notification rules consequently apply when an employer or a public authority, for reasons not related to the individual(s), contemplate the dismissal within a thirty-day period of the following:

- at least ten people in establishments normally employing more than twenty[3] and less than 100 employees;
- at least 10% of the number of employees in establishments normally employing at least 100 but less than 300 employees;
- at least thirty people in establishments normally employing 300 employees or more.

This model was considered to be the most appropriate because of the Danish industrial structure which includes many small and medium-sized companies. These thresholds are more employer-friendly than the other threshold requirements as they only pay regard to the number of contemplated dismissals over a thirty-day period. On the other hand, they are more far-reaching as they apply to the dismissals of as few as ten employees in small employing entities.

In some ways, the Danish regulations go further than the directive's minimum requirements (gold plating), seeing that the Danish rules also include dismissals in the public sector, which is not the case under the directive.

The original directive did not apply to collective dismissals effected in connection with a company ceasing its activities as a result of a judicial decision, bankruptcy/insolvency etc. Following the introduction of Directive 92/56/EEC, insolvency cases were, in general, covered by the directive, although member states were not obliged to apply Article 3 concerning the procedure for collective dismissals in connection with collective redundancies arising from, inter alia, the termination of an establishment's activities as a result of a judicial decision.

The Danish Act provides that some of the provisions do not apply in case of the termination of an employer's activities as a result of a judicial decision. The exception set out in the Act concerning termination of an employer's activities due to a judicial decision has been drafted to the effect that it only includes insolvencies and reconstructions in accordance with the rules set out in the Danish Bankruptcy Act.

2. Act No. 38 of 26 January 1977.
3. The number of employees normally employed is calculated as an average of the four most recent preceding quarters. Every employee is included for the purpose of the calculation without having regard to their working hours, meaning that a part time employee is, for the purpose of the calculation, included as one employee, cf. section 4 of the Computation Statutory Order (Statutory Order No. 1558 of 23 December 2014).

Directive 92/56/EEC required a revision of the Danish rules, and it was therefore decided to transfer the regulation of collective dismissals to a separate Act,[4] colloquially referred to as the 'Collective Dismissals Act' or just the 'Notification Act'. The Act was approved on 1 June 1994 and came into force on 24 June 1994. This is only relevant with respect to collective dismissals. At the same time, specific 'stricter notification requirements' were introduced in Denmark although these did not come into force until 1 July 1996. The stricter notification requirements are specific Danish rules which are not laid down in the directive. These rules are explained in more detail in section 0.

The main aim of the Danish Collective Dismissals Act is to protect the employees. The notification rules – by reference to the obligations arising under EU law – must ensure that a consultation process is commenced as soon as possible so as to find ways and means of avoiding the dismissals or reducing the numbers of these, and of mitigating the consequences of the dismissals. In addition, the relevant authorities (the Regional Labour Market Council) must be given the opportunity to find solutions to any problems created by the dismissals in the region where the employing entities are based.

[B] Implementation under a Collective Agreement

Like other directives from the beginning of the 1990s, Directive 92/56/EEC enables the labour market's parties to implement the provisions of the directive by means of collective agreements.[5] A specific provision in section 1(5)[6] of the Collective Dismissals Act states that the Act does not apply to the extent that the employer is subject to similar obligations under a collective agreement as compared to those set out in the Act. By way of example, the Directive was implemented by Appendix 6 to the Industrial Agreement (*Industriens Overenskomst*) and Appendix 15 to the Collective Agreement for Salaried Employees in Industry (*Industriens Funktionæroverenskomst*). Insofar as any dismissals are covered by these collective agreements, then the rules in these collective agreements apply and not the Act. When a collective agreement, as opposed to the Act, is the relevant legal basis, then this will have an impact on the applicable compensation, procedures etc.

[C] Faroe Islands and Greenland

The Collective Dismissals Act does not apply to the Faroe Islands or to Greenland.

In connection with Denmark's membership of the European Economic Community taking effect on 1 January 1973, the Faroese home rule administration decided that

4. Act No 414 of 1 June 1994 – The Danish Collective Dismissals Act. The most recent changes to the Collective Dismissals Act are set out in Consolidated Act No 291 of 22 March 2010.
5. According to Article 288 TFEU a directive shall be binding, as to the result to be achieved, upon each Member State to which it is addressed, but it is left to the national authorities to decide on the choice of form and methods.
6. Consolidated Act 2010-03-22 No 91 – Collective Dismissals Act.

the Faroe Islands did not wish to become a member of the European Economic Community. The Danish accession as a member state of the European Economic Community did therefore not include the Faroe Islands. Forming part of the Danish Kingdom, Greenland was originally a member of the European Economic Community. After Greenland was given home rule in 1979, and following a referendum, Greenland decided to leave the European Economic Community with effect from 1 February 1985. The Faroe Islands and Greenland are therefore not obliged to implement any EU directives. There are no rules or regulations equivalent to the rules in the directive or the Collective Dismissals Act in either the Faroe Islands or in Greenland.

[D] Danish Terminology

[1] Employees

The text of the Danish directive uses the term 'employed persons' (in Danish: *arbejdstagere*') to describe the individuals protected by the Directive.[7] The Danish Act uses the term 'employees' (in Danish: *lønmodtagere*). The terminology used in the Collective Dismissals Act did not intend to amend the protected group of individuals under the directive. The term 'employee' is just a more commonly used term in Danish employment law as compared to the term 'employed person'. The terms 'employed person', 'employee' and 'employed' are typically used as synonyms in Danish employment law.

Employment law terminology often uses the term 'hourly paid' or 'employees employed on salaried employee terms' to describe individuals who do not carry out salaried employee work (*funktionærarbejde*).[8] It is not uncommon for the term 'hourly paid' to be used irrespective of whether the employee actually receives a monthly salary.

When the directive has been implemented in a collective agreement and the collective agreement is used instead of the Act, it is as a starting point relevant to differentiate between a salaried employee (*funktionær*) and an hourly paid individual, seeing that the two categories of employees are typically subject to different collective agreements. The reason is that the consultation process for these two types of employees is principally carried out by reference to two different sets of rules.

The distinction between 'workers' and 'salaried employees' is further used in Danish Terminology. The Collective Dismissals Act covers both 'hourly paid individuals' and 'salaried employees' and no distinction should be made between the different groups of employees as regards the Act. 'Genuine' directors and consultants who carry out self-employed work are not, however, covered by the regulatory framework.

7. The term used in the directive in English is 'employees'.
8. 'A "salaried employee" (*funktionær*) is a person performing a contract of service and who is employed to do trade or clerical work or perform a labour management role for a minimum of 8 hours (average) per week.'

[2] *Termination of Employment*

The Danish version of the directive uses the term 'termination of employment'. The definition of the term collective dismissals, as set out in Article 1 (1) (a) of the directive, solely includes 'such terminations of employment which occur on the employer's initiative for one or more reasons not related to the individual employee concerned'. The Collective Dismissals Act similarly provides that the Act applies in connection with 'terminations of employment' which are 'contemplated by an employer for one or more reasons which are not related to the individual employee concerned...'.

The term 'termination of employment' is ordinarily synonymous with a 'dismissal' and is typically used to describe circumstances where the employer terminates the employment by giving such notice as required by law or contract. The 'termination of employment' terminology is also synonymous with 'dismissal' with regard to the Collective Dismissals Act.

The reason for an employer's termination of an individual's employment may be related to the employer's circumstances, by way of example cost-cutting measures or a restructuring process. These are the core aspects covered by the Collective Dismissals Act.

A dismissal can also be due to reasons related to the employee him/herself, by way of example an employee's lack of capability, an employee's failure to comply with guidelines covering the way in which work should be carried out, or a failure to comply with internal guidelines in connection with the employer's IT policies, alcohol policies etc. If the employee commits a repudiatory breach of contract, it is open to the employer to choose to terminate the employment contract without the giving of notice, meaning that the employee is required to leave immediately and that the obligation to pay any further salary ceases.[9]

Cases where an employer terminates or rescinds the employment contract due to reasons related to the individual employee should not be included in the calculation of the number of (contemplated) dismissed employees. This is due to the wording of section 1(1) of the Act. The Collective Dismissals Act does not provide any further clarification on how cases should be treated if the employer dismisses the employee unfairly or if the rescission of the employment contract is unjustified. Further information is set out in section 4.

[3] *The Employer*

Article 1(1)(a) of the directive provides that the directive first and foremost applies to collective dismissals effected by an 'employer'. Section 1(1) of the Act similarly provides that the Act applies in connection with dismissals which are contemplated by an 'employer'.

Generally, the term 'employer' should be interpreted as the natural person or legal entity having the power to exercise control over the employees, and the power to

9. Cf. by way of example section 4 of the Danish Salaried Employees Act.

effect the dismissals. This will typically be the company (natural person or legal entity) having employed the employee in question, or the public authority which is employing the individual insofar as it concerns dismissals within public administration. The directive and the Act also apply in circumstances where the decision to effect the dismissals are made by a parent company etc., cf. section 1(3) of the Act (Article 2(4) of the directive).

An employer is obliged to comply with the requirements to inform and consult even though the decision to make the collective dismissals has not been made by the employer, but e.g. by a company with the controlling influence over the employing entity, e.g. a parent company.[10]

[4] The Company (Establishment)

The Danish version of the directive uses the term 'company' but the directive does not contain a further definition of how the term 'company' (establishment) should be construed. The term is used in connection with the calculation of the number of employees to be made redundant, seeing that the application of the rules depends on whether a specified number of employees, as compared to the company's overall number of employees, are to be dismissed over a certain period of time.

The term 'company' is also not further defined in the Collective Dismissals Act, but the Order on the computation of the number of employees pursuant to the Collective Dismissals Act etc. in connection with collective dismissals (the 'Computation Regulations')[11] contains input on how the term 'company' should be interpreted as a matter of Danish law. Having regard to this, it is evident that both private and public entities authorized to effect dismissals are covered by the rules. The regulations further include a review of the circumstances in which smaller entities can make up a company (an employer).

[5] Establishment (Place of Work)

Determining the place of work (establishment) is important in order to determine whether the increased notification rules apply. The increased notification rules are aimed at dismissals effected by large entities which are of crucial commercial- and employment-related importance to the local community. Further details are set out in section 2.7 below. Section 2 of the Collective Dismissals Act provides that an 'establishment' should be interpreted as a 'unit' of the employer's business and in which one or more of the employer's employees are employed. If the employer has more than one establishment within one municipality, then these establishments are considered as one joint establishment.

10. Case No. C-44/08, Akavan Erityisalojen Keskusliitto AEK ry and others v Fujitsu Siemens Computers Oy concerning an employer's duty to inform and consult. The decision also contains guidelines on when the information and consultation process with the employees in the subsidiary should be carried out.
11. Statutory Instrument No. 1558 of 23 December 2014.

If an employer has several local units/establishments (e.g. shops, workshops, bank branches, police stations, crèches, kindergartens or nursing homes), then regulation 2(1) of the Computation Regulations provides that that these should be considered as one establishment to the extent that they are situated in the same labour market council region. If the dismissals in a local unit have reached the limits set out in section 1(1)-(3) of the Act, then the individual local unit is, however, to be considered as the employer who is required to comply with the procedures set out in the Act, cf. regulation 2(2) of the Computation Regulations.

§7.02 THE PROCEDURE

The rules set out in the Collective Dismissals Act must be complied with if the amount of dismissals set out in section 1.1 is contemplated within thirty consecutive days (running days).[12] The computation must be made when the employer intends to make the dismissals, and not on the effective date of termination.

If the employer has several divisions in different geographical locations, then the number of individuals ordinarily employed must be calculated separately for each of the divisions if the divisions are situated in different labour market council regions.[13] Even if the employing entity forms part of a group company which has several group companies, the companies cannot be considered to be one joint unit, irrespective of the fact that the companies may have entities in the same labour market council region. This also applies if the companies are ultimately controlled by the same owner.

[A] Notice Periods

The Collective Dismissals Act does not regulate the employees' notice periods, and Denmark does not have a universal statutory minimum notice period. Notice periods vary in the different workplaces, but it is very common for notice periods to increase in line with an employee's period of continuous employment. In addition, it is required that an employee's individual employment contract set out the rules governing notice periods.

The Salaried Employees Act contains the following statutory notice periods: one month' notice to dismiss a salaried employee before the expiry of the employee's five month of employment, three months' notice to dismiss a salaried employee before the expiry of two years and nine months of employment, four months' notice to dismiss a salaried employee before the expiry of eight years and seven months of employment, and six months' notice to dismiss a salaried employee following eight years and seven

12. This is calculated as thirty running days, irrespective of a turn of the month. This means, by way of example, that if an employer who has approximately fifty employees dismiss five people on 12 October, three people on 22 October and one person on 2 November, then an additional five people can be dismissed on 11 November without the need to comply with the collective dismissal rules.
13. Denmark has eight regional labour market councils: RAR Northern Jutland, RAR Western Jutland, RAR Eastern Jutland, RAR Southern Jutland, RAR Funen, RAR Zealand, RAR Capital and RAR Bornholm.

months of employment. If the parties have agreed on a probationary period, then the employer's notice period must be fourteen days during the first three months of employment.

[B] The Selection of Employees to be Dismissed (Selection for Redundancy)

In Denmark an employer is, in general, free to dismiss its employees. In general, the employer will therefore assess whether the dismissals are needed and, if so, which employees should be dismissed. In some circumstances there is, however, an exception to this rule because of certain employment law provisions and also due to individual and collective agreements.

When selecting employees for redundancy, one ought to consider whether there are any employees with specific protection against dismissal. This could, by way of example, be shop stewards/employee representatives, work environment representatives, pregnant employees, employees who are on maternity/parental leave etc. However, for practical purposes, an employer will primarily consider the company's needs following the restructuring, rather than social considerations vis-à-vis the individual employee.

Generally, it will be considered fair to have regard to a combination of criteria such as the length of service, qualifications, ability, job flexibility, sickness absence, previous warnings and the reduction of high-cost employees. Generally speaking, the criteria must, however, be looked at as a whole and they will depend on a specific assessment.

Before dismissals are made, an employer furthermore ought to consider whether there is any way of avoiding the dismissals, or some of them, by relocating/redeploying employees to other duties or jobs, e.g. following a brief period for re-training/upgrading of skills. There is a more far-reaching obligation to seek to redeploy/relocate employees to other duties/jobs when dealing with long-serving employees or employees who are of advanced age.

The Collective Dismissals Act does not set out specific sanctions if the criteria used for one or more of the dismissals turn out to be unfair. The determining factor for any sanction, including the award of any compensation, is consequently whether this is warranted by any other legislation, collective agreement or any other contract. *See* further section 0.

[C] Information Given to the Employees: Section 6 of the Collective Dismissals Act

An employer will need to prepare written documentation for the purpose of the consultation processes (about the contemplated dismissals) with the employees or the employee representatives. As a minimum, the following information should be provided:

- The reasons for the contemplated dismissals. This could, by way of example, be due to cutbacks for financial reasons or a restructuring process in connection with a change of ownership etc.
- The number of employees normally employed and the employees whose dismissals are being contemplated, and also which categories they belong to. This could, by way of example, be done by grouping into semi-skilled employees, administrative personnel and academics, or it could be done by means of a grouping into hourly paid employees, salaried employees and managers.
- The time frame (period) during which the dismissals are to be effected. This could, by way of example, be stated to be during the next month.
- The criteria intended to be used for the selection of the employees to be made redundant. This could, by way of example, be all the employees in a certain department, the employees who have the shortest length of service or any employees who do not have the required qualifications or the required flexibility as regards the work which needs to be carried out in future. It is important that the criteria do not breach the rules in e.g. the Danish Employment Non-discrimination Act (*forskelsbehandlingsloven*) or the Danish Equal Treatment Act (*ligebehandlingsloven*).
- Information about whether there are any employees who are entitled to redundancy payments, and if so, how these are to be calculated.

The information must be given to the employee representatives before the consultation is initiated. The documentation will, in practice, often not be very comprehensive.

Management can call on the employees to elect representatives if they have not already elected employee representatives/shop stewards or any other representatives to represent the employees. There are no specific rules governing how the representatives should be elected, but it should be done in a satisfactory manner and the representatives must be able to represent all the affected employees. Insofar as employee representatives have not already been elected, such representatives could be elected in a 'town hall meeting', by email or in any other satisfactory (reassuring) manner. Steps should be taken in advance to ensure that the proposed candidates are willing to accept the election. If any employees insist on the vote taking place in writing and by means of a secret ballot, then this should be generally accepted.

The relevant regional labour market council(s) must receive a copy of the written material received by the employee representatives. Communication with the regional labour market council can take place by ordinary post or by email.

[D] Consultation: Sections 5 and 7 of the Collective Dismissals Act

When the employees or their representatives have received the written information material, then the consultation process with the employee representatives should begin. The purpose of the consultation should be to reduce the number of contemplated dismissals. It could, by way of example, be relevant to discuss a deal to reduce the number of employees to be made redundant, a pay cut for all employees during a transitional period, the options to be retrained/redeployed etc.

In actual practice and if no way out of the redundancies can be found, then the consultation can be more in the nature of a process of providing information and clarifying any matters of dispute in connection with the contemplated dismissals.

The employee representatives must be given the opportunity to make their views known during the consultation. If no way of avoiding the redundancies can be found other than dismissing the necessary number of employees, then the consultation process can be relatively short, but the consultation must have been meaningful whatever happens.

Minutes of the consultation meetings should be drawn up to document that a genuine consultation process has actually taken place between the employee representatives and the management. It is recommended that there is a note of the people who participated in the meetings and the questions and solutions discussed by the parties. The regional labour market council must be notified in writing of the outcome of the consultation, including whether the employer can reduce the number of contemplated dismissals or whether the employer insists on the planned number of dismissals. Insofar as the stricter notification requirements apply, then a different procedure applies. The rules governing this are described in section 0.

Pursuant to section 5 of the Act, the consultation process typically lasts for two to three weeks, except in circumstances where the stricter notification requirement rules apply. During the consultation process it is common for the management and the employee representatives to enter into framework agreements regulating the employees' terms and conditions in connection with the dismissals. A further description is set out in section 0.

[E] Notification to the Regional Labour Market Council – Section 7 of the Collective Dismissals Act

Within ten days of the regional labour market council having been notified and informed of the consultation process (pursuant to sections 5 and 6), the regional labour market council must also be informed of the identities of the individuals to be dismissed, cf. section 7(3) of the Collective Dismissals Act. The notification can also be given on the day when the consultation process ends. Finally, and pursuant to section 7(4) of the Collective Dismissals Act, the employer must notify the regional labour market council about the final result of the consultation process under section 5 of the Act. This must be done as soon as possible. This additional notification can, for practical purposes, be sent off at the same time as the notification to the regional labour market council about the identities of the employees to be dismissed, meaning that a total of three notifications will need to be sent off.

Any employees who are to be dismissed must be notified no later than at the time when the third notification document (containing the names of the exact employees who are to be dismissed) is submitted to the regional labour market council. For practical purposes, this individual notification should be followed by the employer having a conversation with the affected employees who are to be made redundant and/or by providing the affected employees with a termination letter. Insofar as the employer does not want to effect the dismissals within a ten-day period after the consultation process has ended, then the employer can inform the employees that their names are on the list sent to the regional labour market council and that they will be dismissed at a later point in time.

When the dismissals of the affected employees are to be effected, it would be wise to give the termination letter directly to the individual employee, who will then countersign to acknowledge receipt. If there are any employees who are off sick or for any other reason are not present at the place of work, then the termination letter should be sent by recorded delivery (where the post office obtains a signature to confirm delivery). Alternatively, the termination letter can be sent by email insofar as communication with the employee ordinarily takes place by email and one can be certain that the employee reads his or her emails. A termination (dismissal) is, as a matter of Danish law, an 'order' which takes effect when the notification has arrived, irrespective of whether it has been brought to the recipient's attention. If a termination letter is sent by email, the courts will, other things being equal, require more evidence of the email actually having been received, as compared to a situation where a termination letter is sent by recorded delivery and where there is third party (the post office) acknowledgement of the fact that the termination letter (dismissal) has reached the recipient's address.

In addition to complying with the notification rules, an employer must also ensure that the ordinary employment law rules governing a dismissal are complied with. This means that the termination letter must have sufficiently clear contents. Furthermore, section 2(7) of the Salaried Employees Act stipulates that the dismissal of a salaried employee must be done in writing. Case law has interpreted this to mean that the requirement for written communication is not an actual precondition of the termination being valid. The significance of section 2(7) is rather that it increases the burden of proving that the termination letter was actually issued at the correct time, if there are any doubts about this.

When dealing with public sector dismissals, it is important to comply with the specific rules governing consultation with the parties involved (in Danish: *partshøring*) before the termination letter is sent off. As a general rule this means that the public authority must provide the employee with a written statement explaining the basis for the contemplated dismissal and also the public authority's preliminary understanding of the matter. If there are any evidential assessments, the statement must also set out the public authority's evidential assessments, and the statement must also contain the public authority's views on the judicial questions in the case, including the legal rules intended to be used in the individual circumstances.

Some collective agreements furthermore contain specific consultation requirements or rules governing the notification to the employees' trade unions etc. Naturally, such rules must be complied with in addition to the rules set out in the Collective Dismissals Act.

[F] The Date on Which the Dismissals Take Effect: Section 8 of the Collective Dismissals Act

The Collective Dismissals Act provides that the dismissals will be effective thirty days, at the earliest, after notification has been sent to the labour market council (or eight weeks if the stricter termination rules apply). With the exception of employees in the manufacturing industry, most employees will ordinarily have a notice period of at least three months. In such a scenario the thirty-day deadline (or eight weeks) has no practical effect if the notification rules have otherwise been complied with.

[G] The Stricter Notification Requirements

If the number of dismissals being contemplated during a thirty-day period amounts to at least 50% of the employees in one establishment (as defined above in section 1.4.5) and the establishment ordinarily employs at least 100 employees, then the stricter notification requirements will apply under section 7(1)(2) of the Collective Dismissals Act.

The argument for the introduction of the stricter notification requirements was, inter alia, an attempt to ensure that there was more time for a meaningful consultation process, and to ensure that the regional labour market councils were given more time to put in place relevant arrangements in circumstances where there were large-scale redundancies. This could have a particular impact in minor regional communities where the business opportunities and employment options are relatively restricted.

As a consequence of the stricter notification requirements, the notification to the labour market council that the employer continues to intend to effect the dismissals can be sent in twenty-one days, at the earliest, after the consultation process commenced – unless a collective agreement provides otherwise. The twenty-one-day limit is therefore not calculated by reference to the date when the first notification was sent to the regional labour market council, but rather from the date when the actual consultation process began, i.e. generally from the first meeting date.

The employer's management will generally be required to use a minimum of twenty-one days to consult with the employees or their representatives. This may result in longer notice periods for certain groups of employees, seeing that the employees' (individual) notice periods may not expire until eight weeks after the second notification letter was sent in the labour market council (at the very earliest). In this connection, it must be assumed that the individual dismissals cannot be effected until the time when the second notification letter has been sent to the regional labour market council (at the earliest), meaning that the individual dismissals cannot be effected before the expiry of the twenty-one-day time limit.

When planning the sequence of events, the employer must pay attention to whether the employees are subject to a collective agreement preventing them from being dismissed whilst they are, by way of example, on holiday or are off sick. If the consultation process is planned during the holiday season, then this could give rise to challenges if the employee representatives are not present.

If the stricter notification requirements are not complied with, then the employer will be obliged to pay compensation. Depending on the circumstances this could, however, turn out not to be of any actual importance, because it is possible to set off any salary paid out during the individual notice period, if any, against the compensation payment.

The stricter notification rules can be derogated from by way of a collective agreement whereby the parties have agreed under the terms of a collective agreement that the twenty-one-day consultation process and the minimum notice of eight weeks do not apply. The Confederation of Danish Industry (*Dansk Industri*) and the Central Organisation of Industrial Employees in Denmark (*CO Industri*) have taken advantage of the power to derogate from the Act by way of a collective agreement, and thus entered into the Industrial Agreement (*Industriens Overenskomst*). Under the terms of an appendix to the collective agreement,[14] it has been agreed that notification must be given within twenty-one days[15] after the consultation process commenced, and compensation of eight weeks' salary can only be awarded to employees who are subject to the collective agreement and who have, at the time of the dismissal, at least nine months' continuous employment. Similar rules apply under the Collective Agreement for Salaried Employees in Industry.

7.03 SUPPORT MEASURES IN FAVOUR OF EMPLOYEES

As set out in section 2.4, management and employee representatives often enter into a framework agreement in connection with the consultation process under sections 5 and 6 of the Collective Dismissals Act. A framework agreement will govern a number of the employees' terms and conditions in connection with the dismissals and it will also contain provisions which put the employees in a more favourable position as compared to an ordinary dismissal.

[A] Retention Bonus

So as to ensure that a transition period goes smooth, all projects/tasks are transferred or terminated in a satisfactory manner, and customers can be sure to receive the customary high levels of service, a framework agreement can also contain separate agreements concerning the payment of a retention bonus to the company's employees. It is a condition for the payment of the retention bonus that the individual employee:

(i) Solves/finishes the individually agreed tasks in an effective and flexible manner and that the employee continues to work to ensure high quality levels of the employer's products and services; and

14. *See* the appendix to the Industrial Agreement dated 20 February 1995 'Notification in connection with large scale dismissals'. Appendix 6 to the Industrial Agreement 2012-2014 and Appendix 16 to the Collective Agreement for Salaried Employees in Industry 2012-14.
15. That is, not 'at the earliest' of twenty-one days. The parties in industry have thus elected to derogate from the obligation set out in section 7(1)(2) of the Act and which deals with the stricter notification requirements.

(ii) Does not make any arrangements/carry out any acts which would entitle the employer to terminate or rescind the individual's employment contract as a result of the employee's fundamental breach.

It might be important for the employee to clarify whether he or she has met the agreed targets. Insofar as it is possible to determine this, the assessment will be carried out by the company's managing director.

The retention bonus will typically be the same for everyone, but there might also be differentiation. By way of example, an employee who is released from his or her duties (garden leave) will typically not be paid a retention bonus.

[B] Garden Leave (Release from Duties)

In Denmark, an employer is entitled to release an employee who has been terminated from his or her duties (garden leave). The release from duties means that the employee is not required to work during the notice period, but the employer cannot terminate the employee's benefits, meaning that the employee is entitled to his or her salary during the garden leave period. A framework agreement can contain a provision whereby the redundant employee is put on garden leave. Typically, the garden leave will only commence when the work-related tasks allocated to the individual employee have been satisfactorily completed as decided by management in its discretion. To the extent possible, the individual employee will be told, which tasks should be completed as a condition of the employee being released from his or her duties (put on garden leave).

The ordinary default option is that an employee who has been released from his duties is entitled to take up other employment with another company during the notice period, insofar as the new employer is not in competition with the existing employer. The parties can, however, agree under the terms of the framework agreement that the employee is released from his or her ordinary duty of loyalty from the date of commencing the garden leave, meaning that the employee will be entitled to take up employment with a competing business, subject to the Danish Marketing Practices Act and its prohibition against the use of a company's trade secrets.

[C] Holiday

The framework agreement will typically contain rules about an employee's taking of holidays. By way of example, it could be agreed that the employer will not ask the employee to take any remaining holidays during a garden leave period, if any, even though the employee could be ordered to do so according to Danish law. The employee will instead receive a payment of any outstanding but accrued holiday pay into the Danish Holiday Account (*FerieKonto*).

[D] Training and Outplacement

It is customary to agree on the provision of certain training or outplacement sessions which might benefit the dismissed employee and improve his/her chances of finding a new job.

[E] Counter-Resignation

Even though the employee will always be entitled to counter-resign, the framework agreement will contain a provision governing this, if relevant. The employee will thus be able to counter-resign from his/her position on the giving of his/her individual period of notice.

In this connection, it can also be agreed that the employer is willing to accept the employee's counter-resignation on the giving of a reduced period of notice if the employee's role is not of vital importance to the employer during the transition period, or until the activities (duties) have been transferred to another employee. Such an agreement will be made on an individual basis. If the employer accepts the reduced notice period, the obligation to pay any salary will cease when the reduced notice period expires.

[F] Full and Final Settlement

The parties will often agree that the framework agreement is in full and final settlement of the dismissed employee's potential claims against the employer as a result of the collective dismissals. It will often be a condition of the agreement that each and every employee acknowledges receipt of a copy of the framework agreement and that the employees acknowledge that they agree that the framework agreement has been entered into in full and final settlement of all and any claims in relation to their termination of employment. These conditions must be fulfilled before the employees become entitled to the rights and entitlements set out in the framework agreement.

§7.04 JUDICIAL CONTROL AND SANCTIONS

The consequences of breaching the procedural rules vary, depending on whether the rules are breached by a public authority, an employer in the collective agreement system or an employer in the individual system (i.e. an employer which does not have a collective agreement). A common feature of all of these spheres is, however, that the dismissals will, in principle, not be held to be invalid. The employee would rather be awarded a financial compensation payment – varying in nature – and the employer may be issued with a fine.

[A] Sanctions Against the Employer

Section 12 of the Collective Dismissals Act contains a punitive provision under which the employer can be ordered by the ordinary courts in Denmark to pay a fine if the provisions of the Collective Dismissals Act have not been complied with. The fine can be issued at the same time as the employer being penalized in another way, for example by being ordered to pay compensation to the redundant employee(s).

The punitive provision (fines against the employer) set out in section 12 of the Collective Dismissals Act have, however, hardly ever been used in actual practice.

[B] Orders for Setting Aside a Dismissal (Reinstatement) and Compensation for an Infringement of the Collective Dismissals Act

If a public authority have breached the provisions of the Collective Dismissals Act it will, in very special cases and dependent on the basis of the collective agreement, be possible to set aside the dismissal (reinstatement). It is, however, a condition (of such an order for reinstatement being made) that there was a clear judicial flaw and that the order can be warranted by other legislation, e.g. if the dismissal is in breach of the Equal Treatment Act.

Consequently, the most commonly used sanction against employers is an order for compensation to the employee, insofar as the employer breaches the provisions of the Collective Dismissals Act. This is specifically warranted by section 11 of the Collective Dismissals Act. Any employees who have been dismissed can consequently demand compensation of up to thirty days' salary (or eight weeks' salary). Depending on the circumstances, this provision can, however, turn out to be of no real significance, seeing that it is possible to set off any salary paid out during the individual notice periods, if any, when calculating the compensation payment.

The Confederation of Danish Industry (*Dansk Industri*) and the Central Organisation of Industrial Employees in Denmark (*CO Industri*) have agreed under the terms of an appendix[16] to the Industrial Agreement (*Industriens Overenskomst*) that compensation equivalent to eight weeks' salary can only be awarded to employees who are subject to the collective agreement and who have at least nine months' continuous employment at the time of the dismissal. Similar rules apply under the Collective Agreement for Salaried Employees in Industry.

[C] Sanctions and Procedure: Unfair Dismissal

As mentioned in section 2.2, the Collective Dismissals Act does not set out any stand-alone penalty provisions governing an employer's unfair dismissal of an

16. Appendix to the Industrial Agreement dated 20 February 1995 'Notification in connection with large scale dismissals'. Appendix 6 to the Industrial Agreement 2012-2014 and Appendix 16 to the Collective Agreement for Salaried Employees in Industry 2012-14.

employee. The legal basis for any unfair dismissal sanctions should therefore be found in other legislation, collective agreements or in an agreement.

[1] The Salaried Employees Act

If the dismissal of a salaried employee who has been continuously employed (by the employer in question) for at least a year before the dismissal cannot be judged to be reasonably attributable to reasons related to the salaried employee or the employer, then the employer needs to pay compensation under section 2(b) of the Salaried Employees Act.

Compensation is calculated by reference to the salaried employee's length of continuous employment and the other facts of the case.

If the salaried employee has reached 30 years of age at the time of the dismissal, the compensation can, however, amount to up to three months' salary. After ten years of continuous employment the compensation can amount to up to four months' salary and after fifteen years' of continuous employment the compensation can amount to up to six months' salary.

As a matter of practice, compensation is typically fixed at an amount representing between one half and two thirds of the maximum compensation payment - unless there are very specific circumstances (justifying a higher award).

[2] General Agreement Between the Danish Employers' Federation and the Danish Confederation of Trade Unions and Other Collective Agreements

The General Agreement[17] between the Danish Employers' Federation (*Dansk Arbejdsgiverforening (DA))* and the Danish Confederation of Trade Unions (*Landsorganisationen Danmark (LO)*) is a collective agreement which contains a number of basic rules governing the relationship between the parties on the Danish labour market. The contents have been widely copied to other spheres outside the Employers' Federation/Trade Union Federation sphere. Article 4(3) of the General Agreement provides that there must be no capriciousness involved in the dismissal of an employee. An order for reinstatement or compensation can only be awarded to an employee who has nine months' continuous employment with the employer in question.

The provisions mean that if an employee claims that he or she has been unfairly dismissed, and not due to reasons related to the employee or the employer, then the dispute can be heard by way of arbitration before the Unfair Dismissals Board[18] (*Afskedigelsesnævnet*). In this connection, the dismissal may be set aside (order for reinstatement) or the dismissed employee may be awarded compensation, the size of

17. The General Agreement of 1973, most recently amended on 1 January 1993.
18. The Unfair Dismissals Board is a specific tribunal within the collective sphere, which is equivalent to industrial arbitration.

which will depend on the facts of the case and the employee's continuity of service. The compensation payment cannot exceed fifty-two weeks of salary calculated by reference to the dismissed employee's average earnings during the previous year.

When deciding whether to make an order for reinstatement, the Unfair Dismissals Board will consider the extent to which the working relationship between the employer and the employee has suffered, or whether it could be assumed to suffer significantly if the employment were to continue. As a matter of practice, orders for reinstatement are seldom made in the private sphere.

[3] Dismissal of Shop Stewards/Employee Representatives

Many collective agreements contain specific rules governing the dismissal of employee representatives/shop stewards, who will typically have longer notice periods, a right to be informed in advance by the relevant trade union and who can only be fairly dismissed when the dismissal is absolutely necessary. If the General Agreement applies, an employees' representative/shop steward can only be dismissed if there are 'compelling reasons', cf. paragraph 8 of the General Agreement. The requirement for compelling reasons cannot be disregarded because of a collective redundancy situation. If it is necessary to close down an entire department because the department is not financially viable, then there will be compelling reasons.

The assessment of the fairness (of a dismissal) will be made by reference to the circumstances prevailing at the time of the dismissal. If the employer, by way of example, is facing an imminent insolvency situation, where all efforts to sell the business appear to have been exhausted, then it will be possible to effect a dismissal of all the employees, including employee representatives/shop stewards even if it should subsequently transpire that a sale might be possible and that it might be possible to have some re-engagements after all.

Compensation awards for the unfair dismissal of employees' representative/shop steward vary in size but will typically be in the region of DKK 100,000-150,000. There have, however, been occasions where the compensation sum awarded significantly exceeded or fell below this range.

[4] Dismissal of Other Categories of Employees Who Have the Same Protection as Employee Representatives/Shop Stewards

Company representatives elected by the employees to become board members of the relevant entities, either in direct or indirect elections and in accordance with sections 140-141 of the Danish Companies Act and the Danish Act on Employee Representation in Limited Companies[19] are covered by a number of rules. However, the, employee nominated board members are protected against dismissal in the same way as employee representatives/shop stewards, cf. regulation 21 of the Government Order.

19. Statutory Instrument (Order) No. 344 of 30 March 2012.

If there is a situation in which more substitutes (alternate members) than employee representatives have been elected, then it is only the number of substitutes which is equivalent to the number of employee representatives who will be protected in the same way as shop stewards. The number of protected substitutes (alternate members) will therefore depend on the number of employees' representatives. The substitutes (alternates) who are protected will depend on the number of votes cast. If, by way of example, only two representatives have been elected, then it is only the two substitutes (alternates) who have received most votes who will receive the same protection as shop stewards.

It is only the substitutes (alternate members) having the same protection as shop stewards who will be registered with the Danish Business Authority (*Erhvervsstyrelsen*). When a substitute (alternate member) for an employees' representative resigns from the board, e.g. because the individual's employment terminates, and a new substitute is appointed instead, then this must be registered with the Business Authority, and the new name(s) will appear in the complete company report.

The above mentioned principles governing the protection of substitutes (alternate members) similarly apply when an employee board representation has been set up on a voluntary basis.

A work environment representative is also protected against dismissal and any other unfavourable treatment in the same away as employee representatives/shop stewards, cf. section 10(2) of the Danish Working Environment Act (*arbejdsmiljøloven*).

The compensation levels for the unfair dismissal of employee nominated board members, substitutes (alternate) employee nominated board members and work environment representatives will typically be in the same range as for shop stewards/employee representatives.

[5] Dismissal of a 'Spokesperson'

It follows from a collective bargaining agreement comprising managers ('Manager's Agreement'[20]) that a 'spokesperson' (representative) may be appointed if an undertaking employs at least ten managers. A manager's status as a spokesperson does not in itself trigger an extended notice period, but paragraph 14(4) of the Manager's Agreement provides that the fact that a manager functions (undertakes work) as a spokesperson will not give rise to the dismissal of the manager, nor will his or her position be significantly impaired as a result thereof. If an employer intends to dismiss a spokesperson, then the Danish Association of Managers and Executives must be notified in advance of the dismissal, cf. section 14(5) of the Manager's Agreement.

Any dispute about the unfair dismissal of a manager subject to the Manager's Agreement between the Danish Association of Managers and Executives and the

20. The Manager's Agreement is an agreement between the Danish Association of Managers and Executives (*lederne*) and the Danish Employers' Confederation (*DA*). The Danish Association of Managers and Executives is a professional body, trade union and unemployment insurance fund for managers and individuals employed in a position of trust.

Danish Employers' Confederation must be heard by the Managers' Arbitration Court pursuant to paragraph 21 of the Manager's Agreement. It will be considered an aggravating factor in any dispute if the manager has been dismissed because he or she undertook duties as a spokesperson.

The compensation levels for the unfair dismissal of a spokesperson are typically lower than for employee representatives/shop stewards. In practice, compensation is in the range of one to three months' salary, although there may be cases where the compensation levels awarded are either significantly lower or significantly higher.

[D] Jurisdiction

Employees' claims for compensation under section 11 of the Collective Dismissals Act can be brought before the ordinary courts, the Labour Court, the industrial arbitration tribunal and the unfair dismissal tribunal, just like any disputes concerning the directive can be brought before the Court of Justice of the European Union.[21]

If there is a breach within the collective system, the employee will need to bring the dispute before the unfair dismissals tribunals. However, any breaches of collective agreements which contain obligations similar to those found in the Collective Dismissals Act can also be brought before the Labour Court. Any disputes about the interpretation of a collective agreement will typically be referred to industrial arbitration.

If there is a breach in the individual system (i.e., where there is no collective agreement) the employer will need to bring the case before the ordinary courts, and any sanction against the employer will be the payment of compensation to the employee.

§7.05 CONCLUSION

In recent years there has been a significant increase in the notifications made in connection with collective redundancies. The majority of the cases which have been notified to the authorities as being 'contemplated dismissals' have also resulted in the dismissals being effected. The primary aim of the notification rules in the Act – to prevent or limit the redundancies – would therefore not appear to have been met, even though the notification requirements have been complied with.

From an employer's perspective, it is a determining factor that any collective dismissals are planned and effected by having due regard to the rules in the Collective Dismissals Act and any applicable collective agreements, seeing that the employer will otherwise risk financial sanctions in the form of compensation, a fine and/or penalty.

21. All national courts can make a reference for a preliminary ruling before the Court of Justice of the European Union ('CJEU'). This entails that the Danish Supreme Court, the High Courts, the City Courts and the Labour Court can make references for preliminary rulings before the CJEU. The European Court of Justice (as it was then) has also decided, in case No C-109/88 Danfoss, that an industrial arbitration board should be construed as a 'court or tribunal' for the purposes of Article 267 of the TFEU (formerly 234).

CHAPTER 8

Collective Dismissal in Estonia

Merle Erikson

§8.01 INTRODUCTION

[A] Formation of the Regulation

The association agreement between Estonia and the European Communities and their Member States (the Europe Agreement) was signed on 12 June 1995. The Europe Agreement imposed an obligation on Estonia to adjust and harmonize its legislation with the EU, particularly in the spheres of commerce and the economy, and in related spheres, including the protection of employees (Articles 68-69).[1]

The conclusion of the Europe Agreement gave an impetus to transpose, among other employees' protection instruments, the EU Directive 75/129/EEC of 17 February 1975 on the approximation of the laws of the Member States relating to collective redundancies[2] into Estonian law. On 20 July 1998, the Council adopted the consolidated version of the Directive and after that the corresponding area has been regulated by Directive 98/59/EC on the approximation of the laws of the Member States relating to collective redundancies.[3]

It should be mentioned that during the Soviet period[4] there were no special rules on the protection of employees' rights in the case of collective dismissals in Estonia.[5]

1. *Euroopa Ühenduste ja nende liikmesriikide ning Eesti Vabariigi vaheline assotsieerumisleping (Euroopa leping)* / Association Agreement between the European Communities and their Member States and the Republic of Estonia (Europe Agreement) – RT (*Riigi Teataja*/State Gazette) II 1995, 22-27, 120.
2. OJ L 48, 22 February 1975, 29-30. This Directive was amended by Directive 92/56/EEC (OJ L 245, 26 August 1992, 3-5).
3. OJ L 225, 12 August 1998, 16-21.
4. Estonia was a part of the USSR from 1940 to 1991.
5. *See Eesti NSV töökoodeks* / Labour Code of the Estonian Soviet Socialist Republic. Adopted on 5 July 1972. Tallinn: Eesti Raamat, 1985, §§ 33-42.

Neither the USSR nor the Republic of Estonia has ratified the ILO Convention No. 158 concerning Termination of Employment at the Initiative of the Employer (1982)[6] the third part of which provides for the supplementary provisions concerning terminations of employment for economic, technological, structural or similar reasons.

After regaining its independence in 1991 Estonia adopted the first Employment Contracts Act (EVTLS)[7] in 1992. The EVTLS did not establish norms about collective redundancies in the meaning of Directive 75/129/EEC. However, EVTLS § 89 set forth some protection for employees when an employer decided to dismiss a greater number of employees.[8] EVTLS § 89 introduced the principle that if an employer intends to terminate employment contracts with ten to twenty employees during a three month period due to a lay-off of employees and job placements for the released employees are not ensured, the organization or person representing the employees may suspend termination of the contracts for up to one month. If more than 20 employees are released during a three-month period due to a lay-off and job placements are not ensured for the released employees, the organization or person representing the employees may suspend termination of the contract for up to two months.[9]

In addition, the employer had the obligation to inform the employment office about the termination of employment contract. Under EVTLS § 88, upon termination of employment contracts due to the liquidation of a legal person, or the lay-off of employees, the employer was required to submit information regarding the released employees to the employment office not later than on the day after the employer notified the employees of the termination of their employment contracts.[10] However, that duty of the employer was not directly related to the collective termination of employment contracts.

As regards the practical value of these rules (EVTLS §§ 88 and 89), it is not known that the implementation of these provisions would have been very topical.

It is interesting to note that on 31 May 2000, the *Riigikogu* (the Estonian Parliament) ratified the Revised European Social Charter[11] that entered into force in respect of Estonia on 1 November 2000. Among other provisions, Estonia accepted

6. http://www.ilo.org/dyn/normlex/en/f?p = NORMLEXPUB:12100:0::NO:12100:P12100_INSTRUMENT_ID:312303:NO (accessed 1 July 2015).
7. *Eesti Vabariigi töölepingu seadus* / Republic of Estonia Employment Contracts Act. Adopted on 15 April 1992 - RT 1992, 15/16, 241; RT I 2009, 11, 67. This Act is no longer in force as from 1 July 2009.
8. M. Muda. *Töötajate õiguste kaitse tööandja tegevuse ümberkorraldamisel* / Protection of Employees' Rights in the Event of the Reorganisation of the Employer's Activities. *Dissertationes iuridicae universitatis Tartuensis* 5. Tartu: TÜ Kirjastus, 2001, at 21.
9. Proceeding from EVTLS § 87 (3), upon giving an employee the advance notice, an employer was also required to give advance notice in writing to the organization or person representing the employee and to present the reason for termination of the contract and communicate the measures taken to provide work for the employee. However, that was the general obligation of the employer that was not connected with collective dismissals.
10. If employment contracts were terminated due to the declaration of bankruptcy of the employer, the employer had the obligation to submit information regarding the employees to the employment office on the date following termination of the employment contracts (EVTLS § 88).
11. *Parandatud ja täiendatud Euroopa sotsiaalharta ratifitseerimise seadus* / Revised European Social Charter Ratification Act. Adopted on 31 May 2000 - RT II 2000, 15, 93; 29.05.2012, 1. The date of deposit of the instrument of ratification was 11 September 2000.

Article 29 of the Charter that lays down the right to information and consultation in collective redundancy procedures. Consequently, Estonia was required to ensure that employers inform and consult employees' representatives in good time prior to collective redundancies, despite the fact that there was no the regulation on the collective termination of employment contracts.[12]

On 18 December 2002, the *Riigikogu* adopted the Unemployment Insurance Act, the EVTLS and the Employees' Trustee Act Amendment Act[13] that, among other things, transposed Directive 98/59/EC into Estonian law. This act took effect on 1 January 2003.[14] Thus, § 89 of the EVTLS was abolished and new provisions concerning collective redundancies (§§ 89^1-89^3) were introduced into the EVTLS. Also, as of the entry into force of the Unemployment Insurance Act (TKindlS)[15] on 1 January 2002, TKindlS §§ 15-18 provided for the obligation of the Estonian Unemployment Insurance Fund (*Eesti Töötukassa*) to pay benefit upon collective termination of employment contracts in the case of collective redundancies.[16] The aim of these rules was not clear (to implement the idea of solidarity of employers in the case of collective redundancies?).[17] Directive 98/59/EC does not lay down the state's obligation to pay benefit to employees when a greater number of employees are dismissed. On the contrary, the state benefits may promote the enforcement of collective redundancies because in such situation the employer gets rid of the duty to pay severance allowances.[18]

On 17 December 2008, the *Riigikogu* passed the new Employment Contracts Act (TLS)[19] that includes, in comparison with the EVTLS, slightly amended regulation on collective dismissals that is based on Directive 98/59/EC. The new act abolished the rules of the TKindlS pertaining to the obligation of the Estonian Unemployment Insurance Fund to pay benefit upon collective termination of employment contracts in the case of collective redundancies.[20] The TLS entered into force on 1 July 2009. In next

12. As in comparison with Directive 98/59/EC, Article 29 of the Revised European Social Charter establishes more general rule, in this paper, that provision of the Charter is not dealt with in greater detail.
13. *Töötuskindlustuse seaduse, Eesti Vabariigi töölepingu seaduse ja töötajate usaldusisiku seaduse muutmise seadus* / Unemployment Insurance Act, the Republic of Estonia Employment Contracts Act and the Employees' Trustee Act Amendment Act. Adopted on 18 December 2002 – RT I 2002, 111, 663.
14. Estonia became the member of the EU on 1 May 2004.
15. *Töötuskindlustuse seadus* / Unemployment Insurance Act. Adopted on 13 June 2001 – RT I 2001, 59, 359; 29.06.2014, 109. The act is available in English at <https://www.riigiteataja.ee/en/eli/509072014020/consolide> (accessed 1 July 2015).
16. The TKindlS established the definition of the collective termination of employment contracts, the amount of benefit upon collective termination of employment contracts; and the application for and grant and payment of benefit upon collective termination of employment contracts.
17. The unemployment insurance premiums of employers and the income received from investment thereof formed the trust fund for benefits upon collective termination of employment contracts.
18. *Supra* n. 8, at 30. M. Muda. *Töölepingute kollektiivne lõpetamine* / Collective termination of employment contracts. - Juridica, 2003, No. 8, at 555.
19. *Töölepingu seadus* / Employment Contracts Act, passed on 17 December 2008 – RT I 2009, 35, 5; 12.07.2014, 1. The act is available in English at <https://www.riigiteataja.ee/en/eli/509012015006/consolide> (accessed 1 July 2015).
20. It is important to mention here that, by contrast with the old regulation, upon termination of an employment contract due to lay-off, the TLS diminishes the employer's responsibility and enlarges the responsibility of the state. In the case of lay-off of employees, the employer must

paragraphs of this paper, the author analyses which the definition of and procedure for the collective termination of employment contracts is according to the TLS.

[B] Situation in Practice

Although in Estonia the regulation on collective dismissals that is in line with Directive 98/59/EC has been in force since 2003, there are no significant court cases concerning these rules. The *Riigikohus* (the Estonian Supreme Court) has not discussed any case pertaining to the collective termination of employment contracts.[21] Pursuant to the database of the county and circuit courts decisions,[22] few cases are related to the collective redundancy but in these cases, usually, an employee demands from an employer unpaid wages and different compensations (e.g., the redundancy compensation, the compensation for the termination of an employment contract without advance notice) due to the incorrect (individual) termination of employment contract.[23]

However, from 2011 to 2014 the Estonian Labour Inspectorate has detected several violations pertaining to the employer's obligation to inform and consult employees and/or notify the Estonian Unemployment Insurance Fund in the event of collective terminations of employment contracts.[24]

Thus, it is not possible to argue that there are no (or are only few) collective dismissals in Estonia. As from 2003 to 2009[25] the Estonian Unemployment Insurance Fund paid to employees benefit upon collective termination of employment contracts in the case of collective redundancies, the reliable data about the number of collective dismissals is available concerning that period. According to statistics, there were approximately 180 collective terminations of employment contracts per year.[26] The majority of collective redundancies took place in the following sectors: manufacturing

pay compensation equivalent to only the average monthly wage to the employee (TLS § 100 (1)). In addition, the TKindlS sets forth a new type of state benefit – redundancy pay, or benefit upon lay-off – that the Estonian Unemployment Insurance Fund pays to the employee upon termination of an employment contract due to lay-off (§§ 141-144). This new benefit replaces, to some extent, the benefit upon collective termination of employment contracts.

21. *See* the database of the Supreme Court decisions (in Estonian): http://www.riigikohus.ee/?id=11 (accessed 1 July 2015).
22. *Kohtulahendite otsing (alates 2006. aastast)* / Search for Court Decisions (since 2006) (in Estonian). https://www.riigiteataja.ee/kohtuteave/maa_ringkonna_kohtulahendid/main.html (accessed 1 July 2015).
23. To the best of the author's knowledge, the similar situations could be found in labour dispute committees.
24. Author's correspondence (13-16 June 2015) with the Labour Inspectorate's Deputy Director General in the Field of Inspection of Labour Relations and Labour Law Ms. M. Miidla-Vanatalu and Head of Law Service Ms. E. Soomets (in possession of the author). *See* paragraph 5 for greater detail.
25. Namely until 30 June 2009.
26. It should be mentioned that during the economic crisis (2008-2009) the number of collective dismissals was bigger in comparison with previous years. Benefit upon collective termination of employment contracts and insurance benefit upon lay-off 2003-2015. Statistics. Estonian Unemployment Insurance Fund. https://www.tootukassa.ee/sites/tootukassa.ee/files/kkhjak_mai2015.xls (accessed 1 July 2015).

industry; wholesale and retail trade; repair of motor vehicles, motorcycles and personal and household goods; and construction.[27]

As regards the period 2011[28]-2014, also, the Estonian Unemployment Insurance Fund has the data about collective dismissals because from the entry into force of the new TLS the Fund is a competent public authority[29] that an employer must notify of the collective termination of employment contracts. Pursuant to the data given by the Estonian Unemployment Insurance Fund, during the period 2011-2014 there were approximately 126 collective redundancies annually. The following sectors were most affected by the collective termination of employment contracts: manufacturing of oil products; electronic equipment manufacturing; and carriage of goods and passengers.[30]

Thus, although during last years the number of collective dismissals has been decreased to some extent, in practice, the collective redundancy is a fairly common phenomenon. In this paper, the author tries to ascertain why in Estonian legal practice the implementation of the provisions about the collective termination of employment contracts has been insignificant.

§8.02 COLLECTIVE DISMISSAL: THE CASE

As mentioned above, the rules on the collective dismissal have been provided by the TLS. Under TLS § 90 (1), collective termination of employment contracts means termination, within thirty calendar days due to lay-off, of the employment contract of no less than:

(1) five employees in an enterprise where the average number of employees is up to nineteen;
(2) ten employees in an enterprise where the average number of employees is 20-99;
(3) 10% of the employees in an enterprise where the average number of employees is 100-299;
(4) thirty employees in an enterprise where the average number of employees is at least 300.

In order to understand the definition of the collective termination of employment contracts, it is important to explain what 'lay-off' and 'enterprise' mean pursuant to Estonian law.

27. *Ibid.*
28. There are no statistics concerning the period as of 1 July 2009-31 December 2010. Author's correspondence (15-26 June 2015) with the Estonian Unemployment Insurance Fund's Chief Specialist Ms. K. Savisto (in possession of the author).
29. Before the entry into force of the new TLS, the competent public authority was the Labour Inspectorate.
30. *Supra* n. 28.

TLS § 89 allows an employer to terminate the employment contract for economic reasons. According to TLS § 89 (1), lay-off is a situation where an employer extraordinarily terminates an employment contract if the continuance of the employment relationship on the agreed conditions becomes impossible due to a decrease in the work volume or reorganization of work or other cessation of work. Lay-off is also extraordinary termination of an employment contract: upon cessation of the activities of employer; and upon declaration of bankruptcy of employer or termination of bankruptcy proceedings, without declaring bankruptcy, by abatement (TLS § 89 (2)). Thus, the lay-off covers all cases when an employer terminates the employment contract due to economic reasons: cessation of work, liquidation or insolvency of the employer.[31] Dismissals for economic reasons tend to be collective more often than not and the opposite is the case for dismissals for reasons arising from employee.[32]

However, pursuant to the information given by the Labour Inspectorate, in order to avoid the performance of obligations that result from the collective termination of employment contracts, instead of lay-offs, Estonian employers try to arrange that employment contracts end on other bases, e.g. by mutual agreement, or due to ordinary or extraordinary termination of employment contract by employee.[33] Such behaviour of employers reduces the number of collective redundancies and prevents potential disputes.

The definition of enterprise has been established by the General Part of the Civil Code Act (TsÜS).[34] Proceeding from TsÜS § 66^1, an enterprise is an economic unit through which a person operates. In the context of obligation law, the meaning of 'enterprise' has laid down in the Law of Obligations Act (VÕS).[35] Under VÕS § 180 (2), an enterprise comprises the things, rights and obligations relating to and in the service of the management of the enterprise, including contracts relating to the enterprise.

31. In addition to lay-off, the employment contact may come to an end by virtue of: mutual agreement, expiry of term, death of employee, ordinary or extraordinary termination of employment contract by employee, and extraordinary termination of employment contract by employer for reason arising from employee (i.e., due to the employee's performance or conduct). These bases for termination of employment contract are not considered in case of defining collective dismissals.
32. J. Rojot, *Security of Employment and Employability*, in *Comparative Labour Law and Industrial Relations in Industrialized Market Economies*, p. 529 (R. Blanpain ed., 11th ed., Kluwer Law International, 2014).
33. According to the Taxation Act (MKS), as of 1 July 2014 a person providing work (incl. employer) is obligated to register in the employment register the commencement, suspension and termination and type of employment of a worker (incl. employee) (*see* MKS §§ 251-258 for greater detail). *Maksukorralduse seadus* / Taxation Act, passed on 20 February 2002 – RT I 2002, 26, 150; 17.03.2015, 3. The act is available in English at <https://www.riigiteataja.ee/en/eli/519032015001/consolide> (accessed 1 July 2015). The employment register shows that, with same employer, employment contracts terminate in a short period on identical bases, but not due to lay-off. *Supra* n. 24.
34. *Tsiviilseadustiku üldosa seadus* / General Part of the Civil Code Act, passed on 27 March 2002 – RT I 2002, 35, 216; 12.03.2015, 5. The act is available in English at <https://www.riigiteataja.ee/en/eli/517062015011/consolide> (accessed 1 July 2015).
35. *Võlaõigusseadus* / Law of Obligations Act, passed on 26 September 2001 – RT I 2001, 81, 487; 23.03.2015, 3. The act is available in English at <https://www.riigiteataja.ee/en/eli/516062015006/consolide> (accessed 1 July 2015). The VÕS sets forth the rules about the transfer of an enterprise (§§ 180-185).

Thus, following both the TsÜS and the VÕS, the enterprise is the economic unit, not a legal person. Such approach is in conformity with Directive 98/59/EC that also has in view a specific unit where an employee works.[36]

When comparing the definition of the collective termination of employment contracts provided for in TLS § 90 (1) to the definition established in Article 1.1 (a) (i) of Directive 98/59/EC, it can be concluded that these concepts are almost identical. However, in addition to the principles of the Directive, TLS § 90 (1) 1) states that the collective dismissal is also the situation where an employer terminates the employment contract of no less than five employees in an enterprise where the average number of employees is up to nineteen. Thus, unlike Directive 98/59/EC, the TLS sets forth that the collective redundancy may take place in the enterprise where at least five employees work.[37] The reason for such regulation is that as most of Estonian employees work in micro- or small-sized enterprises,[38] the legislator decided to give protection for bigger amount of employees.[39]

TLS § 90 (2) specifies that upon determining the (average) number of employees, § 18 (2) of the Employees' Trustee Act (TUIS)[40] is applied. Pursuant to that provision, upon determining the number of employees, the employer is required to take into account the six months' average number of employees as of the date on which the obligation to inform and consult arises. In the case of the collective termination of employment contracts, the TLS does not establish the date on which the obligation to inform and consult arises.[41] Following TLS § 101 (1), before an employer decides on collective dismissal he or she must consult in good time employees' representatives. For employees' representatives to be able to make proposals in consultations, the employer is required in good time to provide them with all necessary information about the planned collective dismissal (TLS § 101 (2)). In the author's opinion, the employer can ascertain the average number of employees thereafter when he or she has decided to reduce the number of employees due to lay-off and determined the number of employees to be made redundant and the period over which the projected redundancy is to be effected.

---

36. In this question, the EVTLS was not in line with Directive 98/59/EC. According to the EVTLS, the collective dismissal took place with an employer, i.e. in order to determine whether redundancies constitute a collective termination of employment contracts, the total number of employees of the employer was taken into account.
37. The same rule was in the EVTLS too.
38. *See* for example, A. Heinlo. *Innovation in Small and Medium-Sized Enterprises*, in *Changes in the Economy and Labour Market*, pp. 49, 60 (R. Eamets ed., Statistics Estonia, Tallinn, 2014), b http://www.stat.ee/72567 (accessed 1 July 2015).
39. *Supra* n. 18, at 551. Article 5 of Directive 98/59/EC states that the Directive does not affect the right of Member States to apply or to introduce laws, regulations or administrative provisions which are more favourable to employees.
40. *Töötajate usaldusisiku seadus* / Employees' Trustee Act, passed on 13 December 2006 – RT I 2007, 2, 6; 12.07.2014, 1. The act is available in English at <https://www.riigiteataja.ee/en/eli/519012015010/consolide> (accessed 1 July 2015).
41. In the context of the TUIS, the date on which the obligation to inform and consult arises is also vague. *Töötajate usaldusisiku seadus. Kommenteeritud väljaanne* / Employees' Trustee Act. Commented Issue, Commentaries by T. Kaadu, Juura, 2008, at 90.

As regards the exceptions to the scope of Directive 98/59/EC (Article 1.2), the regulation of the collective termination of employment contracts applies to all employees in Estonia.[42] Hence, the rules on the collective dismissal must be implemented in relation to employees[43] employed by public administrative bodies or by establishments governed by public law and the crews of seagoing vessels. If an employment contract entered into for a specified term expires upon the expiry of the term, this is not considered in case of defining the collective termination of employment contracts. The situation is different when a fixed-term employment contract ends due to lay-off.

§8.03 PROCEDURE

[A] Informing and Consulting Employees

[1] General Principles

According to TLS § 101, Estonia has transposed Article 2 of Directive 98/59/EC into national law as follows. TLS § 101 (1) establishes that before an employer decides on collective termination he or she is required to consult in good time the employees' representative[44] with the goal of reaching an agreement on prevention of the planned terminations or reduction of the number thereof and mitigation of the consequences of the terminations, including contribution to the seeking of employment by or re-training of the employees to be laid off.[45]

Proceeding from TLS § 101 (2), for the employees' representative to be able to make proposals in consultations, the employer is obliged in good time to provide the employees' representative with all necessary information about the planned collective termination. The employer must submit, in a format which can be reproduced in writing,[46] at least the following information:

(1) the reasons for the collective termination;
(2) the number and official titles of the employees of the employer;
(3) the number and official titles of those employees and the selection criteria determining the persons whose employment contracts are to be terminated;
(4) the period of time during which the employment contracts are to be terminated;
(5) the method of calculation of the compensation to be paid to the employees in addition to the benefits prescribed by law or the collective agreement.

42. As already mentioned, Article 5 of Directive 98/59/EC allows such deviations.
43. The rules on collective redundancies do not apply to officials.
44. In every subsection that lays down the rights of the employees' representative (TLS § 101 (1)-(4); and § 102 (2)), the TLS specifies that in the absence of the employees' representative the employer must perform his or her duties towards all employees.
45. About the employer's possibilities to mitigate the situation of employees, *see* paragraph 3.1.4.
46. For example, by e-mail or on the intranet.

The employer is required to send a transcript of the information specified above to the Estonian Unemployment Insurance Fund concurrently with the submission of the information to the employees' representative (TLS § 101 (3)). This employer's obligation gives the Estonian Unemployment Insurance Fund the possibility to prepare effectively for the alleviation of the consequences of redundancy.

Upon consultation, the employees' representative has the right to meet with the representatives of the employer and make proposals[47] relating to the measures planned with regard to the employees at least within fifteen days as of the submission of the information, unless a longer term is agreed on. Employer is obligated to justify disregard for the proposals (TLS § 101 (4) and § 113 (3)).

[2] Meaning of Informing and Consulting

In order to realize how informing and consulting employees could take place in Estonian practice, it is necessary to clarify the background of the employer's corresponding duty. It should be mentioned that the employer's obligation to inform and consult employees is quite a new phenomenon in Estonian law. Before Estonia decided to join the EU, the subject matter of employee involvement[48] was unfamiliar to the national practice. Thus, the EU law has the direct impact on the development of employees' right to information and consultation.

The first national act that established the employer's duty to inform and consult employees was the Trade Unions Act (AÜS)[49] that took effect in 2000. According to AÜS § 22, an employer was required to inform and consult the representatives elected by the trade union. However, that provision did not elaborate on the concept of these terms, only listing the areas in which informing and consulting was obligatory. The content of the information and consultation was based on the requirements of different Directives that stipulated such obligation.[50]

The existing wording of AÜS § 22 was abolished by the TUIS[51] that transposed Directive 2002/14/EC establishing a general framework for informing and consulting employees in the European Community[52] into Estonian law. Proceeding form that Directive (Article 2 (f) and (g) and Article 4), TUIS § 19 lays down the definition of informing and consulting. Under TUIS § 19 (1), informing means provision of

47. In a format which can be reproduced in writing.
48. Besides informing and consulting employees, the employee involvement also includes the participation of employees.
49. *Ametiühingute seadus* / Trade Unions Act, passed on 14 June 2000 - RT I 2000, 57, 372; 12.07.2014, 1. The act is available in English at <https://www.riigiteataja.ee/en/eli/519012015011/consolide> (accessed 1 July 2015).
50. *Ametiühingute seadus. Kommenteeritud väljaanne* / Trade Unions Act. Commented Issue, Commentaries by K. Pärnits, M. Tuch. The Confederation of Estonian Trade Unions, 2001, at 24.
51. *Supra* n. 40. Pursuant to the new wording of AÜS § 22, an employer must inform the shop steward and consult with him or her under the conditions and pursuant to the procedure prescribed in the TUIS (AÜS § 22 (1)).
52. OJ L 80, 23 March 2002, 29-34.

information to a trustee[53] on an appropriate level which allows the employees to receive in due course a clear and sufficiently detailed overview of the structure and economic and employment situation of the employer and the possible development thereof and of other circumstances affecting the interests of employees, and also to understand the effects of the situation and other circumstances on the employees. TUIS § 19 (2) states that consulting means exchange of views and the establishment of a dialogue between the trustee and the employer on an appropriate level which allows the trustee to express opinions and obtain from the employer reasoned responses to the expressed opinions for the purposes of reaching an agreement on the decisions pertaining to employees.[54] Both the employer and employees' representatives must follow these definitions in the event of the collective termination of employment contracts too.

[3] Employees' Representatives

Who are these employees' representatives whom the employer is required to inform and consult?[55] In Estonia, employees play a relatively insignificant role in shaping of employment and social relationships. This is primarily due to the historical development of organizations representing employees.[56] Also, as in many other countries, the interest of employees to join trade unions has been reduced in Estonia.[57] According to statistics, approximately 6% of employees belong to trade unions.[58] In addition to trade unions, the institution of employees' trustee was introduced into the system of collective labour relations in 1993.[59] Since then, there is a dual-channel system of

53. In every subsection that sets forth the rights of the trustee (TUIS § 19 (1) and (2); and § 21 (2) and (5)), the TUIS specifies that in the absence of the trustee the employer must perform his or her duties towards all employees.
54. TUIS § 21 provides for the manner of informing and consulting.
55. Under Article 1.1 (b) of Directive 98/59 /EC, the laws or practices of the Member States determine who the employees' representatives are.
56. The first classic trade unions in Estonia were formed by the 1930s, but their activity was concluded by the occupation of Estonia by the Soviet Union in 1940. The aim of the trade unions operating in the Soviet era had to do with executing party policy rather more than with fighting for the rights and interests of employees. The restoration of traditional trade unions was only started in Estonia in 1990. About the history of Estonian trade unions, *see* M. Muda, *Estonia*, in *Handbook on Employee Involvement in Europe* pp. 7-11 (M. Weiss & M. Sewerynski eds, Kluwer Law International 2004).
57. *See* for example, G. P. Cella & T. Treu, *National Trade Union Movements*, in *Comparative Labour Law and Industrial Relations in Industrialized Market Economies*, p. 568 ff (R. Blanpain ed., 11th ed., Kluwer Law International 2014).
58. Trade Union Density 2012. OECD.StatExtracts. Organization for Economic Co-operation and Development. https://stats.oecd.org/Index.aspx?DataSetCode=UN_DEN# (accessed 1 July 2015); T. Treier. Trade Union Membership 2008-2013. Industrial relations in Estonia – current situation and a way forward. The Estonian Ministry of Social Affairs, 2014. Presentation at the workshop *Going up the High Road. Rethinking the Role of Social Dialogue to link Welfare to Competitiveness*, Tallinn, 9 October 2014 (in possession of the author).
59. After the restoration of Estonia's independence in the year 1991, the *Riigikogu* adopted the first Employees' Trustee Act in 1993. *Töötajate usaldusisiku seadus* / Employees' Representatives Act, passed on 16 June 1993 – RT I1993, 40, 595; 2002, 111, 663. This Act is no longer in force as from 1 February 2007.

employees' representation in Estonia: employees participate in the forming of labour relations via trustees and trade unions. Similarly to the trade union membership, employees' trustees have been elected in few companies only.[60]

Pursuant to Estonian version of the TLS, in the case of the collective termination of employment contracts, the employer is obliged to inform and consult the *trustee* (*usaldusisik*). It is important to explain that, due to the dual-channel system of employees' representation, there are two types of trustees (employees' representatives) in Estonia: trustees elected by the general meeting of employees[61] and trustees elected by the trade union - shop stewards.[62] Thus, in the event of the collective redundancy, the employer must inform and consult both the trustee and shop steward. Usually, there is only one of these employees' representatives in the enterprise but they also may operate simultaneously.

TLS § 101 (1) and (2) provide that in the absence of the trustee or shop steward, the employer is obligated to inform and consult the employees. Such regulation can be considered justified, because in most Estonian companies, there is no trade union and the trustee has not been elected, thus, the right to be involved must be ensured for all employees. It is, however, a matter of some question how the informing and consulting of all employees would occur in practice. Informing the employees is probably easier to accomplish, for example, by displaying the relevant information on a notice board or by means of electronic notification. But how can consultation with all employees be arranged? The employer has the possibility of obliging the employees to create a representation system as necessary for conducting consultations. In smaller undertakings, negotiations can be conducted also by means of a general meeting of employees. Another question regards ensuring the knowledge and skills of the employees' representatives elected *ad hoc*, so that they could successfully protect their interests during the consultations.[63]

[4] Informing and Consulting in Practice

According to TLS § 101 (1), the aim of the consultation between the employer and the employees' representatives is to reach an agreement[64] on prevention of the planned

60. In 2009, employees' trustees have been elected in 11% of companies. E. Kallaste, *Kollektiivsed töösuhted* / Collective Employment Relations in *Eesti tööelu-uuring 2009 / Estonian Work Life Survey 2009* (M. Masso ed., Series of the Ministry of Social Affairs, 2011, No. 3), at 66. In comparison with the year 2009, the current situation has not changed significantly.
61. The legal status of the trustee has been provided by the TUIS. Under TUIS § 2 (1), a trustee is an employee of an employer who is elected by the general meeting of the employees of the employer as their representative in the performance of the duties arising from the law in relations with the employer.
62. The legal status of the shop steward has been provided by the AÜS. Following AÜS § 16 (4), a shop steward is an employee of an employer who is elected by a trade union (as its representative in the performance of the duties arising from the law in relations with the employer).
63. *Supra* n. 18, at 556; M. Muda, *Impact of European Union Law on the Involvement of Employees in Estonia*, Juridica Intl. L. Rev. U. Tartu II 29 (2008). Available at http://www.juridicainternational.eu (accessed 1 July 2015).
64. TUIS § 19 (2) and § 21 (4) set forth the same goal.

terminations or reduction of the number thereof and mitigation of the consequences of the terminations, including contribution to the seeking of employment by or re-training of the employees to be laid off. This provision grants the employees' representatives relatively broad rights in making decisions related to the staff policy of the employer, allowing them to participate in the enterprise's business-related matters. However, it does not give them the right of veto, i.e. the employer may carry out the collective dismissal without the consent of the employees' representatives but he or she is required to justify disregard for the employees' proposals.[65] Another question is taking into account the less-developed tradition of interaction at the enterprise (collective) level, how aware of their rights employees are.

As already mentioned, no court actions regarding the collective termination of employment contracts have been brought and it seems that in the event of collective redundancies the system for informing and consulting employees has been activated without problems. The author is not sure about this. While the informing of employees is relatively easily arranged, conducting efficient consultations with employees requires good will and the existence of preliminary knowledge from the employer as well as the employees' representatives. No surveys have been conducted in Estonia as to how the conducting of negotiations with employees in the event of collective redundancy works in practice (what the content of the discussions is, what proposals employees usually make, to what extent employers consider the opinions of employees, etc.).[66] Theoretically, the employer has a lot of possibilities to alleviate the situation of employees (the employer may stop hiring; cut overtime; reduce working hours below the usual norm or short work schedule; grant a compulsory holiday during slow business periods or sabbatical leave or unpaid additional days off; stop to the use of temporary staff and short-term contracts or withdraw work contracted out; postpone the pay increase; promote internal mobility transfers of employees, with or without training, or external relocation; favour early retirement, help to set up own business, etc.).[67] Considering, however, the scant experience of employees and employers with intercommunication, one can conclude that such negotiations probably remain quite often formal.

TLS § 101 (1) and (2) state that the employer is required to inform and consult the employees' representative in good time. What does 'in good time' mean? In the timing of the informing and consulting, the employer must keep an eye on different aspects. First, the employees' representative has the right to make proposals relating to the measures planned with regard to the employees at least within fifteen days as of the submission of the information (TLS § 101 (4) and § 113 (3)). It is logical that the employer meets with the employees' representatives and conducts negotiations after receiving the proposals from them. Next, after consultations the employer is obliged to inform the Estonian Unemployment Insurance Fund[68] and, thereupon, he or she may

65. E. Käärats, T. Treier, S. Suder, M. Pihl & M. Proos, *Selgitused töölepingu seaduse juurde* / Comments on the Employment Contracts Act. Ministry of Social Affairs (Juura, 2013), at 166.
66. *Supra* n. 63, at 32.
67. *Supra* n. 32, at 532-533.
68. *See* paragraph 3.2 for greater detail.

terminate employment contracts (TLS § 102 (1) and § 103 (1)). However, collective termination of employment contracts enters into force upon the expiry of the term for advance notice of termination,[69] but not sooner than thirty calendar days after notification of the Estonian Unemployment Insurance Fund (TLS § 103 (2)). Moreover, the Estonian Unemployment Insurance Fund may extend that thirty-day period to up to sixty calendar days (TLS § 103 (4)).[70] Proceeding from the above, it is difficult to determine the exact date when the information and consultation procedure should start but the employer must consider that the period from the notification of employees' representatives to terminations of employment contracts may commonly last at least three months.[71]

According to the information given by the Estonian Labour Inspectorate, the obligation to inform and consult employees in the case of the collective termination of employment contacts is infringed often in the framework of bankruptcy proceedings. The Estonian Chamber of Bailiffs and Trustees in Bankruptcy and the Ministry of Justice are of opinion that the trustee in bankruptcy is not required to inform and consult employees as provided for in TLS §§ 101 and 102 – in the event of bankruptcy of the employer only the Bankruptcy Act (PankrS)[72] applies.[73]

Under PankrS § 1 (1) and (2), bankruptcy means the insolvency of a debtor (employer) declared by a court ruling. A debtor is insolvent if the debtor is unable to satisfy the claims of the creditors and such inability, due to the debtor's financial situation, is not temporary. At the beginning of bankruptcy proceedings, the court appoints a trustee in bankruptcy who perform, among other things, the employer's obligations. Although the PankrS establishes detailed principles how the bankruptcy proceedings must be carry out, including the rules on the communication between the trustee in bankruptcy and creditors (employees), it does not make any exception to norms of the TLS concerning informing and consulting employees in the case of collective redundancy.[74] Directive 98/59/EC also does not allow any deviations. Thus, if the trustee in bankruptcy is contemplating collective redundancies, he or she must start the information and consultation procedure at the earliest opportunity.[75]

69. It should be emphasized that in the case of the collective redundancy, the employer must also follow the rules on the individual dismissal. Nevertheless, pursuant to TLS § 100 (5), if an employer gives advance notice of termination later than provided by law or a collective agreement, the employee has the right to receive compensation (i.e., the average wages) to the extent to which he or she would have been entitled to upon adhering to the term for advance notice.
70. *See* paragraph 4.1. for greater detail.
71. This period may be shorter if employment contracts are terminated collectively due to termination of the activities of the company on the basis of a court judgement which has entered into force. *See* paragraph 4.1. for greater detail.
72. *Pankrotiseadus* / Bankruptcy Act, passed on 22 January 2003 – RT I 2003, 17, 95; 29.06.2014, 109. The act is available in English at <https://www.riigiteataja.ee/en/eli/511072014018/consolide> (accessed 1 July 2015).
73. *Supra* n. 24.
74. However, the intention of trustees in bankruptcy is understandable – they want to carry out collective dismissals as quickly as possible (sometimes with a view to protect the interests of other creditors).
75. The author of the TLS (the Estonian Ministry of Social Affairs) has the same position. *Supra* n. 24.

[B] Notification of the Estonian Unemployment Insurance Fund

[1] General Principles

As previously discussed, in addition to the obligation to provide the employees' representative with all necessary information about the planned collective termination of employment contracts, the employer is required to notify the Estonian Unemployment Insurance Fund as well. The employer's duty to notify the competent public authority has been provided by Article 3 of Directive 98/59/EC and, in the national context, TLS § 102 transposes these rules into Estonian law.

TLS § 102 (1) states that after consultations with employees' representatives an employer must submit[76] the information about the collective dismissal[77] and the information about the consultations to the Estonian Unemployment Insurance Fund. Thus, following TLS § 101 (3) and § 102 (1), the employer is required to inform the Estonian Unemployment Insurance Fund about the same circumstances twice: before and after consultations with employees. Such regulation can be considered justified, because as a result of consultations the data may change.[78]

Under TLS § 102 (2), the employer is obliged to send a transcript of the information specified above to the employees' representative[79] concurrently with the submission of the information to the Estonian Unemployment Insurance Fund. The employees' representative may submit to the Estonian Unemployment Insurance Fund his or her opinion on the collective termination within seven calendar days as of receiving the transcript of the information.

[2] Competent Public Authority

Article 3.1 of Directive 98/59/EC provides that the employer must notify the competent public authority. According to Estonian law, the competent public authority has been changed in the course of time. Before the harmonization of Estonian law with Directive 98/59/EC, the employer was required to inform the employment office, that was a regional structural unit of the Labour Market Board, about the termination of employment contract.[80] From 2003 to the first half of 2009, the competent public authority was the Labour Inspectorate. From the entry into force of the new TLS, the employer has the obligation to notify the Estonian Unemployment Insurance Fund. In order to answer

76. In a format which can be reproduced in writing.
77. The employer is obliged to submit at least the following data: the reasons for the collective termination; the number and official titles of the employees; the number and official titles of those employees and the selection criteria determining the persons whose employment contracts are to be terminated; the period of time during which the employment contracts are to be terminated; the method of calculation of the compensation to be paid to the employees in addition to the benefits prescribed by law or the collective agreement.
78. *Supra* n. 65, at 167.
79. As regards the meaning of 'employees' representative', *see* paragraph 3.1.3.
80. *See* paragraph 1.1. for greater detail.

the question - which is the most competent organ - the functions of the public authority must be examined.

Proceeding from Article 4.2 of Directive 98/59/EC, the competent public authority seeks solutions to the problems raised by the projected collective redundancies. TLS § 103 (2) specifies that the Estonian Unemployment Insurance Fund seeks solutions to the employment problems relating to the collective dismissal.[81] Thus, the public authority must be competent in employment issues.

The main task of the Labour Market Board was to organize labour market services that helped unemployed persons find new employment.[82] Section 8 of the Statutes of the Labour Inspectorate[83] establishes that the main functions of the Labour Inspectorate are: the implementation of the work environment policy; state supervision in the work environment over compliance with the requirements of legislation regulating occupational health and safety and labour relations; informing general public, employees and employers of the dangers in the work environment; and resolving of individual labour disputes in extra-judicial labour dispute resolution body. In 2009, the Labour Market Board was merged with the Estonian Unemployment Insurance Fund. Under TKindlS § 23 (1), one of the objectives of the unemployment insurance fund is implementation of the labour market policy.[84] In order to achieve this objective, the unemployment insurance fund performs, among other tasks, the following functions: organize the provision of labour market services and provide labour market services; pay labour market benefits; keep records of unemployed persons, persons who seek employment, the provision of labour market services, labour market benefits, etc. (TKindlS § 23 (2)).

It can be concluded from the above that, although the Labour Inspectorate is very competent at work environment and labour law issues, in the event of the collective termination of employment contracts, it is necessary to notify the public authority that is able to help persons not in employment. Thus, the transfer of the competent public authority's functions from the Labour Inspectorate to the Estonian Unemployment Insurance Fund is entirely justified.

[3] About Exceptions

Unlike the regulation of Article 3.1 (the second sentence) of Directive 98/59/EC, the TLS does not stipulate that in the case of planned collective redundancies arising from termination of the establishment's activities as a result of a judicial decision, the employer is required to notify the competent public authority in writing only if the latter so requests. According to Estonian law, termination of the activities of the company on the basis of a court judgment may take place in two cases: in the event of

81. *See* paragraph 4.2. for greater detail.
82. About *Töötukassa* (26 August 2014). Estonian Unemployment Insurance Fund. https://www.tootukassa.ee/eng/content/about-tootukassa (accessed 1 July 2015).
83. *Tööinspektsiooni põhimäärus* / Statutes of the Labour Inspectorate, passed on 17 October 2007 - RTL (Appendix to the State Gazette) 2007, 80, 1382; RT I, 16.01.2015, 3.
84. Another objective is organisation of unemployment insurance.

compulsory dissolution[85] and bankruptcy[86] of the employer. As the employer must inform and consult employees irrespective of the reason of the collective termination of employment contracts, he or she can also notify easily the Estonian Unemployment Insurance Fund, although the collective dismissal arise from termination of the company's activities on the basis of a court judgment. This is not a time-consuming duty. Thus, in comparison with Directive 98/59/EC, the rules of the TLS are more favourable to employees[87] but in the case of compulsory dissolution and bankruptcy of the employer, employees need similarly the assistance provided by the Estonian Unemployment Insurance Fund.[88]

As previously discussed, the obligation to inform and consult employees in the event of the collective termination of employment contracts is violated often in the framework of bankruptcy proceedings.[89] Trustees in bankruptcy also fail to comply with the duty to notify the Estonian Unemployment Insurance Fund.[90] As TLS § 102 does not make any exceptions, such activity of trustees in bankruptcy is not in line with the law.

§8.04 SUPPORT MEASURES IN FAVOUR OF EMPLOYEES

[A] General Principles

Pursuant to TLS § 103 (1), an employer may terminate employment contracts after consultations with employees and notification of the Estonian Unemployment Insurance Fund.

---

85. Proceeding from TsÜS § 40 (1), a legal person is dissolved by a court ruling if:

    (1) the objective or activities of the legal person are contrary to law, public order or good morals;
    (2) the legal person was founded in material violation of the law or if the memorandum of association was entered into or the foundation resolution was adopted under circumstances due to which the memorandum or resolution is void, and the corresponding violation cannot be subsequently eliminated;
    (3) the articles of association of the legal person are contrary to law to a significant extent;
    (4) the legal person does not comply with the requirements established for the legal person by law;
    (5) the authority of the management board or a body substituting for the management board of the legal person terminated more than two years ago and a new management board or substituting body has not been elected;
    (6) there is any other basis provided by law.

    The compulsory dissolution of legal persons does not occur frequently in practice.
86. PankrS § 29 (8) provides that if a court terminates bankruptcy proceedings by abatement by a ruling without declaring bankruptcy, the trustee in bankruptcy liquidates the legal person within two months after the entry into force of the ruling on termination of the proceedings. In the case of declaration of bankruptcy, a general meeting of creditors may decide to terminate a legal person. The decision to dissolve the legal person must be approved by the court and, thereupon, the trustee in bankruptcy liquidates the legal person (PankrS § 130 (1) -(3)).
87. As mentioned before, Article 5 of Directive 98/59/EC allows such deviations.
88. *See* paragraph 4.2. for greater detail.
89. *See* paragraph 3.1.4. for greater detail.
90. *Supra* n. 24.

TLS § 103 (2), sets forth that the collective termination of employment contracts enters into force upon the expiry of the term for advance notice of termination, but not sooner than thirty calendar days after the time when the Estonian Unemployment Insurance Fund received the information about the collective dismissal. During that term, the Estonian Unemployment Insurance Fund seeks solutions to the employment problems relating to the collective termination.

TLS § 103 (3) and (4) give the Estonian Unemployment Insurance Fund the right to both shorten and extend the above-mentioned thirty-day period considering the importance of employment issues. The Fund is entitled to shorten the term if the employment problems can be resolved within a shorter term. The Estonian Unemployment Insurance Fund may extend the term up to sixty calendar days if the Fund finds that it cannot resolve the employment problems relating to the collective termination within thirty calendar days. The extension of the term is the exceptional case that may occur in the event of large-scale dismissals, the difficulty of finding new jobs, etc.[91]

The Estonian Unemployment Insurance Fund communicates[92] a decision to change the term to the employer within fourteen calendar days[93] as of the receipt of the information about the collective dismissal (TLS § 103 (5)). The decision to change the term is a discretionary decision that the Fund must justify.[94] The author shares the opinion that it is especially important to motivate the decision to extend the term because it restricts the rights of employers and postpones the time of termination of employment contracts.[95]

The term of entry into force of the collective termination of employment contracts is not applied if employment contracts are terminated collectively due to termination of the activities of the company on the basis of a court judgment[96] which has entered into force (TLS § 103 (6)). Thus, in the event of compulsory dissolution and bankruptcy of the employer, the latter is required to notify the Estonian Unemployment Insurance Fund[97] but may terminate employment contracts immediately after the notification.

[B] Solution of Employment Problems

As already mentioned, the Estonian Unemployment Insurance Fund has usually 30 calendar days[98] in order to seek solutions to the employment problems relating to the collective termination. Thus, the aim of the activity of the Fund is to help employees to get back into employment at the earliest opportunity. Neither the TLS nor the TKindlS

91. *Supra* n. 65, at 169.
92. In a format which can be reproduced in writing.
93. During this time, the Estonian Unemployment Insurance Fund has received the employees' representative's opinion on the collective termination of employment contracts (TLS § 102 (3)) and the Fund can consider it when making a decision.
94. *Supra* n. 65, at 168.
95. *Ibid.*
96. About the termination of the activities of the company on the basis of a court judgement, *see* paragraph 3.2.3.
97. *Ibid.*
98. The Fund has the right to both shorten and extend this period; *see* paragraph 4.1. for greater detail.

that establishes the objective and basis of functioning of the Estonian Unemployment Insurance Fund lay down the guidelines about which measures the Fund must take with a view to alleviate the negative effects of collective redundancies.

Nevertheless, the Estonian Unemployment Insurance Fund explains its services in the case of the collective termination of employment contracts on the Fund's website.[99] According to the information given on the website, a rapid response team is assembled when the notification of a collective redundancy reaches the Estonian Unemployment Insurance Fund. The rapid response team can organize a prompt response to major redundancies. The services of the rapid response team are free of charge.[100]

The rapid response team visits the employer's location before the last working day and sets up activities in order to:

- inform employees about the labour market, training opportunities, registering as unemployed, unemployment benefits and redundancy benefits, social services and benefits, and personal revenue and expenditure planning in light of a reduced income;
- help employees with their job search and organize outplacement activities such as meetings with potential employers;
- make employees aware of active labour market policies and what services they can benefit from.[101]

It can be concluded from the above that the Estonian Unemployment Insurance Fund has created the effective system that determines how to react in the case of collective dismissals. The activity of the rapid response team when it helps employees into new employment is very diverse and this provides quite likely that the employee finds a new job after the lay-off.

[C] Combining of the Collective and Individual Dismissal

In the event of the collective termination of employment contracts, an employer must take into account that he or she is obliged to adhere concurrently to the rules on individual dismissals. As already mentioned, an employer may terminate employment contracts after consultations with employees and notification of the Estonian Unemployment Insurance Fund (TLS § 103 (1)). Hence, only after the discharge of these tasks, the employer may make declarations of termination (give employees an advance notice).

If the employer has not informed and consulted employees and/or notified the Estonian Unemployment Insurance Fund before making declarations of termination, the termination of employment contracts is, under TLS § 104 (1), in conflict with the

99. Outplacement and other services (4 February 2014). Estonian Unemployment Insurance Fund. https://www.tootukassa.ee/eng/content/employers/outplacement-and-other-services (accessed 1 July 2015).
100. That site also contains the contact information of the rapid response team.
101. *Supra* n. 100.

law and, therefore, null and void. In such case, an employee may file an action with the court or an application with a labour dispute committee[102] for establishment of voidness of termination within thirty calendar days as of the receipt of the declaration of termination (TLS § 105 (1)).[103] However, as previously discussed, although employers infringe the obligation to inform and consult employees and/or notify the Estonian Unemployment Insurance Fund in the event of collective dismissal, the employees do not challenge individual terminations of employment contracts.[104] From the author's viewpoint, this is explained by the fact that, in the case of the collective termination of employment contracts, employees are not aware of their competence and rights.

As mentioned before, the collective termination of employment contracts enters into force upon the expiry of the term for advance notice of termination, but not sooner than thirty calendar days after the time when the Estonian Unemployment Insurance Fund received the information about the collective dismissal (TLS § 103 (2)). Following this rule, the employer is able to notify employees of termination at least thirty calendar days in advance, if he or she wants to terminate employment contracts at the first opportunity after informing the Fund. In such case, the employer must notify the Estonian Unemployment Insurance Fund and employees at the same time.

Pursuant to TLS § 97 (2), an employer is obliged to give an employee advance notice of termination if the employment relationship with the employer has lasted less than one year - fifteen calendar days; one to five years - thirty calendar days; five to ten years - sixty calendar days; ten or more years - ninety calendar days.[105] If the employer is required to notify employees of termination at least sixty or ninety calendar days in advance but he or she notifies only thirty calendar days in advance, the termination of employment contract is still lawful. However, if an employer gives advance notice of termination later than provided by law or a collective agreement, the employee has the right to receive compensation (i.e. the average wages) to the extent to which he or she would have been entitled to upon adhering to the term for advance notice (TLS § 100 (5)).

In practice, there may be situations where the employer is not able to provide the employee with the work agreed sooner than thirty calendar days after the time when the Estonian Unemployment Insurance Fund received the information about the collective redundancy. In that case, the employee has the right to require the providing of work (VÕS § 108) or payment of wages (TLS § 35) until the end of the thirty-day mandatory period.[106]

102. Proceeding from § 10 (1) of the Individual Labour Dispute Resolution Act, a labour dispute committee is a pre-trial independent individual labour dispute resolution body. *Individuaalse töövaidluse lahendamise seadus* / Individual Labour Dispute Resolution Act, passed on 20 December 1995 -- RT I 1996, 3, 57; 29.06.2014, 109. The act is available in English at <https://www.riigiteataja.ee/en/eli/503072014007/consolide> (accessed 1 July 2015).
103. *Supra* n. 65, at 168.
104. *See* paragraph 1.2.
105. These are minimum periods.
106. *See* also *supra* n. 65, at 168.

Proceeding from the above, the employer should rethink the rules on both individual and collective dismissal thoroughly in order to guarantee that the collective termination of employment contracts would be legitimate and successful.

§8.05 JUDICIAL CONTROL AND SANCTIONS

Article 6 of Directive 98/59/EC obligates the Member States to ensure that judicial and/or administrative procedures for the enforcement of obligations under the Directive are available to the employees' representatives and/or employees. Under TLS § 115, state supervision of the fulfilment of the requirements provided for in TLS § 101 (1)-(3)[107] and § 102 (1)-(2),[108] is exercised by the Labour Inspectorate under the conditions and pursuant to the procedure provided for in the Occupational Health and Safety Act (TTOS).[109]

The TTOS, in turn, refers to the Law Enforcement Act (KorS).[110] KorS § 6 (1) states that a law enforcement agency is an authority, body or person authorized by law or a regulation to perform the function of state supervision. Thus, the Labour Inspectorate is one of the law enforcement agencies in Estonia. According to KorS § 23 (4), law enforcement agency has the right to issue a precept to a subject of supervision and apply penalty payment.[111] In the case of a failure to comply with a precept, the upper limit of penalty payment is EUR 3,200 (TTOS § 26^1).

TLS § 128 (1) establishes that failure by an employer to perform the obligation to inform and consult upon collective termination of employment contracts is punishable by a fine of up to 100 fine units.[112] The same act, if committed by a legal person, is punishable by a fine of up to EUR 1,300 (TLS § 128 (2)). The body conducting

107. These subsections are about the information and consultation of employees upon collective termination of employment contracts.

108. These subsections are about the notification of Estonian Unemployment Insurance Fund of collective termination.

109. *Töötervishoiu ja tööohutuse seadus* / Occupational Health and Safety Act, passed on 16 June 1999 – RT I 1999, 60, 616; 26.02.2015, 1. The act is available in English at <https://www.riigiteataja.ee/en/eli/525022015005/consolide> (accessed 1 July 2015).

110. *Korrakaitseseadus* / Law Enforcement Act, passed on 23 February 2011 – RT I, 22.03.2011, 4; 23.03.2015, 4. The act is available in English at <https://www.riigiteataja.ee/en/eli/516062015011/consolide> (accessed 1 July 2015).

111. Challenge proceedings concerning precept has been laid down by the Administrative Procedure Act. *Haldusmenetluse seadus* / Administrative Procedure Act, passed on 6 June 2001 – RT I, 2001, 58, 354; 23.02.2011, 3. The act is available in English at <https://www.riigiteataja.ee/en/eli/530102013037/consolide> (accessed 1 July 2015). A penalty payment is applied on the basis of and pursuant to the procedure provided by the Substitutive Enforcement and Penalty Payment Act. *Asendustäitmise ja sunniraha seadus* / Substitutive Enforcement and Penalty Payment Act, passed on 9 May 2001 – RT I, 2001, 50, 283; 12.07.2014, 1. The act is available in English at <https://www.riigiteataja.ee/en/eli/522012015001/consolide> (accessed 1 July 2015).

112. According to § 47 (1) of the Penal Code, a fine unit is the base amount of a fine and is equal to four euros. Hence, the value of 100 fine units is 400 euros. *Karistusseadustik* / Penal Code, passed on 6 June 2001 – RT I 2001, 61, 364; 12.03.2015, 7. The act is available in English at <https://www.riigiteataja.ee/en/eli/519032015003/consolide> (accessed 1 July 2015).

extra-judicial proceedings pertaining to the misdemeanours provided for in TLS § 128 is the Labour Inspectorate (TLS § 130 (2)).[113]

As regards other norms of the TLS concerning collective redundancies (that are not mentioned in TLS § 115) – these are not subject to state supervision and, in the case of disputes, the parties to the employment contract may have recourse to the courts or a labour dispute committee for the establishment of voidness of termination.[114]

As previously discussed, despite the fact that employers always do not comply with duties to inform and consult employees and/or notify the Estonian Unemployment Insurance Fund, there are no individual labour disputes regarding collective dismissals.[115] However, from 2011 to 2014 the Estonian Labour Inspectorate has detected twenty-five violations pertaining to the employer's obligation to inform and consult employees or notify the Estonian Unemployment Insurance Fund in the event of collective terminations of employment contracts in sixteen companies.[116] According to the Labour Inspectorate, the employers know their tasks but they are of the opinion that the implementation of these rules is not important – this is expensive for the company and, in comparison with the costs that corresponding obligations entail, a fine is so small that the payment of it does not cause problems.[117]

Thus, it seems that legal measures are not effective enough to ensure that the regulations are complied with. In the author's view, it is necessary to raise the awareness and competence of employees' representatives in employees' rights in the event of the collective termination of employment contracts, as well as to increase employers' responsibility for violation of the law.

§8.06 CONCLUDING REMARKS

In Estonia, the regulation on the collective dismissals that has been elaborated according to Directive 98/59/EC has been in force more than twelve years. Corresponding norms of the TLS are entirely in conformity with the Directive. Some principles (the meaning of 'collective redundancy', the exceptions to the scope of the regulation and the employer's obligation to notify the Estonian Unemployment Insurance Fund in the case of termination of the activities of the company on the basis of a court judgment) are even more favourable to employees.

However, in Estonian legal practice, the implementation of provisions on the collective termination of employment contracts is not very topical. Consultations with employees are often formal, there are no significant court cases, and supervision

113. The rules on misdemeanour proceedings have been established by the Code of Misdemeanour Procedure. *Väärteomenetluse seadustik* / Code of Misdemeanour Procedure, passed on 22 May 2002 – RT I 2002, 50, 313; 19.03.2015, 1. The act is available in English at <https://www.riigiteataja.ee/en/eli/530032015002/consolide> (accessed 1 July 2015).
114. *See* TLS §§ 104-109 for greater detail.
115. *See* paragraphs 1.2., 3.4.1. and 4.3.
116. The Estonian Unemployment Insurance Fund informs the Labour Inspectorate about the violations. *Supra* n. 24.
117. *Ibid.*

proceedings are conducted quite rarely. From the author's viewpoint, the effective enforcement of the regulation of collective dismissals depends largely on the level of development of collective labour relations. As in Estonia, employees and employers' experiences of intercommunication are scant, they do not pay particular attention to collective redundancies.

CHAPTER 9

Collective Dismissal in Finland

Jorma Saloheimo

§9.01 THE COLLECTIVE DISMISSAL: THE CASE

[A] The Finnish Economy and Labour Market

Finland is a highly industrialized Nordic country with a population of just over 5.4 million. The economy of the country operates on a largely free-market basis. The per capita output equals to that of other western economies such as France, Germany, Sweden or the United Kingdom. The largest sector of the economy is services at ca. 66%, followed by manufacturing and refining at 31%. Primary production is 3%. In services the sectors employing the largest number of people are commerce, transport, hotel and restaurant services, education, health and social services and other services. The largest industries are electronics, machinery, vehicles and other engineered metal products, forest industry, and chemicals. The public sector is large in terms of both its share of the GDP (gross domestic product) and its number of employees. Some 28% of the labour force is employed in public administration and services.

In recent years, the global financial crisis has had a heavy impact on the Finnish economy. Special difficulties have hit electronics, with Nokia giving up its production of mobile phones, and forestry, where the cost-effectiveness of production of has collapsed, leading to closing down pulp and paper mills. As a result, the number of workers dismissed on economic grounds has been on the rise. In August 2016, the level of unemployment was around 7.2% of the total labour force of just under 2.5 million workers. This in turn has led to an increasing importance of the rules protecting workers from the threat of redundancies.

The Finnish labour market and its regulation have been described as an example of the so-called Nordic model for industrial relations. This implies that there are certain common features in the industrial relations and in the labour law systems of the Nordic countries. Characteristic for these systems is the strong role of labour market parties and also their interplay with the state. This role manifests itself in many ways. At the work place level, workers' participation and settling disputes over the application of terms of work is based on negotiations between the employer and the representative of the local trade union, the shop steward. Disputes which are not solved at the company level are transferred to negotiations between the employers' association and the workers' federation, which are parties to the collective agreement in question. The labour market parties also participate in the preparation of labour laws and their application in several public bodies, such as the Labour Court. This is referred to as a system of tripartite cooperation.

The basis of the system lies in the high level of organization on both sides of industry. The union density in Finland is around 65% of the active work force, and on the employer side the level of organization is roughly the same. Collective bargaining relationships in all sectors are long-standing and established. As a result, about 75.5% of the workers in the private sector are within the ambit of normally binding collective agreements, meaning that the workers are employed in companies, which are bound by the collective agreement in question on account of the company's membership in the employers' association that has concluded the agreement. The coverage of collective agreements is further complemented by a procedure in which a collective agreement, which fulfils certain criteria concerning *inter alia* representativeness, is declared as generally binding in the field in question, so that also the non-organized employers operating in that field must follow the agreement. This way more than 84% of the work force in the private sector is covered by collective agreements. The collective agreements concluded for the public sector are applied to all workers employed by the government and the municipalities.

As explained, collective agreements play an important role in the regulation of terms and conditions of work. In addition, Finland has traditionally had a comprehensive set of statutory labour laws in place. These are complemented by collective agreements and sometimes replaced by them, where an Act allows for a derogation from its provisions by means of an agreement, collective or individual, as the case may be. Also procedures applied in redundancy situations and grounds for collective dismissals are subject to this two-tier regulation. This has its consequences for example on the judicial enforcement processes and sanctions applied in dismissal cases, as we will soon discover.

[B] The Regulatory Framework

The rules concerning collective dismissals can be divided according to various criteria. There are rules, which regulate legal grounds for a collective dismissal, and others, which apply to all collective dismissals regardless of the validity of the ground. This division roughly coincides with the difference made between material and procedural rules. Furthermore, there are rules, which must be followed prior to the termination, and rules concerning the protection of workers already made redundant. In the following overview we will first take a look at material rules concerning especially dismissal grounds, and then move on to the procedural rules.

Already the Constitution of Finland provides that 'No one shall be dismissed from employment without a lawful reason' (section 18.3).[1] The main import of this provision is that dismissal grounds must be laid down in mandatory law enacted by the Parliament. Such a statute is the Employment Contracts Act.[2]

The *grounds for termination* of the employment contract by means of notice are regulated in Chapter 7 of the Employment Contracts Act. Different conditions apply to termination on grounds relating to the employee's person, and collective grounds, which are in the Act defined as financial and production-related grounds for termination. The basic reason for a collective termination is lack of work.

Common for both cases of termination is that the ground must be 'proper and weighty' (section 1 of the Chapter 7 of the Act). In the case of collective dismissal this means for example that even if the financial and production-related criteria are met, the termination must not be discriminatory vis-à-vis the employee or employees chosen to be dismissed.

Another common feature for the grounds for termination by notice is that they apply only to employment contracts made for an indefinite period. A fixed-term contract cannot be terminated on these grounds. Such a contract can be terminated before the end of the contract period only by means of *rescinding* the contract with immediate effect. Under section 1 of Chapter 8 of the Employment Contracts Act, this requires an extremely weighty cause, which relates to the conduct or other personal circumstances of the employee. Consequently, an employment contract cannot be rescinded on collective grounds; a period of notice must always be observed in these cases.

For the purposes of this presentation, it is appropriate here to cite the relevant provisions of Chapter 7 of the Employment Contracts Act. The provisions on collective grounds for termination read as follows:

> **Section 3. Financial and production-related grounds for termination**
>
> The employer may terminate the employment contract if the work to be offered has diminished substantially and permanently for financial or production-related reasons or for reasons arising from reorganization of the employer's operations. The employment contract shall not be terminated, however, if the employee can be placed in or trained for other duties as provided in section 4.
>
> The employer shall provide employees with training required by new work duties that can be deemed feasible and reasonable from the point of view of both contracting parties.
>
> If an employer which in fact exercises control in personnel matters in another enterprise or corporate body on the basis of ownership, agreement or some other arrangement cannot offer an employee work as referred to in subsection 1, it must find out if it is possible to meet the employer's obligation to provide work and training by offering the employee work in other enterprises or corporate bodies under its control.

1. Suomen perustuslaki 11.6.1999/731.
2. Työsopimuslaki 26.1.2001/55.

These provisions apply to financial and production-related grounds for termination regardless of the number of the employees to be made redundant. So even a dismissal of only one employee may be effected by an employer and assessed by a court according to these provisions. The interpretation of the conditions for a collective dismissal is further discussed below in section §9.04 of this presentation.

A less severe alternative to collective dismissal is *lay-off*. Laying off means temporary interruption of work and remuneration on the basis of an employer's decision or an agreement made on the employer's initiative, while the employment relationship continues in other respects. Thus, employees laid off can keep their jobs and hope to be invited back to work as the economic situation of the employer company improves. In many cases, however, a lay-off is just a measure which precedes dismissal. The grounds for an indefinite lay-off are the same as those, which apply to dismissal on economic or production-related reasons. A somewhat lower threshold is applied in cases where the employer's potential to offer work is deemed to have diminished temporarily for a period of ninety days at maximum, which is then also the maximum length of a fixed-term lay-off (sections 1 and 2 of Chapter 5 of the Employment Contracts Act). Yet another alternative to collective dismissal is *changing the employment relationship into a part-time relationship*. The employer is entitled to change the employment relationship unilaterally into a part-time relationship on the termination grounds applicable to collective dismissal, and observing a period of notice (section 11, Chapter 7 of the Employment Contracts Act).

The terms of notice are regulated in section 3, Chapter 6 of the Employment Contracts Act. The notice periods to be observed by the employer vary from fourteen days to six months according to the length of the employment relationship. The longest notice period is granted to employees with a service of more than twelve years. In lay-off cases the term of notice is fourteen days. The provisions on notice periods are, however, optional and allow for shorter periods if so determined in an individual or collective agreement.

The procedure applied in the context of collective dismissals is in the main regulated in the Act on Co-operation within Undertakings.[3] There are a number of issues, which have to be handled within the co-operation procedure, such as practices of recruitment, principles of temporary agency work, various changes in business operations affecting the personnel and arrangement of work, and redundancies. *The organisation* for the co-operation has been adapted to the line organisation at the work place and to the negotiation systems already in use at the work places. Thus, the parties to co-operation are the employer and the personnel, which are normally represented by the shop stewards of the personnel groups affected by the measure the employer is contemplating. If the measure concerns only an individual employee or a few employees, the negotiations can be conducted directly with the employees in question.

3. Yhteistoimintalaki 30.3.2007/334. This Act repealed the former Co-operation within Undertakings Act (22.9.1978/725), which in many respects contained the same principles as those adopted in the new Act. Therefore, case law concerning the interpretation of the old Act is still in many respects relevant and is utilized also in this presentation.

Collective redundancies are, however, subject to *intensified co-operation with minimum periods of negotiation*. If the measure is a collective dismissal, lay-off or changing employment relationships into part-time ones, the employer has various duties of information and negotiation regulated in detail in Chapter 8 of the Act. The Act prescribes certain minimum negotiation times, which have to be followed prior to announcing reductions of the work-force. If the reduction concerns less than ten employees or involves a lay-off of more than ten employees for ninety days at maximum, the negotiation period is fourteen days, unless otherwise agreed in the negotiations. The same applies to undertakings with a staff of at least twenty but fewer than thirty employees regardless of the number of employees to be reduced. If the number of employees is higher or the length of a lay-off is longer than those explained above, the negotiation period is six weeks counted from the start of the negotiations.

As a main rule, the Act is applicable to undertakings normally employing at least twenty persons, subject to certain exceptions, of which one is mentioned above. Within the scope of application of the Co-operation Act there are just under 900,000 wage-earners, who are employed with approximately 8,000 undertakings. As for smaller undertakings, the Employment Contracts Act contains simplified rules of procedure. Prior to terminating the employment contract on a collective ground, the employer must at the earliest possible stage explain to the employees to be dismissed the grounds for termination of employment and the alternatives, as well as the employment services available from the employment and economic development office (section 3, Chapter 9 of the Employment Contracts Act).

If an employee, who is dismissed on a collective ground, has worked for the same employer for at least three years, the employer must *notify the employment authority* regarding the termination without delay. This notification shall, with the consent of the employee, contain information on the education, work tasks and work experience of the employee. The employee is also entitled to be informed by the employer of a so-called employment programme, which is drawn up by the employment authorities. The employee must further be informed of an employment supplement available to him or her from public unemployment funding (sections 3a and 3b of Chapter 9 of the Employment Contracts Act).

The above-described regulation concerning the material and procedurals aspects of protection in redundancy situations apply to employees having a private law contract of employment. The employment relationships of civil servants and municipal officers are governed by public law. The protection of these employees is regulated in much the same way as has been explained above, but will not be further handled in this presentation. There are also certain groups, such as employees' representatives and employees on parental leave, who enjoy special job protection. Also these aspects of protection are left without further discussion in this text.

The account given above concerns the statutory regulation of collective dismissals. Alongside with this regulation several *collective agreements* apply to the same situations. It is common to include provisions on job security in collective agreements or in separate confederation-wide agreements governing protection against unwarranted termination of employment contracts. For the most part these provisions and agreements reproduce the appropriate rules of the Employment Contracts Act. Some variation may occur concerning for instance the length of notice periods or the amount of the compensation to which an employee, who is dismissed without valid ground, is entitled. The co-operation procedure is not so commonly regulated in collective agreements.

An aspect concerning collective dismissals, which is regulated solely in collective agreements, is *the sequence of redundancies*. Under statutory law, the employer is in principle free to choose the employees to be dismissed, as far as the decision is not discriminatory. Collective agreements, however, limit the employer's freedom in this respect. The provisions in collective agreements, concluded for various fields, are very similar. The preference to remain in employment is afforded to those employees, who are *deemed important to the operation of the undertaking*. Secondary criteria are the length of service and the employee's family support responsibilities. An employer's omission to observe this sequence constitutes a violation of the collective agreement and is sanctioned accordingly, but does not render the dismissal unfounded. On the contrary, the provisions discussed here are applied only to dismissals, the grounds of which are not challenged.

The import of the collectively agreed regulation of redundancies is that disputes arising from the application of the provisions can be brought before the Labour Court instead of regular courts of justice. This alternative is available to parties to employment contracts who are bound by the collective agreement in question. Litigation in the Labour Court provides several advantages, which will be discussed in more detail below in section §9.04[B][2].

§9.02 THE PROCEDURE PRECEDING COLLECTIVE DISMISSALS

[A] The Co-operation Procedure

The main features of the negotiation procedure under Chapter 8 of the Co-operation in Undertakings Act have been described in the previous chapter. Next, a more detailed account of the employer's duties will be given in a chronological order. The procedure includes a number of measures, which must be taken in undertakings normally employing at least twenty persons if the employer is planning collective dismissals, lay-offs or reducing a contract of employment into a part-time contract. The regulation is intended to implement the requirements of the Directive on Collective Redundancies 98/59/EC and the Information and Consultation Directive 2002/14/14 into the Finnish legal order.

Employer's proposal for negotiations (section 45 of the Act). The employer shall give a proposal for negotiations to all affected employees or their representatives in order to commence the co-operation procedure and employment measures. The proposal has to be issued at the latest *five calendar days* prior to the negotiations in writing. The proposal shall include at least the time and place of the negotiations and an outline of the issues to be discussed.

The proposal for negotiations or its material contents shall be delivered, in writing, also *to the employment office* no later than at the commencement of the co-operation negotiations (section 48).

Information provided by the employer (section 47). If the planned measure affects *at least ten* employees, the employer is to provide the representatives of the employees concerned with information, in writing, available to him as follows:

- the grounds for the intended measures;
- initial estimate of the amount of reductions in the work-force;
- report of the principles used to determine which employees are going to be affected; and
- time estimate for implementation of the planned reduction measures.

The information has to be attached to the proposal for negotiations. Information obtained by the employer after this point can be given in the first meeting of the negotiations. Thus the negotiations can be commenced, even though all relevant information is yet not available when making the proposal for negotiations. The purpose is to begin the negotiations as early as possible.

If the planned reduction measure concerns *less than ten* employees, the employer may provide the information to the employees concerned or their representatives verbally, unless otherwise requested by the employee side.

Plans and principles for action (section 49). The provision purports to improve the co-operation between the employer, the personnel and the employment office in *collective dismissal* situations. If *at least ten employees* are affected, the employer shall in the beginning of the negotiations provide the representatives of the personnel groups with a report on a plan of action to promote employment. In preparing the plan of action the employer shall together with the employment authorities examine how the public employment services can be used to support employment. The action plan shall include:

- the intended timetable for the negotiations;
- the procedures to be followed in the negotiations; and
- the planned principles of action to be applied during the notice period; this involves use of the services of the employment authorities to advance training and applying for work.

If the employer contemplates terminations of contracts of *less than ten employees,* a somewhat more simple procedure can be followed. In these cases the employer shall present the principles according to which the employees can have support from public employment services in applying for other work or education during the notice period. The Employment Contracts Act provides for an employee's right to employment leave with full pay during the notice period (*see* below in section §9.03[A]).

Contents of the duty to negotiate (section 50). Matters concerning the reduction of the number of employees have to be discussed in the spirit of co-operation to obtain consensus. The content of the duty to negotiate is the same regardless of how many employees are within the employer's reduction plan. Contents of the negotiations include:

- the grounds and effects of the measures;
- principles or plans of action;
- ways to limit the number of people affected by reductions; and
- alleviation of the consequences of the reductions to the employees.

Matters to be discussed in the negotiations include in particular opportunities for training and relocation and work and working time arrangements. Training possibilities have to be examined together with the employment authorities. For example taking a study leave or pension options can be considered as an alternative to redundancies. If reduction in the use of the work force cannot be avoided, the opportunities to minimize the social harm and financial loss have to be discussed in the negotiations.

Fulfilment of the duty to negotiate (section 51). The minimum duration of the negotiations is fourteen days or six weeks since the commencement of the negotiations, depending on the number of the affected employees, the length of the lay-off and the size of the undertaking (*see* section §9.01 above).

Although the negotiations must aim at obtaining consensus on the measures to be taken, the Act does not require the parties to agree on the measures. After the prescribed time for negotiations has elapsed, the employer is entitled to decide unilaterally on the reductions in the work force.

The employer must, however, *register the outcome* of the negotiations (section 52). Furthermore, the employer shall within a reasonable time provide the employees and the representatives of the personnel groups who participated in the negotiations with a *report on the decisions* the employer is considering on the basis of the negotiations (section 53). The report shall provide at least:

- the number – but not necessarily the names – of the employees affected by the reduction measures;
- duration of the lay-offs; and
- an estimate of the time during which the planned reductions are intended to be carried out.

On request of the representative of the personnel group the employer has to present the report jointly to the employees of the personnel group concerned.

[B] Problems of Interpretation

The regulation described above has given rise to legal proceedings and different interpretations. *The correct timing* of the co-operation negotiations is one of the crucial issues.

On the one hand, there is a point when the negotiations must be initiated *at the latest*. In its Judgment 1997:55 the Supreme Court held that the employer does not have an obligation to commence the negotiations before the necessity of the dismissal has become *obvious*. In this case the reason for the dismissals was that the company had lost the dealership of a certain make of cars. On the other hand, consultations held before the expected changes in business operations have come to a concrete stage, can be *premature*. The effects of the change cannot be usefully discussed on such a basis. Later dismissals may then require new consultations (*see also* the ECJ's statement in C-44/08, referred to below).

Also the Labour Court has dealt with these issues. One case concerned the outsourcing of the mail handling functions of a municipal energy utility to a private company. The preparations for the reorganization project had started in the summer of 2001, negotiations between the utility and the company had commenced, and the first offer of the company was made in November 2001. Soon after that a new offer was asked and was presented in January 2002. The first cooperation meeting was held in March 2002, and the employee representatives were informed of the forthcoming arrangement and its effects on the personnel. The Court considered this to be too late and said that the negotiations should have been initiated in November at the time when the last offer, which was later on also accepted, was requested. At a later stage the opportunity to real interaction was missed, and the grounds and effects of and the alternatives to the intended changes could not be discussed meaningfully.

A specific problem of *evidence* may come up in these kinds of cases. There may be uncertainty as to *when* the employer has in fact made the decision on the business operation or other arrangement, which is the cause of redundancies. The point of departure in Finnish law is that such a decision may not be taken prior to discharging the negotiation duty. In this respect the domestic law is perhaps stricter than Article 2(1) the Collective Redundancies Directive, according to which the consultation duty is triggered when the employer is *contemplating redundancies*.

The problem arose in the context of the *Fujitsu Siemens* case, which was referred to the European Court of Justice by the Finnish Supreme Court. Fujitsu Siemens Computers Ltd, based in Finland, was a subsidiary of Fujitsu Siemens Computers BV, the parent company, which in February 2000 decided to terminate most of its operations and proceeded to make 450 workers in a factory in Finland redundant. The parent company had already considered the divestment of this factory in December 1999, although without specifying what was finally to become of it.

The ECJ recalled that, as is clear from Articles 2 and 3 of Directive 98/59/EC, the obligations of consultation and notification imposed on the employer come into being prior to the employer's decision to terminate employment contracts, when there is still a possibility of avoiding or at least reducing collective redundancies, or of mitigating the consequences. The Court specified that, on the one hand, it would be premature to start consultations when collective redundancies are only a possibility contemplated by the employer and the relevant factors for the consultations are not known. On the other hand, a consultation which began when a decision making such collective redundancies necessary had already been taken, could not usefully involve any examination of conceivable alternatives with the aim of avoiding them and would therefore be too late to achieve the objectives of the obligation. The Court concluded that the consultation procedure must be started by the employer once he adopts strategic decisions or changes in activities which compel him to contemplate or to plan for collective redundancies.

Upon receiving the ECJ's preliminary ruling, the Supreme Court heard witnesses, went through the records of meetings of the boards of both companies and conducted a thorough analysis of the evidence presented. The Court noted that in the minutes for the December meeting of the board of the parent company contained no express mention of closing down the factory in question. The next day the daughter company issued a proposal for holding co-operation negotiations on collective redundancies resulting from the planned closure of the factory. After these events the board of the parent company did not get back to the matter. The Court came to the conclusion that the decision had in reality been made by the parent company in December, so already before the co-operation procedure had even been launched. The co-operation within Undertakings Act had thus been violated.

The Labour Court was faced with very similar problems in its Judgment 2011:73. The co-operation negotiations, concerning the closing down of a paper mill, had come to an end in January 2008. An official decision on the closure was subsequently announced. However, no real alternatives to this solution had been discussed in the negotiations. Instead, press releases issued by the company, public statements of the management, and internal information given by the company over the autumn of 2007 revealed, that the decision had already been taken by the end of the year 2007. The Labour Court held that the company was in breach of the Co-operation Agreement concluded for the paper industry.

The case law described above indicates that in the assessment of observing the consultation duty, the time of the factual decision-making is decisive, and not for example the date formally entered in the minutes of the company board or the like.

§9.03 THE SUPPORT MEASURES IN FAVOUR OF WORKERS

A major part of measures designed to support employees, who are under a threat of redundancy or who have already been dismissed, are governed by a set of rules which is called *the change security operating model.* These measures are taken by the employer and the employment authorities. They are available regardless of the validity of the dismissal ground.

In section §9.02[A] above we have already discussed *the action plan for promotion of employment*, which the employer is obliged to prepare with the staff during the consultations preceding collective redundancies. In preparing the plan the employer shall without delay together with the employment authorities examine the public employment services supporting employment. The proposal for negotiations or its material contents shall also be delivered, in writing, to the employment office no later than at the commencement of the co-operation negotiations, unless the said information has been previously provided in some other context (section 48 of the Co-operation within Undertakings Act).

In situations requiring change security, the services of the employment office will offer:

- information events for the employees;
- job seeking and job exchange services;

- labour market training;
- work trials;
- advice on enterprising and support for a new entrepreneur;
- other services that will improve the job seeker's professional capabilities.

The regional mobility of job seekers can also be supported, for example by reimbursing expenses arising from travel to look for a job.

After the termination has been effected, there is support available during the term of notice while the employment relationship is still in force. An employee dismissed on a collective ground is entitled to *employment leave with full pay* during the notice period for the purposes of gaining new employment. The duration of the employment leave is determined by the duration of the period of notice and varies from five to twenty working days (section 12, Chapter 7 of the Employment Contracts Act). Before taking employment leave or part thereof, the employee shall inform the employer regarding the leave and the grounds therefore as early as possible, and shall, upon request, present a reliable account on the grounds for each leave. Taking employment leave shall not cause substantial inconvenience to the employer.

During the employment leave the employee may for example take part in drawing up a *personal employment plan* with the authorities, engage in job seeking and attend job interviews. The employment plan will contain details of the client's independent job search and measures to support it, and measures that will optimally promote chances of finding a permanent new job as soon as possible. The client can get *basic unemployment allowance at a higher rate* for the time he or she participates in services facilitating placement in a job, supposing there has been an agreement about the service in the personal employment plan.

Another kind of protection, *the right to re-employment*, concerns employees, who have already been made redundant due to collective grounds and whose employment relationship has come to an end. If the employer needs *new employees within nine months* of termination of the employment relationship for the *same or similar work* that the employee given notice had been doing, the employer shall offer work to this former employee. This presupposes that the employee is seeking work via the official channel, the employment office, which can on request inform the employer of such job seekers (section 6, Chapter 6 of the Employment Contracts Act). Fulfilling the duty of re-employment means that a new contract of employment is concluded between the parties. The terms and conditions work, such as pay, do not have to be the same as in the previous employment relationship. In relation to other job-seekers, former employees have a privilege to be hired, but in relation to employees who have been laid off by the same employer, former employees are in a secondary position.

The duty of re-employment is not actualized, if the employer decides to have the former work done by external work force, such as temporary agency workers or a subcontractor (Judgment 2007:6 of the Labour Court). In some collective agreements, however, there are restrictions on the use of temporary agency work in these situations.

§9.04 JUDICIAL CONTROL AND SANCTIONS

[A] Control of the Validity of a Collective Dismissal

[1] Decrease in the Amount of Work

The basic condition for a lawful collective dismissal is that *the amount of work has decreased substantially and permanently* (section 3, Chapter 7 of the Employments Contract Act).

These criteria cannot always be considered separately, but an overall assessment is needed. It is clear, however, that if the decrease concerns only a part of the work tasks of an employee, the employer may not terminate the contract without first finding out, if there are other tasks which can be offered to the employee. Even if this is not possible, the employer can reduce a full-time employment contract to a part-time time contract instead of terminating the whole contract.

Decrease of work is easy to establish if the work tasks of the dismissed employee no longer exist. This is the case when an undertaking simply ceases to run some of its operations as non-profitable or for some other reason. The amount of work can also be reduced so that the position of an employee is abolished and his or her tasks are divided and assigned to the remaining staff. This was found for example in Judgment 2014:185 of the Labour Court, where the number of staff in the finance department of an undertaking was permanently reduced from four to three as a result of the dismissal of one person. Altogether, the reason for the decrease of work may be *external*, such as decline of the demand of the products of a company, or *internal*, such as the company's decision to reorganize its functions.

Permanent decrease of work refers to a certain period of time within which there is no longer need for the employee's work input. As a rule of thumb, the time of ninety days has certain relevance. At least if the time of lack of work is estimated to be shorter, only the criteria of a temporary lay-off under section 2(1), Chapter 5 of the Act may be fulfilled. Also the length of the term of notice of the employee in question has a bearing in the discretion. The longer the term, the longer the foreseeable lack of work must last.

In this discretion, the employer must make certain that the shortage of work exists also at the end of the period of notice. If new work emerges within this period, the employer has to call back the notice (Judgments 1993:97 of the Supreme Court and 2015:107 of the Labour Court). On the other hand, the employer has a certain 'right of anticipation' in this respect. Even if the decrease in the amount of work has not yet become current at the time of giving a notice, but can be expected to materialize by the end of the notice period, the notice can be issued.

The decrease in the amount of work relates to *work done in an employment relationship*. It is part of the employer's managerial prerogative to decide what forms of labour he uses to carry out the business operations. Consequently, the employer may have the right to terminate employment contracts and continue to have the same work tasks performed by external labour, such as temporary agency workers. The Labour Court has expressed this principle cautiously by saying that 'the use of temporary agency work does not in itself indicate that work available to employees has not decreased substantially and permanently' (Judgment 2007:103). In that case the terminations of four employees in these circumstances were deemed to have a valid ground.

There are, of course, cases which imply that there has been an attempt to circumvent of the law on job security. An example is found in the Labour Court's Judgment 2011:144. The employer company, which operated in manufacturing furnishing elements for ships, had terminated the contract of employment of an employee who had worked in warehouse and maintenance tasks. The employee had, however, training and experience also in metal work. At the time of the co-operation negotiations the company had open vacancies for metal workers. The company had taken on two temporary agency workers to do this work and subsequently, after four months, regularized them as permanent employees of the company. The employer was deemed to have no legal ground to terminate the contract of its warehouse worker.

It is another matter that several collective agreements include provisions, according to which the use of temporary agency work is not permitted in work normally done by the permanent staff of the company. In Judgment 2007:103 of the Labour Court, mentioned above, the company was found to have violated such a provision, although the terminations as such were regarded as legal. Recently the validity of collectively agreed provisions restricting the use of temporary agency work in these and certain other circumstances was challenged under Article 4(1) of the Temporary Agency Work Directive 2008/104/EC. The case was referred to the European Court of Justice for a preliminary ruling by the Finnish Labour Court. According to the ECJ's ruling in AKT C-533/13, the Directive does not impose an obligation on national courts not to apply any rule of national law containing prohibitions or restrictions on the use of temporary agency work which are not justified on grounds of general interest within the meaning of Article 4(1). Having received the ruling, the Labour Court tried the case and found that the company in question had not restricted the use of temporary agency workers to dealing with peaks of work or to other special situations permitted in the collective agreement. Thus the use of temporary workers was deemed to constitute unfair practice and a violation of the agreement (Judgment 2016:11).

[2] The Reasons for the Decrease of the Amount of Work

The grounds for collective dismissal are defined in the Employment Contracts Act as *financial or production-related reasons or reasons arising from reorganization of the employer's operations*. As opposed to grounds for individual dismissals, these reasons are not related to the conduct or other qualities of the dismissed employee. There may be borderline cases, where for example work or production methods are changed so that the employee no longer can tackle the new work tasks. A good example is found in the Labour Court's Decision 2014:152. The sales operations of a company had been essentially reorganized. As a result, the contract of an employee, who had been working in sales support activities, was terminated. His work tasks had changed so that the simple routines he had taken care of had been abolished. Another employee was hired and assigned the new tasks, which required high level of expertise and a very good command of English. Since the former employee could not be reasonable trained to do this work, the termination was found to be valid.

It may also happen in court proceedings that the plaintiff asserts that the termination was in reality based on an individual reason, such as the employee's trade union activity or long sick leaves. Such an allegation is intended to undermine the credibility of the collective ground presented by the employer, but is in practice difficult to prove (*see* for example the Decision of the Labour Court 2012:21).

The basis of the grounds for collective dismissal lies in the employer's freedom of business administration. Any genuine decision made within this area can in principle be a just cause for collective terminations. The expediency or necessity of such a decision is not for the court to assess in legal proceedings following a termination. To justify a collective dismissal, the decision must, however, always lead to an actual reduction of work (section 3.2, Chapter 7 of the Employment Contracts Act). This condition must be fulfilled even at the end of the period of notice. If new work emerges during that period, the termination must be cancelled.

Financial reasons for termination refer to the economic situation of the employer undertaking. If the undertaking is making losses for example due to diminished demand and is necessitated to cut its operations, it is rather obvious that it also has a ground to reduce the number of its employees. To warrant dismissals in such cases, the undertaking is usually able to show that the dismissals bring about savings and promote the profitability of the activities of the undertaking. Even a profit-making company is allowed to reduce its work force on the basis of a reliable prognosis according to which the company is about to face with problems of cost-effectiveness in the near future (Judgment 2005:29 of the Supreme Court). Also the unit, in which redundancies are made, can be profitable, but if the economic situation of the undertaking as a whole calls for saving measures, the redundancies may be justified (Judgment 2002:87 of the Supreme Court). The measures must, however, be such that they also promote the profitability of the undertaking in reality.

Production-related reasons for dismissal often relate to the employer's own decisions to change the business idea, production methods or the organization of the undertaking. If the employer decides to reduce the portfolio of its products or to close down a whole unit, the need for work force is understandably reduced. In organizational change work tasks can combined or re-divided among the staff. If such an arrangement results in a substantial and permanent decrease of the work of one or more employees, redundancies can be valid. This presupposes that the employees cannot be reassigned or trained to other work within the enterprise, which is a general condition concerning all collective dismissal grounds (*see* section §9.04[A][4] below).

In section 3, Chapter 7 of the Employment Contracts Act, *reorganization of the employer's operations* is mentioned as a separate ground for collective dismissal. Reorganization of operations may be difficult to keep apart from production-related reasons, discussed above. As an example of reorganization, one could mention the decision of the owner of a company to add his or her work input and to take over work tasks which were previously performed by an employee. Another example is *outsourcing* some of the activities of a company. Such a measure may not, however, be taken in order to get rid of an employee who is regarded as difficult in one way or another.

This was the case in Decision 2006:43 of the Labour Court. The employer had outsourced the office activities of the company, including the calculation of pay, which was the work of an employee who was also the office workers' shop steward. The plaintiff trade union was able to prove that the real reason for the outsourcing decision was the employer's aim to get rid of the payroll worker, who had not even under pressure agreed to leave the company voluntarily. One of the plaintiff's evidence was a discussion, recorded by the employee, which revealed the owner's real motives and the pressure he had exercised. – If outsourcing constitutes a transfer of a part of an undertaking, the transferor may not, under the general rules governing transfer of undertakings, terminate employment contracts merely on this ground (section 5.1, Chapter 7 of the Employment Contracts Act).

[3] Replacing a Dismissed Employee with a New One

The Employment Contracts Act contains express provisions on situations in which a collective dismissal is not deemed valid. An important restriction concerns *hiring a new employee either before termination or thereafter for similar duties* even though the employer's operating conditions have not changed during the equivalent period (section 3.2, Chapter 7 of the Employment Contracts Act).

The purpose of the provision is to prevent circumventing the job protection in existing employment relationships. The meaning of 'new employee' is usually clear. First, the expression refers to persons who are recruited from outside the undertaking. However, transferring another employee within the undertaking to replace a dismissed employee is also against the purpose of the provision (Judgment 2015:29 of the Labour Court). Internal transfers are usually not justifiable even on economic grounds. Furthermore, renewing fixed-term contracts of employees performing similar duties as the dismissed employee is comparable with hiring a new employee for these tasks.

In all these cases the court will have to decide if the duties of the new employee are of similar kind as those performed by the dismissed person. This is assessed on a case-by-case basis. For instance in one case, decided by the Supreme Court, the work of a shop assistant, whose job was to sell shoes, was not considered similar to the much heavier work of a shop assistant selling flooring. Also differences in the formal qualifications concerning for example language skills or training needed for the work may have relevance.

On the other hand, hiring a new employee for similar duties for a short period of time only does not render the dismissal invalid. The same applies to hiring temporary agency workers on a non-permanent basis (Decision 2007:103 of the Labour Court).

The employer's *operating conditions* may have changed before or after the termination, so that new personnel can be recruited for similar duties. Such recruitment may have taken place before the economic situation of the undertaking deteriorated unexpectedly, necessitating dismissals. The economic prospects of the undertaking may respectively improve after the end of the employment relationship of the dismissed person. In the last-mentioned cases the employee can, however, present a claim on *re-employment* under section 6, Chapter 6 of the Employment Contracts Act (*see* Chapter 3 above).

[4] The Employer's Duty to Offer Other Work or Training

To avoid making redundancies, the employer shall first find out if the employee can be placed in or trained for other duties. Employees under threat of redundancy shall primarily be offered work that is equivalent to that defined in their employment contract. If no such work is available, they shall be offered other work equivalent to their training, professional skill or experience (section 4, Chapter 7 of the Employment Contracts Act).

In legal proceedings, the employer's omission to discharge his duty in this respect is among the most commonly used grounds of action. It is often presented in a situation in which, at the time of the termination, there are open vacancies in the undertaking, and the plaintiff argues that the vacancy should have been offered to the dismissed employee. Convincing evidence according to which the employee would have been suitable to do that work is respectively one of the common means of winning a dismissal case. In general, actions in collective dismissal cases are difficult for the employee side to carry on successfully. It is relatively easy for the employer side to show an economic or production-related ground for redundancies with a reference to financial statements showing loss, decline in the order book etc. Without much exaggeration one could say, that an employer is at liberty to decide the number of the employees with whom he wants to run the operation of the undertaking. But if the undertaking actually has work on offer but nevertheless effects redundancies, the legal protection against collective dismissals may have been violated.

The first issue to be resolved in these cases is whether there has been work on offer that was suitable to the dismissed employee. In court proceedings it is for the plaintiff to identify the work that can be considered in this regard. *The burden of proof* is then shifted and the employer must show that the employee could not have mastered the work tasks even after reasonable training (Judgment 2000:59 of the Supreme Court). The employer may, for instance, show that the qualifications for the work, as described in a job advertisement, were such that the employee could not fulfil them, unlike the person who was finally recruited to the post. Such was the case in Judgment 2014:152 of the Labour Court. After restructuring the operations of a company also the amount and nature of sales support work had changed and an employee doing this work was dismissed. The employer was able to show that the new tasks in that work were much more demanding and versatile than the previous routines the dismissed employee had carried out. The new tasks involved direct contacts with foreign customers and required better command of English than the dismissed employee had. The new employee hired to do the work had the necessary qualifications. On the other hand, a fixed-term contract on warehouse work was made with the dismissed person. The case was dismissed on the merits.

The alternative work may also be less demanding than the work of the dismissed employee. Thus, in its Judgment 1993:145 the Supreme Court held that instead of termination, work as a physiotherapist should have been offered to the manager of a rehabilitation centre, who had the necessary education for also this kind of work. Respectively the Labour Court decided in its Judgment 2011:86 that work in an assembly line should have been offered to a white-collar worker, who earlier in her work career had done such work. In cases where there is considerable but maybe not full evidence of the suitability of the alternative work in question, the court often says that the employer should at least have given the dismissed employee *an opportunity to try* if he or she can manage in that work (*see* Judgment 2006:70 of the Labour Court as an example). *The length of the training*, which the employer is required to offer, depends much on the circumstances of the case, mainly the size and other resources of the undertaking.

The employer's duty to offer work covers the whole undertaking and all its units in the country. This is, however, one of the duties in the field of job protection which can be limited by means of a collective agreement concluded by nation-wide federations. For example in the collective agreement concluded for the construction industry this duty is restricted to an area where the employee can daily go to work from home.

On the other hand, *in concerns and other groups of companies* the duty to offer work is not necessarily limited to the company which is the formal employer. If an employer which *in fact exercises control* in personnel matters in another enterprise or corporate body on the basis of ownership, agreement or some other arrangement cannot offer an employee work as an alternative to dismissal, it must find out if it is possible to meet the employer's obligation to provide work and training by offering the employee work in other enterprises or corporate bodies under its control (section 4.3, Chapter 7 of the Employment Contracts Act). Normally this provision obliges the mother company to find out if its worker can be employed in a daughter company. In Judgment 2014:162 of the Labour Court this obligation was, however, held to apply also to a daughter company in relation to the other companies of the group, which were controlled by the same owner.

To fulfil its obligation to offer work the employer must *actively and of its own initiative* find out both the availability of such work and its suitability to the employee. It is not sufficient, for example, to give general information during co-operation negotiations on how employees can report of their interest to transfer to other work (Judgment 2011:86 of the Labour Court). The employer must make a concrete work offer personally to the employee(s) in question and inform that the work is an alternative to dismissal.

[B] Judicial Process, Sanctions and Remedies

[1] Proceedings in Regular Courts

When an action is based on a violation of the provisions of the Employment Contracts Act, concerning unfair dismissal, the case is brought before a regular court of justice. There are twenty-seven such Courts of First Instance in Finland. The appeals from the decisions of the court of first instance go to one of the five Courts of Appeal, and from these courts to the Supreme Court, provided that the latter grants leave to appeal. The central precondition to the granting of such leave is that a decision of the Supreme Court is necessary for the application of law in identical or similar cases or for the consistency of case law. In other words, the most important function of the Supreme Court is to establish judicial precedents in leading cases, thus ensuring uniformity in the administration of justice by the lower courts. This means in practice that only a few of the roughly 100 judgments, which the Supreme Court passes per year, are given in dismissal cases.

The remedy available in dismissal cases is the employer's liability for damages. Reinstatement of the employment relationship cannot be awarded in court proceedings.

The compensation afforded to an employee who is found to be dismissed unfairly is determined basically according to the same criteria regardless of the individual or collective ground for the dismissal. The criteria are provided for in section 2, Chapter 12 of the Employment Contracts Act. The provision reads as follows:

> **Section 2. Compensation for groundless termination of an employment contract**
>
> If the employer has terminated an employment contract contrary to the grounds laid down in this Act, it must be ordered to pay compensation for unjustified termination of the employment contract. If the employee has cancelled the employment contract on the grounds laid down in chapter 8, section 1, arising from the employer's intentional or negligent actions, the employer must be ordered to pay compensation for unjustified termination of the employment contract. The exclusive compensation must be equivalent to the pay due for a minimum of three months or a maximum of 24 months. Nevertheless, the maximum amount due to be paid to shop stewards elected on the basis of a collective agreement or to elected representatives referred to below in chapter 13, section 3, is equivalent to the pay due for 30 months.
>
> Depending on the reason for terminating the employment relationship, the following factors must be taken into account in determining the amount of compensation: estimated time without employment and estimated loss of earnings, the remaining period of a fixed-term employment contract, the duration of the employment relationship, the employee's age and chances of finding employment corresponding to his or her vocation or education and training, the employer's procedure in terminating the contract, any motive for termination originating in the employee, the general circumstances of the employee and the employer, and other comparable matters.

Under subsection 3 of the provision, the minimum of three months' pay is, however, not applied to collective dismissals.

As can be seen, the amount of compensation under the provision can be fixed with consideration to various elements, such as financial and non-material damage suffered by the employee. Also the length of service of the employee and the size of the employer company are considered in the overall assessment of a just compensation to be awarded. In collective dismissal cases, clearly the most important element is the financial loss caused to the employee, usually in the form of unemployment and loss of earnings. Consequently, the period of unemployment is decisive in the calculation of the amount of the compensation. It seldom happens that the compensation awarded exceeds this amount, because a collective dismissal, although unjustified, is usually not considered to have caused non-material damage for example in the form of personal insult to the employee. Neither is the compensation meant to have any particular deterrent effect on the employer. No statistical data on the amount of compensations awarded in collective dismissal cases is available, but the general idea of a practical judge is that compensations equivalent to the pay of six to twelve months are commonly ordered.

An employee who is made redundant is entitled to unemployment allowance. In the case of unjustified dismissal, the employee would gain extra benefit if he or she could receive full compensation for the loss of earnings in addition to the unemployment allowance. To prevent this, a certain portion (normally 75%) of the unemployment allowance is deducted from the compensation. On the other hand, to secure the employer's full liability the court must order the employer to pay the sum deducted from the compensation to the Unemployment Insurance Fund (section 3, Chapter 12 of the Employment Contracts Act).

The court may, if warranted by the amount of the compensation, the employee's financial and social circumstances and the insult suffered by him, reduce the amount deductible from the compensation or waive the deduction fully. Such a reduction is made more often in individual dismissal cases than in cases concerning collective dismissal.

Also *breaches against the co-operation duties* under the Co-operation within Undertakings Act may lead to the employer's liability. The remedy is called *indemnity* and is order by a regular court. The conditions for indemnity under section 62 of the Act are the following:

- the employer has deliberately or negligently failed to observe the duties concerning Co-operation procedure in reducing the use of personnel (*see* above in section §9.02[A]); and
- as a result of the employer's decision, an employee's contract has been terminated or reduced to a part-time contract or he or she has been laid off.

The remedy is ordered as a sanction of a procedural neglect. It does not require, for example, that the redundancies have been effected without a valid ground. The maximum sum of the indemnity to be paid to the employee is EUR 30,000. When determining the amount of the indemnity, consideration is given to the degree of neglect in respect of the co-operation obligation, the general circumstances of the employer, the nature of the measure applied in respect of the employee and duration of his employment relationship.

[2] Proceedings in the Labour Court

As was explained above in section §9.01[B], the provisions on protection against unfair dismissal of the Employment Contracts Act are included in several collective agreements as well. To a lesser extent, collective agreements also regulate the co-operation procedure within undertakings. This means that within the scope of application of these collective agreements, disputes over terminations of employment and observance of co-operation duties can be heard and tried also in the Labour Court.

There are, however, certain differences between the regular courts and the Labour Court as bodies administering justice. The Labour Court is a special court with a jurisdiction restricted to disputes arising from collective agreements. It is a tripartite body with a regular composition, in which there are two members representing the employer side, two representing the employee side, and two neutral members. The members representing the labour market parties are in practice experienced lawyers, who have their full-time jobs in nation-wide employers' associations and workers' federations. The competence and the composition of the Labour Court provide the court with special expertise in the field of labour law cases. This may also contribute to the confidence that the Labour Court's decision-making enjoys in the labour market.

On account of the features just explained, there has been no need to provide an opportunity to appeal from the decisions of the Labour Court to a higher instance. Consequently, it is possible to get a final decision from the Labour Court in a much shorter time than from the system of regular courts. The average time of handling a case in the Labour Court is five to six months.

As *parties to the litigation* in the Labour Court are the parties to the collective agreement in question. Thus, for instance in a dismissal case the plaintiff is the trade union whose member has been dismissed. This way the individual employee does not have to bear the trial costs either.

The remedies awarded by the Labour Court are the same as those explained in the previous chapter. Provisions on compensation and indemnity are regularly included in collective agreements, which regulate dismissal grounds or the co-operation procedure. In addition, the Collective Agreements Act[4] contains a special sanction, *the compensatory fine*, which can be ordered if the provision of a collective agreement has been violated (sections 7-9 of the Act). The maximum amount of the compensatory fine is EUR 29,500. It is paid to the other party of the collective agreement, such as the trade union in a dismissal case.

Such a fine is inflicted upon an employer who wittingly violates, or should reasonably have known that he violates, any provision in a collective agreement. The same sanction applies to omissions of the so called *surveillance duty*. Associations which are bound by the agreement are required to ensure that their member associations, employers and employees do not contravene the provisions of the collective agreement in any manner. An omission is deemed to have taken place, if a provision of the collective agreement has been clearly violated and if, taking account of the circumstances, the incorrect application is not adjusted quickly, when the association has received knowledge of it.

In dismissal cases, the compensation paid to the employee is in established practice regarded to *exclude* the possibility of imposing the employer to pay a compensatory fine for the same violation. The opposite applies to cases concerning

4. Työehtosopimuslaki 7.6.1946/436.

violation of *the sequence of redundancies* (*see* section §9.01[B] above). In these cases the compensatory fine is the only sanction available.

It is, however, possible that the employers' association is ordered to pay a compensatory fine for neglecting its duty of surveillance also in dismissal cases. This does not happen often, because the association is seldom aware of the events and circumstances at the company level, when the decision to dismiss an employee is taken. On the other hand, if the period of notice has not yet elapsed and the trade union challenges the ground for the dismissal, the employers' association must interfere and, if necessary, correct the situation.

Bibliography

Markus Äimälä, Johan Åström, Hannu Rautiainen & Mikko Nyyssölä, *Finnish Labour Law in Practice* (Vantaa 2005).

Seppo Koskinen, Kimmo Nieminen, Mika Valkonen, *Työsuhteen Päättäminen (Termination of Emloyment Relationship)* (2nd ed., Helsinki 2012).

Antti Suviranta, *Labour Law in Finland* (3rd revised ed., Kluwer Law International, Helsinki 2000).

CHAPTER 10

Collective Dismissal in France

Michel Blatman

§10.01 FRENCH SYSTEM FEATURES OF COLLECTIVE DISMISSALS FOR ECONOMIC REASONS

[A] Distinction Between Dismissal for Personal Reasons and Dismissal for Economic Reasons

The French law envisages several ways of termination of the employment contract; some derive from the unilateral will of the employer (cessation of an unsuccessful trial, dismissal, proceedings for judicial termination of an apprenticeship contract, employee early retirement); others follow an individual decision of the employee (resignation, acknowledgement of contract termination to the detriment of the employer, retirement); and others derive from the common will of both parties (mutual termination agreement).

One should distinguish essentially between two categories of dismissals, depending on the employer's purpose: 'dismissal for personal reasons' and 'dismissal for economic reasons'.[1]

The dismissal for personal reasons is inherent in the employee, who is either reproached for a mistake in the performance of the work contract (disciplinary dismissal), or is faced with a fact or situation that leads to the termination of the employment relations (e.g., dismissal for incompetence or lack of results, dismissal for prolonged illness disrupting the company operations or for medical unfitness to work and impossibility of redeployment).

1. A 'sui generis' dismissal also exists, in the case that the employee exerts the right to refuse a contract modification resulting from a new law or collective agreement. This is considered an individual dismissal for economic reasons, even if several employees are involved (*Cf. infra* section §10.01[B][3]).

On the contrary, the dismissal of an employee for economic reasons is unrelated to the individual. This type of dismissal is, in fact, defined by Article L. 1233-3 of the Labour Code as being: '*carried out by an employer for one or more reasons unrelated to the employee as an individual, resulting from the job's suppression or transformation, or a substantial modification of the contract refused by the employee, consequential to economic difficulties or technological changes.*'.

Three criteria for economic dismissals are therefore identified: first, the *absence of a relation* between the reason of dismissal and the employee; then a *material element* constituted by the job's suppression or transformation – at company level (Soc. 5 April 1995, n° 93-42690, bull. civ. 1995, V, n° 123) – and the contract modification refused by the employee; finally a *causal element* which includes economic difficulties or technological changes.

With respect to such last criterion, the Court of cassation has admitted two other economic reasons for dismissal which were not envisaged by the Labour Code: the *reorganization or restructuring of the company* as well as the *cessation of its activity*. In the first case, the jurisprudence required the reorganization to be necessary for the '*safeguard of the competitiveness*' of the company (Soc. 5 April 1995, n° 93-42690, bull. civ. 1995, V, n° 123), with respect to the *activity sector* of the company or group to which it belongs (Soc. 23 September 2015, n° 14-11663). In the second case, the company's cessation of activities can be a valid cause for economic dismissals, except if it is due to the employer's fault or culpable carelessness ('légèreté blâmable') (Soc. 16 January 2001, n° 99-44647, bull. civ. 2001, V, n° 10).[2]

The economic dismissal, as that for personal reasons, must, on the one hand state the reasons on which it is based, and on the other, be justified by a *real and serious cause* (Labour Code Article L. 1233-2). The judge's role, therefore, when hearing a dispute on such two points, is to verify: *the form*, i.e., whether the dismissal letter includes the above-mentioned material and causal elements, and *the substance*, i.e., the existence of a real and serious economic reason for the dismissal (Soc. 12 May 1998, n° 96-16406, bull. civ. 1998, V, n° 243).[3]

Thus, for example, keeping in mind that 'the letter of dismissal submitted for economic reasons must mention the economic reasons envisaged by law **and** their impact on the job or the employment contract', the Court of cassation held that the dismissal merely due to the employee's refusal to be transferred to other cities, without specifying the economic reasons for such contract modification, did not satisfy the legal requirement of motivation; so that such dismissal was considered without a real and serious cause (Soc. 17 October 2001, n. 99-44393).

It is true that the so-called El Khomri law n° 2016-1088 of 8 August 2016, concerning employment, the modernization of social dialogue and the securing of career paths (JORF n° 0184 of 9 August 2016), has recaptured the two criterions of

2. 'The employer's error of evaluation of the risk inherent in all management choices does not itself alone characterize culpable carelessness.' (Soc. 11 December 2015, n° 14-25676; Soc. 14 December 2005, n° 03-44080, bull. civ. 2005, V, n° 365).
3. *See* in particular Jean-Yves Frouin, *La légalité du licenciement pour motif économique*, Semaine sociale Lamy of 5 September 2005, n° 1226, p. 7.

reorganization of the company necessary for the safeguard of its competitiveness, as well as of the cessation of its activity, in Article L. 1233-3 of the Labour Code. However, this law, harshly disputed within the society and in Parliament, aims to relax the rules of the jurisprudence and the role of the judge, in order to make contract terminations secure and reach legal certainty. Therefore, the 'economic difficulties' are now legally characterized, *either by the significant evolution of at least one economic indicator such as the decrease of orders or turnover, operating losses or a deterioration of the cash flow or gross operating profit, or by any other element the nature of which justifies such difficulties.*

Furthermore, in order to take into account the size of the company and to facilitate dismissals in very small enterprises, the new Article L. 1233-3 provides that: '*There is a significant decrease of the orders or turnover when, compared to the same period of the previous year, its duration is of at least:*

(1) three months for a company of at least eleven employees;
(2) two consecutive quarters for a company of at least eleven and less than fifty employees;
(3) three consecutive quarters for a company of at least fifty and less than 300 employees;
(4) four consecutive quarters for a company of 300 or more employees.'

Thus, the smaller the company, the fewer months are required for such difficulties to arise.

It is to be noted that, anyway, the Government had to give up the part of its bill setting forth that the economic difficulties criterion would not be envisaged at the level of foreign subsidiaries within the group, should these be performant. In other words, the foreign level of assessment of these difficulties requested by the jurisprudence remains.

[B] Field of Application of the Legislation on Economic Dismissals

[1] The Legislation on Economic Dismissal Applies to the Company and Not to a Particular Employer

The provisions regarding dismissals for economic reasons are not applicable to the employer of household domestic staff (Soc. 10 October, 1989, n° 86-45069) or of a private property caretaker (Soc. 4 April 2001, 98-40275), nor to a co-ownership property representative ('Syndic de copropriété') (Soc. 10 October 1990, n° 87-45366). However, if the domestic staff is employed by a 'société civile immobilière' (non-trading joint property ownership company), the rules of economic dismissals apply due to the fact that the employer is in this case a *legal entity* (Soc. 21 January 2015, n° 13-17850, bull. civ. 2015, V, n° 5).

[2] *The Legislation on Economic Dismissals Does Not Apply to Employees with a Fixed-Term Contract ('contrat à durée déterminée' – 'CDD')*

Indeed, this type of temporary contract cannot be terminated prematurely, except for in the cases of: mutual agreement, grave misconduct by the employee, force majeure or the employee's inability recorded by the company doctor (Article L. 1243-1 of the Labour Code). The company's financial difficulties (Soc. 20 February 1996, n° 93-42663, bull. civ. 1996, V, n° 59) or the suppression of the replaced employee's job (Soc. 26 March 2002, n° 00-40652, bull. civ. 2002, V, n° 103) do not constitute cases of force majeure.

[3] *Special Treatment of Certain Employee Refusals to Modifications of Their Contract*

The employee's refusal to accept a contract modification can, in certain cases, provide the grounds for a dismissal which, although not of an economic nature *stricto sensu*, is legally assimilated as such.

Refusal of Modification of the Employment Contract Resulting from the Application of a Working Time Reduction Agreement

Since 1996,[4] the judicial jurisprudence distinguishes between changes of the '*employment conditions*', which the employer can unilaterally apply within his management powers, and changes of the '*employment contract*', for which the employer requires the employee's agreement, in view of the bilateral and immutable nature of the contract. The *working time and remuneration* have been considered by the Court of cassation as the 'pillars' or 'bases' of the employment contract, and thus not modifiable without the agreement by the two parties. With the introduction in 2000 of the legislation reducing the legal working time to thirty-five hours per week, the issue arose for the legislator regarding those employees who refused a contract modification resulting from the application of a collective agreement implementing such time reduction.

So as to avoid that the employer be in a position of having to proceed with economic collective dismissals, it was therefore decided:

- first, that 'the mere decrease of the number of hours stipulated in the employment contract in application of a working time reduction agreement does not constitute a modification of the contract.' (Law n° 2000-37 dated 19 January 2000 so-called Aubry II concerning the negotiated reduction of the work time, Article 30, recodified as Article L. 1222-7 of the Labour Code);
- then, that in the case that one or more employees refuse a contract modification resulting from the application of such an agreement, their dismissal '*is not based on an economic reason*' and '*is subject* to *the provisions relating to the*

4. Soc. 10 July 1996, n° 93-40966, bull. civ. 1996, V, n° 278.

termination of the employment contract for personal reasons.' (Article L. 1222-8).

Refusal of a Modification of the Employment Contract Resulting from the Application of a Job Security Agreement

In the case of '*serious economic difficulties of the company*', the employer may propose a company agreement whereby, in exchange of its commitment to maintain jobs for the duration of the agreement's validity, the concerned employees agree to a change in their work time, organization and distribution as well as their remuneration (Article L. 5125-1 of the Labour Code). Each employee must be informed of the right to accept or refuse the application of the provisions of such agreement to the employment contract. However, in the case of refusal by various employees, '*their dismissal is based on an economic reason, and announced according to the modalities of an individual dismissal for economic reasons and is based on a real and serious cause*' (Article L. 5125-2).[5]

Refusal of a Modification of the Employment Contract Resulting from the Application of a 'Job Preservation or Development Agreement'

Another objective of the 'El Khomri' law of 8 August 2016 is to allow for the conclusion of offensive agreements, in order to promote employment growth, should employees' contractual rights in terms of wages and work duration be decreased. The new Article L. 2254-2 (I) of the Labour Code strongly provides thereby that: '*In the case of a company agreement stipulated in view of the preservation or development of employment, its provisions shall automatically substitute those of the employment contract which are contrary and incompatible, including those relating to the remuneration and working hours (...)*'. The law, moreover, provides that such an agreement, which can therefore modify the employment contract in terms of the work organization and working hours, '*cannot however result in the decrease of the employee's monthly salary*'. Under the same Article L. 2254-2 (II):

> *The employee can refuse the contract modification resulting from the application of the agreement (...). Such refusal must be in writing. / If the employer adopts a dismissal procedure against the employee who refused the application of the agreement (...), such dismissal is deemed to be based on a specific reason constituting a real and serious cause and will be subject only to the terms and conditions (...) applicable to individual dismissals for economic reasons as well as to articles L. 1234-1 to L. 1234-20 (notice or dismissal indemnity). The dismissal letter must include a statement regarding the specific grounds on which such dismissal is based.*[6]

---

5. On these two social support measures, cf. *infra* section §10.03[B].
6. Cf. *infra* section §10.03[A][4].

Refusal of a Modification of the Employment Contract Resulting from the Application of an Internal Mobility Agreement

In order to establish a certain degree of 'flexi-security' ('flexi-sécurité'), the national Inter-professional Agreement of 11 of January 2013 and later Law No. 2013-504 of 14 June 2013 relating to job security, envisaged the possibility for the employer to negotiate an agreement with the unions on the *professional or geographical mobility within the company*. Such agreement is within the framework of common practice collective organization measures without a workforce reduction plan (Article L. 2242-17 of the Labour Code).[7] In the case of refusal by various employees of the application of the provisions of such agreement to their contract, their dismissal is based on an *economic reason*, and announced according to the modalities of an *individual dismissal for economic reasons* (Article L. 2242-19).

[4] Economic Dismissal in Case of Company Transfer

According to Article L. 1224-1 of the Labour Code, '*in the case of a change of the employer's legal situation, such as through succession, sale, merger, transformation of company assets, or vesting in a company or partnership, all current contracts of employment on the day of the change remain between the new employer and the company's staff*'. From such provision of public order, interpreted in the light of Directive n° 77/187/CEE of 14 February 1977, the jurisprudence has established the non-authorization by the transferor to proceed with a dismissal for economic reasons of those employees concerned by the transfer. The reason for this is the following: once the economic entity has been transferred to the buyer who will carry on its activity, the employee's work contract continues in full right under the new employer, so that in the case of a dismissal made prior to the transfer of the company, this will be without effect (Soc. 22 January 2002, appeal n.° 00-40756, bull. civ. 2002, V, n° 24, p. 17). In the same way: '*Given the invalidity of a dismissal made prior to the transfer of the entity, the employee, at its choice, can request: to the buyer the continuation of the employment contract which was illegally terminated, or to the author of the illegal dismissal the repair of the suffered damage*' (Soc. 20 March 2002, n° 00-41651, bull. civ. 2002, V, n° 94, p. 102).

The 'El Khomri' law of 8 of August 2016 has brought some nuances to this solution with respect to companies of at least 1000 employees: in the case when the employment safeguard plan ('PSE') envisages, in order to avoid the closure of one or more establishments, the transfer of one or more economic entities to protect a part of the jobs and when such companies accept a buyer offer, the provisions of Article L. 1224-1 concerning the transfer of the employment contracts apply only 'within the limit of the number of jobs which have not been cut following the dismissals, from the effective date of such transfer' (Article L. 1233-61).

7. Cf. *infra* section §10.03[A][2].

[C] The Difference Between Individual and Collective Dismissals for Economic Reasons

[1] Differentiation Criteria

These criteria regard the number of employees affected by a dismissal for economic reasons or those who refused a modification of their employment contract proposed for such reasons.

Number of Employees Affected by a Dismissal for Economic Reason

One refers to a *collective* dismissal for economic reasons in the case of two or more employees being dismissed.

Refusal by at least Ten Employees of a Modification of Their Employment Contract

The refusal, by at least ten employees, of the modification of a substantial element of their employment contract proposed by the employer for an economic reason, leads their dismissal to be subject to the provisions applicable in the case of collective dismissals for economic reasons (Article L. 1233-23 of the Labour Code).

[2] Inclusion of Voluntary Redundancies and Mutual Termination Agreements Within the Context of Collective Economic Dismissals

Voluntary Redundancy Plans

In the attempt to '*take into account the global nature of an employment reduction plan irrespective of the types of termination for which it takes place*' (annual report of the Court of cassation, 2011, section 4) the social chamber considers the employer free to privilege voluntary redundancies, which can be legitimately negotiated so as to reach a common agreement of contract termination. However, in such case, if the employer's social plan envisages the suppression of more than ten employees, via dismissal where necessary, this is viewed as a human resource management operation possibly leading to, for an economic reason, the suppression of numerous jobs to be analysed within a collective redundancy plan (Soc. 10 April 1991, n° 89-18485, bull. civ. 1991, V, n° 179).

Mutual Termination Agreements

In the light of the Council Directive 98/59/EC of 20 July 1998 concerning the Member States legislation approximation related to collective dismissals and reflected in the French legal texts, the Court of Cassation judges that mutual termination agreements, when due to an *economic reason* and within a workforce reduction process of which they constitute a modality, must be taken into account to determine the information and consultation procedure of the concerned employee representatives, as well as the employer's obligations with regard to the employment safeguard plan (Soc. 9 March 2011, n° 10-11581, bull. civ. 2011, V, n° 70).

[D] Collective Economic Dismissal Ordering Criteria

The issue of the selection of the employees to be dismissed is crucial and has given rise to an extensive jurisprudence. Many laws have succeeded themselves in this area, notably the so-called law of social modernization of 17 January 2002,[8] and the 'Macron law' of 6 August 2015. Moreover, the subject matter is regulated by Articles L. 1233-5 à L. 1233-7 of the Labour Code.

[1] Identification of Dismissal Ordering Criteria

Sources and Selection of the Criteria

The definition of the dismissal ordering criteria can result from a company-specific, or collective bargaining agreement. In the case of the latter, the employer is not authorized to envisage any other criteria. Thus, as according to a collective agreement '*dismissals (...) will be carried out taking into account the family situation and the seniority within the company as well as the job qualifications of the concerned employees*', the employer cannot use the 'holding of a diploma' as a criteria (Soc. 20 January 1993, n° 91-42032, bull. civ. 1993, V, n° 18).

However, in the absence of an agreement defining the dismissal ordering criteria, it is up to the employer to identify them following consultations with the works council or, failing that, with the employee representatives (Article L. 1233-5, paragraph 1). *In particular,* these criteria take into account (same Article, paragraph 2):

(1) the family responsibilities, especially those of single parents;
(2) the seniority within the company or its establishments;
(3) the employee's situation, which would make finding new employment particularly difficult, notably in the case of disabled and elderly employees;
(4) the job qualifications evaluated by category.

Since the law *does not establish a hierarchy* between the criteria, the employer can *favour one,* provided that the *totality of all the other criteria* envisaged in Article L. 1233-5 is *taken into account.* This is the highest recognition of a longstanding need of the jurisprudence (Soc. 8 April 1992, n° 89-40739, bull. civ. 1992, V, n° 259; Soc. 20 January 1993, n° 91-42032, bull. civ. 1993, V, n° 32; Soc. 23 October 2014, n° 13-22008).

8. Pierre-Yves Verkindt, *L'ordre des licenciements après la loi de modernisation sociale,* Gazette du Palais, 21 September 2002, n° 264, p. 22.

Notion of Professional Category

According to the Court of cassation '*a professional category, at the basis to establish the order of dismissals, applies to all the company's employees who carry out functions of the same nature assuming a common professional training*' (Soc. 3 March 1998, n° 95-41610, bull. civ. 1998, V, n° 84). A trial judge cannot differentiate between *full-time and part time* within a same category (same sentence). An assessment has to be made as to whether the employee included in the collective dismissal carried out tasks of the same nature as those, his equivalent, who were not dismissed (Soc. 5 November 2014, n° 13-1966). Moreover, the employer is not allowed to *artificially split a same activity*, as could be the case in a factory, into different professional categories ruled by separate dismissal ordering criteria on the grounds that different generations of machinery are being utilized, *without demonstrating that the use of the one or the other machine requires a specific or supplementary training exceeding the employer's obligation of adaptation*. (Soc. 27 May 2015, n° 14-11688, FS-P + B).

[2] *The Loyalty Obligation by the Employer*

The employer is under an *obligation of loyalty* when applying the dismissal ordering criteria. A decision by the social chamber recalls such obligation in a case whereby the employer had not taken into account the employees of a company which had been acquired a year earlier (Soc. 8 October 2014, n° 13-14979, bull. civ. 2014, V, n° 228).

[3] *Employee Information on the Criteria Applied*

The employee may request in writing to the employer to be informed on the dismissal ordering criteria used for the selection of the dismissed employees (Articles L. 1233-17 and L. 1233-43). The employer must inform of such criteria within a period of ten days (Article R 1233-1). Further on we will see the sanctions applied in case of non-adherence to such obligation.[9]

[4] *Unlawful Criteria*

The Court of cassation prohibits discriminatory dismissal ordering criteria based on the Constitution's Preamble of 4 October 1958 and Article L. 1132-1 of the Labour Code. The banned criteria include the foreign (Soc. 10 February 1998, 95-42315, bull. civ. 1998, V, n° 78) or non-European (Soc. 8 April 1992, n° 90-41276, bull. civ. 1992, V, n° 256) origin of the employee, the fact of working part time rather than full time, considering that part time employees should benefit by law from the same rights as those working full time (Soc. 3 March 1998, n° 95-41.610, bull. civ. V, n° 113). Another banned criterion is constituted by the situation of an employee with parental childcare leave (Soc. 7 October 1992, n° 89-45503, bull. civ. 1992, V, n° 503).

9. Cf. *infra* section §10.01[D][6][c].

[5] *The Issue of the 'Perimeter' of Application of the Ordering Criteria*

In order to understand at what *minimal* level the economic dismissal ordering criteria should be considered, on the one hand, one should distinguish whether or not the criteria result from a collective agreement; on the other, examine the dismissals which are accompanied by an employment safeguard plan ('Plan de sauvegarde de l'emploi' – 'PSE'); and finally, take into account the specific level of the 'economic and social unit' ('unité économique et sociale' – 'UES').

[a] *Perimeter of Application in the Presence or Absence of a Collective Agreement*

In the Absence of a Collective Agreement on the Perimeter, the Latter Cannot be Lower than the Level of the Company

The principle, as stated by the Court of cassation, is that the dismissal ordering criteria '*must apply to the whole of the company's workforce*'. This requirement is not applied by an employer who, on the grounds of the closure of an entire establishment, suppresses all its jobs and consequently dismisses all its employees, and thus does not apply the dismissal ordering criteria (Soc. 15 May 2013, n° 11-27460, bull. civ. 2013, V, n° 121).

The Council of State adopts the same position in its judgment that 'unless a collective agreement exists at company level or higher, the dismissal ordering criteria must apply to the whole of the company's workforce' (C.E., 4th and 5th SSR, 7 December 2015, n° 386582, recueil Lebon).

Possible Setting of the Perimeter Via a Collective Agreement

The social chamber generally considers that a collective agreement made *at company level* can envisage a perimeter for the application of the dismissal ordering criteria. Therefore, an *agreement at the level of the establishment*, being of a lower level, cannot limit the application of the criteria only to the employees of such establishment concerned by the job cuts (Soc. 10 February 2010, n° 08-41109), unless *an agreement at company level or higher* explicitly envisages such possibility (Soc. 15 May 2013, n° 08-41109). Such was the case whereby the dismissal ordering criteria were applied within the geographic perimeter '*of the agency, office or technical site, social headquarters, technical platform*', envisaged by a collective agreement signed by a company and seven unions and approved by the works council (Soc. 14 October 2015, n° 14-14339, published).

[b] *Perimeter of Application and Employment Safeguard Plan ('plan de sauvegarde de l'emploi' – 'PSE')*

The solution varies according to whether the PSE results from a collective agreement or a unilateral document by the employer.

Setting of the Perimeter via a Collective Agreement on the PSE

Law n° 2015-990 of 6 August 2015, so-called 'Law Macron', has introduced two provisions in the Labour Code according to which *the agreement on the PSE* (envisaged for companies with at least fifty employees and a dismissal plan concerning at least ten employees within a same thirty-day period) can indicate the perimeter of application of the dismissal ordering criteria (Articles L. 1233-5 and L. 1233-24-2, 2°).

Unilateral Document by the Employer and 'Employment Zone'

The same texts authorize the employer to set the perimeter of the order of dismissals within the *unilateral document* prepared in order to establish the PSE. However, in such case, Article L. 1233-5 specifies that '*the perimeter cannot be lower than that of each employment zone where one or more establishments of the company concerned by the job cuts are located*'. Such '**employment zones**' ('zones d'emploi') are defined by decree n° 2015-1637 of 10 December 2015 (creating Article D. 1233-2 of the Labour Code) as '*those indicated in the atlas of employment zones established by the National Institute of statistics and economic studies ("INSEE") and the statistical services of the minister responsible for employment*'. The INSEE ('Institut national de la statistique et des études économiques') website specifies the sense of such notion: '*An employment zone is a geographical area within which most of the labour force lives and works, and in which establishments can find the main part of the work force necessary to occupy the offered positions*'.

[c] The Perimeter of the Criteria at the Level of the Economic and Social Unit ('unité économique et sociale' – 'UES')

The UES is a legal concept which aims to avoid the break-up of a company so as to allow it to subtract itself from the social obligations related to a certain workforce threshold.

The Court of cassation defines it as follows: '***An economic and social unit between various legally distinct entities*** *is characterized, firstly by the concentration of its management powers within the concerned perimeter as well as by the similarity or complementarity of the activities carried out by the different entities, and secondly by a community of workers with similar social status and work conditions which can allow a certain permutability of the employees*' (Soc. 18 June 2000, n° 02-60033, bull. civ. 2003, V, n° 299).

The jurisprudence considers such grouping as a valid level of application of the dismissal ordering criteria: such was the case of a PSE which envisaged that the dismissal ordering criteria applied within the perimeter of the UES and not of the companies (Soc. 19 January 2011, n° 09-41171).

[6] *Judicial Review of the Dismissal Ordering Criteria and Sanctions Incurred*

[a] *Judicial Competence of the Dismissal Ordering Criteria Concerning Protected Employees*

The dismissal of 'protected employees', particularly employee representatives, must be authorized by the labour inspector. Any challenge to this authority falls within the jurisdiction of the administrative courts (administrative tribunal, Administrative Court of Appeal and Council of State). The principle of separation of the judicial and administrative authorities prohibits the judicial judges to evaluate the legality or validity of the decision by the Administration. However, exceptionally, even in the presence of an administrative authorization for the employer to proceed with the dismissals granted by the labour inspector, only the judicial judge can assess the implementation of the dismissal ordering criteria (Soc. 10 December 2003, n° 01-47147).

In other words, '*the authorization by the Labour inspector prior to the dismissal for economic reasons of a protected employee has no effect on the assessment of the respect, on occasion of this measure, of the rules setting the dismissal ordering criteria and the consideration of such criteria*' (Soc. 9 July 2003, n° 01-40016).

[b] *The Extent of the Judge's Review on the Dismissal Ordering Criteria*

In case of any dispute, the employer, obliged to consider the dismissal ordering criteria as a whole, is responsible to inform the judge of the objective elements on which he based his choice (Soc. 24 February 1991, n° 91-45859, bull. civ. 1993, V, n° 66). Failing to do so, the employer is liable to be condemned for damages for violation of the order of dismissals (Soc. 24 February 1993, n° 91-45859, bull. civ. 1993, V, n° 66).

Regarding the implementation of the dismissal ordering criteria, the Court of cassation establishes the principle according to which, *the judge cannot substitute its assessment of the employee's professional qualities to that of the employer* (Soc. 4 December 1991, n° 89-45937, bull. civ. 1991, V, n° 552). However, in case of dispute, it is up to the judge to verify whether the assessment of the employee's professional skills derives from an *abuse of power* (Soc. 4 December 1993, n° 89-45937, bull. civ. 1991, V, n° 552) or a manifest error (Soc. 24 September 2014, n° 12-16991, bull. civ. 2014, V, n° 201). An example of abuse of power is in the case that the assessment of the employee's professional qualities is distorted by the employer's desire to avoid the dismissal of a more junior employee, due to the cost of dismissal for the company. In such case, the employee whose job was maintained had been hired in the framework of a 'work initiative' contract ('contrat "initiative-emploi"') for which the employer received a State subsidy of up to 46% of the salary; the dismissal of such employee would have required the company to pay back the full subsidy amount received.

[c] *Compensatory Sanctions in the Case of Failure of Stating the Ordering Criteria and 'Unjustified Loss of Employment'*

An Indemnity in the Case of Failure of Stating the Ordering Criteria

Failure to provide information on the dismissal ordering criteria upon request of the employee constitutes an irregularity liable for damages. On the one hand, the Court of cassation considers such irregularity to '*necessarily*' cause a prejudice against the employee which the judge must resolve within the scope of his function (Soc. 26 January 1999, n° 97-40463, bull. civ. 1999, V, n° 39). On the other hand, the indemnity awarded on this basis is combinable with the indemnity for dismissal without a real and serious cause as they cover distinct prejudices (Soc. 24 September 2008, n° 07-42200, bull. civ. 2008, V, n° 178).

Indemnity for Violation of the Dismissal Ordering Criteria

Failure to comply with the rules of the economic dismissal ordering criteria is not subject to the sanctions envisaged in the case of dismissal without a real and serious cause, but constitutes, with respect to the employee, an '*illegality leading to a prejudice, which can lead to an unjustified job loss, which must be fully recovered by the trial judge*' (Soc. 14 January 1997, appeal n° 95-44366, bull. civ. 1997, V, n° 16; Soc. 2 February 2006, n° 03-45443, bull. civ. 2006, V, n° 57). Such assessment of the prejudice is *final* and therefore not subject to review by the Court of cassation (Soc. 15 May 2013, n° 27-460, bull. civ. 2013, V, n° 121, above mentioned). The compensation awarded under the *violation of the dismissal ordering criteria cannot be combined* with the compensation for dismissal without a real and serious cause, which is due when the dismissal declared for economic reasons has no economic cause (Soc. 5 October 1999, n° 98-41384, bull. civ. n° 366): otherwise a case of duplication would arise.

§10.02 PROCEDURE FOR COLLECTIVE DISMISSALS FOR ECONOMIC REASONS

The modalities of the procedure vary *depending on the number of dismissals* envisaged during a fixed period of time and according to the *company's workforce*. The Labour Code distinguishes, with respect to the representative bodies' consultation rules, among companies with *less than fifty employees* and those with *at least fifty*. As far as the other rules are concerned, a distinction is made according to whether the dismissal affects *less than ten employees* within a thirty-day period, or *ten or more employees* within the same above-mentioned period.

[A] Dismissal of Less Than Ten Employees Within a Same Thirty-Day Period

The Labour Code distinguishes three types of persons concerned by such procedure: the employee representatives, the employees and the administrative authority.

[1] Employee Representatives Consultation Procedure

The employer who envisages a collective dismissal for economic reasons of less than ten employees within a thirty-day period must meet and consult with: the *works council* in the case of companies of at least fifty employees (Article L. 1233-8 of the Labour Code); the *employee representatives* in those of less than fifty employees (same Article and Article L. 2313-7);[10] the *central works council*, if it exists, and/or the committees of the establishments concerned by the dismissals in such cases where the envisaged measures exceed the power of the head(s) of the concerned companies or cover various companies at the same time (Article L. 1233-9).

The employer provides the employee representatives, via the *notification* to attend the meeting, with all the *necessary information* regarding the collective dismissal plan. Such information should indicate the economic, financial or technical *reason(s)* of the dismissal plan; the *number of dismissals* envisaged, the *professional categories* concerned and the proposed *dismissal ordering criteria*; the *number of permanent or non-permanent employees* within the establishment; the *estimated timeframe of dismissals*; the proposed *economic measures* (Article L. 1233-10).

[2] Procedure Regarding the Employees

Pre-dismissal Meeting

Prior to any decision, the employer must *call* a pre-dismissal meeting with each employee to be dismissed (Article L. 1233-11). The notification letter must indicate: the meeting's object (Article L. 1233-12), the possibility to seek the assistance of an adviser as well as the address of such services or alternatively the list of such advisers should be put at the disposal of the employees (Article L. 1233-13, al.3). *The pre-dismissal meeting is individual.* During the meeting, the employer informs of the reasons for the proposed decision and takes note of the employee's observations (Article L. 1233-12). Moreover, in the case of a company with at least 1000 employees, the employer must also indicate the *redeployment leave* conditions (Article R. 1233-19).[11]

During the meeting, the employee may choose to be assisted by a person within the company, or by an adviser chosen from a list compiled by the administrative authority (Article L. 1233-13).

Notification of the Dismissal

The employer who decides to dismiss, must *notify* the employees of their dismissal via registered letter against signed receipt (Article L. 1233-15). Such letter cannot be sent before *seven working days* from the date of the pre-dismissal meeting, and must state the *economic reasons* put forward by the employer (Article L. 1233-16) and inform of the right of *priority for re-employment* which the employees can benefit from within a

10. Employee representatives are elected in companies with at least eleven employees (unless there is a collective agreement which envisages a lower number).
11. Cf. *infra* section §10.03[E].

time limit of one year, as well as the conditions for implementation (Article L. 1233-16, al.2 and L. 1233-45 of the Labour Code).[12]

Moreover, upon written request by the employee, the employer must inform in writing on the *criteria* utilized for the order of dismissals (Article 1233-17).[13]

[3] Information to the Administrative Authority

The employer must inform the administrative authority of the pronounced dismissals (Article L. 1233-17), in particular the *Regional Directorate for Companies, Fair Trading, Consumer Affairs, Labour and Employment* (the 'Direccte' – *'Directeur régional des entreprises, de la concurrence, de la consommation, du travail et de l'emploi'),* within eight days from submittal of the dismissal letters to the employees concerned (Article D. 1233-3). The minutes of the meeting held with the employee representatives consulted on the economic collective dismissal plan are also submitted to the Direccte (Article L. 1233-20).

[4] Criminal and Civil Sanctions

The act of proceeding with an economic collective dismissal of less than ten employees within a thirty-day period without informing the administrative authority, or without providing the required information, is punished through a *fine* (Article R. 1238-2).

Moreover, noncompliance with the procedure concerning: the consultation with employee representatives, or the information to the administration, entitles the dismissed employees to an *indemnity* for the prejudice caused by such irregularity (Soc. 25 April 2007, n° 06-40267).

[B] Dismissal of Ten or More Employees Within a Same Thirty-Day Period

For convenience sake, the clear plan adopted by the Labour Code will be hereby followed in order to determine the, sometimes complex, applicable rules in the case of such a 'large dismissal'.

[1] General Provisions

The law envisages that a company agreement or, failing that, a unilateral decision by the employer, can concern the consultation modalities of the employee representative bodies on the economic plans and the proposed dismissal measures, as well as on the employment safeguard plan (PSE). The law also specifies the circumstances for the reintegration of certain dismissals in the context of economic collective dismissals.

12. Cf. *infra* section §10.02[B][3][c].
13. On such criteria, cf. *supra* section §10.01[D].

[a] Possibility of a Collective Agreement and the Resulting Specific Procedures (L. 1233-21)

Further on, company and higher level agreements as well as majority agreements regarding the PSE, will be examined.

[i] Company, Group or Branch Agreement Concerning the Information and Consultation Procedures of the Works Council

In companies with at least fifty employees, when an employer envisages a dismissal for economic reasons of at least ten employees within a same period of thirty days, a company, group or branch ***agreement*** can set, **in *derogation*** ('accord dérogatoire') to the employee representative consultation rules, the *information and consultation procedures of the works council*. Such agreement sets the conditions by which the works council:

(1) meets and is informed of the company's economic and financial conditions;
(2) can make some alternative proposals regarding the economic plan at the basis of a restructuring affecting employment and obtain a reasoned reply ('réponse motivée') from the employer to its proposals (Article L. 1233-22).

However, such agreement cannot derogate from:

(1) the general information and consultation rules of the works council;
(2) providing the employee representatives with the relevant information regarding the collective dismissal plan;
(3) the consultation rules applicable in the case of a company judicial reorganization or liquidation (Article L. 1233-23).

[ii] Majority Company Agreement on the Content of the Employment Safeguard Plan and the Implementation of the Dismissals

In companies with fifty or more employees, a collective agreement signed by one or more majority representative unions may determine the content of the employment safeguard plan and the implementation modalities of the dismissals (Article L. 1233-24-1).

Such agreement can also include:

(1) the information and consultation procedures of the works council;
(2) the weighting and the perimeter of application of the dismissal ordering criteria;

(3) the timetable of the dismissals;
(4) the modalities for implementing training, adaptation and redeployment measures.

The Administration must be informed immediately of the opening of a negotiation in view of such agreement.

[b] Unilateral Document by the Employer (Article L. 1233-24-4)

In the absence of a collective agreement, a *document prepared by the employer* following the last meeting of the works council, sets the *content of the employment safeguard plan* and specifies the same elements as those envisaged in the majority agreement mentioned above.

[c] Modifications of the Employment Contract Resulting in Ten or More Refusals

In the case of refusal by at least ten employees of the modification of a substantial element of their contract proposed by the employer for one of the economic reasons envisaged by the Labour Code and whose dismissal is envisaged, such dismissal is *subject to the provisions applicable in case of collective dismissals for economic reasons* (Article L. 1233-25).

[d] Consecutive Dismissals

When a company or establishment, subject to the legislation regarding works councils, has proceeded:

- either during three consecutive months to economic dismissals of more than ten employees, without reaching ten employees within a same thirty-day period; or
- during a calendar year to economic dismissals of more than eighteen employees in total, without having had to present an employment safeguard plan;

any new economic dismissal envisaged during the following three months in the first case, or during the first three months of the following calendar year in the second case, are subject to the provisions on economic dismissals (Articles L. 1233-26 and L. 1233-27).

[2] Consultation Procedure for Employee Representatives

The employer who envisages a collective dismissal for economic reasons of at least ten employees within a same thirty-day period meets and consults with, accordingly, the works council or the employee delegates (Article L. 1233-28).[14]

[a] Companies of Less Than Fifty Employees

The employer meets and consults with the *employee delegates*, to whom all the *relevant information* on the collective dismissal plan must be provided. The employer provides the same information as that mentioned above regarding the dismissal of less than ten employees (Article L. 1233-31)[15] and informs of the planned *measures to avoid or limit the number of dismissals* and to *facilitate* the *redeployment* of those employees whose dismissal is unavoidable (Article L. 1233-32).

[b] Companies or Establishments of at least Fifty Employees

In companies or establishments with at least fifty employees, the employer meets and consults with the works council ('CE'), the health and safety committee ('comité d'hygiène, de sécurité et des conditions de travail' – 'CHSCT') as well as with the central works council ('CCE'), if present.

[i] Information-Consultation of the Works Council

The works council must be duly notified of any '*restructuring and workforce reduction plans*' (Article L. 2323-31). Subsequently the council will issue an *opinion* on the proposed plan and its application procedures, especially with respect to the employment safeguard plan. The conditions and deadlines for such consultation are strictly defined and set (Article L. 1233-30). The opinion is transmitted to the administrative authority.

The employer must *study* the suggestions of the works council regarding the social measures envisaged and the alternative proposals to the restructuring plan. The employer must provide a *reasoned response ('réponse motivée')* (Article L. 1233-33).

In the case of absence of a works council and submittal of a deficiency statement ('process-verbal de carence') to the labour inspector, the dismissal plan must be provided to the employee delegates (Article L. 1233-30 *in fine*).

The works council can request the *assistance of an accountant* at its first meeting (Article L. 1233-34). Moreover, it can mandate an accountant to make all the necessary

---

14. The reader is reminded hereby that works councils are compulsory for companies of at least fifty employees (Article L. 2321-1) and employee representatives are compulsory for companies of at least eleven employees (Article L. 2312-1).
15. Cf. *supra* section §10.02[A].

analyses in order for the unions to be able to *carry out a collective negotiation* to reach an agreement on the content of the employment safeguard plan.

In order to avoid that the recourse to such assistance does not cause serious delays in the economic dismissals procedure, the legislator has set *precise deadlines* regarding the request for information to the employer, the response of the latter, and the submittal of the report to the works council and the unions.

[ii] Consultation with the Hygiene and Safety Committee ('Comité d'hygiène, de sécurité et des conditions de travail' - 'CHSCT')

Consultation with the CHSCT on the Restructuring and Workforce Reduction Plan

The CHSCT is consulted prior to all '*important management decisions which modify the conditions of health and safety or those of employment*' and, in particular, prior to any significant work transformation deriving from: a change of utilization, a change of product or work organization, and prior to any changes in the timetable and productivity norms whether or not they are linked to employment remuneration (Article L. 4612-8-1). The notion of 'important management decision' envisaged by the jurisprudence also concerns '*the restructuring and workforce reduction plan*' within Article L. 4614-12-1. It is easily understood that a collective economic dismissal can lead to issues of health and safety as well as of the employment conditions of both the employees who were dismissed and those not dismissed. During the consultation on the plan, the CHSCT can seek the *assistance of an expert* recognized by the administrative authority (Article L. 4614-12).

Consultation with the CHSCT on the Employment Safeguard Plan

The employer must consult with the CHSCT on the *employment safeguard plan* (Articles L. 1233-57-2 and L. 1233-57-3). Only after having ensured the regular and effective information and consultation procedure with the CHSCT, can the Direccte validate the collective agreement or approve the unilateral document by the employer in relation to the PSE.[16]

Jurisdictional Competence and Sanctions in Case of Irregular Procedure

As will be described further below,[17] only the administrative judge has the material *competence ('competence matérielle')* to rule on the *lawfulness of the administrative decision validating the collective agreement or approving the unilateral document* prepared by the company in the context of an economic collective dismissal plan. In this context, the Administrative Court of Appeal of Versailles ruled the irregularity of the procedure under judgment, as the employer had *not provided sufficient information to the CHSCT so as to* allow it to make a full *assessment of the impact of the reorganization on the health and safety of the workers* (CAA Versaille, 22 October 2014,

16. Cf. *infra* section §10.02[B][4][b].
17. Cf. *infra* section §10.03[C][5].

n° 14VE02351, Chapter 4, B). Similarly, the Administrative Court of Marseille cancelled the administrative approval of a unilateral document regarding a large economic collective dismissal plan, due to the irregularity of the composition of the consulted CHSCT – the mandate of two of its members had expired – and the insufficiency of the redeployment plan proposals within the PSE (CAA Marseille, 26 August 2015, n° 15MA02165, Chapter 7, A3).

However, as noted by the same Administrative Court, it is not up to the administrative judge, in charge of the legality of the administrative decision, to cancel the employment safeguard plan. Such dispute is in fact, under the jurisdiction solely of the judicial judge.

[iii] Consultation with the Central Works Council

In companies with a central works council, the employer consults the latter and the council(s) of the concerned establishment(s) in the case that the proposed measures exceed the responsibility of the establishment(s) head(s) or affect one or more establishments at the same time. In such case, the establishment council(s) hold their meetings following those of the central works council. The central works council can designate an expert accountant (Article L. 1233-36).

[3] Procedure Regarding the Employees

Such procedure differs from that regarding the dismissal of less than ten employees within a thirty-day period.

[a] Absence of a Pre-dismissal Meeting

Pre-dismissal meetings are not applicable in the case of economic dismissals of at least ten employees within a same thirty-day period and in the presence of a works council or employee delegates (Article L. 1233-38).

[b] Notification of Dismissal

In such case also, the rules differ according to whether or not the company's workforce is of less than fifty employees.

[i] Notification Procedures and Deadlines

Companies with Less than Fifty Employees

The economic dismissal notification letter cannot be sent prior to the expiry of *a certain period from the dismissal plan notification to the administrative authority*. The expiry period cannot be of less than *thirty days*, however collective bargaining or company agreements ('convention ou accord collectif') can envisage a deadline more favourable for the employees (Article L. 1233-9).

Companies with Fifty or More Employees

In the case that the dismissal plan concerns ten or more employees within a same thirty-day period, the employer must notify of the dismissal according to the procedures indicated below. This can only occur, however, *following* the administrative authority's notification of its decision to validate the collective agreement or approve the unilateral document, both relating to the PSE – *or at the expiry of the deadlines* for the Direccte to provide an opinion. The employer cannot terminate the employment contracts prior to such deadlines, or otherwise such terminations can be declared null (Article L. 1233-39).

[ii] Content of the Dismissal Letter: Reasons and Dismissal Ordering Criteria

In this case the rules are the same as those for individual or collective economic dismissals concerning less than ten employees in a same thirty-day period. The dismissal letter must explain *the economic reasons* put forward by the employer and mention the *priority of re-employment* as well as its implementation procedure (Article L. 1233-42). The employer, upon written demand by the employee, must indicate the dismissal ordering criteria utilized (Article L. 1233-43).

[c] Priority of Re-employment

An employee who has been dismissed for economic reasons has a right of priority for re-employment (Article L. 1233-42) for one year after the dismissal, if the employee makes a written request during such period to use such right (Article L. 1233-43). In such case, the employer informs of any position available which is compatible with the employee's qualifications (Article L. 1233-45).

The employee who has acquired a *new qualification* can also benefit from the priority for re-employment as long as the employer is thereof informed.

This will be discussed in more detail below (section §10.03[F]).

[d] Internal Redeployment Measures

Within companies of fifty or more employees and following the works council's favourable opinion, the employer can propose internal redeployment measures (Article L. 1233-45-1). Redeployment will be examined in more detail further on, in the section regarding social support to the dismissal measures.[18]

18. Cf. *infra* section §10.03[B].

[4] Information and Intervention of the Administrative Authority

[a] Information to the Direccte

The employer must notify the administrative authority of any economic *dismissal plan* of at least ten employees within a same thirty-day period (Article L. 1233-46). In the presence of employee representatives, the notification takes place, at the earliest, the day after their first meeting. The notification includes all the information concerning the convocation, the agenda and the meeting proceedings. At the latest on such date, the notification will indicate, if the case, the employer's intention to open negotiations to reach an agreement on the PSE and the works council consultation procedures.

All the information provided to the employee representatives when called to attend the envisaged meetings, is communicated simultaneously to the administrative authority (Article L. 1233-48). The employer must also provide the latter with the *minutes of the meetings* including the opinions, suggestions and proposals of the employee *representatives*.

In the absence of a works council or employee delegates, a company which is subject to the establishment of an *employment safeguard plan* must submit *such plan as well as the information for the employee representatives* to the administrative authority at the same time as the notification of the dismissal plan. Moreover, the employees must be made aware of the plan by all means available at the workplace (Article L.1233-49). If the works council seeks the assistance of an *accountant,* the employer must inform the administrative authority. The employer must also provide the accountant's *report* together with *any changes to the dismissal plan* (Article L. 1233-50).

In the case that the planned dismissals give rise to *consultations with the central works council,* the administrative authority of the company's headquarters must be informed of such consultation as well as, if the case, of the designation of an accountant (Article L. 1233-51).

[b] Intervention of the Administrative Authority

The role of the Direccte[19] is to act, in the course of the information-consultation procedure, as 'a privileged interlocutor, facilitator of social dialogue in the respect of the responsibilities and rights of each'. To this end, it has two 'levers' at its disposal: observation and proposal letters on the regularity and content of the employment safeguard plan; and the power to issue injunctions with respect to the employer so as help 'resume a peaceful dialogue between the parties'.

The role of the administrative authority varies according to whether or not the companies are obliged to establish an employment safeguard plan.

19. According to ministerial instruction n° 2013-10 of 26 June 2013 relating to the new responsibilities of the Direccte.

[i] Role of the Direccte Regarding Companies Which Are Not under the Obligation to Establish an Employment Safeguard Plan

In companies with less than fifty employees, *the Direccte verifies*, in compliance with the legal and conventional provisions, that: the employee representatives have been informed, reunited and consulted; social measures have been set up to avoid or limit the dismissals and facilitate redeployment; and that such measures have effectively been implemented (Article L. 1233-55). In the case of irregular procedure, a *notice* will be sent to the employer specifying the nature of the irregularity identified. A copy of its observations must be sent simultaneously to the works council or, in its absence, to the employee delegates.

The administrative authority may provide *its observations* on the social measures mentioned above. The employer responds and sends copy of its response to such observations to the employee representatives. If such response occurs after the deadline for sending the dismissal letters, the dismissal is delayed until the date of submittal of the response to the administrative authority. *The dismissal letters cannot be sent to the employees until from such date* (Article L. 1233-56).

[ii] The Role of the Direccte Regarding Companies Subject to the Obligation to Establish an Employment Safeguard Plan

[a] Changes or Additions to the PSE (Article L. 1233-57)

The administrative authority can make proposals to *complete or modify the employment safeguard plan*, taking into account the company's economic situation. Such proposals are made prior to the last meeting of the works council. They are communicated to the employer and the works council or, failing the latter, to the employee representatives. The employer submits a reasoned reply ('réponse motivée') to the administrative authority. In the absence of employee representatives, the proposals, together with the employer's reply submitted to the administrative authority, are communicated to the employees via posting at the work place.

[b] Administrative Procedure of Validation of the Agreement or Approval of the Unilateral Document Establishing the Employment Safeguard Plan

Diligent Review by the Direccte

The majority collective agreement or the unilateral document by the employer including the employment safeguard plan are submitted to the administrative authority for validation of the agreement or approval of the document (Article L. 1233-57-1). The competent Direccte is that where the company or establishment concerned by the collective dismissal plan is located (Article L. 1233-57-8). The Direccte *validates the collective agreement* once it has ensured its compliance and regularity. This will be explained later in relation to the Direccte's review of the employment safeguard plan. In the absence of a collective agreement or in the case of a partial agreement, the Direccte *approves the document* prepared by the employer. This occurs after having verified the compliance of its content to the above-mentioned obligations, and having ensured that the employer has envisaged recourse to a job security contract or the implementation of redeployment leave (*see* below). According to the Council of State, *the administrative authority must ensure*, under the supervision of the judge of abuse of power ('juge de l'excès de pouvoir'), the regularity of the works council information and consultation procedure. Thus, the administrative authority cannot provide any legal approval until the *works council has been put in a position to be able to provide its opinion*: first on the proposed operation and its application procedures, and second on the collective dismissal and employment safeguard plans. It is up to the administrative authority to ensure that the employer has provided the works council with *all the relevant information* and, if appropriate, responded to any requests, in *order for it to be able to provide its two opinions in full knowledge of the facts* (Council of State, Assembly, 22 July 2015, n° 385816, recueil Lebon).

Injunction and Observations

The administrative authority's active role is all the more evident by the likelihood of receiving claims, prior to the submittal of the validation or approval request, *ordering the employer* to provide the information relating to the ongoing procedure or to comply with a procedural rule envisaged by law or by collective bargaining or company agreements. Its decision must be provided within five days (Article L. 1233-57-5). Moreover, the administrative authority may, at any time during the procedure, make *all the necessary observations or proposals to the employer* concerning the procedure or the social measures envisaged by law. At the same time it sends a copy of its observations to the works council, or in its absence, to the employee delegates and, in the case of negotiations on a social plan, to the company union representatives. The employer must respond to such observations and submit copy of its response to the employee representatives and, where appropriate, to the unions (Article L. 1233-57-6).

Explicit or Implicit Validation and Approval of the PSE

The administrative authority *notifies the employer of its validation decision* within fifteen days from the receipt of the majority collective agreement, and of *its approval* within twenty-one days from the receipt of the complete document prepared by the employer (Article L. 1233-57-4). At the same time, the administrative authority must notify of its decision the works council as well as the signatory representative unions, in the case of a collective agreement. The decision made by the administrative authority must be *reasoned ('motivée')*.

The administrative authority's *silence* within the above time limits is *equivalent to acceptance of validation or approval*. In such case, the employer submits a copy of the validation or approval request, accompanied by the administrative authority's confirmation of receipt, to the works council as well as to the signatory representative unions, in the case of a collective agreement.

The employees are informed of the validation or approval or, failing those, of the above-mentioned documents and the modalities and deadlines for appeal, *via posting at their work place or through any another means* so as to set a sure date to access such information.

Refusal of Validation or Approval

In case of refusal of validation or approval, the employer who wishes to *re-propose its plan* may resubmit a new request after having made the necessary changes and consulted the works council (Article L. 1233-57-7).

[C] Obligation to Seek a Buyer in Case of Planned Closure of an Establishment

Such obligation was established by Law n° 2014-384 of 29 March 2014 *aimed at recovering the real economy*. Thus, when an establishment's closure resulting in a collective dismissal plan is envisaged, the company with at least *1000 employees* must meet with and inform the works council, no later than at the start date of the information and consultation procedure envisaged for companies normally employing at least fifty employees (Article L. 1233-57-9 of the Labour Code).

The application decree n° 2015-1378 of 30 October 2015 specifies the procedures for the concerned companies to seek a buyer, so as to find an alternative solution to the prospect of closing the establishment, and must inform the administrative authority, the concerned elected parties and the employee representative bodies thereof.

[1] Information to the Employees, the Administrative Authority and the Local Authorities on the Intention to Close the Establishment

Preliminary Definitions

The new Article R. 1233-15 of the Labour Code defines the terms 'establishment' and 'closure': an establishment is '*An economic entity subject to the obligation of constituting an establishment works council*'; a closure is defined as '*the termination of all the establishment's activities resulting in the implementation of an employment safeguard plan leading to a collective dismissal plan at the establishment or company level*'. The closure of an establishment is constituted also by '*the merging of various establishments outside of their employment zone, or by the transfer of an establishment outside of its employment zone, when resulting in the implementation of an employment safeguard plan leading to a collective dismissal plan*'.

Information to the Employees

The employer must provide the *employee representatives*, via the notification to attend the meeting, all the relevant information on the establishment's closure plan. The following information must be included (Article L. 1233-57-10):

(1) the economic, financial or technical reasons for the proposed closure;
(2) the actions the employer envisages taking to try and identify a buyer;
(3) the possibilities for employees to make an offer, the different takeover models, and the right for the employee representatives to seek an expert's assistance.

The works council, if it exists, must also be consulted and informed (Article L. 1233-57-11).

Information to the Administrative and Local Authorities

The prefect of the department ('département') of the establishment's headquarters must be informed of the closure plan. *The Direccte* must also be informed and receive, in addition to the same information provided to the employees, the works council minutes of meeting (Article L. 1233-57-12). The employer must also inform *the mayor of the commune* where the establishment is to be closed. In any case, the mayor is also informed by the departmental prefect ('Il l'est en tout état de cause par le préfet de department') (Article L. 1233-57-13).

[2] The Search for a Buyer

Obligation by the Employer to Search for a Buyer

The employer, after having informed the works council of the establishment's closure plan, must *seek a buyer* (Article L. 1233-57-14). The employer must:

(1) inform *potential buyers*, by all possible means, of its intention to sell the establishment;
(2) immediately prepare a *presentation document* of the establishment aimed at the potential buyers;
(3) undertake an '*environmental survey*', if appropriate, to examine potential pollution levels due to the establishment's activity and present pollution abatement solutions, as well as their cost;
(4) give access to all the relevant information to any potential buyer companies, except for such information the nature of which would damage the establishment's interests or put at risk its activities. In fact, the potential buyer companies have an obligation of confidentiality;
(5) review any offers received;
(6) provide a reasoned response ('réponse motivée') to each of the offers received, within the required deadlines.

Role of the Works Council

The works council must be *informed of any formal offers* no later than eight days from receipt. The information received must be treated as *confidential*. The works council can provide an opinion on the offer, participate in searching for a buyer, and make proposals (Article L. 1233-57-15).

The works council can seek the *assistance of an expert* of its choice paid for by the company, and must inform thereof immediately the administrative authority. The expert's mission is to analyse the buyer search procedure, its methodology and field, evaluate the information available to the potential buyers, study the buyer offers and provide assistance to the works council in seeking a buyer and in preparing takeover plans (Article L. 1233-57-17).

The employer *must consult the works council on any offer* which the employer wishes to pursue as well as, in particular, indicate the reasons for its acceptance, especially with respect to the *proposed buyer's capacity to guarantee the activity's sustainability and employment in the establishment*. The works council issues an opinion on such offer.

End of the Period to Search for a Buyer

Prior to the end of the information and consultation procedure of the works council, if no offers have been received or the employer does not wish to pursue any of the offers, the employer must meet with the works council and present a report, which is submitted to the administrative authority (Article L. 1233-57-20). Such report indicates:

(1) the actions undertaken to seek a buyer;
(2) the offers received and their details;
(3) the reasons, if applicable, why such offers were refused.

The actions by the employer in seeking a buyer are taken into account in the *revitalization agreement* ('convention de revitalisation') between the company and the administrative authority (Article L. 1233-57-21).[20] In view of the employer's capacity, demonstrated by the above-mentioned reports, to avoid or limit the number of dismissals through the handover of the concerned establishment, the *departmental prefect* (Article R. 1233-15-2) *can claim reimbursement of the subsidies* regarding the installation, economic development, research or public job assignment ('emploi attribuées par une personne publique à l'entreprise'), received on behalf of the concerned establishment, during the two years preceding the meeting of the works council on the economic dismissals plan (Article L. 1233-57-21, paragraph 2).

[D] Economic Dismissals and Collective Procedure (Safeguard, Judicial Reorganization or Liquidation)

The economic dismissal regime, in the case of safeguard, judicial reorganization ('redressement') and judicial liquidation ('liquidation judiciaire') is provided for under Article L. 1233-58 and following, of the Labour Code.

20. On the 'convention de revitalisation', cf. *infra* section §10.03[E].

The bodies of the collective procedure assist or replace the employer, depending on the gravity of the commercial jurisdiction's measures towards the company, with the various information or consultation procedures of the employee representative bodies, in informing the administrative authority, and in the preparation of an employment safeguard plan, when it is required.

Without going into detail regarding the applicable regulations, it is noteworthy to mention that: the deadlines of the procedure and available remedies are generally shortened; the administrative authority verifies the employment safeguard plan's compliance with respect to the company means; and the provisions of the Labour Code on the cancellation of dismissals in case of absent or insufficient plan, or due to the cancellation of the administration's validation or approval decision of respectively the unilateral document or the PSE, are not applicable to the companies under judicial reorganization or liquidation (Article L. 1235-10).

§10.03 PREVENTION OF DISMISSALS AND SUBSIDY MEASURES IN FAVOUR OF THE WORKERS

A first approach for a company to avoid further dismissals consists in introducing some internal *flexibility* via collective mobility or job security agreements in order for the company to be able to adopt measures which are less favourable than those of individual employee contracts.

At a later stage, dismissals for economic reasons can only be declared subject to the existence of such economic reasons and to the impossibility of redeployment by the employer.

[A] Collective Agreements for the Upstream Prevention of Economic Dismissals

In order to prevent the risk of job cuts, and even to promote job development, the social partners and the legislator have envisaged various mechanisms in consideration of the different contexts and allowing for a certain degree of employment 'flexi-security' ('flexi-sécurité').

[1] Employment and Skills Planning Programme ('Gestion Prévisionnelle des Emplois et des Compétences' – 'GPEC')

Conceived as a mechanism to maintain and safeguard employment which benefits, under certain conditions, from public financial aid, the GPEC is a '*global anticipation approach*' (Agreement of 11 January 2008 on the labour market modernization, Article 9) which aims to *secure the employees' professional careers*. Indeed, the GPEC aims to adapt the latter to the changes in jobs, skills and qualifications (Article L. 5221-1 of the Labour Code). It is subject to a triennial collective negotiation (Article L. 2241-4) and can give rise, under certain conditions, to a training plan to ensure the employees' adaptation to the changes in their jobs (Article D. 5121-4).

[2] Internal Mobility Agreements[21]

Such agreements were originally envisaged by the national Inter-professional Agreement of 11 January 2013, then taken up by the job security Law n° 2013-504 of 14 June 2013, and leading to a new Article L. 2242-21 of the Labour Code. The 'mobility agreements' aim at the professional or geographical mobility within the company. Such mobility is intended to put in place '*common collective organization measures without a job reduction plan*', resulting in the changing of jobs or locations within the same company'.

Mobility agreements include *mobility support measures* for the employees, particularly in terms of training and geographical mobility assistance. The agreement also envisages limits to the geographical mobility outside the geographic area of employment, as well as provisions to take into account the *conciliation of the professional and family life* (Article L. 2242-22, paragraphs 1, 2).

The envisaged mobilities *must never lead to a decrease in the employee's salary or personal classification*, and must guarantee either to maintain or improve the employee's professional qualification.

In the case of refusal by various employees of the application of internal mobility agreements to their contract, their dismissal, as indicated above, '*is based on economic grounds, and is declared according to the procedures of an individual dismissal for economic reasons and thus gives the right to support and recovery measures which must be envisaged in the agreement*' (Article L. 2242-23).

[3] 'Job Security Agreements': A Temporary Negotiated Solution to Face the Companies' 'Grave Economic Difficulties'

Still in the context of job flexibility, the national Inter-professional Agreement of 11 January 2013 has authorized the stipulation of *majority company agreements*, the so-called job security. Such agreements envisage a temporary commitment by the employer with respect to the concerned employees, to maintain their jobs in exchange of their acceptance to certain changes of their contract. This measure has been provided for by Law n° 2013-504 of 14 June 2013 relating to job security (Articles L. 5125-1-L. 5125-4 of the Labour Code).

Such agreements are subject to the existence of 'grave cyclical economic difficulties', the diagnostic of which must be analysed together with the employee representative unions. The works council may designate an expert accountant to support such analysis as well as the negotiation.

Whilst the employer who commits to job conservation for the duration of the agreement –maximum five years in virtue of the 'Law Macron' of August 2015 – avoids any *economic dismissals* of the concerned employees; on the other hand, the employees must *adapt their working hours, work organization and distribution, as well as their*

21. Regarding the mobility and job security agreement, *see Rencontres de la Chambre sociale 2014* [of the Court of cassation], Round table n° 2 information bulletin, n° 807, 15 September 2014.

remuneration. The employer who does not respect the above commitment is liable to pay damages. A limit has meanwhile been set, which must respect the minimum guaranteed salary ('Salaire Minimum Interprofessionnel de Croissance' – 'SMIC') increased by 20%, as well as some legal thresholds and limits regarding the number of hours of work and rest (Article L. 5125-1, I).

Each employee is *informed of the right to accept or refuse* the application of the agreement to their work contract (Article L. 5125-2). In the case of acceptance by the employees, the agreement is applicable to their work contract, whilst the *contract clauses contrary to the agreement are suspended* during the period of the agreement's application.

In the case of refusal by one or more employees of the application of the agreement to their work contract, their dismissal is grounded on an *economic reason*, and declared according to the *modalities of an economic individual dismissal*, based on a *real and serious cause*. The employer does not have to respect its obligations of adaptation and redeployment, however the employee (in companies of at least 1000 employees) benefits from either the redeployment leave or from a job security contract.

[4] Offensive Company Agreements for Job Preservation and Development

According to Article L. 2252-4.-I resulting from the 'El Khomri' law of 8 August 2016, in the case an employer envisages to undertake negotiations for the conclusion of a so-called offensive agreement, it must transmit all the necessary information to the employee trade unions so as to establish a 'shared diagnosis' between the employer and the unions. An expert can be appointed, at the expense of the employer, to assist in negotiating the employee portion (Article L. 2254-2). The agreement, of a maximum duration of five years, must include a 'foreword' indicating its objectives in terms of employment preservation and development, and must specify:

- the modalities of how to deal with a situation in which the expectations of the employees are disproportionate to their personal or family life;
- the information procedure with respect to the employees, on its application and follow up during the whole duration of the agreement.

The agreement may also envisage the conditions by which the employees should provide efforts in proportion to those requested to other employees:

- the managers acting within the perimeter of the agreement;
- the corporate representatives and shareholders, in the respect of the competencies of the administrative and supervisory organs.

Moreover, the agreement may envisage the conditions by which the employees benefit from an improvement of the company's economic situation as a result of the agreement.

As mentioned above, the employee who refuses the modification of the employment contract resulting from such agreement risks a dismissal. Article L. 2254-2 of the

Labour Code specifies that in such case the employer is obliged, during the pre-dismissal interview, to propose the benefit of a 'personalized support system' mentioned in Article L. 2254-3 and to inform the employee in writing of the specific reason for the termination in case of acceptance by the employee of such support system. In fact, acceptance by the employee results in contract termination, without notice or payment in lieu of notice, however it gives the right to various other types of indemnities. The 'process', whose terms are set by decree, begins with a pre-assessment phase, skills evaluation and career guidance for the development of a career plan. In particular, it includes some accompanying and support measures for the career plan, as well as training and working periods. Such measures are ensured by the Job centre, according to conditions set by decree (Article L. 2254-3).

The beneficiary is placed under the *statute of vocational training intern* and, if with a seniority of more than twelve months, receives, for a maximum period of twelve months, an allowance higher than that to which such beneficiary would have been entitled in respect of unemployment benefits during the same period (Article L. 2254-4).

The employer contributes to the financing of such allowance through a transfer representative of the payment in lieu of notice, within the limit of three months salary increased by the combination of dues and related mandatory contributions (Article L. 2254-5).

[B] Social and Local/Support of the Dismissal Procedures

In the absence of a justification by the employer regarding the economic reason or the attempt of redeployment of the concerned employee, the dismissal shall be judged as lacking a real and serious cause. It is also necessary that the employer previously envisaged the employees' adaptation to the evolution of their jobs.[22] Moreover, certain collective agreements require the employer to consult a joint commission of employment equal treatment ('commission paritaire de l'emploi'[23]) prior to the envisaged dismissal.

[1] The Obligation by the Employer to Adapt Employees to the Evolution of Their Jobs

The Judge and the Law on Adaptation

The obligation for the employers to adapt their employees to the evolution of their jobs has been set, since an early stage, by the social chamber of the Court of cassation. The respect of such obligation is under the employer's responsibility, who '*must respect in*

22. Marie-José Gomez-Mustel, L'adaptation et la reconversion: deux figures de l'obligation de reclassement lors du licenciement économique, Revue de droit du travail, 2009, p. 655.
23. Michel Morand, 'Licenciements économiques et commissions paritaires de l'emploi', Les Cahiers du DRH n° 207, 1 March 2014.

good faith the work contract' (Soc. 25 February 1992, n° 90-44466, bull. civ. 1992, V, n° 90-44466).

The legislator has endorsed such jurisprudence. Article L. 1233-4 of the Labour Code, thus, states that: '*The employee's economic dismissal can only take place when all training and adaptation efforts have been made and no redeployment was possible within the context of jobs of the same category or equivalent, or failing that, and subject to the employee's explicit agreement, of jobs of an inferior category within the company or, if the case, within the companies of the same group (...)*'. Moreover, the first paragraph of Article L. 6321-1 of the Labour Code, regarding professional training, states the following: '*The employer ensures the employees' adaptation to their jobs. He monitors their capacity of job maintenance, especially with respect to the evolution of their jobs, technologies and organizations*'.

Supplementary or Initial Training?

The adaptation envisaged by the Court of cassation implies a duty of *supplementary training* for the employees. However, there is a limit to such obligation: it cannot be imposed on the employer to provide a *new qualification* which would allow the employee to access an available position of a higher category (Soc. 17 May 2006, n° 04-43022). Moreover, the employer cannot be forced to provide initial training to the employee who lacks it, as it would be *long and costly* (Soc. 6 December 2007, n° 06-43346). Thus, the owner of a pharmacy cannot be accused of failing his loyalty obligation by not offering certain job posts to an employee, without verifying if the latter, secretary to the director, had received an initial training for such posts of pharmaceutical assistant or pharmacist (Soc. 2 July 2014, n° 13-13876, bull. civ. 2014, V, n° 165).

Basically, if it is ascertained that the training that the employee should have received to cover the position filled after his departure, superseded the level of training and adaptation obligation by the employer, the latter must be considered as having fulfilled the obligation of redeployment[24] (Soc. 17 March 2015, n° 13-26698).

On the contrary, the employer will have failed such obligation, in the case of failure to inform the dismissed employee (for economic reasons), of available jobs of a lower category requiring only a 'slight adaptation' (Soc. 27 May 2015, n° 13-18313).

[2] Obligation of Redeployment

The employer's obligation of redeployment originates from the constitutionally recognized *right to employment* (Constitutional Council, decision n° 2004-509 DC of 13 January 2005, recital 28). It is not an obligation of result but only an '*obligation of means*'. Such obligation is characterized by the attempt to seek a solution of redeployment in order to avoid dismissal.

24. On condition that the employer made a precise and personalized attempt to redeploy the employee within the company or group. Cf. *infra*.

The employer can prove the impossibility, notwithstanding its efforts, in finding another job for the employee.

Such obligation of means is however 'strengthened', as the employer must comply with certain restrictions, particularly regarding the proof.

[a] *Guiding Principles for Seeking Redeployment*

First of all, the principles applicable to the obligation of redeployment in the case of economic dismissals are more or less the same as those regarding the obligation of redeployment of an employee who is declared physically or mentally unfit by the company doctor. The jurisprudence of the Court of cassation therefore generally treats these two obligations in a similar way, subject to the specific features of each.

Second, the obligation of redeployment of the employee is, in principle, exercised '*internally*'. The employer is, therefore, not obliged to seek a solution of redeployment in other companies prior to the dismissals taking place, unless there is an opposing collective or company agreement (Soc. 26 February 2013, n° 11-27608) or a unilateral commitment by the employer. The employer, however, could be deemed responsible for not having respected a mechanism aimed at facilitating the professional reconversion of the employees following their dismissal (Soc. 21 November 2006, n° 05-40656).

An important exception to the internal nature of the redeployment concerns the companies belonging to the same group as the employer company or connected otherwise.

[i] The Need to Seek an Available Job Within the Company, Group, or Co-employer Companies ('entreprises coemployeurs')

[a] Available Jobs of the Same or Equivalent Category, and, Failing that, of a Lower Category

Availability of Employment

In the case of an employee's claim against a lack of redeployment, the judge's first task is to verify whether the employer can justify the absence of available jobs (Soc. 27 February 2013, n° 11-28835; Soc. 2 July 2014, n° 13-13876). In this regard, evidence that there were no job losses arose in the case of an employer who systematically hired independent workers under *fixed-term contracts*, following the dismissal of two employees (Soc. 12 February 1997, n° 95-41694, bull. civ. 1997, V, n° 58, p. 38). Similarly, the *systematic use of temporary workers*, before and after the dismissals, for a number of hours corresponding to the employment of several employees, proved that jobs were available and that the employer had not satisfied its obligation of redeployment nor the priority for reemployment. (Soc. 1 March 2000, n° 98-46233, bull. civ. 2000, V, n° 82).

The temporary nature of a job should not, therefore, stop it from being proposed within a redeployment plan (Soc. 5 March 2014, n° 12-24456). Moreover, the employer can transform an employee's full time job into a *part time* job (Soc. 4 July 2000, n° 98-44626), and fails its obligation if he does not offer a mid term job when available (Soc. 18 November 1998, n° 96-42991, bull. civ. 1998, V, n° 499 p. 372). Finally, the employer can, in order to make a job available for redeployment, propose a modification of another employee's contract (Soc. 14 December 2005, n° 04-40021), but such modification cannot be imposed (Soc. 15 November 2006, n° 05-40408, bull. civ. 2006, V, n° 339). However, the employer cannot oblige an employee to pre-retirement in order to include such job in another employee's redeployment plan (Soc. 28 November 2000, n° 98-46140).

Employment Category

As per Article L. 1233-4 of the Labour Code, the employee's redeployment can take place within the *same category* of his job or of an equivalent job and remuneration. Failing that, and subject to the employee's explicit agreement, the redeployment can take place within a job of a lower category.[25]

The jurisprudence specifies that the proposal to the employee of a lower job category '*is conditional upon there being no other job of the same category within the company*'. (Soc. 27 October 1998, n° 96-42843, bull. civ. 1998, V, n° 458 p. 342). Thus, the case of a department store which recruited a fashion press agent immediately prior to the dismissal of an employee, head of press, after having offered to redeploy her as saleswoman at a 75% reduced salary, is clearly not an example of respect of its loyalty obligation (same sentence).

[b] The Redeployment Perimeter: The Company, the Group, the Co-employer and the Franchise

The Company and the Group

The employee's dismissal for economic reasons cannot take place without the double condition that: all efforts of training and adaptation have been made and, that no redeployment is possible within the available jobs in the company or companies of the same *group* (Article L. 1233-4 of the Labour Code).

Whereas the legislator does not provide a definition of group, the social chamber of the Court of cassation has done so since a long time. It applies the criteria of *interchangeability* of employees between companies: '*the employees' redeployment options must be considered within the group, between the companies whose activities, organization or place of operation allows for an interchangeability of all or part of the staff*' (Soc. 5 April 1995, Thomson Vidéocolor, n° 93-42690, bull. civ. 1995, V, n° 123). Such *interchangeability* does not necessarily imply the existence of capital sharing between the companies considered. In fact, the partial detention of capital by a company of one or more other companies does not imply the possibility to interchange

25. For further details on the notion of category, cf. Pascal Burchkalter, '*Obligation de reclassement l'obligation de rechercher des postes disponibles (acte I)*', JCP La semaine juridique, édition sociale n° 48, 25 November 2014.

all or part of their personnel and does not characterize the existence of a group within which the redeployment can take place (Soc. 27 October 1998, bull. civ. 1998, V, n° 459; Soc. 10 February 2009, n° 07-4572).

The judicial jurisdictions must, therefore, verify whether the activities, the organization or the place of operation of the various companies allow an interchangeability of all or part of their staff. Such requirement, however, was not satisfied by the Court of Appeal which ruled the existence of a group solely based on the adherence of a health insurance company to a national federation, without seeking possible group linkages with other member insurance companies (Soc. 11 February 2015, n° 13-23573, bull. civ. 2015, V, n° 26).

Co-employers or Joint Employers

In the case of co-employment – whereby the responsibility of proof falls on the employee (Soc. 16 May 2013, n° 11-25.711) – the dismissal declared by one of the co-employers terminates the work contract. In such case, each of the co-employers has to bear the consequences, especially with respect to the obligation of redeployment (Soc. 28 September 2011, n° 10-12299). It is of little matter to note that the role of co-employer was recognized only after the dismissals (same sentence).

In order to identify a *situation of co-employment,* the social chamber refers to the criteria of '*common interests, activities and management*' between various companies. Such criteria are demonstrated by the *interference* of one company in the personnel management of the other, regardless of whether or not there is a relation of subordination of the employees with respect to the latter (Soc. 28 September 2011, n° 10-12278).

The social chamber later restricted the scope of such definition by requiring that the *interference be in the economic or social management* of one of the companies by the other. The interpretation of the social chamber is, thus, the following: '*irrespective from the existence of a relation of subordination, and apart from the necessary financial coordination between same group companies and the economic dominant status that can arise thereof, a company of the same group cannot be considered as co-employer with respect to the staff employed by another, unless there are common interests, activities and management which manifest themselves through an interference in the economic and social management of the latter*. (Soc. 2 July 2014, société Molex, n° 13-15208 et s, bull. civ. 2014, V, n° 159). The Court, thus, assumed, the non-existence of a situation of co-employment in a particular case whereby the subsidiary managers belonged to the group, and the parent company took some group policy decisions leading to the subsidiary's closure and job suppression, whilst committing to provide the related social financial support. In a more recent case, the social chamber judged that a Court of Appeal could not determine a situation of co-employment simply based on the fact that the subsidiary managers belonged to the group and were in close collaboration with the parent company, and that the latter, a few months later, taking over the decisions of the subsidiary, aimed at its reorganization, then gave up its financial assistance which could have avoided the subsidiary's judicial liquidation, whilst however seeking to redeploy the employees' within the group (Soc. 10 December 2015, n° 14-19330, FS-P + B).

Franchise

In this case the responsibility of proof falls on the employer, and the social chamber of the Court of Cassation judges that the activity within a franchising contract is not sufficient to demonstrate the absence of possibilities of staff interchangeability between the various companies included in the same franchise. It is, therefore, up to the employer to justify that the obligation of redeployment has been satisfied (Soc. 25 May 2011, n° 10-14897). In the same way: Soc. 15 January 2014, n° 12-22944; Soc. 10 December 2014, n° 13-18679.

[ii] Possibility for Collective Agreements to Envisage External Redeployment (Outplacement)

Some collective bargaining agreements extend the perimeter of redeployment outside the company or group. Thus, the metal industry national employment agreement of 12 June 1987 (Article 28) imposes on the employer who envisages economic dismissals to '*seek the support from the local labour commission ('commission territoriale de l'emploi') for possibilities of redeployment outside the company*'. The Court of cassation deems that in a situation where the employer does not respect such obligation, the dismissals lack a real and serious cause (Soc. 16 May 2013, n° 12-10065). A more recent ruling points out that it is only when a 'Commission territoriale de l'emploi' has been created by a collective agreement and was expressly assigned the mission to assist external redeployment, that the employer should seize it prior to any dismissal for economic reason (Soc. 11 July 2016, n° 15-12752, FS-P + B + R + I).

[iii] The Issue of Redeployment Abroad

In view of the Court of cassation's decision which does not limit redeployment obligation to companies or groups on the national territory, employers have sometimes proposed job posts abroad according to the local conditions, resulting therefore in salaries much lower than the French legal minimum. So as to avoid such poor conditions, Law n° 2010-499 of 18 May 2010 which '*aims to guarantee fair salaries for employees subject to redeployment*', established a special procedure for redeployment offers abroad, by integrating the notion of equivalent remuneration.

The so-called Macron Law n° 2015-990 of 15 August 2015 provides for such situation by restricting the perimeter of the redeployment obligation only to '*jobs available on the national territory*', and considers redeployment abroad as an exceptional situation, conditional upon the employee's request (Article L. 1233-4-1). The employee must therefore specify any restrictions, in particular regarding the remuneration and location, of the offered jobs. The employer then transmits the corresponding offers to the employee who made the request. Such offers must be 'written and precise'.

Article D. 1233-2-1 of the Labour Code, via decree n° 2015-1638 of 10 December 2015, details the procedures for informing the employees - individually and collectively - regarding the possibility to request such offers, and which the employer must submit. In particular, the new text states that an *offer* is *'precise'* when it indicates at least the employer's name, the location, the job title and salary, the nature of the employment contract, and the working language.

[b] Redeployment Search and Proposals

The search for redeployment by the employer must be above all serious, personalized and loyal. Moreover, it must be accompanied by written, precise, and firm offers guaranteeing the employees' redeployment.

[i] A Serious, Personalized and Loyal Search

Serious Search

The seriousness of the employer is demonstrated when he acts in an effective and reasonable way in the search for an available post in view of redeployment (Soc. 10 March 2010, n° 09-40288).

Personalized Search

The issue of a personalized search for redeployment mainly concerns the group. The jurisprudence requires the employer to provide sufficient information to the group companies, so as to enable them to make the requested searches, as well as to the employees concerned by the dismissals. The jurisprudence therefore ensured that the employer called upon the group companies in a precise and personalized way (Soc. 10 March 2010, n° 09-40288 et s). In fact, it was judged that a circular letter submitted to the group companies, failing to indicate the employee's age and professional versatility, did not allow the concerned companies to properly respond to the redeployment request (Soc. 10 February 2010, n° 08-45267).

On the other hand, the redeployment obligation is respected when the job description in the redeployment request letter includes the job's nature, the employee's seniority and qualification (Soc. 23 October 2014, n° 13-16009), the employee's name, the job classification and nature (Soc. 22 October 2014, n° 13-20403). More recently, the Court of Cassation reduced the level of its demands. It was thus ruled that such job searches within the group's companies did not need to match the personalized profile of the concerned employees in order to establish the redeployment plan integrated within the employment safeguard plan. The latter needs only to specify the number, the nature, the location, the status and the remuneration of the jobs available within the group (Soc. 28 October 2015, n° 14-17720, ongoing publishing).

Loyal Search

According to the jurisprudence, the employer must carry out its redeployment obligation in a *loyal* way. Such is not the case, for example, if one of the group companies offers a job to someone recruited externally, rather than to the concerned employee whilst the dismissal procedure is ongoing (Soc. 7 April 2004, n° 01-44191, bull. civ. 2004, V, n° 114). Another example, is the case of an employer proposing that the employee accept jobs at a salary lower than the minimum wage (SMIC) (Soc. 5 December 2012, n° 11-21849, bull. civ. 2012, V, n° 318). Moreover, a redeployment offer reserving the right to pay at the employer's discretion upon estimation of the work done and with no reference to the minimum wage, certainly does not respect the loyalty obligation (Soc. 28 October 2014, n° 13-11852).

The Social chamber ruled that an employer had not loyally satisfied its redeployment obligation as he had made only one offer which meant a strong declassification and salary decrease for the employee. Furthermore, such employer was not able to demonstrate the non-availability of other jobs, more compatible with the employees functions (Soc. 13 February 2013, n° 11-21074, F-D).

[ii] Written, Precise, Firm Offers Guaranteeing the Employee's Effective Redeployment

The redeployment offers made to the employee must be *written and precise* (Article L. 1233-4 of the Labour Code). The jurisprudence requires them also to be *firm*. It was thus ruled that the redeployment offers specifying that the employees' recruitment was subject to the validation by a group director and by the department manager, did not respond to the legal requirements, as they were not firm and did not guarantee the effective redeployment of the employees in the case of available posts within the group (Soc. 28 January 2015, n° 13-23440).

[c] The Judge's Role in the Case of Redeployment

It is up to the judge to assess whether the employer respects its obligation of redeployment. Thus, the judge's decision cannot base itself merely on the declarations of the employer contested by the employee (Soc. 28 February 1998, n° 95-42841). Furthermore, the judge's decision must specify whether the employer sought possibilities of redeployment (Soc. 30 May 2007, n° 05-44210). Such assessment is final, and not subject to review by the Court of cassation (Soc. 29 February 2012, n° 10-28781).

[3] Prior Referral to the Employment Joint Commissions ('commission paritaires de l'emploi')

The national Inter-professional Agreement of 10 February 1969 on job security obliges the employers of various professions to refer to the *employment joint committees* (*'commission paritaires de l'emploi'*) in the case of economic dismissals of over ten employees within a thirty-day period and which pose an issue of redeployment. Such referral is compulsory and if ignored, the dismissals are considered without a real and serious cause (Soc. 30 September 2013, n° 12-15940, bull. civ. 2013, V, n° 223; Soc. 8 July 2014, n° 13-14611 and following, bull. civ. 2014, V, n° 181). It is up to the employer to justify its impossibility to refer to the competent local employment commission prior to the dismissal (Soc. 13 September 2012, n° 11-22414).

[C] The Employment Safeguard Plan ('Plan de sauvegarde de l'emploi' Article – 'PSE'), Key Point of the 'Great Dismissals for Economic Reasons'

In *the companies of at least fifty employees* where the dismissal concerns less than ten employees in a same thirty-day period, the employer must prepare and implement an *'employment safeguard plan to avoid or limit the number of dismissals'* (Article L. 1233-61, paragraph 1 of the Labour Code). Such plan, like the 'social plan' which historically preceded it, integrates a *'redeployment plan'* so as to facilitate the redeployment of those employees whose dismissal could not be avoided. This is the case especially of the older employees and of those with social or qualification characteristics which would make their professional reinsertion particularly difficult (Article L. 1233-61, paragraph 2).

[1] Who Establishes the Employment Safeguard Plan (PSE)?

In the past, the PSE was prepared *unilaterally* by the employer. However, Law n° 2013-504 of 14 June 2013 on job security envisaged that the plan could also result from a *majority collective agreement* (Article L. 1233-24-1 of the Labour Code). The unilateral aspect of the employer's document establishing the PSE is mitigated, as in the case of the majority collective agreement, by the participation of the works council which must always be *informed and consulted for an opinion*. Such opinion is *twofold*, as it must cover both *the envisaged operation and application procedures, as well as the collective dismissal (number of job cuts, professional categories, ordering criteria, and the dismissals' timing) and its accompanying social support measures* (Article L. 1233-20, I).

On the other hand, in order to be enforced, the unilateral document and the collective agreement are both subject, to the *prior authorization by the administrative authority* by way of validation of the first or approval of the second.

[2] Conditions for Establishing a PSE

In the presence of a company satisfying the double condition concerning the number of employees (*at least fifty employees*) and the number of economic dismissals (*ten or more employees over the same thirty-day period*), the establishment of an employment safeguard plan is compulsory. The assessment of such two conditions is made either at the company level (Soc. 28 January 2009, n° 07-45481) or at the level of the economic and social unit ('unité économique et sociale' – 'UES') (Soc. 16 November 2010, n° 09-69489).

Reference should be made to the above paragraphs on the inclusion of voluntary dismissals or mutually agreed terminations for the determination of the number of job cuts. It is important to note, however, that the use of mutually agreed terminations as a means of workforce reduction for economic reasons assumes that the *employment contracts have been terminated after the approval of the mutually agreed terminations by the labour administration*. Thus one cannot consider agreements which, failing their approval, did not lead to the termination of the employment contract (Soc. 29 October 2013, n° 12-15382; n° 12-27393).

[3] Content of the PSE: Measures for Internal and External Redeployment

According to Article L. 1233-62 of the Labour Code, the employment safeguard plan envisages, without limitations, the following *measures*:

- the employees' *internal redeployment* with respect to relevant jobs of the same category or equivalent, or of a lower category subject to the employee's explicit agreement;
- *development* or support *of new activities* by the company, or recovery of existent activities by the employees;
- *external redeployment*, in particular through actions to support the revitalization of the employment area;
- training, job accreditation ('validation des acquis de l'expérience' – 'VAE'), and job reconversion so as to facilitate the employees' internal or external redeployment on equivalent jobs; *work time reduction or reorganization measures* as well as measures to *reduce the number of extra hours worked* on a regular basis as such overtime clearly indicates that the company is not respecting the weekly thirty-five hours or yearly 1600 hours, and its reduction could possibly maintain all or part of the jobs envisaged to be cut.

The PSE must include, amongst others, a *redeployment plan*. However, no redeployment plan is envisaged in the case of voluntary departures in the framework of amicable mutually agreed terminations, as the redeployment only concerns job cuts which occur through 'dismissals', (Soc. 25 January 2012, n° 10-23516, bull. civ. 2012, V, n° 22, FS-P + B + R + I).[26]

[a] The Employment Safeguard Plan Must be Exempt from Discrimination and Respect the Principal of Equal Treatment

Measures Reserved to Certain Employees

Based on the Labour Code's provisions on discrimination (Article L. 1133-2), interpreted 'in the light' of Article 6 of Directive n° 2000/78/CE of 27 November 2000, the Court of cassation rules that *'an employment safeguard plan can include measures reserved to certain employees conditional that all the company's employees who are in an identical situation can benefit from such measures, unless a difference in treatment is justified by objective and relevant reasons and that the rules determining such conditions be defined in advance and are controllable'* (Soc. 12 July 2010, n° 09-15182, bull. civ. 2010, V, n° 166). A termination which respects the principal of equal treatment of the employees of the different establishments of a same company is demonstrated: on the one hand, by the PSE measures encouraging voluntary departures only of the employees of a *specific establishment* and, on the other, if such measures did not succeed in reaching the workforce reduction objective, it was envisaged that the economic dismissal plan would go ahead exposing all the employees belonging to the concerned professional categories without them being able to benefit from the support of the initial voluntary departure alternative.

The Paris Administrative Court of Appeal made the same assessment regarding the respect of the principle of equal treatment on occasion of its judicial review of the legality of a Direccte's decision (CAA of Paris, 12 March 2015, n° 14PA05025, 'Comité d'établissement' of the company France Télévisions and others).[27] However, the circumstance by which the employees from an activity due to decrease or be outsourced were given priority in the case of multiple candidatures for the same available post, was not considered as unequal treatment.

Measures Concerning Age

The jurisprudence has been called upon to decide on the legality of the inclusion in the employment safeguard plan of varying measures according to the employees' age. In order to make such assessment with respect to the above-mentioned criteria, the judges take into account: the specificities of the unemployment benefits, which can be more favourable for the older employees, as well as the possibility of access to a retirement pension. Thus, the setting of the age limit at 57 years and over as a limiting criteria for

26. 'The PSE itself does not include any dismissals, however it sets a method and framework which must respect the envisaged dismissals' (Jean Lessi and Louis Dutheillet de Lamothe, Maîtres des requêtes Council of State, 'Le contrôle du juge administratif sur les plans de sauvegarde de l'emploi', AJDA 2015, p. 1632).
27. *See in* Florian Roussel, Rapporteur public, *Le contrôle des plans de départs volontaires par le juge administratif*, Revue de droit du travail 2015, p. 315.

the employees affected by the PSE to receive an indemnity was justified by the fact that for such age category the unemployment indemnity limits the loss of revenues following the dismissal. Therefore, when such employees were encouraged to envisage professional reinsertion '*the means utilised to reach the legitimate objective of job maintenance and balance between the employee categories which do not benefit from the same advantages following the loss of their job, were appropriate and necessary*' (Soc. 18 March 2014, n° 12-28275, D).

Similarly, to avoid the accusation of discrimination towards a 60-year-old worker, it was taken into account that the *less senior* employees, if dismissed, would have found themselves in a *greater state of precariousness* than those older than them who could have access, either immediately or within less than two years, to their pension or job return allowance (Soc. 15 April 2015, n° 13-18849, D). The crosscheck of such reasoning is demonstrated by a case in which the PSE, intending to encourage employees of at least 55 years old to early retirement, envisaged that the dismissal benefits of the latter in case of their refusal would be less than those of the other dismissed employees who did not fulfil the conditions to be able to claim such early retirement. In view of the above, the Court of cassation approved the Court of Appeal's decision which considered, with respect to the 55-year-old employee, that such *difference in treatment was not justified by objective and relevant reasons.* (Soc. 9 July 2015, n° 14-16009, published).

[b] The Employment Safeguard Plan Does Not Replace the Employer's Obligation of Redeployment

Notwithstanding the inclusion of a redeployment plan in the PSE, the employer's general obligation of redeployment in the case of an economic dismissal remains. The Court of Appeal had rejected an employee's claim for indemnity for absence of real and serious cause, as it considered the employer to have satisfied its redeployment obligation through the proposal of redeployment offers within the employment safeguard plan. Such decision was annulled on the grounds that '*it is the responsibility of the employer, even if an employment safeguard plan is established, to seek possibilities of redeployment, whether or not they are envisaged in the plan, and to propose available jobs to the employees whose dismissal is envisaged*'. (Soc. 14 March 2012, n° 10-26613).

As explained by a specialist: '*Such solution is understandable in view of the different objectives of each of the two obligations: in the context of redeployment, the obligation is of an individual nature, the employer having to seek available jobs within the company or group. On the other hand, the employment safeguard plan has a collective character as its objective is to avoid or limit the number of dismissals* (Labour Code, Article L. 1233-61)'.[28]

28. François Taquet, '*Coordination du plan de sauvegarde de l'emploi et de l'obligation de reclassement*', Revue des procédures collectives n° 5, September 2012, comm. 150.

[4] The Administration's Review of the Preparation and Content of the PSE

The role of the Administration, as mentioned above, is to either validate the majority company agreement inclusive of the employment safeguard plan or approve the unilateral document by the employer. Such validation or approval can only take place following the Administration's review of the procedure leading to the preparation of the above documents.

The review by the Administration, in this case the Direccte, *changes intensity*[29] according to whether it applies to the majority company agreement or the unilateral document by the employer. In the first case, the review is limited, whilst in the second it is much heavier. This difference in treatment is due to the greater legitimacy conferred to the plan through collective bargaining from which it originates.

However, in both cases, the administrative review procedure '*has not been devised on a demand-decision basis, but on an ongoing logic of improvement, where possible, of the employer's plan so as to ensure its compliance with the legal and conventional requirements*'.[30]

[a] 'Limited' Review of the Majority Company Agreement

According to Article L. 1233-57-2 of the Labour Code, the Administration *validates the collective agreement* as soon as it has ensured the following:

(1) its conformity to the legal provisions in relation to the signature conditions and its content;
(2) the regularity of the works council information and consultation procedures and, if the case, of the hygiene and safety committee (CHSCT), as well as the coordination body of the latter;
(3) the presence of a *redeployment plan*, within the employment safeguard plan, regarding the employees whose dismissal cannot be avoided, as well as the *monitoring modalities* of the implementation of the redeployment plan's measures;
(4) that the obligations, where appropriate, to call and inform the works council of the *closing* of the envisaged establishment have been met.

Law n° 2013-504 of 14 June 2013 has transferred the competence on such matters from the judiciary to the administrative jurisdictions. It is therefore the decisions of the latter which determine the role of the Administration when it is called upon to rule on a demand for validation of the collective agreement in relation to the PSE.

29. *Change d'"objet"*, according to professeur Alexandre Fabre, in *Validation des PSE négociés: contrôler moins ou... autrement?*', in Semaine sociale Lamy, 28 December 2015, n° 1704, p. 10.
30. Jean Lessi and Louis Dutheillet de Lamothe, Maîtres des requêtes au Conseil d'Etat, '*Le contrôle du juge administratif sur les plans de sauvegarde de l'emploi*', AJDA 2015, p. 1632.

First of all, the Direccte has to assess, 'under the supervision of the administrative judge', whether the company agreement under examination has actually been established by a '*majority*', i.e., whether it has been signed on behalf of one or more union representatives with at least 50% of approvals in their favour at the first round of the last professional elections within the company.

Next, the Direccte must ensure that the agreement's signatory is in the *position ('qualité')* to do so. Thus the agreement signed on behalf of a union by a person who was not formally in the legal position to do so (central union delegate), was considered null and therefore without a majority agreement (C.E. 22 July 2015, société Pages jaunes, appeal n° 385668, recueil Lebon).

[b] 'Heavy' Review of the Unilateral Document of the Employer

[i] Textual Elements

In the absence of a collective agreement or in the case of a partial agreement, the administrative authority *approves* the document prepared by the employer. Such approval, as per Article L. 1233-57-2 of the Labour Code, takes place after having verified:

- the *compliance of its content* to the legal and conventional provisions in relation to the: works council information and consultation procedures, dismissal ordering criteria weighting and perimeter, dismissal calendar, number of job cuts and professional categories concerned, training implementation modalities, adaptation and redeployment as envisaged by law;
- the *regularity of the information and consultation procedure* of the works council and, where appropriate, of the CHSCT and its coordinating body;
- the respect, where appropriate, of the legal obligations concerning the *closure* of an establishment;
- the inclusion of a *redeployment plan* within the PSE and the planning of the various measures to allow the redeployment.

Such assessment is made on the basis of the following criteria:

- the means available to the company, the social and economic unit ('unité économique et sociale') and the group;
- the envisaged accompanying measures according to the dismissal plan's importance;
- the training and adaptation efforts required by law.

Moreover, the Administration must also ensure that the employer has envisaged the recourse to a job security contract or the implementation of redeployment leave (*see* below).

[ii] Elements of Jurisprudence

The administrative jurisprudence highlights the importance of the information and consultation procedure of the employee representative bodies.

[a] Regularity of the Works Council Information and Consultation Procedure

According to the Council of State, *the Administration must ensure*, under the supervision of the 'judge of abuse of power' (*'juge de l'excès de pouvoir'*), the regularity of the works council information and consultation procedure. Therefore, approval can only be granted *if the works council has been able to regularly issue an opinion* on both: the planned operation and its application modalities, as well as on the collective dismissal and employment safeguard plans. In view of the above, the administrative authority must ensure that the employer has provided the works council, through the first meeting notification and eventually its response to any demands, *all the relevant information in order to be able to provide its two opinions with the full knowledge of the evidence* (CE, Assembly, 22 July 2015, Heinz France, appeal n° 385816, recueil Lebon).

In the case that the works council has sought the assistance of an accountant, the administrative authority must ensure that the latter was able to properly carry out its mission to allow for the works council to provide its *opinions with the full knowledge of the evidence* (CE, 21 October 2015, Union CFDT social health of Seine-Saint-Denis and others, n° 382633, A).

[b] Regularity of the Composition and Consultation of the Hygiene and Safety committee (CHSCT)

The employer must ensure the *regular composition* of the Hygiene and safety committee (CHSCT) which has been consulted on the employment and safeguard plan. The Administrative Court of Appeal of Marseille specifies the effects of an irregular composition of the CHSCT on the validity of the Direccte's approval decisions and applies the rules set by the Council of State on the employer's search for redeployment (CAA Marseille, 26 August 2015, n° 15MA02165).

[c] Conditions of 'Sufficiency' of the PSE: A Global, Analytical and Balanced Approach

The employment safeguard plan set by the unilateral document of the employer must be '*sufficient*' (Article L. 1235-10 of the Labour Code). With reference to the previous judicial jurisprudence, and for the sake of coherence and lawfulness, the administrative jurisprudence set the Administration's responsibility to ensure, through a *global assessment*, that the PSE is *sufficient* with respect to its objectives. In particular, according to the extent of the dismissal plan, the administrative authority must assess whether the plan's *measures* are *precise and concrete*. Moreover, in view of each measure's *contribution to the objectives* of job security and employee redeployment, the administrative authority must also assess whether, *on the whole*, they directly or indirectly satisfy: the training and adaptation efforts on the part of the employer, the means of the company and, if the case, of the economic and social unit ('UES') as well as of the group.

In a case submitted to the Council of State, the latter considered the approval of the employer's unilateral document was justified by its inclusion of measures which, directly or indirectly, contributed to job security or employee redeployment, even if some benefited from public financing. Such measures comprised: the company's participation to job security contracts, the priority of reemployment of the dismissed employees by another company, the maintenance of the company's contribution to the complementary social protection system of the dismissed employees or the setting up of a psychological support unit. Taken *as a whole*, these *measures* are considered '*sufficient*' to ensure the respect of the legal provisions, *taking into account the means of the company and of the group* to which it belongs (CE. 22 July 2015, Calaire Chimie, n° 383481, recueil Lebon).

On the contrary, the Administrative Court of Marseille refused the approval of a unilateral document setting a PSE, notwithstanding the employer had identified some redeployment posts within the company and indicated their number and nature; however *no indication of their location* had been provided, not even implicitly (CAA Marseille, 26 August 2015, n° 15MA02165).

[c] The Decision of the Administrative Authority Must Be Reasoned ('Motivée')

The administrative authority's validation of the majority agreement or approval of the unilateral document setting the PSE '*must be reasoned*' *('motivé')* (Article L. 1233-57-4, paragraph 2 Labour Code). According to the Council of State, in order to be considered sufficient, such motivation must '*state the legal and factual grounds, in a way that, the persons notified of such decisions can read it and clearly be informed of the reasons*' (CE, 22 July 2015, *Heinz France*, appeal n° 385816, recueil Lebon). In its conclusions regarding the above decision, the public 'rapporteur' specifies that such rule applies also in the case of a decision of *refusal* of validation or approval.

There is however a *limit to the motivation obligation*: the administrative authority is not obliged neither to explicitly rule on the respect of each of the rules it is responsible to review, nor to indicate in its motivation the steps leading to its decision. The Direccte is, thus, not obliged to specifically mention the injunction issued to the employer or the response by the latter.

[d] Legal Recourse Against the Decision of the Administrative Authority

In order to ensure a rapid procedure, the legislator of 2013 put a stop to the possibility of hierarchical recourse, contrary to the decision of the Direccte. Such recourse is only possible in cases of abuse of power.

Functional Authority ('qualité') and Interest to Act: Who Can Have Recourse?

Although the Labour Code (Article L. 1235-7-1) limits itself to mention that recourse is lodged by the employer, the unions and the employees, the Council of State *extends such right* to the works council, the unions who are not signatory of the majority agreement as well as to the union of unions.

In the case of the employees, the latter must justify an *interest to act*. whilst in the case of the CHSCT, the latter *does not have the functional authority ('qualité')* to contest a decision of approval, or of validation of a PSE (CE, 21 October 2015, Union CGT SKF Montigny and others n° 386123, B).

Setting of the Appeal and Sentence Periods

In order to accelerate the litigation procedure in the case of economic collective dismissals, the legislator has set very strict deadlines. The appeal by the employer must be presented within two months from the notification of the administrative authority's decision, whilst that by the unions and employees must be presented starting from the date of the formal notification of such decision. The administrative court must pronounce its judgment within three months. If, after such period, no decision has been taken, not even in the case of appeal, the dispute is brought before the Administrative Court of Appeal, which must rule within three months. If, after such period, no decision has been taken, not even in the case of an appeal in cassation, the dispute is brought before the Council of State. The latter, however, is not restricted by such deadline.

[5] Sanctions in the Case of Irregularities and Non-performance of the PSE

The PSE and the procedure leading to its establishment can present various types of irregularities, some of which can lead to its invalidation by the judge. With the law of June 2013 which has substituted on various issues the competence of the judiciary judge by that of the administrative judge (Article L. 1235-7-1 of the Labour Code), it is here opportune to specify the respective competences of the two orders of jurisdiction on the subject.

[a] Competence of the Administrative and Judiciary Courts

Although the law of 14 June 2013 on job security has deprived the judiciary court of most of its functions in favour of the administrative courts – professor Patrick Morvan[31] evokes, in this respect, the '*removal of the judicial court and the enthronement of the*

31. Jurisclasseur de droit du Travail, Traité, fascicule 31-3: Licenciement pour motif économique. – Accompagnement social. – Plan de sauvegarde de l'emploi et dispositifs d'accompagnement, n°117.

administrative court'- the first remains competent on various issues. Thus, as remarked by the same author, an '*unprecedented explosion of disputes*'[32] has resulted thereof.

[i] Administrative Competence

[a] The Administrative 'Block of Competence'

The collective agreement and the unilateral document establishing the employment safeguard plan, its content, the administration's decisions on behalf of the injunction procedure, and the regularity of the collective dismissal procedure, *cannot be the object of disputes independent from that in relation to the validation or approval decision of the plan* (Article L. 1235-7-1 of the Labour Code).

These different areas constitute an important 'block of competence' which affect, in particular, the procedural aspects of the PSE's establishment and the collective dismissal, as well as the validity of the administrative decision. The disputes concerning such issues are of the competence of the first instance administrative court.

In view of this recent transfer, administrative court decisions are starting to take place, and the Council of State's jurisprudence to be set. The latter has to be 'coherent' with respect to: its own jurisprudence concerning the dismissal of protected employees (employee representatives or union delegates) subject to the work inspector's authorization, and the Court of cassation's jurisprudence in the areas currently attributed to the administrative order.

[b] Possibility of Administrative Temporary Suspension Orders Subject to Conditions

Notwithstanding the legislator of 2013 already envisaged an accelerated judgment procedure of the administrative decisions regarding the PSE (agreement validation, employer unilateral document approval, decision to refuse), the Council of State has allowed the possibility to submit a case to the *judge in chambers ('juge des référés')* on the grounds of Article L. 521-1 of the Code of administrative justice, so as to obtain the suspension of the implementation of the Administration's decision. The legislator defines the conditions of admissibility of such action and defines the judge's role.

The Assessment of the Urgency

Whilst excluding a presumption on such matter, the Council of State first of all establishes the principle that '*the urgency justifies the suspension of an administrative act when it seriously and immediately affects a public interest, the claimer's status or the interests he wishes to defend*'. In addition, '*in view of the justifications provided by the*

32. *Ibid.* n° 127.

claimant, it is up to the judge in chambers to concretely assess whether the effects of the disputed act are of such an urgent nature to justify, without awaiting the judgment on the merits, the suspension of the decision'. Moreover, '*the urgency must be objectively assessed, taking into account all the circumstances of the case. This is particularly true in the case of a request of suspension made to the judge in chambers of the implementation of the decisions (...) which validate the collective agreement or approve the employer's document in relation to the employment safeguard plan*'.

Its Control

In application of such principles, the High administrative court approved a judge in chambers who assessed that the condition of urgency was not fulfilled unless: the dismissals planned by the employer in a period of observation of receivership were authorized by the bankruptcy judge of the commercial court for the reason of its urgency, inevitability and absolute necessity; and notwithstanding the gravity of the consequences of the planned job cuts on the professional and financial situation of the concerned employees, the company had to proceed with the dismissals so as to *avoid the status of cessation of payments and, eventually, a judicial liquidation which would seriously prejudice its activity and employment.* (CE. 21 February 2014, IPL Atlantique-Aquitaine, n° 374409).

A commentator of such decision highlights the difficult task of the administrative judge in chambers, who has to respect the deadline constraints (obligation to rule within three months from the request's submittal), and cannot infringe neither on the decision of the judicial jurisdiction on the economic reason of the dismissal, nor on that of the trial judge.[33]

[ii] Judicial Competence: The Dismissal Judge

The judicial court, in such case the first instance Labour court ('conseil de prud'hommes'), is competent for resolving *individual disputes*, particularly concerning: indemnity and reinstatement, cancellation of the administrative decision validating the company agreement or approving the employer's unilateral document, and the review of the existence of the economic grounds for dismissal. In this respect, the Council of State recalls that '*when called to rule on a request to ratify a document setting an employment safeguard plan, the administration is not entitled to rule on the validity of the economic grounds of the dismissals, as this is the role of the dismissal judge*' (CE, 22 July 2015, Heinz France, n° 385816, above mentioned). In the context of a claim for abuse of power, the administrative judge can, in fact, only rule on the lawfulness of the contested administrative decision.

33. Caroline Mayeur Carpentier, Le juge administratif de l'urgence et le plan de sauvegarde de l'emploi, Revue de droit du travail 2014, p. 353.

Thus, a request to the administrative judge aiming at the cancellation of a PSE is *inadmissible* (Administrative Court of Marseille, 28 August 2015, appeal n° 15MA02165).

Apart from the cancellation of the plan, Professor Morvan (*supra*) lists, here below, other areas of competence of the judicial judge, counterposed to those of the administrative judge:

- assessment of the regularity of a consultation and information procedure leading exclusively to a restructuring plan, without a workforce reduction;
- determination of the number of contract terminations over a same thirty-day period, in the absence of a social plan by the employer due to the fact that the legal threshold was not reached;
- disputes on the implementation and follow up of the PSE, particularly with respect to whether the employer respected the commitments therein;
- disputes regarding the dismissals declared by companies not legally bound to establish an employment safeguard plan;
- disputes regarding actions against co-employers.

Whereas the same author also includes disputes regarding any discriminatory clauses of the employment safeguard plan, others consider that such review of equal treatment ('égalité de traitement') is of competence of the Direccte.[34] A decision on this point is awaited by the Council of State, the Court of cassation or the Jurisdictional court ('Tribunal des conflits').

Finally, a case is to be noted whereby, notwithstanding the administrative authority's approval of the employer's unilateral document establishing an employment safeguard plan accompanied by job cuts and a phase of voluntary departures, the Court of Appeal, on the basis of the obligation of security, attributed the judicial jurisdiction to suspend a restructuring plan leading to possible psychosocial risks for the employees. In such case, the Direccte's role was, therefore, strictly interpreted to be limited to the assessment of the PSE content and the regularity of the employee representative bodies' consultation procedure. (Versailles, Chapter 6, 1 December 2015, n° 15/01203, Observations Michel Morand, Dictionnaire Permanent Difficultés des entreprises, 7 January 2016).

[b] Nullity of the Dismissal

> *The cornerstone of redeployment in case of large collective dismissals is constituted by the establishment of an employment safeguard plan which includes a redeployment plan accompanied by a particularly harsh sanction, i.e. the nullity of the dismissals* (Comment of Labour Code Dalloz).

34. Judith Krivine et Stéphanie Guedes da Costa, 'Que peut-on attendre du juge administratif dans le contentieux des plans de sauvegarde de l'emploi?', Revue de droit du travail 2015, p. 438.

[i] Limited Application of the Nullity of Dismissals

Areas of Nullity

The nullity of the dismissal procedure or of the dismissals themselves can be declared in the following cases:

- dismissal in the *absence of any decision* relating to the employment safeguard plan's validation or approval (Article L. 1235-10, paragraph 1);
- dismissal, irrespective of the Direccte's *negative decision* (same text);
- dismissal declared by virtue of a validation or approval decision which was *later cancelled due to a lack or deficiency of the employment safeguard plan* (Article L. 1235-10, paragraph 2);
- dismissal declared by virtue of an administrative decision later cancelled due to a *reason other than that of the plan's lacking or deficiency* (Article L. 1235-16, paragraph 1).

Limits of Nullity

With respect to the nullity envisaged in the first two above situations, a *first limit* is constituted by the inapplicability to companies going into receivership or judicial liquidation (Article L. 1235-10, paragraph 3). A *second limit* avoids that the employer be held responsible for an irregularity by the administrative authority. This results from the 'Macron' law which aims to *prevent the nullity of an administrative authority decision for insufficient motivation*. In this case, the legislator invites the administrative authority (Direccte) to make *a new decision which is sufficiently motivated.* This must take place within fifteen days from the notification of the sentence to the administration. The employer must inform the employees who were dismissed following the initial validation or approval decision, of such decision (Article L. 1235-16, paragraph 3). Once the administrative authority has issued its new decision, the nullity of the initial decision is without incidence on the validity of the dismissal, giving no right to reinstatement, nor to payment of an indemnity by the employer (Article L. 1235-16, paragraph 4).

A *third limit* derives from a noteworthy decision by the Court of cassation in 2012, which by virtue of Article L. 1235-10 of the Labour Code, declared that *only the absence or deficiency of the employment safeguard plan* submitted to the employee representatives, and *not the absence of a real and serious cause*, can lead to the nullity of an economic dismissal. In fact, the High jurisdiction explains that '*the dismissal procedure cannot be annulled in consideration of the economic reason of the dismissal, as the plan's validity is independent from the cause of the dismissal*' (Soc. 3 May 2012, Viveo, n° 11-20741, bull. civ. 2012, V, n° 129).

As highlighted by some authors, the Council of State is in line with such jurisprudence as it removes any element concerning the dismissal's economic reason from the control of the administrative jurisdiction.[35]

35. J. Lessi et L. Dutheillet de Lamothe, 'Le contrôle du juge administratif sur les plans de sauvegarde de l'emploi', AJDA 2015, p. 1632.

[ii] Effects of the Nullity of the PSE

[a] Nullity of Subsequent Acts

The Nullity of the PSE Results in *the Cancellation of the Amicable Terminations (Voluntary Departures)* Deriving from Such Plan

Such was the decision following the cancellation of a PSE due to the invalidation of the information and consultation procedure of the employee representatives (Soc. 9 March 2011, n° 10-11581). In fact, as noted by the Court of cassation on such matter, '*mutual termination agreements on economic grounds and within a workforce reduction process of which they constitute a modality, must be taken into account to determine the information and consultation procedure of the applicable employee representatives as well as the employer's obligations regarding the employment safeguard plan*'. Having established that many mutual termination agreements had occurred in a context of job cuts related to economic difficulties and that they took place in the framework of a global agreed workforce reduction plan within a social and economic unit ('unité économique et sociale'), the Court of Appeal could not refuse the works council's and union's request for damages on the basis that mutual termination agreements for economic reasons are legally out of the realm of the economic dismissal law (same sentence). In a later decision, the Court of cassation states more specifically that '*the nullity of an employment safeguard plan which is legally non compliant, extends to all subsequent acts and that, in particular, a contract termination due to voluntary departure for economic reasons and within a workforce reduction process giving rise to such plan, is itself null*' (Soc. 15 May 2013, n° 11-26414, bull. civ. 2013, V, n° 122). This decision was applied in a case where the employee's voluntary departure was clearly in the framework of and employment safeguard plan which encouraged voluntary departures.

Justification of the Employee's 'Acknowledgement' ('prise d'acte') of Contract Termination

In the case of absence or deficiency of an employment safeguard plan, the employee's acknowledgment of contract termination by fault of the employer in a context of dismissals for economic reasons results in the *dismissal's invalidity* (Soc. 25 January 2012, n° 10-23516, bull. civ. 2012, V, n° 22, FS-P + B + R + I). Such was the case of an employee's dismissal following a plan of outsourcing by the employer who had not, however, envisaged any redeployment plan.

[b] Reinstatement of the Dismissed Employees

The judge may order either the *continuation of the employment contract*, or declare the *invalidity of the dismissal and order the employee's reinstatement* upon request by the latter, in the case of a dismissal taking place notwithstanding the invalidity of its procedure (either due to the absence of an administrative decision or notwithstanding its negative decision, or in the case of invalidity of the validation or approval decision due to the absence or deficiency of the PSE) (Article L. 1235-11, paragraph 1 of the Labour Code).

However, such reinstatement cannot occur in the following cases (Article L. 1235-11, paragraph 2):

- in the absence of a request by the employee;
- in the case of the establishment's or site's closure or in the absence of an available job;
- if the employee is not able to justify at least *two years of seniority* or if the employer normally employs *less than eleven employees* (Article L. 1235-14). The Constitutional council validated such seniority condition, on the one hand due to it being founded on '*an objective and rational criterion directly linked to the object of law*', and on the other, due to the fact that by setting such two year requirement, the legislator created '*a conciliation between the right to employment and the freedom to undertake a business*' which was '*not* patently unbalanced'. (Constitutional council, decision n° 2012-232 QPC of 13 April 2012).

[c] Dismissal Indemnity

In the absence of a request for contract continuation or in the impossibility of a reinstatement, the employee has the right to an indemnity. The indemnity amount is set by the judicial jurisdiction and varies according to: the cause of invalidity of the dismissal procedure, the employee's seniority and the company's workforce.

Invalidity of the Administrative Decision due to the Absence or Deficiency of the PSE (L. 1235-10, paragraph 2)

In such situation, the judge orders the employer to pay an indemnity to the dismissed employee, of an amount which cannot be less than the *salaries of the last twelve months* (Article L. 1235-11, paragraph 2). Such provision is not applicable to the dismissal of an employee with less than two years of seniority in the company, and to the dismissal by an employer who normally employs less than eleven employees. In the latter case, the employee has the right to an indemnity corresponding to the *prejudice incurred* (Article L 1235-14).

Invalidity of the Decision due to Incorrect Procedure or Irregularity of the Works Council Information-Consultation Procedure (L. 1235-16)

The employee who does not make a request for reinstatement or does not obtain it, has the right to an indemnity which cannot be less than the *salaries of the last six months*. Such indemnity is due, irrespective of any seniority, and without prejudicing the legal dismissal indemnity. Moreover, as mentioned above, in case of improper dismissal, an employee with less than two years of seniority dismissed by a company of less than eleven employees can expect an indemnity corresponding only to the prejudice incurred.

[c] *Responsibility of the Employer for the Failure to Implement the PSE*

The employer failing his obligation to respect the commitments within the employment safeguard plan is liable to pay damages to the concerned employees. Such was the case whereby an employee was prejudiced in as so far he never benefited from the technical and financial support, envisaged in the PSE, necessary for the creation of his own company (Soc. 12 June 2001, n° 99-43329, bull. civ. 2001, V, n° 218, FS-P).

[d] *Reduced Time Limit of Action*

The legislator's intent to set strict deadlines for any claims against the decision on the regularity or the validity of a dismissal is again clearly shown by the twelve month time lapse set for the court's action. (Article L. 1235-7 Labour Code).

[D] Social Support Measures for the Employees Concerned by a Collective Dismissal for Economic Reasons

The Job Security Contract

Since 2011, such contract has replaced the 'personalized redeployment convention'. The job security contract is a reinforced and personalized measure to support employees to be dismissed for economic reasons. It applies to *companies with less than 1000 employees*, and to those in receivership or judicial liquidation whereby the redeployment leave provisions are not applicable, irrespective of their workforce (Article L. 1233-75 Labour Code). The objective is '*the development of an employment recovery process, whether through a company reconversion, creation or recovery*'. Its implementation measures are defined by an approved collective agreement, the *Unédic convention of 19th July 2011*, which specifies the conditions of: seniority, age, residence and physical aptitude to benefit, as well as the contract duration, the measure's means of financing and the employee's compensation. The employee's agreement *leads to the termination of the employment contract* without, however, depriving the employee from the right to contest the regularity of the dismissal procedure (absence of employee delegates or failure to mention the priority of reemployment benefit) or its legitimacy (failure to declare the economic reasons or absence of a real and serious cause), as in any case it is within the context of a dismissal for economic reasons. (Soc. 17 March 2015, n° 13-26941, FS-P + B);[36] (Soc. 22 September 2015, n° 14-16218, FS-P + B).

36. Thibault Lahalle, *Portée de l'adhésion à un contrat de sécurisation professionnelle*, La semaine juridique Social n° 22, 2 juin 2015, 1192.

The Redeployment Leave

This measure is applicable in companies or establishments with at least 1000 employees (except for those in receivership or liquidation). Such redeployment leave is proposed by the employer to each employee whose dismissal for economic reasons is envisaged, after having informed and consulted the works council or the employee delegates on the implementation conditions of such measure (Article R. 1233-17 Labour Code). The objective of such leave, of a maximum of twelve months, is to favour the employee's redeployment in a regular and personalized way through an accompanying *cell ('cellule')* supporting the employee's job search and training, financed by the employer (Articles L. 1233-71 and R. 1233-23). Such support leads to a *skills assessment* allowing to develop a *professional plan* for the employee (Article L. 1233-71). The employer *finances* the employee's training and remuneration. The social partners may, in the framework of a national Inter-professional Agreement, envisage a contribution in the context of such leave.

The implementation conditions of the redeployment leave are set in PSE established by the employer.

It will be quickly mentioned that such a leave is, as mentioned earlier, available to employees refusing the modification of their contract due to a job preservation or development agreement (cf. *supra* sections §10.01[B][3] and §10.03[A][4]).

Mobility Leave ('conge de mobilité')

In companies of *at least 1000 employees,* the employer who has concluded a collective agreement in relation to the employment and competences planned management ('gestion prévisionnelle des emplois et des competences' – 'GPEC') may propose mobility leave to the employee (Article L. 1233-77). Such leave, taken by the employee during the notice period which he is dispensed from carrying out, aims to promote the employee's return to a stable job through support measures, training and *periods of work* that can be completed *within or outside the company* which proposed it (Article L. 1233-78). This can take place through either a permanent or fixed-term contract. In the case of the latter, the mobility leave is suspended until a new contract for the duration of the remaining leave is concluded. The employee's acceptance of the mobility leave frees the employer from having to propose redeployment leave (Article L. 1233-81) and immediately results in the contract termination by mutual agreement (Article L. 1233-80). However, according to the Court of cassation, such acceptance does not deprive the concerned employee from the possibility to contest the economic motive (Soc. 12 November 2015, n° 14-15430, FS-P + B + R).

[E] A Means of Indirect Prevention and Compensation for Collective Dismissals: The Revitalization of Employment Areas

Companies of *at least 1000 employees* proceeding with a collective dismissal which necessarily affects the balance of the employment areas where they are established must contribute to *the creation of activities and the development of jobs as well as mitigate the dismissal's effects on the other companies in the area(s) of employment* (Article L. 1233-84 Labour Code). This is done on the basis of an *agreement between the company and the administrative authority*, following: the notification of the dismissal plan to such authority, a study on the *social and territorial impact* ordered by such authority (Article L. 1233-85), and consultation with the concerned local communities. The company must pay a contribution which cannot be less than twice the monthly minimum growth salary for each job cut. However, the administrative authority can set a lower amount when the company is not able to face the financial burden of such contribution.

The 'El Khomri' law of 8 August 2016 adds that in the case of job cuts concerning at least three 'départements', a 'national revitilisation framework agreement' ('*convention-cadre nationale de revitalisation*') will be concluded between the Minister in charge of employment and the company. Such agreement must result in one or more local agreements between the State representative and the company, in conformity with the content of the framework agreement (Article L. 1233-90-1 of the Labour Code).

[F] Priority of Reemployment of the Employee Dismissed for Economic Reasons

As mentioned above, the dismissal letter by the employer must mention the employee's right of 'priority for reemployment' for one year from the date of contract termination. In such case, the employer informs the employee of 'any job which has become available and compatible with his qualification' (Article L. 1233-45, paragraph 2), as well as inform the employee representatives. The employee benefits from the reemployment priority also in the case of acquisition of a *new qualification*, if the employer is informed thereof (Article L. 1233-45, paragraph 3). Such provision has given ground to various disputes and thus to the establishment of a jurisprudence on the matter. A few solutions provided by the Court of cassation are herein recalled.

[1] Extent of the Reemployment Priority

The employee's right to the priority of reemployment is exercised with respect to *the company which has dismissed him* (Soc. 6 April 1994, n° 92-41782, bull. civ. 1994, V, n° 134) or a company of the group in the case that the available job post is in common between the two companies (Soc. 6 July 2001, n° 99-43024, bull. civ. 2001, V, n° 253). The priority does *not concern house domestic workers ('employés de maison')* (Soc. 8 July 1992, n° 91-40915) and is applicable only in the case of dismissals for economic reasons (Soc. 14 May 1996, n° 93-40447, bull. civ. 1996, V, n° 188). The *lack of a real and serious cause of an economic dismissal does not deprive it from its legal status of a dismissal for economic reasons*, and thus, does not result in the inapplicability of the priority (Soc. 13 April 1999, n° 96-45028, bull. civ. 1999, V, n° 271; Soc. 30 November 1999, n° 97-41431, bull. civ. 1999, V, n° 464; Soc. 14 February 2007, n° 05-40504, bull. civ. 2007, V, 25).

The priority weighs on the employer from the moment that the employee requests to benefit from such priority (Soc. 30 March 1999, n° 97-41265, bull. civ. 1999, V, n° 146). It is applicable on all contract terminations for economic reasons, especially in the case of voluntary departures, which are governed under the provisions relative to dismissals (Soc. 10 May 1999, n° 96-19828, bull. civ. 1999, V, n° 202). The priority also applies:

- in the case of a takeover, but only to the employees affected by the transfer to another company. (Soc. 5 March 2002, n° 00-41429, bull. civ. V, n° 85);
- to employees who are dismissed due to their refusal of a contract modification (Soc. 20 January 1998, n° 95-42177);
- to employees who regained a job following their departure from the company (Soc. 5 March 2002, n° 00-41429, bull. civ. V, n° 85);
- to employees who adhered to a personalized redeployment agreement (Soc. 30 November 2011, n° 09-43184, bull. civ. 2011, V, n° 282).

[2] Available and Compatible Job Posts

The issue often arises, regarding to which posts the priority of reemployment applies, and more specifically, on how to determine their 'availability' and 'compatibility' as per the legal provisions. A jurisprudence has therefore developed grounded on such matters.

The employer must first of all inform the employee as soon as a job is available (Soc. 6 April 1994, n° 92-42108). The priority of reemployment is not limited only to the availability of jobs identical to that of the dismissed employee, but can also apply to other jobs as long as they are compatible with the employee's qualification (Soc. 6 April 1994, n° 92-42259).

The priority can **only** be applied when the employer is in a *hiring* process: thus the offer of 'internal' jobs does not imply their 'availability' (Soc. 6 July 1999, n° 97-40546, bull. civ. 1999, V, n° 334).

The jobs which are *momentarily vacant*, as in the case of maternity leave (Soc. 26 November 1997, n° 95-44308) or annual leave (Soc. 17 June 1992, n° 91-45.458, bull. civ. 1992, V, n° 404) are not available for the purpose of the reemployment priority.

Moreover, the continual hiring of temporary workers, prior and after a dismissal and for *a number of hours corresponding to the employment of various employees*, demonstrates that job posts were available and that the employer did not satisfy its obligation of redeployment nor the priority of reemployment (Soc. 1 March 2000, n° 98-46233, bull. civ. 2000, V, n° 82).

[3] Sanctions for Violation of the Priority of Reemployment

A differentiation must be made between the formal failure to declare the priority of reemployment and the actual failure to enact it.

Sanction in the Case of Failure to Mention the Priority of Reemployment in the Dismissal Letter

Such omission constitutes a fault of the employer giving rise to the employee's right to an indemnity, the amount of which is set by the trial judge without appeal (Soc. 30 March 1993, n° 91-42266). In the case that the contract termination results from the employee's acceptance of a personalized redeployment agreement (currently 'job security contract' – 'contrat de securitisation professionnelle'), the priority of reemployment must be mentioned in the written document stating the economic reason for the contract termination, and thus must be made known at the latest at the time of the employee's acceptance. (Soc. 30 November 2011, n° 10-21678, bull. civ. 2011, V, n° 276).

Sanction in the Case of Non-respect of the Priority of Reemployment

If the priority of reemployment is not respected, '*the judge agrees to an indemnity to be paid to the employee of an amount which cannot be less than two months salary*' (Article L. 1235-13 of the Labour Code). Exceptionally, such rule does not apply to the dismissal of an employee with less than two years of seniority, nor to the dismissal within a company normally employing less than eleven employees: in case of improper dismissal, the concerned employee can request an indemnity corresponding to the prejudice incurred (Article L. 1235-14), which shall be assessed by the trial judge, without appeal (Soc. 6 April 1994, n° 02-42459).

The prejudice resulting from a dismissal without a real and serious cause and that resulting from the non-respect of the reemployment priority are distinct (Soc. 5 October 1995; Soc. 3 February 1998, n° 95-42914, bull. civ. 1998, V, n° 57): each can therefore be resolved through two combinable indemnities (same sentence and Soc. 12 January 1999, n° 96-43422).

§10.04 JURISDICTIONAL CONTROL AND SANCTIONS

The company which does not respect certain of its obligations in terms of collective economic dismissals can be subject to civil and penal sanctions.

[A] Civil Sanctions

The employer is subject to sanctions in relation to the following violations, already mentioned above:

- the dismissal ordering criteria;
- the priority of reemployment;
- the conditions of validity and respect of the employment safeguard plan.

Other causes for sanctions can be envisaged.

[1] Sanction of Non-respect of the Procedures of Consultation with the Employee Representatives or of Information to the Administrative Authority

In the case that the employer does not respect the procedures of consultation with the employee representatives or of information to the administrative authority, the judge orders the employer to pay an indemnity to the dismissed employee which is *calculated according to the prejudice incurred* (Article L. 1235-12). For an application of this principle *see*: Soc. 28 October 2015, n° 14-16519, published).

Such assessment cannot give rise to appeal and can result in the payment of an indemnity in principle ('indemnité de principe') (Soc. 16 September 2015, n° 14-20491).

A dismissal procedure for economic reasons is irregular in a company where *no works council or employee representatives have been set up,* whilst they are so obliged, and whereby *no statement of insolvency ('proces-verbal de carence')* has been established (Article L. 1235-15). The employee has the right to an indemnity to be paid by the employer which cannot be less than *one month's net salary*, without prejudicing the dismissal and notification indemnities (Article L. 1235-15).

[2] Sanction in the Case of a Collective Dismissal Whereby the Economic Motive is Neither Real nor Serious

In addition to the notification and dismissal indemnities, the employees also have a right to an *indemnity* in the case their dismissal lacks a 'real and serious cause'. Such indemnity is paid by the employer to the employee for an amount which cannot be less than that of *the salaries of the last 6 months* (Article L. 1235-3). Moreover, the judge orders the *employer to reimburse the unemployment management agencies* of all or part of the unemployment indemnities paid to the employee from the day of dismissal to that of the judge's negative sentence, for an amount of up to six months of unemployment indemnity for each concerned employee. The above provisions are not applicable to the dismissal of employees with less than two years of seniority within a company and to the dismissal by a company which normally employs less than eleven employees: in the case of 'improper dismissal' the law mentions and specifies the right to an indemnity 'corresponding to the *prejudice incurred*' (Article L. 1235-5).

Such employees can, unlike the others, add the damages from the indemnity for irregular procedure envisaged by Article L. 1235-2, with an amount which cannot be higher than one month's salary.

[3] Extra-contractual Responsibility of a Third Party with Respect to Employees of an Insolvent Company

According to the Court of cassation, employees dismissed for economic reasons can request compensation for the prejudices incurred to third parties who are indirectly responsible for their dismissal. In this respect, the Court of cassation, within the context of *criminal responsibility* envisaged by Articles 1382 and 1383 of the civil code, approved the payment of damages claimed by the employees against both: the company buyer of the employer company's shares, as well as the company sole shareholder of such buyer company. The reason for such ruling takes into account the fact that the failures, negligence or culpable carelessness ('légèretés blâmables') of such third parties, had: on the one hand contributed to the employer company's insolvency and consequent job losses, and on the other deprived the employer company from the employment safeguard plan's financial support, thus depriving the employees from benefiting from such measures which could have favoured their redeployment or reconversion, and giving rise to a prejudice distinct from that suffered by the creditors of the collective procedure (Soc. 8 July 2014, n° 13-15470 – 1 judgment, and n° 13-15573 – 2 judgment, bull. civ. 2014, V, n° 180, FS-P + B).

[B] Penal Sanctions

The Labour Code Envisages and Punishes Certain Violations in the Context of Dismissals for Economic Reasons

A sanction of EUR 3,750 is applied each time an employee is affected by a violation in the following cases:

- when a dismissal is declared in the absence of the required consultation of the employee delegates and the works council (Article L. 1238-2);
- when the deadline for the dismissal letters for economic reasons is not respected (Article L. 1238-3);
- when a dismissal takes place without notifying the administrative authority as per legal requirements (Article L. 1238-4);
- in the case of receivership or judicial liquidation, when the employer, administrator or liquidator do not respect certain provisions in relation to the information-consultation regarding the employee representatives, the establishment of the employment safeguard plan or the information to the administrative authority (Article L. 1238-5).

The Hindrance Offence ('délit d'entrave') is Likely to Arise at the Time of a Collective Dismissal for Economic Reasons

Such offence consists in hindering or trying to hinder the proper functioning of the employee delegates (Article L. 2316-1), the works council (Article L. 2328-1) or the CHSCT (Article L. 4742-1). It can arise when the employer omits to provide such bodies with the relevant information and material for the accomplishment of their mission, or fails its obligation to meet with them. The sanction amount is of EUR 7,500.

§10.05 BRIEF CONCLUSION

The French legal system concerning collective dismissals for economic reasons certainly has a keen inclination towards employee protection, however also appears as particularly complex. Fortunately, the substantial transfer of disputes from the judicial court to the Administration and administrative judge has not given rise to legal ruptures. In fact, the administrative jurisdiction has demonstrated, at all its levels (administrative tribunals, courts of appeal, and Council of State), a clear concern of coherence, with respect to the previous judicial jurisprudence, and of clarity with respect to the demarcation of the two jurisdiction orders' respective missions. In this respect, it is well known that the Court of cassation and Council of State organize consultation meetings between themselves with the aim to avoid any distortions of the law which may arise due to the multiplicity of the fields of concurrent competences. The fact that collective agreements are privileged, thus implying an egalitarian approach of the social partners for the establishment of the employment safeguard plan, seems to have quashed a part of the disputes.

Meanwhile, the present study gives us a feel of how difficult it can be, considering the current Labour Code whose rules are often followed by derogations, to immediately understand the sense of certain provisions without seeking assistance from specialist sources.

In view of the simplification of the labour law and Labour Code which is to take place soon, a clear integration by the legislator of the achievements of the jurisprudences of the two orders, would be opportune. In fact, in our opinion, the issue is not so much that of the Labour code's dimensions, but rather of its readability and understanding.

CHAPTER 11

Collective Dismissal in the Federal Republic of Germany

Mario Eylert & Reinhard Schinz

§11.01 COLLECTIVE REDUNDANCIES: THE CASE

[A] Introduction

If an employer intends to dismiss a larger amount of employees on account of redundancy within a certain period of time (collective redundancies) there are a number of legal requirements to be observed. These are: Information of the economic committee (§ 106 Act on Works Constitution - Betriebsverfassungsgesetz - BetrVG), information and consultation of works council (§§ 111, 112, 102 BetrVG), the need of social justification according to § 1 Act on Protection of Employment - Kündigungsschutzgesetz - KSchG[1] and - above all - the particular rules of procedure in case of collective redundancies according to §§ 17 to 22 KSchG. These provide the core of special regulations for collective redundancies.

[B] The Law

§§ 17 - 22 KSchG read as follows:

> *Chapter 3.*
>
> *Redundancies Requiring Notification*
>
> *§ 17 Duty of Notification*

1. BAG 6.12.1973 - AP KSchG 1969 § 17 Nr. 1; Schaub/Linck: Arbeitsrechtshandbuch, 15 Edition, 2015, § 142 paras. 1 and 2.

(1) The employer shall notify the Agency for Employment within 30 calendar days prior to dismissing

1. *more than 5 employees in establishments with regularly more than 20 and fewer than 60 employees,*
2. *10 per cent of the regularly employed employees or more than 25 employees in establishments with at least 60 and fewer than 500 employees,*
3. *at least 30 employees in establishments with regularly at least 500 employees.*

Any other termination of an employment relationship brought about by the employer shall be assimilated to redundancy.

(2) Where an employer intends to make redundancies which are notifiable pursuant to para. (1), he must inform the works council in writing and in a timely manner of, in particular,

1. *the reasons for the planned redundancies,*
2. *the number and occupational group of the employees to be dismissed,*
3. *the number and occupational group of the employees regularly employed,*
4. *the period of time over which these redundancies are to take place,*
5. *the intended criteria for the selection of the employees to be dismissed,*
6. *the criteria for calculating any severance payments.*

Employer and works council shall, in particular, have the opportunity to discuss ways in which the redundancies can be prevented or limited and their consequences can be mitigated.

(3) The employer must, at the same time, send the Agency for Employment a copy of the notification to the works council; this notification must at least contain the information set forth in para. 2 sent. 1 nos. 1-5 above. The notification pursuant to para. (1) must be in writing and include the works council's comments regarding the redundancies. Where the works council has not given its comments, the notification shall be effective if the employer can demonstrate that he informed the works council at least two weeks prior to submitting the notification pursuant to para. (2) sent. 1 and describes the status of the discussions. The notification shall give the employer's name, the seat and nature of the establishment, the reasons for the planned redundancies, the number and occupational group of employees to be dismissed and of those regularly employed, the period of time over which the redundancies are to take place and the intended criteria for the selection of the employees to be dismissed. Further, in agreement with the works council, for the use of the Agency for Employment, the notification should give the sex, age, occupation and nationality of the employees to be dismissed. The employer shall send a copy of the notification to the works council. The works council may submit further comments to the Agency for Employment. It shall send the employer a copy of such comments.

(3a) The duty to provide information, to consult with the works council and to notify the Agency for Employment pursuant to paras. (1) to (3) shall apply even if the decision on the redundancies was made by a Company controlling the employer. The employer cannot invoke the fact that the Company responsible for the redundancies did not convey the necessary information.

(4) The right of dismissal without notice shall remain unaffected. Redundancies without notice shall not be counted in the calculation of the minimum number of redundancies pursuant to para. (1).

(5) The following shall not be deemed to be employees within the meaning of this provision:

1. *in establishments of a legal entity, members of the body appointed to legally represent that legal entity,*
2. *in establishments of a partnership, the persons appointed by law or in the articles of association or by-laws to represent the partnership,*
3. *managers, directors of establishments and similar persons exercising management functions insofar as they have the authority to independently hire or dismiss employees.*

§ 18 Period Before Dismissal Takes Effect

(1) Redundancies which are notifiable pursuant to § 17 shall not become effective sooner than one month of the date of the Agency for Employment's receipt of the notification without its consent; such consent may also be granted with retroactive effect as of the date of application.

(2) The Agency for Employment may, in individual cases, determine that redundancies shall not become effective before at most two months have elapsed following the date of the Agency for Employment's receipt of the notification.

(3) (repealed)

(4) If the redundancies are not carried out within 90days following the date as from which they are permissible pursuant to paras (1) and (2), a new notification must be made which conforms to the requirements of § 17 para. (1).

§ 19 Permissibility of Short-Time Work

(1) Where the employer is not able to occupy the employees fully up to the time described in § 18 paras. (1) and (2), the Federal Agency for Employment may permit the employer to introduce short time work for the interim period.

(2) In the case of short-time work, the employer shall be entitled to reduce proportionately the wages or salaries of employees occupied on a short-time work basis; this reduction shall, however, only be effective as from the time when the employment relationship would have ended under general statutory or contractual provisions.

(3) Provisions of collective bargaining agreements relating to the introduction, duration and remuneration of short-time work shall not be affected by paras. (1) and (2).

§ 20 Decisions of the Agency for Employment

(1) Decisions of the Agency for Employment pursuant to § 18 paras. (1) and (2) shall be reached by its management or a committee (decision-maker). The management may only decide if less than 50 redundancies are involved.

(2) The committee shall consist of the chairperson of the management of the Agency for Employment, or an employee of the Agency for Employment appointed by him or her, as chairperson and two representatives each for the employees, the employer and public bodies, to be nominated by the administrative committee of the Agency for Employment. The committee shall arrive at its decisions by a simple majority of votes.

(3) The decision-maker shall hear the employer and the works council before reaching its decision. The committee shall receive, in particular from the employer and the works council, all Information it considers necessary for evaluations the case.

(4) The decision-maker shall take into account the interests of the employer as well as those of the employees to be dismissed, the public interest, and the entire employment market Situation, particularly taking into consideration the branch of industry to which the establishment belongs.

§ 21 Decisions of the Headquarters of the Federal Agency for Employment

For establishments belonging to the area of business for which the Federal Minister of Transport or the Federal Minister of Post and Telecommunications is responsible, if more than 500 employees are to be dismissed, a committee to be formed pursuant to § 20 para. (1) by the Headquarters of the Federal Agency for Employment shall make the decisions pursuant to § 18 paras. (1) and (2). The competent Federal Minister may appoint two representatives in an advisory capacity to the committee. Notifications pursuant to § 17 shall, in this case, be submitted to the Headquarters of the Federal Agency for Employment. Otherwise § 20 paras. (1) to (3) apply mutatis mutandis.

§ 22 Exempted Establishments

(1) The provisions of this chapter shall not apply to seasonal and project-orientated establishments in the case of redundancies made necessary by special nature of such establishments.

(2) Establishments in the construction industry, in which year-round occupation pursuant to the Third Book of Social Security Code is promoted, shall not be deemed to be seasonal or project-orientated establishments. The Federal Minister of Labor and Social Affairs shall be empowered to issue provisions by decree defining which establishments are deemed to be seasonal or project-orientated enterprises within the meaning of para (1).

§ 1 subsection 5 KSchG reads:

If, in the event of a termination on the basis of a change in business pursuant to § 111 of the Works Constitution Act, the employees who are to be dismissed are designated by name in a reconciliation of interests between the employer and the works council, then it shall be presumed that the dismissal is due to compelling operational requirements within the meaning of para. (2). The social selection of the employees may only be reviewed for gross errors. Sentences 1 and 2 shall not apply to the extent that the situation has materially changed after the reconciliation of interests came about. The reconciliation of interests pursuant to sent. 1 shall replace the works council's comments pursuant to §17para. (3) sent. 2.

[C] Rationale of the Law

§§ 17 ff KSchG are much older than the European Directives 75/129/EWG and 98/59/EG ('the Directive') on the approximation of the laws of the Member States relating to collective redundancies. The German regulations were one of the reasons for creating the directive.[2] They have remained virtually unchanged since 1951. However, the purpose and emphasis of the German law on collective redundancies has traditionally been to enable the 'competent public authority', that is, the Federal Agency for Employment (Bundesagentur für Arbeit – BfA), to cope with larger numbers of redundant employees seeking occupation, whereas the directive was hailed to improve

2. Directive 75/129 results from the AKZO case and the varying national rules on collective redundancy. The international company AKZO wanted to restructure their business. Collective redundancies were executed mainly in Belgium as the company deemed that such dismissals would be more complicated in Germany due to the higher level of employment protection.

employment protection[3] and to assimilate national rules on such protection and provide fair competition between the Member States.[4]

The German view of the regulations on collective redundancies had to change drastically after the ECJ's decision in the Junk case from 2005. Before the Junk case the interpretation of the German law was mainly based on the wording of the KSchG and the traditional understanding of the terms 'Kündigung' (dismissal as the act of notifying the employee of the termination of the contract) and 'Entlassung' (time of legal ending of the contract after the expiry of the period of notice). After the Junk decision the aspect of individual employment protection has become the focus of the German law[5] as well following the ECJ's interpretation of the directive according to its purpose.[6]

The German law provides mainly rules on procedure for employers, that is, the duty to inform and consult with the employees' representatives, the works council.

[D] Scope of the Law on Collective Redundancies

Dismissals are deemed collective redundancies within the meaning of the act if the employer plans to dismiss the number of employees stated in § 17 KSchG within the period given.

[1] Establishment

The provisions of §§ 17 KSchG apply to establishments and administrations constituted under private law and to establishments operated by a public administration insofar as they pursue commercial objectives (e.g., providers of energy, water). They do not apply to workers employed by public administrative bodies or by establishments governed by public law exercising sovereignty administration or to seagoing vessels and their crews.

The Federal Labour Court now applies the definition of the term 'establishment' as set by European law and the jurisdiction of the ECJ.[7] For the purposes of the application of Directive 98/59, an 'establishment', in the context of an undertaking, may consist of a distinct entity, having a certain degree of permanence and stability, which is assigned to perform one or more given tasks and which has a workforce, technical means and a certain organizational structure allowing for the accomplishment of those tasks. By the use of the words 'distinct entity' and 'in the context of an undertaking', the Court specified that the terms 'undertaking' and 'establishment' are

3. ECJ 8.6.1994 – C-383/92 1994, I-2479, para. 27; 18.10.2012 – C-583/10, para. 38 (Nolan); 13.5.2015 – C-182/13, para. 43, NZA 2015, 731 (Lyttle).
4. ECJ 13.5.2015 – C-182/13, para. 43, NZA 2015, 731 (Lyttle).
5. BAG 13.7.2006 – 6 AZR 198/06 - para. 19.
6. Cf. Spelge: Massenentlassung – Büchse der Pandora oder Panazee, in: Heinrich (editor): Insolvenz- und Arbeitsrecht als Bausteine des Unternehmenserfolgs, Baden-Baden, 2015, pp. 151-152.
7. ECJ 30.4.2015 – C-80/14 – ZIP 2015,1041 (Wilson); 13.5.2015 – C-392/13, ECLI:EU:C:2015:318 (Rabal Cañas).

different and that an establishment normally constitutes a part of an undertaking. The ECJ, in the judgment in Rockfon,[8] held that the term 'establishment' in Article 1(1)(a) of Directive 98/59 must be interpreted as designating, depending on the circumstances, the unit to which the workers made redundant are assigned to carry out their duties. It is not essential in order for there to be an 'establishment' that the unit in question be endowed with a management that can independently effect collective redundancies.

This contravenes the traditional German understanding of the term 'Betrieb' as used in § 17 KSchG. Under German law, for example, the manager of a supermarket who has no authority to hire or fire staff but is entitled and by virtue of his contract obliged only to assign work and generally execute the employer's prerogative would not be considered 'Betriebsleiter' which consequently means that the unit he is in charge of would not be deemed 'establishment' for the purpose of collective redundancies. Here – as in a number of other instances – German jurisdiction had to learn that technical terms used in German legislation might have to be understood differently if interpreted in the light of European legislation and the different and occasionally erratic methodological approaches of the ECJ.

In small establishments (i.e., less than twenty-one employees) the employer is not obliged to adhere to the legal procedures of §§ 17 ff KSchG. Since the number of employees per establishment (and not per undertaking) is relevant this results in the perplex situation that for example in a case of closing down five local stations of an airline only one which had more than twenty employees fell within the scope of §§ 17 KSchG. However, this is in line with the ECJ's understanding of the Directive. In the judgment in Athinaïki Chartopoiïa,[9] the Court held that since Directive 98/59 concerns the socio-economic effects that collective redundancies may have in a given local context and social environment, the entity in question need not have any legal autonomy, nor need it have economic, financial, administrative or technological autonomy, in order to be regarded as an 'establishment'. Consequently, where an 'undertaking' comprises several entities meeting the criteria set out above, it is the entity to which the workers made redundant are assigned to carry out their duties that constitutes the 'establishment' for the purposes of Article 1(1)(a) of Directive 98/59, and the number of dismissals effected at that establishment must be taken into consideration separately from those that take place at the other establishments of that same undertaking.

[2] Employee

§§ 17 ff KSchG protect only employees. The term comprises all kinds of employees regardless of the type of employment contract (e.g., fixed-term contracts), including apprentices and persons who, while not receiving remuneration from the employer, perform real work within the undertaking in the context of a traineeship – with financial support from, and the recognition of, the public authority responsible for the

8. C-449/93, EU:C:1995:420.
9. C-270/05, EU:C:2007:101.

promotion of employment – in order to acquire or improve skills or complete vocational training.[10] Part time workers are counted per head not per quota of working time.

According to § 17 subsection 5 Nr. 3 KSchG senior executives are not covered by the regulations on collective redundancies although they are employees in the general sense of the norm. This contravenes the Directive.[11] According to the ECJ senior executives in Italy ('dirigenti') fall within the scope of the Directive regardless of whether or not they are entitled to hire and fire staff.[12]

The same applies to the provision in § 17 subsection 5 Nr. 1 KSchG according to which the following shall not be regarded as workers for the purposes of this paragraph: '1. in establishments of one legal person, the members of the body that is responsible for the legal representation of that person'. The ECJ has ruled that the directive must be interpreted as meaning that it precludes a national law or practice that does not take into account, in the calculation provided for by that provision of the number of workers employed, a member of the board of directors of a capital company, who performs his duties under the direction and subject to the supervision of another body of that company, receives remuneration in return for the performance of his duties and does not himself own any shares in the company.[13] Because of the clear wording of the German definition of the term 'employee' German Labour Courts will have to consider whether it is possible to interpret § 17 subsection 5 Nr. 1 KSchG in the light of Union Law as seen by the ECJ.

[3] Dismissal

Following the ECJ's ruling in Junk, the German jurisdiction now understands the term 'dismissal' as the unilateral declaration of the intention to terminate the employment relationship at a given time.[14] Unlike the Directive the German law does not limit its scope to dismissals effected by an employer for one or more reasons not related to the individual workers concerned. Therefore ordinary dismissals (with notice) regardless of the employer's reason (be they operational, personal or on grounds of conduct) are to be taken into account. Outside the scope of § 17 KSchG are expiries of fixed-term contracts[15] and extraordinary dismissals without notice.[16]

Since § 17 KSchG provides that redundancies shall be equivalent to other terminations of the employment relationship which are brought about by the employer, German jurisdiction regards a termination of the employment contract by the employee as a dismissal within the meaning of § 17 KSchG if the employer causes the

10. ECJ 9.7.2015 – C-229/14, ECLI:EU:C:2015:455 (Balkaya).
11. Kiel, in Erfurter Kommentar zum Arbeitsrecht, 15 Edition, 2015, § 17 KSchG para. 10.
12. ECJ 13.2.2014 – C-596/12, Commission/Italy.
13. ECJ 9.7.2015 – C-229/14, ECLI:EU:C:2015:455 (Balkaya).
14. BAG 23.3.2006 – 2 AZR 345/02 – para. 18, BAGE 117, 281; 21.3.2013 – 2 AZR 60/12 – para. 13, BAGE 144, 366; 20.2.2014 – 2 AZR 346/12 – para. 31, BAGE 147, 237; cf. Schwarze/Eylert/Schrader: KSchG, 1st edition, 2012, § 17 para. 15.
15. ECJ 13.5.2015 – C-392/13, ECLI:EU:C:2015:318 (Rabal Cañas).
16. Cf. Schwarze/Eylert/Schrader: KSchG, § 17 para. 19 ff.

termination ('constructive dismissal'). The same applies to agreements of termination if they are instigated by the employer.[17] 'Brought about' by the employer are such terminations if the employer gives to understand that the employment relationship will be terminated anyway because there is no further opportunity for occupation.

Dismissals with the option of altered conditions of employment ('Änderungskündigung') are considered to be dismissals for the purpose of §§ 17 KSchG regardless of whether the employee accepts the altered conditions (in which case the employment relationship is continued) or not (in which case the employment relationship is considered to be terminated by the dismissal).[18]

[4] Number of Redundancies

The number of dismissals necessary to qualify as collective redundancies under §§ 17 ff KSchG differ to some extent from the numbers given in the Directive. The threshold level is in most cases lower than in the Directive. This was a conscious decision by the legislator as adopting the numbers of the Directive would have meant lowering the protection level granted by the earlier German law.

When § 17 KSchG refers to the 'regular' number of employees it does not mean the average number occupied in an establishment but rather the number which signifies the establishment over a longer period of time, the amount which is 'normally' occupied. Therefore neither short-time temporary workers nor times of unusually high or low (seasonal) employment[19] are taken into account.

Having established the 'regular' number of employees at the time of issuing the dismissals the necessary number of dismissals to qualify as 'collective' has to be reached within a period of thirty days. Therefore the terms of §§ 17 ff KSchG apply if the necessary amount of employees have received the notice of termination within this period.[20] The process is revolving: Every new dismissal starts a new thirty-days-period so that if dismissals are issued over a longer stretch of time it has to be tested whether or not at any given thirty-days-period within the process of issuing dismissals the required number has been reached. For example: If an employer in an establishment with 300 employees plans to issue dismissals for thirty employees on 30 June these are held to be collective redundancies. However, if he will issue twenty dismissals on 30 June and another ten on 31 July these are outside the scope of § 17 KSchG.

§11.02 THE PROCEDURE

§§ 17 ff. KSchG lay down the rules of procedure to be observed by the employer in a case of collective dismissals.

17. BAG 1.3.1999 – NZA 1999, 761; 28.6.2012 – 6 AZR 780/10 – para. 47, BAGE 141, 202.
18. BAG 20.2.2014 – 2 AZR 346/12, BAGE 147, 237.
19. BAG 22.3.2001 – NZA 2002, 1349; 13.4.2000 – NZA 2001, 144.
20. BAG 18.10.2012 – 6 AZR 41/11.

[A] Consultation

The consultation procedure is commonly regarded as the centre piece of the proceedings.[21]

The information, consultation and notification requirements laid down by the law presuppose the existence of a body of workers' representatives. Under German law this body is the works council ('Betriebsrat') under the Betriebsverfassungsgesetz (Act on Works Constitution). Since there is no legal obligation to establish and elect such a works council collective redundancies may take place without any consultation procedure if no such works council is in existence. In German doctrine it is commonly held that the Directive does not demand the creation of a body of workers' representatives for the sole purpose of consultations.[22]

On account of the rather complicated structure of works councils on the different levels of establishment, undertaking and group and their competences (original or conferred) the employer has the difficult task to identify the 'correct' body (local works council, works council of undertaking, group works council) with which to enter into the consultation process. According to the Federal Labour Court's jurisdiction, depending on the scope of the intended restructuring either the works council of undertaking or the group works council may be competent to execute these consultations instead of the local works councils.[23]

[1] Information

According to Article 2 (3) of the Directive, § 17 KSchG provides that the employers shall in good time during the course of the consultations:

(a) supply them with all relevant information; and
(b) in any event notify them in writing of:
  (i) the reasons for the projected redundancies;
  (ii) the number of categories of workers to be made redundant;
  (iii) the number and categories of workers normally employed;
  (iv) the period over which the projected redundancies are to be effected;
  (v) the criteria proposed for the selection of the workers to be made redundant;
  (vi) the method for calculating any redundancy payments.

According to the purpose of the duty to consult the works council, namely to enable workers' representatives to make constructive proposals, the necessary information shall be provided 'in good time'. Timely is such information only if any proposals made by the works council can be taken into account by the employer before

21. Cf. Spelge, aaO, S.159; Salamon, NZA 2015, 789; BAG 13.12.2012 – 6 AZR 752/11.
22. Cf. Wißmann RdA 1998, 221, 224; Ascheid/Preis/Schmidt, Kündigungsrecht, 4th edition, 2012, § 17 KSchG para. 58.
23. BAG 20.9.2012 – 6 AZR 155/11.

he has made his final decision on the planned collective dismissals. § 17 subsection 3 (3) KSchG demands that the works council is informed at least two weeks prior to submitting the notification to the Agency for Employment.

In addition of his obligation under §§ 17 ff KSchG the employer has to observe the works council's rights of participation under the provisions of the Works Constitution Act (BetrVG). If an employer's economic decisions may cause substantial disadvantages to the workforce of the establishment according to §§ 111 ff BetrVG the management has to provide information akin to § 17 KSchG, consult with the works council and – in excess of the demands of the directive and § 17 KSchG – try to reach a 'compromise of interests (Interessenausgleich)'. This means that management must try to come to an agreement with the works council on whether the measures planned by the employer should be carried out at all and if so how disadvantages to the workforce can be minimized. If no agreement can be reached the employer has to refer to an arbitration committee in order to facilitate a compromise. However, since the works council has no right of co-determination proper in economic matters the arbitration committee has no authority to decide on the envisaged measures. If it is established in the committee's proceedings that a compromise cannot be reached the employer is deemed to have fulfilled his obligations and may go ahead with the intended measures. Since these obligations under collective law are not identical with but for the purpose of collective redundancies and mutatis mutandis similar to those under § 17 KSchG both procedures may be carried out simultaneously provided that the employer indicates clearly that he wants to fulfil his obligations under both collective and employment protection law.[24]

[2] Consultation

In accordance with EU law § 17 KSchG obliges the employer to discuss ways in which the redundancies can be prevented or limited, and their consequences can be mitigated. The law does not require an understanding or agreement to be reached between employer and works council. Under German law there are no precise rules on when the employer may regard further negotiations as futile or how long such consultations/negotiations must be held to be deemed sufficient for the purpose of the law by the courts. An indication may be the two-weeks-rule in § 17 subs. 3 (3) KSchG;[25] however, we believe that such a rigid time frame might not take into account the specific needs of all manners of collective redundancies and might not suffice considering the rationale of the directive as seen by the ECJ. If employer and works council have reached a compromise of interests according to §§ 111, 112 BetrVG it is commonly accepted that the employer has fulfilled his obligations to inform and consult under § 17 KSchG. In practice this is an incentive for employers to seriously try to reach such a compromise with the works council.

24. BAG 13.12.2012 – 6 AZR 752/11, AP KSchG 1969 § 17 Nr. 44.
25. BAG 28.6.2012 – 6 AZR 780/10, BAGE 142, 202.

[3] Works Council's Comments Regarding the Redundancies

The works council is supposed to comment in writing on the employer's intentions. This comment must be attached to the notification of the Agency for Employment. This requirement exceeds the demands of the directive. The purpose of this provision is that the Agency can assess if there might be any alternatives to the intended dismissals or which measures have been considered to mitigate disadvantages to the workforce.[26]

Therefore the works council's comment must at least contain:

- the council's declaration that his rights of information and consultation have been observed;
- that this is the definite and final comment of the council; or
- that the council waives his right to comment on the measure.

[B] Notice to the Agency

The notice must at least contain the employer's name, the seat and nature of the establishment, the reasons for the planned redundancies, the number and occupational group of employees to be dismissed and of those regularly employed, the period of time over which the redundancies are to take place and the intended criteria for the selection of the employees to be dismissed. Further, in agreement with the works council, for the use of the Agency for Employment, the notification should give the sex, age, occupation and nationality of the employees to be dismissed. It is to be noted that any dismissal within the scope of §§ 17 ff. KSchG is deemed null and void if the notification suffers from any incorrect or incomplete information on these 'hard' criteria.

The employer must, at the same time, send the Agency for Employment a copy of the notification to the works council and include the works council's comments regarding the redundancies. Where the works council has not given its comments, the employer is deemed to have fulfilled his obligations if he can demonstrate that he informed the works council at least two weeks prior to submitting the notification and describes the status of the discussions. The same applies in case of a faulty or incomplete comment by the works council.[27]

§11.03 THE SUPPORT MEASURES IN FAVOUR OF WORKERS

[A] Delay of Dismissals

The Agencies' powers in cases of collective dismissals are marginal. According to § 18 KSchG dismissals shall not become effective sooner than one month of the date of the Agency for Employment's receipt of the notification without its consent. This period can be extended to two months. Becoming 'effective' means that the employer may

26. BAG 22.11.2012 – 2 AZR 371/11, BAGE 144, 47.
27. BAG 28.6.2012 – 6 AZR 780/10, BAGE 142, 202.

issue the notice of dismissal immediately after having notified the Agency without waiting for their decision. Therefore the Agencies' power of delay means that the period of notice must be at least one month. Even this minimum period of notice does not necessarily mean that the employees will receive their full wages for this period. § 19 KSchG provides the permissibility of short-time work with the entitlement to reduce proportionately the wages or salaries of employees occupied on a short-time work basis.

§§ 17 ff. KSchG can thus not be regarded as providing any kind of substantial material employment protection but only some limited protection by procedure. However, in German court practice the legal snares of the necessary procedures result in the cassation of a fair number of collective redundancies.

[B] Material Protection of Employment

Under German law material protection of employment is provided in individual as well as in collective dismissals by §§ 1 ff. KSchG. Accordingly, the termination of the employment relationship of an employee who has been employed by the same employer without interruption for more than six months is legally invalid if it is socially unjustified. A dismissal is socially unjustified if it is not due to reasons related to the person, the conduct of the employee, or to compelling operational requirements which preclude the continued employment of the employee in the establishment or the undertaking. For the purpose of collective redundancies only compelling operational requirements can justify such dismissals. Therefore the employer has to submit facts to the effect that due to external or internal causes the need to employ all or a significant part of the workforce has ceased and – if contested – prove these facts.[28] Furthermore the dismissal is held to be socially unjustified if, in selecting the employee, the employer has not, or has not sufficiently, considered the employee's seniority, age, duty to support dependents or severe disability.

[C] Compromise of Interests and Compensation Plan

As pointed out under section §11.02[A][1], the employer is obliged to seek a compromise of interests with the works council before he executes collective dismissals. Moreover, according to §§ 112, 112a BetrVG, the works council can demand that a compensation plan ('Sozialplan') is put up to provide financial compensation for those employees who shall be or have been made redundant. Here the law provides a right of co-determination proper, that is if employer and works council do not agree on the modalities of distributing such monies or – which in practice is usually the case – on the total amount to be provided by the employer for the purposes of the compensation plan either party can refer to compulsory arbitration. The arbitration committee has the legal power to determine bindingly both the overall amount to be provided and the scheme of distribution. In practice the anticipation by the management of possible

28. BAG 20.2.2014 – 2 AZR 346/12, BAGE 147, 237.

costs of collective redundancies provides a certain amount of de facto employment protection – up to a point.

§11.04 JUDICIAL CONTROL AND SANCTIONS

[A] Faulty Notification of Agency

Following the Junk decision of the ECJ the Federal Labour Court now holds dismissals which have been issued without any notification of the Employment Agency or before the notification has been handed in to be null and void.[29] Before Junk case, the Federal Labour Court held that according to the traditional German terminology and the differentiation between 'Kündigung' and 'Entlassung' a dismissal was only null and void (or more precisely: could not legally terminate the contract of employment) if the Agency was not notified before the expiry of the period of notice. After the Junk decision the Federal Court changed its jurisdiction accordingly. However, the Court granted protection for reliance on existing case law for dismissals issued before the publication of the Junk judgment.[30] Granting this protection was held to be unconstitutional by the Federal Constitutional Court (after seven years duration of proceedings at the Constitutional Court) on the grounds that the Federal Court were not empowered to grant such a protection if this contravened the effet utile of the Directive;[31] by virtue of the European treaties and the German Constitution only the ECJ were empowered to limit the effet utile by granting exemptions.

A faulty notification can also render a dismissal null and void.[32] A notification is held to be faulty in this context if it does not contain all the obligatory information as set out earlier. However, failure to adhere to the directory provisions in § 17 subs. 3 (5) KSchG does not effect the validity of the notice. In principle, the employer could complete his notification after having submitted it. Since the notification has to be correct at the time at which the employee receives the declaration of dismissal the dismissal remains null and void even if the Employment Agency states that the notification had – at the end – been complete and correct.[33]

The notification is also deemed faulty if it does not contain the works council's comments[34] or if these comments do not fulfil the legal requirements.[35]

29. BAG 22.11.2012 – 2 AZR 371/11; 21.3.2012 – 2 AZR 60/12, ZIP 2013, 1589; 20.2.2014 – 2 AZR 346/12 – BAGE 147, 237.
30. BAG 23.3.2006 – 2 AZR 343/05, BAGE 117, 281; 13.7.2006 – 6 AZR 25/06.
31. BVerfG 10.12.2014 – 2 BvR 1549/07 – ECLI:DE:BVerfG:2014:rk20141210.2bvr154907.
32. BAG 28.6.2012 – 6 AZR 780/10, DB 2012, 2167; 22.11.2012 – 2 AZR 371/11, BAGE 144, 47; 26.2.2015 – 2 AZR 955/13 – NZA 2015, 881.
33. BAG 21.3.2013 – 2 AZR 6/12, BAGE 144, 366; 26.2.2015 – 2 AZR 955/13 – NZA 2015, 881.
34. BAG 28.6.2012 – 6 AZR 780/10, BAGE 142, 202; 22.11.2012 – 2 AZR 371/11 –, BAGE 144, 47.
35. BAG 21.3.2013 – 2 AZR 60/12, BAGE 144, 366.

[B] Faulty Procedure of Consultation

The Federal Labour Court has not yet fully clarified in which cases failures in the consultation process has an effect on the dismissals. Having regard to the rationale of the need to consult with the workers' representatives and considering the effet utile of the directive the Court has decided that a total lack of consultation before issuing collective dismissals renders these dismissals null and void.[36]

36. BAG 21.3.2013 – 2 AZR 60/12, BAGE 144, 366; 22.11.2012 – 2 AZR 371/11; cf. Spelge, *ibid.*, p. 171.

CHAPTER 12

Collective Dismissals in Greece

Andriani Papadopoulou

In the last five years Greece has been going through tremendous changes, not all of them positive. In the mist of the hurricane of the economic crisis and the uncertainty it has generated in regards to the future economic stability and growth of the country, several essential modifications have occurred in Greece's legal framework pertaining to labour relations. These changes were adopted under the direction and the pressure of the foreign creditors of the country (the 'troika' or as it is today named, 'the institutions') and for the most part these changes may be considered as regressive, to the detriment of the rights of the workers.

As it will be developed below, the aforementioned changes in labour relations emerge as real digression, or as a threat, to long upheld principles of the European society: principles concerning the sustenance, or the establishment, of just and favourable working conditions, the setting up mechanisms for protection against unemployment, of ensuring adequate pension provision, of providing fair social welfare benefits for the vulnerable and of universal health coverage for all Europeans. Fair remuneration for work offered is also affected by these changes.

In the absence of such commonly upheld principles, there could never be a unified Europe. If the notion of European society entails uniformity in the principles and values governing labour relations, a convergence in the standard of living of its citizens, a common ethic established and represented in the social and cultural rules operating in the different states,[1] then the changes endorsed to be carried out by Greece do not seem to be in that direction. The opposite in fact occurs.

The situation occurring today in Greece displays the process of the establishment of an unstable labour relations system, whereby the balance between the rights of the employee and those of the employers appears to tilt over to the side of the employers, ostensibly benefiting their individual interests rather than the common good. For this

1. This is something which the Directives are supposed to promote.

reason it will be of importance to consider in this work if the changes now advanced in Greece pertaining to the issue of *collective dismissals*, are on line with the principle of the EU concerning fair labour relations and convergence of labour rules amongst the European Members States.

§12.01 THE LEGAL FRAMEWORK PERTAINING TO COLLECTIVE DISMISSALS IN GREECE

As a general rule, albeit with many exceptions, in the Greek labour law, employee dismissal, or precisely, the termination of the employment contract by the employer, has two basic characteristics:

(a) It does not depend on the existence of a 'good cause', that is, on a legally significant fact, such as wrongful conduct from the part the employee. It is rather an exercise of 'managerial prerogative of the employer', which may be carried out at the will of the employer, without legal, judicial or administrative, control of the employer's judgment.
(b) It has been built in the institution of compensation, as a mechanism of deterrence of the aforesaid, possibly very harmful arbitrary behaviour from the part of the employer. The amount of compensation is determined, first, by the amount of the employee's earnings during the dismissal time period and, second, on the length of service of the employee with the same employer.

This legal framework concerns, first, employees who posses permanent or 'indefinite time' contracts. For the employees who are on fixed-term contracts different rules apply.

Particularly, what is the case in Greece regarding *collective dismissals*?

[A] Limits

In the existing Greek legislation, not yet completely adapted to the corresponding European Community legislation (Directive 92/56), *collective dismissals* are considered to be the mass redundancies performed by companies, or other establishments, *which employ more than twenty workers,*[2] for reasons that have nothing to do with the performance, or the person, of the workers, *but are performed solely on logistical grounds of the business or enterprise.* The status of the ownership of enterprises plays no role in the regulation of the issue, as under this legislation all types of enterprises are included, private and public businesses, local administration companies and holdings that belong to public law legal entities.

2. Small businesses (with fewer than nineteen employees) do not have collective redundancies limits.

In accordance with Article 74 of Law 3863/2010 (which revised the subparagraphs a and b of paragraph 2 of Article 1 of Law 1387/1983), the boundaries which determine when *dismissals* are to be considered *collective* are as following:

(a) For companies or enterprises that employ twenty and up to 150 workers the upper limit is *six workers*. (This number is lower that the upper limit provided in the Directive 92/56).
(b) For companies or enterprises that employ more than 150 workers the upper limit is *a percentage of 5% of all personnel, up to the number of thirty workers*.
(c) If such a company wishes to dismiss workers beyond the limits specified, the procedure to be applied is different and will be described below, as specific approval is required.

It should be mentioned here that, in regards to the category of people that belong to the age group 55-64, the law provides that their number being dismissed must not exceed the percentage of 10% of the total number of the redundancies performed (while any fraction that may occur is rounded to the nearest integer). Below, reference will be made to the additional measures that are provided in the law for the protection of this vulnerable category of workers from collective dismissals.

Finally, in order to determine the number of workers of the establishment upon which the calculation of the number of dismissals will be based, the entire staff of the company or enterprise is taken into account, that is, both the central establishment and any branches the company/enterprise might operate.

[B] Exemptions

The process of collective dismissals does not apply:

- to employees who hold a fixed-term contracts or contracts for temporary work or project ('contract for definite time'); this is due to the fact that the act of dismissal is already pre-determined, *unless it occurs before the end of the contract period or the completion of the project*;
- to civil servants, local administration employees and the personnel of public law entities engaged in private law employment relationship;
- to the workers made redundant by contractors, due to the suspension or interruption of activities, crucial, evidently, to the main body of the project, when the developer is the State or a public entity;
- the crews of the ships;
- in the instance when the redundancies are made for reasons related to the actions or behaviour of the dismissed employees, such as unconventional behaviour, lawsuit, retirement, illness, unsuitability, etc.;
- to the workers dismissed due to interruption of business following a First Instance Court judgment.

[C] Obligations of the Employer Prior to the Decision for Collective Dismissal

Prior to the decision for collective dismissals, the employer is obligated to follow a procedure of notification and consultation.

Specifically, the employer is required to undertake consultations with the representatives of workers representatives. This is demanded so that the *possibility of circumventing the need for collective dismissals,* or for reducing their number of intended redundancies, *is explored.* In particular, the employer, in accordance with paragraphs 3, 4 and 5 of Article 1 of Law 1387/1983, is required:

- To notify in writing the workers' representatives *of the reasons* for which the company plans to proceed with collective dismissals, as well as, *the number of the employees* considered to be dismissed, classified by gender, age, specially vis-à-vis the total number of workers employed in the enterprise.
- To provide all the necessary information which is likely *to facilitate the dialogue* between the employers and the workers, for the purpose of finding a commonly accepted solution which could circumvent collective dismissals (i.e., to show that he/she acting in 'good faith').
- Submit for approval copies of all required documents to *the Labour Inspectorate and the Prefect.* If the business or the enterprise has branches in more than one region, these copies are submitted to the Minister of Labour and to the Labour Inspectorate, of the place of business or branch where the redundancies, or where most of them are to be carried out.

[D] 'Real Employment'

In the process of labelling dismissals as *collective*, it is significant to underline that what is taken into account is the 'real employment time' of workers. As such it may be considered, in addition to the time prescribed in the contract, the work offered with an invalid labour contract. The opposite may also occur, a reduction of 'real employment time', under the pretence of a time period deemed as 'probationary work'.

In fact, in paragraph 2 A of Article 74 of Law 3863/2010, is prescribed that '*the employment contract of indefinite duration is treated as probationary employment period for the first twelve (12) months of work from the date of its validity, and it can be denounced without notice and without severance pay, unless there is other agreement between the parties*'.

The probationary period starts from the day the contract takes effect. This provision, which modified the previous law, was introduced in 2010 (Law 3899/2010) and has altered an essential, long established right of the worker, that is, the right to obtain all the benefits accrued from his/her holding a long-term employment contract, after having passed all the prerequisites to do so. In other words, what is at stake with this type of provision is the establishment of an unstable, insecure work environment, whereby the personal performance of the worker is secondary or even irrelevant to the needs of the employer. As the system is at present, a worker may be moved from one working place to another, without justification, without notice or compensation; he/she may encounter 'probationary periods' for the rest of his/her productive life. The employer on the other hand has the flexibility and the economic profit which may ensue from not having to provide its staff with the mandatory benefits provided in the law for employing personnel on long-term employment contracts.

This provision constitutes a great departure from the previous legislation, which in general terms sought to balance the needs of the workers with those of the employers. As it is now the worker has to rely on the good will of the employer while feeling threatened that his long-term contract could be revoked at any time during the so-called 'probationary period', without any justification, notice or compensation. As such the present provision seems to be a serious departure from the aforementioned principles of European Labour Law of fairness, of due remunerations and benefits earned through work offered within a framework of a legal, long-term employment contract.

[E] *Due Notification*

Once the 'probationary' twelve-month period is passed and the private employee is of the status of 'real employment' time, the revocation of his/her permanent ('indefinite time') labour contract may be legally revoked only after the worker has been properly notified in writing and is paid the required compensation. The dismissal takes affect the day after the notification.

The time required for legal notification to take effect is:

(a) For employees who have served from twelve completed months up to two years, one month of notice period is required before the dismissal.
(b) For employees who have served from two years up to five years, two-month notice is required.
(c) For employees who have served from five years up to ten years, three-month notice is required.
(d) For employees who have served ten completed years and more, four-month notice is required.

The law provides that the employer who gives notice to a worker must simultaneously, with the handing over of the notice, pay half of the amount of the compensation the worker is entitled. However, this provision was also modified in 2012 (Law 4093/2012), and now the payment of compensation by the employer is as follows: when the compensation, due to a revocation of a long-term labour contract, supersedes the amount of two months' earnings of the worker, the employer is obligated to pay only a part of the compensation which corresponds to that amount. The rest the employer must pay in instalments, every two months. Each instalment may not be less than the sum of two months' earnings of the employee unless the amount left to clear the total sum of compensation is less.

Therefore, in the situation of collective dismissals, the revocation of permanent labour contracts would be valid, if:

(a) the employees are notified in writing;
(b) the employees are paid the legal compensation;
(c) the employer has notified, within the specified in the law dates, the competent institutions for the dismissal (e.g., unemployment Agency);
(d) the dismissals have not been considered unlawful by the Supreme Labour Court and/or have the approval of the Minister of Labour.

It is also underlined that if a company wishes to dismiss workers beyond the limits specified above the following procedure must be followed: mandatory consultation between employer and employee, opinion of the Special Administrative Committee (Supreme Labour Council) and decision (approval or rejection) or of the General Secretary of the Ministry of Labour.

The situation in Greece regarding *collective dismissals* is still fluid, undetermined. That is why the Directive 92/56 is not typically and officially transposed into national legislation, while the government still persists to resist the full implementation of all the demands the creditors pertaining to changes in labour relations. However, from the aforementioned it ensues that the prevalent trend in Europe today is towards obliterating long established rights for the benefit of the workers and their re-fashioning for the worse in the name of an abstract notion of the 'needs of the marketplace' or of the 'health of the economy', as if the marketplace and the economy are something separate from the well-being of the people the relations of whom it must regulate. Our interest is to attend to the changes promoted in regards to the issue of *collective dismissals* because they disclose a change in the core of European labour relations and workers rights. That is, we must attend to what these changes mean for the well-being of the Europeans and of the quality of our culture and democracy.

CHAPTER 13

Collective Redundancies in Hungary

Tünde Handó

§13.01 REGULATIONS ON COLLECTIVE REDUNDANCY

[A] Introduction

The peculiarity of the Hungarian regulation on labour law is that the rules on several work-related legal relationships are governed by comprehensive codes. In fact, besides the Labour Code, separate acts contain the Labour regulations on unique and various sectors of civil service. Among these there are certain ones that govern collective redundancies by referring to the Labour Code for example, Act XXXIII of 1992 on the Status of Public Officials and others that govern collective redundancies independently for example, Act CXCIX on Public Service Officials. These are separate Acts that do not refer to the relevant EU directive as a governing basis, but the jurisprudence uses interpretation of the directive on definitions and procedure.

Collective redundancy as a phenomenon governed by the law appeared in Hungary in 1991. The social regime change at the turn of the decade substantially affected the economic life of the country. By way of privatization or due to the economic insolvency of the existing state-owned companies, collective redundancies became significant throughout the country. This caused such confusion in the Labour market that immediate regulation of the phenomenon was called for. Regulation came under Act IV of 1991 on Employment Promotion and Provisions for the Unemployed (hereinafter referred to as the Act on Employment Promotion). In defining the rules, also with respect to the future joining of the EU, the provisions of Directive 75/129/EEC were taken into consideration.

The regulations on collective redundancies moved to Act XXII of 1992 on the Labour Code (hereinafter referred to as the former Labour Code) in 1995 as part of fulfilling legal harmonization commitments. The next substantial change to the Labour Code was made, in 2012, with respect to Council Directive 98/59/EC. Before this change, the Act on Employment Promotion included tasks and possibilities concerning employers' announcements and reduction of the effects of collective redundancies among the duties of the government employment agency.

[B] Present Regulation

Act I of 2012 on the Labour Code (hereinafter referred to as the Labour Code) came into effect on 1 July 2012. The peculiarity is that the Code contains regulations both for individual legal relationships and the collective one. The Labour Code contains relevant regulations under the title 'Collective Redundancies' in 71-76 § The Labour Code refers specifically to collective redundancies in other Articles:

- under regulations on protection from termination of the legal relationship – 65.§ (4) and 68.§ (3) of the Labour Code; and
- under regulations on temporary agency work – 222.§ (4) of the Labour Code.

Furthermore, the Labour Code contains several regulations that relate indirectly to the course of collective redundancies and interpretations of definitions specified in them. These are regulations on the Labour connections and works council. Reference to conformity with Council Directive 98/59/EC can be found under closing provisions.

Besides legislation, employment regulations shall mean collective agreements and work agreements (13.§ of the Labour Code). Therefore the subject of these agreements has legal relevance for collective redundancies. 85.§ (1) c) of the Labour Code enables the parties to expressly derogate in the collective agreement to the benefit of workers. Many collective agreements contain regulations with considerable protection for employees' groups from possible collective redundancies.

Powers and duties of the government employment agency related to collective redundancies are furthermore contained in Act IV of 1991 on Employment Promotion and Provisions for the Unemployed.

§13.02 CHARACTERISTICS OF COLLECTIVE REDUNDANCIES

[A] The Definition

The definition of collective redundancy is given in the Code in accordance with Council Directive 98/59/EC. The Code defines collective redundancies with respect to the relevant number of workers, the period of action and the method of termination of the employment relationship. According to 71.§ (1) of the Labour Code:

> Collective redundancy shall mean when an employer, based on the average statistical workforce for the preceding six-month period, intends to terminate the employment relationship:
>
> a) of at least ten workers, when employing more than twenty and less than one hundred employees,

b) of 10 per cent of the employees, when employing one hundred or more, but less than three hundred employees,
c) of at least thirty workers, when employing three hundred or more employees,

in accordance with Subsection (3), within a period of thirty days, for reasons in connection with its operations.

According to regulations of 71.§ (4) of the Labour Code, the provisions on collective redundancies shall not apply to the crews of sea-going vessels. According to 222.§ (4) these regulations shall not apply either to temporary agency work.

The Hungarian regulation did not and does not contain alternative regulation than that contained in Article 1 (a) (ii) of Council Directive 98/59/EC. In the Hungarian regulation, the thirty-day period has relevance, although the thirty-day period is not only defined by the calendar but is also restricted by the first and last action.

[B] Specific Features

[1] Methods and Grounds for Termination of a Legal Relationship

Former regulation contained a positive formulation of the ground for termination of a legal relationship by using 'reason in connection with operation' (94/A.§ (1) of the former Labour Code). The Labour Code also uses this expression but according to a subsequent regulation thereof (73.§ (4)-(5) of the Labour Code) this cannot be interpreted restrictively in connection with the actual method of termination.

It is essential to underline that according to Hungarian regulation (64.§ and 66.§ of the Labour Code), the employment relationship may be terminated by:

- mutual consent;
- notice; or
- dismissal without notice.

[2] Dismissal

Essential characteristics of the dismissal are the requirement of justification, notice period, elements of protection and allowances. An employee may be dismissed only for reasons in connection with his/her behaviour in relation to the employment relationship, with his/her ability or in connection with the employer's operations. An uncertain case could arise, when, in spite of the general rule, justification can be ignored. The employer is not required to give reasons for terminating an employment relationship if the worker affected is:

- a pensioner (66.§ (9) of the Labour Code); or
- an executive employee (210.§ (1) b) of the Labour Code).

Regulation under 73.§ (5) of the Labour Code corresponds fully to Council Directive 98/59/EC, according to which, termination for reasons in connection with the employer's operations shall cover such notice of dismissal, until proven otherwise.

It is worth noting that a fixed-term employment relationship can be terminated by notice only in exceptional cases (66.§ (8)), if undergoing liquidation or bankruptcy proceedings or if maintaining the employment relationship is no longer possible due to unavoidable external reasons.

[3] Dismissal Without Notice

An employment relationship shall be terminated without notice basically in the case that the other party commits a severe violation of any substantive obligations arising from the employment relationship. The employer shall be entitled to terminate without notice in two further cases (79.§ (1) a)-b) of the Labour Code) without giving reasons:

- during the probationary period; or
- during a fixed-term employment relationship.

In the latter case the employee shall be entitled to absentee pay for twelve months, or if the time remaining from the fixed period is less than one year, for the remaining time period.

Employees whose employment relationship has been terminated without notice before the end of the fixed term shall be affected by collective redundancy, unless it is stated that the termination was not for reasons in connection with the employer's operations (73.§ (5) of the Labour Code).

The wording of the Labour Code that refers to 'reasons in connection with employer's operations' differs apparently from the wording of Council Directive 98/59/EC: 'dismissals effected by an employer for one or more reasons not related to the individual workers concerned'. The Hungarian legislator assumes the legal fiction that every measure is in connection with an employer's operations, unless referred to otherwise by the justification, or for lack of justification, if the contrary has not been proven.

[4] Mutual Consent

The essential feature of the termination of an employment relationship by mutual consent is that it can be initiated by either party. It has to be in writing but the agreement shall not contain the initiating party and nor the reason why. Parties shall be free to define the due date of the termination.

Uncertainty of interpretation may arise in connection with employees affected by the agreement because of two circumstances. On the one hand, it is hard to prove subsequently who initiated the termination by mutual consent and for what reason. On the other hand, there is the question of the due date of the termination. In particular, whether employees should be counted as employees affected by the collective redundancy only if the effective date of the termination falls within the thirty-day period.

According to the law, the employees shall be counted as employees affected by the collective redundancy if the termination by mutual consent was initiated by the employer (73.§ (4) b) of the Labour Code). With respect to the date of the termination, whether the effective date of the termination falls within the thirty-day period is only partly significant. The employee shall be counted in the affected headcount only if already listed in the first employer's notification. As a result, an employee affected by termination with mutual consent shall be counted in the headcount even if his/her employment relationship has been terminated before or after the thirty-day period, or within thirty days subsequent to the last action within the thirty-day period.

Hungarian regulation, similar to Article 4(1) of Council Directive 98/59/EC includes the obligation to notify the government employment agency and the employee thirty days before communication of the termination statement only in the case of employment relationships terminating by notice. Similarly, the Supreme Court decided that in the case of collective redundancy the employer shall not be obliged to notify formerly the employee whose employment relationship terminates by mutual consent (Court Decision 1999/146). However, many court decisions (Court Decision 2009/89 and 2008/130) confirm that mutual consent shall be taken into consideration regarding collective redundancy if it is in connection with the employer's operations.

[5] Other Methods of Termination

An employment relationship terminates in certain cases without any separate legal statement. This can be, among others, in the case of fixed-term employment or the expiration of the fixed period or in the case of the end of the employer without a successor.

The latter case may occur as a result of a liquidation proceeding resulting from insolvency. The former Labour Code used the more favourable regulation recommended by Article 4(4) of Council Directive 98/59/EC when regulating the proceeding in case of insolvency in details (former the Labour Code 94/H.§). The Labour Code does not contain any such regulations. No court case on this question has arisen since the new Labour Code entered into effect. It is a fact that Council Directive 98/59/EC does not contain any obligation to insert such matters into Member State regulations. However, legal practice, based upon former regulations gives the green light to a favourable interpretation for employers, because the Code does not contain any excluding regulations. In liquidation proceedings, the liquidator exercises the employer's rights and obligations, therefore the liquidator has to act on collective redundancy in this quality, as a normal employer. This kind of interpretation is underlined in the judgment of the European Court of Justice in Joined Cases C-235/10-C-239/10. According to this judgment, Council Directive 98/59/EC has to be interpreted in such a way that it has to be applied when a company is under winding-up or liquidation due to insolvency.

The Hungarian Supreme Court took a guiding decision in 2005 concerning expiration of a fixed-term employment. In accordance with this decision, the expiration of the employment relationship due to termination of the fixed term, cannot be taken into consideration in relation to collective redundancy proceedings (Court Decision 2005/1341).

[6] *Average Headcount, Number and Rate of Affected Employees*

Resulting from the provisions of Council Directive 98/59/EC, in defining the collective redundancy thoughtful mathematical operations have to be performed. Above all, when transposing it into the Hungarian legal order how to fill the expression 'normally employing' with actual content had to be clarified. Using 'average statistical workforce' was obvious. The Central Statistical Office defines, namely year by year, how a company or another legal entity may register its average statistical workforce. According to this, an employee shall be regarded as employed when he/she is in an employment relationship with the employer and is obliged to work at least sixty hours a month on average. Statement No. 3/2010 (IV.2.) KSH of the Central Statistical Office gives a guideline, pointing out the categories not to be counted in average statistical workforce (e.g., employees on childcare or unpaid leave or those employed by temporary agency work) and how to calculate the monthly, half-yearly and yearly average.

According to 71.§ (1) of the Labour Code the average statistical workforce for the preceding six-month period before the decision has relevance. In the case that company existed for less than half a year and no such statistical average workforce can be calculated thereupon, the average statistical workforce has to be defined for the period of existence.

Furthermore the regulation (71.§ (1) of the Labour Code) follows staff number and ratios and also the recommendation of Council Directive 98/59/EC concerning minimal affected number. The Hungarian regulation deals specially with summation of number of places of business and number of affected employees. The Hungarian regulation does not contain the last sentence of Article 1(2) of Council Directive 98/59/EC:

> For the purpose of calculating the number of redundancies provided for in the first subparagraph of point (a), terminations of an employment contract which occur on the employer's initiative for one or more reasons not related to the individual workers concerned shall be assimilated to redundancies, provided that there are at least five redundancies.

It seems to be a contradiction between Council Directive 98/59/EC and the Hungarian regulation, because according to the definitions of the Labour Code, under a specific size or rate these special regulations shall not apply to collective redundancies. If half-yearly statistical workforce of an employer is nineteen, the regulations on collective redundancies shall not even apply to all of the employment relationships terminated. Although, special regulations will apply even if less employment relationships are terminated than planned, due to negotiations. In the case only one employment will be terminated compared to ten as planned by an employer of twenty-one employees, the process shall be followed also in his/her case until closing.

The Labour Code's peculiarity is that it governs many atypical employment forms as an employment relationship (e.g., call for work, employee sharing) but, except for temporary agency work, no special regulations apply to them concerning collective redundancies.

[7] The Employer, Place of Business

Hungarian regulation uses, in accordance with Council Directive 98/59/EC, the definition of employer. However, the Labour Code also calculates the possibility that the employer operates more branches of the same business. The Code does not provide any definition on place of business but there are decades of legal practice on this question. Place of business is every business unit of the employer that operates outside the place of incorporation of the employer and whose executive exercises employer's rights concerning establishment and termination of employment relationships independently.

Place of business has importance in relation to the possible summation of redundancies, employer's representation and employer's obligations. 71.§ (3) of the Labour Code provides the following:

> Compliance with the requirements specified in Subsection (1) shall be ascertained, where applicable, separately for each place of business; however, the number of workers employed at various locations, but within the jurisdiction of the same county (Budapest) shall be calculated on the aggregate. The employee shall be accounted at the location where he/she works in the position registered at the time when the decision on collective redundancy was adopted.

Hungarian regulation eliminates thereby all attempts to assert that an executive of a place of business did not become aware of the owner's or central decisions, or did not have sufficient knowledge or authority. The Code places fulfilment of employer's rights at the responsibility of the employer. Summation is required in order to improve employment market measures, because the government employment agency has to solve the large number of new job applicants in one geographical region.

Reference must be made to 47.§ (5) of the Act XLIX of 1991 on Bankruptcy Proceedings and Liquidation Proceedings, according to which from the time of the opening of liquidation proceedings, employer's rights shall be exercised and obligations shall be fulfilled by the liquidator within the framework of the relevant legislation, the collective agreement, and internal regulations and contracts of employment.

[8] Relevant Period

According to the Labour Code, the thirty-day period shall be relevant when terminating employment relationships, which corresponds to Article 1(1)(a) of Council Directive 98/59/EC. The legislator integrated experiences of jurisdiction into the regulation when, independently from the employer's scheduling it gave importance to the actual situation concerning summation of measures of various times. 73.§ (3) of the Labour Code provides the following:

> The number of workers shall be calculated on the aggregate, if within thirty days from the date of disclosure of the legal act for the termination of the last employment relationship or from the date of reaching an agreement, the employer communicates another statement or concludes an agreement for the termination of employment in a given period.

The Code underlines which methods of redundancy shall have special importance during summation. The Code highlights termination based upon the employer's operations, mutual consent initiated by the employer and termination of fixed-term employment without notice.

[9] Representatives of Employees

According to former regulation, with regard to negotiations, representatives of employees were the works council, or if there was no works council, the committee formed from the representatives of the local trade union branch and employees.

According to the new Labour Code only the works council is the possible representative of the employees. The works council can be established in order to ensure cooperation between the employer and the employees and to ensure the participation in the employer's decisions. Concerning the establishment of a works council 236.§ (1) of the Labour Code provides the following:

> A shop steward, or a works council shall be elected if, during the half-year prior to the date when the election committee was established, the average number of employees at the employer or at the employer's independent establishment or division (hereinafter referred to as 'fixed establishment'), is higher than fifteen or fifty, respectively.

The works council established at each fixed establishment may form a central works council, and central works councils may set up a corporate-level works council at a recognized or de facto group of companies.

The establishment of works councils is not a legal obligation. There is no provision of law that envisages direct sanctions if employees do not establish a works council. With respect to the exclusive wording of the Labour Code, the absence of a works council might end in a situation in which the employer will not have any negotiating party during collective redundancies. The case law may refer here only to the provisions of Council Directive 98/59/EC, according to which employees' representatives shall be who is the representative of the employees under Member State law or practice. In other words, present regulation could be an incentive to the establishment of works councils, because employees are directly interested in the operation of works councils. If jurisdiction applies an interpretation near to the wording of the Labour Code, this can indicate that no collective redundancies shall be carried out by employers having no works council.

It is a special question whether a shop steward – the provisions pertaining to work councils shall apply to shop stewards – shall be deemed as negotiator during collective redundancies. This could be a real situation in companies employing between twenty and fifty employees, where it is not possible to elect a shop steward.

[10] *Government Employment Agency*

State employment bodies are the organs both of the government office of the capital and the county government offices providing employment policy and labour market duties. The organs dealing with employer's notifications and with mitigation of results of redundancies are county employment centres and their branches. The Act on Employment Promotion deals with the main tasks of these organizations.

§13.03 COURSE OF COLLECTIVE REDUNDANCIES

[A] Employer's Intention

The procedures of collective redundancies begin with the employer's planning. With respect to the fact that a notification of a determined content shall be given about the plans, this content specifies the essence of the planning.

The formation of the plans can be influenced, if there are relevant general provisions in the collective agreement or in the work agreement concluded with the works council. In these agreements it is possible to provide extra protection for certain employees.

[B] Employer's Notification and Consultation

[1] *Industrial Relations*

The peculiarity of the Labour Code is that it contains general provisions on industrial relations. This is of importance because its regulations shall apply also to negotiations about redundancies. Regulations defining notification and consultation are highly important. Notification shall be the handing over of information defined by the law in connection with industrial relations and the employment relationship, in a way that enables recognition and analysis thereof and the creation of an opinion thereon. Consultation is the exchange of views and conversation between the employer and the works council or trade union. Consultation has to be carried out in favour of the agreement, according to the defined goal specified in the initiative, in order to ensure:

- the due representation of parties;
- the direct personal exchange of opinions; and
- real negotiations.

[2] *Notification*

According to 72.§ of the Labour Code the employer shall, at least seven days before the discussions, inform the works council in writing regarding:

- the reasons for the projected collective redundancies;
- the number of workers to be made redundant broken down by categories or the number of workers employed during the half-period before the decision;
- the period over which the projected redundancies are to be effected, and the timetable for their implementation;
- the criteria proposed for the selection of the workers to be made redundant; and
- the conditions for and the extent of benefits provided in connection with the termination of the employment relationships, other than what is prescribed in employment regulations.

Within this scope, the regulation is in accordance with Article 2(3) of Council Directive 98/59/EC. Although the wording does not contain the passage 'supply them with all relevant information', it results from the general obligation of notification that the employer has to do so.

It is very important that notification has to be given to the works council simultaneously to the government employment agency (74.§ (1) of the Labour Code).

This should be proven towards the works council by giving them the receipt of the notification forwarded to the government employment agency.

[3] Negotiations

With respect to the proceeding of negotiations, duration and content are of real importance. With respect to the latter 72.§ (4) of the Labour Code provides minimal requirements:

- the possible ways and means of avoiding collective redundancies;
- the principles of redundancies;
- the means of mitigating the consequences; and
- the reduction of the number of employees affected.

Negotiations may start on the eighth day subsequent to the first notification and shall be continued until an agreement is reached but at least for fifteen days. With respect thereto, the employer's decision can be taken only on the twenty-fourth day subsequent to the first notification or on the sixteenth day subsequent to the beginning of the negotiations.

There are no other provisions concerning the proceedings of the negotiations, but following the general obligation of the parties on cooperation, negotiations must be seriously carried out. In the case that the parties fulfil their obligations on negotiations only formally, this can be judged illegal by the court in out-of-court proceedings.

The Code does not contain any reference to the fact that the government employment agency could have any role during the negotiations. In practice, representatives of the government employment agency may participate in negotiations or may be in contact with the parties, because search and representation of the labour market possibilities to the parties can already begin in this part of the process. This has importance, because the Code does not refer to concrete measures in order to mitigate consequences such as re-education or relocation. As a consequence – if provided otherwise by a collective agreement or work agreement – parties could feel alone in the formulation of possible solutions. Without assistance, finding potential avoidance possibilities and defining selection criteria carefully would be made extremely difficult, especially without knowing possible best practices or assistance available. With respect to the latter, the last phrase of Article 2 (2) of Council Directive 98/59/EC is very interesting because it deems it possible for a Member State to prescribe that representatives of the employees might use experts' services according to national legislation and/or practice. This possibility is provided by the Act on Employment Promotion in Hungary.

[4] Agreement

The conclusion of an agreement is not an obligation but a possibility for the parties. According to the practice, even negotiations may foster the employer to take more points of view into consideration when taking its decision.

The agreement is legally binding. Such a work agreement shall be an employment regulation according to 13.§ of the Labour Code. With respect to employees' rights it is of major importance which selection criteria shall apply to affected employees. This is underlined by 76.§ of the Labour Code that provides indirectly that an employee may raise a claim against the employer if selection happens against the agreement.

The agreement has to be sent to the governmental employment agency. This has importance because the agency may take its own measures in this respect.

[5] Employer's Decision

According to 73.§ (1) of the Labour Code, the written decision for the implementation of collective redundancies shall specify:

- the number of workers affected, broken down by job categories; and
- the date of commencement and conclusion and the timeframe of collective redundancy, or the timetable for implementing the said redundancies.

The employer shall notify the governmental employment agency in writing of its decision regarding collective redundancies by disclosing the identification data, the position and the qualification of the employees to be made redundant (74.§ (2) of the Labour Code).

Workers affected shall be notified about the employer's decision. This notification shall be sent to the works council and the government employment agency as well (75.§ (1)-(2) of the Labour Code).

It is important that the above-mentioned notification shall be sent thirty days before the employer's effective action. Dismissal of the employee or termination of the fixed-term employment shall be made only on the thirty-first day subsequent to the decision. If the employer does not comply with this deadline, the dismissal shall be considered unlawful. In this regard, in Decision no. 1999/146, the Supreme Court declared upon a similar regulation of the former Labour Code, that no preliminary notification shall apply to the worker whose employment relationship has been terminated by mutual consent.

There is no provision in the law that would authorize the governmental employment agency to shorten or extend the above deadlines. At the same time – lacking a prohibitory provision – parties shall have the right to extend deadlines during negotiations, therefore it is possible that negotiations in connection with redundancies exceed [fifteen?] days. The question of whether the continuance of a negotiation or the execution of an employer's decision after the thirty-day period means an infringement to the workers or not, would need to be clarified in litigation.

§13.04 MEASURES IN FAVOUR OF THE EMPLOYEES

Regulations that ensure protection from dismissal shall be deemed as measures in favour of employees. These regulations of the Labour Code mean protection for workers of a specific nature or for those that are in a specific situation in general.

Such protection shall apply to the worker who is inside the five-year period before the date of reaching the age limit for old-age pension and to the mother or single father until her/his child reaches three years of age. In their case, the employment relationship might be terminated in connection with the employer's operations if the employer has no vacant position available at the workplace suitable for the worker affected in terms of skills, education and/or experience required for his/her previous job, or if the worker refuses the offer made for his/her employment in that job (66.§ (5)-(6) of the Labour Code). A trade union official shall be subject to protection by requiring prior consent to his/her dismissal.

The employer shall be protected from notification of dismissal:

- during pregnancy;
- during maternity leave;
- during an unpaid leave taken for caring for a child;
- during any period of actual reserve military service; and
- in the case of women, while receiving treatment related to a human reproduction procedure, for up to six months from the beginning of such treatment.

With respect to collective redundancies, prior notification about termination shall be prohibited (65.§ (4) of the Labour Code). Resulting therefrom, in connection with collective redundancies, the employee shall be notified about termination only following the expiration of the protection period.

With respect to the beginning of the notice period, a protection shall be applied if at the beginning of the measure one of the following applies to the employee:

- duration of incapacity to work due to illness, not to exceed one year following expiration of the sick leave period;

- absence from work for the purpose of caring for a sick child; and
- unpaid leave for providing home care for a close relative.

If a worker affected by redundancy is in one of the above situations at the moment of prior notification, the notice period shall commence only subsequent to the expiry of the period (68.§ (3) of the Labour Code). If no protection existed at the time of the notification, the actual situation at the moment of the termination has no importance with reference to protection.

Under the Labour Code, the employer is not obliged to take concrete measures mitigating the effects of redundancy (e.g., social plan). The governmental employment agency has such obligations and possibilities. According to the Act on the Employment Promotion and the Decree of the Ministry of Employment 6/1996 (VII. 16) on subsidies promoting employment and on subsidies to be provided from the Labour Market Fund for handling employment crisis, such subsidies shall be among others:

- a subsidy for education;
- a subsidy for establishment and keeping of workplaces;
- the Labour market programs; and
- a subsidy for wage costs.

The subsidy for mitigation of the negative effects of collective redundancy is specified in the decree independently. From the employment fund, part of the National Employment Fund subsidies can be provided in order to mitigate the negative effects of collective redundancy for employees subject to the Labour Code and other employment laws. The criterion of the subsidy is that the employer:

- has initiated the consultation prescribed by the law related to collective redundancies;
- undertakes – according to the government office's principles - to establish a committee which aims to promote the employment of workers affected by redundancy (hereinafter referred to as the Employment Committee) at branches affected by redundancy;
- declares how and to what extent the employer contributes to the operation of the Employment Committee; and
- undertakes during the operation of the Employment Committee and at the closing of its operation – at moments defined in the official contract concluded with the government office – to prepare a calculation and evaluation about the use of the subsidy.

For each place of business affected by the collective redundancy a maximum of HUF 1 million non-refundable subsidy can be given for up to twelve months to the employer for the operation of the Employment Committee(s). The district office shall be entitled to define the quantity of the subsidy with respect to the Labour market situation of the region, the number of workers affected by collective redundancy and the relevant budget.

The request for a subsidy shall be submitted by the employer, until the notification to the first employee affected by the collective redundancy about the measures related to the termination of the employment and other occupational relationship or until the conclusion of the agreement with the first employee, to the competent district office competent for the branch affected by the redundancy. The request shall contain the employer's:

- data (name, place of business, place(s) of business affected by collective redundancy, address, tax number, NACE code);
- declaration about establishment of the Employment Committee;
- method and extent of its contribution to the operation of the Employment Committee;
- plans about services to be provided for workers affected by the collective redundancy; and
- preliminary budget prepared for the operation of the Employment Committee and programs organized by the Committee.

Both the written notification to the participants of the consultation and the preliminary cooperation agreement concluded by the participants of the consultation on the establishment of the Employment Committee shall be attached to the request for a subsidy. The subsidy can be used for expenses in connection with the operation of the Employment Committee. The subsidy can be granted if the employer has fulfilled its obligations concerning notification on redundancies prescribed in a separate law towards the district office.

§13.05 REMEDIES, SANCTIONS

[A] The Employee

The employee shall be entitled to apply to the administrative and labour court in order to enforce his/her claims resulting from wrongful measures of the employer. According to 75.§ (3) of the Labour Code the employer's measure in connection with collective redundancies shall be unlawful if preliminary notification has not been given prior to dismissal or has not been duly given. The employee shall have the right to challenge the employer's measures if aspects of the agreement upon redundancies have not been observed. A precondition of the measures is to give relevant information about the employee during selection (76.§ (2) of the Labour Code).

Beyond that, general provisions of the Labour Code shall apply to individual employer's measures on redundancies. Therefore, employer's measures can be challenged for many reasons, for example:

- violation of the rules of protection from dismissal;
- improper legal practice; and
- violation of requirements of equal treatment.

The provision of the Labour Code according to which a claim may be filed against a decision adopted by the employer within its right of discretion, may legitimate also requests of the employee challenging the regularity of the process of redundancies.

Claim enforcement shall be limited by time if enforced against a measure in connection with termination of an employment, because such a claim shall be submitted within thirty days following the notification.

The employee shall be entitled to monetary compensation if his/her employment relationship has been wrongfully terminated. The employee shall be entitled to reimbursement of his/her claims in connection with the measure, but compensation for loss of income from employment payable to the employee may not exceed twelve months' pay. The employee is entitled to severance pay if he/she did not receive any severance pay at the time that his/her employment relationship was terminated because of lack of dismissal or subsequent untruthfulness of the dismissal. Instead of the aforementioned monetary compensation, the employee shall be entitled to request the paid leave covering a period that would otherwise be due in the event of dismissal.

In the case of wrongful termination of employment, the employment relationship shall be reinstated only exceptionally, in the following cases:

- if it was terminated in violation of the principle of equal treatment;
- if it was terminated in violation of protection from termination;
- if the employee was a trade union official and former consent has not been provided; or
- if the employee served as an employees' representative at the time that his employment relationship was terminated.

The time between the termination of the employment relationship and the day of reinstatement shall be regarded as time spent in employment.

The employee shall be compensated for any lost wages and for damages in excess thereof.

[B] Works Council

In 94/F.§ the former Labour Code expressly mentioned the possibility of claim enforcement for the works council in connection with collective redundancies. According to this provision, if the employer had violated the rights of the works council to be notified and consulted, the works council was entitled to go to court. The court had to take a decision within eight days in an out-of-court procedure. Such claims were rarely filed to courts, however, the decisions stating a violation of the law could also have an impact in separate legal disputes of employees. A final decision of the court was binding in a lawsuit filed under the subject 'unlawful termination'.

The possibility of claim enforcement of the works council can be found today among general provisions of the Labour Code. In the case of a violation of the regulations on notification or consultation, according to 285.§ (1) of the Labour Code the works council shall have the right to go to the court within five days. The court shall take a decision within fifteen days about the claim in an out-of-court proceeding. The decision shall be subject to appeal. In such cases, also the court of appeal shall take its decision within fifteen days.

In such cases, the administrative court and the Labour court competent in relation to the place of incorporation of the works council shall have jurisdiction.

[C] Governmental Employment Agency

According to 56/A.§ of the Act on Employment Promotion the employer shall pay a fine in case of a violation of his obligation on notification under 74.§ of the Labour Code or fulfilling this obligation in an improper way or late. The amount of the fine shall be between HUF 5,000 and HUF 500,000 (about EUR 16-EUR 1,600).

The fine has further consequences as it serves as a ground for excluding the employer from state subsidies and tenders.

§13.06 SUMMARY

Council Directive 98/59/EC has been duly adopted in Hungary. The Labour Code is in accordance with the Directive concerning the definition and process of collective redundancies.

Published court decisions give a good example that in the case of a dispute Hungarian courts intend to interpret legal regulations in accordance with the Directive. Changes to legal regulations in previous years have been initiated by legal interpretation in accordance with EU law as also represented in the case law.

Hungarian case law intends to follow rules of interpretation defined by the European Court of Justice, among which the decision in Case C 12/08 *Mono Car Styling SA, in liquidation, v. Dervis Odemis and Others* should be highlighted:

> 60 However, when it applies domestic law, a national court is bound to interpret that law, so far as possible, in the light of the wording and the purpose of the directive concerned in order to achieve the result sought by the directive and consequently comply with the third paragraph of Article 249 EC (see, to that effect, *Pfeiffer and Others*, paragraph 113).
>
> 61 That obligation to interpret national law in conformity with Community law concerns all the provisions of national law and is limited by the general principles of law, particularly those of legal certainty and non-retroactivity, and that obligation cannot serve as the basis for an interpretation of national law *contra legem* (see, to that effect, Case 80/86 *Kolpinghuis Nijmegen* [1987] ECR 3969, paragraph 13; Case C-212/04 *Adeneler and Others* [2006] ECR I-6057, paragraph 110; *Impact*, paragraph 100; and Case C-378/07 *Angelidaki and Others* [2009] ECR I-0000, paragraph 199).
>
> 62 The principle of interpreting national law in conformity with Community law thus imposed by Community law, requires the national court to consider national law as a whole in order to assess to what extent it may be applied so as not to produce a result contrary to that sought by the directive at issue (see, to that effect, *Pfeiffer and Others*, paragraph 115).

> 63 If the application of interpretive methods recognised by national law enables, in certain circumstances, a provision of domestic law to be construed in such a way as to avoid conflict with another rule of domestic law or the scope of that provision to be restricted to that end by applying it only in so far as it is compatible with the rule concerned, the national court is bound to use those methods in order to achieve the result sought by the directive at issue (see, to that effect, *Pfeiffer and Others*, paragraph 116).
>
> 64 In this instance, that principle thus requires the referring court to do whatever lies within its jurisdiction, having regard to the whole body of rules of national law, to ensure that Directive 98/59 is fully effective, so as to avoid the obligations binding an employer who intends to proceed with collective redundancies being reduced below those laid down in Article 2 of that directive.

Courts are supported in decision making by Article 28 of the Hungarian Fundamental Law as follows:

> In the case law, the courts shall in principle interpret the laws in light of their purpose and in accordance with the Fundamental Law. When interpreting the Fundamental Law or any other law, it shall be presumed that they are reasonable and of benefit to the public and are pursuing virtuous and economical ends.

CHAPTER 14

Collective Dismissal in Ireland

Anthony Kerr

§14.01 INTRODUCTION

The legislative provisions governing 'collective redundancies' are contained in the Protection of Employment Act 1977[1] ('the Act of 1977') which came into operation on the 10 May 1977.[2] This Act was designed to satisfy Ireland's obligations under Council Directive 75/129/EEC on the approximation of the laws of the Member States relating to collective redundancies.[3]

Directive 75/129 was amended by Council Directive 92/56/EEC[4] and, consequently, the Act of 1977 should have been amended by 23 June 1994 at the latest, principally by ensuring that workers had at their disposal 'administrative and/or judicial procedures' in order to ensure that the information and consultation obligations laid down in the Directives were fulfilled. Amendments to the Act of 1977, however, were not made until 9 December 1996.[5] The European Commission subsequently issued a Reasoned Opinion that, despite these amendments, Ireland was still in breach of its obligations.[6] Further amendments were then made by the European Communities (Protection of Employment) Regulations 2000,[7] with effect from

1. No. 7 of 1977.
2. Protection of Employment Act 1977 (Commencement) Order 1977 (S.I. No. 139 of 1977).
3. [1975] O.J. L48/29.
4. [1992] O.J. L245/3. The two Directives were consolidated by Council Directive 98/59/EC ([1998] O.J. L225/16).
5. Protection of Employment Order 1996 (S.I. No. 370 of 1996).
6. *See* europa.eu/rapid/press-release_IP-99-526_en.doc (accessed 24 May 2015).
7. S.I. No. 488 of 2000. Further technical amendments have been made by the Protection of Employment (Exceptional Collective Redundancies and Related Matters) Act 2007, the Protection of Employees (Temporary Agency Work) Act 2012 and the Local Government Reform Act 2014. The collective citation is now the Protection of Employment Acts 1977 to 2014: *see* section 1(7) of the Local Government Reform Act 2014.

21 December 2000, which finally introduced a procedure whereby individual complaints could be made that an employer had contravened the information and/or consultation requirements imposed by the Act of 1977.

§14.02 COLLECTIVE DISMISSAL

Section 6(1) of the Act of 1977[8] defines 'collective redundancies' as meaning dismissals effected by an employer 'for one or more reasons not related to the individual concerned' where, in any period of thirty consecutive days, the number of dismissals is:

(a) at least five in an establishment normally employing more than 20 and less than 50 employees;
(b) at least ten in an establishment normally employing at least 50 but less than 100 employees;[9]
(c) at least 10% of the number of employees in an establishment normally employing at least 100 but less than 300 employees, and
(d) at least 30 in an establishment normally employing 300 or more employees.[10]

Section 6(3) then provides that, in this section, 'establishment' means 'an employer or a company or a subsidiary company or a company within a group of companies which can independently effect redundancies'.[11]

Section 7(1) provides that the Act of 1977 applies to 'all persons in employment in an establishment normally employing more than 20 persons' save that subsection (2) then provides that the Act does not apply to:

(a) dismissals of employees engaged under a contract of employment for a fixed term or for a specified purpose where the dismissals occurred only because of the expiry of the term or the cesser of the purpose;

8. The present wording of section 6 was substituted for the original wording by Article 5 of the Protection of Employment Order 1996 (S.I. No. 370 of 1996).
9. Section 6(2) of the Act of 1977 provides that, for the purpose of calculating the number of redundancies where the number of dismissals is at least ten in an establishment normally employing more than twenty and less than 100 employees, terminations of a contract of employment which occur to the individual workers concerned shall be assimilated to redundancies provided that there are at least five redundancies.
10. Section 8 of the Act of 1977 provides that the number of employees 'normally employed in an establishment' shall be taken to be 'the average of the number so employed in each of the 12 months preceding the date on which the first dismissal takes effect'.
11. This definition applies also to the use of the term 'establishment' in section 7: *see* section 7(5) of the Act of 1977. This definition must now be interpreted in light of the decision of the Court of Justice in Case C-182/13, *Lyttle v. Bluebird UK Bidco 2 Ltd*, on an Article 267 reference from the Industrial Tribunal (Northern Ireland). *See also* Case C-80/14, *USDAW v. WW Realisation 1 Ltd* and Case C-392/13, *Cañas v. Nexea Gestión Documental SA*. All three decisions are reported at [2015] I.R.L.R. 577.

(b) a person employed by or under the State;[12]
(c) officers of a local authority;[13]
(d) employment under an employment agreement pursuant to Part II or Part IV of the Merchant Shipping Act 1894.[14]

Although the Directive refers to 'workers', the scope of the Act of 1977 applies to 'employees'. An employee is defined by section 2 (1) of that Act as meaning a person who is or was employed under a 'contract of employment'. A 'contract of employment' is defined as meaning either 'a contract of service or of apprenticeship' or 'any other contract whereby an individual agrees with another person, who is carrying on the business of an employment agency within the meaning of the Employment Agency Act 1971, and is acting in the course of that business, to do or perform personally any work or service for a third person (whether or not the third person is a party to the contract)'. It would not appear from that definition that a contract whereby an individual agrees with another person personally to execute any work or service for that person is necessarily a 'contract of employment'. Accordingly, in light of the Court of Justice decision in *Balkaya v. Kiesel Abruch und Recycling Technik GmbH*,[15] the definition of 'employee' may be under inclusive.

The concept of dismissals effected 'for one or more reasons not related to the individual concerned' has not yet been judicially considered. It is probable, however, that it would be construed in accordance with the provisions of section 7(2) of the Redundancy Payments Act 1967[16] ('the Act of 1967') which provides that an employee who is dismissed shall be taken to be dismissed by reason of redundancy if, 'for one or more reasons not related to the employee concerned', the dismissal is attributable wholly or mainly to:

(a) the fact that his or her employer has ceased, or intends to cease, to carry on the business for the purposes of which the employee was employed by him or her, or has ceased or intends to cease, to carry on that business in the place where the employee was so employed; or
(b) the fact that the requirements of that business for employees to carry out work of a particular kind in the place where he or she was so employed have ceased or diminished or are expected to cease or diminish; or

12. *See Central Bank of Ireland v. Gildea* [1997] 1 I.R. 160 where the Supreme Court had to consider whether a security guard of the bank was 'employed by or under the State' for the purposes of the Unfair Dismissals Act 1977.
13. Within the meaning of the Local Government Act 2001, as amended by the Local Government Reform Act 2014.
14. Article (2)(c) of Directive 98/59/EC permits the exclusion of 'crews of seagoing vessels'.
15. Case C-229/14, reported at [2015] I.R.L.R. 771.
16. This subsection was amended by section 19 of the Redundancy Payments Act 1971 (following the High Court decision in *Limerick Health Authority v. Ryan* [1969] I.R. 194) and by section 5 of the Redundancy Payments Act 2003 (in light of the determination of the Employment Appeals Tribunal in *St Ledger v. Frontline Distribution Ireland Ltd* UD 56/1994 (reported at [1995] E.L.R. 160)).

(c) the fact that his or her employer has decided to carry on the business with fewer or no employees, whether by requiring the work for which the employee had been employed (or had been doing before his or her dismissal) to be done by other employees or otherwise; or

(d) the fact that his or her employer has decided that the work for which the employee had been employed (or had been doing before his or her dismissal) should henceforward be done in a different manner for which the employee is not sufficiently qualified or trained; or

(e) the fact that his or her employer has decided that the work for which the employee had been employed (or had been doing before his or her dismissal) should henceforward be done by a person who is also capable of doing other work for which the employee is not sufficiently qualified or trained.

This definition of 'redundancy' goes beyond an excess of manpower resulting from mechanization, rationalization or from a decrease in business activity which requires a permanent reduction in the number of persons employed. The focus is not just on the kind of work but also on the type of employee.

In *St Ledger v Frontline Distribution Ireland Ltd*,[17] the Employment Appeals Tribunal said that the statutory definition of 'redundancy' had two important characteristics, namely 'impersonality' and 'change':

> Impersonality runs throughout the five definitions in the Act. Redundancy impacts on the job and only as a consequence of redundancy does the person involved lose his job. It is worthy of note that the EC Directive on Collective Redundancies uses a shorter and simpler definition: 'one or more reasons not related to the individual workers concerned'. Change also runs through all five definitions. This means change in the workplace. The most dramatic change of all is a complete close down. Change may also mean a reduction in needs for employees, or a reduction in numbers. Definitions (d) and (e) involve change in the way the work is done or some other form of change in the nature of the job.

The impersonality of 'redundancy' was emphasized by the High Court in *JVC Europe Ltd v. Ponisi*,[18] where Charleton J. described it as the 'economic or technological reorienting of an enterprise whereby the work of employees needs to be shed or to be carried out in an entirely different manner'.

If the dismissals come within the meaning of 'redundancy' in the Act of 1967 then, regardless of their entitlements under the Act of 1977, the dismissed employees are entitled to a statutory redundancy lump payment calculated in accordance with the provisions of the former Act.[19] Depending on the circumstances, they might also be able to claim that they had been unfairly selected for redundancy contrary to section 6(3) of the Unfair Dismissals Act 1977. This subsection provides that, if the

17. UD 56/1994 (reported at [1995] E.L.R. 160).
18. [2011] IEHC 279; [2012] E.L.R. 70, 72.
19. Subject to each individual employee satisfying the service and other conditions of the Act of 1967, Schedule 3 to that Act and the Redundancy Payments (Lump Sum) Regulations 2004 (S.I. No. 695 of 2004) provide that the amount of the lump sum shall be equivalent to the aggregate of:

selection of an employee for dismissal for redundancy resulted wholly or mainly from the employee's membership of a trade union or from his or her race, colour, sexual orientation, age or pregnancy or was in contravention of a collectively agreed procedure, then the dismissal is deemed to be an unfair dismissal.[20]

The opening up of the Irish labour market in May 2004, by permitting direct access by citizens of the then ten accession States, gave rise to concerns about 'the possibility of the collective compulsory replacement of workers by lower paid workers from those states'.[21]

Accordingly, and to assuage the concerns of the trade unions, legislation designed to deal with so-called exceptional collective redundancies was enacted in 2007.[22] Section 4 of this Act provides that proposed dismissals would constitute 'exceptional collective redundancies' if the dismissal was one of a number of dismissals that, together, would constitute 'collective redundancies' as defined by section 6 of the Act of 1977 and:

(a) the dismissals concerned were effected on a compulsory basis;
(b) the dismissed employees were, or are to be, replaced, at the same location or elsewhere in the State, (except where the employer has an existing operation with established terms and conditions) by:

(a) the product of two weeks normal weekly remuneration (capped at EUR 600) and the number of years of continuous employment, and
(b) a sum equivalent to the employee's normal weekly remuneration (capped at EUR 600).

It is customary for employers, particularly those that are unionised, to agree to pay those employees who are made redundant an *ex gratia* sum over and above their statutory entitlement. The annual review of severance settlements for 2014 published in *Industrial Relations News* (IRN 15, 23 April 2015, pp. 21-29) instances Diageo offering its administrative staff eight weeks' pay per year of service plus statutory entitlements, Pallas Foods offering three weeks' pay per year of service plus statutory entitlements and ACC Bank offering five and a half weeks pay per year of service inclusive of statutory entitlements. Their annual review of severance settlements for 2015 instances Bulmers offering six and a half weeks pay per year of service, inclusive of statutory entitlements, capped at EUR 150,000 or two years' pay whichever was greater: *see Industrial Relations News* (IRN 8, 25 February 2016, pp. 16-21). In their review of severance settlements for the first eight months of 2016, it is noted that, while severance terms in some firms held up, others were offering terms lower than historic precedents such as Intel whose severance package was five weeks pay per year of service in contrast to its 2009 package of six weeks pay per years of service: see *Industrial Relations News* (IRN 37, 13 October 2016, pp. 18-22).

20. Under section 7 of the Unfair Dismissals Act 1977, the redress which may be awarded for an unfair dismissal is reinstatement, re-engagement or compensation (capped at two years gross remuneration calculated in accordance with S.I. No. 287 of 1977).
21. *Per* the Minister of State at the Department of Enterprise, Trade and Employment when introducing the legislation (the Act of 2007) to the Seanad and the Dáil: 186 *Seanad Debates* Col. 1238 and 634 *Dáil Debates* Col. 1572.
22. Protection of Employment (Exceptional Collective Redundancies and Related Matters) Act 2007 ('the Act of 2007') which came into operation on 8 May 2007. Part 2 of this Act (namely sections 4 to 10) had effect only for the three years following commencement unless that period was extended by the Minister. These provisions were extended initially to 7 May 2013, then to 7 May 2016 and then again to 7 May 2019: *see* Protection of Employment (Exceptional Collective Redundancies and Related Matters) Act 2007 (Duration of Part 2) Orders 2010, 2013 and 2016 (S.I. Nos. 197 of 2010, 153 of 2013 and 224 of 2016).

(i) other persons who are, or are to be, directly employed by the employer; or

(ii) other persons whose services are, or are to be, provided to that employer in pursuance of other arrangements;

(c) those other persons perform, or are to perform, essentially the same functions as the dismissed employees; and

(d) the terms and conditions of employment of those other persons are, or are to be, materially inferior to those of the dismissed employees.

The Act of 2007 goes on to provide that a proposal to create collective redundancies may be referred to the Redundancy Panel (a body established by this Act).[23] This body is then empowered, if it so decides, to give a notice in writing to the Minister for Jobs, Enterprise and Innovation requesting the Minister to seek an opinion from the Labour Court as to whether the proposal amounts to 'exceptional collective redundancies'.[24] If the Labour Court subsequently issues an opinion that the proposed dismissals are 'exceptional collective redundancies', and the employer nevertheless proceeds with the dismissals, the compensation awardable is increased to 208 weeks gross salary in the case of an employee who had less than twenty years service and to 260 weeks gross salary in the case of an employee who had more than twenty years service.[25]

§14.03 THE PROCEDURE

Section 9(1) of the Act of 1977[26] provides that, where an employer proposes to create 'collective redundancies', he or she shall, 'with a view to reaching agreement', initiate consultations with 'employees' representatives'.

The term 'employees' representatives' is defined in section 2(1) of the Act of 1977[27] as meaning, in relation to employees who are affected, or are likely to be affected, by proposed collective redundancies:

(a) a trade union, staff association or excepted body with which it has been the practice of the employer to conduct collective bargaining negotiations; or

23. The panel consists of a senior civil servant (as chairman) and nominees from the Irish Congress of Trade Unions and the Irish Business and Employers Confederation: *see* section 5 of the Act of 2007.
24. The panel must be satisfied that the party making the reference had unsuccessfully sought to resolve the matter through established dispute-resolution, or ordinary consultative, procedures; had acted reasonably and not in a manner that had frustrated the possibility of agreement to restructuring, or other changes, necessary to secure the viability of the business and best possible levels of employment and conditions; and had not had recourse to industrial action: *see* section 6(3) of the Act of 2007.
25. *See* section 9 of the Act of 2007. The normal cap on compensation for an unfair dismissal is 104 weeks gross salary: *see* section 7(1)(c)(i) of the Unfair Dismissals Act 1977 (as amended by section 6 of the Unfair Dismissals (Amendment) Act 1993).
26. As amended by Article 7 of the Protection of Employment Order 1996 (S.I. No. 370 of 1996).
27. This definition was substituted by regulation 3 of the European Communities (Protection of Employment) Regulations 2000 (S.I. No. 488 of 2000).

(b) in the absence of such a trade union, staff association or excepted body, a person or persons chosen (under an arrangement put in place by the employer) by such employees from amongst their number to represent them in negotiations with the employer.[28]

Consequently, where a trade union is recognized for collective bargaining purposes, the employer cannot establish alternative or parallel consultation mechanisms drawn directly from representatives of the workforce.

The term 'collective bargaining negotiations' is not defined in the Act of 1977. The term was also used in the Industrial Relations (Amendment) Act 2001[29] and, because it was not defined in that Act either, the Labour Court initially took the view (when hearing complaints under that Act) that the term should be assigned 'the meaning which it would normally bear in an industrial relations context'.[30] Collective bargaining, the Labour Court said, comprehended more than mere negotiation or consultation on individual employment related issues. In *Ryanair Ltd v Labour Court*,[31] however, the Supreme Court said that the Labour Court were incorrect in so interpreting the term. In their view, 'collective bargaining negotiations' in what Geoghegan J. described as a 'non unionised company' did not have to take the same form and adopt the same procedures as would apply in collective bargaining with a trade union.

28. The terms 'trade union', 'staff association' and 'excepted body' are defined as follows in section 2(1) of the Act of 1977 (as amended by S.I. No. 488 of 2000):

> 'trade union' means a trade union which is the holder of a negotiation licence granted under the Trade Union Acts 1941 to 1990;
> 'staff association' means a body of persons all the members of which are employed by the same employer and which carries on negotiations for the fixing of the wages or other conditions of employment of its own members only;
> 'excepted body' has the meaning assigned to it by section 6(3) of the Trade Union Act 1941 (as amended).

29. This Act gave new dispute-settling powers to the Labour Court in cases where it was not the practice of the employer to engage in collective bargaining negotiations. Although this Act cannot be used to force employers to engage in collective bargaining with trade unions, it does provide a measure of protection to employees in employments where pay and conditions are not freely determined by collective bargaining. *See* Doherty, *Representation, Bargaining and the Law: Where Next for the Unions?* 60 N.I.L.Q. 383 (2009); Kerr, *The Trade Union and Industrial Relations Acts* pp. 269-288 (5th ed., Dublin: Round Hall, 2015) pp. 269-288 (5th ed, Dublin: Round Hall, 2015); and Gibbons, 44 I.L.J. 472 (2015).
30. *See Ashford Castle Ltd v. SIPTU* DECP 2/2003 (reported at [2004] E.L.R. 214). The Industrial Relations (Amendment) Act 2015 amends the 2001 Act by defining 'collective bargaining' as comprising 'voluntary engagements or negotiations between any employer or employers' organisations on the one hand and a trade union of workers or excepted body to which this Act applies on the other, with the object of reaching agreement regarding working conditions or terms of employment, or non-employment of workers'. An excepted body to which the Act applies is defined as a body, all of the members of which are employed by the same employer, that is independent and not under the domination or control of the employer. *See Freshways Food Company v. SIPTU* LCR 21242 on this point.
31. [2007] IESC 6; [2007] 4 I.R. 199.

Section 9(2) of the Act of 1977[32] provides that 'consultations' must include the following matters:

(a) the possibility of avoiding the proposed redundancies, reducing the number of employees affected by them or mitigating their consequences by recourse to accompanying social measures aimed, *inter alia*, at aid for redeploying or retraining employees made redundant; and
(b) the basis on which it will be decided which particular employees will be made redundant.

Consultations must be initiated 'at the earliest opportunity and in any event at least 30 days before the first notice of dismissal is given'.[33] The Employment Appeals Tribunal has made it clear that consultations under this section must be 'meaningful'. Merely informing the employees of the employer's decision did not amount to consultation.[34]

The question of precisely when an employer can be said to be proposing to create collective redundancies was considered by the High Court in *Tangney v. Dell Products*.[35] In 2009, the company embarked on a worldwide rationalization and reorganization of its activities which eventually saw the cessation of computer manufacturing in Ireland which had previously been carried out at its premises in Limerick. On 8 January 2009, the employees received a written communication from the company furnishing information as to its plan. On the same day, a staff meeting was held at which the employees were briefed by senior management. Thereafter, the company engaged in a consultation and discussion process with the employees and their designated representatives until 27 March 2009. This process resulted in a number of employees being redeployed, the actual leaving dates for several production lines being changed and there was also a significant improvement in the severance package available to employees.

Twenty-eight of the employees presented a complaint that Dell was in breach of section 9 of the Act of 1977 because what occurred on 8 January 2009 constituted notice of dismissal and, accordingly, that any discussions which took place afterwards came too late to comply with the company's statutory obligations. Birmingham J. identified the question as being whether the required consultation process commenced on 8 January 2009 or whether a breach of section 9 occurred by the reason of the fact that the company made a decision to dismiss the employees prior to that date and merely communicated that decision which had been taken in the absence of consultation.

32. As amended by Article 8 of the Protection of Employment Order 1996 (S.I. No. 370 of 1996) and Regulation 4 of the European Communities (Protection of Employment) Regulations 2000 (S.I. No. 488 of 2000).
33. Section 9(3) of the Act of 1977, as amended by section 12 of the Act of 2007; which amendment was necessitated by the decision of the Court of Justice in Case C-188/03, *Junk v. Kuehnel* [2005] E.C.R. 1-885.
34. *See Stonearch Branch Roadstone Ltd v. O'Brien* PE 1/2003.
35. [2013] IEHC 622; [2014] E.L.R. 61.

The Employment Appeals Tribunal, having been referred to and considered the decision of the Court of Justice in *Akavan*,[36] concluded that the meeting on 8 January 2009 was the commencement of the required consultation process and ruled that the company was not in breach of section 9. The employees appealed to the High Court but the appeal was dismissed on the basis that no point of law had been identified which would provide a basis for overturning the Tribunal's finding of fact that the events of 8 January 2009 did not constitute notice of dismissal. It seemed to Birmingham J. that the Tribunal had taken the view that 'the employer had, as it was obliged to do, embarked on consultation when a strategic commercial decision compelling it to contemplate or plan for collective redundancies had been taken'.

For the purpose of consultations under section 9 of the Act of 1977, the employer concerned is required, by section 10, to supply the employees' representatives with 'all relevant information relating to the proposed redundancies'. Section 10(2) of the Act of 1977 provides that the information supplied must include the following, of which details must be given in writing:

(i) the reasons for the proposed redundancies;
(ii) the number and description of categories of employees whom it is proposed to make redundant;
(iii) the number of employees, and description of categories, normally employed;
(iv) (a) the number (if any) of agency workers to which the Protection of Employees (Temporary Agency Work) Act 2012 applies engaged to work for the employer;
(b) those parts of the employer's business in which those agency workers are, for the time being, working; and
(c) the type of work that those agency workers are engaged to do;
(v) the period during which it is proposed to effect the proposed redundancies;
(vi) the criteria proposed for the selection of the employees to be made redundant; and
(vii) the method of calculating any redundancy payments other than those methods set out in the Redundancy Payments Acts 1967 to 2014 or any other relevant enactment for the time being in force or, subject thereto, in practice.

The Act of 1977 does not specify the degree of particularity as to the reasons for the proposed redundancies but, clearly, there should be sufficient information to enable the employees' representatives to make constructive proposals.

Both sections 9 and 10 of the Act of 1977 apply to an employer irrespective of whether the decision regarding collective redundancies is being taken by the employer or by an undertaking which controls the employer.[37]

36. Case C-44/08, *Akavan Erityisalojen Keskusliitto AEK ry v. Siemens Computers Oy* [2009] E.C.R. 1-8163. Birmingham J. was also referred to, and considered, the subsequent opinion of the Advocate General in Case C-583/10, *United States of America v. Nolan* [2012] I.R.L.R. 1020.
37. *See* section 10A of the Act of 1977, inserted by Article 10 of the Protection of Employment Order 1996 (S.I. No. 370 of 1996). This implements Article 2(4) of Council Directive 98/59/EC. The section further provides that it shall not be a defence on the part of the employer that the

In Case C-235/10, *Claes v. Landsbanki Luxembourg SA*,[38] the Court of Justice confirmed that the obligations to consult and inform applied even where a company had been wound up by a court, with those obligations devolving on the liquidator. So in *Tobin v. OCS Operations Ltd (in liquidation)*[39] an adjudication officer awarded 61 claimants sums ranging between EUR 394 to EUR 3,408 in respect of the liquidators' failure to comply with sections 9 and 10 of the Act of 1977.[40]

Section 10(3) of the Act of 1977 requires the employer, as soon as possible, to supply the Minister for Jobs, Enterprise and Innovation, with copies of all information supplied in writing under section 10(2). Section 12(1) of the Act of 1977 also requires an employer, who proposes to create collective redundancies, to notify the Minister in writing of its proposals 'at the earliest opportunity and in any event at least 30 days before the first dismissal takes effect'.[41] Section 12(3) requires the employer to supply a copy of the notification to the employees' representatives affected who may forward to the Minister in writing any observations they have relating to the notification. Section 15 of the Act of 1977 then provides that, for the purpose of seeking solutions to the problems caused by the proposed redundancies, the employer, if the Minister so requests, is required to enter into consultations with the Minister's authorized officer and to supply such information relating to the redundancies as that officer might reasonably require.

§14.04 SUPPORT MEASURES IN FAVOUR OF WORKERS

To date, Ireland has submitted ten successful applications under the European Globalisation Adjustment Fund (EGF) for co-financing of active labour market measures in support of workers made redundant as a result of the adverse impacts of globalization. All applications established a link between the redundancies and major

---

necessary information had not been provided to the employer by a controlling party, or parties, which took the decision leading to the collective redundancies.

38. [2011] E.C.R. 1-1113.
39. r-157441-pe-15/RG. The decision is noted in *Industrial Relations News* (IRN 7, 18 February 2016).
40. This case concerned the sudden closure of the Clerys Department Store on O'Connell Street in Dublin in June 2015. The particular circumstances of the closure are set out in the Report to Government prepared by the Minister for Business and Employment and available at https://www.djei.ie/en/Publications/Sale-and-Liquidation-of-Clerys-A-Report-to-Government.html (accessed 17 January 2016). *See also* the decision of Twomey J in *Foley v. Workplace Relations Commission* [2016] IEHC 585 at paragraphs 10 and 11.
41. The particulars to be specified by an employer in a notification under this section are prescribed by the Protection of Employment Act 1977 (Notification of Proposed Collective Redundancies) Regulations 1977 (S.I. No. 140 of 1977). The particulars include not just the number and descriptions or categories of employees whom it is proposed to make redundant and the reasons for the proposed collective redundancies but also the date on which consultation with relevant trade unions or staff associations commenced 'and the progress achieved in those consultations to the date of the notification'. Section 12(4) of the Act of 1977, inserted by Article 11 of the Protection of Employment Order 1996 (S.I. No. 370 of 1996), provides that, in the case of collective redundancies arising from the employer's business being terminated following bankruptcy or winding up proceedings or for any other reason as a result of a decision of a court of competent jurisdiction, the person responsible for the affairs of the business need comply with section 12(1) 'only if the Minister so requests'.

structural changes in world trade patterns due to globalization and co-financing of 50% (decreasing from 65% as and from the 1 January 2012) was received from the European Union in respect of the first nine programmes. Matching national funding came from Exchequer and National Training Fund sources.

The first seven programmes encompassed some 14,000 workers and are now closed. The first three programmes completed saw 10,514 individual supports being provided to 3,894 of the 4,628 affected workers. These involved a range of guidance, education, training and enterprise supports. In the case of the Dell computer manufacturing plant, 2,606 workers benefitted from an expenditure amounting to EUR 13.62 million out of a possible EUR 22.82 million fund. In the case of the Waterford Crystal factory, 532 workers benefitted from an expenditure amounting to EUR 3.09 million out of a possible EUR 3.96 million fund. In the case of the SR Technics aircraft maintenance facility at Dublin Airport, 756 workers benefitted from an expenditure amounting to EUR 4.5 million out of a possible EUR 11.46 million fund.[42] The seventh programme – that for the Talk Talk call centre facility in Waterford – provided 350 workers with additional employment services supports and advice, training courses, bespoke graduate programmes at Waterford Institute of Technology and training grants from a fund of EUR 5.4 million.[43]

The eighth and ninth programmes concern 171 workers made redundant at the Andersen Ireland fashion jewellery manufacturing plant in Rathkeale, Co. Limerick and 427 workers made redundant at Lufthansa Technik Airmotive Ireland's aircraft maintenance, repair and overhaul facility at Rathcoole, Co. Dublin. The only open programme concerns 108 workers made redundant at PWA International's aircraft maintenance, repair and overhaul facility at Rathcoole, Co. Dublin.[44]

In these three applications, the required 500 redundancy threshold normally required for an EGF application was not met, but sufficiently strong cases were made that the redundancies were of an exceptional nature impacting significantly on the local and regional economy.

§14.05 JUDICIAL CONTROL AND SANCTIONS

The enforcement mechanism established by the Act of 1977 (as amended) is a mixture of criminal and civil sanctions, neither of which have proved effective in practice.

Section 11 provides that an employer who fails to initiate consultations under section 9 or who fails to comply with section 10 is guilty of an offence and is liable on

42. Details of the first six programmes are set out in the Department of Education's Value for Money Review: *see* https://www.education.ie/en/Publications/Value-For-Money-Reviews/egf_review_aug2012.pdf (accessed 28 May 2015).
43. Details of this programme are set out at https:/www.egf.ie/egf-programmes/closed-programmes/talk-talk-application/ (accessed 28 May 2015).
44. Details of these three programmes are set out at https:/www.egf.ie/egf-programmes/open-programmes (accessed 1 January 2016). In the case of the PWA International application, the total cost of the proposed active labour market measures is EUR 737,156. The application for 60% funding from the EGF was approved by the European Commission on 6 November 2015: *see* COM (2015) 555 final. The European Parliament's and the Council's approval was given on 16 December 2015.

summary conviction to a fine not exceeding EUR 5,000. A similar penalty is provided by section 13 in respect of an employer who fails to notify the Minister contrary to section 12.[45]

Section 14 provides that collective redundancies shall not take effect before the expiry of the period of thirty days beginning on the date of the relevant notification under section 12. Where collective redundancies are effected by an employer before the expiry of that thirty-day period, the employer is guilty of an offence and is liable on conviction on indictment to a fine not exceeding EUR 250,000.[46] The section, however, does not state that any purported dismissals before the end of the thirty-day period are void. Consequently, it is uncertain whether the High Court would grant an interlocutory injunction restraining a breach of what appears to be a mandatory requirement of the Act.[47]

Section 22 of the Act of 1977 provides that, where an employer is convicted of an offence under either section 11 or section 14, the employer may plead, in mitigation of the penalty for that offence, that there were 'substantial reasons related to his business which made it impracticable for him to comply with the section under which the offence was committed'. The combination of 'substantial reasons' and 'impracticability' suggests that employers who are going into the process of bankruptcy or liquidation cannot avoid their responsibilities under the Act of 1977 by being unreasonably late in coming to a decision. This section, however, does not apply to a conviction under section 13 of the Act of 1977.

Section 41 of the Workplace Relations At 2015 enables an employee to present a complaint to the Director General of the Workplace Relations Commission that the employer has contravened either section 9 and/or section 10 of the Act of 1977.[48] Section 11A of the Act of 1977[49] empowers an adjudication officer of the Commission to require the employer to comply with the relevant provision and/or require payment of compensation. That compensation, however, is required to be of an amount that is just and equitable having regard to all the circumstances but is limited to a maximum

45. No sanction is prescribed in respect of a failure to comply with section 15. An offence under section 11 is a 'relevant offence' for the purposes of section 36 of the Workplace Relations Act 2015 which empowers a labour inspector to issue a 'fixed payment notice'.
46. Section 14(3) of the Act of 1977 provides that subsections (1) and (2) do not apply in the case of collective redundancies arising from the employer's business being terminated following bankruptcy or winding up proceedings or for any other reason as a result of a decision of a court of competent jurisdiction.
47. Although, to obtain such an injunction, a plaintiff is only required to show that there is a serious question of law or fact to be tried pending trial, the High Court also has to consider whether damages would be an adequate remedy and, overall, where lies the balance of convenience: *see Campus Oil Ltd v. Minister for Industry and Energy (No. 2)* [1983] I.R. 88.
48. Prior to 1 October 2015, a complaint was made, in the first instance, to a rights commissioner with an appeal to the Employment Appeals Tribunal. Under the Workplace Relations Act 2015, the Director General of the Commission refers the complaint to one of his/her adjudication officers for hearing and an appeal lies to the Labour Court. For an analysis of the changes brought about by the 2015 Act *see* Kerr, *The Workplace Relations Reform Project 7 European Employment Law Journal* 125 (2016).
49. Section 11B of the Act of 1977 empowers the Labour Court on appeal to 'affirm, vary or set aside' the adjudication officer's decision. Both sections were inserted by section 52 of the Workplace Relations Act 2015.

of four weeks' remuneration.[50] In *Lakelands Nursing Home Ltd v. Costelloe*,[51] the Employment Appeals Tribunal awarded compensation limited to one week's remuneration because the company's failure to comply with section 9 was 'technical in nature only' in that consultations would not have changed the outcome in any way.

Appeals from decisions of the Labour Court can be brought, on a point of law only, to the High Court (whose decision is 'final and conclusive').[52]

Labour Inspectors also have considerable powers under section 17 of the Act of 1977 and section 27 of the Workplace Relations Act 2015 to enter premises, require the production of records and make any examination or enquiry necessary for ascertaining whether the Act of 1977 has been complied with. The scope of these powers was considered by the High Court in *Foley v. Workplace Relations Commission*.[53] The applicant submitted that the premises to which an Inspector is allowed to gain entry under section 27(1) of the 2015 Act must be a place of work of the employees the subject of the investigation. Twomey J, however, said that the Inspector was entitled to enter 'any place of work or premises' that he or she had reasonable grounds for believing is being 'used in connection with the employment of persons'. These expressions were very expansive and supported the Inspectors' interpretation that they had the right to enter the applicant's premises on the basis that it was a place of work of persons, even though it was not the place of work of the employees, the subject of the investigation.

§14.06 CONCLUSION

At the height of Ireland's economic crisis, there were 77,001 redundancies notified in 2009, reducing to 58,731 in 2010 and to 49,762 in 2011.[54] Of those, it would appear that only the twenty-eight Dell employees involved in the *Tangney* proceedings instituted complaints concerning breaches of the Act of 1977. In large measure this can be attributed to the low visibility which the Act of 1977 enjoys, which is undoubtedly due to the fact that, for the first twenty-three years of its operation, the only sanction for failure to inform and/or consult was by means of a criminal prosecution of the employer; a sanction rarely availed of. Originally, the maximum fine on summary

50. Remuneration is calculated in accordance with the Unfair Dismissals (Calculation of Weekly Remuneration) Regulations 1977 (S.I. No. 287 of 1977) and includes 'average weekly overtime earnings'.
51. PE 1/2013.
52. The only case to have gone to the High Court is *Tangney v. Dell Products* [2013] IEHC 622; [2014] E.L.R. 61 discussed *supra*. The circumstances in which the High Court will overturn a decision of a specialist tribunal such as the Labour Court were considered by Noonan J. in *Nano Nagle School v. Daly* [2015] IEHC 785 who emphasised that, in considering whether to allow an appeal, the High Court must consider whether that body based its decision on an identifiable error of law or on an unsustainable finding of fact.
53. [2016] IEHC 585.
54. In 2014, that figure had dropped to 6,883. The previous lowest figure was 7,793 in 1996. For 2015, the figure was 4,324 and for the first eight months of 2016, the total number of redundancies notified was 3,323: *see* http://www.welfare.ie/en/Pages/Actual-Redundancies---General-Statistics.aspx (accessed 21 October 2016).

conviction was IRP 500 (EUR 634.87) which was then increased, in 2000, to IRP 1,500 (EUR 1,904.61).[55] The current fine of EUR 5,000 was set in 2007.[56]

To date, the only reported prosecution under the Act of 1977 was against Dunnes Stores (Newbridge) Ltd in 1992 and fines totalling IRP 300 (EUR 380.92) were imposed on the company with two IRP 50 (EUR 63.49) fines imposed on one of the company's directors.[57]

Although a process whereby individual workers can bring complaints that their employer is in breach of its information and/or consultation obligations has been in place since December 2000,[58] it is hardly ever availed of. This is undoubtedly due to the fact that, by the time the complaint comes on for hearing, it will be too late for an order requiring the employer to comply with the relevant provision of the Act of 1977. Furthermore, the compensation that may be awarded is limited to four weeks' remuneration. This cannot be described as a meaningful sanction.[59]

It is also clear that much better use could be made of EGF funds which were underspent by 40% in the case of the Dell workers and by 61% in the case of the SR Technics workers.

§14.07 AFTERWORD

Following the sudden closure of the Clerys Department store in June 2015,[60] the Department of Jobs, Enterprise and Innovation commissioned a twin-track examination of protections in law for employees with a particular focus on ways of ensuring that limited liability and corporate restructuring were not used to avoid a company's obligations to its employees. All of the staff of Clerys, most of whom had accrued significant service, were made redundant when the company by which they were employed became insolvent and was placed in liquidation. The principal disquiet stemmed from the fact that the insolvency was preceded by a corporate restructuring which involved a separation of the enterprise into two different companies; one holding the principal property asset and the other operating the business.

55. By the European Communities (Protection of Employment) Regulations 2000 (S.I. No. 488 of 2000).
56. By section 13 of the Act of 2007.
57. *See Industrial Relations News* (IRN 36, 24 September 1992).
58. Originally under Regulation 6 of the European Communities (Protection of Employment) Regulations 2000 (S.I. No. 488 of 2000) and now under section 41 of the Workplace Relations Act 2015.
59. This cap on compensation is the same as that imposed by section 7 of the Terms of Employment (Information) Act 1994 (transposing Council Directive 91/533/EEC) for failure to give a written statement of the particulars of the terms of an employee's employment and is significantly lower than the cap of twenty weeks' remuneration imposed by section 32 of the Maternity Protection Act 1994 (transposing Council Directive 92/85/EEC) and by section 21 of the Parental Leave Act 1998 (transposing what is now Council Directive 2010/18/EU). The normal cap on compensation for breach of employment rights is two years remuneration: *see* section 27 of the Organisation of Working Time Act 1997 (implementing what is now Council Directive 2003/88/EC) and section 14 of the Protection of Employees (Fixed Term Work) Act 2003 (implementing Council Directive 1999/70/EC).
60. Referred to at fn 40 *supra*.

As a result of the transfer of the property asset, the monies owing to the employees (such as redundancy lump sums, payment in *lieu* of notice, accrued holiday entitlements) will have to be paid out of the Social Insurance Fund.[61]

As part of the examination process, an expert group[62] was appointed to examine the legal protections available for employees' interests in situations where assets of significant value were separated from the employer in advance of liquidation. The stated focus of their examination was on 'how the legitimate interests of employees could more effectively be safeguarded in situations in which collective redundancies arise from the liquidation of an employer following corporate restructuring in which assets that might otherwise have been available to protect those interests are transferred to a related person'.

The expert group delivered its report on 11 March 2016, and it was published the following month.[63] It recommended that consideration be given to deleting the exemption at section 14(4) of the Act of 1977 from the prohibition against the giving effect to collective redundancies until the expiry of thirty days after the notification to the Minister in circumstances of insolvency. As a consequence, consideration should also be given to expressly providing that a dismissal in contravention of section 14(1) was legally null and void.

Another proposal was to amend the Act of 1977 so as to provide that, where a decision is in contemplation by a person in relation to an asset of significant value over which it exercises control and it is known, or ought to be known, that collective redundancies will arise in a related person in consequence of that decision, if implemented, that person must notify the employer, who in turn is obliged to commence the thirty-day consultation period. This proposal should ensure that if a 'related person'[64] intends to refuse to renew a lease or intends to sell the property in which the employer's business is transacted there must at that stage be a period of consultation where it is known (or could reasonably be known) that this decision will result in collective redundancies.

The expert group were also of the opinion that the maximum compensation that might be awarded for a breach of sections 9 and 10 of the Act of 1977 – currently four weeks' remuneration – did not provide adequate redress and did not have a sufficient deterrent effect. Consideration should therefore be given to increasing the amount that could be awarded to a maximum of two years' remuneration.

61. Established pursuant to the Protection of Employees (Employers' Insolvency) Acts 1984 to 2012 (implementing Parliament and Council Directive 2008/94/EC).
62. The group consisted of the then Chairman of the Labour Court, Kevin Duffy, and a company law expert, Nessa Cahill BL.
63. Available at http://www.djei.ie/en/Publications/Duffy-Cahill-Report.html (accessed 25 April 2016).
64. It is suggested that the definition of 'related companies' in section 2(1) of the Companies Act 2014 be adapted to define a 'related person'.

CHAPTER 15

Collective Dismissals in Italy

Filippo Curcuruto

§15.01 INTRODUCTION

The first rules and regulations on collective dismissals in Italy were not dictated by law but rather by the social partners. The notion of collective redundancies is already, though indirectly, present in the agreement called *Accordo Interconfederale* (lit. Inter-union Agreement) of 7 August 1947, on the establishment and functioning of internal Committees, aimed at regulating individual dismissals through special restrictions by forcing the employer to justify it, yet excluding such an obligation in cases of collective redundancies, defined as the dismissal due to a need for reduction or conversion of the operation or work. The very first regulation on collective dismissal came with the Inter-union agreement of 20 December 1950 regarding dismissals due to staff reductions, renewed with marginal changes fifteen years later with the Inter-union agreement of 5 May 1965.[1] We would still have to wait nearly thirty years for the first law on redundancies, Law 223/1991.

The aforementioned agreements were intended to regulate the hypothetical situation where 'the management' considers it necessary to reduce the 'number of staff of the company for reduction or conversion of the operation or business',[2] this latter terminology being taken up again in Article 24 of the above-mentioned Law 223/1991. The general lines of these agreements deserve to be briefly recalled because in them we can find some of the rules later transformed into legal standards codified by law.

As a matter of fact, the Agreement of 1950 provided for a mandatory consultation phase between the company and the union and, according to its result, an attempt at conciliation aimed at avoiding layoffs or, in case of a negative outcome, at determining

1. GHERA, GARILLI, GAROFALO, *Diritto del lavoro* (TORINO, 2015), 572.
2. On the agreements and the events related to them, *see* extensively: GIGLIO, *I licenziamenti collettivi* (MILANO, 2014), 3 and fol.

the criteria on the basis of which workers to be made redundant would be chosen. These criteria would be modified in the subsequent agreement of 1965 and, later, implemented in the mentioned Law of 1991.[3]

The Agreement of 1965 confirmed the requirement for the company to activate a procedure of trade-union conciliation and gave this phase a more precise structure. First of all, the company was compelled to communicate the intention to dismiss and indicate the reasons, the number of workers involved and the time needed for implementation. After this informative step, the union would have the opportunity to request a meeting aimed at analysing the grounds for the reduction and possible means to avoid it. A negative conclusion of this stage – due to failure in reaching an agreement or because of the expiration of the term of twenty-five days since the communication – allowed the dismissal, provided that three criteria had been met, namely the technical and production requirements, seniority and dependants, all at the same time, as later confirmed by Article 5 paragraph 1 of Law 223/1991.

The scope of both agreements was, on the one hand, conditioned by the size of the company and, on the other hand, limited to companies in the industrial sector. The agreements bound companies in this sector to the minimum number of twenty-five employees, and their contractual nature estopped extension by analogy to different sectors, since they were contractual clauses and not legal provisions.[4]

The protection of workers in cases of collective dismissals was hence entrusted to the collective source. This situation did not undergo any changes, not even with the entry into force of the first general law on the protection of workers against dismissal, Law 604 of 15 July 1966. The matter of collective redundancies was in fact expressly excluded from the scope of the new legislation (Article 11, last paragraph of the mentioned law) as this type of dismissal was conceived as the manifestation of an entrepreneurial power which should dispense with the decision of the judge.[5] More specifically, collective dismissals were regarded as the manifestation of the entrepreneur's organizational power, ascribable to the right to free economic initiative protected by Article 41 of the Constitution.[6]

At the same time, however, the legislative choices were intended to prevent cases of staff reduction and to keep the employment relationship alive under a suspension regime. On the one hand, in fact, financial support to the workers' income was guaranteed during the period of restructuring of the company through the intervention of the fund for laid-off workers (the Italian *Cassa Integrazione Guadagni*, CIG, Law

3. The Agreement of 1950, (Article 2 e) made reference to: (1) technical and production requirements; (2) seniority; (3) dependants; (4) economic situation of the laid-off-to-be's family. The following Agreement of 5 May 1965 (Article 2) reduced the number of selection criteria to (3) and reworded them with the same terminology later used by Article 5 paragraph 1 of the cited Law 223/1991, which refers to the technical and production requirements, seniority, and dependants.
4. Cf. MAMMONE, La regolazione dei licenziamenti collettivi: itinerari legislativi e orientamenti giurisprudenziali, in COSIO, CURCURUTO E FOGLIA, Il licenziamento collettivo in Italia nell'ambito del diritto dell' Unione Europea (MILANO, 2016), 114.
5. MAMMONE, 113.
6. GHERA-GARILLI-GAROFALO, 573.

1115/1968). On the other hand, other procedures were provided for with the aim of enabling the passage of the workers from the enterprise facing difficulties to other enterprises (Law 675/1977), and the dismissals for staff reductions were suspended until the conclusion of the procedure.

When EEC Directive 75/129 of 17 February 1975 on the approximation of Member States' legislations on collective redundancies entered into force, the Italian system was thus characterized by the presence of rules intended not so much to regulate, as rather to avoid collective redundancies or, in any case, to try and guarantee the continuity of employment. Most likely, this situation was one of the reasons for the long delay of Italy in transposing the Directive of 1975. The Italian system is certainly characterized by a tight link between mobility procedures, which are governed by two above-mentioned regulations, and collective redundancies.[7]

Yet the non-applicability of the individual dismissal's rules and regulations to collective dismissals, expressly enshrined in the cited Law 604/1966, was mainly deemed as a gap to be necessarily filled with a law. The Directive of 1975 could not be of help since the jurisprudence did not consider it as a source of law but as a mere recommendation to Member States,[8] as it had not yet been transposed into national law.

The decisive push to transpose the directive came from the sentence against the Italian State for remaining in default on the obligation to comply once the deadline had expired. The sentence was passed by the Court of Justice in the judgment of 8 June 1982, Case 91/81, followed by a subsequent sentence (judgment of 26 November 1985, Case 131/84) for prolonging the non-fulfilment after the first judgment.

In this regard, it is worth pointing out that in the first of two judgments the Court fully detected that the protection of the workers in case of collective dismissal was basically entrusted to the inter-union Agreements, and that this represented insufficient protection. Layoffs in the agricultural and commercial sectors were, in fact, not considered and there was no requirement for the active involvement of the public authority, to which the project of redundancies was not notified.[9]

A subsequent sentence[10] was passed by the Court of Justice to sanction the non-inclusion of redundancies made by those employers who, during their activities, did not pursue profit making. These redundancies would need to be included among those to which the law on collective redundancies should apply.

Finally, a recent judgment of the Court of Justice[11] has once again convicted Italy for excluding executives from the scope of the protective rules.

7. MAMMONE, 118.
8. Court of Cass. 6736/1986; Court of Cass. 5601/1990; MAMMONE, 115.
9. MAMMONE, 116; GIGLIO, 10: 35.
10. *See* decision C-32/02/2003 following which the legislative change of Article 24 of Law 223/1991 were carried out with the introduction of paragraph 1 b providing for the applicability of the provisions regarding collective dismissal for entrepreneurs also to private non-entrepreneur employers.
11. *See* decision C-596/12/2014 discussed below.

§15.02 THE COLLECTIVE DISMISSAL: THE CASE. GENERAL REMARKS

Collective dismissals, as now regulated by Law 223/1991,[12] fall in the layoffs due to reasons unrelated to the employee and instead ascribable to the organization of the enterprise, together with individual dismissal for objective reasons (defined by law as the redundancies determined by 'reasons pertaining to production, work organization and its normal functioning': Article 3 second part of Law 604/1966).

What makes the two situations different from one another is primarily the repetitiveness of the phenomena from which the need for collective redundancies arises. The necessity for shrinking the workforce is a regular story as a result either of the enterprise's failure or even just because of the increasingly less need for labour. Very often automation processes actually allow getting the same amount of product with fewer workers.[13] Another difference is also in the social importance of collective dismissal, bound to negatively affect a number of workers concentrated in certain geographic areas.

In the event that leads to collective redundancies, several conflicting interests are therefore involved and the authority of the employer to determine the level of labour force in his/her own business is at stake, this being an expression – as already recalled – of the freedom of economic initiative, also guaranteed at the constitutional level (Article 41 of the Constitution), as recognized by the case law (Sentence no. 191 of 1985 by the Constitutional Court) against which the interest of the worker to keeps his/her job arises.

Since the organizational choices through which the freedom of economic initiative is expressed are unappealable and cannot be obstructed, a body of contractual or legal standards was arranged in order to avoid layoffs or, at least, to reduce the number of workers involved.[14] These rules and regulations aim at offering protection to workers in a particularly critical moment. However, they come up against the difficulty to oppose business decisions, which become difficult to change at a certain point.[15]

None of these profiles can be found in the individual dismissal, even though they are not related to reasons regarding the worker. In this case, the conflict of interests concerns only the employer and the worker affected.

This is why collective redundancies have been governed by a complex and intricate specific set of regulations – both in terms of collective clauses first, and by a set of legal provisions then – different from those that would apply to a sum of individual dismissals, even when each of these is based on reasons unrelated to the individual worker.

---

12. *See* below.
13. GIGLIO, 1.
14. VALLEBONA, Istituzioni di diritto del lavoro, II, (PADOVA, 2015), 637.
15. DEL PUNTA, 670.

[A] The Features of the Collective Dismissal

Law 223 of 23 July 1991, which introduced rules and regulations concerning all cases of over-staffing, has implemented Directive 75/129/EEC of 17 February 1975 in Italy.[16] On the one hand, in fact, it has regulated the case of those enterprises that – during the support period of the 'extraordinary' fund for laid-off workers (also CIGS) and suspension from work of certain employees – were not able to guarantee the re-employment of the suspended workers. On the other hand, it has considered the possibility of staff reduction because of a choice of the entrepreneur independent of the previous intervention of the CIGS.

In both cases, it is possible to lay off redundant staff, and the procedure for their dismissal is the same. With regards to terminology, however, we speak of 'placement into mobility' (lit. *collocamento in mobilità*) in the first case, and of 'collective dismissal for staff reduction' in the second one. The most significant difference between the two subjects is that in the 'placement into mobility' there is no requirement for a minimum number of layoffs in a given unit of time in order to make it mandatory to start off the procedure. This has therefore to be set up also in the event of the dismissal of an individual worker who cannot be otherwise reinstated.[17]

Article 24 of Law 223/1991 decrees that companies, which employ more than fifteen employees and face a reduction or conversion of their operation or of their business, and which intend to carry out at least five redundancies over a period of 120 days in each production unit or in several production units within the territory of the same province[18] as a consequence of the aforementioned reductions or conversions, should activate the procedure provided for in the foregoing Articles 4 and 5 of the Law, that is to say the procedure of collective dismissal.

Collective dismissal therefore implies the presence of a core element, which is made up of the aforementioned reduction or conversion and of getting through a triple access threshold: dimension, time and space.[19]

The regulatory reference to 'reduction or conversion of operation or business' is not, however, to be interpreted as a need for stable reduction of the economic activity nor for changes to the material structures of the company.[20] The reduction or conversion may result from the decision to change the organization of production even only by reducing the work force when this has a real and not merely temporary impact.[21] If layoffs are related to the need to rationalize the productive activity and are

16. GHERA-GARILLI-GAROFALO, 576.
17. TATARELLI, 420: 3. The difference between the two branches regarding the number of laid-off workers comes from the lack of reference to Article 4 paragraph 1 of Law 223/1991, which regulates the 'placement into mobility' of those workers who result to be redundant during or at the end of a period of CIG (fund for laid-off workers), giving the company the right to dismiss in Article 24 paragraph 1 of the same law defining the minimum number of workers and the reference period for collective redundancies, independent of an earlier period of CIG.
18. The Province is the administrative unit, which encompasses all the municipalities present on the territory.
19. TATARELLI, 421.
20. *See* Court of Cass. 24566/2011.
21. *See* Court of Cass. 84/2009.

then connected to an increase or the prospect of an increase – instead of being connected to a decrease in the productive activity – they should be considered as a collective and subject to the relevant procedure, provided they reach the threshold numbers prescribed by law.

This criterion shows all its importance when applied to the so-called technological dismissal.

In this case, the company is not in crisis, it does not suffer from revenue declines but is able to maintain the achieved production levels with less workforce supply because of/thanks to the technological innovations adopted. Even in this case the company, by activating the collective dismissal procedure, may initiate a generalized reduction in the workforce with real and not temporary impact [even if only] on the [single] element of the staff employed.

The mentioned law (Article 24 of Law 223/1991) considers the necessity of dismissal as a result of the reduction or conversion of the operation or business. This does not mean, however, that in assessing the legitimacy of the dismissal one can scrutinize the reasons for the reduction or conversion.

The law connects the decision of reducing or transforming the operation or business and of carrying out redundancies which result from this, to the requirement of activating a specific procedure but it does not assign any relevance to the reasons because of which the company intends to implement these changes: the changes must be real but the reasons why they are adopted have no importance to deciding whether the dismissal is legitimate or not. Corporate policy choices leading to a reduction or conversion can be erroneous or with no justification whatsoever (it does not matter whether the decision of transforming or reducing the operation is economically wrong, totally unjustified, or even insane). The dismissal cannot be challenged on the ground that the decision to reduce or transform the operation and consequently decrease the number of employees is unjustified.

Therefore, the downsizing of the company is not to be disputed in court. The control over it is instead exercised in advance, by subjecting the power/right to cancel of the employer to certain formal accomplishments, and by involving the union and the public administration in the affair. As previously mentioned (*see* above), collective redundancies are recurrent and of considerable social importance phenomena, characterized by the conflict between the interest of the individual worker to preserve his/her jobs and the entrepreneur's right to make organizational decisions which are deemed to be the most appropriate. It was therefore considered appropriate to involve the union and the public administration in the matter with the task of seeking solutions aimed to avoid layoffs or to reduce their number and to cope with their consequences.

The following control in court relates to the legitimacy of the notified individual layoffs at the conclusion of the procedure.

In particular, it concerns:

(a) the effect of the reduction or conversion and the existence of a causal link between the reduction or conversion and the decision to dismiss, which means making sure that the layoffs have affected employees involved in the reduction or conversion and not those who were not involved;

(b) the observance of the procedure;
(c) the compliance with the selection criteria;
(d) the conditions of effect of the withdrawal.

The consequences arising from the lack of one of these conditions will be discussed later.

In addition to the dismissal due to a reduction or conversion of operation or business, Law 223/1991 Article 24 paragraph 2 considers as collective and subject to the relevant procedure also the redundancies stemming from the termination – featuring effectiveness and finality – of the company's business or of the work of the non-entrepreneur employer.[22] This is explained by considering the possible social security or welfare benefits granted to the collectively dismissed workers. The law has considerable importance when one bears in mind that the termination was previously considered as a matter different from the reduction of operation and therefore allowed only to notify multiple individual dismissals on a justified objective ground.[23]

The collective procedure is also needed in case of a termination of the business due to judicial decisions, as in bankruptcy proceedings.[24] (Issue of business closing-down resulting from judicial decisions (Article 3 paragraph 2 of the Directive provides in this case for a possible exception to the obligation to notify the public authority). Examine the national/Italian solution.)

§15.03 PREREQUISITE REGARDING THE EMPLOYER

[A] Issues Concerning the Dimensional Profile of the Enterprise in General

Article 24 paragraph 1 of Law 223/1991 makes the provisions on collective dismissal applicable to 'enterprises employing more than 15 employees'. To determine whether this number is reached the entire corporate complex has to be taken into consideration, regardless of its possible single territorial extensions, since the law makes reference to the enterprise without further specification. Accordingly, it has no importance whether in each of these extensions there are a number of employees below the aforementioned threshold.

The law lacks specific provisions about the time period to be taken into account in order to assess the number of workers employed.

In this regard, it is considered mostly useless to make reference to the time of activation of the procedure or to the time the layoffs are notified, because both of these criteria might be applied in a manner aimed at evading the law obligations. In particular, taking into consideration the time of activation of the procedure would make the applicability of the legislation random. On the contrary, we usually make use

22. Article 24 paragraph 2 of Law 223/1991.
23. AMOROSO, DI CERBO, MARESCA, Diritto del lavoro – Lo Statuto dei lavoratori e la disciplina dei licenziamenti (MILANO, 2015), 1807.
24. Article 3 paragraph 3 of Law 223/1991. Court of Cass. 19405/2011; Court of Cass. 12465/2004.

of the criterion of the average employment of more than fifteen employees, in the semester preceding the date of notification of the layoffs, as resulting from the company's organization chart and without taking into account incidental and occasional staff reductions. The legislation on collective redundancies is therefore also applicable to the enterprise that at the time of dismissal has fewer than sixteen employees but has exceeded – in the previous months – its dimensional limit. The criteria set out in Article 1 of Law 223/1991 to determine which enterprises may benefit from the intervention of wage subsidy is thus applied in a systematic way.[25]

Speaking of the dimensional prerequisite, a peculiar issue arises when a single entrepreneurial subject is organized in several corporate facilities employing more than fifteen employees altogether. When one of these facilities, with less than fifteen employees, carries out more/a certain number of layoffs in the time unit considered by law, it must be determined whether that facility is obliged to the mentioned collective procedure.

A positive response implies the determination of a single centre entrusted with the company's interests. To ascertain its existence, we have to consider the fundamental criteria formulated by law in this regard, such as the uniqueness of the organizational and productive structure, the integration among the activities of the various facilities, the existence of a single management oriented to a common goal, the undifferentiated performance of work tasks in favour of the facilities of the group. Whenever these conditions are satisfied, the collective dismissal procedure is mandatory. Those advocating the collective character of the dismissal also have also to prove the existence of such indications.

[B] The Non-entrepreneur Employers

Article 4 of Law 223/1991 makes reference to the 'enterprise' admitted to the extraordinary treatment of wage supplement and Article 24 of the same law considers the 'enterprises' with more than fifteen employees. These references have technical features and lead to the conclusion that – according to the original wording of the cited law – the dismissal procedure concerns entrepreneur employers only.

However, as previously said, the Court of Justice considered this limitation to be non-compliant with the Directive, which refers generically to employers, without any distinction, and covers only specific exclusions. Legislative Decree no. 110 of 8 April 2004, intended to comply with the decision of the Court, provided for the extension of the most significant provisions of Law 223/1991 to the non-entrepreneur employers as well, provided they exceed the numerical threshold of fifteen employees.

These employers will therefore be subjected to the regulations on the prerequisites of collective dismissal, those on the consultation with union representatives, those on the criteria for selecting workers to be dismissed (criteria established in the union agreements and subsidiary legal criteria); the restrictive provisions on the

25. *See* Court of Cass. 1465/2011; *see also* Court of Cass. 12592/1999.

dismissal of female employees; the provisions on the consequences of the errors of the dismissal.

As to the latter [provisions], it must be recalled that the cited Legislative Decree 110/2004 has identified – within the category of non-entrepreneur employers – a subcategory of employers 'who perform non-profit activity [of a nature that can be] political, in the unions, cultural, educational or [dealing with] religion or worship'. These employers are still subject to the regulations on the procedure for collective dismissal, without being required to reinstate the employee in case of the procedure is unlawful. This regulation is consistent with the same exclusion provided for in the individual dismissal ordered by one of these organizations,[26] finding grounds in the choice of not obliging the employer who operates in sectors characterized by a specific social value to forcibly resume cooperation with workers possibly unconnected with the organization's trends.[27]

§15.04 ISSUES REGARDING PARTICULAR CATEGORIES OF WORKERS

[A] The Issue of Executives

Workers with managerial status have been excluded, under Italian law, from the application of the regulations of Law 1991/223 concerning collective dismissal. According to Article 4 of the law, in fact, [the subjects] to be considered collectively dismissible were only those workers who were recipients of mobility allowance under Article 16 of the law, and therefore only the workers, employees and executives. Executives were explicitly included by Article 24 paragraph 1 of the cited law in the minimum number of employees necessary to make the rules on collective dismissal applicable. On the contrary, they were left out of the minimum number of workers making up the prerequisite for the collective dismissal procedure, and this was even for when the grounds for their dismissal was the same economic crisis that had led to the exclusion of the other non-executive employees.[28]

At the root of this choice there was the consideration that executives were excluded from the application of the rules on individual dismissals introduced by Law 604 of 15 July 1966, therefore it would have been inconsistent to extend to them protection of the regulations on collective dismissal. In addition, the element of trust peculiar to the managerial employment contract would have been hard to reconcile with the protective provisions laid down for this kind of layoffs.[29]

By the judgment of 14 February 2014, Case C-596/2012, the Court of Justice found, however, the Italian regulations contrary to Directive 59/1998, so – by the enforcement of that judgment – Article 24 of Law 223/1991 was amended by Law 161 of 30 October 2014, which introduced paragraph 1d on the collective layoffs of executives.

26. VALLEBONA, 672.
27. TATARELLI, 136.
28. TATARELLI, 15.
29. GIGLIO, 43.

At present, executives are thus to be considered both in the number of employees needed to reach the dimensional threshold and in the number of those 5 layoffs making up the prerequisite for the collective dismissal procedure.

In the collective dismissal involving executives, we mostly apply the same regulations laid down for collective redundancies in general.

As for the procedure, we should also highlight that the joint examination of the parties, provided for by Article 4 paragraphs 5 of Law 223/1991 must be carried out in 'special meetings', apparently enabling a consultation, which would be separate compared to the one of the other workers.

In addition, the violation of the selection criteria determines only the right to some compensation in favour of the executive, consistent with the general principle that debars the fired executive from the right to reinstatement.[30]

[B] Issues Regarding Other Categories of Workers

In principle, as mentioned, in order to apply the regulations on collective dismissal, we must be considered all forms of employment.

Article 24 paragraph 4 of Law 223/1991 also sets out some exceptions. The non-applicability of the collective dismissal is primarily provided for cases of expiry of fixed-term employment contracts. There is debate over this, on whether collective dismissal may still cover also those types of contract when the term has not expired yet,[31] as envisaged by the Directive, for that matter.

Cases of expiry due to the end of work in construction are also excluded, not in the sense of a closing-down of the company's business or a the end of a construction but in the sense of the fulfilment of the work phase for which the person had gotten hired[32] such as, for example, a specific job order. It must also be emphasized that it should be workers absolutely unrelated to the permanent staff of the company.[33]

Finally, seasonal and occasional works are excluded.[34]

A problematic exception seems to be the one decreed by Article 22 of Legislative Decree no. 276 of 10 September 2003, with respect to employees coming from staff leasing companies, in case of a supply termination. The related layoffs must therefore be traced back to dismissals for just cause, this resulting in a difference in their treatment, which could violate European directives.[35]

30. TATARELLI, 426: 17.
31. In a negative sense, *see* GALANTINO, 551; on the matter in general, *see* TATARELLI, 426.
32. *See* Court of Cassation Case 4349/2015.
33. GALANTINO, 552.
34. It should be highlighted in this regard that the hotel industry is not included in the excluded businesses because, despite being characterized by seasonal rhythms, it does not have a nature featuring precariousness and discontinuity: *see* Court of Cass. 15290/2000.
35. TATARELLI, 432.

[C] The Dismissal of Workers in Critical Situations Requiring Specific Protection

Even workers hired compulsorily because of their disability are subject to collective dismissal for staff reduction.[36] However, since the law provides for a certain number of positions specifically for these workers, in proportion to the size of the company, the dismissal of a disabled worker becomes illegitimate if it cuts down to a number below the required quota the amount of workers to be compulsorily employed.[37]

Female workers approaching their marriage and working mothers are also protected against collective dismissal. However, the protection is not active in case of dismissal for total closing-down of the business.[38]

§15.05 LAYOFF AND OTHER FORMS OF EMPLOYMENT TERMINATION

In order to integrate the collective dismissal cases, Article 24 paragraph 1 of the cited Law 223/1991 considers the minimum number of five layoffs within the period of 120 days. This assessment seems in line with the one in Article 1 of Directive 98/59/EC on the extent of staff reductions. The Directive provides for a higher access threshold and establishes that, in order to reach it, we must assimilate to redundancies those employment terminations due to one or more reasons not related to the individual worker, provided - nonetheless - there are at least five redundancies.

So, giving an interpretation of domestic law in conformity with each word and with the spirit of the Directive,[39] the law has repeatedly pointed out that the term 'dismissal' used by the law has to be regarded as a technical term, which does not allow to make layoffs equal to any other type of employment termination, even if determined also or only by a choice of the employee, as in the cases of resignation, termination agreed upon by both parties or early retirement, and even if such forms of termination are ascribable to the same operation of reducing the surplus of labour that justifies the recourse to redundancies.[40]

§15.06 THE COLLECTIVE DISMISSAL PROCEDURE

The collective dismissal procedure is mainly regulated by paragraphs 2-12 and paragraph 15 bis of the Article 4 of the Law 223/1991 as well as paragraphs 1-5 of the following Article 5 of the same Law 223/1991. These provisions were laid down for dismissal following the granting of the extraordinary wage integration period but Article 24 of the same law extended their application also to dismissals due to a staff reduction.

36. *See* Court of Cass. 1201/2000.
37. Article 5 paragraph 2 of Law 223/1991; GIGLIO, 43.
38. GIGLIO, *ibid.*
39. GALANTINO, 548.
40. *See* Court of Cass. 3866/2006; Court of Cass. 7519/2010.

According to the above-mentioned Article 4 if in the course of the implementation of the program set forth by Article 1 of the law, the company deems impossible to guarantee the reinstatement of all the laid-off workers and to provide alternative measures it is then authorized to start the collective dismissal procedure. The application of the said procedure is conditional to the obligation of issuing a previous communication. The communication must be in written form, expressing the intent to collectively dismiss.

The Trade Unions are the recipients of the communication.

Several cases may arise in this regard.

If the company includes corporate union groups of representative, the communication is to be transmitted to these groups and to the respective professional association.[41]

If only one RSA (internal union representatives) was set up the obligation is fulfilled with a communication to the latter and the employer is under no obligation to ascertain its representativeness.[42]

If there are no RSA the communication is to be provided to the professional associations belonging to the most representative Confederations.[43]

Article 4 paragraph 3 of the cited Law 223/1991 states, literally, that the communication must indicate 'the reasons determining the redundancy and the technical, organizational or productive issues which led to the conviction that it was impossible to adopt remedying measures in order to partially or totally avoid the collective dismissal; the number of corporate placement and the professional profiles of the redundant staff as well as the staff usually employed and the timeline of the staff reduction; the potential measures devised to face the social impact of the reduction programme implementation; the calculation of any other sums of money due to the workers other than those already provided for by the legislation and the ones resulting from collective bargaining.

The opening communication of the procedure has a pivotal relevance for a fruitful and productive participation of the union in co-management of the crisis and for the transparency of the decision-making process and draws the conclusion that the dismissed employee is therefore entitled to invoke the incompleteness of the information as incomplete information prevents the union from such participation.[44]

The communication being considered here, like the one provided for in the subsequent paragraph 9 of Article 24, refers to the conditions in which the company finds itself at the very opening of the procedure and it cannot concern future arrangements and potential re-organizational processes. Hence the staff reduction procedure can be activated only by the employer and not by a future and potential company assignee, also as the transfer of a part of the company could impact on the

41. *See* Article 4 paragraph 2 of the Law 223/1991.
42. *See* Cass. 24025/2013.
43. *See* again Article 4 paragraph 2 of the Law 223/1991.
44. *See* Cass. 6959/2013. *See* above for a possible regularization (or s.c. sanatoria) of procedural defects.

parameters of reference used to calculate the actual number of the personnel to be made redundant.[45]

The Public Authority must be informed of the commencement of the procedure and must receive the same communication already sent to the unions (Article 4 paragraph 4 of the Law 223/1991).

Once the requirements allowing performance of an analysis of the situation are met, there is the possibility of conducting a joint assessment which must commence within seven days from the notice of receipt of the communication by the Union counterparts. The latter must request the assessment.

In compliance with the law object of assessment, are the causes which determined the personnel redundancy, the possibility of allocating them to alternative duties within the same company maybe considering other forms of contract or other modes of labour time management. In case none of these solutions proved to be feasible and the personnel reduction is unavoidable then the focus of the assessment must shift on the so-called social measures, i.e. re-skilling and requalification of the employees.

The joint assessment takes place between the parties. In this phase the Public Authority, already informed of the situation by a copy of the communication sent to the Trade Union, is not yet involved.

The unions might avail themselves of expert professional assistance (Article 4 paragraph 5 of the Law 223/1991) as permitted by the Directive (Article 2).

A similar provision is not dispensed to employers but it is usually believed that they also have the same possibility.

Regarding the timing of the procedure, its conclusion is expected to within forty-five days from the date of receipt of the communication by the company/the employer.

The joint assessment can be completed with or without the parties reaching an agreement.[46] The law provides that the company informs the public authority on the result and on a potential negative outcome, by explaining the reasons of the latter. (Article 4 paragraph 6 of the Law 223/1991). Therefore the result must be communicated[47] in any case but whereas negative, reasons must be provided.

The failure in reaching an agreement opens the way to the PA's intervention.

The PA shall summon the parties again and the issues at the core of the meeting will be the same ones already discussed by the parties, of which a copy of the communication which opened the bargaining had also been notified to the authority in advance.

This second bargaining phase has a shorter deadline than the first one. The bargaining must be completed within thirty days after the receipt of the communication.

45. *See* Cass. 16805/2003; 3603/2010.
46. It is to be noted that the unions' agreement reached in these situations might envisage the reinstatement of the laid-off employees and it can decide that they will be allocated to perform duties other than those they previously did. As generally recognized also by the Lower Courts the workers might be assigned to lesser duties but having to choose between dismissal and the loss of the previously acquired professional skills the law chooses the latter.
47. The omitted communication in case of reached agreement it is not relevant. *See* below n. 64.

The employer cannot dismiss before this deadline meaning that his power to lay off is suspended until a final attempt for the parties to reach an agreement is performed with the intervention of the Public Administration as provided in substance by the Article 4 paragraph 1 of the Directive. No extensions to the above-mentioned thirty-day limit are allowed for the completion of the new phase of the bargaining, something which the Directive would allow the Member States to consider.

The company now can avail itself of right to dismiss the individual employees considered as redundant. Among them, as previously said, executives shall now also be included.

The right to dismiss follows the general rules and it is to be notified within the terms of notice (which may vary from worker to worker).

Concurrently with the individual dismissal notice, the employer must also inform the Public Administration. In the previous communication the employer needed only to indicate the number of workers deemed redundant because it was still considered as a dismissal project. At the time of the second communication the dismissals have been decided and the Public Authority shall therefore be informed on the data allowing the identification of the dismissed workers. Therefore the employer shall indicate the name, the residence, rank, pay grade, the age and the dependants of these workers. Furthermore the criteria of selection applied to the workers shall also be clearly specified (promptly indicated, the law reads).

This communication allows the administrative bodies to control the fairness of the operation and the respect of the agreements, if any. For this reason, according to jurisprudence, sending the list of the laid-off workers and the reasons justifying the selection criteria agreed with the unions is not sufficient; not even the setting up of a sequential mechanism of application of the several criteria. It is necessary to control that all workers possessing the required characteristics have been included into the category to scrutinize and, furthermore, when the number of employees is higher than the numerical projections of dismissals, it is also necessary to check if the comparative criteria of assessment for identifying the workers to dismiss were applied correctly.[48]

The notifications of dismissal to workers and to the Public Administration must be preceded by the above-mentioned procedure and must be in written form.

The consequences of the noncompliance with the obligation of using the written form will be debated below.

The law identifies the employing company as the subject responsible for the foregoing obligations of information, consultation and communication. In compliance with similar provisions of the directive (Article 2 paragraph 4), the law does not consider as relevant the relation between the employing company and external controlling parties. Even if these parties having control on the employing company took the decisions regarding the staff reduction, the latter shall still comply with the aforementioned obligations and is responsible for any lack of compliance with regards to these obligations. The risk stemming from the absence of information due to the

48. *See* Cass. 16805/2003;3603/2010.

choices of the controlling party still remains a burden to be carried by the official employer.

§15.07 SELECTION CRITERIA APPLIED IN THE CHOICE OF WORKERS TO BE DISMISSED

While Article 4 of the Law 223/1991 outlines the procedure which starts with the decision of reducing the personnel and ends with the conclusion of the employment relationship, the following Article 5 deals with the crucial matter of the rules adopted to choose the workers to be laid-off describing, as said, (*see* above) a fair selection procedure.

With regards to Article 5 paragraph 1 cited, it provides that 'the identification of workers to be laid off must occur in relation to the technical, productive and organizational needs of the company, within the respect of the criteria laid out in the collective contracts agreed with the unions (*see* Article 4 paragraph 2), or, in absence of these contracts, within the respect of these joint criteria: (a) dependants; (b) seniority; technical, productive and organizational needs'.

The reference to the collective contracts (*see* Article 4 paragraph 2) could instil the doubt that the law would like to call attention on the national collective bargaining instead that on the criteria laid out in the negotiation with the corporate Union bodies, but considered the role of the provision we tend to believe that the criteria to which the regulation refer are those laid out following a specific negotiation at corporate level having as subject matter the power to dismiss and being effective only for the contracting parties.[49]

The technical-productive and organizational needs are referred to twice, with a view to several different aims. In the first part of the regulation, due to the reasons at the basis of the staff reduction, the reference encompasses and delimitates the selection scope of the workers to be laid-off. Once determined this scope, the second reference pertains to the veritable criteria of choice and it operates in relation with the identification of the remaining jobs after the closedown.[50]

In other words the 'audience' of workers who might be chosen is decided on the basis of the technical-productive and organizational needs of the corporate complex. This is totally consistent with the premise that the dismissal shall be a 'consequence of a reduction or conversion of the work or activity conducted' as provided for by Article 24 paragraph 1 of the Law 223/1991.

The reference to the technical-productive and organizational needs basically allows on the one hand, to define the limits within which it is possible to operate the selection and, on the other hand, provides a tool for conflicts resolution among several workers who are all interested in the protection of their jobs.

Of special interest is the case when the restructuring concerns exclusively one productive unit or a specific sector of the company. In this case the scope of the workers

49. MAMMONE, 135.
50. *See* Cass. 1938/2011.

involved might be limited to the employees of a specific unit or sector if this is an objective consequence of the organizational needs at the basis of the personnel reduction and did not stem from a unilateral decision of the employer. These requirements must be adequately explained in the communication to the trade unions indicating the reasons why it is not possible to avoid the dismissals by relocating the workers to other productive units geographically close to the one suppressed or downsized, insomuch as the trade unions could verify the need of planned dismissals which then has to be proven by the employer.

The choice of workers cannot be limited to those working in the unit or sector whose closure or reduction have been planned if by virtue of their professional skills, they can be employed in other positions previously assigned to colleagues working in other units and departments[51] who shall then be involved in the choice of whom to dismiss.[52] If an agreement on the selection criteria was not reached and the foregoing legal criteria are applied in compliance with the above-mentioned Article 5 paragraph 1, it is not relevant – in order to rule out the comparison with workers of equivalent skills employed in still operational units – the fact that keeping in service workers operating in determined premises would imply their relocation into an other site, with an obvious increase in costs for the company.[53]

As previously highlighted the Article 5 paragraph 1 of the Law 223/1991 makes reference to the possibility of an agreement between the Union and the employer aimed at regulating the power to dismiss and at setting forth selection criteria other than the legal ones. As underlined by the Constitutional Court[54] the agreement has a regulatory function entrusted to the law, therefore the criteria set out in the agreement shall respect the imperative rules expressed in it and meet the requisites of objectivity and rationality. They must operate without discrimination amongst the employees trying to minimize as much as possible the so-called social impact and choosing, within the limits compatible with the reasons causing the personnel reduction, to dismiss the workers that – also due to several reasons (personal ones amongst others) – will be subject to a relatively less serious damage.[55]

For example is it rationally justified the criterion of the requisites to benefit from the pension? It is certainly an objective criterion allowing choosing, on a fair ground, the worker that is victim of a relatively lesser damage, being able to replace the salary with the pension.[56]

The criteria must be objective and verifiable so as to be controlled during the application phase; they shall not imply any discretional evaluations not even as an exception to the application of intrinsically objective criteria. Therefore, as an example,

51. For example as recently decided by the Supreme Court, in case of shut down of the vehicle maintenance unit the dismissal only of the workers allocated to this unit cannot be considerate as legitimate, let alone the fact that they previously worked as drivers in the transport unit and therefore they could also been employed there: *see* Cass. 203/2015.
52. Cass. 4678/2015; Cass. 22655/2012; Cass. 13705/2012; Cass. 2429/2012.
53. Cass. 17177/2013.
54. Const. Court decision 268/1994.
55. Cass. 6959/2013.
56. Cass. 4186/2013.

once established the objective criteria which meet all seniority requirements during a specific period of time, it is not legitimate to also adopt – as an exception – the criteria of the professional skills required to manage a company, discretionally identified by the latter.[57]

The agreement might encompass criteria other than those provided by the law or give more relevance by only one set forth by the law, as for example, the one related to the productive and organizational needs of the corporate complex.

If the parties do not reach an agreement the criteria provided by the law shall be applied directly; it is relevant to note that in this case the criteria are to be applied jointly. However this does not mean that they should be necessary given the same relevance. They could as well be given a priority order.[58] The employer is entitled to prioritize them, giving a different importance to each one of them.

The application of the aforementioned criteria is limited due to the protection of female workers. Article 5 paragraph 2 provides that the percentage of laid off female workers (or placed in labour mobility) cannot be higher than the percentage of female personnel performing the same duties.

With regards to the protection of disabled workers or female workers about to get married or in maternity leave, *see* above §14.04[C]paragraph 4.3.

§15.08 JUDICIAL CONTROL AND SANCTIONS

[A] General Remarks

First of all it is worth underlining that one of the main principles regarding judicial control on collective dismissal is that the judge cannot challenge the specific reasons pertaining to the personnel reduction but only check the procedural correctness of the operation which led to the reduction.

Therefore it is not possible to ask to the Courts to verify that the reduction or conversion of the activity or work meet real and objective needs.[59] This control is entrusted solely to the union-related phase of the collective dismissal, through the explication of the reasons of the company and the subsequent bargaining action of the Union,[60] both in the case of dismissal due to personnel reduction and also with regards to a dismissal following a labour mobility procedure.

In both cases no judicial control is foreseen on the reality of the reduction or conversion needs.[61] The 'unjustified nature of the personnel reduction is totally irrelevant.

However, one thing is that the reduction or conversion of the work activity constitute the consequence of judicial undisputable choices, and another one is that the reduction or conversion are truthful as they constitute the prerequisites for accession to

57. Cass. 12544/2011.
58. GALANTINO, 563; Cass. 2008/21138.
59. Cass. 4653/2009; Cass. 19576/2013.
60. Cass. 2012/10126.
61. Cass. 2009/82; 2013/ 5145.

the collective dismissal procedure; the evaluation of the correctness of the procedures includes the verification of the existence of such reduction or conversion.

Moreover, provided that the law (Article 24 paragraph 1 of the Law 223/1991) foresees that the dismissals have to be a consequence of the change or reduction in activity or work, it is also appropriate to verify that the laid-off workers fall within the scope of those involved into the conversion or reduction.

If one or the other requirements are not met the dismissal of several workers, even if presented by the employer as collective, it is not considered as such. It is considered as a group of individual cases of dismissal due to economic reasons. The employer will then have the burden of proving that for each one of them there were reasons in connection to the productive activity, the work organization and the ordinary function of the activity as set forth by Article 3 of the Law 604 of 15 July 1966.

Second it is also important to observe that the infringement of procedural rules is considered as a breach in the exercise of the power to the right of withdrawal.

Therefore the judicial control of the legitimacy of the dismissal involves the power of verifying the compliance to such rules over the course of the entire procedure. It is to be noted that some procedural rule are devised to protect the role of the Union during the negotiation and that, in principle, only the Union is legitimate to directly invoke the noncompliance of said rules, using for this purpose the special repression procedure of anti-union discrimination.

However the noncompliance with the procedural rules aimed at granting the negotiating role of the Union can negatively impact on the quality of the Union negotiation and by consequence prejudicing the workers themselves.

The workers, in this case, can prove the negative impact of the omissions and irregularities on the quality of the negotiation and the prejudice they have been subjected to.

The flaws present in collective dismissals must be distinct in procedural flaws, which in the terms indicated then translate into flaws in the dismissal (procedure) and in flaws directly and exclusively related to the dismissal in the above-mentioned terms. In the following paragraph the procedural flaws will be examined.

[B] Procedural Flaws

[1] The Opening Communication

Among the procedural rules great importance hold those related to the Opening Communication as set forth by Article 4 paragraph 3 of the Law 223/1991.

This Communication, whose content is accurately stated by Article 4 paragraph 3 of the Law 223/1991,[62] constituting an essential step for a fruitful and productive participation to the joint management of the crisis with the Union and for the transparency of the decision-making process performed by the employer.[63] The

62. *See* above §15.06.
63. Cass. 5582/2012; Cass. 6959/2013.

Communication shall provide the foreseen information insomuch as to allow the Union to knowingly perform an effective control on the staff reduction planned by the employer, assessing as well the possibility of adopting alternative measures to the redundancy plan. If the information presented is inadequate and this inadequacy has influenced the conclusion of the agreement, the dismissals are then invalid due to the irregularity of the procedure.[64] Generally speaking, in providing information to the Union the employer must act in good faith by providing truthful and complete data even without disclosing details and clarifications which can be debated during the negotiation.[65]

Regarding the possibility of solving communication flaws, until a recent legislative amendment which will be examined below, there were jurisprudence uncertainties but the prevailing idea was that reaching an agreement between the Union and the employer was not sufficient to solve the initial flaw of communication.

The agreement however could have been considered as a fundamental element to assess the completeness of the communication. In this regard, considering what said above regarding the burden falling upon the worker to prove the detrimental effects due to an inadequate or incomplete opening communication; it is understandable that such type of burden is interpretable as an indirect tool of recognition of the Union's role. Actually, regardless the lack of adequate information if the Union has reached an agreement with the counterpart and if not proved that the agreement has been prejudicial to the workers, the Union cannot be held responsible for not having realized the inadequacy of the information provided as far as it managed to reach a non detrimental agreement for the workers.

A recent legislative innovation amended this subject matter. Article 1 paragraph 45 of the law of 28 June 2012 has actually modified the paragraph 12 of Article 4 of the Law 223/1991 stating that the potential flaws contained in the communication provided by the company could be solved in the framework of a Union's agreement reached during the collective dismissal procedure.

The new norm introduces the possibility for the parties to solve the opening communication flaws by including into the agreement–even if concluded only with some of the Unions to which the communication was addresses – a specific clause aimed at agreeing on the s.c. *sanatoria* (regularization), which by the way cannot solve the most serious of all flaws: the total lack of a prior communication.[66]

According to the prevailing interpretation[67] the clause should contain an explicit declaration recognising the flaw and the intent of overcoming it. In alternative, i.e. in the case of a generic clause, the remedying effect occurs only when from the

64. Cass. 880/2013. This decision considered the dismissal as flawed in a case where the Opening Communication did not indicate that a redundancy incentive plan had already been initiated. *See also* Cass. 10424/201 which deemed as insufficient the indication of the redundant categories of personnel (labourers, intermediates, employees, managers and executives) in order to realise the company restructuring plan given that the Article 4 paragraph 3 of the Law 223/1991 states that 'the professional profiles of the redundant personnel must be specified'.
65. VALLEBONA, 654.
66. MAMMONE, 138.
67. TATARELLI, 447.

contracting parties' behaviour emerge that during the assessment the missing elements in the opening communication have been discussed and examined. The remedying clause cannot be expressed only with refined turns of phrase.

[2] The Communication to the Public Administration and the Communication of the Union Negotiation Result

The law (Article 4 paragraph 4 and 6 of the Law 223/1991) set forth some communication obligations to the Public Administration.[68] Even the noncompliance with these obligations is to be deemed as a reason to invalidate the dismissals, considering 'the importance that these public offices hold in the framework of the procedure as social mediation bodies'.[69]

[3] The Final Communication

According to Article 4 paragraph 9 of the Law 223/1991 'once the union agreement is reached or the procedure mentioned in paragraph 6, 7 and 8 is concluded, the company might lay-off the redundant workers by communicating the dismissal in writing to each one of them, within the respect of the notice deadline'. The notification must be sent simultaneously to the Public Authority and the Unions; the finality is to make the correctness of the employer regarding the application of the selection criteria visible and therefore controllable by the Unions (and through them by each single worker) and as well to allow the Public Authority to manage the measures of support in favour of the workers.[70]

These communications, until the amendments introduced by Law 92 of 28 of June 2012, were to be sent simultaneously with the notice of dismissal; following such amendments they shall now be sent within seven days from the laying-off communication.

The subsequent paragraph 12 of the above-mentioned Article 4 contains a clear provision according to which the communications foreseen by the preceding paragraph 9 of the same article are 'invalid whereas performed in noncompliance with the written form or the procedures set forth by the previous article'.

The general reference to the 'procedures' includes all the forms in which the collective dismissal can be expressed[71] regarding therefore also the conclusive communication, whose flaws are sanctioned with the invalidity of the dismissal as it is now accepted also by the jurisprudence even if after some debate.[72]

---

68. *See* above §15.04.
69. MAMMONE, 139; *See* Cass. 10187/1996. However when the parties reach the agreement, the failure to send the communication on the outcome of the consultation becomes irrelevant.
70. Cass. 1722/2009.
71. Such reference is to be attributed to procedural norms and does not include the failure in respecting the notice deadline, which is a substantial principle and not part of the procedure *See* Cass. 2013/23183; Cass. 2000/3271.
72. Cass. 2000/302.

The violation of the rules of the final Communication might mainly consist in a total omission of such Communication or the Communication might not be in writing. These hypotheses are mainly theoretical and rarely occur.

More relevance has, in fact, the content of the Communication.

According to paragraph 9 of Article 4 cited, the Communication to the Authority and the Union must contain 'the list of laid-off workers, specifying for each one of them the name, place of residence, position, type of contract, age, dependants' and 'an accurate indication of the modality of selection criteria application'.

Among such requirements the most frequent problems stemmed from the selection criteria modality of application.

It is to be remembered that the obligation to accurately indicate such modalities has the aim of allowing the interest workers, the Trade Unions, and the Administrative bodies to control the correctness of the operation and the compliance with the reached agreements. Therefore it is not sufficient to communicate the list of laid-off workers and the selection criteria agreed with the trade unions or setting up a sequential mechanism of application of the several criteria as it is first and foremost important to check if all the workers possessing the foreseen requirements have been included in the categories to be scrutinized and moreover if the number of employees is higher than the number of planned dismissals and if the comparative assessment criteria to select the employees to be laid-off[73] have been correctly applied.

The application modality must be indicated even if there is only one criterion so that the worker might be able to understand why the choice of termination fell upon him instead of others and eventually challenge the legitimacy of his/her dismissal.[74]

Finally it must be kept in mind the case in which the final Communication, even if in compliance with the provisions of law regarding the contents, comes from an author other than the one of the initial communication. In this hypothesis, which could happen, for example, in a company transfer situation, the jurisprudence considers as flawed such Communication and by consequence invalid the dismissal even vis-à-vis to the assignee.[75]

[4] The Anti-union Discrimination

The employer behaviour can also be prejudicial to the role of Trade Unions recognized by the law in the dismissal procedure.

The Trade Union representation might, for example, have not been previously informed of the reasons hindering the implementation of measures alternative to dismissal.

73. GIGLIO Cass. 2009/14943.
74. Cass. 2011/12196; however Cass. 19576/2013 stated that even the communication of the list of laid-off workers and the selection criteria regarding the possession of the requirements to access seniority or old age pension benefits can be appropriate as the objective nature of this criterion does not require a comparison with workers not meeting this requirement.
75. Cass. 2009/14943.

The employer might have infringed upon the obligation imposed by the collective contract to solve staff redundancy issues with measures alternative to laying-off the personnel. Furthermore he/she might have violated the obligation to act in good faith and honesty during the negotiations and therefore jeopardising the Union's right to initiate a useful debate on the possibility to avoid or limit the dismissals.[76]

In all these cases the dismissal procedure is flawed and the flaw can be used by the Union with the specific appeal provided by Article 28 of the cited Law 300/1970 (so-called Workers' Statute). In such case, as provided by the above-mentioned article the judge should remedy to the effects, which are harmful to the Union's interest, and he/she might order the reinstatement of laid-off workers whereas he/she deems such reintegration to be the best remedy given the situation.[77]

[C] Dismissal Flaws

The dismissal flaws can be divided as follows.

The most serious formal flaw expressly provided for by Article 5 paragraph 3 of the Law 223/1991 and it is the defect in the written form.

The most serious substantial flaw, also explicitly stated in the same paragraph, consists in the violation of the selection criteria.

The flaw of the written form occurs rarely and as it shall be examined more in details in the following chapters; it determines the applicability of the strongest protection against the illegitimate dismissal, i.e. the reinstatement and the compensation of the damage incurred in a measure equal to the lost wages. *See* below regarding the protections related to the violation of the selection criteria. It is to be remembered that the above-mentioned criteria are those stated primarily in the agreements reached with the employer in the course of the Union negotiation and additionally, i.e. in absence of such agreements, those provided for directly by the law. (Article 5 paragraph 1 of the Law 223/1991).

Equally important is the fact that the criteria application preliminarily requires the identification of the entire scope of application of the said criteria; such scope is defined 'in relation to the technical and productive needs of the company.

This reference highlights the link between the restructuring programme as indicated in the Opening Communication and the individual cases of dismissal.

The company's needs, as described in the Opening Communication of the collective dismissal procedure, delimitate the scope within which the selection of personnel of interest shall be performed. Once identified the scope, the choice of staff to be laid-off shall be carried out on the basis of agreed upon criteria, or in absence of the latter, in compliance with the law, which encompasses the criterion of the technical and productive needs.

Therefore if the choice of workers to be dismissed falls within an area not impacted by the technical and productive requirements outlined in the Opening

76. GIGLIO, 166.
77. TATARELLI, 470.

Communication then the worker employed into said areas, if laid-off, might challenge the dismissal by claiming that the group of people selected has no relation with the organizational needs mentioned in the restructuring programme; even though the scope of dismissal selection is correctly identified, there are other types of procedural flows or infringements, which consist of violations of legal or negotiation criteria.

In all these cases, included the one in which the group of workers to be laid–off was determined in a manner not consistent with the restructuring plan, the worker also carries the burden of proving the illegitimacy of their own dismissal by identifying the workers who were supposed to be laid-off instead of him/her and that, on the contrary, benefitted from an illegitimate selection criteria application.

[D] The System of Sanctions

In the previous paragraph the potential procedural flows which impact on the final action, i.e. the dismissal, were examined as well as the flaws related to the dismissal itself.

The consequences, which, according to the law, stem from these flaws are now to be examined.

In this regard, relevant amendments have been introduced over the last few years in Italy mainly with the Law 92/2012 and more recently with the legislative Decree n. 23 of 23 March 2016. In order to understand them it is necessary to dwell upon the system of sanctions in force previously to the cited law.

In accordance to that system the right of withdrawal/dismissal was to be considered invalid if in contrast with the selection criteria regarding the workers to be laid off.

The noncompliance with the procedural rules was externally impacting on the dismissal by depriving the employer of the power to collectively dismiss. The violation of the selection criteria impacted instead on the legitimacy of the individual dismissal.[78]

In these cases the flaw was sanctioned with the reinstatement of the employee in his/her workplace; basically a complete application of Article 18 of the Law 300 of 20 May 1970 was enforced (so-called Workers' Statute). In the system introduced by the Law 92/2012, a more detailed sanctions system has been provided for with regards to the individual cases of dismissal. The collective dismissal has been, in turn, referred to the essential guidelines of the new discipline.

In the new system, under the sanctions-related standpoint a distinction is drawn between the dismissal due to a noncompliance with the written form, dismissal in breach of procedure and dismissal in breach of selection criteria.

78. In determining the amount of said compensation the law provides for different criteria as the workers' seniority, the number of people employed by the company, the size of the economic activity, the conduct and conditions of the parties: Article 18 subsection 5 of the Law 300/1970, which is made reference to in the third sentence of the subsection 7 of the same article, to which reference is made again in Article 5 subsection 3.

The dismissal which is not ordered in writing is subjected to the most severe sanction; the reinstatement of the worker and a compensation having a minimum threshold of five months' pay but not having a maximum cap.

The dismissal ordered following the conclusion of a procedure in breach of the employment relationship procedure can be finalized but the worker has right to a compensation ranging from a minimum of twelve months' pay to a maximum of twenty-four months' pay.[79] Finally the dismissal ordered in breach of selection criteria is annullable and gives right to reinstatement and a compensation equal to the pay which would have been received during the dismissal period but to be capped at twelve months' pay.

Substantial amendments to the sanctions system have been introduced by the legislative Decree n. 23 of 4 March 2015 ('Provisions regarding the permanent contract with increasing protections, in implementation of the Law 183 of 10 December 2014, so-called Jobs Act).

Presently however they regard only a limited numbers of workers as the law can be enforced only to permanent employment relationships which started as of 7 March 2016, as clearly stated by the law under assessment by Article 1 paragraph 1.

In the framework of the new system the dismissal procedural flaws can be originated only in two cases; the dismissal lacking a written form on the one hand and the dismissal ordered in breach of the procedures or in breach of selection criteria on the other one.

In the first instance the reinstatement and the compensation starting from a minimum of five months 'pay is foreseen.

In the second instance (which actually encompasses the two hypothesis so far considered as distinct) the dismissal determines the termination of the employment relationship and the employee has right to a compensation of two months' pay for each year of service, considering a minimum of four and a maximum of fourteen months' pay.

The collective dismissal system was characterized by the parallelism of the consequences originating from the illegitimacy of the employer's conduct regardless the type of violation in terms of breach of procedure or breach of criteria; this occurred until the reform introduced by the Law 223/91.

With the Law 92/2012 the procedural flaws were regulated in a differentiated manner by ruling out the possibility of reinstatement, with an obvious weakening of the protections for the invalid cases stemming from procedural flaws and a parallel loss of relevance of unions' negotiation.[80]

The Decree 23/2015 impacted even more on the sanctions-related aspects of collective dismissal; it unified in the same system the non-compliance with the procedures and the selection criteria with a further downsizing of the Unions' role.

The system of sanctions is different according to the date of the first employment of workers with the peculiar consequence that in the same dismissal procedure the very same flaws are sanctioned in a different manner.

79. MAMMONE, 144.
80. In general GIGLIO, 171 and foll.

§15.09 THE SUPPORT MEASURES IN FAVOUR OF WORKERS

The system of support measures in favour of the workers was essentially based until recently on a direct financial support given on a monthly basis for a certain period of time following the dismissal and on the projection of several incentives of different content in order to favour the re-employment of the laid-off worker.[81]

In order to understand the direct financial support system it must be kept in mind that when companies of a certain size need restructuring, reorganizing or reconverting their production - should they arrive to consequently suspend from work a certain number of workers - the Law 223 of 23 July 1991 (Article 1) provides that a financial support is to be given to suspended workers for a certain period of time following to the presentation of a specific programme of reorganization subject to the approval of the relevant Authority. (s.c. Extraordinary Redundancy Fund- *Cassa integrazione guadagni straordinaria)*.

As above-mentioned (*see* §15.02[A]) if at the end of the period foreseen by the programme it is not possible to re-employ all the suspended workers, the collective dismissal procedure might be initiated. Until the Act n. 82 of 28 June 2012 came into force, the workers laid-off due to a collective dismissal procedure were registered into a so-called 'Labour mobility list' and were entitled to receive a mobility allowance for a fixed period of time, twelve months for the majority of workers and twenty-four months for workers over 40 and twenty-four months for those over 50, considering the age-related lower likelihood of re-employment. The amount of the said indemnity was anchored to the amount of the indemnity received by the workers during the period of time they benefitted from the so-called *Cassa Integrazione*-Temporary Lay-off Fund.

Thus the employee of a company in crisis who was then dismissed was receiving an indemnity during the suspension period that was then replaced with a so-called mobility indemnity after the dismissal equal to the previous supplementary benefits for the first twelve months and to 80% of this amount starting from the thirteenth month up to the thirty-sixth month (a timeline during which only workers over 40 and 50 were entitled to benefit from this supplementary treatment). The system was funded by a general contribution provided by all the employers meeting the size requirements to have access to the Lay-off Fund and with additional amounts which had to be paid by employers who were dismissing staff and in relation to the number of laid-off workers, to the amount of mobility indemnity to be paid to laid-off workers and to other circumstances like reaching or not an agreement with the Trade Unions.[82]

The above-mentioned system was repealed and the mobility indemnity replaced by the Occupational Social Insurance - *Assicurazione sociale per l'impiego, see* Article 2 paragraph 71 (b) which repealed the Articles 6-9 of the Law 223/1991.

Even this insurance is funded by a general contribution paid by all employers and not only by those who could have benefitted from a Lay-off Fund contribution charged

81. GIGLIO, 172.
82. GIGLIO, 173.

to employers reducing personnel and meaningfully named 'termination contribution' or 'dismissal ticket'.[83]

In the framework of this new insurance a monthly unemployment indemnity has been foreseen, called 'Nuova prestazione di Assicurazione Sociale per l'impiego – New occupational social security insurance scheme', whose aim, as literally stated by the law is to 'provide support to employees who unwillingly lost their jobs'.

The prerequisites to obtain the right to access to this indemnity are: the unemployment; a minimum period of paid social security contributions in the four years prior to unemployment and a period of work in the twelve months preceding such period.

The indemnity regards all the workers under subordinate employment contracts, with certain limited exceptions and it is therefore not necessarily linked to restructuring and subsequent collective dismissals.

It is worth noting that the previous provisions on the mobility indemnity shall be repealed (not immediately but as of 1 January 2017 and they shall apply to the authorized collective dismissals until 31 December 2016.

The measures that give indirect support to the laid-off workers on one hand are constituted mainly by economic incentives provided to the employer in case of re-employment and on the other hand they provide to the workers a pre-emption right in case the employer who collectively dismissed will start new employments. The first ones consist of social security contribution reliefs in case of re-employment of the workers laid-off and registered into the 'mobility' lists. Similarly, for the employment of workers benefitting from the indemnities of the 'Social Insurance for the Employment', a monthly contribution to the employer is foreseen in the measure of half of the indemnities that the worker shall be receiving.

The second ones provide to the laid-off worker the right to be re-employed in case the employer offered new employments as of six months from their dismissal. This right is recognized as well when the employer dismissed due to the close down of operations.

In summary the incentives' system is organized by providing advantages to the employers in order to promote occupation and as well financial support given to the laid-off workers according to several different parameters.

83. Facilitations have been devised for the employment of workers in 'mobility' with a fixed term contract or an internship, regardless of age limits and with a reduced contributive burden: *see* GIGLIO, p. 176.

Chapter 16

Collective Dismissals in Latvia

Dana Rone

§16.01 INTRODUCTION

The association agreement between Latvia and the European Communities and their Member States (the Europe Agreement) was entered into force on 12 June 1995. This Agreement imposed an obligation on Latvia to adjust and harmonize its legislation with the EU, particularly in the spheres of commerce and economy, and in related spheres, including the protection of employees (Articles 68-69).[1]

The conclusion of the Europe Agreement gave an impetus to transpose, among other employees' protection instruments, EU Directive 75/129/EEC of 17 February 1975 on the approximation of the laws of the Member States relating to collective redundancies[2] into Latvian law. On 20 July 1998, the Council adopted the consolidated version of the Directive, and after that the corresponding area has been regulated by Directive 98/59/EC on the approximation of the laws of the Member States relating to collective redundancies.[3]

During the Soviet period[4] there were no special rules on the protection of employees' rights in the case of collective dismissals in Latvia. The then USSR had not ratified the ILO Convention No 158 concerning Termination of Employment at the

1. Available at: http://www.mfa.gov.lv/data/file/l/01_Eiropas_Ligums_txt.pdf Eiropas līgums par asociācijas izveidošanu starp Eiropas Kopienām un to Dalībvalstīm, no vienas puses, un Latvijas Republiku, no otras puses / Association Agreement between the European Communities and their Member States and the Republic of Latvia (Europe Agreement).
2. OJ L 48, 22 February 1975, pp. 29-30. This Directive was amended by Directive 92/56/EEC (OJ L 245, 26 August 1992, pp. 3-5).
3. OJ L 225, 12 August 1998, pp. 16-21.
4. Latvia was a part of the USSR from 1940 to 1991.

Initiative of the Employer (1982),[5] the third part of which provides for the supplementary provisions concerning termination of employment for economic, technological, structural or similar reasons.

After regaining its independence in 1991, the Employment Code adopted in Soviet times continued to be in force. However in 2002 new Latvian Labour Law came into effect.[6] The Labour Law established norms about collective redundancies in the meaning of Directive 75/129/EEC and set out some protection for employees when an employer decides to dismiss a greater number of employees.

§16.02 REGULATION OF COLLECTIVE DISMISSALS

Collective redundancy is a specific case of and procedure on dismissal of employees.[7] Articles 105, 106 and 107 of the Labour Law stipulate rules on collective dismissal or, as termed in the official translation of the Labour Law, collective redundancy. The term 'redundancy' will be used in this article, in keeping with the terminology of the law. The Articles provide:

> Section 105. Collective Redundancy
> (1) Collective redundancy is a reduction in the number of employees where the number of employees to be made redundant within a 30-day period is:
> 1) at least five employees if the employer normally employs more than 20 but less than 50 employees in the undertaking;
> 2) at least 10 employees if the employer normally employs more than 50 but less than 100 employees in the undertaking;
> 3) at least 10 per cent of the number of employees if the employer normally employs at least 100 but less than 300 employees in the undertaking; or
> 4) at least 30 employees if the employer normally employs 300 and more employees in the undertaking.
> (2) In calculating the number of employees to be made redundant, such employment legal relation termination cases shall also be taken into account as which the employer has not given notice of termination of the employment contract, but the employment legal relations have been terminated on other grounds, which are not related with the conduct or abilities of the employee and which have been facilitated by the employer.
> (3) The provisions of this Law regarding collective redundancy shall not apply to:
> 1) crews of sea-going ships; and
> 2) employees employed in State administrative institutions.
>
> Section 106. Information and Consultations, when Carrying out Collective Redundancy
> (1) An employer who intends to carry out collective redundancy shall in good time commence consultations with employee representatives in order to agree on the number of employees subject to the collective redundancy, the process of the collective redundancy and the social guarantees for the employees to be made redundant. During consultations the employer and the employee

5. http://www.ilo.org/dyn/normlex/en/f?p=NORMLEXPUB:12100:0::NO:12100:P12100_INSTRUMENT_ID:312303:NO (accessed 30 November 2015).
6. *Darba likums* / Republic of Latvia Labour Law. Adopted on 20 June 2001 – 'Latvijas Vēstnesis' No. 105 (2492) 06. July 2001. In force since 20 June 2002.
7. Slaidiņa Velga. Skultāne Ilze. Darba tiesības. – Zvaigzne ABC. 2011. 136. lpp.

representatives shall examine all the possibilities of avoiding the collective redundancy of the employees employed in the undertaking or of reducing the number of employees to be made redundant and how to alleviate the effects of such redundancy by taking social measures that create the possibility to further employ or retrain the employees made redundant.

(2) In order to ensure that the employee representatives have an opportunity to submit proposals, the employer shall in good time inform the employee representatives regarding the collective redundancy and notify in writing regarding the reasons of the collective redundancy, the number of employees to be made redundant including the occupation and qualifications of such employees, the number of employees normally employed by the undertaking, the time period within which it is intended to carry out the collective redundancy and the procedures for calculation of severance pay if they differ from the procedures specified in Section 112 of this Law.

(3) The duties set out in Paragraphs one and two of this Section shall be performed irrespective of whether a decision on collective redundancy is taken by an employer or a dominant undertaking of the employer as a dependent company. An objection that the failure to fulfil the duty of information, consultation and notification is related to the fact that the dominant undertaking has not provided the necessary information, is not permitted.

(4) An employer who intends to carry out collective redundancy shall, not later than 30 days in advance, notify in writing thereof the State Employment Agency and the local government in the territory of which the undertaking is located. The notification shall include the given name, surname (name) of the employer, location and type of activity of the undertaking, reasons for the intended collective redundancy, number of employees to be made redundant stating the occupation and qualifications of each employee, number of employees normally employed by the undertaking and the time period within which it is intended to carry out the collective redundancy, as well as provide information regarding the consultations with employee representatives referred to in this Section. The employer shall send a duplicate of the notification to the employee representatives. The State Employment Agency and the local government may also request other information from the employer pertaining to the intended collective redundancy.

Section 107. Commencing Collective Redundancy

(1) An employer may commence collective redundancy not earlier than 30 days after the submission of a notification to the State Employment Agency, unless the employer and the employee representatives have agreed on a later date for commencing the collective redundancy.

(2) In exceptional cases the State Employment Agency may extend the time limit referred to in Paragraph one of this Section to 60 days. The State Employment Agency shall notify in writing the employer and employee representatives regarding extension of the time period and the reasons for it two weeks before expiry of the time period referred to in Paragraph one of this Section.

A definition of collective redundancy is included in the first part of Article 105. In terms of quantity the definition provides for an exact number of employees in redundancy in points 1, 2 and 4 of the first part of Article 105. Point 3 of the first part of Article 105 in its turn provides for a percentage of employees in redundancy. When the amount of employees is determined according to the percentage rule included in Point 3, the rounding up of the number is not allowed. For instance, if the employer employs 150 employees and dismisses ten employees, that is, 6.66%, this is not a case of collective redundancy.[8]

The time limitation of the collective redundancy is thirty days in any period of time. However, artificial division of the number of employees in redundancy is not permitted. For instance, the employer employs fifty employees and dismisses five employees within one period of thirty days and five more employees in the next period of thirty days, this case would be considered as collective redundancy.

Collective redundancy is considered within one undertaking in the meaning of Article 5 of the Labour Law, namely: 'Within the meaning of this Law, an undertaking shall mean any organisational unit in which an employer employs his or her employees.' The meaning of undertaking in the Labour Law differs from this term in the Commercial Law,[9] because both laws have different objectives. The aim of the Commercial Law is to regulate relations among merchants and improve commercial relations, but the aim of the Labour Law is to regulate legal relations between employer and employees and to protect employees. The Labour Law provides imperative norms for the protection of employees as the socially vulnerable party, but the merchants in terms of Commercial Law are equal parties and also in terms of Civil Law.[10] The term 'undertaking' in the meaning of the Labour Law also includes enterprises that are not merchants or part of merchants, but are involved in other activities.[11] For instance, the employer has two shops in different cities. Each of the shops are undertakings in the meaning of the Labour Law. Therefore the term 'undertaking' in the meaning of the Labour Law does not mean only organizational units of persons, but instead organizational units, which have necessary resources to reach particular goals.[12]

When the amount of employees to be dismissed is calculated, employees who have had their employment relations terminated without notice of termination from their employer must also be taken into account, if their employer is responsible for the grounds for such termination.

Regarding information about collective redundancy, in the majority of cases the information is given in written form, but consultations proceed in oral form, so the social partners can as effectively as possible formulate their opinions on technological, organizational and social issues.[13] The aim of information is to eliminate the risks of

8. Darba likums ar komentāriem. Zvērinātu advokātu birojs 'BDO Zelmenis & Liberte'. 2010, p. 207. Available at: http://www.lbas.lv/upload/stuff/201102/dl_ar_kom.pdf.
9. Komerclikums. Adopted on 13 April 2000, in force since 1 January 2002. Published in 'Latvijas Vēstnesis' on 4 May 2000, No. 158/160 (2069/2071). Available at: http://likumi.lv/doc.php?id=5490.
10. Kalnina I., *Transfer of Undertakings in Latvia. The Comparative Law Yearbook of International Business*, Volume 28a, 2006, Special Issue: Employment Law, Kluwer Law International: Center for International Legal Studies, 2007, pp. 415-417. ISBN 978-90-411-2440-1.
11. Balodis K. Komersanta uzņēmums kā civiltiesību objekts. Likums un Tiesības, 2005, Nr. 3, 68. lpp.
12. Darba likums ar komentāriem. Zvērinātu advokātu birojs 'BDO Zelmenis & Liberte'. 2010, pp. 17-18. Available at: http://www.lbas.lv/upload/stuff/201102/dl_ar_kom.pdf.
13. *Ibid.*, 209. lpp.

sudden, unexpected collective redundancy.[14] The term 'in order to agree' used in Part 1 of Article 106 is interpreted in the case law. Namely, it can be considered that consultations have been organized (even if mutual agreement is not reached), when consultations have proceeded in a *sufficient amount*.[15] During consultations the employer and the representatives of employees review all possibilities on how to avoid collective redundancy or to decrease the number of dismissed persons, or to mitigate the consequences of the redundancy by social measures, re-qualification, etc. The employer must provide all possibilities for the representatives of employees to submit proposals.[16] Therefore the employer must inform them about collective redundancy in a timely way and notify them in written form about the reasons for collective redundancy, the number of employees to be dismissed, their profession and qualification, the number of employees normally employed in the undertaking, the time period within which it is intended to carry out the collective redundancy and the procedures for the calculation of severance pay if they differ from the procedures specified in the Labour Law. The employer is not forced to agree with all demands of representatives of employees. However reasoned answers to all questions and proposals shall be provided. It is the employer's responsibility to prove that consultations have been made efficiently and in a sufficient amount. The length, circumstances and other terms of consultations depend to a great extent on the activity of the representatives of the employees involved.

The aim of Article 106 of the Labour Law, which regulates the obligation of the employer to organize consultations and provide information in the case of collective redundancy, is to provide social protection for employees in the case of disputed circumstances in which the employer wants to terminate the employment agreement with employees and the grounds for the termination are essential. The purpose of Articles 105-107 of the Labour Law is not to restrict the freedom of the employer to organize its activities, when there are no objective possibilities to eliminate or reduce the amount of employees to be dismissed. However, according to the case law, a lack of consultations as such cannot be a sufficient ground to render collective redundancy null and void.[17] In the case of dispute the court examines the circumstances of the collective redundancy and determines whether the information and consultations have been sufficient to eliminate or mitigate the consequences of the process.

14. Gailums Ingus. Darba likums. Komentāri. Tiesu prakse. 3. grāmata. C (100. – 129. pants) un D daļa. – Rīga, 2004. 60. lpp.
15. Judgment in Case No. C31157103 on 19 March 2003 in Riga city Zemgale district court, and further in Case No. CA-3339/10 on 10 June 2003 in Riga Regional court.
16. Renbuša Daiga. Burkevics Andis. Par visu var un vajag vienoties (II). 26.04.2011. 'Latvijas Vēstnesis'. Available at: http://www.sorainen.com/UserFiles/File/Publications/article.on-all-can-and-should-be-agreed.2009-04-21.lv.lv.lat.andisb.pdf.
17. Judgment of the Supreme Court of Latvia in Case No. SKC-1106/2013 (C33329011) dated 26 April 2013. Available at: http://at.gov.lv/lv/judikatura/judikaturas-nolemumu-arhivs/senata-civillietu-departaments/tiesibu-aktu-raditajs/2013/1-latvijas-republikas-tiesibu-akti/12-likumi/#8.

CHAPTER 17

Collective Dismissals in Lithuania

Diana Labokaite

This overview consists of two parts. The first part deals with the regulation of legal collective dismissals in Lithuania, since the restoration of independence in 1990 until 2011, when it reached its current wording. A short history is presented of how laws have undergone change in this period, with a particular emphasis on the main concepts that are used to regulate legal relations when dismissing a group of employees, and how these are defined by law. The second part deals with examples from legal practice regarding the dismissal of groups of employees, where the court had to decide if the employer was keeping to the additional requirements or not. In connection with this process, the courts had to interpret the most essential concepts found in the law, such as who can be recognized as representatives for the employees, what qualifies as being an active union within a company, how to solve disputes among various representatives of the employees, and how many employees must be involved in a case before it can be considered a collective dismissal. This article gives examples from a time span of five recent years of legal practice, starting from the time when not only specific requirements for employers regarding collective dismissals were first introduced in Lithuanian law, but also the responsibility for employers who neglected to adhere to the new requirements.

§17.01 REGULATION BY LAW

The termination of work relations is always of a very high significance for both parties in a legal dispute regarding labour relations, and the laws of the Lithuanian Republic therefore strictly regulate the termination of work relations. More specifically, separate lists are issued where all legal grounds for termination of work relations or public service relations are specified, and the procedure for carrying out such termination is also regulated in detail. Strict regulation is necessary because the act of dismissing an employee from work is considered 'the most negative action an employer can take towards an employee in the workplace, both in financial and psychological terms, and also the one that carries with it the most serious consequences in the sphere of individual relations between employee and employer'.[1]

All the aspects of legal relations of work in the Republic of Lithuania are regulated by the Labour Code, the Law of State Civil Service, and other laws. The Labour Code of the Republic of Lithuania was passed by Seimas (the Parliament) and took effect in 1 January 2003. Furthermore, the Labour Code determines in which order, and with what procedure individual labour agreements can be terminated. There are requirements for employers in those cases where there is a plan to dismiss larger number of employees. The motive, from the point of view of the Legislator, is to reduce the negative consequences that such actions might produce. Such as, for instance, a surge of unemployed work seekers into the job market, a tougher situation for family members depending on the salaries of the workers being laid off, and a general worsening of the situation in society as a whole.

The attempts to create such laws, through which it was possible to mitigate the consequences of collective dismissals, were corrected after the restoration of Independence of Lithuania, in 1990. Following the spirit and principles of the International Labour Organisation (ILO) Convention 'Concerning Termination of Employment at the Initiative of the Employer' 1982 (No. 158), the Citizens' Activity or Unemployed Support law was approved in 1 January 1991. This law imposes a duty on the employer to inform the Labour Exchange Office and municipality three months in advance, that there are plans to dismiss a group of employees (defined as ten or more people in companies, offices and organizations of up to 100 employees, or 10% or more of the overall staff in companies, offices and organizations, that employ in excess of 100 people) over a period of thirty days. Municipalities were given, via a proposal from the Labour Exchange Office, the right to suspend dismissals temporarily for up to six weeks. The territorial Labour Exchange Office, after receiving notification about a future group dismissal, were to evaluate the reverberations of dismissals for the local job market, and predict possibilities to soften the consequences of such, by applying measures of active work market policy (professional education, supportive employment, support in creating work places, work rotation, etc.), and in addition to organize meetings with employees, in which they would be informed about the situation in the employment market, workers' rights and duties. If the Labour Exchange Office would suspend procedures of dismissals, the employers would have additional costs. Parts of those costs had to be compensated from the Employment fund or budgets of municipalities, provided that the employer would lay off a group of workers without taking into consideration the procedure described in the first part of this article, these layoffs could be rescheduled until the deadline on the dismissal slip.

Since 28 July 1999, in the law of Support for the Unemployed of the Republic of Lithuania, there has been an additional requirement for employers to notify about collective dismissal, or about the upcoming disruption of the activity of the company, not only to the municipality and labour exchange office, but also to the professional

1. Petrylaite D., Davulis T., Petrylaite V., *The Implementation of European Union Legislation in the Lithuanian Labour Law*, 292 (Vilnius: Center of Registers, 2008).

union. A clause was included stating that collective dismissal does not qualify when a group of employees are working by fixed term agreements, or are seasonal workers and are laid off, provided that the terms of their work agreements are not violated. This clause is still present in the Labour Code.

The Ministry of Social Security and Labour regulated the procedures of collective dismissals in more detail. By the order from the minister, the structure of the dismissal of a group of workers and its prevention was confirmed. This provided the form of notice, the order of submission, consultations with the unions, meetings with employees in case the unions are absent, the structure for how such consultations should be carried out, and terms and conditions.

Article 130 of the Labour Code, which came into effect on 1 January 2003, specified how one is supposed to notify the employee about the imminent termination of the work agreement. In Part 5 of said article it was additionally stated that 'when reducing a number of employees, or when disrupting the activity of a company, the employer must notify the territorial Labour Exchange Office, municipality and representatives of the employees' (Labour Code Article 19) about this in written form two months in advance that in thirty calendar days it is planned to dismiss: (1) ten or more employees, if there are up to 99 workers; (2) more than 10% of the work force, if the company has from 100 to 299 workers; (3) thirty and more workers, if the company has 300 and more workers.

However, when a group of employees working by fixed-term agreements, or as seasonal workers, are laid off without violating the terms of their work agreements it is not considered group dismissal. The procedure and peculiarities of group dismissals still need to be defined by the Government. Moreover, the Government hesitated to define the necessary procedures, and the previously mentioned Social Security and Labour minister's determined group dismissal procedure in the legal sense became inadequate, because it was adopted by an unauthorized subject, namely the minister, not the Government.

Only setting the duty to notify the Labour Exchange Office, municipality and representatives of the workers, two months in advance was not an acceptable implementation of European Union Directive 98/59 EB.[2] Primarily because, from the text of the law, it was possible to draw the conclusion that the duty of the notification appears only when reducing the number of employees, or when disrupting the activity of the company. However, in those cases such as the disruption of an activity in the case of the employer's death, or disruption of the company's activity by court order, remained beyond the commitment boundaries. Besides, the employer only had the duty to notify, but no duty to hold consultations with representatives of the employees and take into consideration employees', municipalities', and possible labour exchange propositions. The term itself, namely, two months prior to the dismissal, was too short in order to carry out any consultations, and most importantly it coincided with the

2. Council Directive 98/59/EC of 20 July 1998 on the approximation of the laws of the Member States relating to collective redundancies. *Official Journal L 225, 12/08/1998 P. 0016 - 0021.* http://eur-lex.europa.eu/legal-content/EN/TXT/?uri=uriserv:OJ.L_.1998.225.01.0016.01.ENG (accessed 8 February 2015).

primary notification term before the layoff. Therefore, the notice was only a formality, and could not have any real positive influence for the work market. Moreover, there was no sanction in the Labour Code to the employer for failure to give notice, and the Unemployed Support (or Citizens' activity) law was invalid from 1 August 2006. The absence of a real sanction in the law did not allow courts to react more strictly to those cases, when employers did not keep their duty to notify the Labour Exchange Office and municipality about the group dismissal at all.

In essence, all the mentioned imperfections of the law were corrected in 2008, when the Labour Code was amended with Article 130 (this took effect on 1 July 2008). It was specially designed for cases where groups of employees are being laid off. In this article it was determined that: '1. The dismissal of a group of employees is considered when, during the thirty calendar days, due to economic and technological reasons, workplaces' structural rearrangements or other reasons, not connected with individual employee, it is planned to lay off:

(1) Ten or more employees in companies where there are twenty and up to 99 employees;
(2) No less than 10% of employees in companies, where from 100 to 299 employees work;
(3) Thirty or more employees in companies with 300 and more employees;
(4) It is not considered a group dismissal when employees are laid off after the termination of a work agreement (fixed term, seasonal and temporary work).
(5) The employer has to notify the planned termination of a work agreement in a written form to the territorial Labour Exchange Office following the procedure set down by the government when the consultations with the representatives of the workers are over, and no later than before notification of the termination of the work agreement.
(6) The work agreement cannot be terminated if the duty to notify the territorial Labour exchange office about the dismissal of group of employees, or the duty to consult with representatives of employees has been violated'.

With the introduction of this new law, the transfer of the Directive 98/59/EB to Lithuanian national law was successfully completed. The duties of the employer to hold consultations with representatives of employees, to notify local institutions, and clear prohibition to terminate work agreements until these requirements were carried out, were defined in more detail. The law also clearly laid down the sequence of employers' actions: (1) after the decision to reduce the number of employees, due to one or another reason, had been taken the employer first has to present information about his/her decisions, and hold consultations, which have to be constructive rather than formal. (2) After these consultations, the employer takes the final decision about the dismissals, about which he notifies the territorial Labour Exchange Office; and (3) after that, the procedure of notifying each employee individually must be carried out. The Labour Code, Article 130, determines the terms of individual notification. The standard notification term is two months, however, certain groups of employees (those who provide for children, those who have five years left until their retirement, and those who have disability) have to be notified four months in advance.

Longer notification terms can be set out in collective agreements. In certain cases, longer notification terms can be set out by specific laws. For example, in the Law of additional activity and social guarantees of the employees of the Republic of Lithuania State Company Ignalina Atomic Plant, it was defined that employees at the plant are to be informed every year about possible staff reductions and lists of positions and professions at the soon-to-be-closed plant within the nearest twelve months. The employees that are to be dismissed are to be informed ten months in advance in a written form.[3]

Although the procedure of collective dismissals is outlined in the Labour Code, and in its essence is valued as consistent with Directive 98/59/EB, Professor Tomas Davulis nevertheless states that there are some aspects that are not problem free.[4] For example, the meaning of 'company' is not really clear. In Lithuanian labour law, a 'company' is understood as the employer, the entire company, establishment or organization, but not a structural unit, as it is understood by the court of European Justice. If we understand only the entire company as an employer, we can find ourselves in the situation where in one subdivision, which is in a smaller city, half of the employees are made redundant, but from the point of view of the whole company this will not correspond to the concept of group dismissal. Thereby not triggering the mechanisms of consultation and information. Another common problem for Lithuanian labour market is that there are quite often no professional unions in companies, therefore; as a consequence, there are no strong representatives of the employees. In this case, as Article 19 of the Labour Code determines, the representative of the employees can be a Work Council, that has been elected during secret voting in a general staff meeting. If employees do not have a Work Council, the employer is exempt from the duty to consult with the representatives of the employees, and it is sufficient that he, during the meeting with employees, informs them about the decision to reduce their numbers.

In Labour Code Article 130^1, the concept of consultations with employees is being used. What the consultations are, and how they should be carried out, is defined in the same Labour Code Article 47. It states there that informing is information (data) transmission to the employees' representatives, when striving to get them acquainted with the main points of the case. Consultation is an exchange of opinions and the establishment and elaboration of the dialog between representatives of the employees and employers. This Labour Code defines that before making a decision about group dismissal, the employer has a duty to inform the employees' representatives and hold consultations with them. The information given has to cover the reasons for planned layoffs, the number of redundant workers, the number of employees according to the

3. The law on Lithuanian Republic State company of Ignalina Atomic Plant employees additional employment and social guarantees. Article 6, https://www.e-tar.lt/portal/lt/legalAct/TAR.6686E2AF9EFE (accessed 8 February 2015).
4. Petrylaite D., Davulis T., Petrylaite V., The Implementation of European Union Legislation in the Lithuanian Labour Law, 292 (Vilnius: Center of Registers, 2008).

categories that are about to be laid off, the period during which work agreements will be disrupted, the criteria for the selection of redundant employees, the conditions of disruption of work agreements and other important information. The aim of consultations should be to avoid group dismissals, to lessen their number or to alleviate the effects of the dismissals.

The duty to hold consultations with the representatives of employees is determined in other cases too, such as before making a decision to reorganize the company, the takeover of a business or part of it, and other decisions that can have effects for work organization in the company and the employees' legal position. The employer has to inform the employees' representatives and hold consultations with them about the reasons for such decisions, inform them about the legal, economic and social effects for the employees, and about the measures that will be used to reduce the effects of the layoffs.

Other ways of information and consultation, as well as conditions and procedures can be provided in the laws, in collective agreements, or in representative agreements between employer and employee.

The law also determines that consultations have to take place on time, by creating the opportunity for the employees' representatives to meet with competent employer's representatives. Such representatives must be authorized to make decisions, and capable of giving well founded answers. The aim of these consultations is to achieve decisions that satisfy both parties. The results of the consultations are documented in a protocol.

In the case of the absence of representatives of the employees, as is defined in the Labour Code Article 47(3) and 47(4), the employer has a duty to inform the workers in advance, directly or during a general employees' meeting, about the date of the taken decision, the reasons, legal, economic and social effects, and the foreseen measures.[5]

During periods when the economy is being shaken by various crises, employees experience not only collective dismissals but even bankruptcies or liquidations of entire companies. The bankruptcy of a business is also considered as a collective dismissal because in such instances often all of the employees lose their jobs. However, bankruptcy is regulated by a special Enterprise Bankruptcy Law of the Republic of Lithuania. The company's insolvency practitioner ('Enterprise Administrator to provide bankruptcy services' as is stated in the Law) has a duty to warn employees in written form within three working days after the court' order institute bankruptcy proceedings come to effect about the disruption of the work agreement and after fifteen days after such warning to disrupt work agreement with them. The bankruptcy administrator has to notify the Labour Exchange Office, the municipality and the representatives of the employees about the coming reduction of staff no later than three

5. Labour Code of the Republic of Lithuania. Lietuvos Respublikos Darbo kodeksas, 47 str., http://www3.lrs.lt/pls/inter3/dokpaieska.showdoc_l?p_id=169334&p_tr2=2 (accessed 24 February 2015). Translations of one of the older version of Labour Code: http://www3.lrs.lt/pls/inter3/dokpaieska.showdoc_l?p_id=191770.

working days from the time that the courts' decision to institute bankruptcy proceedings comes into effect.[6] It is obvious that the enterprise administrator has no duty to hold consultations with the representatives of the employees, because the administrator only appears in the insolvency when the above-mentioned court's decision comes into effect, or the creditors decide to start insolvency procedures and appoint an administrator. In the mind of a law maker, when the decision to start insolvency is taken, consultations with employees are pointless. It is possible to dispute that in this case the consultations with the representatives of employees could help find outcomes that are less harmful to employees, perhaps even rescue the business or find the ways to restructure. Legal scientist Ingrida Mačernytė-Panomariovienė raises the question of whether competent institutions can take effective steps during such a short time margin, in order to tone down the consequences of dismissals on such a scale, and to form presumptions for further employment of such employees?[7] The question is rhetorical, but reveals the problem that, in the case of the insolvency of a company, neither information nor consultation has any effect on the fate of the employees and is only a formality.

As the data of the third quarter of 2014 shows, 6.15% of the work force of Lithuania worked in public administration, defence or the compulsory social insurance sector.[8] For that reason, it is important to consider that the work relations of these professionals are being regulated not only by the Labour Code, but also by special laws. Public Service law defines the rules of work relations in state and municipal institutions and offices for employees considered as civil servants, who perform duties of public administration or implement state governance politics in certain spheres.

Not only are requirements for civil servants quite specific, but civil servants also acquire special status and responsibilities, as well as other guarantees. The legal status of separate groups of employees can be determined by other specific laws, such as the Lithuanian Republic Law of Prosecutors' office (it regulates the work relations of prosecutors), Domestic service statute (police and similar), Court law (to regulate the working relationships of judges), the statute of the Prison Department under the Ministry of Justice of the Republic of Lithuania, and similar. All mentioned special laws (statutes) that regulate the work relations of separate groups of employees, civil servants and officers deal with various ways of terminating work agreements. The above-mentioned special laws regulate the legal relationships of a group of professionals and describe a way of terminating work agreements when due to reorganizing work organization a position was simply lost. However, not a single act defines any

6. Enterprise Bankruptcy Law of the Republic of Lithuania. Lietuvos Respublikos įmonių bankroto įstatymas, 13 straipsnis, 19 straipsnis, http://www3.lrs.lt/pls/inter3/dokpaieska.showdoc_l?p_id=493988 (accessed 8 February 2015). Translation of the older version of Law could be accessed: http://www3.lrs.lt/pls/inter3/dokpaieska.showdoc_l?p_id=136576.
7. Ingrida Mačernytė-Panomariovienė. Kolektyvinio darbuotojų atleidimo iš darbo reglamentavimas Lietuvoje/Regulation of the collective dismissals from work in Lithuania. Jurisprudencija.2007.Nr.10, http://www.mruni.eu/lt/mokslo_darbai/jurisprudencija/archyvas/?l=96090.
8. Official statistics portal. Employed persons. http://osp.stat.gov.lt/en/statistiniu-rodikliu-analize?portletFormName=visualization&hash=3f638a42-aaf4-490d-bcc0-472165d55a48 (accessed 8 February 2015).

additional requirements for the employer in those cases if there is the removal of more than one position. In all the special laws it is defined that Labour Code norms can only be applied in those cases where a specific case is not regulated by a specific law. Moreover, a state or municipal institution, or office, or another employer acting in the name of the state, has no duty to consult with civil servants' representatives, or to inform the Labour Exchange Office. Legal scientists, such as T.Davulis, state that laying off civil servants from state service, when the number of positions is reduced, does not mean that the employer has any duty to consult with representatives of civil servants and inform the respective Labour Exchange Office or municipality. Such an opinion is based on the fact that Directive 98/59/EB determines an exception for public administration and state institution employees. Besides, State Service law and other public sector service regulating laws calls for the duty of the employer to first find possibilities to transfer the civil servant, whose position has been eliminated, to another analogous or lower position.

Court practice, however, has gone along another path. Work disputes among civil servants and officers are being examined, not in general competence courts, but in administrative courts (the system of administrative courts in Lithuania consists of five regional administrative courts and one Supreme Administrative Court, which investigates regional administrative court's decisions in appellate order). Administrative courts consistently follow Article 5 of the Law on Public Service, where it is stated that other laws regulating work relations and social guarantees are applied to civil servants to such an extent as their status and social guarantees are not regulated by the Law on Public Service. The courts have derived a rule from Article 5 that in all cases where legal relations are regulated by Public Service Law (PSL), norms of this Law are applied. Labour Code (LC) norms are applied only when an established relationship is not regulated by the PSL. On 20 March 2007 the Constitutional Court of the Republic of Lithuania concluded that the state service relationship, although not identical to work legal relations, has some similarities, state service legal relations are treated as legal relations between state servants and the state, which from the point of view of the civil servant plays the role of the employer. One of the principles of work relations is the stability of these relations (Labour Code Article 2, paragraph 1.8), more specifically, work relations have to apply the criteria of permanence, they should not be changed too often, only introduced out of necessity, and employees should be informed about them in advance, following the required terms. Administrative courts keep to the opinion that this principle has to be taken into consideration in state service legal relations. That is why, in the practice of the administrative courts, there are quite a number of cases where civil servants or statute officers, dispute dismissal from work on the grounds that the employer has violated the determined duties found in the Labour Code to hold consultations with employee representatives, and to notify the Labour exchange office and municipality.

The definition of who can be representatives of the employees is defined in Article 19 of the Labour Code: 'In labour relations the rights and interests of employees may be represented and protected by the trade unions. Where an enterprise, agency or undertaking has no functioning trade union, and if the staff meeting has not transferred the function of employee representation and protection to the trade union of the appropriate sector of economic activity, the employees shall be represented by the Works Council elected by secret ballot at the general meeting of the staff'.[9] Trade unions can be established by guidance of a special Lithuanian Republic Law on Trade Unions, and can be organized according to various principles, such as professional, official, industrial, territorial or other. To establish trade unions, it is necessary to have no fewer than twenty founding members, or that those members must make up not less than one-tenth of the company, office or organization (and one-tenth of all employees would not be less than three employees). Furthermore, internal statutes and management bodies within the union have to be established at its first meeting, and the locality of the union should also be indicated.[10]

Very often trade unions are being established based on a territorial, sectorial principle, when twenty founders, who work in different companies, establish a trade union. In that case, even if there is no one-tenth ratio of employees who make up the members of that trade union, the employer has to acknowledge that the company has a trade union with which he has a duty hold consultations prior to collective dismissals.

A very special representative of employees is the Work Council, whose rules of establishment are determined by the special Lithuanian Republic Law of Work Councils that came into effect on 26 October 2004.[11] A Work Council is to be set up in cases where an undertaking has no functioning trade union, and where a staff meeting has not transferred the function of employee representation and protection to the trade union of the respective sector of economic activity. Only one Work Council may be set up in an undertaking, irrespective of whether it has any branches, representative offices or other structural divisions. A Works Council shall be set up in an undertaking where the number of employees, calculated in accordance with the procedure laid down in Article 5 of this Law, is at least twenty. The number of employees, is the number of employees on the day of the receipt of their proposal to select a Work Council (when the proposal is presented to the employer) is the number of employees currently working irrespective of their length of service in that undertaking. When determining the number of employees, employees of all branches, representative offices and structural divisions, shall be counted with the exception of employees who are on parental leave until their children reach the age of three; employees undergoing active national defence service; employees employed under temporary employment contracts; and the employer himself (company head or his/her representatives). In a company that has fewer than twenty employees, Work Council functions are put into the hands of the representative of employees elected in a general meeting of employees. Elections of a Work Council are called by the employer after receiving the written proposal for the establishment of a Work Council signed by one tenth of the employees

9. Labour Code of the Republic of Lithuania. Lietuvos Respublikos Darbo kodeksas, 47 str., http://www3.lrs.lt/pls/inter3/dokpaieska.showdoc_l?p_id=169334&p_tr2=2 (accessed 24 February 2015). Translations of one of the older version of Labour Code: http://www3.lrs.lt/pls/inter3/dokpaieska.showdoc_l?p_id=191770.
10. Law on Trade unions, http://www3.lrs.lt/pls/inter3/dokpaieska.showdoc_l?p_id=21129 (accessed 19 February 2015).
11. Law on Works Councils, http://www3.lrs.lt/pls/inter3/dokpaieska.showdoc_l?p_id=301239 (accessed 19 February 2015).

of the undertaking. It transpires that Works Council election procedure can only start at the initiative of no less than one tenth of the employees. The employer neither has a duty to initiate Work Council elections, nor to put effort into founding such a representative body for the employees.

§17.02 LEGAL PRACTICE

The Legal practice is presented by reviewing examples of legal cases. The cases that are presented here are from the year 2009 till present. Earlier legal practice is not presented in this article, because although the law required the employer to keep to the demands when going through collective dismissals, it is not until 2008 that the Lithuanian Labour Code determined any negative consequences if the demands of the Code are not followed. It is interesting to note that even after changing the law in 2008, when collective dismissals were regulated by the Labour Code, which corresponded to European Union Directive 98/59/EC, collective dismissal cases were few in numbers. The most often quoted plaintiff's reason for addressing the court was that the employer did not keep to Labour Code Article 130^1, which regulates the demands for collective dismissals. The courts, however, after hearing the case would conclude that there was no need to keep to those requirements, as the situation did not correspond to the definition of collective dismissals. Other problems that arose while applying Labour Code Article 130^1 were related to determining whether there were any representatives of the employees that had a legal right to consultations, who to recognize as such representatives, and at which point a layoff process is to be considered a collective dismissal. In other words, identifying when the duty to hold consultations and notifying the Labour Exchange Office and municipality arises.

[A] Election of the Work Council Does Not Constitute Duty of the Employer

The Supreme Court concluded that if there is no elected Work Council, the employer does not have a duty to initiate the election of such a council to later hold consultations with. If there is no Work Council, it is sufficient to inform the employees.

The Lithuanian Supreme court was hearing a case, where a dismissal was disputed based on an argument that the employer did not follow the requirements of Article 130^1 of the Labour Code while dismissing a group of employees.[12] While hearing the case, the Lithuanian Supreme court had a chance to determine whether employers are obligated to put an effort into 'creating' representatives for the employees in cases where they themselves do not take such an initiative.

The facts of the case were as follows: the plaintiff worked at a Lithuanian State Fish Breeding and Fishery Research Centre (later – Centre) as an advisor to the general

12. Civil case 'L. K. v. Žuvininkystės tarnyba prie Lietuvos Respublikos žemės ūkio ministerijos', case No. 3K-3-198/2012, Supreme Court of Lithuania, Magazine of the Court practise 'Teismų praktika' Nr.37, http://www.infolex.lt/tp/375575#.

director. On 1 July 2009 he received a notice concerning his dismissal. On 11 August 2009, by the order of the minister of agriculture of the Republic of Lithuania, it was decided to reduce the number of positions at the Centre from 231 to 155. On 18 January 2010, the plaintiff was laid off. He filed a complaint about his dismissal to court, claiming that it was unfair, and pointing to the fact that, at the time of the delivery of the notice about his dismissal, the decision to reduce the number of employees was not yet issued. Since he was also partially handicapped, he had the right to be prioritized when selecting employees for further employment, and was also entitled to a longer term of notice. These rights were not observed, and no other position was offered even though the employer had such an opportunity. The court of first instance satisfied the complaint in part and acknowledged that the dismissal was unfair, but in its motives the court did not base its reasoning on collective termination provisions. The court of appeal, who heard the complaint from the defendant, drew attention to the fact that there was a procedure of collective dismissals being carried out at the Centre. For that reason, the employer had to hold consultations with the union, and if there was no such union, with another representative of the employees, the election of which the employer had to take care of.

The defendant, although he explained that there was a meeting during which employees were informed, could not prove that there were real negotiations during which they offered the opportunity to the employee representatives to present their suggestions concerning other and possibly less restrictive ways, and more compromising approaches, to changing the structure of the company. After indicating that in the absence of the professional union, employees are to be represented by a Work Council (Article 9 of the Labour Code), whose election is announced by the employer following the initiative of employees (Law on Work Councils Article 6(1)), the board of judges decided, that in those cases when the obligation of consultations is imperatively determined in the law, in the absence of a union, the employer has to announce the election of Work Council despite the absence of application from the determined 10% employees. After determining the fact that, until 29 May 2009, when the minister of agriculture decided to change the structure of the Centre, the defendant did not fulfil his duty to hold consultations. The board of judges acknowledged him to have violated rights of the plaintiff when dismissing him, according to Article 129 of the Labour Code.

The violation of the duty to hold consultations was one of the reasons that the plaintiff was returned to work. The defendant submitted a cassation complaint to the Supreme Court of Lithuania, where they explained that in the absence of representatives of employees in the Centre, they, as the employers, informed about the coming structural reorganizations in advance in a meeting (in which the plaintiff took part). They therefore claimed to have fulfilled the duty to inform found in the law. The defendant, in the absence of employee representatives, did not have a duty to negotiate with employees. For that reason, in the opinion of the employer, when court stated that there were no real negotiations, it is not acknowledged as the violation of imperative laws that could be the basis claiming that the plaintiff's dismissal was unfair. In the ruling of 27 April 2012, the Lithuanian Supreme Court discussed the employer's duty to hold consultations with representatives of employees, stressing that the duty of the employer to hold consultations with the representatives is determined as a measure to assure the rights of employees, and to stimulate the dialogue between them and the employer. On the other hand, it is possible to have a situation when the company, entity or organization has no representatives of employees who can represent them legally. In such cases the employer has to inform the employees during a general meeting, directly and in advance, about the date of decisions, the reasons for dismissals, as well as the legal, economic and social implications of the changes. The law also determines the outcomes of a violation of the employers' duty to hold consultations with the representatives in case of collective dismissals. Such actions are punishable by a ban from terminating the work agreement (Labour Code Article $130^1(4)$). The jurisprudence of Lithuanian Supreme court draws attention to the fact that, in most general sense, the failure to hold consultations with the employees would be considered as legal grounds to treating the dismissals as unfair. Provided that it is determined that the failure to organize consultations with employee representatives, or failure to keep to the regulations while organizing consultations, could have influenced the dismissal of a particular employee (the decision of the board of judges in Civil cases department of Lithuanian Supreme Court 26 March 2008, in the civil case *V.V. v. AB 'Jonavos grūdai'*, Case No. 3K-3-186/2008). The board of judges of the Court of Cassation explained that in those cases when a company, or organization, has no employee representation, who could represent and defend the rights and interests of the employees against the employer (Labour Code Article 19), the employer can, before the dismissal of employees, (it also concerns the reorganization of a company) inform and consult employees directly or in a general meeting. In the meeting the employer has to indicate the date, reasons, legal and economical outcomes for employees following the termination of work agreements. The Supreme Court decided that the employer is not obligated to ensure that a Work Council (which according to labour law represents the rights and interest of the employees and defends them in work relations) is elected if there is no proposal from employees to establish such. The court determined that the employer of the Centre informed its employees about the coming reorganization during a meeting with employees. The Court of Cassation decided that the employer did not commit serious violation as they held consultations with the employees, and the employer is in addition exempt from the duty to initiate elections of a Work council for employees. The plaintiff's complaint was returned to the Court of Appeals. The Vilnius district court heard the complaint again and decided that the plaintiff was laid off without any reasonable ground, as the employer did not try to move the claimant to another job. The court did not base its decision on the fundamentals of collective dismissals.

[B] Duty to Transfer Employees to the Newly Formed Company

The court admitted that the employer did not keep to the requirement to notify the Labour Exchange Office and municipality about the collective dismissal. But what the plaintiff indicated as a collective dismissal due to company liquidation, was considered by the court as a taking over of the business. In the end, the court admitted the dismissal to be unfair because in the take-over employees were not transferred to the newly formed company.

Šiauliai district court heard a case[13] where it was decided that the employer, prior to dismissing employees, failed to notify the Labour Exchange Office and in this way violated the requirements of Labour Code Article 130[1]. The court went even further and said that when liquidating the company where the plaintiff worked, a new company was established that carried out analogous activity. Into which, according to the law, all the employees had to be transferred. In other words, it was not a collective dismissal from work, but rather a company takeover. A takeover is not a basis to lay off the employees as the law claims. The case started when two plaintiffs filed complaints because their work places were liquidated. Up until the time they were dismissed, they worked in the Raseiniai municipal budget institution 'Raseiniai Social Services Center'. In 2 August 2011, Raseiniai district municipality council decided to liquidate the budget run institution, lay off all the employees, and set up public institution by the same name. The municipality of Raseiniai did not overtake the duties of the liquidated budget institution with all its legal interconnection with former employees, nor did it transfer them to a public institution. The municipality disputed that automatic transfer of all employees to the public institution was impossible at the alteration of work organization when employer dismissed all of the employees because of the liquidation of a budget institution. The public institution had a legal right to choose new employees. The decision about the liquidation of the budget institution was taken by Raseiniai district municipality council and was announced publicly. The territorial Labour Exchange Office has a duty to monitor the territory for which it is responsible and register all dismissals. Therefore, municipality concluded that it had no obligation to notify the Labour Exchange Office as it had to follow the announcements about dismissals in internet and in the press. Municipality did not need to notify anyone because the municipality itself performed the dismissals. The absence of a formal written notification cannot be the basis to apply Labour Code 130[1] Article, on the basis of which the disruption of work agreements could be considered as unfair. Besides, the municipality explained in court that since the budget institution had no active professional union, there was no opportunity to inform the representatives of employees about the termination of work. As a consequence, the employer informed each employee individually. It is important to mention that upon receiving the information, any of the employees, including the plaintiffs, had a right to dispute the decision of the municipality council about the liquidation of the budget institution. After the municipality decided to liquidate the budget institution, and after the budget institution itself publicly announced about the liquidation, the Labour Exchange Office were informed about the dismissals of all the employees.

The first instance court, i.e., the Raseiniai district court, satisfied the complaint of both plaintiffs, claiming that they were dismissed from work unfairly. The court did not return them to work, however, but instead awarded them monetary compensations payable both by municipality and a newly set-up public institution. In addition, the

13. Civil case ' D. Y. B. ir A. K. v. VšĮ "Raseinių socialinių paslaugų centras", Raseinių rajono savivaldybė', case No. 2A-518-124/2011, Šiauliai regional court, 18 September 2012.

plaintiffs were awarded LTL 2000 (about EUR 600) each in non-pecuniary damages. The court concluded that the budget institution was not liquidated, but reorganized by changing its legal form of activity. Therefore, the plaintiffs dismissal following Labour Code Article 136(1.6) concerning employer's liquidation, was unfair. The court also indicated that the budget institution 'The social Center of Raseiniai' did not submit information to Kaunas territorial Labour Exchange Office, or to its Raseiniai department, about the anticipated dismissal of a group of employees. For that reason, the employer was considered to have violated the requirements of Labour Code Article 130^1.

The plaintiffs appealed the decision to Šiauliai district court. In its ruling, given on 18 September 2012, the court analysed the factual situation even more closely and determined that the Raseiniai district municipality transferred all the assets of the liquidated budget institution to the newly established public institution, and that newly established public institution overtook all of the functions and tasks of the liquidated budget institution, adding only a few additional functions. In the end, the tasks of both institutions remained the same. The public institution 'Raseiniai Center of Social Services' received not only the activity of the budget institution, but also all the assets and resources necessary to carry out these activities. Half of the employees from the former institution were employed as well. The positions and the number of them remained relatively the same, if not a bit bigger. The plaintiffs' positions were retained in the newly set up institution. The regulations of both institutions reveal that the owner of the liquidated institution was Raseiniai district municipality, and the municipality was also the founder of the newly set-up public institution. The duties of the liquidated institution's owner were performed by Raseiniai district municipality council, and the duties of the newly set-up institution - by Raseiniai district municipality administration director. The transfer of the rights and duties between of the two companies, in spite of how it was formalized, shows the relations with other employees. In the new institution ninety-seven employees were employed, almost all of them form the former institution. Therefore, the successor of legal duties of the liquidated institution had no basis to terminate work agreements with the plaintiffs. Article 138 of the Labour Code of Lithuania regulates that the change of ownership of a company, institution or organization, their leadership, founder or name, the merging of institutions, organization or splitting, distribution or joining to another institution, company or organization, the transfer of business or a part of it, cannot be legitimate reason to terminate work relations. This provision is applied not only to private institutions, but also to state institutions which carry out various activities, whether they are profit driven or not. The principle is also applied to legal persons that are established and run according to the norms of public law. The aim of this norm is to protect and ensure that employee's rights are protected in case there is an alteration of employer, so that they get a possibility to stay employed with the new employer on the same conditions that were agreed with the first employer. When transferring employer duties, assets and commitments to the public institution 'Raseiniai Social Service Center', the employees had to also be transferred, including the plaintiffs. Therefore, Šiauliai district court changed the decision of the first instance court and returned the plaintiffs to their former positions in the new institution. The district court agreed with the first instance court's opinion that the plaintiffs experienced emotional distress, worsening of health and humiliation due to the fact that, unlike them, a large group of employees were employed in a new institution. The judges' board agreed that illegal acts on the part of the employer caused the claimants distress, a feeling of instability in the work place, and concerns for their future. They concluded that there is causality between the harm experienced by the plaintiffs and defendants' illegitimate acts. For that reason, the decision concerning non-pecuniary damages was kept valid.

The district court agreed with the reasoning of the First Instance Court that when the claimants were dismissed from work, the rules of dismissal outlined in Labour Code Article 130^1, were violated due to the fact that the territorial Labour Exchange Office was not notified about the imminent dismissal of a group of employees. This violation cannot be disregarded by the fact that the decision about the liquidation of the institution was announced publicly. As Article 130^1(3), and the decision of Lithuanian government of 14 October 2008 No. 1032 outlines, a notification in a written form is required.

[C] Consultations with the Representatives of Employees Are Neccesary

The validity of dismissal was debated on different grounds. The court, however, after hearing the case, decided that the employer did not hold any consultations with the representatives of employees before laying off ten employees.

Plaintiff V.B. worked in the municipal company, 'Vilniaus miesto būstas', as a manager. She was laid off on 14 October 2011 due to structural reorganizations in the company. She filed a complaint indicating that there was no actual reorganization, as her functions were retained within the company. Furthermore, only five years were left until her retirement. In such a situation, the work agreement could have been terminated only if her staying at work would have violated the interests of the employer. The plaintiff also indicated that when disrupting the work agreement, the provisions of the collective agreement functioning in the company were violated. First of all, it was provided in the collective agreement that when reducing the number of staff and laying off more than three employees per month, a commission consisting of the employer and a Work council should be formed, which would coordinate work agreement disruptions. But such a commission was not formed and the conditions of the plaintiff's disruption of work were not discussed. Second, in the collective agreement it was stated that, upon the employer's initiative, the work agreement with employees could be disrupted only due to very important reasons, specified in the Labour Code Article 129(2), and after receiving the consent of the Work council. Such consent from the Work council was not received. Third, it was determined in the collective agreement that when laying off employees according to the Article 129 of the Labour Code the precautionary period is increased up to four months for all the employees instead of two months, and respectfully up to six months for those who have a precautionary period of four months. According to the plaintiff, she had a right to be warned six months in advance instead of the four months that were granted by the law. Fourth, it was determined in the collective agreement that the employer will pay severance compensation to employees that are being laid off, with amounts varying in relation to the duration of employment in the company in each employee's case. Based on this assumption, the plaintiff had a right to receive six month size severance payment instead of the received two month payment. The defendant acknowledged that they changed the structure of the company and approved a new staff list, according to which the number of employees in the company was reduced from 41 to 27, and the number of departments from 7 to 3. When the new structure of the company was ratified, on the 15 June 2011 together with the new list of staff, the company had to lay off thirteen employees. The functions of the plaintiff remained only partially, while other parts were transferred to an employee of another department, who had longer work experience. No new vacancies were opened, and consequently there were no other positions to offer the plaintiff. She reproached the employer for not keeping to the provisions of the collective agreement. To that the representative of the defendant answered that in 11 July 2011, there was a collective work dispute investigation. During this meeting with the reconciliation commission, the representatives of the Work council and the employer's representatives decided to recognize that the collective agreement is invalid from the day it was signed, and the representatives of the Work council resigned their authority. Such a decision was taken due to the fact that when electing the Work council the order of its election was violated, and therefore, all of the decisions taken by the council are in consequence invalid. Because the collective agreement is invalid from the moment it was formed, the requirement of the claimant to be awarded compensations and payments is also not sound.

The court of first instance, that is, Vilnius city second district court, after hearing the case determined that the plaintiff was laid off unfairly.[14] The court did not return her to her former job and ruled that the work agreement was to be terminated on a date set by the court. She was awarded payment for work for the forced truancy from the illegal dismissal day until the day the court took the decision to lay her off. The court took the arguments of claimant V.B. about the violation of the work agreement that the employer disrupted according to the Article 129(4) of the Labour Code as well-based. Namely that the plaintiff V.B. at the time of the dismissal had four years, seven months and sixteen days left until the retirement, that is, less than five years. Therefore, the employer could have laid her off only in very special circumstances, and provided that leaving her at work would have violated the interests of the employer. The court of first instance noted that in this case, the employer did not prove that the plaintiff's qualification did not correspond to the position of a newly found specialist. There is no basis to construe that the plaintiff could not have retained the employee by giving her this position, nor that her staying at work would have harmed the interests of the employer. This means that there were no legal grounds to disrupt the work agreement with the plaintiff, and she should not have been notified about the disruption of the work agreement. The court also determined that when carrying out structural reorganization, during which more than ten employees (thirteen in all) were laid off, the

14. Civil case '*V.B.v. Vilniaus miesto būstas*', No. 2A-764-661/2012, Vilnius regional court, 17 April 2012.

employer did not keep to the Labour Code Article 130[1] requirements to hold consultations with the representatives of the employees. It is interesting to note that the court did not mention the fact that after deciding to dismiss a group of employees the employer failed notify the Labour Exchange office and municipality about the planned layoffs. The court also drew attention to the fact that the employer, when disrupting the work agreement, following the Article 129 of the Labour Code, should be seeking opportunities to transfer the employee to another position and upon the consent of the employee, do so. This duty the employer has to carry out during all of the notification period, up and until the factual date of the layoff. In this case it was determined that during the plaintiff's notification period, the employer 'Vilniaus miesto būstas' recruited a new employee to the position of administrator without raising any special requirements. The court rejected the arguments of the defendant that there was an inscription printed on the slip claiming that the plaintiff agreed to be laid off prior to the notification term for her dismissal this way relieving the employer of the duty to offer her another position. The court indicated that the reconciliation commission that was formed by the defendant during the meeting on 11 July 2011, on the agreement of parties, decided that the collective agreement of the Municipal company 'Vilniaus miesto būstas' No. 1 of 8 April 2011 should be held invalid from the date it was signed. This decision of the reconciliation commission is obligatory and enforceable for parties. Since the collective agreement is invalid from the date it was signed, there is no reason to support any provisions from this agreement. The case following the appeal complaint of the plaintiff came before the Vilnius district court, which in essence agreed with the motives of the first instance court.

The Vilnius district court stressed that the defendant's company had a collective agreement, but that the employer viewed it as illegitimate and in violation of the laws and legal interests of the company. Following the Article 68 of the Labour Code a collective work dispute is a dispute between the employees and their representatives, as well as employers and their representatives arising about the establishment or changing of work, social and economic conditions when conducting the negotiations or when concluding and implementing the collective agreement (conflict of interests), in case of failure to meet the demands made and submitted by the parties according to the procedure established by this Code, because of which collective interests and rights of employees are being violated. When the employer started disputing over the collective agreement being invalid, the differences were at first solved by a reconciliation commission consisting of an equal number of parties (in this case employee and employer) representatives. According to Article 74(1) of the Labour Code a decision made by a reconciliation commission is upheld if both parties agree, and is then ratified by writing a protocol and becomes obligatory for both parties. The reconciliation commission on the date 11 July 2011, decided by the agreement of the parties to declare the collective agreement No. 1 signed 8 April 2011, illegal from the day it was signed, due to violation of laws while preparing it. The decision of this commission is not annulled, it is in effect. For this reason, the court did not agree with the statements of the plaintiff that in her case the provisions of the collective agreement had to be applied, although the plaintiff was warned about the lay off and remained laid off until the reconciliation commission took the decision about the collective agreement being illegitimate. The reconciliation commission in addition determined that the Work council which signed the collective agreement was elected illegally. Also, there was no preliminary commission formed to create the outlines of the collective agreement, and the project of collective agreement was not discussed in any meeting with employees. The provisions of the collective agreement regarding the payment for work, awarding of bonuses and one-off payments, was not approved by the company's board. Nor were the provisions of the collective agreement approved by the institution that played the role of the company's owner, more specifically, the institution that puts into effect the rights and duties of the owner, the Vilnius city municipality director of administration. The Court of Appeal stated that it has no basis to deem the reconciliation commission's decision of 11 July 2011 void, in conflict with Labour Code or other laws and regulations. If a normative act is considered illegitimate it cannot be applied, that is why the first instance court was right to refuse to award monetary payments based on the provisions of the collective agreement.

[D] The Work Council Needs to Be Invited to Consultations

Although the dismissal was disputed on several other grounds, the court emphasized that the employer did not hold consultations with the company's Work Council. This constitutes the essential violation of Labour Code Article 130^1, which consequently makes the plaintiff's dismissal unfair.

In the case complaint was filed by the plaintiff Č.R. against the defendant, the company 'Vilniaus miesto būstas'. The court was hearing a case about the changes in the same company carried out by the same decision (ref. II. paragraph 3), during which it was decided to lay off fourteen employees out of forty-one, and to remove the plaintiff from his position as the head of the Loans administration department. The first instance court, Vilnius city second district court, on 7 November 2011, took a decision that satisfied the complaint only partially: it acknowledged the fact that the plaintiff was laid off unfairly, but did not return him to his former position.[15] The court awarded him the salary for the forced period of absence, starting from the time when he was laid off and ending at the time when the decision was made by the court. The court further decided that during the structural reorganization, Č.R. had a right to be kept at work according the Labour Code Article 135(1.2). The municipal institution 'Vilniaus miesto būstas', had to take into consideration the fact that the plaintiff supported a disabled wife, with a disability percentage of 75, and supported two teenage children. Thus in comparison with other employees, whose qualifications were equal to those of the plaintiff, he qualified for the priority right to be kept at work. However the defendant did not consider the question of the priority right to retain the plaintiff at work. By offering the plaintiff only a part time position in the House care department, the defendant violated their essential duty to offer the plaintiff another job. By seeking to keep a different employee at work, the defendant acted illegally and violated the

15. Civil case '*Č.R.v. Vilniaus miesto būstas*', No. 2A-1556-262/2012, Vilniaus regional court, 29 March 2013.

plaintiff's rights. The defendant did not prove that the employee who was kept at work had a priority right over the plaintiff. This way the municipal institution 'Vilniaus miesto būstas' followed Labour Code Article 129(1.2) provisions only formally and when there was a vacant work place, it did not offer the plaintiff a full position. The court also indicated that the employer did not address the then active Work Council about consultations, and this way violated Labour Code Article 130[1] provisions concerning the termination of the work agreement with the plaintiff. With regards to the additional rights the employees were entitled to at the time of the layoffs, the court rejected the demands of the plaintiff, stating that the collective agreement was considered invalid by the reconciliation commission. As a consequence, the plaintiff cannot claim payments based on the collective agreement. The decision of the court was appealed to the higher court of the Vilnius region, but this court upheld the previous decision and agreed with all of the motives indicated by the first instance court.

[E] The Definition Depends on the Number of Dismissed Employees

Out of 458 employees the employer decided to lay off eight. The courts decided that a lay-off of such small proportions does not qualify as what is in the Labour Code Article 130[1] defined as collective dismissal. For that reason, there was no need to keep to the additional requirements.

The courts were hearing a case where they tried to answer the question of whether employer had a duty to fulfil the requirements found in Labour Code Article 130[1]. In other words, whether there was such a dismissal as is described by that article.[16] The facts of the case were as follows: the plaintiff F.K. filed a complaint against the defendant, the Joint-Stock Company 'Philip Morris Lietuva', claiming that she had been laid off unfairly from her position as an ancillary worker. In the plaintiff's opinion her lay-off was unfair because the employer neither organized consultations with representatives of the employees, nor took into consideration the fact that five years were left until the plaintiff was set to retire. For this reason the layoff was especially harmful for the plaintiff. The court of first instance determined that on 8 October 2009, 458 employees worked in the Joint stock company 'Philip Morris Lietuva'. As a result of structural changes (the reorganization of the canteen) the defendant decided to dismiss eight employees, including the plaintiff. Due to the fact that the number of dismissed employees was very small, the court rightfully concluded that when laying off only eight employees the defendant was not obliged to keep to the requirements of Labour Code Article 130[1] – to hold consultations with the representatives of the employees and inform the territorial Labour Exchange office about the dismissals. The fact was that the extent of the layoffs did not correspond to the notion of a group dismissal (when there is 458 employees, the layoffs are only to be considered a group dismissal if the number of dismissed workers exceed thirty). The court

16. Civil case '*F.K. v. Joint stock Company Phillips Morris Lietuva*', No. 2A-661-513/2011, Klaipeda regional court, 21 November 2011.

determined that even without a duty to hold consultations with the representatives of the employees, the defendant, as it is clear from the case material, carried out the dialogue with the representatives of employees, met labour union representatives on a number of occasions, provided explanations about the structural reorganization, and answered questions posed by employee representatives. Besides, the court determined that the notification that the plaintiff received clearly indicated the reasons why she was being laid off. The parties of the dispute do not oppose the fact that the Joint Stock Company 'Philip Morris Lietuva' underwent structural changes. There is also no proof that these structural changes were of a fictitious nature. The court pointed out that it does not have the authority to evaluate whether the reduction of positions was justifiable on economic grounds. In other words, it cannot evaluate if the employer had a sound basis to get rid of one or another position, because it is not within the competence of the court. For that reason it should not be questioned if the defendant purposefully reduced the positions and employed a third party to provide catering services. In this respect according to the evaluation of the lawyers' board, the essence is whether the defendant was offering the plaintiff another job and under which circumstances was the offer presented. As it is visible from the announcement presented by the defendant and the signature of the plaintiff on it, the plaintiff was informed about the vacant positions of technical and project engineer in the company. After evaluating these positions and the description, the board of judges found that at the time claimant was being laid off it was not possible to transfer her to another job. The regional court of Klaipeda agreed with the decision of the first instance court and upheld it as valid.

[F] Two Unions in the Company

Sometimes the employees have two professional unions in the same company. The employer starts consultations with both, but later only makes agreement with one of them. The other union is unhappy with this agreement and wants to have it appealed. The courts are saying that such a dispute first has to be solved by a reconciliation commission formed in the company.

In another case the court was pondering the question of how to resolve a dispute concerning the lawfulness and legitimacy of a decision taken during the consultations with employee representatives.[17] The case was that of the Kaunas transport companies' employees union versus the joint company 'Autrolis' and the Kaunas trolleybus driver's professional union. The facts of the case were such: in the joint stock company 'Autrolis' two professional unions were formed and were active: The transport workers' professional union and The trolleybus drivers' professional union, in other words, the company had two representatives of employees. In June 2009, the company 'Autrolis' began consultations with both professional unions about the deteriorating financial situation and the ways to make it better. During later

17. Civil case '*Kaunas transport companies' employees union v. Joint company "Autrolis" and 'Kaunas trolleybus drivers union*', No. 2S-1603-413/2011, 21 July 2011.

consultations on 1 September 2009, one of the professional unions did not take part. This union was that of the transport workers professional union, to which the plaintiff belonged. A decision was made during these consultations to follow certain criteria when laying off group of employees. The first to be let go would be pensioners who already possess the right to full retirement benefits and those already receiving benefits (in spite of the fact that they are members of professional unions), but with an exception made for professional union committee members. Second priority was to be given to employees with valid demerits, whose term of complaint is already passed, and to those with the shortest experience at work. Third priority would be those employees with the shortest experience and the largest number of demerits, whose complaint term is not yet passed. Provided that enough employees qualified for dismissal could not be found in the two first categories. The agreement also stated that the employer cannot lay off members of Kaunas trolleybus drivers' professional union, who do not have valid demerits.

On 1 September 2009, the defendant, limited company 'Autrolis', submitted a notification to the Kaunas Labour Exchange office about the dismissal of a group of employees. The notification was produced after the consultations with employees were held. In the notice to the Labour Exchange office, the defendant indicated that in the period from 10 November 2009 to 1 February 2010, there were plans to dismiss 220 employees. In reality, in the period from 1 September 2009 until 28 February 2011, only 178 employees were laid off, out of which thirty-five were returned to work following the court's decision. The court pointed out that the employer's duty to hold consultations with the employee representatives about the group dismissals is regulated in Article 130^1(3) of the Labour Code. In this case, however, the employer only made an agreement with one of the professional unions, and this agreement did not satisfy members belonging to other professional unions within the company. The agreement seemed discriminatory to the members of this union because it planned to ban the dismissal of employees of belonging to the union with which the employer had made an agreement. The law does not describe the procedures the dissatisfied party should follow to appeal an unsatisfactory agreement achieved during consultations. Article 68 of Labour Code determines that a collective labour dispute is a disagreement between a union and an employer or a subject that can form collective agreements. The disagreements can arise due to social and economic conditions, their change when negotiating, formulating and carrying out collective agreement (conflict of interest). The conflict between the parties can also arise when requirements that were demanded were not satisfied. Based on the norm of this law, the court decided that the plaintiff's complaint concerning the situation when one professional union disputes the decision of another union is a collective labour dispute according to Article 68 of the Labour Code. Collective labour disputes are solved by the procedure determined in part two, section ten of the Labour Code. According to Article 71 of Labour Code, the collective labour disputes are investigated by: (1) reconciliation commission; (2) work arbitration or the third party court. The court drew attention to the fact that the plaintiff did not initiate the procedure of collective dispute in his workplace and he neither addressed the employer nor the reconciliation commission. Instead the plaintiff addressed the court directly on 9 December 2010, asking the court to declare the agreement which expired on 1 February 2010, invalid. During consultations it was decided to lay off 220 employees over a period stretching until 1 February 2010. The court decided that during the consultations, the legitimacy of the reached agreement was limited from the point of view of time and number of employees being laid off. The agreement expired on 1 February 2010, and as a consequence there were no grounds to apply the collective dispute procedure, since there no longer was any active and valid agreement between the two parties.

The court concluded that the plaintiff did not keep to the regulations of pre-court dispute and will not be able to use these regulations to his advantage because the disputed act stopped being valid. That is why the court decided that there was a basis to dismiss the case.

[G] The Dismissal of Small Part of Employees Does Not Fall under the Scope of Collective Dismissal

The court repeatedly declared that if seventeen employees are dismissed out of total 424 employees, the employer does not have to fulfil the duties of Article 130[1] of the Labour Code, because it is not a collective dismissal in the sense of the law.

Vilnius district court was hearing a case in which the plaintiff V.S.V. filed a complaint concerning his dismissal from work at the limited company 'Lietuvos paštas'.[18] The plaintiff claimed that the Labour Code Article 47 assign a duty for employers to inform employees and hold consultations with employee representatives when reducing positions. The plaintiff had signed a collective agreement with the Lithuanian Communications Workers' Union in 2005. According to this agreement, point 17 dictates that if employees are laid off due to economic or technological reasons, structural reorganization or similar, the defendant has a duty to hold consultations with the before mentioned union to avoid negative consequences of the reorganization. The defendant held consultations about the dismissals with the afore-mentioned professional union following the requirements, on 10 December 2008, and on 6 January 2009. However, the defendant had no agreement with another union that is mentioned by the plaintiff.

The latter union, as the documents of the case show, was not known to the defendant, therefore the defendant did not have any duty before that union. The notice presented to the plaintiff fulfilled the requirements provided in Article 130(2) of the Labour Code. The deadline of notification was met. The plaintiff refused the defendant's offer of another job on 24 January 2009 and 24 March 2009. For that reason it is accepted that there were no opportunities to transfer the plaintiff to another job. Therefore his dismissal procedure was not violated. Vilnius district court upheld the decision of the first instance court and rejected the plaintiff's demand to deem his dismissal from work unfair. The court also established the fact that there were 424 employees in the company. And in 17 March 2009, only seventeen employees were laid

18. Civil case '*V.S.V. v. Joint company Lietuvos paštas*', No. 2A-716-611/2010, Vilnius regional court, decision of 16 September 2010.

off. For that reason, the plaintiff's argument that the defendant had to notify the Labour Exchange office about the planned dismissal of a group of employees in advance is unfounded as according to LR Labour Code Article 130^1, since the defendant laid off fewer than thirty employees.

[H] The Notification of the Labour Exchange Office Should Be in Advance

The municipality did not notify the labour exchange office about the dismissal of 10% of its administration employees. The court agreed that the municipality violated the requirements of a group dismissal outlined in the Labour Code. However, the court concluded that this violation was not essential. The plaintiff's complaint was satisfied on the different grounds.

On 7 May 2013, Šiauliai district administrational court was hearing a case where claimant D.V. was complaining that his lay off was unfair.[19] Up until the dismissal the plaintiff worked in Joniškis district municipality administration as a head of a department. The municipality of Joniškis region decided to reorganize the structure of the administration and to remove some of the positions, including the position of the plaintiff. The municipality, however, did not offer the plaintiff any new job. During the hearing of the case, the defendant, i.e., Joniškis district municipality, agreed that on 1 September 2012, in the administration of Joniškis district there worked 110 employees with work agreements and seventy-nine civil servants, all in all 189 employees. On 3 September 2012, the director of the municipality decided to remove nine employee positions and twenty-eight career civil servant positions, in total thirty-seven positions, starting from 7 January, 2013. The court determined that during the structural reorganization the municipality decided to dismiss more than 10% of its employees. For that reason, according to Labour Code Article 130^1, first and second parts, it was qualified as a dismissal of a group of employees. The court decided that the municipality, when deciding to lay off more than 10% of its employees, failed to inform the Labour exchange office about the upcoming group dismissal. During the court hearing the municipality explained that the reason they did not inform the Labour exchange was that they in reality only laid off four career state servants and four employees who worked according to labour agreements during the structural reorganization in 7 January 2013. The court rejected the defendant's arguments as unsound because the Labour Code requires to notify the territorial Labour Exchange office about the *planned* dismissal of the group of the employees not the already carried out dismissal. Finally, the court decided that the violation is not substantial, and consequently it was not possible to apply Article 89 Part 1 subpar. 3 of the Law on Administrative Proceedings,[20] that is, to admit the decision about the removal of positions as invalid. In this

19. Administrative case '*D.V. v. Joniškis district municipality*', No I-377-257/2013, Šiauliai regional administrative court, 7 May 2013.
20. Law on Administrative Proceedings, http://www3.lrs.lt/pls/inter3/dokpaieska.showdoc_l?p_id=91191, accessed 10 May 2015.

case the claim was satisfied because the plaintiff was not offered another position by the municipality.

[I] Small Number of Employees

Director of municipal administration decided to lay off fifteen employees in his municipality, but in reality laid off only four. The court has ruled that the number of laid off employees was very small, and did not make ten employees in total. For that reason it was not necessary to hold consultations with representatives of the employees and it was not necessary to notify the labour exchange office about the lay-off.

On 11 February 2011, the Supreme Administrative Court of Lithuania was hearing a case according to a plaintiff's E.G. complaint concerning her unfair dismissal from work as a civil servant.[21] The plaintiff worked in the administration of Kalvarijos as a senior specialist in the department of Economic Development and Investment. At home she was raising two children, who both had light disabilities. According to the plaintiff, the director of Kalvarijos municipality administration decided to remove two positions of senior specialists in the department of Economic Development and Investment on 1 June 2009. By the same administrative order, the list of newly established positions revealed that there was being established two new senior positions in the department. For that reason, according to the plaintiff, the number of positions in the department was not actually reduced. Those state servants were left to work in the municipal administration of Kalvarijos for whom there is no basis to apply Article 129(4) of the Labour Code where guarantees for more vulnerable employees are determined. Besides Article 43(1) of the Law on Public Service has a reinforced guarantee for civil servants, whose positions are removed, that they are to be appointed to other positions of the same level and category. In case there are no such positions, and the state servant agrees, he or she can be transferred to a lower position. At the order of the Kalvarijos municipality administration director, eleven new positions were established on 1 June 2009, but none of them were offered to the plaintiff. The plaintiff also based her claim on Labour Code Article 130^1 by saying that the order concerning her lay off was carried out in violation of the requirements found in Article 130^1 of the said Code, because the director of Administration of Kalvarijos municipality, when taking the order on 1 June 2009, No. A-74, where he decided to remove fifteen positions of state servants, did not hold neither consultations with the representatives of the employees and nor notified the Labour Exchange office. The disputed order was found to be taken in violation of the requirements of the collective agreement point 83, ratified on 4 April 2007, because at the time of implementation there was no agreement made with the professional union concerning the dismissals. The defendant said that he had no such duty as described in Labour Code Article $130^1(3)$ to inform territorial Labour exchange office about the coming lay off, because the dismissal were of a minor scale. The order of 1 June 2009, outlined the dismissal of fifteen civil servants and other

21. Administrative case *E.G. v. Kalvarijos municipality administration*, No A143-756/2011, Supreme Administrative Court of Lithuania, 22 February 2011.

employees. It does not reflect the real number of laid off employees, because among the reduced number of positions were also non-existent positions. Non-existent positions were called such positions into which nobody was employed. From the day the decision came into effect, on 21 May 2009, Kalvarijos municipality council laid off only four employees in total. The defendant pointed out that they held consultations with the representatives of the employees, namely, with the then operating professional union of Kalvarijos municipality administration state servants. This was confirmed by the protocol of the consultations. The professional union committee of the Kalvarijos municipality administration informed the administration of Kalvarijos municipality about the agreement to dismiss the plaintiff, and therefore it did not violate the paragraph 83 of the collective agreement.

The court, after hearing the case decided that the plaintiff was laid off unfairly. The motive for this: the employer did not check whether the plaintiff had better reasons to be left in the state service as opposed to the other employees who remained. The court determined that in total there were three analogous positions in the municipality, one of which was occupied by the plaintiff. Since it was decided to remove one of the three positions, the employer had to check which one of the employees had better grounds to be kept in the work place. The arguments for keeping the plaintiff were that she was raising kids younger than 14 years old of age, therefore she should have been laid off only in very special circumstances. This decision was based not on the law of State service but on Labour Code Part 4, Article 129. When it was decided that the dismissal of the plaintiff was unfair, she was reinstated in the state service in the position she had before the lay-off. Also she was awarded average salary for the forced absenteeism from the day she was unfairly laid off until the day the court's decision came into effect (Labour Code Article 297 (1) and (3)). The court also made a conclusion that the defendant did not violate Labour Code Article 130^1 requirements because in reality until 10 December 2009, the work relations were disrupted concerning only four employees, therefore, taking into consideration requirements of Article 130^1, the defendant did not have the duty to hold consultations with the representatives of the employees and to notify the territorial Labour Exchange office about the dismissals. Since these requirements only call for such steps if the dismissal concerns ten or more employees. The defendant also organized consultations about the structural changes in Kalvarijos municipality administration and reduction of employees.

[J] Who Could Be Defined as Representative of the Employees

Lithuanian Police Forensic Research Centre decided to remove twenty-two positions. Although among the employees of the Centre there were members of two professional unions, the court decided that the employer did not have a duty to consult with neither of them, because they were not actively performing the functions of employee representation and defence at the Lithuanian Police Forensic Research centre.

The Supreme Administrative court of Lithuania heard a case concerning the dismissal of the civil servant R.J.[22] The plaintiff worked as a senior specialist in the Lithuanian Police Forensic Science Centre, Identification Committee, Department of Biological Research. Her position was A level, 11th category according to the Law on Public Service of the Lithuanian Republic. The positions of civil servants are classified according to levels and categories which are decisive as to what requirements must be met in order to occupy the position and consequently what salary is paid. The plaintiff was complaining that she was not offered any other position, and also pointed out that a group of civil servants was laid off without holding any consultations with the professional unions. The court determined that Lithuania's commissioner general through the order issued on 3 February 2009, effective from 1 July 2009, removed all (twenty-two) Lithuanian Police Forensic Science Centre Identification Committee Department of Biological Research positions: five statute civil servants and seventeen career civil servants (out of them – three chief specialist positions). By the same order there were established twenty-two new positions: five statute civil servants and seventeen career civil servants (out of them: three – chief specialists, ten senior specialists, and four specialists). However none of the newly established positions in the Lithuanian Police Forensic Science Centre Identification Committee Department of Biological Research were A level and 11th category on 1 July 2009. Therefore there is no basis to doubt that after the Biological Research Department was reorganized, the plaintiff's position was removed. When comparing the newly confirmed Biological Research Department Description of career civil servants positions with previously existing positions in this department of career civil servants, it is obvious that in reality not only the plaintiff's position disappeared, but also other positions of career civil servants at the Biological Research Department were removed and replaced by new positions which had different or additional functions. Therefore the court decided that the plaintiff's claim that after reorganization of the Lithuanian Police Forensic Science Centre Identification Committee Department of Biological Research structure, positions and their allotted functions in essence stayed the same is unfounded. What concerns the plaintiff's claim that the defendant, while reorganizing Identification Committee Biological Research Department, did not consult with the representatives of employees, as it is required based on Article 23 (1.2) and Article 47 of the Labour Code. The court stressed that in the previously heard case the courts have determined that the Lithuanian Police Forensic Science Centre and Police Department in this case did not have to consult with the professional union of Vilnius district pre-trial research institution and the professional union of Lithuanian police officers, because they were not performing the functions of representation and defence that the employees of the Biological Research Department employees had bestowed on them. Besides, the courts determined from the documents in the case that the defendant prior to reorganizing the Centre, held meetings both with the Police department's leaders and with the employees, in which they touched upon the questions of the reorganization of the Lithuanian Police Forensic Science Centre Identification Committee Department of Biological

22. Administrative case '*R.J. v. the Lithuanian Police Forensic Research Centre*', No.A756-332/2011, The Supreme Administrative Court of Lithuania, decision of 27 January 2011.

Research. The chairman of the professional union of Vilnius district pre-trial research institutions and the chairman of Lithuanian police officers professional union took part in some of the meetings. The information about the change of position descriptions of the centre's civil servants' was submitted to the professional union of Vilnius District Pre-Trial Research Institutions. In the Article 43(1) of the Law on Public Service is regulated that a career civil servant whose position is removed should be appointed to another position of the same level and category. Or if there is no such position and the civil servant agrees, to a lower position. If until the removal of the position a career civil servant is not appointed to another position, he is laid off.

The court determined that after the reorganization at Lithuanian Police Forensic Science Centre Identification Committee Department of Biological Research from 1 July 2009 there remained no career civil servants of A level 11th category at the department. Therefore, the plaintiff could not be appointed to the same department and the same level and category position. The plaintiff was offered an A level 10th category position, but she refused. Therefore she was laid off legitimately and on a fair basis.

[K] Whether Consultations with the Union Be Successful?

The court agreed that before dismissing a group of employees no consultations were held with the professional union. But the fact that such consultations could have stopped the plaintiff from being laid off was not proved.

Šiauliai district Administrative Court was hearing a case following the complaint of the plaintiff A.M. concerning the order of 22 December 2009, No. TR-225, 'About A.M.'s dismissal from interior service', signed by the Šiauliai selection commander of Lithuanian Republic interior ministry.[23] The plaintiff called for the abolishment of the above-mentioned order and also had other requirements. He was serving in the Šiauliai Selection as a specialist at the Technical department (statute civil servant, level B, category 7). He was asking the order from the commander of the selection, through which he was laid off, to be abolished as unfair and without any legal basis. The plaintiff received the dismissal slip, in which he was informed that he will be laid off from the position, although it was not said specifically that his position was being removed. A number of positions were removed in the Šiauliai Selection due to structural reorganizations. The plaintiff was motivating his right to be left at work by pointing out that he had spent twelve years in the service. Besides, the plaintiff claimed that the duties of the Labour Code Articles 23, 47 and 130^1(4) were not carried out. The defendant not only failed to provide detailed or at least minimal information, on how the reorganization would be carried out in the Šiauliai Selection, but also how the reorganization would affect the employed civil servants. Although the professional union did express a wish to provide consultations, the Šiauliai Selection did not take it

23. Administrative case '*A.M. v. State Border Guard Service at the Ministry of the Interior of the Republic of Lithuania Šiauliai selection office*', No I-102-621/2010, Šiauliai regional administrative court, decision of 14 June 2010.

into consideration. A third party, the Professional Union of Lithuanian Republic Pre-trial Research Institutions, commented that the State Border Guard Service under the Ministry of the Interior of the Republic of Lithuania (later-SBGS), Šiauliai Selection, carried out the reorganization and laid off a group of employees, among which there were Professional union members, including the plaintiff. In this way they violated the demands of Article 130[1] of the Labour Code and Article 47 of the Law on Trade Unions, as the defendant did not inform and did not hold consultations with the Professional union. According to the data provided by the professional union, the dismissal slips were distributed over a period of time starting from 30 September 2009. There were no consultations held with the professional union, and the union also did not receive neither any information about the present and future activity of the company (structural unit) nor any information about the economic situation or work relations. In addition, no written notification was submitted to the Labour Exchange office about the planned dismissal of the group of employees. The professional union claimed that SBGS, being in specific relations with the defendant (because only he has a right to take a decision concerning reorganization and a number of positions), had a duty before taking a decision about reduction of positions to notify the Professional union about the dismissals before 27 August 2009. The Šiauliai Selection, as an employer, had a duty to inform and hold consultations in a period stretching from 27 August 2009 until 30 September 2009 (that is, until the slips were delivered to the employees). But the case material holds no proof that it was actually done. The fact that consultations were held could have been proved if the defendant had been able to present the protocol of consultations, but such was not presented by the defendant. Since the protocol does not exist, a conclusion can be drawn that there were no consultations. The same can be said about the information. The defendant cannot submit, and did not submit, the objective proof to the court of what specific information it handed over to the professional unions. And in contrast, the third interested party presented all the information that it had received.

The court did not satisfy the plaintiff's complaint. It decided that there was no realistic opportunity to offer the plaintiff another position. He was offered a lower category position, but since he refused he was reasonably laid off from the service. Concerning the arguments that the defendant did not keep to the duties when carrying out the collective dismissal, the court admitted that, as Article 130(4) of the Labour Code determines, the employer had an obligation to hold consultations with the employee representatives before presenting the employees with dismissal slips. The purpose of the consultations is to ensure that the rights of the employees are observed and that the dialogue between the employees and employers is kept alive. The court agreed with the argument of the plaintiff that there were no consultations held with Lithuanian Republic Pre-trial Investigation Institutions' Professional Union, but this circumstance in itself is not sufficient basis to acknowledge that the plaintiff was laid off unfairly. The court made the conclusion that the absence of consultations would not have had any consequence for the plaintiff's dismissal. It was not proved that the dismissal could have been avoided through organizing consultations.

§17.03 CONCLUSION

In conclusion, it can be seen from the presented examples of court practice that employers do not keep closely to the Labour Code requirements when dismissing groups of employees. In practice, consultations with the representatives of employees are often of a rather formal nature, if indeed they are held at all.

The courts are not inclined to take the violations of these requirements as serious infringement or as reason to deem the dismissal of one or several employees as unfair. It is difficult to agree with the court's decision mentioned in Part II.11, that consultations, even if they were held, would not have had any consequences when laying off the plaintiff. Such a conclusion only shows that the court does not believe in the importance of consultations, and disregards their meaning or benefit. Even in those cases when the courts agree that the requirements to consult with the employee representatives, or to announce about the dismissal to the Labour Exchange office and municipality, weren't carried out before laying off a group of employees, such a violation, in the eyes of the courts is not viewed as being a substantially serious basis to acknowledge the concrete dismissal from work as unfair. The courts, when satisfying or rejecting the requirements of the plaintiffs, usually base their decisions on other arguments. In the case of a group employee dismissal, the failure to carry out the requirements is mentioned only as the additional secondary motive.

CHAPTER 18

Collective Dismissals in the Grand-Duchy of Luxembourg

Tom Moes

§18.01 PART ONE: THE LEGAL FRAMEWORK

The 31 July 2006 Law creating a Labour Code, abrogating a number of relevant laws and other legal texts concerning the relationship between employers and employees, such as the 24 May 1989 Law on the employment contract ('Loi du 24 mai 1989 sur le contrat de travail'), has come into force on 1 September 2006.

Article L. 166-1 to L. 166-9 of the above-mentioned Labour Code deal with collective dismissals. Article L. 166-1 refers to the definition of collective dismissals and the scope of application of the legislation, whereas Article L. 166-2 and L. 166-3 concern the negotiations preceding the establishment of a social plan ('plan social') and Articles L. 166-4 to L. 166-8 deal with the procedure of a collective dismissal. Finally, Article L. 166-9 relates to damages and compensation.

> Article L. 166-1:
>
> The legislation concerning collective dismissals comes to application when the employer decides several dismissals on one or several non-inherent grounds in the employees: when the number of dismissals amounts to 7 for a period of 30 days or to 15 dismissals for a period of 90 days. For the calculation of the mentioned dismissals the employment contracts terminations on the initiative of the employer are assimilated to dismissals on one or several non-inherent grounds in the employees provided that the explicit dismissals are at least four in number.
>
> Articles L. 166-2 and L. 166-3:
>
> Prior to take the decision of collective dismissals the employer has to negotiate with the representatives of the employees in order to achieve a social plan (' plan social') which will deal with the social accompanying measures, the possibilities of re-conversion of the workers, the immediate re-insertion on the labour market and

the financial compensation measures. Under penalty of nullity, the negotiations have to refer in the first place to the possibilities of avoiding or reducing collective dismissals and the possibilities of mitigating the consequences by using social accompanying measures such as redeployment and retraining measures or the possibilities of an immediate reintegration into the labour market.

The employees' representatives within the meaning of Article L. 166-2 are the staff delegates, the mixed committees if they exist or, in the case of enterprises bonded by a collective agreement, the trade unions being parties to this agreement. The employees and their representatives are allowed to solicit experts in legal, fiscal, social, economic and accountant matters.

At the latest fifteen days after the beginning of the negotiations the parties record the result of the negotiations in a duly signed convention which is designated as 'social plan' ('plan social'). This convention is transmitted without delay to the Employment administration with a copy to the Employment Inspection ('Inspection du Travail et des Mines'). The contract documents either the agreement of the parties on the social plan or the disagreement of the parties; in latter case the document is to be transferred without delay to the Employment administration with a copy to the Employment Inspection.

In case of disagreement the parties will jointly refer to the National conciliation office ('Office national de conciliation') at the latest three days after the signing of the disagreement protocol. The chairman of the National conciliation office convenes within two days the members of the joint commission which sits at the latest three days after the convocation. The deliberations of the commission are closed at the latest fifteen days after the first hearing and the result of these deliberations is recorded in a protocol which is transmitted without delay to the Employment administration and the Employment Inspection.

Any dismissal notified for a non-inherent ground in an employee before the date of the signature of the social plan or the ruling of the National conciliation office would be null and void.

Article L. 166-2 (8) provides the possibility for an employee in case of dismissal to refer in fifteen days to the Chairman of the Labour court ('Président du Tribunal du travail') who will establish the illegal nature of this dismissal or the ineffectiveness ('nullité') and decide that the employee will remain on his working place. If the employee has not invoked the nullity or the ineffectiveness of his dismissal and has not requested the continuation of the working relationship in the above mentioned term he is entitled to the damages and compensation referred to in paragraph (1) of Article L. 124-7 of the Labour Code. Furthermore, he can exercise a legal action on the basis of unfair dismissal provided by Articles L. 124-11 and L. 124-12 of the same Code.

Article L. 166-3 of the Labour Code provides that in order to give the employees' representatives the possibility to formulate constructive suggestions concerning the conclusion of the social plan the employer has the obligation to deliver them all useful information about the motives of the project of collective dismissals, the number and the employees' categories affected by the dismissals, the number and the categories of the employed workers, the period during which the collective dismissals are due to take place, the criterions considered for the choice of the employees to be dismissed and, if appropriate, the calculation method for any compensation for a dismissal exceeding the one provided by the law or the collective agreement. The employer has to transmit a copy of this written communication to the Employment administration which transmits it to the Employment Inspection.

Articles L. 166-4 to L. 166-8:

At the latest at the beginning of the negotiations concerning the conclusion of a social plan the employer has to give a written notification of the collective dismissal project to the Employment administration which delivers a copy to the Employment Inspection. The employer has in addition the obligation to transmit to the employees' representatives a copy of the aforesaid notification and the representatives can address their possible observations to the Employment administration which transmits a copy to the Employment Inspection. The present Article (L. 166-4) is also applicable to a collective dismissal project linked to a cessation of activities of the enterprise resulting from a court decision.

The employer can only notify individual dismissals to the concerned employees after the signature of the social plan or the protocol of the National conciliation office and the notifications notified in violation of the aforesaid rule are null and void.

The collective dismissals operated respectfully to the provisions of the afore mentioned Articles shall take effect with regard to the employees at the expiration of a seventy-five days term, regardless of possible longer terms provided by legal or conventional provisions governing individual rights in the field of periods of notice. However, the Minister of Labour can extend the term to a period of ninety days when the problems caused by the collective dismissals seem to get no solution within the initial term.

It is to be added that the above mentioned provisions are not applicable to intervening collective dismissals following the cessation of activities of the enterprise resulting from a court decision. However, Article L.166-7 of the Labour Code provides that if the total or partial cessation of activities of a company within the meaning of Article 16 of the modified Law of 27 July 1993 on 1. the economic development and diversification 2. the improvement of the general structure and the regional balance of the economy intervenes without a justification of objective reasons the Minister of Labour can exceptionally extend the term of seventy-five days to ninety days.

It is also to be underlined that provisions concerning the collective dismissals apply regardless the fact that the decision concerning the collective dismissals emanates from the employer or from a company controlling the employer. Concerning the breaches of the obligations of information, negotiation and notification provided by the legislation applicable to collective dismissals, any justification by the employer based on the fact that the company which took the decision of collective dismissals did not give him the necessary information will not be taken to account.

Article L. 166-9:

Without prejudice to the nullity or the ineffectiveness of dismissals described above the employees having been subject to collective dismissals not corresponding to the rules applicable to collective dismissals are entitled to, outside the compensation provided by law, damages for unfair termination of the contract.

§18.02 PART TWO: THE LUXEMBOURGISH AND EUROPEAN JURISPRUDENCE

[A] The Definition of a Collective Dismissal

As related in Part One the collective dismissal characterizes itself by the number of dismissed persons and the nature of the motives at the bases of the dismissal. We are talking about collective dismissal when the number of considered dismissals by the employer concerns either at least seven employees for a period of thirty days, or at least fifteen employees for a period of ninety days.

> In order to get the number of seven workers or of fifteen workers one has to count not only the dismissals in the proper sense but also the other terminations of working contracts which are not linked to the person of the employee and result from the initiative of the employer.

The jurisprudence takes also into account retirements and negotiated departures *(cf. judgment of the Court of Appeal of 27 April 2006, n° 30194)*.

Nevertheless, the procedure of collective dismissals applies only to the dismissals in the proper sense and not to the other terminations of contract. One judiciary decision has even taken into account the global number of dismissals pronounced by the employer, that the dismissal took place in Luxembourg or not:

- Court order of 20 March 2002, n° 1567/02:

> In this case the employee has been dismissed on economic grounds. He states that during the same period of thirty days his employer, a Belgian company, has dismissed more than twenty employees for rationalization and restructuration motives of the enterprise without complying with the collective dismissals legislation, notably the employer did not engage negotiations with the employees' representatives. The company does not contest the dismissals of more than seven employees on one or several non-inherent grounds in the employees, specifying that the restructuration of the enterprise on a world level would lead to twenty-three dismissals in Belgium and four in Luxembourg. It is clear that the legislation on collective dismissals does not distinguish between an employer established on the national territory and the one established abroad.
>
> *The judges therefore deem that it is necessary to take into account, by reference to the Luxembourgish law which is clear, the global number of the dismissals pronounced by the employer, the Belgian company, and not to consider therefore only those concerning the employees of the Luxembourgish branch. Since then it is to be noted that the threshold of seven dismissed employees during the reference period of thirty days has been exceeded and that, according to the collective dismissals legislation, the employer should have started negotiations in the Grand-Duchy of Luxembourg in order to establish a social plan for the four employees of the Luxembourgish branch of the Belgian company. As this did not happen the dismissal of the employee has been declared null and void and he has been reinstated in the enterprise.*

The conditions of information and consultation of the workers during an intra-group restructuring: The Court of Justice of the European Union (CJEU) delivered a judgment that has a direct impact on Luxembourgish Labour law:

• Judgment of the Court of Justice of the European Union (CJEU) of 10 September 2009 (Case C-44/08) (Akavan Erityisalojen Keskusliitto AEK ry and Others v/s Fujitsu Siemens Computers Oy):

Following the merger of certain IT businesses of Fujitsu Ltd and Siemens AG into a joint undertaking, the Fujitsu Siemens Computers group started trading on 1 October 1999.

FSC is a subsidiary of Fujitsu Siemens Computers (Holdings) BV (the 'parent company'), a company established in the Netherlands. At that time, the group had production plants in Espoo (Kilo) (Finland) and in Augsburg, Paderborn and Sömmerda (Germany).

At a meeting held on 7 December 1999, the executive council of the parent company, which consists of the executive members of its board of directors, decided to make a proposal to the board of directors for the divestiture of the Kilo factory.

At a meeting of 14 December 1999, that board of directors decided to support the proposal, but no specific decision was taken in relation to that factory.

On the same day, FSC proposed consultations, which took place between 20 December 1999 and 31 January 2000.

On 1 February 2000 FSC's board of directors, mainly consisting of directors of the group and chaired by the deputy chairman of the parent company's board of directors, took a decision to terminate FSC's operations in Finland with the exception of computer sales. On 8 February 2000 FSC began making employees redundant. In total, some 450 of the 490 employees were made redundant.

Some employees claimed that FSC has infringed the Law on cooperation in the course of decisions taken at the end of 1999 and beginning of 2000 with regard to the closure of the Kilo factory. Those employees assigned their claims for compensation under that law to the appellants in the main proceedings, who are trade unions, so that they could seek recovery. The appellants brought an action before the Espoon käräjäoikeus (Court of first instance in Espoo) for that purpose.

During the proceedings before that Court, the appellants in the main proceedings claimed that a final decision to run down the activity of the Kilo factory and to separate it from the group's activity before transferring it to Germany, so that that production plant would no longer be part of the group, had in fact been taken by the parent company's board of directors by 14 December 1999 at the latest. According to the appellants in the main proceedings, the real decision had been taken on 14 December 1999, before the consultations with the workforce required by the Law on cooperation had taken place. The respondent in the main proceedings had therefore, intentionally or through manifest negligence, failed to comply with that law.

FSC for its part asserted, first, that no decision on the production plant had been taken at the meeting of the parent company's board of directors on 14 December 1999 and, second, that possible alternatives existed, such as the continuation of the activity, as it was or in a reduced form, its sale or its continuation in partnership with another undertaking. FSC further contended that the concept of a decision by the employer implies action by the competent body of the company concerned, namely, in this case, its board of directors, and that the decision on termination had been taken by the board of directors on 1 February 2000, in other words after conclusion of consultations.

The Espoon käräjäoikeus held that the appellants in the main proceedings had not shown that the parent company's board of directors had decided to close the Kilo factory in such a way that the interaction between the employer and the employees within FSC could not take place in the manner prescribed by the Law on cooperation. In the opinion of that court, the alternatives to closure of that factory were genuine and those alternatives had been examined in the course of consultations. The court held that the decision on closure had been taken at the meeting of FSC's board on 1 February 2000, after it had proved impossible to find another solution, and that the consultations had been genuine and appropriate, and accordingly dismissed the action.

On appeal, the Helsinki hovioikeus (Helsinki Court of Appeal) stated that the final decision referred to by Paragraph 7(1) of the Law on cooperation could only have been taken by the employer, namely the respondent in the main proceedings, and that the proposals made by the parent company were not within the scope of the obligation to hold consultations imposed by the law. It accordingly upheld the decision of the Espoon käräjäoikeus.

The Korkein oikeus, before whom an appeal was then brought by the appellants in the main proceedings, held that there were differences both of structure and content between the provisions of Directive 98/59 and of the Law on cooperation and that, consequently, the connection between them was not entirely clear.

The Korkein oikeus considered that an interpretation of the provisions of Directive 98/59 was necessary for its decision and therefore decided to stay the proceedings and to refer the following questions to the Court of Justice for a preliminary ruling:

' (1) Is Article 2(1) of Directive 98/59/EC to be interpreted as meaning that the obligation under that provision to embark on consultations when "contemplating collective redundancies" of employees and "in good time" requires consultations to be started when it is established from strategic decisions or changes that have been made relating to the activity that a need for collective redundancies of employees follows? Or is the provision in question to be interpreted as meaning that the obligation to start consultations already arises on the basis of the employer contemplating measures or changes affecting the activity, such as a change in production capacity or a concentration of production, as a consequence of which a need for collective redundancies is to be expected?

(2) Having regard to the fact that the first subparagraph of Article 2(3) of Directive 98/59 refers to the supply of information in good time during the course of the consultations, is Article 2(1) of (that) directive to be interpreted as meaning that the obligation under that provision to start consultations when "contemplating" collective redundancies and "in good time" requires consultations to be started already before the employer's intentions have reached the stage at which the employer is required to identify and supply to the employees the information specified in Article 2(3)(b) (of that directive)?

(3) Is Article 2(1) in conjunction with Article 2(4) of Directive 98/59 to be interpreted as meaning that, in a situation in which the employer is controlled by another undertaking, the employer's obligation to start consultations with the representatives of the employees originates when either the employer or the parent company controlling the employer contemplates action for collective redundancies of employees in the employer's service?

(4) In the case of consultations to be carried on in a subsidiary belonging to a group, and in assessing in the light of the provisions of Article 2(4) of Directive 98/59 the obligation under Article 2(1) to enter into consultations when "contemplating"

collective redundancies and "in good time", does the obligation to start consultations already arise when the management of the group or the parent company contemplates collective redundancies but that intention has not yet taken concrete form as concerning the employees in the service of a particular subsidiary under its control, or does the obligation to embark on consultations within the subsidiary arise only at the stage when the management of the group or the parent company contemplates collective redundancies specifically in that subsidiary company? (...)"

The Court ruled as follows:

"1. Article 2(1) of Council Directive 98/59 of 20 July 1998 on the approximation of the laws of the Member States relating to collective redundancies must be interpreted to mean that the adoption, within a group of undertakings, of strategic decisions or of changes in activities which compel the employer to contemplate or to plan for collective redundancies gives rise to an obligation on that employer to hold consultations with workers' representatives.

2. Whether the obligation has arisen for the employer to start consultations on the collective redundancies contemplated does not depend on whether the employer is already able to supply to the workers' representatives all the information required in Article 2(3)(b) of Directive 98/59.

3. Article 2(1) of Directive 98/59, read in conjunction with the first subparagraph of Article 2(4) of that directive, must be interpreted to mean that, in the case of a group of undertakings consisting of a parent company and one or more subsidiaries, the obligation to hold consultations with the workers' representatives falls on the subsidiary which has the status of employer only once that subsidiary, within which collective redundancies may be made, has been identified.

4. Article 2(1) od Directive 98/59, read in conjunction with Article 2(4) of that directive, must be interpreted to mean that, in the case of a group of undertakings, the consultation procedure must be concluded by the subsidiary affected by the collective redundancies before that subsidiary, on the direct instructions of its parent company or otherwise, terminates the contracts of employees who are to be affected by those redundancies".

As the motives underlying the dismissals are concerned one has to note that these reasons have to be of an economic nature (restructuration of the enterprise leading to a dismantling of work places, bad financial situation of the company forcing it to reduce its personnel costs...).

A collective dismissal can never be based on grounds inherent to the employee's aptitude or his conduct in the enterprise:

- Judgment of the Labour Court of Luxembourg of 15 November 1999, n° 4907/99):

The disputed dismissal occurred within a collective dismissal procedure. However, even if the employee is protected by a special legislation in the case of collective dismissals, it has been decided that such an employee, victim of a dismissal within a collective dismissal, has the same rights as the one being victim of an individual dismissal. So the employer has to provide the employee, if he asks the grounds, a precise and concrete motivation justifying his dismissal. In the present case the employer did not provide the reasons of the dismissal of the employee with the requested precision, the social plan stating besides only briefly that " (...) due to the termination of several important building sites and regarding the situation of the order book the company is forced to reduce a significant number of the personnel."

As the imprecision of the reasons is equivalent to an absence of motives the disputed dismissal is to be declared unfair.

Dissolution and liquidation of an enterprise: The immediate termination of employment contracts following a judicial decision ordering the dissolution and winding up of a legal person is assimilated to a collective dismissal for the application of Articles 1-3 of Council Directive 98/59/EC of 20 July 1998 on the approximation of the laws of the Member States relating to collective redundancies. The procedure of the collective dismissals has therefore to be respected by the management of the company if it remains in place, even with limited executive powers, or by its liquidator insofar as the management has been taken over by the latter. These obligations have to be respected until the definitive extinction of the legal personality of the enterprise whose dissolution and winding up has been ordered:

- Judgment of the Court of Justice of the European Union (CJEU) of 3 March 2011 (Joined Cases C-235/10 to C-239/10):

The references for a preliminary made by the Cour de Cassation of Luxembourg relate to the interpretation of Articles 1 to 3 of Council Directive 98/59/EC of 20 July 1998 on the approximation of the laws of Member States relating to collective redundancies (OJ 1998 L. 225, p. 16). The references were made in the course of proceedings between Mr Claes, Mrs Jeanjean, Mr Rémy, Mr Schneider and Mrs Tran and Landsbanki Luxembourg SA (' Landsbanki '), in liquidation, concerning the immediate termination of their employment contracts following a judicial decision ordering the dissolution and winding up of Landsbanki. It is to be specified that Landsbanki is a credit institution established in Luxembourg.

By judgment of 8 October 2008, the Tribunal d'arrondissement de Luxembourg (Luxembourg District Court), upon application by Landsbanki, made Landsbanki subject to the suspension of payments procedure for a maximum duration of six months and appointed Deloitte SA as administrator to monitor the management of the assets.

By application of 27 November 2008, the State prosecutor of the Tribunal d'arrondissement de Luxembourg applied for the dissolution and winding up of Landsbanki. The financial sector supervisory commission also sought an order for the judicial winding up of Landsbanki.

By judgment of 12 December 2008, the Tribunal d'arrondissement de Luxembourg held that Landsbanki's situation could not be rectified and that it was not in a position to meet its commitments and ordered its dissolution. It also announced the winding up of Landsbanki and appointed two liquidators.

By letter of 15 December 2008, the liquidators informed the employees of Landsbanki of the dissolution and winding up of that institution and that their employment contracts had been terminated in accordance with Article L. 125-1 of the Luxembourg Labour Code.

On 19 December 2008, Landsbanki's banking authorisation was withdrawn.

By application of 24 December 2008, the applicants in the main proceedings sought from the President of the Tribunal du travail (Labour Court) a declaration that their redundancies were of no effect, since, in four of the cases, they were staff representatives and, in one, a pregnant woman. They applied for their immediate reinstatement.

By orders of 10 February 2009, the President of the Tribunal du travail dismissed the applications as unfounded, given the circumstances making that reinstatement literally impossible.

The applicants in the main proceedings appealed against those orders.

By orders of 4 June 2009, the President of the chamber of the Cour d'appel (Court of Appeal) having jurisdiction dismissed those appeals as unfounded and upheld the orders under appeal, on the ground that the reasons which led the legislature to provide in Article L. 125-1(1) of the Luxembourg Labour Code for the termination with immediate effect of employment contracts following a declaration of the employer's insolvency held good in this case. The termination of activities was the result of a factual situation which was comparable to insolvency and so the judicial winding up can be compared to the insolvency referred to in Article L. 125-1(1).

The applicants in the main proceedings appealed against the orders of 4 June 2009 to the Cour de Cassation which, finding that interpretation of Articles 1 to 3 of Directive 98/59 was necessary to enable it to give judgment in the cases of which it is seised, stayed the proceedings and referred to the Court the following questions for a preliminary ruling, which are worded identically in each of the three cases:

'(1) Are Articles 1, 2 and 3 of Directive 98/59 ... to be interpreted as applying to a termination of activities as a result of a declaration that the employer is insolvent or a judicial decision ordering the dissolution and winding up, on grounds of insolvency, of the credit institution which is the employer on the basis of Article 61(1)(a) and (b) of the Law ... of 5 April 1993 relating to the financial sector, (as amended by the Law of 19 March 2004), in respect of which termination national legislation provides for the termination of employment contracts with immediate effect?

(2) If the answer to the first question is in the affirmative, are Articles 1, 2 and 3 of Directive 98/59 to be interpreted as meaning that the administrator or liquidator is deemed to be in the same position as an employer who is contemplating collective redundancies and who is able to carry out, to that end, the acts referred to in Articles 2 and 3 of (that) directive and of effecting such redundancies (Case C-323/08 Rodriguez Mayor and Others (2009) ECR I-11621, paragraphs 39, 40 and 41)?'

The Court ruled as follows:

"1. Articles 1 to 3 of Council Directive 98/59 of 20 July 1998 on the approximation of the laws of the Member States relating to collective redundancies must be interpreted as applying to a termination of the activities of an employing establishment as a result of a judicial decision ordering its dissolution and winding up on grounds of insolvency, even though, in the event of such a termination, national legislation provides for the termination of employment contracts with immediate effect.

2. Until the legal personality of an establishment whose dissolution and winding up have been ordered has ceased to exist, the obligations under Articles 2 and 3 of Directive 98/59 must be fulfilled. The employer's obligations pursuant to those provisions must be carried out by the management of the establishment in question, where it is still in place, even with limited powers of management over the establishment, or by its liquidator, where that establishment's management has been taken over in its entirety by the liquidator."

The Cour de Cassation than stated that by retaining that the work contract had been duly terminated with immediate effect by reference to Article L. 166-1 (1) of the Labour Code, on the ground that the reasons which led the legislature to provide in Article L. 125-1(1) of the Luxembourg Labour Code for the termination with immediate effect of employment contracts following a declaration of the employer's insolvency held good in this case and that the termination of activities was the result of a factual situation which was comparable to insolvency and so the judicial winding up can be compared to the insolvency referred to in Article L. 125-1(1), the President of the chamber of the Cour d'appel having jurisdiction has violated Articles 2 and 3 of Council Directive 98/59/EC of 20 July 1998 and Articles L. 166-1 to L. 166-5 of the Labour Code. Thus, this order is liable to cassation (Judgment of Cour de Cassation of 10 October 2011, N° 58 to 61/11).

[B] The Collective Dismissal and Protective Measures Against the Discharge of a Staff Representative

The issue comes down to answer the following question: Protection against the discharge of a the staff representative or freedom of commerce and industry: which principle prevails?

According to Article L. 415-11 of the Labour Code during their mandate the staff representatives or equality and security representatives cannot be dismissed.

What it is the incidence of a collective dismissal on such a protection?:

• Order of the President of the chamber of the Cour d'appel (Court of Appeal) (8th Chamber) of 27 October 2005:

"The adoption of a negotiated social plan between the employer and the employees' representatives is certainly a prerequisite to the considered dismissals. However, the law, in its provisions regarding the collective dismissals, has not the effect for the staff delegates of losing their protection against dismissal, this specific protection being attached to their function.

Thus, the employees having a representative mandate enjoy, in the interest of the whole of the employees who are represented by them and whose interests are preserved by them, an exceptional and exorbitant protection which prohibits the employer, even in the case of a collective dismissal, to dismiss them prior to the expiration of their social mandate. The conclusion of a social plan does therefore not exempt the employer to respect the compulsory provisions of Article L 415-11 of the Labour Code which allow no derogation, except the dismissal for serious misconduct. The first degree order having declared the dismissal of the staff representative null and void is thus to be confirmed."

• A judgment of the Constitutional Court (Cour Constitutionnelle) of 26 March 2010, Reg. N° 56, has confirmed the primacy of the staff representatives' protection in face of the managing power of the employer:

The facts were the following:

An employee was employed by a transportation company as a lorry driver. By 12 November 2008 he has been elected a staff delegate of the company's personnel. However, by a registered letter of 15 March 2009 he has been dismissed with a six months' term on the ground of the permanent cessation of the goods' transportation business of the company. But the subsidiary activities of the company did not cease. The first degree judge retained that, even if the company has ceased the goods' transportation business it did not cease its other activities, as the accommodation of goods, export or administrative management, and has not been liquidated, so that the continuation of the work relationship had not become materially impossible. He concludes that the employee should have been reassigned by the employer to another activity within the establishment.

Consequently, the President of the Labour Court (Président du Tribunal du travail) declared the dismissal of that employee null and void and ordered his reinstatement in the company.

Procedure before the Court of Appeal (Cour d'appel):

By 25 August 2009 the company appealed against the above mentioned order before the President of the Court of Appeal (Président de la Cour d'appel) in order to declare the requests of nullity of the dismissal and of reinstatement in the company not founded and argued that the legal protection of the staff delegates, provided for by the Labour Code, cannot override the constitutional principles of equality:

- Art. 10bis. (1) "Luxembourgers are equal before the law. (...) "

- Art. 11 (6) "Freedom of commerce and industry, the exercise of a non-salaried profession and of an agricultural work are guaranteed, except the restrictions established by law."

Indeed, the delegates' protection may not cause a discrimination favouring the personnel's delegates compared to the employees not provided with that protection. Then, according to the employer, that protection should not violate the principle of the free enterprise of the employer at the basis of the managing power of the company's CEO. As the first argument is concerned, the Court rejects it as being without any justification. As the respect of the constitutional principle guaranteeing the freedom of commerce and industry is concerned, the Court considers that, even if the Labour Code installs an absolute protection of the staff delegate against dismissal during the exercise of his mandate, this protection is in conflict with the managing power of the employer who is entitled to organize or to restructure his enterprise, especially by redundancies linked to economic necessities.

Since then, before deciding, the Court of Appeal submits to the Constitutional Court following question:

"Article L. 415-11 (1) of the Labour Code as it prohibits the employer to dismiss the personnel's delegate during his mandate, protecting him of any measure of personnel reduction, specifically in case of a total suppression of the enterprise's activity to which he was affected, is it corresponding with Article 11 (6) of the Constitution guaranteeing the freedom of commerce and industry?"

Position of the Constitutional Court:

The Constitutional Court considers that the protection against dismissal available to the members of the personnel's delegation is not contrary to the principle of freedom of commerce and industry instituted by the Constitution. The decision of an employer to remove a branch of its activities does not eliminate the protection against dismissal of the employees being staff delegates of this branch. The Court of Appeal has thus to consider this decision of the Constitutional Court in order to render its judgment.

[C] The Effects of the Social Plan on Following Individual Dismissals

One has to remember that no dismissal can take place:

- before signing the social plan;
- before signing the protocol of the National conciliation office in case of failure of negotiations;
- before the establishment of a personnel's delegation or a joint committee where these institutions are lacking instead of the legal obligation.

If a dismissal is pronounced prior to one of these dates it is declared null and void. As we saw above, the employee can refer in fifteen days to the Chairman of the Labour Court (Président du Tribunal du travail) who will establish the illegal nature of this dismissal or the ineffectiveness ('nullité') and decide that the employee will remain on his working place. Furthermore, if the employee has not invoked the nullity or the ineffectiveness of his dismissal and has not requested the continuation of the working relationship in the above-mentioned term he is entitled to the damages and compensation referred to in paragraph (1) of Article L. 124-7 of the Labour Code. He can even exercise a legal action on the basis of unfair dismissal provided by Article L. 124-11 and L. 124-12 of the same Code *(this principle was confirmed by a judgment of the Court of Appeal of 27 January 2011, n° 34096)* and is entitled to a severance pay.

It is to be repeated that even if the dismissal intervenes in the full respect of the legal obligations applicable to collective dismissals, the employee retains the right to attack this dismissal by a legal action in order to request financial compensation for unfair dismissal. The fact that it is a collective dismissal does indeed not relieve the employer of his obligation to deliver to the employee the precise grounds and motives of the discharge.

In the case for instance that the motivation is lacking or is not sufficiently precise, the dismissal will be considered as unfair by the judge.

The non-acceptance by an employee of the social plan signed by the social partners:

- Judgment of the Court of Appeal (Cour d'appel) of 9 November 2006, N° 29736:

In this case the employee was hired by the company in 1990. The employer projects to dismiss 195 employees in order to replace them by robots. In 2003, as part of the collective procedure leading to the discharge of 179 persons, a social plan has been negotiated and signed. This social plan limits its scope to those employees having expressly accepted the provisions of the social plan and waiving expressly and irrevocably all other legal actions against the dismissals. The employee did not expressly accept the provisions of the social plan and did not expressly waive all legal actions against the dismissal. By error, the employer paid her compensation resulting from the social plan and the employee considered that the willingly paid compensation is to be interpreted as a recognition of the unfairness of the dismissal and is accepted as interim damages receivable for this unfair dismissal. So she brought a legal action before the Labour Court (Tribunal du travail) in order to declare the discharge unfair.

The employer pretended that the employee had accepted the compensation as resulting from the social plan without reservations so that there was a transaction between the parties leading to the inadmissibility of the action. The Court of Appeal did not follow this reasoning. For her, the unconditional acceptance as a transaction of the proposed amounts was not established.

The employer had terminated the work contract of the employee with a notice period of six months and by referring to the social plan. By a letter of 6 February 2004 he provided the employee the reasons of her dismissal.

For the Court the reasons of the dismissal fall within the accuracies character by law and jurisprudence. Furthermore, these reasons, forming the basis of the dismissal of 179 persons, have been accepted as serious and grounded by the staff representatives, these reasons being the profound causes of the restructuration of the company deemed necessary by all the parties of the social plan to ensure the economic survival of the enterprise.

In the absence of criticism of the announced reasons from the employee the Court considered them as serious and established and declared the dismissal with notice justified on economic grounds.

The unanticipated dismissal in the social plan:

- Judgment of the Court of Appeal (Cour d'appel) of 10 January 2008, n° 30986:

The Court held that in the motivation letter of 16 September 2004 as in the dismissal letter mention is made of serious financial difficulties forcing the employer to negotiate a social plan foreseeing numerous discharges. The reference to the negotiated social plan between the staff delegations, the trade unions LCGB and OGBL and the representatives of the companies of Group C and signed on 22 December 2003, is a sufficiently precise motive meeting the legal and jurisprudential requirements in this field. The reality of these economic reasons and the extent of financial difficulties justifying a dismissal on economic grounds are resulting to the requisite legal that a social plan had to be established foreseeing an important number of dismissals.

It has no impact on the regularity of the dismissal when the employer refers in the dismissal letter of 30 July 2004 to the provisions of the social plan even if this plan is not applicable to the dismissal of employee Z. Besides that, no legal provision prohibits dismissal on economic grounds after the expired term of a social plan.

It is clear from the dismissal letters of 30 July and 16 September 2004 that the dismissal of employee Z intervened for economic grounds, even if this dismissal did not intervene in the framework of the social plan. Consequently, the dismissal of employee Z of 30 July 2004 is to be declared regular and his legal action for compensation is to be rejected so that the judgment of first instance is to be confirmed:

CHAPTER 19

Collective Dismissal in Malta

Paul Gonzi

§19.01 COLLECTIVE REDUNDANCIES

[A] The Legal Framework

In Malta, the general rules on termination of an employment relationship, including those on *collective redundancies*, are regulated primarily by the *Employment and Industrial Relations Act* (Chapter 452, Laws of Malta),[1] hereinafter referred to as '*the Act*'.

These general rules on *collective redundancies* are further substantiated by means of the *Collective Redundancies Regulations (Protection of Employment) Regulations* (Subsidiary Legislation 452.80 of 2003, as last amended in 2004), hereinafter referred to as '*the Regulations*'.

These rules on collective redundancies provided for in Maltese Law are transposed from EU Directive Council Directive 98/59/EC of 20 July 1998 on the approximation of the laws of the Member States relating to collective redundancies.[2] This means that an understanding of the framework regulating collective redundancies must necessarily comprise an understanding of the interpretation given to the Directive in judgments of the Court of Justice of the European Union (the 'CJEU' or 'ECJ') which have direct applicability in Malta as an EU Member State.

Indeed, local Industrial Tribunal or Court jurisprudence also has a bearing on the interpretation of these rules, although it must be stated at the outset that there is as yet

1. The Employment and Industrial Relations Act, Chapter 452, Laws of Malta as last amended by means of ACT IV of 2015.
2. Council Directive 98/59/EC of 20 July 1998 on the approximation of the laws of the Member States relating to collective redundancies (OJ L 225, 12.8.1998, p. 16).

no local jurisprudence on the interpretation on the Regulations on collective redundancies per se, and it must be noted that in any case the Maltese judiciary is not bound by the doctrine of precedent (other than in respect of judgments of the CJEU).

[B] Termination of an Employment Relationship

The collective redundancy rules transposed into Maltese Law must not be seen in a vacuum. On the contrary, they must be seen in light of the broader framework of legislation governing the field of employment and industrial relations in Malta – in particular the rules relating to the termination of an employment relationship.

By way of general introduction, Maltese Law provides different rules on the termination of an employment relationship which will vary depending on the nature of the employment, the cause giving rise to the termination and of course any specific terms that may be agreed to between the employer and employee in any contract or collective agreement.

For instance, the law provides different rules when terminating indefinite-term contracts as opposed to fixed-term contracts. Specific rules apply if the employee is still engaged during a probationary period at the time of termination, or if the employee has suffered an injury at work or if the employee has reached retirement age. Similarly, different procedures apply depending on whether the employee is choosing to resign, as opposed to the employer terminating the employment as a result of a 'good and sufficient cause' (such as gross misconduct) or otherwise as a result of cost-cutting exercises, restructuring or a redundancy scenario where the employer is abolishing the post of the employee.

Summarily, fixed-term contracts can only be terminated prior to the stipulated termination date if the employees mutually agree to terminate or if a party has a 'good and sufficient cause' to terminate. Otherwise, early termination good give rise to liability and payment by the terminating party.

Indefinite-term contracts, on the other hand, can also be terminated by mutual agreement or by either party in the event of a 'good and sufficient cause'. Otherwise, the employee may terminate such employment by resigning and giving prior notice (the duration of which will, generally, depend on the length of continuous employment with the employer), whereas the employer would be entitled to terminate the employment by giving prior notice only in the event of a 'redundancy', in which case the duration of the notice will also, generally, depend on the length of continuous employment with the employer.

Terminating employment on the grounds of 'redundancy' is a concept specifically referred to in the Act but is, as such, not defined in the law. In fact, what constitutes a redundancy, and what circumstances permit an employer to claim cause for redundancy, has been the subject of many Industrial Tribunal and Court judgments, several of which have been conflicting over the years. That said, the most recent trend over past years is one which saw the Tribunal and Courts take a somewhat restrictive stance and more protective approach towards the employee. Thus, the circumstances that would entitle the employer to terminate by giving notice on the grounds of a redundancy are those where the employer has abolished the position held by the employee, not out of any cause related to the employee himself, but because of a situation where the employer can no longer afford to maintain that position or no longer requires that position as a result of a necessary restructuring. Indeed, the Tribunal and Courts seem to have established the principle that a genuine redundancy is not one which arises merely out of a restructuring process undertaken merely to cut increase profits, but rather must constitute a measure intended either to avoid further losses or as a reorganization to render the employer's operations sustainable. In addition, a further principle adopted by the Tribunal and Courts is that a genuine redundancy is one where the position of the employee is in fact abolished, and not one where the duties previously carried out by an employee are distributed amongst other employees or merged into a new post having a different designation.

If an employer does have a genuine redundancy scenario, and proceeds towards laying off employees on this basis, then the Act provides that the employer must, in addition to the requirement of giving prior notice (depending on the length of the continuous employment, or as may be outlined in the employment contract) comply with two additional requirements. First, the employer must respect the 'Last-In-First-Out' principle, that is, the last person to have been employed in a 'class' of employment must be the first to be made redundant. Second, if the employer reinstates the position within one year from the date of the redundancy, then the employee previously made redundant must be offered that position first before it is offered to any other person.

If an employer does not terminate according to the applicable rules, whether in the case of a dismissal for 'good and sufficient cause' (in which case the employee must also be afforded a 'fair process' prior to dismissal) or in the context of a redundancy, then the employee is entitled to certain remedies provided in the Act. Essentially, the employee may claim that the termination constituted an unfair dismissal and may raise a complaint before the Industrial Tribunal within four months from the termination, requesting that the Tribunal confirms the dismissal to be unfair and awards compensation and/or in certain circumstances, reinstatement.

[C] Collective Redundancies

The previous section provides an outline of the general rules under Maltese Law that govern the termination of employment.

As mentioned already, as from the year 2004, when Malta became a member of the European Union, new provisions where transposed into Maltese Law in order to regulate collective redundancies – that is a situation whereby an employer terminates (or rather lays off) a grouping of employees during a particular period of time.

Since the European Union legislated on this matter by means of a Directive (rather than, for instance an EU Regulation which generally has direct effect in EU Member States), the Member States – including Malta – were required to adopt certain minimum harmonized rules in relation to collective redundancies, but were also allowed certain leeway in determining other related conditions. This means that certain requirements provided for in the Maltese Law may vary when compared to other EU Member States.

In fact, for purposes of Maltese Law, as defined in the Regulations, the term 'collective redundancy' means the termination by an employer on the grounds of redundancy, over a period of thirty days, of either ten or more employees in establishments normally employing twenty to ninety-nine employees, or 10% or more of the employees in establishments employing 100-299 employees, or thirty employees or more in establishments employing more than 300 employees.

Article 37 of the Act provides the general principle that an employer is prohibited from terminating the employment of any employee on grounds of collective redundancy before he has notified in writing the employees' representatives recognized by him of the termination of employment contemplated by him and has provided the said representatives with an opportunity to consult with the employer.

The Act also grants powers to the Minister responsible for employment who may, after due consultation with the Employment Relations Board, make regulations prescribing the circumstances when redundancies are to be deemed collective redundancies, the manner in which consultations between the employer and the employees' representatives are to take place, the procedure to be adopted, the categories or classes of employment that are exempted from the effects of such regulations and any other matter that is related or ancillary thereto.

The Act establishes also that any person who fails to comply with the provisions of this Article 37 or of any regulations shall be guilty of an offence against the Act.

[1] The Number of Terminations

An exercise to determine whether a number of layoffs will meet the requirements to comprise a 'collective redundancy' must take into account the termination of any employment contract which occurs '*on the employer's initiative for one or more reasons which are beyond the control of the individual employees*' provided that there are at least five redundancies.

Therefore, so long as the employer lays off five employees on the grounds of 'redundancy', then all other terminations, that are beyond the individual employees' control, are to be assimilated to redundancies for purposes of the Regulations, and thus computed as part of the aggregate.

What the phrase '*beyond the control of the individual employees*' means in practice is yet to be defined since the Regulations do not provide an express definition or parameters with which to determine whether a situation falls within the employee's control or not. In this context, it is interesting to note that the EU Directive refers to wording which varies slightly as follows: '*terminations of an employment contract which occur on the employer's initiative for one or more reasons not related to the individual workers concerned*'.

Arguably, there is a distinction between the termination being beyond the control of an individual, as opposed to the termination being for reasons not related to the individual. For instance, one might argue that a termination based on the basis of the employee reaching retirement age (which under Maltese law, permits the employer to force retirement without liability) may be beyond the employee's control, but would nonetheless be a reason related to the individual.

[2] The Five Redundancies

The Regulations do not provide a definition of the term 'redundancy', and whilst they do establish, that the '*terms and expressions used in these regulations shall, unless the context otherwise requires, have the meaning assigned to them in the Act*', the Act itself does not expressly define the term 'redundancy', as previously described. Indeed, local jurisprudence appears to have taken the restrictive approach - effectively that a redundancy must bring about the abolition of the post and duties previously held by the employee.

Whether this interpretation will hold for purposes of these Regulations or not is yet to be conclusively determined. Presently there is no local jurisprudence establishing what the term 'redundancy' is to mean for purposes of these Regulations. That said, it is likely that the required five redundancies would be deemed to comprise the laying off of employees, by an employer, who abolishes the employees' posts and duties for reasons that do not relate to the individual employee himself, in each case adhering to the relative notice periods and 'Last-In-First-Out' rule.

A question which however remains subject to further interpretation is whether, in the context of a collective redundancy whereby a majority of the layoffs might not necessarily comprise a pure 'redundancy' as interpreted by the Maltese Tribunals so far (such as early termination of a fixed-term contract which would not normally give rise to prior notice, or termination during the probationary period, or termination based on the employee reaching retirement age), the employer must treat such terminations in accordance with the general rules on 'redundancy' including, therefore, the rule on granting prior notice, the Last-In-First-Out rule or the one-year reinstatement rule. This matter remains subject to debate and no doubt will be the subject of case law in the future.

[3] The Term 'Establishment'

As mentioned above, the Regulations make reference to the term 'establishment' when determining whether a number of layoffs, in a particular period, would give rise to a collective redundancy. However, neither the Regulations nor the EU Directive itself define the term 'establishment'.

Therefore, reference should be made to case law of the CJEU wherein, for instance in the Rockfon case[3] the CJEU clarified that whereas the Directive does not preclude two or more interrelated undertakings in a group, neither or none of which has a decisive influence over the other or others, from establishing a joint recruitment

3. CJEU Case C-449/93; Judgment of 07/12/1995, Rockfon / Specialarbejderforbundet i Danmark, acting on behalf of Søren Nielsen and others (Rec.1995, p. I-4291).

and dismissal department so that dismissals on grounds of redundancy in one of the undertakings could take place only with that department's approval, the term 'establishment' must, however, be understood as designating the unit to which the workers made redundant are '*assigned to carry out their duties*'. The CJEU clarified that it was not necessary to construe establishment as meaning a unit endowed with a management which could independently affect collective redundancies. That would be incompatible with the aim of the Directive, because it would allow companies belonging to the same group to try and make it more difficult for the Directive to apply by conferring the power to take decisions concerning redundancies on a separate decision making body.

Also in the *Athinaiki Chartopoiia AE v. Panagiotidis*[4] case the CJEU held that an establishment need not have any legal autonomy, nor need it have economic, financial, administrative, or technical autonomy to be regarded as an establishment and in fact found that one of several production units each of which had distinct equipment and a specialized workforce and a chief production officer could be deemed to be an 'establishment' even if decisions concerning operating expenses, purchase of materials and product cost were taken at the company's head office. The Court added that it is not essential for the unit to be endowed with a management that could independently impact collective redundancies.

In the more recent judgment handed down by the CJEU in the *Woolworths Case,*[5] the Court clarified that where an undertaking comprises several entities, the term 'establishment' must be interpreted as referring to the entity to which the workers made redundant are assigned to carry out their duties. Therefore, the CJEU clarified that when an undertaking comprises several entities it is not necessary to take into account the dismissals in each establishment considered separately as such interpretation would be contrary to the directive's objectives of ensuring comparable protection for workers' rights in the different Member States and of harmonizing costs which these rules entail for EU undertakings.

[4] Exclusions

The aforementioned rules on giving information and consultation in collective redundancies are excluded only in certain circumstances. The Regulations provide that Article 37 of the Act and the Regulations themselves do not apply to terminations of employment effected under contracts of employment concluded for limited periods of time or for specific tasks, except where such terminations take place prior to the date of expiry or the completion of such tasks and the reason for such prior termination is the 'redundancy' of the employees so terminated.

4. CJEU Case C-270/05; Judgement of 15/02/2007, *Athinaiki Chartopoiia AE v. L. Panagiotidis and Others, third party Geniki Sinomospondia Ergaton Elladas (GSEE).*
5. CJEU Case C-80/14 *Union of Shop, Distributive and Allied Workers (USDAW) and B. Wilson v. WW Realisation 1 Ltd (in liquidation), Ethel Austin Ltd and Secretary of State for Business, Innovation and Skills.*

As a side note, this reference to 'redundancy' in the context of a fixed-term contract gives rise to a significant matter for debate. Under normal circumstances, that is, circumstances not giving rise to a collective redundancy scenario, Maltese Law (or perhaps better, jurisprudence) has excluded the possibility of an employer to terminate a fixed-term contract prior to the original expiry date on the grounds of redundancy by merely giving notice. The law establishes that premature termination of a fixed-term contract not based on a 'good and sufficient cause' will automatically give rise to liability. The employer will have to pay a sum of money to the employee, irrespective of whether notice is given and irrespective of whether the Last-In-First-Out rule was complied with by the employer. This begs the question as to whether the inference in these Regulations (that there may be the possibility to terminate a fixed term contract on the grounds on redundancy) opens up the possibilities for employers to terminate fixed-term contracts on the grounds of redundancy and if so what the conditions, implications and possible liabilities are.

Apart from these rules on fixed-term contracts, Article 37 of the Act and the Regulations are also excluded for persons employed on ships falling under the provisions of the Merchant Shipping Act.[6] For sake of clarity, it is not only the rules on collective redundancies that do not apply to seafarers, but also rules on the protection of employees in transfer of undertakings[7] and the general rules on termination of employment for seafarers, the reason being that other specific rules regulate the employment and discharge of seamen under the Merchant Shipping Act and subsidiary legislation.[8]

[5] The Right to Information and Consultation

The standard rules on termination of employment and redundancies provided under Maltese Law do not specifically establish that employees have a right to be consulted on or given information about prospective terminations or prior to receiving notice of redundancy. This applies to the extent that such rights are not otherwise granted to the employees, perhaps in the individual employment contract, or by means of company policy or applicable collective agreement. Having said this, certain Tribunal judgments have emphasised the importance of guaranteeing a fair process leading up to any redundancy, even if one person is being made redundant, and this should include some form of information and consultation with the employee who may be declared redundant. Employers should act 'fairly' and not suddenly surprise employees with the redundancy.

Certain information and consultation obligations do however arise for undertakings established in Malta which employ fifty employees and over or where a Works

---

6. Chapter 234, Laws of Malta.
7. Regulated under Article 38 of the Employment and Industrial Relations Act, Chapter 452, Laws of Malta.
8. Article 39 of the Act provides that the provisions of Articles 36, 37 and 38 shall not apply in respect of seamen employed on ships under the provisions of the Merchant Shipping Act; and in the event of any conflict between any of the provisions of the Merchant Shipping Act and any of the provisions of Act, the former shall apply.

Council is established, and these obligations may include a requirement to provide information and/or consultation on redundancies or threats of employment termination.[9]

The issue is more clearly defined in the context of a collective redundancy where the Regulations expressly provide that the employer is bound to enter into consultations with the employees and to give them certain minimum information.

In fact, in all cases of collective redundancies, the employer proposing to declare the redundancies is prohibited from terminating the employment of such employees before he has notified in writing the employees' representatives, of the termination of employment contemplated by him and has provided the said representatives with an opportunity to consult with the employer.

The consultations between the employer and the employees' representative must begin within seven working days from the day on which the employees' representatives have been notified of the intended collective redundancies.

In fact, within the aforementioned seven-day period and prior to the commencement of the consultation period, the employer must supply the employees' representatives with a statement in writing giving all relevant information and shall in any event give such employees' representatives the reasons for the redundancies, the number of employees he intends to make redundant, the number of employees normally employed by him, the criteria proposed for the selection of the employees to be made redundant, details regarding any redundancy payments which are due and the period over which redundancies are to be effected.

The above obligations apply irrespective of whether the decision regarding collective redundancies is taken by the employer or an undertaking controlling the employer. The Regulations provide that in the event of alleged breach of the information, consultation and notification requirements, account will not be taken of any defence on the part of the employer that the necessary information had not been provided to the employer by the undertaking which took the decision leading to the collective redundancies. This obligation, however, does not apply in those cases where the collective redundancy is the result of a judicial decision. The CJEU also specified, in a later case *Akavan Erityisalojen Keskusliitto AEK ry and Others v. Fujitsu Siemens Computers Oy*,[10] wherein it held that the adoption, within a group of undertakings, of strategic decisions or of changes in activities which compel the employer to contemplate or to plan for collective redundancies gives rise to the obligation on that employer to hold consultations with workers' representatives. Therefore, the obligation for the employer to start consultations does not depend on whether the employer is already able to supply to the workers' representatives all the information required. In the case of a group of undertakings consisting of a parent company and one or more subsidiaries, the obligation to hold consultations with the workers' representatives falls on the

9. The *Employee (Information and Consultation) Regulations*; Subsidiary Legislation S.L.452.96 as last amended by Legal Notice 427 of 2007. Similar obligations may arise also where a Works Council is established (The European Works Councils Regulations S.L.452.86 and S.L.452.107).
10. CJEU Case C-44/-08; *Akavan Erityisalojen Keskusliitto AEK ry and Others v. Fujitsu Siemens Computers Oy* (reference for a preliminary ruling).

subsidiary which has the status of employer only once that subsidiary, within which collective redundancies may be made, has been identified and the consultation procedure must be concluded by the subsidiary affected by the collective redundancies before that subsidiary, on the direct instructions of its parent company or otherwise, terminates the contracts of employees who are to be affected by those redundancies.

Apart from the above-mentioned obligations, the employer must also forward to the Director responsible for Employment and Industrial Relations, a copy of the written notification given to the employees' representatives together with a copy of the written statement on the same day that these are notified to the employees' representatives. This obligation also does not apply in those cases where the collective redundancy is the result of a judicial decision.

At such point the consultation process may begin. The Regulations provide that the consultations are to cover ways and means of avoiding the collective redundancies or reducing the number of employees affected by such redundancies and for mitigating the consequences thereof. In practice, this means that the employer cannot approach the employee representatives with a *fait accompli*. Final decisions to terminate must not have been taken, and the employer must allow scope for real consultation to seek ways to mitigate the negative impact of the potential redundancies.

It is to be noted that the Regulations do not stipulate a maximum or minimum duration for an effective consultation to take place. That said, the burden to prove that a genuine opportunity to consult was given to the employees representatives would ultimately rest on the employer - and this would require proof about the degree of information supplied to the representatives and the degree of opportunity to consult on the basis of that information. In practice, therefore, it is important for the employer to maintain sufficient documentation as evidence of his effort to inform and consult.

[6] When Does Notice of Termination Begin to Run

The Regulations provide that, without prejudice to the right of employees regarding notice of dismissal (which, as mentioned above, is not clear whether it applies to all employees or not being laid off in a collective redundancy), any projected collective redundancies notified to the employees' representative and to the Director responsible for Employment and Industrial Relations may only take effect on the lapse of thirty days after the said notification.

The Director responsible for Employment and Industrial Relations may, in exceptional circumstances, grant the employer a shorter period of notification or may also extend the said period by a second period of thirty days if it appears to him that such extension may provide further opportunity for the resolution of the reasons for the redundancies or for the identification of solutions to the benefit of those employees who are being declared redundant. If the Director responsible for Employment and Industrial Relations extends the time limit of thirty days accordingly, the employer must be informed of such extension by notice in writing which is to reach him prior to the lapse of the initial period.

The Regulations also provide that in the context of collective redundancies, the notice of termination of employment '*may begin to run from the date when the consultations referred to above commence*', with the implication therefore that any notice of termination given before the consultations begin would be a breach of the Regulations.

This matter however does not appear to be straightforward and such provision under the Maltese Regulations may possibly become a matter of a dispute in the future. The key issue is that, on the one hand, the employer must not present a *fait accompli* prior to commencement of consultation, but on the other hand, the Regulations seem to allow the employer to give notice of termination based on the redundancy even during the thirty-day period, at any point after the consultation commences, even if the consultation has not concluded.

Reference to CJEU jurisprudence must necessarily be made, in particular to the judgment of the CJEU in *Irmtraud Junk v. Wolfgang Kühnel.*[11] In this judgment the CJEU decided that Articles 2-4 of the Directive which impose the consultation and notification obligations on employers must be construed as meaning that the event constituting 'redundancy' consists in the declaration by an employer of his intention to terminate the contract of employment. The notification to a worker that his or her contract of employment has been terminated is the expression of a decision to sever the employment relationship. The actual cessation of that relationship on the expiry of the period of notice, therefore, is no more than the effect of the employer's decision to carry out the redundancy.

The CJEU therefore seems to clarify that an employer is entitled to carry out collective redundancies '*after the conclusion of the consultation*' procedure and after notification of the projected collective redundancies - and possibly, therefore, not necessarily when consultations commence. This interpretation of the CJEU was tied to the scope of the Directive, as set out in Article 2(2), which is to avoid terminations of contracts of employment or to reduce the number of such terminations, so the achievement of that purpose would be jeopardized if the consultation were to be subsequent to the employer's decision.

Therefore, it would appear that one cannot merely interpret the Maltese Regulations at face value as the findings of the CJEU may prevail and may, therefore, impose a more restrictive obligation to give notice once consultations have been concluded or at least come closer to an end. An employer entertaining the possibility of collective redundancies is best advised to entertain and conclude effective consultation prior to the giving of, and the commencement of, any notice periods, even if the thirty-day period would have commenced, this to reduce the risks of a claim that the consultation was not genuine.

Ultimately, the employer must act with utmost caution prior to giving notice of termination, taking into account the above regulatory timeframes and weighing them out with the operational needs of the business. For instance an employer must consider whether employees may be required to continue performing duties for a specific period

11. CJEU Case C-188/03; *Irmtraud Junk v. Wolfgang Kühnel* (reference for a preliminary ruling).

of time, or to deliver a handover of pending work. This must be considered in light of the rule that an employee has an option at law, upon receiving notice, to not work the notice period and instead get paid fifty percent of that basic salary which he would have earned had he worked the notice in full. Thus, the employer must be cautious in planning how and when to give notice periods, considering other options to protect its needs, such as the offering of retention incentives to safeguard its operational needs, rather than offering very long notice periods which could result in the employer having to pay large pay-outs in lieu of the notice period if the employee chooses to not work the notice period.

[D] Protection for Employees

As may be noted, the Directive and the Regulations establish the obligation on the employer to provide information and to consult with the employees' representatives and not with individual employees directly.

In fact, in the judgment of the *Mono Car Styling SA*[12] case, the CJEU clarified that the rights to receive information and to be consulted are intended for workers' representatives and not for workers individually. Consequently, without prejudice to remedies in domestic law intended to ensure protection of the individual rights of workers in the case of improper dismissal, these rights (of information and consultation) are to be exercised limitedly through workers' representatives and the laws of Member States may limit employees from acting individually, for instance, if the workers' representatives failed to raise any objections with the employer during the consultation procedure.

Therefore, it would appear that individual employees who are not represented by any union or employee representative may, in practice, encounter difficulty in requesting information and/or being consulted. This could be the case, for instance, where an employer employs more than twenty employees, but less than fifty employees, in which case there is no obligation to elect an employee representative from amongst the employees in terms of the Employee (Information and Consultation) Regulations,[13] but the employer would nonetheless be governed by the Regulations on collective redundancies in the event that ten or more employees are made redundant within a period of thirty days.

Notwithstanding this, it is interesting to remember that in terms of the Regulations,[14] terms and expressions used in the Regulations have, unless the context otherwise requires, the meaning assigned to them in the Act. To this end, Article 2 of the Act expressly provides that the term 'employees' representative' for the purposes of Article 37 on collective redundancies is to mean either the recognized union representative, or, where there exists no recognized union, such representative of the union

12. CJEU Case C-12/08; Judgment of the 16 July 2009; *Mono Car Styling Sa, in liquidation, v. Dervis Odemis and Others* (reference for preliminary ruling).
13. Such obligation would arise in terms of the Employee (Information and Consultation) Regulations; Subsidiary Legislation S.L.452.96 as last amended by Legal Notice 427 of 2007.
14. Regulation 2(2).

representing the employees, or, in the case of non-unionized employees, the terms shall mean such representative duly elected from amongst the non-unionized employees, by means of a secret ballot called for such purpose by the employer.

Therefore, although yet to be tested before the local Industrial Tribunal or Courts, there seems to be a strong argument that even if no obligation to elect a representative arises in terms of the Employee (Information and Consultation) Regulations or in the regulations governing Works Councils, the employer may nonetheless, by reference to the definition in Article 2 of the Act, be required to elect from amongst any non-unionized employees, a representative by means of a secret ballot for purposes of Article 37.

Thus, upon a reading of the Act and pursuant to certain Decisions of the Industrial Tribunal, any employer willing to err on the side of caution should encourage the employees to elect a representative from amongst them even in cases where there may be no express obligation to do so. In addition, if the employees refuse or decline to elect a representative, the employer should nonetheless consider undertaking some form of information and consultation process with all the employees that may be declared redundant.

Where an individual employee is not duly represented, that individual employee may have recourse to other remedies, in practice, if his employment is prejudiced following a collective redundancy.

First, employees may raise a formal complaint with the Department of Industrial and Employment Relations about the breach, or potential breach, of the Act or of any regulations enacted pursuant to the Act.

The Department, through its inspectors, is empowered to carry out examinations, tests or inquiries[15] and may also collaborate with the executive police for action to be taken against the employer, or may in certain circumstances also act as prosecutor, in the event of a breach of the Act or regulations enacted pursuant to the Act. In practice, it is not uncommon for the Department to first intervene by inspecting any complaint and issuing a formal caution to the employer to abide by the law, failing which legal action would be instituted. Such a caution could take the form of instructing the employer to hold a secret ballot to elect an employee representative and/or to fulfil the information and consultation obligations.

Second, by way of precautionary measure, an employee who feels aggrieved may consider applying to the Courts to seek an interim order to protect his rights provided he can prove that such right exists, that requesting the order is necessary (and therefore that no other remedy exists) and that failing to obtain the order would cause irremediable prejudice to him. Such an order can be issued in the form of a Warrant of Prohibitory Injunction which is a form of interim measure provided for under the general principles of law contained in the Code of Organisation and Civil Procedure.[16]

15. The Department is empowered in terms of Article 43 of Chapter 452, Laws of Malta. Any impediment shown towards an inspector who is carrying out his duties in terms of Law constitutes an offence.
16. Chapter 12, Laws of Malta.

Indeed, civil law procedural requirements will have to be considered, and the employee will have to prove to the court on a prima facie basis that the requirements at law to uphold such an order exist. Once the Court issues such an order, the employee will then have twenty days within which to file a case before the Civil Courts or the Industrial Tribunal requesting a final confirmation on the dispute giving rise to the breach of his rights. It must be noted, however, that whereas such warrants have been successfully applied before the local Courts by employees, this has only been in limited cases[17] and not in the specific context of collective redundancies. Therefore the applicability thereof and the practical implications arising from such requests to the Court in this particular context are yet to be tested.

Third, in the case of improper dismissal (resulting from a breach of the Act or the Regulations) employees will have the right to contest their dismissal should they consider it to have been unfair or unjust – including if the employee consider the termination not to constitute a genuine redundancy. Employees have four months from the effective date of the alleged breach within which to file a complaint before the Industrial Tribunal.[18] The employee has a right to request the Tribunal to order compensation and in some cases to order reinstatement.

Finally, another alternative that may be availed by employees is to call upon their recognized union and/or any other union registered in terms of Maltese Law to act on their behalf, in which case they can either proceed against the employer according to legal remedies, including for instance call issuing directives for industrial action.

[E] Penalty for Offences

As already mentioned above, the breach of the Act or of the Regulations is an offence at law, prosecutable by the police with the assistance of the Director responsible for employment and industrial relations.

By way of general rule, Article 45 of the Act provides that any employer who contravenes or fails to comply with any provisions of this Act or any regulations made thereunder shall, unless a different penalty is established for such offence, on conviction be liable to a fine (multa) of not less than EUR 232.94 and not exceeding EUR 2,329.37.

In addition to this general rule, the collective redundancies Regulations provide[19] that any person contravening the provisions of the Regulations shall be guilty of an offence and shall, on conviction, be liable to a fine (multa) of not less than one thousand and EUR 1,164.69 for every employee that is declared redundant.

Finally, in terms of the Act,[20] where an offence against the provisions of the Act or of any regulations made thereunder is committed by a partnership, company,

17. Such as, in the case of *Sandra Diacono v. Deutsche Bank (Malta) Ltd and Deutsche Holdings (Malta) Ltd*; Warrant Number 1861/2014/1 decided on 19 December 2015 by the Maltese Civil Courts.
18. This right arises in terms of Article 75 of the Act.
19. Regulation 11, Collective Redundancies (Protection of Employees) Regulations S.L.452.80.
20. Article 46, Chapter 452 Laws of Malta.

association or other body of persons, every person who, at the time of the commission of the offence, was a director, manager, secretary or other similar officer of such partnership, company, association or other body of persons or was purporting to act in any such capacity shall be deemed to be guilty of that offence unless he proves that the offence was committed without his knowledge and that he exercised all due diligence to prevent the commission of the offence.

CHAPTER 20
Collective Dismissal in the Netherlands

Gerrard Boot & Yvonne Erkens

§20.01 INTRODUCTION

In this chapter we will first point out the definition of collective dismissal according to Dutch law. We will use the term collective dismissal for the dismissal on economic reasons of at least twenty employees within three months by one employer within one of six restricted area in the Netherlands. If we use the term collective dismissal in another way, we will mention that. After some preliminary remarks on dismissal, we will describe a collective dismissal case. Step by step we apply the rules and regulations regarding collective dismissal to an individual case. On 1 July 2015 a major change has taken place in dismissal law. We will explain the consequences of this reform for collective dismissal law and throw light on the right of advice of the Works Council regarding the decision to dismiss more than twenty employees. Both the procedure at the Institute for Employee Benefit Schemes (UWV) and the procedure at the Cantonal judge will be described as well as the support measures in favour of workers that often go with a collective dismissal. We conclude this chapter with the judicial control and sanctions.

[A] Collective Dismissal Versus Individual Dismissal

According to one generally accepted definition, collective dismissal is the dismissal of at least twenty employees within three months by one employer within one restricted area in the Netherlands. Other definitions are possible. In Dutch dismissal law a distinction is made between the grounds for dismissal: economic reasons versus personal reasons and reasons regarding the personality of the employee. An example of the latter (personal reasons) is disfunctioning. Normally a collective dismissal will be necessary for economic reasons. Suppose an employer wants to dismiss thirty employees for economic reasons. If one of these employees is disfunctioning, and the dismissal of that employee is accepted on this ground, there only remains the need to dismiss twenty-nine employees for economic reasons. So dismissal on economic and on personal grounds can interfere. If an employer wants to dismiss at least twenty employees within three months within one restricted area in the Netherlands (there are six of these areas), the employer needs to inform the trade unions and the Ministry of Social Affairs. This obligation is laid down in the Dutch Collective Redundancy Act (Wet Melding Collectief Ontslag, 'DCRA'). For the application of this Act it is not important on which ground the dismissal is asked. Even if an employer and an employee decide to separate by mutual agreement, this termination counts for one in the applicability of the DCRA. Another approach however is to look to the ground for the termination. As mentioned before a distinction is made between termination for economic reasons, and termination for other (that means: personal) reasons. This distinction has become very important because from 1 July 2015, a dismissal for economic reasons must be decided by an administrative body (the Institute for Employee Benefit Schemes, UWV), with the possibility to appeal at the Cantonal judge and afterwards the Court of Appeal. A dismissal on personal grounds directly has to be decided by the Cantonal judge.

[B] Preliminary Remarks on the Dismissal of Employees in the Netherlands

If an employer wants to terminate an employment agreement for an indefinite period, he needs (with a few exceptions) the prior approval of a public administrative body (UWV) or the court. This is called a *preventive* system, opposed to a *repressive* system. In a preventive system the employment agreement remains valid, unless the employer has got this approval. There are a few exceptions. No prior approval is necessary in case of a dismissal within the probation period of one or two months, a dismissal for an urgent cause and, of course, termination with mutual consent (the employee accepts the dismissal). Besides these exceptions the employer needs a prior approval to dismiss an employee with a contract for an indefinite period.

Until 1 July 2015 the employer had the choice to ask preventive approval at the UWV or at the Cantonal judge. In practice the way through the UWV appeared to be slower and slightly more applications were rejected, but the UWV could not attribute a severance payment to the employee so this way of dismissal was cheaper for the employer. If the employee did not accept the dismissal or the severance payment that the employer voluntary had offered, the employee had to go to the cantonal judge on the ground of manifestly unreasonable dismissal (with the possibility to appeal). Even in case the cantonal judge decided that the dismissal could be qualified as manifestly unreasonable, the payments attributed to the employee were quite low (due to some verdicts of the Supreme Court in 2009 and 2010). The other way to dismiss an employee was to ask the termination at the cantonal judge. This was a fast way to terminate the employment contract, there was no possibility to appeal (with a few restrictedly interpreted exceptions), and the cantonal judge used a so-called cantonal court formula, in which the starting point was to attribute the employee one month severance pay per year of service. This implicates there was a big difference between the two ways of dismissals, and it was the employer who had the choice which way was followed. From 2002 till 2009 the UWV dealt with on average as much cases as the cantonal judges. As from 2009 the percentage of cases through the UWV raised. There are a few reasons for that. First, per October 2006 it was not necessary anymore to contest a dismissal on economic grounds in order to get an unemployment benefit. Until 2006 lots of employees went to court because they were afraid of not getting an unemployment benefit if they did not. When it became clear that this was not necessary anymore, more employees agreed with the termination of the contract. Second, the number of dismissals on economic grounds raised, whereas the dismissals for the personal motives decreased. Historically most economic cases were handled by the UWV, the personal cases by the cantonal judge.

From 1 July 2015 this system changed dramatically. The preventive system remains, but the employer cannot choose freely between the UWV and the cantonal judge anymore. Dismissal for economic reasons as well as dismissal if the employee is ill for more than two years must be decided by the UWV (with the possibility to appeal to the cantonal judge and afterwards to the court of appeal). All other dismissals (misconduct, disfunctioning, a disturbed working relation, other personal grounds) must be decided directly by the cantonal judge (with the possibility to appeal to the court of appeal). A second major change has to do with the severance payment. Every employee, who has a service of at least two years, is entitled to a severance payment (called Transition Payment) if the employer dismisses him or if the employer does not want to extend a temporary contract after two years. The level of this Transition Payment is about one-third of the former cantonal court formula: for the first ten years of employment the employee gets one-third month salary per year of service; after ten years of employment the employee receives for these years one-half month per year of service. There are some positive – meaning higher payment – exceptions for older employees and some negative – meaning lower payments – exceptions for employers with financial difficulties. If the employer is highly culpable for the dismissal, the employee might claim a higher severance payment ('billijke vergoeding', which means: reasonable payment). If the employee is highly culpable for the dismissal, he will receive nothing, or less than the normal Transition Payment.

Instead of going to the UWV with dismissals on economic grounds, it is possible to sign a collective labour agreement ('CLA'), in which is stipulated that instead of the UWV a CLA-commission will decide on these applications for dismissal. This CLA-commission must have an independent chair. In the CLA other dismissal criteria can be applicable than the official, legal, criteria.

Because the system as per 1 July 2015 differs dramatically from the system used before, there are some transitional provisions ('overgangsrecht'). One temporary rule (effective until 1 July 2016) is that if a Social Plan – which often contains measures facilitating the employee after his dismissal, such as outplacement and severance pay

– has been signed with the trade unions, the employees will receive the payment according to the Social Plan instead of the legal Transition Payment. If a Social Plan has been signed with others than trade unions (e.g., with the Works Council), the employee may choose which payment he wants to receive: the payment according to the Social Plan, or the legal Transition Payment.

[C] Collective Dismissal: The Case

In this section we will describe the situation that a company wants to dismiss 100 employees for economic reasons on a rather short term (e.g., before the end of the year) in one restricted area. Which steps have to be taken? The company has to act on three levels: (i) inform the trade unions and the UWV; (ii) get the approval of the Works Council; and (iii) realize the 100 individual dismissals. Every level has its own specific elements.

In this case the employer wants to dismiss more than twenty employees within three months in one restricted area. As to the area: a dismissal is only considered as a collective dismissal according to the DCRA when it takes place within one area, defined by Royal Decree, in which all twenty employees are working (Article 3(1) DCRA). Sometimes an employer limits the number of dismissals within the period of three months to nineteen employees, to realize that no obligation is due in this respect. The obligation to inform the UWV has its origins in the fact that the UWV also distributes unemployment benefits. The UWV has an interest to know what future developments in this field can be expected. According to Article 3(3) DCRA trade unions with members in the company have to be informed of the collective dismissal. They might try to reduce the number of dismissals the employer wants to realize (Article 3(2) DCRA). Because of this obligation trade unions will also be able to go into action to conclude a Social Plan, although a collective dismissal can be realized without such Plan. A Social Plan often deals with the financial compensation for the employees. It is not necessary to enter into a Social Plan. After having informed the trade unions, the employer cannot terminate the employment agreements with the employees involved, unless the trade unions explicitly agree and not earlier than one month after the intention for the collective dismissal is reported (Article 5a DCRA). The employees involved can nullify the termination of employment (whether by notice of by mutual agreement) within six months after the notice was given or the termination agreement was concluded, if the employer does not consult the trade unions although it was compulsory to do so. If the termination is successfully nullified, the employee is restored to his position with retroactive effect, and is entitled to claim his wages (Article 7(1) DCRA). Instead of calling upon the nullity, the employee may claim a reasonable payment ('billijke vergoeding'), Article 7(2) DCRA. These sanctions make it recommendable for a company to comply with the obligations of the DCRA.

Normally the dismissal of 100 employees within a short period is considered as an important company decision (Article 25 Work Councils Act, WCA). If a company wants to make such an important decision, it needs the prior advice of the Works Council. If the employer does not ask that advice, although he is obliged to do so, the Works

Council may ask the nullity of this decision. There is a special Court to deal with these cases (Enterprise Section of the Court of Appeal in Amsterdam). This Enterprise Section is quite strict on the applicability of the law: if no advice was asked although this had to be done, the company decision is null and void. In practice, this means that the company cannot continue the reorganization. If the Works Council gives a negative advice, and the company ignores this advice, the Works Council can address the Enterprise Section and request to decide whether the company could reasonably take this decision. If the Works Council has given a negative advice or no advice at all (after it was asked to give such an advice), the company has to postpone the decision for one month (Article 26 WCA). This period of one month is to enable to Works Council to start a procedure at the Enterprise Section. *See* further section §20.01[D].

If the company has got a positive advice of the Works Council, or if the period of one month after giving no or a negative advice has passed or if the Enterprise Section has decided that the company could reasonably take its decision, the company can ask for permission for the individual dismissals at UWV. Instead of going to the UWV, the company might ask individual employees if they agree with the dismissal. If the employee agrees, since the change of law in 2006 this has no (negative) consequence on his Unemployment Benefits (Article 24(2) Unemployment Act, 'Werkloosheidswet'). Sometimes the company gives the employee a slightly higher severance payment ('quick decision bonus') if the employees agree with the dismissal. Such an agreement is lucrative, because it prevents the company for making the costs (and risks) of a dismissal procedure. For the employee this can be profitable too: because of the small financial advantage and the wish to avoid a procedure which he may consider difficult to win.

[D] The Procedure at the Enterprise Section of the Court of Appeal in Amsterdam

On the basis of Article 26 WCA the Works Council has the right to appeal to the company's decision for a collective dismissal, if that decision deviates from the Works Council's advice or if new facts come up after the advice was given that would have affected the Works Council's advice. The Works Council should address the Enterprise Section within a month after the company has announced its decision. In the procedure at the Enterprise Section the Works Council can only put forward objections that have been made before. The company has to postpone the realization of its decision in order to give the Works Council the opportunity to go to the Enterprise Section. It is the competence of the company to take strategic decisions, the judge would not interfere with the company's autonomy on economic matters. If the Enterprise Section however decides that the company did not decide on reasonable grounds, provisions will be made, possibly enforced by a penalty payment. The Enterprise Section can oblige the company to withdraw its decision or to rectify the effects of that decision, although third-party's rights will be respected.

[E] Which Employees Can Be Dismissed?

The first question is whether UWV or the cantonal judge will be convinced of the necessity of the reorganization. This question will be answered in sections §20.01[F] and §20.01[G]. If the reorganization as such, and the number of employees involved, are accepted, the next question is which employees can be dismissed. The rules regulating this choice are laid down in the Dismissals Decree ('Ontslagregeling') of 11 May 2015. Article 11 of this Dismissals Decree ('DD') includes the 'proportionality principle'. According to this principle redundancies must affect all age groups of the employed staff equally. On the basis of the proportionality principle, employees who hold interchangeable positions are divided into 5 age groups (15-25 years, 25-35, 35-45, 45-55 and 55 up). First must be decided how many employees from each age group can be dismissed. Second, it is necessary to determine for every age group which employees entered the company's employment most recently. These employees will be the first that qualify to be made redundant per group ('last in, first out'). However, the employees who are entitled to retirement under the Dutch General Old Age Pensions Act (AOW) will be the first to be dismissed. Equally, employees with a temporary contract which will take less than six months or agency workers, have to be dismissed first. If an employee is ill for less than two years, it is very difficult to dismiss him for economic reasons. A dismissal for that reason during the first two years of illness is not possible. There are some exceptions: (i) the illness started after permission from the UWV was asked; (ii) the employee did not fulfil his obligations to try to recover; or (iii) all activities of the enterprise are stopped. If the employee is pregnant or recently has given birth no dismissal on economic grounds is allowed.

[F] The Procedure at the UWV

The proceedings at the UWV require well-ground reasons and evidence for terminating the employment agreement. The employer must substantiate these reasons with documentary evidence. The procedure is mostly in writing, an oral hearing is rare. Dutch is the working language. The employer sends in his request. If the request is not complete, the UWV will ask for the missing information. After the request is completed, the employee is asked for a reaction, which must be given within fourteen days. Normally the UWV will come to a decision based on this information. Most decisions will be taken within four weeks after the compete request is received. However, it is possible that the UWV decides that extra written information is necessary. In that case the employer is asked to give his reaction to the employees defence within seven days, and after which the employee may give a (second) written defence within seven days. In exceptional cases an oral hearing will be held. If necessary, two representatives of both the employer's organization and the trade union can be heard, if UWV deems this to be necessary for the knowledge of the specific branch. The UWV can decide to give or refuse permission for dismissal. If the permission is given, the employer can give notice. This period is at least one month, and sometimes longer depending on the period of employment. If the UWV refuses the permission, the employer can abide by this decision or ask the termination of the contract through the court. If the employer decides to do so, the request must be sent in within two months after the refusal of the UWV.

[G] The Procedure at the Cantonal Judge

The employer requests the termination of the contract. The request must contain information about the employer, the employee and of course the reason for the termination. Normally the court will fix a date for the (oral) hearing, normally four or five weeks after the request has been sent in. The employee is asked to send in his written defence ten days before the oral hearing. The employer may send in additional information until five days before the hearing. The hearing takes about 1.5 hour. After the hearing the court will take its decision within on average three weeks. The decision of the cantonal judge can be to terminate the contract or to refuse the termination of the contract. If the contract is terminated, in most cases a Transition Payment must be paid. In case the conduct of the employer is considered severely culpable, an additional reasonable payment is due. Both parties may appeal this decision. The Court of Appeal can, in short, take the same decisions as the Cantonal judge could have done.

[H] Support Measures in Favour of Workers

As written above, the protective system for employees in case of a collective dismissal consists of three elements: (i) the trade unions are informed first. This makes it possible for them to negotiate about the intended collective dismissal and bring down the number of dismissals involved, or agree about a financial and other compensation for the employees involved. The trade unions do not have the power to slow down the process: if the information has been given, and the company does not want to come to an agreement, the role for the trade unions (apart from starting a strike) has ended. On an informal level the unions could try to influence (members of) the Works Council or individual employees. (ii) The second element is the Works Council. A company normally needs the advice of the Works Council in case of an intended collective dismissal. If the Works Council gives a negative advice, the Works Council can ask the Enterprise Section of the Court of Appeal in Amsterdam to forbid the decision to come to a reorganization. The Enterprise Section judges whether the company could reasonably come to this decision. If the company could not, the decision cannot validly be taken. If the company does anyway, the decision can be declared null and void. To persuade the Works Council to give a positive advice, the company might give some advantages (financial or otherwise) to support the employees. This creates more protection for the employees on an informal basis. (iii) The third element is the preventive individual system. If the employee does not agree with the dismissal (termination by mutual agreement), the employer has to ask the UWV for permission to terminate the contract, and can address the cantonal judge after a refusal of the UWV. So the individual employee may try to avoid the dismissal. If the dismissal is accepted, the employee is entitled to a standard severance payment, since 1 July 2015 called the Transition Payment, of at least one-third month salary per year of employment. Apart from the protection of labour law and unemployment law, protection can be derived from collective labour agreements. These CLAs can be declared generally binding, which means that they are applicable to every employee in the branch involved.

The Unemployment Act entitles the employee to an unemployment benefit. The employee is entitled to this benefit for a maximum of three months, if he has worked during the so-called reference-period, which means that he has worked for at least one hour in twenty-six weeks out of thirty-six weeks before becoming unemployed. If the employee has worked for at least 208 hours in 4 or 5 of the previous years before getting unemployed, the maximum period is extended: the period becomes as long as the years of employment the employee has had in his life, after the age of 18 years. The maximum period of an unemployment benefit was thirty-eight months. This maximum period will be reduced from 1 January 2016 and step by step come to a maximum of twenty-four months. The unemployment benefit is 70% of the last salary, with a maximum of 70% of approximately EUR 200 gross per day. The unemployment premiums are, until now, paid by the employers.

Most CLAs have an education fund. This fund is financed by employers. Employees are entitled to follow education, paid by the fund. Sometimes the CLA entitles the employee to an addition to the normal legal unemployment benefits. For example the unemployment benefit of 70% of the last salary (with a maximum of 70% of approximately EUR 200 gross per day) is lifted up to for example 80%.

[I] Judicial Control and Sanctions

The judicial control and sanctions have shortly been described above. Normally the government or the judiciary does not take any action by itself, the parties involved (trade unions, Works Council or employees) have to take the first step. As an exception the government acts itself if working conditions are dangerous or if the national minimum wage is not paid. In the case of a collective dismissal this normally does not play a role. Trade unions can not stop the business decision by legal means; the Works Council has a right to advise on the business decision to reorganize. The employees involved can fight their individual dismissals. The judicial measure (does the judge accept the business decision) differs from the different steps. The Enterprise Section decides whether it was reasonable that the company has taken the decision for a collective dismissal. So the Enterprise Section does not judge what the best decision would have been: if the company's decision is reasonably defendable, it cannot be stopped. The company must explain why the decision is taken ('what was the problem'); what effect the decision should have ('are you going to solve the problem with this decision') and what the consequences of that decision are for the employees. In the individual case the UWV (and afterwards the cantonal judge and the court of appeal) considers whether the business decision was reasonably defendable and if this is reasonable for this employee. Possibly the employer chose the wrong employee, or extra efforts should have been taken towards this employee.

CHAPTER 21

Collective Dismissals in Poland

Agata Ludera-Ruszel

§21.01 INTRODUCTION

The system of legal protection from collective dismissals originated in the socio-economic transformations following the system transformation occurring in 1989 in Poland and other countries of the former Eastern Bloc. Mass dismissals of employees as part of the policy of employment rationalization became a common phenomenon in the emerging free market economy in Poland. As a result, in 1991, 12.2% of people able to work were unemployed, which was twice as many as in 1990 (then the percentage of the unemployed was 6.5%).[1] The act on special terms of terminating employment relationships for employer-related reasons adopted on 28 December 1989[2] was an attempt to balance the opposing economic and social goals. Regulating collective dismissals was to help employers dismiss larger numbers of employees in cases justified with the economic situation, in return providing a system of extra (as compared to individual dismissals[3]) legal and economic protection from job loss in such cases.[4]

When the 1989 act was adopted, Poland was not a member of the European Union (EU), but the act was evidently modelled on the Council Directive 75/129/EEC,[5] although the objectives of these acts differed. The assumption underlying the regulation of collective dismissals at the EU level in 1975 was the belief that the differences

1. Central Statistic Office, *Polska 1989-2014*, Warszawa 2014, p. 14.
2. Journal of Laws of 2002, No. 112, item 980.
3. Both collective dismissals and individual dismissals rules constitute a system of job security in Poland.
4. L. Florek, *Job and Unemployment Security in Poland*, [in:] American University Law Review 1992, Vol. 7, Issue 3, p. 533.
5. Council Directive 75/129/of 17 February 1975 on the approximation of the laws of the Member States relating to collective redundancies (Official Journal L 48, 22 February 1975, p. 29).

occurring in this regard between Member States were a serious threat for the process of economic integration aimed at creating a common market based on freedom of movement of persons, services and capital.[6] The social aspect of the phenomenon of social dumping, resulting from differences in the level of employees' protection from collective dismissals, was of secondary importance.[7] The currently binding Council Directive 98/59/EC of 20 July 1998[8] balances the economic and social goals, clearly referring to The Community Charter of Fundamental Social Rights for Workers of 1989. The Directive was based on the minimum harmonization principle (Article 5), which makes it possible to eliminate differences between the protection level in Member States within the framework of the minimum protection standards determined in it.[9]

Poland's accession to the EU on 1 May 2004 caused the need of full adjustment of the national law to the European standards, including those concerning collective dismissals included in the Directive 98/59/EC. This was the main goal of the adoption of the Act of 13 March 2003 on special terms of terminating employees' employment for reasons not related to the employees (hereinafter referred to as 'the Act'),[10] which repealed the previous Act of 1989. The valid Act copies the model of legal regulation of collective dismissals adopted in the Act of 1989, following the Directive 98/59/EC. Its aim is to improve the level of employee protection in the case of collective dismissals, preserving the employer's freedom to carry out collective dismissals.[11]

§21.02 THE COLLECTIVE DISMISSAL: THE CASE

From the point of view of regulating collective dismissals, Article 1 of the Act is crucial, as it determines its subjective and objective scope included in the definition of 'collective dismissal', implemented on the basis of Article 1(1) of the Directive 98/59/EC. Article 1 u.z.g. reads as follows:

> Art. 1(1) The provisions of the Act apply when the employer who hires at least 20 employees is forced to end the employment contracts due to the reasons which do not concern the employee by way of termination or agreement of the parties, if within the maximum of 30-day window dismissals encompass:
> 1) 10 employees, if the employer hires less than 100 employees,
> 2) 10% employees, if the employer hires at least 100, but less than 300 employees,

6. R. Blanpain, *European Labour Law*, Kluwer 1999, p. 334. *See*, with regard to the principle of equal pay between men and women, J. Kenner, *EU Employment Law: From Rome to Amsterdam and Beyond*, Oxford, Hart 2003, p. 2.
7. C. Barnard & Deakin S., *'Negative' and 'Positive' Harmonization of Labor Law in the European Union*, [in:] Columbia Journal of European Law 2002, Vol. 8, p. 389.
8. Official Journal of the European Communities L 225, 12 August 1998, pp. 16-21 – hereinafter referred to as the Directive 98/59/EC.
9. C. Gerner-Beuerle, *United in Diversity: Maximum versus Minimum Harmonization in EU Securities Regulation*, [in:] Capital Markets Law Journal 2012, Vol. 7, No. 3.
10. Journal of Laws of 2015, item 192 – hereinafter referred to as Act on collective dismissals or the Act
11. *See* CJEU judgment of 12 February 1985 in the Case C-284/83 *Dansk Metalarbejderforbund and Specialarbejderforbundet i Danmark v. H. Bielsen & Son*, [ECR] 1985, p. 553.

3) 30 employees, if the employer hires at least 300 or more – hereinafter referred to as the 'collective dismissals'.
(2) The numbers that apply to employees, referred to in (1), includes cases, where at least five employees are dismissed by agreement of the parties.

[A] Personal Scope of Application

In the subjective aspect, the Act on collective dismissals applies to persons with the status set forth in Article 2 of the Labour Code,[12] except workers employed on the basis of nomination (Article 1(1) of the Act) and temporary workers (Article 6 of the Act of 9 July 2003 on the employment of temporary workers[13]). Excluding workers employed on the basis of nomination from the application of the Act only partially overlaps with excluding public administration workers from the Directive 98/59/EC (Article 1(2)(b)), because in Poland employment in public administration is not always based on nomination. On the other hand, nomination is also used as the basis of employment relationship in spheres other than public administration (e.g., universities, the judiciary, prosecutor's offices). Therefore, Article 11 of the Act raises some doubts in terms of compliance with the Directive 98/59/EC in the scope it excludes nominated workers not employed in public administration,[14] regardless of the rationality of this exclusion justified with greater employment stability of nominated workers.[15] Excluding temporary workers from the subjective scope of the Act results from the innate 'temporary' character of employment of this category of employees, which by assumption satisfies employers' temporary demand for workforce.[16] The above information shows that the Act on collective dismissals shall also apply to workers employed under employment contracts, nomination, appointment, and cooperative employment contracts. The kind of employment contract does not affect the subjective scope of the Act on collective dismissals. As a result, the act is applied to any notice of termination or employer-initiated termination upon mutual agreement of the parties of any fixed-term contract – for a specific period, for the trial period, or for the time of performing a specific work – before the expiration date of the contract. This interpretation, taking into consideration the provision of Article 1(2)(a) of the Directive 98/59/EC, was approved by the Polish Supreme Court in its judgment of 4 December 2008.[17] Polish regulation of

12. Act of 26 June 1974 Labour Code (Journal of Laws of 2014, item 1502) – hereinafter referred to as the Labour Code. According to Article 2 of the Labour Code, an employed person is a person employed on the basis of an employment contract, appointment contract, postings, election or a cooperative employment contract.
13. Journal of Laws of 2003, No. 166, item 1608 as amended.
14. J. Stelina, [in:] *Grupowe zwolnienia. Komentarz*, K. Jaśkowski, E. Maniewska & J. Stelina, Oficyna 2007, p. 178.
15. L. Kryńska-Wnuk, Regulacja zwolnień grupowych pracowników, Oficyna 2009, Lex.
16. A. Sobczyk, Ustawa o zatrudnianiu pracowników tymczasowych. Komentarz, Zakamycze 2005, Lex.
17. II PK 139/04, OSNP 2010/11-12/134.

collective dismissals does not refer to people with non-employee employment forms, which includes those working under civil law contracts (a mandate contract or another contract for providing services, or a contract for specific work), under tolling agreements,[18] military officers providing work as part of administrative-legal service relationship, and members of agricultural production cooperatives and their family members, as well as professional soldiers.[19] The doctrine points out that the act on collective dismissals shall apply to workers employed on ships, whose employment relationship is regulated by the Act of 23 May 1991 on work on board of merchant ships.[20]

The Act on collective dismissals refers to all employers within the meaning of Article 2 of the Labour Code,[21] regardless of their legal status or the kind of business. In accordance with Article 1(1) of the Act, the Act shall only apply to employers employing at least twenty workers. The Polish legislator, choosing one of the options of defining a collective dismissal specified in the Directive 98/59/EC, set the quantitative employment threshold allowing the application of the provisions of the Act on collective dismissals at a level more beneficial than did the directive. In Article 1.1.(a), the Directive 98/59/EC refers to employers employing more than twenty workers. The number of at least twenty workers refers to all the workers employed by the employers, notwithstanding the basis for the employment relationship, including the type of employment contract (fixed term or indefinite term), working hours (full-time or part-time), and the actual provision of work (e.g., holiday or sick leave). The workforce also includes nominated and temporary workers.[22] However, the Act on collective dismissals does not apply to employers employing fewer than twenty workers, irrespective of the range of planned dismissals. The legislator's intention behind relieving so-called small employers from the application of the Act on collective dismissals was to improve the flexibility of employment and lower the costs of employers' activity.[23] As a result, general regulations of the Labour Code shall apply in the case of dismissals by an employer employing fewer than twenty workers, regardless of their range or reason.

---

18. Employment issues of such categories of persons, including dismissals due to the principal, are governed by the Regulation of the Council of Ministers of 31 December 1975 on employee rights for persons employed under tolling agreement (Journal of Laws of 1975, No. 3, item 19 as amended).
19. K.W. Baran, Komentarz do ustawy o szczególnych zasadach rozwiązywania z pracownikami stosunków pracy z przyczyn niedotyczących pracowników, [in:] Zbiorowe prawo pracy. Komentarz, [in:] Zbiorowe prawo pracy, 2nd edition, Wolters Kluwer, Lex.
20. *See* L. Kryńska-Wnuk, *Regulacja zwolnień* ... .
21. According to Article 3 of the Labour Code, an employer is an organizational entity, even where it has no legal personality, as well as a natural person, if they employ any employees.
22. *See also* T. Liczcz, *Prawo pracy*, LexisNexis 2005, Lex. Different J. Stelina, [in:] K. Jaśkowski, E. Maniewska & J. Stelina, *Grupowe zwolnienia ..., supra*, p. 27 and K.W. Baran, that however considered reasonable to exclude only temporary agency workers, *see* K.W. Baran, *Komentarz ..., supra*, [in:] Zbiorowe ..., *supra*.
23. Ł.M. Pisarczyk, [in:] M. Latos-Miłkowska & Ł.M. Pisarczyk, *Zwolnienia z przyczyn niedotyczących pracownika*, ABC 2005, Lex.

[B] Material Scope of Application

Provisions of the Act on collective dismissals shall apply whenever the employment relationship is terminated for reasons not related to employees. The objective scope of the regulations is broad. On the basis of the quoted provision, it covers any reasons directly and indirectly connected with the employer, as well as any reasons which are not connected with any of the parties to the employment relationship but result from objective causes (force majeure, change of the legal status, political and economic situation in the country) which influence the need of providing work for the employer.[24] The reason justifying the dismissal must be real but it does not have to occur before the termination of the employment relationship. In the judgment of 12 December 2001, the Supreme Court argued that a liquidation of a workplace is a real reason for terminating the employment contract if it is advanced enough not to raise any doubt.[25] The necessity of reducing the workforce, when used as a reason related to the employer, may be justified with economic, organizational, technological or production reasons. Liquidation of a workplace may result from the need to reduce the costs of the conducted business, a change of production technology, lowering production as a result of limited demand for certain products or services, deconcentration of production, the use of outsourcing[26] or changes in the internal structure of the employment establishment. In practice, dismissals justified with organizational changes raise greatest doubts. The goal of internal organizational changes is legally irrelevant and not subject to court evaluation. What matters is only whether the liquidation of the workplace really occurred. An apparent liquidation which does not justify the termination of employment relationship may be recognized by maintaining the previous range of responsibilities, changing the name of the workplace and employing a new worker for the apparently liquidated workplace.[27] A special cause for dismissal pursuant to the Act is the bankruptcy or liquidation of the employer. In its judgment of 2 March 1994, the Supreme Court ruled that a decision of liquidation of the employment establishment alone may be the reason for termination of employment relationship, just like the declaration of bankruptcy.[28] A reason related to the employee does not have to be the only and exclusive reason for termination of the employment relationship but it must be the decisive one. An interesting example of such evaluation is the judgment of the Supreme Court of 11 February 2005, in which the Court argued that if the circumstances resulting in the termination of the employment contract with an employee (e.g., improper performance of employee's responsibilities, the lack of necessary qualifications, negative assessment of the employee's work, the lack of trust,

24. K.W. Baran, *Komentarz ..., supra*, [in:] Zbiorowe ..., *supra*.
25. I PKN 733/00, OSNP 2003/23/569.
26. *See* the Judgment of the Polish Supreme Court of 12 July 2001, I PKN 541/00, OSNAP 2003, No. 11, item 268.
27. *See* the Judgment of the Polish Supreme Court of 12 July 2001, I PKN 680/00, OSNAP 2003, No. 20, item 488. In the Judgment of 4 September 2007, Polish Supreme Court indicated that the assessment as to whether the apparent suppression of the post has occurred involves the comparison of working conditions in a newly created and suppressed position.
28. I PZP 55/93, OSNCP 1994, No. 12, item 229.

or lasting absence from work) did not result in terminating the employment relationship with the employee if the reasons specified in Article 1(1) of the Act did not occur, then this 'co-reason' would not exclude the application of provisions of the Act on collective dismissals.[29]

The number of employees, decisive for the number of employees qualifying a collective dismissal, is determined following the same principles as the number of employees decisive for the application of the Act to the employer. In the objective aspect, the termination of employment relationship for reasons not related to employees should occur by means of a notice of termination given by the employer or an employer-initiated agreement of the parties. In the case of agreement of the parties, the provisions of the Act are only applied if the redundancy covers at least five employees. The Supreme Court, in its judgment of 17 May 2007,[30] decided that the Act on collective dismissals shall also apply to a notice of termination amending the employment contract (Article 42 of the Labour Code) if it is transformed into a notice terminating the employment relationship as a result of the employee refusing to accept the new terms and conditions of work or payment. Thus, the Act on collective dismissals does not apply to the termination of the employment relationship by a notice of termination given by the employee, or the expiration of the employment relationship.

A dismissal is collective if the employment relationships with a specific number of employees are terminated at the same time or within a period of thirty days. This time limit is considered observed if before thirty days the employee is submitted a declaration of will concerning the termination of the employment relationship. The moment of actual discontinuance of the employment relationship is irrelevant.[31] The above-mentioned period begins on the day of the employer submitting the first declaration of will concerning the termination of employment relationship by notice or by mutual agreement of the parties.[32] The period may be shortened in the agreement or the rules concerning collective dismissals. Then the period for collective dismissals specified in such acts is binding for the employer.

§21.03 THE PROCEDURE

The collective dismissal procedure involves three stages: the stage of information and consultation and the stage of notification, preceding the collective dismissal, and the stage of actual collective dismissals. The information and consultation procedure is regulated in Articles 2 and 3 of the Act, and notification is specified by Article 4 of the Act. The conditions of terminating employment relationship as part of collective dismissal, in turn, are provided in Articles 5, 6 and 7 of the Act. Three entities participate in the procedure preceding a collective dismissal: the employer, trade

29. Lex No. 375699.
30. III BP 5/07, OSNP 2008, No. 13-14, item 188 with gloss by Ł.M. Pisarczyk, OSP 2009, No. 3, item 28.
31. T. Liszcz, *Prawo* ... .
32. *See also* the Judgments of the Polish Supreme Court of 4 March 2015, I PK 184/14 and of 20 September 1994, I PRN 63/94, OSNAPiUS 1995, No. 3, item 36.

unions (or representatives of the employees) and the poviat labour office as the public administration body.[33]

[A] Information and Consultation

The information and consultation procedure is obligatory. The obligation to carry it out arises when the employer intends to carry out collective dismissals. Hence, this stage precedes the employer's final decision of collective dismissals.[34]

The employer is obliged to consult the intention of a collective dismissal with all the company trade union organizations[35] (Article 2(1) of the Act). In the scope set forth in the Act of 2 April 2002 on European works councils,[36] the employer is also obliged to consult the intention of a collective dismissal with the European works council. If no company organization functions in the employer's establishment, the consultation obligation only refers to the employee representatives appointed in the mode functioning in the establishment (Article 2(7) of the Act). The act does not define the term 'employee representatives', nor does it specify the mode of their appointment, leaving that to the regulations of each employer. Literal interpretation of Article 2(7) of the Act is that there should be at least two employee representatives, they should be workers employed by the employer in question, and elected by the employees in a free election.[37]

Article 2(2) of the Act provides that the basic aim of the consultation is to avoid or reduce the range of dismissals, and if this is impossible, to determine the ways of assisting the dismissed employees in finding another job, in particular by means of reskilling or professional training. However, the consultations may cover any issues connected with the planned dismissals.

The consultation procedure shall be initiated by the employer informing the company trade union organizations (or employee representatives) in writing of the intention of a collective dismissal. Pursuant to Article 2(3) of the Act, the notification should include information of: the reasons for the intended collective dismissal, the number of workers employed, professional groups covered by the intention of the collective dismissal, the period when the dismissal is to take place, the criteria of choosing the employees to be dismissed, the order of the dismissals, proposals for settling employee matters connected with the intended dismissal, and if they include cash consideration, also the way of determining the amount of payments. Further, Article 2(5) of the Act obliges the employer to provide these entities with other information at their request. With reference to the Directive 98/59/EC, the quoted

33. L. Kryńska-Wnuk, *Regulacja zwolnień* ... .
34. L. Kryńska-Wnuk, *Regulacja zwolnień* ... .
35. Which have the status of company trade union within the Article 251(1) Act of 23 May 1991 on Trade Unions (Journal of Laws of 2001, No. 79, item 854).
36. Journal of Laws No. 62, item 556.
37. In the Judgment of 6 October 2005 Polish Supreme Court indicated that the formation of a new trade union when the procedure of collective dismissals has already been initiated does not require the employer to hold the consultation again (II PK 63/05, unpublished).

provision refers to significant information which may affect the course of the consultation and the content of the agreement on collective dismissals. Ultimately, the employer evaluates the character of information and the need to provide the information. Unjustified refusal to provide the required information is the employer's violation of the mode of consultation. Additional information may be provided in any form.[38]

In practice, the greatest doubts result from the reasons for collective dismissals included by the employer in the notification and the criteria of choosing employees to be dismissed. The Supreme Court judgments indicate that the reason for a collective dismissal should be real and concrete, so that it could be verified and evaluated in terms of justification and range of the planned dismissals. Thereby, the reason for a collective dismissal may not be limited to a general statement of quoted statutory provisions.[39] The criteria for the choice of employees to be dismissed may be determined in a positive or negative way. The parties have a considerable freedom in this respect, limited by the provisions of law concerning collective dismissals, which specify the categories of employees that cannot be dismissed in this mode, the order of equal treatment and lack of discrimination in employment, which means that the applied criteria may not be discriminatory (e.g., regarding sex, age, race, skin colour, trade union membership), and by the principles of community life (Article 8 of the Labour Code).[40] As the Supreme Court argued, the criteria of choosing employees for dismissal should be objective and just[41] and equally apply to all the employees.[42] Furthermore, the criteria must be formulated in a way that allows their verification.[43] It is impossible to establish a general list of acceptable criteria for assigning employees for dismissal; they should always be evaluated individually, with consideration of the individual circumstances. The judgments of the Supreme Court may be helpful in this regard. Basically, the Supreme Court holds the opinion that the employees' performance of their responsibilities, meeting the targets, professional qualifications and work experience should be taken into consideration.[44] However, the personal, family or material conditions of the employee are also taken into account as part of evaluating the choice of employees to be dismissed from the point of view of community life principles. The Supreme Court has found a termination of contract with the best employee having the longest work experience, a family of five and a poor financial situation,[45] as well as the choice of an employee whose personal situation was much worse than that of the other employees,[46] to be contrary to the principles of community life.

38. K.W. Baran, *Komentarz ...*, *supra*, [in:] Zbiorowe ..., *supra*.
39. *See* Judgment of the Polish Supreme Court of 19 May 1978, V PZP 6/77, OSNCP 1978, item 127.
40. T. Liszcz, *Prawo ...*, *supra*.
41. *See* the Judgment of 19 December 1997, I PKN 442/97, OSNP 1998, No. 21, item 630.
42. *See* the Judgment of 14 March 2013, I PK 243/12, Lex No. 1448686.
43. R. Sadlik, *Kryteria zwalniania przy zmniejszeniu zatrudnienia*, [in:] Służba Pracownicza 2007, No. 7, p. 15.
44. *See* the Judgment of 27 June 1985, III PZO 10/85, OSNCP 1985, No. 11, item 164 and the Judgment of 19 December 1997, I PKN 442/97, OSP 1998, No. 21, item 630.
45. *See* the Judgment of 27 February 1997, I PKN 20/97, OSNP 1997, No. 21, item 417.
46. *See* the Judgment of 19 December 1996, I PKN 46/96.

The Act, just like the Directive 98/59/EC, does not precisely determine the time when the employer is obliged to give the trade unions (or employee representatives) a notification of planned dismissals, only specifying in Article 2(4) that it should occur 'at a time that allows these organisations to submit for consultation their proposals concerning the matters specified in the notification'. This leaves a lot of freedom for the employer. Taking into consideration the goal of the information and consultation stage, it can be rightly concluded that the notification should occur without delay. The same refers to additional information provided to the entities specified in Article 2(5) of the Act. Only then can we say that trade unions (or employee representatives) really participate in the consultation procedure and really have impact on the employer's ultimate decision.

At the information and consultation stage, the employer is also obliged to notify the competent labour office of the intention of a collective dismissal, providing in writing the same information that was previously included in the notification addressed at the trade union organizations (or employee representatives), except the information concerning the way of determination of cash consideration the employees shall be entitled to (Article 2(6) of the Act). However, it may be reasonable for the employer to provide additional information concerning the employees to be dismissed (their age, education, or sex), at the labour office's request or on their own initiative.[47] The act does not provide a deadline for notifying the poviat (*local*) labour office. Yet, taking into account the aim of the notification, it is obvious that the notification should be sent at the same time that trade unions (or employee representatives) are notified, or immediately after.[48]

The consultation finishes with the employer and the company trade union organizations concluding an agreement on collective dismissal (Article 3(1) of the Act). The agreement is the preferred way of concluding the consultations. Only if it is impossible to find a consensus with trade unions concerning the content of the agreement (Article 3(4) of the Act) or if there are no company trade union organizations in the employment establishment (Article 3(5) of the Act), is the employer obliged to issue rules concerning collective dismissals – if possible, taking into account the proposals presented by trade union organizations during the consultations, and if there are none, after consulting employee representatives. In its judgment of 25 May 2000, the Supreme Court indicated that 'the obligation to issue the rules only refers to the cases in which the parties are unable to determine the content of the agreement, but not to the cases when it is possible to make the agreement but the parties unanimously waiver that'.[49] The agreement should be concluded within twenty days of the employer notifying the trade union organization of the planned collective dismissal,[50] but the parties may effectively conclude the above-mentioned arrangement even after that

47. K.W. Baran, *Komentarz ..., supra*, [in:] Zbiorowe ..., *supra*; T. Liszcz, *Prawo ..., supra*.
48. T. Liszcz, *Prawo ...* .
49. I OKN 649/99, OSNP 2001, No. 21, item 546.
50. Where more than one trade union is involved in the consultation, such a period shall be determined from the date of notification of the last of such organization.

date, in fact until the moment of the employer issuing the rules[51] or even later, after the abrogation of the rules, if this occurs.[52] The instruction character of the period for the conclusion of agreement was also pointed out by the Supreme Court in its judgment of 2 March 2004, which indicated that the agreement on collective dismissals concluded after that date is not ineffective.[53] The subject of the agreement was defined broadly, as 'principles of proceeding in matters concerning employees covered with the intention of collective dismissal' and 'employer's obligations in the scope necessary to settle other employee matters connected with the intended dismissal'. The agreement should indicate the criteria of choosing employees for dismissal, the order, and the dates of terminating employment contracts. It is also possible to specify in the agreement the names of employees assigned for dismissal. As the Supreme Court argued in its judgment of 15 December 2000, the agreement may also include the employer's obligation to present to the company trade union organization the list of employees assigned for dismissal before handing them the notices of termination. The employer's failure to fulfil this obligation is a violation of the provisions concerning the termination of employment contracts within the meaning of Article 45 of the Labour Code.[54] The Supreme Court, in its judgment of 24 June 2013, also stated that the period within which the collective dismissal will occur can be included in the agreement.[55] Other obligations of the employer related to settling various employee matters may in particular refer to holiday leaves, the equivalent for unused holiday leave, the conditions of repayment of loans taken out by the employees at the employee savings and loan association, etc.[56] Other matters which the parties consider to be important may also be included. The subject of the rules, in turn, is narrower. Obligatorily, the subject of the rules is the determination of principles of proceeding in matters concerning employees covered with the intention of collective dismissal. Other obligations of the employer may but do not have to be specified in the rules of collective dismissals. The agreement and the rules are regarded as the sources of labour law within the meaning of Article 9 of the Labour Code, which means that their provisions may be the subject of individual employee claims and be pursued in court.[57]

[B] Notification

The notification of collective dismissals is written information by the employer for the relevant district employment agency on the arrangements concerning collective dismissals. Pursuant to Article 4(1) of the Act on collective dismissals (the Act),

51. T. Gregorczuk, *Tryb postępowania w sprawie zwolnień grupowych*, [in:] Praca i Zabezpieczenie Społeczne 1991, Nos 7-8, pp. 78-79.
52. T. Liszcz, *Prawo* ... . *See* K.W. Baran who indicated on the rules of interpretation *lex posteriori derogat legi priori* and *lex posterior generalis non derogat legi priori speciali* - K.W. Baran, *Komentarz* ..., [in:] Zbiorowe ..., *supra*.
53. I PK 387/03, OSNP 2005, No. 9, item 124.
54. I PKN 161/00, OSNP 2002, No. 17, item 404.
55. II PK 341/12, Lex No. 1350303.
56. T. Liszcz, *Prawo* ..., *supra*.
57. *See* the Judgments of the Polish Supreme Court of 26 September 2000, I PKN 56/2000, OSNAPiUS 2002, No. 9, item 207 and of 20 June 2005, II PK 323/05, unpublished.

notification is given after the conclusion of agreement with company trade unions or after the employer issuing the regulation on collective dismissals.

Generally, the notification is a compulsory procedure that precedes a collective dismissal. Its relative compulsory character only refers to those cases of collective dismissals that are related to the winding up of the employer's company due to a court decision.[58]

The period for notification has not been stipulated by the law. It is assumed, in practice, that notification should be made immediately after the establishment of conditions of collective dismissals,[59] in accordance with its aim, which is suitable preparation of district agencies to provide adequate support for the potential unemployed.

The notification of the district employment agency should include information about: the number of employed and dismissed employees, the reasons for dismissals, the period within which the dismissals will be carried out, consultation with company trade union or employee representatives. As during the information and consultation procedure, the notice to district employment agency should indicate the information about the dismissed employees, such as their age, gender, the level of education and qualifications.

According to Article 4(2)(3), a copy of the notification has to be sent by the employer to the company trade union or, in their absence, to employee representatives. This has to be done immediately after the notification.[60] The participation of employee representatives in the notification procedure, on the one hand, is targeted at the verification of information provided to the employment agency by the employer,[61] and on the other hand allows for better adjustment of support which is provided to the dismissed employees by the employment agency. Upon receipt of the copy of notification, the entitled subjects may provide to the employment agency their opinions on the collective dismissal, in which they may include any information which may be relevant in that regard but has been omitted by the employer.

[C] The Termination of Employment Relationship Within the Collective Dismissals Procedure

The starting point for further reflections on the rules that govern the termination of employment relationship under the collective dismissals procedure must be Article 12 of the Act. According to the above provision, within the scope not regulated in the Act on collective dismissals, any dispute related to the provisions of this Act shall be governed by the relevant Labour Code provisions. It is therefore clear that the termination of employment relationship as part of collective dismissal has to be carried out in accordance with the relevant general provisions of the Labour Code on the

58. *See* Act of 28 February 2003 on the bankruptcy and composition law (Journal of Laws from 2015, item 233).
59. K.W. Baran, *Komentarz* ..., *supra*, [in:] Zbiorowe ..., *supra*.
60. T. Liszcz, *Prawo* ..., *supra*.
61. K.W. Baran, *Komentarz* ..., *supra*, [in:] Zbiorowe ..., *supra*.

termination of employment relationship by the employer, to the extent to which the Act on collective dismissals, which is *lex specialis* to the Labour Code, does not provide otherwise.

Pursuant to Article 30 § 3 and 5 of the Labour Code, any termination of the employment contract, including termination under collective dismissals, has to be in the written form and provide the information on the right of appeal to a court. Moreover, in the light of Article 30 § 4 of the Labour Code, a justified reason has to be included in the termination of an indefinite term employment contract by the employer. Under the above provision, it does not only mean formal presentation of the reason but also formulating it in a way that is concrete, clear and comprehensible for the employee.

As has been mentioned before, the Act on collective dismissals was based on the model that is an attempt to reconcile conflicting interests of the parties to the employment relationship, where the employer has faced the necessity to dismiss more employees. For this reason, during the collective dismissals procedure, on the one hand the mechanism of job security is being weakened, but on the other hand, certain time constraints as to the moment of termination and dismissals are in force.

The Act on collective dismissals allows for easier termination of the employment relationship (as compared to the Labour Code) by the exemption from the obligation of individual consultation with the trade union and the reduction of specific protection of employees against the termination of employment relationship.[62]

According to general rules set out in Article 38 of the Labour Code, the termination of an indefinite term employment contract by the employer entails the obligation to consult their intention with the relevant trade union that represents the employees. Pursuant to Article 5(1) (2) of the Act, the employer is exempted from this duty when the agreement on collective dismissals with the company is concluded, which is set out in Article 3(1) of the Act. As a result, in the event of issuance of the regulation on collective dismissals, the termination of an indefinite term employment contract by the employer under the collective dismissals procedure has to be preceded by individual consultation with the trade union.

In this way, the Act on collective dismissals in Article 5(1) diminishes the ban on the employer terminating an employment contract during the holiday leave and any other justified absence from work contained in Article 41 of the Labour Code. According to Article 5(3) of the Act, in the above-mentioned situations the termination of employment relationship is allowed during the holiday leave lasting at least three months, as well as during any other absence from work, since the period for the employer's termination of employment relationship without notice has already expired, pursuant to Article 53 of the Labour Code. Under the above provisions, the Polish Supreme Court has emphasized that the condition of three months relates to holiday leave entitlement rather than its actual duration.[63] Pursuant to Article 5(4), termination amending the contract of employment is, however, allowed without any

62. Ł.M. Pisarczyk, [in:] M. Latos-Miłkowska & Ł.M. Pisarczyk, *Zwolnienia z przyczyn niedotyczących pracownika*, ABC 2005.
63. *See* Judgment of 11 December 1996, I PKN 39/96, OSNAPiUS 1997/14/252.

limitations regarding both the duration of holiday leave and any other justified absence from work.

The Act on collective dismissals partly modifies and partly drops the specific protection of employees against termination of employment relationship by reason of performing certain public functions or an exceptional personal situation. Such a waiver of special protection involves, in particular, the following categories of people: members of parliament, senators, members of local government entities, employees – members of professional or business self-government authorities, employees – members of foundation committees of trade unions, young employees during the apprenticeship employment contract, and women – employees whose husbands perform military service. On the other hand, the modification of special protection against termination involves the following categories of people: pre-retirement employees within four years before the retirement age, pregnant employees and employees on maternity leave, employees – members of the works council of a state company, employees – members of a trade union authorized to represent it before the employer, employees – members of a special negotiating body, elected body or a body that represents the employee in the European company, European Cooperative or the supervisory body of a company which was established through a cross-border merger, employees – social labour inspectors, employees called up for military service, alternative service or military training, employees – members of works councils or entitled to obtain information from the employer and carry out consultations with the employer. The above categories of employees are still protected against termination of employment relationship, but in the case of such people the Act on collective dismissals allows termination amending employment relationship, pursuant to Article 42 of the Labour Code. Where the termination amending employment relationship leads to a reduction of their remuneration, the specially protected employees are entitled to compensatory allowance[64] provided for in Article 5(6) of the Act. However, Article 7 of the Act drops the above safeguard mechanisms with regard to: pre-retirement employees, employees on holiday leave or absent from work due to any other justified reasons, pregnant employees and employees on maternity leave, employees raising children during the maternity leave, employees on parental leave, employees entitled to parental leave who apply for the reduction of working time, young employees employed under an apprenticeship employment contract, provided that the collective dismissal results from the employer's declaration of bankruptcy or winding up their business.

The Act on collective dismissals provides for a specific time limit for the termination of employment relationship in this case, which is undoubtedly a sign of improvement of job security.[65] According to Article 6(1) of the Act, the termination of employment relationship can be made no earlier than after the notification by the

64. In the amount provided for in the Regulation of the Minister of Labour and Social Policy of 29 May 1996 on the method of calculating remuneration for a period of inactivity and on the method of calculating remuneration on which compensation, severance payments, compensatory allowance and other benefits provided for in the Labour Code are calculated (Journal of Laws No. 62, item 289 as amended).
65. L. Kryńska-Wnuk, *Regulacja zwolnień ...*, *supra*.

employer to the relevant district employment agency, and if in particular case the notification is not required, no earlier than after the conclusion of an agreement or issuing the regulations on collective dismissals. This period may be extended in the agreement or regulation on collective dismissals. Pursuant to Article 6(2) of the Act, the dismissals may not occur earlier than after the lapse of the period of thirty days from the notification to the relevant district employment agency or from the conclusion of the agreement or issuance of the regulation on collective dismissals, if the notification is not required in the particular case. This period may also be extended in the agreement or regulation on collective dismissals. However, this so-called warranty period does not apply where the dismissal is the result of winding up of the business activity by the employer due to the ultimate court ruling. The Polish legislator has not yet decided to grant district employment agencies the right to reduce or extend such a period, as indicated in the Directive 98/59/EC.

§21.04 THE SUPPORT MEASURES IN FAVOUR OF WORKERS

With a view to the need to balance the conflicting interests of the parties during the collective dismissal procedure, the law in force provides for a few measures, which are intended to alleviate the adverse effects that are related to the termination of employment relationship due to the reasons independent of the employee. Those measures are provided by the Act on collective dismissals and by the Act of 20 April 2004 on employment promotion and labour market institutions.[66] Apart from that, social partners in the agreement on collective dismissals concluded as part of the consultation procedure may grant an employee the right to benefits other than statutory, or modify statutory benefits in a more favourable manner. Below I focus on those measures which are addressed solely to an employee dismissed under the collective dismissals procedure.

The Act on collective dismissals has introduced three so-called warranty periods, which are protective in nature. These are: the maximum period of thirty days within which the employment relationships with a certain number of employees have to be terminated in order to benefit from collective dismissals rules (Article 1(1) of the Act); the period that precedes the notice of termination during the collective dismissals procedure (Article 6(1) of the Act) and the minimum time limit of thirty days after which the employment relationship may be terminated as part of the collective dismissals procedure (Article 6(2) of the Act).[67] The last two periods are of critical importance. They allow the employee to undertake necessary measures to find new employment before the termination of the employment relationship, which is especially important in the case of a short notice period. As indicated in the justification of the Act on collective dismissals, the minimum period for termination of employment relationship 'will allow employment agencies to better prepare to assist the employees that lose their jobs as a result of collective dismissals, thanks to the possibility to

66. Journal of Laws of 2015, item 149 – hereinafter referred to as the Act on employment promotion.
67. L. Kryńska-Wnuk, *Regulacja zwolnień ...*, *supra*.

determine more precisely the time when certain categories of employees would be dismissed'.[68]

In terms of the impact of collective dismissals on the situation on the labour market, the participation of district employment agencies becomes significant in the context of collective dismissals. The information that is given at the time of intended dismissals and immediately preceding collective dismissals, in the legislator's intention, was supposed to better prepare employment agencies to provide comprehensive assistance to the dismissed employees. The same effect is to be achieved by the right to provide an opinion to the employment agency with regard to collective dismissals during the notification procedure, which was given to company trade unions and employee representatives.[69]

An employee that was dismissed under the collective dismissals procedure acquires the right to severance payment, provided for in Article 8 of the Act. The severance payment is intended to compensate for the employee's involuntary unemployment,[70] and thus guarantee the stabilization of employment relationship,[71] at the same time providing the means of subsistence for the employee after having been dismissed.[72] The social nature of severance payment has been indirectly confirmed by the Polish Supreme Court, which has decided that the right to severance payment is independent of the right to compensation for wrongful dismissals under the collective dismissals procedure, pursuant to Article 45 § 2 in conjunction with Article 47^1 of the Labour Code,[73] while in the case of reinstatement of employment relationship, the severance payment, as an undue payment, is subject to reimbursement.[74] The severance payment is one-off in nature. It has to be paid to the employee no later than on the day of termination of the employment relationship.[75] The amount of severance payment is dependent on the length of service in the current employer (regardless of the type and number of employment contracts and intervals between them[76]) and exceptionally on the length of service in the previous employer, if the change of employer was made pursuant to Article 23^1 of the Labour Code, i.e., through the transfer of whole or part of the employer's enterprises to the new employer or where the new employer under separate regulations is a successor in the employment relationship concluded by the previous employer (Article 8(2) of the Act). The severance payment is equivalent to the monthly, two- or three-monthly remuneration with respect to employment lasting shorter than two years, between two and eight

68. *See* justification to the Act of 13 March 2003 on particular principles of dissolution of employment relationship due to reasons independent of employees, http://orka.sejm.gov.pl/Druki4ka.nsf/wgdruku/1155/$file/1155.PDF (16 July 2015).
69. *Ibid.*
70. K.W. Baran, *Komentarz ...*, *supra*, [in:] Zbiorowe ..., *supra*.
71. A. Dral, Powszechna ochrona trwałości stosunku pracy. Tendencje zmian, Oficyna 2009, Lex.
72. K. Jaśkowski, [in:] K. Jaśkowski, E. Maniewska & J. Stelina, *Grupowe zwolnienia ...*, *supra*, pp. 111-112.
73. *See* Judgment of 13 December 1990, III PZP 22/90, OSNCP 1991/5-6/64.
74. *See* Judgment of 3 February 2006, II PK 158/05, OSNP 2006/23-24.
75. K.W. Baran, *Komentarz ...*, *supra*, [in:] Zbiorowe ..., *supra*.
76. *See* Judgment of the Polish Supreme Court of 15 January 2003, III PZP 20/2002, OSNP 2004/1/4.

years, and more than eight years, respectively. Taking into account the financial interest of the employer, the law stipulates the maximum amount of severance payment, which in any case cannot exceed the amount equivalent to fifteen-monthly minimum wage that is valid on the day of termination of the employment relationship.[77]

The employee dismissed within the collective dismissal procedure has the right to reintegration into employment in the same employer (Article 9(1) of the Act). As was emphasized by the Polish Supreme Court in the judgment of 22 February 1994, in this case, an employee is given the right to claim from employer the establishment of employment relationship.[78] The above-mentioned right of the employee is relative in nature, as its occurrence is dependent, first, on reemployment in the same professional group (as well as only one employer[79]), second, on the notification of such employee's request in any form within one year from the termination of employment relationship. The Act on collective dismissals does not define, however, the notion of 'the same professional group' as a condition of reemployment; therefore, it has to be interpreted individually including all the relevant circumstances of the case, especially the situation of the particular employer, their character, type of activities and the employee's qualifications,[80] as well as the aim of the reinstatement due to the changing circumstances that justified collective dismissals. The Polish Supreme Court in the judgment of 7 March 1997 called for a broad interpretation of the above notion, indicating that 'a professional group can be understood as a team of employees with special qualifications to perform a specific kind of work (driver, doctor), or a team whose activities are the same or similar in type, as well as a group of employees with a similar level of education and qualifications needed for the performance of certain tasks at the employer's company'.[81] The reemployment may not involve the same conditions as previously, which was determined by the Polish Supreme Court in the judgment of 4 December 1998.[82] In the event where the number of employees requesting exceeds the number of vacant posts, the employer freely decides on the choice of employees for reemployment; however, the employer cannot use criteria that are discriminatory in nature.[83] Pursuant to Article 9(2) of the Act, the employer is obliged to provide reemployment for the period of fifteen months from the day of termination of employment relationship within collective dismissals.

The Act on promotion of employment introduced the institution of outplacement as a form of support for employees that are at risk of collective dismissals. The outplacement procedure is the termination of employment relationship for reasons related to the employer, due to which labour market services are provided to the

77. *See* Minimum Wage Act of 10 October 2002 (Journal of Laws from 2002, No. 200, item 1679 as amended).
78. I PZP 2/94, OSNAPiUS 1994/1/5.
79. T. Liszcz, *Prawo* ... .
80. *See* Judgment of the Polish Supreme Court of 07 March 1997, I PKN 26/97, OSNAPiUS 1997/24/486.
81. I PKN 26/97, OSNAPiUS 1997/24/486.
82. I PKN 444/98, OSNP 2000/2/45.
83. T. Liszcz, *Prawo* ..., *See also* Judgment of the Polish Supreme Court of 20 January 2015, III PK 52/14, Lex No. 1663409.

employee. This institution will only apply to the cases of collective dismissal that include at least fifty employees within three months (Article 70(1) of the Act on employment promotion). The outplacement is aimed at providing the dismissed employees or those at risk of unemployment certain activities which may help them to move on the labour market.[84] According to Article 70 of the Act on employment promotion, these activities are provided in the form of a programme agreed by the employer with the labour office, which includes, in particular: employment services, vocational guidance and vocational training. These are directed at employees that are envisaged to be made dismissed (at risk of dismissals and during the notice of termination) as well as within the period of six months from the termination of employment relationship. The programme may be implemented by the district labour office, employment agency and training organization.

§21.05 JUDICIAL CONTROL AND SANCTIONS

According to Article 12 of the Act, within the scope not regulated in the Act on collective dismissals, any dispute related to the provisions of this Act shall be governed by the relevant Labour Code provisions. Moreover, pursuant to Article 300 of the Labour Code, in the scope not regulated in the labour law provisions, the relevant civil law provisions shall be alternatively applied. In view of the above, the scope of judicial review of the correctness of the collective dismissals procedure is broad, defined by the provisions of the Act on collective dismissals, the Labour Code and the Civil Code.

By the appeal to labour court an employee may challenge the legality of the agreement on termination of employment contract, justification for the notice of termination of employment contract under the collective dismissals procedure, the legality of collective dismissals, and may claim benefits to which he or she is entitled, showing that the dismissal, in this particular case, was collective in nature.

Where the employment contract is terminated upon mutual agreement of the parties, an employee is allowed to set aside such an agreement by invoking defects of the declaration of intent. In practice the employee may at most refer to errors as to the facts stated by the employer as grounds for the termination of employment relationship under that procedure. According to Article 84 of CC, in the case such a declaration of intent has been communicated to another person, it shall be possible to avoid the legal consequences of one's own declaration of intent, provided that the error has been caused by that person, even with no fault on their part, or if that person knew of the error or could have easily perceived it. Moreover, the error must relate to the contents of a legal act and it must be essential, which means that it justifies the assumption that if the person making the declaration of intent had not been influenced by the error and had considered the matter in the reasonable manner, he or she would not have made such a declaration (Article 86 § 1 of CC). Pursuant to Article 88 of CC, the right of avoidance expires a year after the discovery of the error. In the light of the case law of

84. E. Bielak-Jamaa, [in:] Ustawa o promocji zatrudnienia i instytucjach rynku pracy. Praktyczny komentarz, Lex 2011.

the Polish Supreme Court, an example of declaration of intent made under an error is when the employee was unaware that the winding-up proceeding of the company of his or her former employer had not yet finished.[85] The effective employee's avoidance of the legal consequences of his or her will results in reactivation of the employment relationship and gives rise to the obligation of reimbursement of the severance payment received previously. In this case the employee may also file a claim to confirm the existence of the employment relationship (Article 189 of C.C.P.).

Within the judicial review of the termination of employment contract under the collective dismissals procedure, an employee may challenge its validity. With respect to temporary employment contracts (fixed-term employment contract, employment contract for a trial period), which the employer is not obliged to justify, the labour court is empowered to conduct judicial review in two cases. First, when an employee challenges the criteria of selection for collective dismissals, which in the light of case law of the Polish Supreme Court cannot be arbitrary.[86] Second, when an employee shows that the termination of an employment relationship in that particular case was under the procedure of collective dismissals, thus he or she demonstrates that the real reasons for termination of the employment contract, although not indicated by the employer, were reasons set out in Article 1(1) of the Act. It should also be emphasized that pursuant to the judgment of the Polish Supreme Court of 24 March 2011, in this situation the burden of proof regarding the above lies on the employee; however, the employee does not need to prove that these were the reasons behind the employer's decision.[87] Notwithstanding the above, questioning the validity of termination of an indefinite term employment contract, an employee may argue that the reason indicated by the employer was not the real reason for the termination of employment relationship in this case. An example of such evaluation is the interpretation of Polish Supreme Court provided in the judgment of 18 February 2014, in which this court challenged the reason for dismissing an employee, which was the need for restructuring of the employer's company, where the projected reduction of the workforce set out in the company's regulation on collective dismissals had already been achieved through voluntary leaves of employees.[88] The lack of real cause for the termination also occurs when the indicated liquidation of position is only apparent.

The termination of employment relationship under the collective dismissals procedure is also the subject of judicial review in terms of its formal aspect. Within this judicial control the assessment refers to the lawfulness of the termination, which includes: the Act on collective dismissals, general Labour Code provisions, and the provisions or the regulation on collective dismissals. Not all of the infringements with regard to formal requirements qualify as illegal and entitle the employee to relevant claims.

85. *See* Judgment of 31 August 1989, III PZP 37/89, OSNC 1990/9/108.
86. *See* Judgment of the Polish Supreme Court of 27 February 1997, I PKN 20/97, OSNP 1997/21/417.
87. I PK 185/10, Lex No. 1119478.
88. III PK 63/13, OSNP 2015/ 5/62.

A termination which is not in a written form is unlawful. The lack of information or improper information provided to the employee about the right of appeal to the court shall not, however, have the same effect; it may only give rise to re-establishment of the time-limit to file a claim to the court.[89] Termination of an indefinite term employment contract, in which the employer has not indicated the reason, is unlawful. The Polish Supreme Court has decided that equivalent to the lack of reason is the reason which is unclear, insufficiently specified and hard to understand for the employee.[90] Failure to carry out an individual consultation of the intended termination of employment contract with company trade union organization representing that employee also qualifies as an infringement of the provisions of law on termination. Such individual consultation is obligatory when pursuant to Article 5(2) of the Act the agreement on collective dismissals with the trade union or employee's representatives has not been concluded. The infringement of the provisions of law on termination within collective dismissals could also involve the violation of special protection against collective dismissals under Article 5(3)(4)(5) of the Act. The Polish Supreme Court emphasized in the judgment of 23 January 1991 that the infringement of obligations related to consultations and information procedure set out in Articles 2 and 3 of the Act by an employer who intends to conduct collective dismissals qualifies the termination as unlawful, which constitutes the basis for claims indicated in Article 45 of the Labour Code.[91] The lack of notification of the relevant district labour office pursuant to Article 4 of the Act has the same effect. The legal doctrine argues, however, that the absence of the written form of information given both to the employee representatives and to the relevant district employment agency, as well as the lack of written form of notification to the district employment agency, does not constitute infringement of the provisions of law on termination, since this defectiveness does not affect the legal position of employees based on collective dismissals.[92] For the same reasons, failure to send a copy of notification of the relevant district employment agency to the company trade union or employee representatives pursuant to Article 4(2)(3) of the Act does not mean the infringement of the provisions of the law on termination.[93] Polish Supreme Court, referring to the violation of the collective dismissals rules set out in the agreement or regulation on collective dismissals has decided that it may be the infringement of provisions of the law on termination under Article 45 § 1 of the Labour Code provided that in the particular case it had a real impact on the termination of employment relationship.[94] According to the Polish Supreme Court, the infringement of the criteria for selecting employees for dismissals, the order and dates of dismissals

89. Judgment of the Polish Supreme Court of 23 November 2000, I PKN 117/00, OSNAPiUS 200213/304.
90. Judgment of the Polish Supreme Court of 19 May 1978, V PZP 6/77, OSNCP 1978/8/127; of 27 July 1985, III PZP 10/85, OSNCP 1985/11/164; of 1 October 1997, I PKN 315/97, OSNP 1998/14/427.
91. U PR 450/90, OSP 1992/3/57.
92. K.W. Baran, *Komentarz ...*, *supra*, [in:] Zbiorowe ..., *supra*.
93. E.W. Baran, K.W. Baran, Zwolnienia grupowe w systemie ustawodawstwa polskiego na tle prawodawstwa wspólnotowego, Radca Prawny 2004, No. 3, p. 76.
94. *See* Judgment of 29 June 2005, II PK 342/04, OSNP 2006/9-10/151; of 24 November 2011, I PK 60/11, OSNP 2010/23-24/281.

that are set out in the agreement on collective dismissals has the same effect.[95] Finally, the failure to observe the periods indicated in Article 45 of the Labour Code for termination of employment relationship through collective dismissals also constitutes an infringement of provisions of the law on termination.[96]

According to Article 45 of the Labour Code, unjustified and unlawful termination of an indefinite term employment contract entitles an employee to claim to declare the termination void, and if the employment contract has already been terminated, claim the restoration of the employee or compensation for the amount specified in Article 47^1 of the Labour Code, i.e., the amount equivalent to wages in the period from two weeks to three months, not higher than the wages during the period of notice. The labour court, however, may not uphold the employee's claim to declare the termination void or claim of the restoration of employment if it determines that both are impossible or impracticable (e.g., in the event of liquidation of the post or the organizational unit where the employee was employed). In addition, an employee who begins work due to the restoration of his or her employment is entitled to remuneration for the period of unemployment, but no more than for two months, and if the notice period was three months – no more than for one month (Article 47 of the Labour Code). In the event of unlawful termination of a temporary employment contract, an employee is only entitled to compensation in the amount equivalent to wages in the period for which the contract would last; however, no more than for three months in relation to a fixed-term employment contract (Article 50 of the Labour Code).

If the labour court finds that a reason not related to the employee was the real or decisive reason to terminate an employment relationship, and if all the remaining conditions indicated in Article 1(1) of the Act were met simultaneously, the labour court – upon the request of the employee – will award to the employee all the benefits to which he or she is entitled under the Act on collective dismissals, and additionally under the agreement or regulation on collective dismissals.

An employee who due to collective dismissals has the priority in re-integration into employment relationship according to Article 9 of the Act may claim to establish the employment relationship if the employer waives from this duty. According to Article 64 of CC, in conjunction with Article 300 of the Labour Code, a final court ruling that affirms a duty of a given person to make a determined declaration of intent shall replace this declaration. Polish Supreme Court, in its judgment of 12 July 2011,[97] indicated that instead of a request to establish an employment relationship, an employee may claim compensation for damage that he or she suffered as a result of the employer's breach of their duty under Article 471 of CC in conjunction with Article 300 of the Labour Code, i.e., subject to general contractual liability. Such compensation will be for the period of unemployment. The employee's loss of earnings during such a period has to refer to the remuneration given to the person who has been employed instead of the dismissed employee.

95. *See* Judgment of the Polish Supreme Court of 24 June 2013, II PK 341/12, Lex No. 1350303.
96. *See* Judgment of the Polish Supreme Court of 25 June 2010, II PK 32/10.
97. II PK 19/2011, OSNP 2012/19-20/231.

§21.06 CONCLUSIONS

The restructuring of enterprises was an inseparable element of transformations of Polish economy and adjustment to the requirements of market economy, which occurred after 1989 as part of the system transformations. But currently companies also face the necessity to adapt to the dynamically changing environment. This way restructuring has become an indispensable part of functioning of each organization. It is rightly pointed out that the enterprises of the twenty-first century are in a new stage of operation – the stage of permanent restructuring, forced by the global, competitive environment.[98] In these conditions the instruments of achieving equilibrium between the opposing economic and social goals are of great importance. It is so because restructuring in the sphere of employment, leading to mass dismissals of employees, usually entails negative social effects connected with the increase of unemployment level.

The Polish model of legal regulation of collective dismissals aims at such equilibrium. Leaving the employer some freedom in carrying out collective dismissals, usually forced by economic factors, the Act covers employees with a system of additional protection in case this occurs. The basic right the employee has pursuant to the Act is the right to termination pay and to re-employment. However, in the current labour market conditions, the rights of the employees who are dismissed or about to be dismissed – whose aim is to enable them to stay on the labour market by smooth transition to another employment – are of special importance. These rights and benefits, being an instrument of Corporate Social Responsibility (CSR), are among others career counselling, assistance with finding new jobs, financing training sessions and skills improvement courses, assistance with relocation, or resources for starting one's own business activity.

The institution of outplacement, present in Polish legislation on the basis of the act on promotion of employment and labour market institutions, which evenly divides the encumbrances of collective dismissals between the employer and public administration bodies, does not apply to all the cases of collective dismissals covered by the provisions of the Act on collective dismissals. In practice, the employer who is not obliged to carry out outplacement autonomously decides about the scope and form of assistance for the employees assigned for collective dismissal. Thus, the actual encumbrance of providing assistance for employees covered by collective dismissals is transferred to public administration bodies: labour offices.

Bibliography

Baran E.W. & K.W. Baran, *Zwolnienia grupowe w systemie ustawodawstwa polskiego na tle prawodawstwa wspólnotowego*, [Collective Dismissals in the Polish Law against the European Union Law], [in:] Radca Prawny 2004, Vol. 3.

98. R. Borowiecki, Permanentna restrukturyzacja jako czynnik rozwoju i sukcesu przedsiębiorstw w dobie globalizacji rynku, Zeszyty Naukowe Uniwersytetu Ekonomicznego w Krakowie 2010, No. 836, ss. 28-29.

Baran K.W., *Zbiorowe prawo pracy. Komentarz*, [Collective Labour Law. Commentary], 2nd ed., Wolters Kluwer.
Barnard C & Deakin S., *Negative' and 'Positive' Harmonization of Labor Law in the European Union*, [in:] Columbia Journal of European Law 2002, Vol. 8.
Bielak-Jamaa E., *Ustawa o promocji zatrudnienia i instytucjach rynku pracy. Praktyczny komentarz*, [Act on employment and labour market institutions. Practical commentary], Lex 2011
Blanpain R., *European Labour Law*, Kluwer 1999.
Borowiecki R., *Permanentna restrukturyzacja jako czynnik rozwoju i sukcesu przedsiębiorstw w dobie globalizacji rynku*, [Permanent restructuring as a factor of development of enterprises at the time of the globalisation of the market], [in:] Zeszyty Naukowe Uniwersytetu Ekonomicznego w Krakowie 2010, No 836.
Dral A., *Powszechna ochrona trwałości stosunku pracy. Tendencje zmian*, [The Trends in Job Security Changes], Oficyna 2009.
Florek L., *Job and Unemployment Security in Poland*, [in:] American University Law Review 1992, Vol. 7, Issue 3.
Gerner-Beuerle C., *United in Diversity: Maximum versus Minimum Harmonization in EU Securities Regulation*, [in:] Capital Markets Law Journal 2012, Vol. 7, No. 3.
Gregorczuk T., *Tryb postępowania w sprawie zwolnień grupowych*, [Collective Dismissals Procedure], [in:] Praca i Zabezpieczenie Społeczne 1991, Nos. 7-8.
Jaśkowski K., E. Maniewska & J. Stelina, *Grupowe zwolnienia. Komentarz*, [Collective Dismissals. Commentary], Oficyna 2007.
Justification to the Act 13 March 2003 on particular principles of dissolution of employment relationship due to reasons independent from employees, http://orka.sejm.gov.pl/Druki4ka.nsf/wgdruku/1155/$file/1155.PDF (16 July 2015).
Kenner J., *EU Employment Law: From Rome to Amsterdam and Beyond*, Oxford, Hart 2003.
Kryńska-Wnuk L., *Regulacja zwolnień grupowych pracowników*, [Collective dismissals], Oficyna 2009.
Latos-Miłkowska M. & Ł.M. Pisarczyk, *Zwolnienia z przyczyn niedotyczących pracownika*, [Dismissals for reasons not related to employees], ABC 2005.
Liczcz T., *Prawo pracy*, LexisNexis 2005.
Sadlik R., *Kryteria zwalniania przy zmniejszeniu zatrudnienia*,[The criteria for dismissals in the reduction of employment], [in:] Służba Pracownicza 2007, No 7.
Sobczyk A., *Ustawa o zatrudnianiu pracowników tymczasowych. Komentarz*, [The Act on hiring temporary employees. Commentary], Zakamycze 2005.
The Central Statistical Office, *Polska 1989-2014*, [Poland 1989-2014], Warszawa 2014.

Documents

Act of 20 April 2004 r. on employment promotion and labour market institutions (Journal of Laws of 2015, item. 149).
Act of 23 May 1991 on Trade Unions (Journal of Laws of 2001, No 79, item. 854).
Act of 26 June 1974 Labour Code (Journal of Laws of 2014, item. 1502).

Act of 28 February 2003 on the bankruptcy and composition law (Journal of Laws from 2015 r., poz. 233).
Council Directive 75/129/of 17 February 1975 on the approximation of the laws of the Member States relating to collective redundancies (Official Journal L 48, 22 February 1975, p. 29).
Dyrektywa Rady 98/59/WE z dnia 20 lipca 1998 r. w sprawie zbliżania ustawodawstw Państw Członkowskich odnoszących się do zwolnień grupowych, (Dz. Urz. WE L 225 z 12.08.1998, ss. 16-21).
Minimum Wage Act of 10 October 2002, (Journal of Laws from 2002, No 200, item. 1679 as amended).
Regulation of the Minister of Labour and Social Policy of 29 May 1996 on the method of calculating the remuneration for a period of inactivity and on the method of calculating remuneration on which compensation, severance payment, compensatory allowance and other benefits provided for in Labour Code are calculated (Journal of Laws No 62, item. 289 as amended).
Rozporządzenie Rady Ministrów z dnia 31 grudnia 1975 r. w sprawie uprawnień pracowniczych osób wykonujących pracę nakładczą (Dz. U. z 1975 r., Nr 3, poz. 19 ze zm.).
Ustawa z dnia 13 marca 2003 r. o szczególnych zasadach rozwiązywania z pracownikami stosunków pracy z przyczyn niedotyczących pracowników, (Dz. U. z 2015 r., poz. 192).
Ustawa z dnia 28 grudnia 1989 r. ustawa o szczególnych zasadach rozwiązywania z pracownikami stosunków pracy z przyczyn dotyczących zakładu pracy, (Dz. U. z 2002 r., Nr 112, poz. 980).
Ustawa z dnia 5 kwietnia 2002 r. o europejskich radach zakładowych, (Dz. U. Nr 62, poz. 556).
Ustawa z dnia 9 lipca 2003 r. o zatrudnianiu pracowników tymczasowych, (Dz. U. z 2003 r., Nr 166, poz. 1608 ze zm.).

Judgments

CJEU judgment of 12 February 1985 in the case C-284/83 *Dansk Metalarbejderforbund and Specialarbejderforbundet i Danmark v. H. Bielsen & Son*, [ECR] 1985, p. 553.
Judgment of the Polish Supreme Court of 20 January 2015, III PK 52/14, Lex no. 1663409.
Judgment of the Polish Supreme Court of 18 February 2014, III PK 63/13, OSNP 2015/5/62.
Judgment of the Polish Supreme Court of 24 June 2013, II PK 341/12, Lex no. 1350303.
Judgment of the Polish Supreme Court of 14 March 2013, I PK 243/12, Lex no. 1448686.
Judgment of the Polish Supreme Court of 12 July 2011, II PK 19/2011, OSNP 2012/19-20/231.
Judgment of the Polish Supreme Court of 24 March 2011, I PK 185/10, Lex no. 1119478.
Judgment of the Polish Supreme Court of 4 December 2008, II PK 137/08, M.P.Pr. 2009/1/3.

Judgment of the Polish Supreme Court of 4 December 2008, II PK 139/04, OSNP 2010/11-12/134.
Judgment of the Polish Supreme Court of 17 May 2007, III BP 5/07, OSNP 2008/13-14/188.
Judgment of the Polish Supreme Court of 3 February 2006, II PK 158/05, OSNP 2006/23-24.
Judgment of the Polish Supreme Court of 20 June 2005, II PK 323/05, unpublished.
Judgment of the Polish Supreme Court of 29 June 2005, II PK 342/04, OSNP 2006/9-10/151.
Judgment of the Polish Supreme Court of 6 October 2005, II PK 63/05, unpublished.
Judgment of the Polish Supreme Court of 2 March 2004, I PK 387/03, OSNP 2005/9/124.
Judgment of the Polish Supreme Court of 15 January 2003, III PZP 20/2002, OSNP 2004/1/4.
Judgment of the Polish Supreme Court of 25 May 2000, I OKN 649/99, OSNP 2001/21/546.
Judgment of the Polish Supreme Court of 26 September 2000, I PKN 56/2000, OSNAPiUS 2002/9/207.
Judgment of the Polish Supreme Court of 23 November 2000, I PKN 117/00, OSNAPiUS 2002/13/304.
Judgment of the Polish Supreme Court of 15 December 2000, I PKN 161/00, OSNP 2002/17/404.
Judgment of the Polish Supreme Court of 22 November 2001, I PKN 680/00, OSNP 2003/20/488.
Judgment of the Polish Supreme Court of 24 November 2011, I PK 60/11, OSNP 2010/23-24/ 281.
Judgment of the Polish Supreme Court of 12 July 2001, I PKN 541/00, OSNAP 2003/11/ 268.
Judgment of the Polish Supreme Court of 12 December 2001, I PKN 733/00, OSNP 2003/23/569.
Judgment of the Polish Supreme Court of 4 December 1998, I PKN 444/98, OSNP 2000/2/45.
Judgment of the Polish Supreme Court of 27 February 1997, I PKN 20/97, OSNP 1997/21/417.
Judgment of the Polish Supreme Court of 7 March 1997, I PKN 26/97, OSNAPiUS 1997/24/486.
Judgment of the Polish Supreme Court of 1 October 1997, I PKN 315/97, OSNP 1998/14/ 427.
Judgment of the Polish Supreme Court of 27 February 1997, I PKN 20/97, OSNP 1997/21/417.
Judgment of the Polish Supreme Court of 19 December 1997, I PKN 442/97, OSP 1998/21/630.
Judgment of the Polish Supreme Court of 11 December 1996, I PKN 39/96, OSNAPiUS 1997/14/252.

Judgment of the Polish Supreme Court of 22 February 1994, I PZP 2/94, OSNAPiUS 1994/1/5.

Judgment of the Polish Supreme Court of 2 March 1994, I PZP 55/93, OSNCP 1994/12/229.

Judgment of the Polish Supreme Court of 20 September 1994, I PRN 63/94, OSNAPiUS 1995/3/36.

Judgment of the Polish Supreme Court of 23 January 1991, U PR 450/90, OSP 1992/3/57.

Judgment of the Polish Supreme Court of 13 December 1990, III PZP 22/90, OSNCP 1991/5-6/64.

Judgment of the Polish Supreme Court of 31 August 1989, III PZP 37/89, OSNC 1990/9/108.

Judgment of the Polish Supreme Court of 27 June 1985, III PZO 10/85, OSNCP 1985/11/164.

Judgment of the Polish Supreme Court of 19 May 1978, V PZP 6/77, OSNCP 1978/127.

CHAPTER 22

Collective Dismissal in Portugal

Filipe César Vilarinho Marques & Paula Mendes Ferreira Roberto

§22.01 THE COLLECTIVE DISMISSAL: THE CASE[1]

The Labour legislation in Portugal has suffered major changes in the last decade.

In 2003 (Law 99/2003, of 27 August) came into force the first Labour Code, where for the first time all the main rules regarding labour relationship were condensed in a systematic way. In 2009 (Law 7/2009, of 12 February), a new Labour Code replaced the previous one.

Facing a severe financial crisis in the first years of this decade and having been under a *Financial Assistance Programme* agreed with the *European Union*, the *European Central Bank* and the *International Monetary Fund* (the so-called *Troika*) between 2011 and 2014, Portuguese authorities were pressed by international institutions to change labour laws in order to bring more flexibility and competitiveness to its labour market. The area of collective dismissals was one of the affected by these changes.

Collective Dismissals ('Despedimentos Coletivos') are regulated in Book I (General Part), Title II (Employment Contract), Chapter VII (Termination of Contract), Section IV (Dismissal by Initiative of the Employer), Subsection I (Modalities of Dismissal), Division II (Collective Dismissal) of the 2009 Labour Code - Articles 359-366.

Collective dismissal is defined in Article 359, nr 1, as '*the termination of contracts of employment promoted by the employer and operated simultaneously or successively within three months, covering, at least, two or five workers, if in the case of a micro or small company, on the one hand, or of a medium or large company, on the other, where*

1. In the absence of bibliography in English language, and seen the more practical than theoretical goal of this article, we chose to refer only some of the most relevant texts in this field, although in Portuguese, thus allowing those in need of further deepening to have some general references where to start from.

that occurrence is based on closure of one or more sections or equivalent structure or on the reduction of the number of workers determined on grounds of market, structural or technological motives'.

The definition of micro, small, medium and large company can be found on Article 100 of the Labour Code:

Article 100

Types of companies

1 - *It is considered:*
   a) *micro company the one employing less than 10 workers;*
   b) *small company the one employing from 10 to less than 50 workers;*
   c) *medium company the one employing from 50 to less than 250 workers;*
   d) *large company the one employing 250 or more workers.*
2 - *For the purposes of the preceding paragraph, the number of persons employed corresponds to the average of the preceding calendar year.*
3 - *In the year of the beginning of activity, the number of employees to be taken into consideration for the application of the legal regime is the existing on the day of the event.*

The relevant number of workers does not include temporary workers (placed by temporary work agencies[2]) and the total number must count all the workers of the company and not only those working in the section or structure to be extinct.[3]

Seen the definition above quoted, in order to be in the presence of a collective dismissal, the following three criteria must be met:

(1) termination of contracts of employment operated *simultaneously* or *successively within three months*;
(2) covering, at least, *two workers* (if in the case of a micro or small company) or *five workers* (if in the case of a medium or large company);
(3) based on *closure of one or more sections or equivalent structure* or on the *reduction of the number of workers determined on grounds of market, structural or technological motives*.

Paragraph 2 of Article 359 defines the notion of *'market, structural or technological motives'* in the following manner:

(a) *market motives* – reduction of the company's activity caused by predictable decrease in the demand for goods or services or supervening impossibility, practical or legal, of placing these goods or services in the market;
(b) *structural motives* – economical-financial imbalance, change of activity, restructuring of productive organization or replacement of dominant products;

2. Xavier, Bernardo da Gama Lobo, *O Despedimento Colectivo no Dimensionamento da Empresa*, Verbo, August 2000, p. 376.
3. Ramalho, Maria do Rosário Palma, *Direito do Trabalho, Parte II – Situações Laborais Individuais*, Almedina, Coimbra, July 2006, pp. 867/868.

(c) *technological motives* - changes in manufacturing techniques or processes, automation of instruments of production, control or cargo handling, as well as computerization of services or media automation.

These definitions are mere examples, not excluding other facts that may be included in the notions described.

The definitions given by the law clearly show that the collective dismissal is mainly aimed to help companies facing a crisis to overcome it or to allow companies to strategically redirect their business. In that sense, the Labour Code of 2003 did not include a motive that was previously included in the motives for collective dismissals (Article 16 of Law 64-A/89, of 27 February): the definitive closure of the company. The subsequent 2009 Labour Code does also not include that motive so, in this case, employment contracts cease by expiry, regulated in Article 346, paragraphs 2 and 3,[4] and not by means of a collective dismissal. Although relevant in theoretical terms, the effects of the distinction are not very relevant, seen that paragraphs 3 and 5 of Article 346 state that the procedure to be followed by the employer in the case of expiry of contracts by definitive closure is the same as the one for collective dismissal (except in the case of micro companies - nr 4 of Article 346) and the indemnity due to workers is calculated in the same manner.

This specific nature of the collective dismissal has in its origin a managerial decision - the decision taken by the owner or the managing board of a company to close a section or structure or to reduce the number of workers due to market, structural or technological motives. This is precisely the battlefield of two rights established in the Constitution of the Portuguese Republic - the right to free private economic enterprise (Article 61) and the right to job security (Article 53).[5]

Judicial control of these managerial decisions has been the subject of a doctrinal a jurisprudential debate.[6] According to one opinion, courts should have a minimal control over the managerial decisions that are in the basis of collective dismissals undertaken by companies - courts should not replace managerial decisions by its own assessment of the situation.[7] Although that opinion has been followed by the jurisprudence in the first years, with courts ruling that the decision of dismissing was not subject to judicial control, but only the truthfulness of the motives invoked,[8] the most recent orientation of judicial decisions tends to broaden the control of those managerial decisions, putting under judicial control the link between the motives invoked and the

---

4. Ramalho, Maria do Rosário Palma, *ibid.*, p. 870, clarifying that this does not exclude the possibility of having a collective dismissal in the complex process leading to the definitive closure of a company.
5. For an English version of the *Constitution of the Portuguese Republic see*: http://www.en.parlamento.pt/Legislation/CRP/Constitution7th.pdf.
6. Loureiro, Jorge Manuel da Silva, 'O Controlo Jurisdicional da Decisão de Despedimento Coletivo', in *Prontuário de Direito do Trabalho*, 90, September-December 2011, Coimbra Editora, p. 107.
7. Xavier, Bernardo da Gama Lobo, *ibid.*, p. 682; Ramalho, Maria do Rosário Palma, *ibid.*, p. 878, footnote 420.
8. Supreme Court (*Supremo Tribunal de Justiça*) decisions of 21/09/2000 (*Colectânea de Jurisprudência / Acórdãos do STJ*, 2000, vol III, p. 259) and of 02/11/2005 (*Acórdãos Doutrinais*, 532.°, p. 735).

dismissal and if the decision to dismiss is adequate to fulfil the goals defined by the employer.[9] This orientation is backed by some Labour Law theorists, that sustain that the role of courts cannot be of mere formal control, but of material assessment of the proportionality and rationality of the decision of dismissing.[10]

§22.02 THE PROCEDURE

The procedure for collective dismissal is divided into three different phases: (1) Communications; (2) Negotiation; (3) Decision.

[A] Communications (Article 360)

The employer that decides to carry out a collective dismissal must transmit that decision, in written, to the commission of workers or, in the absence thereof, to the inter-union commission or trade union commissions of the company that represent the workers covered by the dismissal (Article 360, nr 1).

If in the company there is none of these commissions, the employer must communicate the decision, in written, to each of the workers that may be affected by the dismissal, which can designate among them, in the period of five working days counting from the reception of the communication, a representative commission with a maximum number of members ranging from three to five, depending on the dismissal covering up to five or more than five workers (nr 4 of Article 360).

According to nr 2 of Article 360, the communication to be sent (to the commissions referred in nr 1 or to the *ad hoc* commission latter referred) must include:

(a) the motives invoked for the collective dismissal;
(b) the names of all workers of the company, divided by organizational sectors of the company;
(c) the criteria for the selection of the workers to be dismissed;
(d) the number of workers to be dismissed and the professional categories concerned;
(e) the period of time in which the dismissal is to be carried out;
(f) the method of calculation of compensation to be generally awarded to workers to be dismissed, if appropriate, without prejudice to the compensation set out in article 366 or in collective labour regulation instrument.

In the same day, the employer must also send a copy of the communication to the service of the ministry in charge of employment that has the competence to follow and promote collective bargaining (currently the *Direção Geral do Emprego e Relações de*

9. *See* Supreme Court decision of 19/12/2012 in case nr 1222/10.1TTVNG-A.P1.S1, available in http://www.dgsi.pt/jstj.nsf?OpenDatabase.
10. Gomes, Júlio Manuel Vieira, *Direito do Trabalho – Volume I – Relações Individuais de Trabalho*, Coimbra Editora, March 2007, pp. 991-996.

Trabalho of the *Ministério da Solidariedade, Emprego e Segurança Social*) – Article 360, nr 5.

The worker may not be immediately suspended from work after the sending of these communications, otherwise it could be considered a violation by the employer of the worker's right to effective occupation.[11]

[B] Negotiation (Articles 361 and 362)

After the sending of the communications, the period of negotiations begins.

Within five days after the sending of the communications, the employer promotes a phase of information and negotiation with the representative structure of workers, in order to reach an agreement on the extent and effects of the measures to be applied, as well as other measures that reduce the number of workers to be dismissed (Article 361, nr 1).

Article 361, nr 1 includes a non-exhaustive list of alternative measures to be considered in these negotiations:

(a) suspension of employment contracts;
(b) reduction of normal working periods;
(c) conversion or reclassification of workers;
(d) early retirement or pre-retirement.

In the case of the first two (suspension of contracts or reduction of working periods), the lay-off negotiation procedure established in Articles 299 and 300 is not applicable (nr 2 of Article 361), as it is replaced by the collective dismissal negotiation.

Article 361, nr 3 expressly states that the conversion or reclassification of workers or the early or pre-retirement are only possible with the worker's consent.

Either the employer or the representative structure of workers have the right each to be assisted by an expert in the negotiation meetings (Article 361, nr 4).

Written minutes of the negotiation meetings must be elaborated, containing the matters agreed, as well as the divergent positions of the parties and the opinions, suggestions and proposals made by each party (Article 361, nr 5).

Article 362, nr 1 states that the competent service of the ministry responsible for the employment area participates in the negotiation. The scope of this intervention is defined by nr 1 of Article 362 as '*promoting the substantive and procedural regularity of the process and the conciliation of the interests of the parties*'. In that sense, nr 2 of Article 362 establishes that if the governmental body believes there is a substantive and/or procedural irregularity, it must alert the employer and, if it persists, must mention it in the minutes of the negotiation meetings. We must conclude from this that the governmental intervention is only a technical and not decisional one.[12]

11. Roberto, Paula Mendes Ferreira, 'Despedimento Colectivo – Algumas Questões Práticas', *in Prontuário de Direito do Trabalho*, 90, September-December 2011, Coimbra Editora, p. 115.
12. Ramalho, Maria do Rosário Palma, *ibid.*, p. 875.

At the request of either party or on the initiative of the governmental body, the regional employment, professional formation and social security services indicate the measures to be applied in the respective areas, in accordance with the legal framework of the solutions to be adopted (nr 3 of Article 362).

The negotiation phase has a maximum extension of ten days. This is not expressly mentioned in Article 361 or 362, but it's a conclusion drawn from Articles 361 and 363, the previous imposing a maximum of five days from the sending of the communications to the start of the negotiations and the latter imposing a maximum of fifteen days from that same date to the final decision in the case of an agreement not being reached.

In the case of workers who are pregnant, who have recently given birth or are breastfeeding and also in the case of workers that are in parental leave, after the negotiations the employer must send the process to the *Comissão para a Igualdade no Trabalho e no Emprego* (*CITE*) – for the issuance of an opinion (Article 63, nrs 1 and 3, b)). If the opinion of this commission is negative, the employer can only dismiss the worker after a judicial decision that declares the existence of the motive invoked to dismiss (nr 6 of Article 63). In case the employer does not ask for this opinion, the dismissal is legally presumed unlawful.

The commission must give the opinion in thirty days after receiving the process, and if it fails to comply, it is considered that the opinion is favourable to the dismissal (Article 63, nr 4). This period of thirty days is added to the maximum period of extent of the negotiation phase above referred.

[C] Decision (Articles 363-365)

After reaching an agreement or fifteen days after the sending of the initial communications,[13] the employer communicates the dismissal decision to each worker affected, mentioning expressly the motive and the date of termination of the contract and with the indication of the amount, manner, time and place of payment of the compensation, credits accrued and payable by effect of the termination of the contract (nr 1 of Article 363).

This communication must be in written and must be sent with a minimum advance prior to the date of termination of:

(a) fifteen days in the case of a worker with seniority of less than one year;
(b) thirty days in the case of a worker with seniority equal or superior to one year and less than five years;
(c) sixty days in the case of a worker with seniority equal or superior to five years but less than ten years;
(d) seventy-five days in the case of a worker with seniority equal or superior to ten years.

13. This fifteen-days term is also a minimum one, and the employer cannot send the decision before it has completely passed – *see* ROBERTO, Paula Mendes Ferreira, *ibid.*, p. 117.

If the dismissal affects both spouses or persons living in de facto union, the communication must be sent with an advance at least equal to the one laid down in the rank immediately higher than the one that would apply if only one of them was affected by the dismissal (nr 2 of Article 363).

If the minimum period is not respected, the contract only ceases after expiry of the period of notice, counted from the communication of dismissal, and the employer is forced to pay the salary corresponding to this period (nr 4 of Article 363).

In the same day when that communication is sent to workers, the employer must also send (nr 3 of Article 363):

- to the department of the ministry of employment, the minutes of the meetings of the negotiation or, in the absence of them, information on the reasons for such lack, the reasons that hindered agreement and the final positions of the parties, as well as a list with the name of each worker, address, dates of birth and admission in the company, social security situation, profession, category, salary, measure applied and the date set for its implementation;
- to the structure representative of workers, a copy of the list just mentioned.

The payment of the compensation and of credits accrued and payable by effect of the termination of the employment contract must be made until the end of the period of notice, except in the case of bankruptcy or in cases regulated in special legislation on corporate recovery and restructuring of economic sectors (nr 5 of Article 363).

The contract ceases after the period of notice, and Article 366, nr 4 establishes a legal presumption of acceptance of the dismissal by the worker when he receives the full amount of the indemnity paid by the employer.

This presumption is rebuttable and may be contested by the worker in court, as long as the worker, simultaneously, delivers or puts in any way the total compensation paid by the employer at the disposal of the latter (Article 366, nr 5).

§22.03 THE SUPPORT MEASURES IN FAVOUR OF WORKERS

[A] Indemnity

The indemnity due to workers affected by collective dismissal (established in Article 366) has suffered great changes in recent years, intended to lower the costs of dismissal for employers.

[1] Legislative Evolution

Until 1 November 2011, the amount of the indemnity was of one month of basic salary and periodic raises[14] for each full year of seniority (calculated proportionally in the case

14. In Portuguese: *diuturnidades*.

of a fraction of a year), with a minimum amount of three months of salary and periodic raises.

On 1 November 2011 came into force Law 53/2011, of 14 October, that added a new article to the Labour Code (Article 366-A), establishing that for all contracts initiated after 1 November 2011, indemnity would be of only twenty days of basic salary and periodic raises for each full year of seniority (or calculated proportionally in the case of a fraction of a year) and calculated in the following manner:

(a) the value of the basic monthly remuneration and the worker's periodic raises to consider for the purpose of calculating the indemnity may not exceed twenty times the legal minimum monthly wage;
(b) the total amount of compensation may not exceed twelve times the basic monthly remuneration and periodic raises of the worker or, when applicable the limit provided for in the preceding paragraph, 240 times the value of the legal minimum monthly wage;
(c) the daily value of salary and periodic raises to be considered is the result of the division by thirty of the monthly basic salary and periodic raises.

So, after 1 November 2011 there were two different indemnities: for contracts initiated before that date and for contracts initiated after that date.

In 2012, however, a new modification came into force, with Law 23/2012, of 25 June. This law established a transitional scheme for older contracts, in order to cease the complete distinction between old and new contracts, thus revoking Article 366-A.

Compensation remained in twenty days of basic salary and periodic raises for each full year of seniority (calculated proportionally in the case of a fraction of a year), and was calculated in the way just mentioned (previously in Article 366-A, then transferred to nr 2 of Article 366). However, for contracts initiated before 1 November 2011, Article 6 of Law 23/2012, of 25 June, established a specific way of calculating the indemnity:

(a) for the period of duration of the contract until 31 October 2012, the amount of the indemnity corresponds to one month of basic salary and periodic raises for each full year of seniority;
(b) for the period of duration of the contract as from the date referred to in (a), the amount of the indemnity is of twenty days of basic salary and periodic raises for each full year of seniority;
(c) the total amount of compensation may not be less than three months of basic salary and periodic raises.

For the period of duration of the contract after 31 October 2012:

- the value of the basic monthly remuneration and the worker's periodic raises to consider for the purpose of calculating the indemnity may not exceed twenty times the legal minimum monthly wage;

- the daily value of salary and periodic raises to be considered is the result of the division by thirty of the monthly basic salary and periodic raises.

It was also established that:

- when the indemnity based on the time of duration of the contract until 31 October 2012 exceeds twelve times the basic monthly remuneration and periodic raises of the worker or 240 times the value of the legal minimum monthly wage, the period of duration after that date gives no right to compensation;
- when the indemnity based on the time of duration of the contract until 31 October 2012 does not exceed those limits, the global indemnity (including the period after that date) has those maximum limits.

[2] Current Regime

This was not the last change in the indemnity, however. *In 2013, Law 69/2013, of 30 August (that came into force on 1 October 2013), introduced new modifications, further reducing the amount of the indemnity and thus having to establish a new transitional scheme for older contracts – this is the scheme currently in force.*

[a] Indemnity for Contracts Initiated after 1 October 2013

Indemnity established in Article 366 is now of twelve days of basic salary and periodic raises for each full year of seniority (calculated proportionally in the case of a fraction of a year) and is calculated as shown above:

(a) the value of the basic monthly salary and periodic raises to consider for the purpose of calculating the indemnity may not exceed twenty times the legal minimum monthly salary;[15]
(b) the total amount of indemnity may not exceed twelve times the basic monthly salary and periodic raises of the worker or, when applicable the limit provided for in the preceding paragraph, 240 times the value of the legal minimum monthly salary;
(c) the daily value of salary and periodic raises to be considered is the result of the division by 30 of the monthly basic salary and periodic raises.

[b] Indemnity for Contracts Initiated Before 1 October 2013

The transitional regime for older contracts is now established in Article 5 of Law 69/2013, of 30 August, and distinguishes between contracts initiated before 1 November 2011 and contracts initiated between that date and 30 September 2013.

15. The legal minimum monthly salary is of EUR 505.00/month, since 1 October 2014 – Decree-Law 144/2014, of 30 September 2014.

In either case (contracts initiated before 1 November 2011 or between that date and 30 September 2013), when considering the period of duration after 1 November 2011:

- the value of the basic monthly salary and periodic raises to consider for the purpose of calculating the indemnity may not exceed twenty times the legal minimum monthly salary;
- the daily value of salary and periodic raises to be considered is the result of the division by thirty of the monthly basic salary and periodic raises.

[i] Contracts Initiated Before 1 November 2011

For contracts initiated before 1 November 2011:

(a) for the period of duration of the contract until 31 October 2012, the amount of the indemnity corresponds to one month of basic salary and periodic raises for each full year of seniority;
(b) for the period of duration of the contract from 1 November 2011 to 30 September 2013, the amount of the indemnity is of twenty days of basic salary and periodic raises, calculated proportionally to the time worked;
(c) for the period of duration of the contract from 1 October 2013, the amount of indemnity is the sum of the following amounts:
    (I) eighteen days of basic salary and periodic raises for each full year of seniority for the first three years of duration of the contract;
    (II) twelve days of basic salary and periodic raises for each full year of seniority, in subsequent years;
    (III) the provision of point (I) applies only in cases where the contract of employment has not yet reached, in 1 October 2013, the duration of three years.

The total amount of compensation may not be less than three months of basic salary and periodic raises.

If after calculating the indemnity as established in point (a):

- the indemnity exceeds twelve times the basic monthly remuneration and periodic raises of the worker or 240 times the value of the legal minimum monthly salary, the worker has no right to any other value exceeding that one;
- the indemnity does not exceed those limits, the global indemnity (including all the periods) has those maximum limits.

If the sum of the indemnities of points (a) and (b):

- exceed twelve times the basic monthly salary and periodic raises of the worker or 240 times the value of the legal minimum monthly salary, the worker has no right to any other value exceeding that one;

- the indemnity does not exceed those limits, the global indemnity (including all the periods) has those maximum limits.

[ii] Contracts Initiated Between 1 November 2011 and 30 September 2013

For contracts initiated between 1 November 2011 and 30 September 2013:

(a) for the period of duration of the contract until 30 September 2013, the amount of the indemnity corresponds to twenty days of basic salary and periodic raises for each full year of seniority;
(b) for the period of duration of the contract from 1 October 2013, the amount of indemnity is the sum of the following amounts:
    (I) eighteen days of basic salary and periodic raises for each full year of seniority for the first three years of duration of the contract;
    (II) twelve days of basic salary and periodic raises for each full year of seniority, in subsequent years;
    (III) the provision of point (I) applies only in cases where the contract of employment has not yet reached, in 1 October 2013, the duration of three years;

If after calculating the indemnity as established in point (a):

- the indemnity exceeds twelve times the basic monthly remuneration and periodic raises of the worker or 240 times the value of the legal minimum monthly salary, the worker has no right to any other value exceeding that one;
- the indemnity does not exceed those limits, the global indemnity (including all the periods) has those maximum limits.

[B] Credit of Hours and Right to Cease the Contract

During the period of notice, the worker is entitled to a credit of hours corresponding to two working days a week, without loss or reduction of salary, and may terminate the employment contract by simple declaration to the employer, with a previous notice of at least three working days, keeping the full right to the compensation (Articles 364 and 365).

Although not expressly mentioned in law, during this period the contract may also cease by a free agreement between the worker and the employer.[16]

16. RAMALHO, Maria do Rosário Palma, *ibid.*, p. 877.

§22.04 JUDICIAL CONTROL AND SANCTIONS

[A] Sanctions

[1] Regulatory Offences[17]

The legal regime of collective dismissals defines the noncompliance of various aspects by the employer as regulatory offences:

- the dismissal without sending the communication of the intention to dismiss to the workers' representative structures or without including in those communications all the elements demanded by law is considered a severe offence (Article 360, nr 6);
- the dismissal without sending the communication of the intention to dismiss to the service of the ministry of employment is considered a light offence (Article 360, nr 6);
- the dismissal without the negotiation period is considered a severe offence (Article 361, nr 6);
- the conversion or reclassification of workers or the early or pre-retirement without consent of the respective workers is considered a severe offence (Article 361, nr 6);
- the banning of participation in the negotiation meetings of the representative of the ministry of employment is considered a light offence (Article 362, nr 4);
- the dismissal done non-complying with the previous notice period is considered a severe offence (Article 363, nr 6);
- the non-payment of the indemnity and all the credits accrued and payable by virtue of the termination until the date of termination of contract is considered a severe offence (Article 363, nr 6);
- the dismissal done without sending the final decision of dismissal and the list of workers affected to the service of the ministry of labour and to the workers' representative structures is considered a light offence (Article 363, nr 6);
- not allowing the worker to have the credit of hours is considered a light offence (Article 364, nr 4);
- the non-payment of the indemnity established by law is considered a severe offence (Article 366, nr 7).

Labour regulatory offences are classified by Article 553 of the Labour Code as light, severe and very severe, and the economic sanctions vary according to that classification, the fact that they are the result of a voluntary or involuntary conduct and depending on the turnover of the company in the previous civil year (Article 554).

17. In Portuguese, *contra-ordenações*, the equivalent to the German *Ordnungswidrigkeiten*.

[2] Unlawfulness of Dismissal

Article 381 of the Labour Code has a *general rule of unlawfulness of any dismissal* carried out by the employer. It is considered unlawful:

(a) if due to political, ideological, ethnic or religious reasons, albeit with different motive invocation;
(b) if the reason justifying the dismissal is declared unfounded;
(c) if it is not preceded by the corresponding procedure;
(d) in the case of a pregnant worker, worker who has recently given birth or is breastfeeding or during the initial parental leave, in any of its modalities, if not prompted the prior opinion of the competent authority in the area of equal opportunities between men and women.

In Article 383 there are some *specific motives for collective dismissals*. It states that a collective dismissal is considered unlawful when the employer:

(a) has not made the communication referred to in paragraphs 1 or 4 of Article 360 or promoted the negotiation referred to in paragraph 1 of Article 361;
(b) has not observed the deadline to decide the dismissal, referred to in paragraph 1 of Article 363;
(c) has not made available to the worker dismissed, until the expiry of the period of notice, the compensation due as referred to in Article 366 and the credits accrued or payable by virtue of the termination of contract of employment (except in the case of bankruptcy or in cases regulated in special legislation on corporate recovery and restructuring of economic sectors – nr 5 of Article 363).

The *consequences of the declaration of unlawfulness of a collective dismissal* are established in Articles 389-392 of the Labour Code.

Article 389, nr 1 states that in the case of unlawful dismissal, the employer must:

(a) compensate the worker for all damages caused, patrimonial and non-patrimonial;
(b) reintegrate the worker in the same establishment of the company, without prejudice to its category and seniority, except when the worker opts for a substitutive compensation (established in Articles 391 and 392).

Apart from the compensation of all damages, the worker also has the right to receive all the salaries he ceased to be paid between the date of the dismissal and the date when the court sentence that declares the unlawfulness becomes res judicata (Article 390). To these salaries must be deducted (nr 2 of Article 390):

- all the amounts that the worker received subsequently to the termination of the contract and that he wouldn't get if not for the dismissal;
- the salaries due during the period that has elapsed since the dismissal and thirty days before the filing of the action, if it is not proposed in the thirty days following the dismissal;
- the unemployment insurance assigned to the employee in the meantime (the amount of which must be delivered by the employer to social security).

In substitution of reintegration, the worker may opt (until the closure of the public hearing in court) for a compensation to be paid by the employer. The court establishes the amount of the compensation between fifteen and forty-five days of basic salary and periodic raises for each year (complete or fraction) of seniority, with a minimum of three months of basic salary and periodic raises – counting all the time until the court sentence becomes res judicata (Article 391).

In the case of micro companies or of workers that had administration or directive functions, the employer may ask the court to exclude reintegration, invoking facts and circumstances that show that the return of the worker to the company would be seriously harmful and disturbing for the functioning of the company (Article 392, nr 1). This is only not admissible in cases when the dismissal is considered unlawful because based on political, ideological, ethnical or religious motives or when the motive invoked for opposing the reintegration has been voluntarily created by the employer (nr 2). If the court decides not to reintegrate the worker, he has the right to a compensation to be determined between thirty and sixty days of basic salary and periodic raises for each year (complete or fraction) of seniority, with a minimum of six months of basic salary and periodic raises (nr 3).

[B] Judicial Control

The unlawfulness of collective dismissals can only be declared by a court – Article 388, nr 1.

The judicial procedure can only start within the period of six months after the date of termination of contract (nr 2 of Article 388), and in that judicial procedure the employer can only invoke the facts that have been mentioned in the final dismissal decision he has sent to the worker (Articles 387, nr 3 and 388, nr 3).

Although the maximum date for asking for a judicial decision of unlawfulness of the dismissal is of six months counted from the termination of the contract, this does not prevent the worker from demanding his former employer in court to pay amounts he believes are due, after that date, as long as he does not wish to also have a declaration of unlawfulness of the dismissal. The worker has in that case a term of one year after the termination of contract to do so – Article 337, nr 1 of the Labour Code.[18]

18. *See* the decision of the appeal court of Porto (*Tribunal da Relação do Porto*), of 17/06/2013, available in http://www.dgsi.pt/jtrp.nsf?OpenDatabase, case nr: 527/10.6TTMAI.P1.

The Labour Procedure Code[19] has a special process for the judicial assessment of collective dismissals in Articles 156-161. This process is considered of urgent nature (Article 26, nr 1, d) of the Labour Procedure Code).

After the presentation of the petition by the worker, the employer is summoned to present in fifteen days his defence and all the documents showing he has complied with the procedural requirements of the collective dismissal. In the same period, the employer must ask the court to bring to the process all the workers that, not being the author of the process, have also been affected by the dismissal (Article 156).

After the presentation of the defence by the employer, if the motives invoked by the employer to base the collective dismissal have been challenged, the judge nominates a qualified assessor. Notified of that decision, any of the parties may in ten days: require that the judge nominates two other qualified assessors; indicate a technician to assist the assessors in the fulfilment of their task (Article 157).

The assessors have a term of thirty days to present a report containing the material checks carried out, the information collected and their origin, as well as an opinion on the facts that substantiate the collective dismissal and on whether this is or not justified. The technicians appointed by the parties may present in five days a justified declaration of dissent with the report (Article 158).

After the presentation of the report, the judge sets a date for a preliminary hearing and after that hearing has to decide if the legal procedure has been correctly followed by the employer and if the motives invoked for the dismissal are valid or not (Article 160).

If the process does not end after the preliminary hearing, the court may decide to conduct separate hearings for each worker, when deemed adequate (Article 161).

Workers may ask for a court to rule a preliminary injunction against the collective dismissal, on grounds of Articles 34-40 of the Labour Procedure Code. In this case, after receiving the petition, the court immediately sets a date for a final hearing to be held in a maximum of fifteen days, and notifies the employer to present his opposition and bring to the process the documents showing the compliance with all the legal procedural requirements for the dismissal.

According to Article 39, nr 1, c), the court suspends the dismissal when the judge concludes that there probably is a noncompliance with the formalities demanded by the Labour Code for collective dismissals. In this case, until the last day of each month subsequent to the decision, the employer must bring to the process the documents showing the payment of the salary to the worker (Article 39, nr 2).

The decision of the court in this process assesses only the formal aspects of the dismissal and not the motives which were invoked by the employer to do it, which can only be judicially controlled in the main process.[20]

19. Approved by Decree-Law 480/99, of 9 November, and subsequently modified by: Decree-Law 323/2001, of 17 December; Decree-Law 38/2003, of 8 March; Decree-Law 295/2009, of 13 October (rectified by Declaration 86/2009, of 23 November); Law 63/2013, of 27 August.
20. *See* the decision of the appeal court of Lisbon (*Tribunal da Relação de Lisboa*), of 21/11/2012, available in http://www.dgsi.pt/jtrl.nsf?OpenDatabase, case nr: 2816/11.3TTLSB-A.L1-4.

The preliminary injunction expires if the worker does not file the action for the declaration of unlawfulness of the collective dismissal within thirty days from the date of notification of the decision of the preliminary injunction (Article 40-A, a)).

CHAPTER 23

Collective Dismissal in Romania

Aurelian Gabriel Uluitu

§23.01 THE APPLICABLE LEGISLATION

The Romanian Labour Code – Law no. 53/2003[1] (Articles 68-74) transposed Council Directive 98/59/EC of 20 July 1998 on the approximation of the laws of the Member States relating to collective redundancies into national legislation.

Law no. 53/2003 is the first Labour Code since the political regime changed in 1989. Since its enforcement, the Labour Code has been modified several times, the most important legislative interventions being passed in 2005, 2006 and 2011 (the last one also included some changes to the collective dismissal regulation).

Romania has also transposed other directives, which regulate incidental aspects concerning collective dismissal:

- Directive 91/533/EEC of the Council of 14 October 1991 on an employer's obligation to inform employees of the conditions applicable to the contract or employment relationship was transposed by Labour Code Articles 17-19.
- Directive 2001/23/EC of the Council of 12 March 2001 on the approximation of the laws of the Member States relating to the safeguarding of employees' rights in the event of transfers of undertakings, businesses or part of undertakings or businesses was transposed by Law no. 67/2006.[2]
- Directive 2002/14/EC of the European Parliament and of the Council of 11 March 2002 establishing a general framework for informing and consulting employees in the European Community was transposed by Law no. 476/2006.[3]

1. Republished in the Official Gazette, first part, no. 345 of 18 May 2011.
2. Published in the Official Gazette, first part, no. 276 of 28 March 2006.
3. Published in the Official Gazette, first part, no. 1006 of 18 December 2006.

- Directive 2008/94/EC of the European Parliament and of the Council of 22 October 2008 on the protection of employees in the event of the insolvency of their employer was transposed by the legislative acts that subsequently amended Law no. 200/2006.[4]

Romania has not ratified the International Labour Organization's Convention no. 158 (1982) concerning the termination of employment.

Some particular aspects concerning collective dismissal are regulated by:

- Emergency Government Ordinance no. 98/1999 on social protection of persons subject of redundancy.[5]
- Emergency Government Ordinance no. 36/2013 that is applicable between the years 2013 and 2018 and introduces social protection measures for employees laid-off as a result of collective dismissals.[6]
- Law no. 85/2014 on the procedures for preventing insolvency and on insolvency.[7]

§23.02 THE CASES

According to Article 58, paragraph 2 of the Labour Code, dismissal may be ordered for *reasons pertaining to the employee's person* or *for reasons that do not pertain to the employee's person.*

Dismissal for *reasons not pertaining to the employee's person* represents the termination of the individual labour contract, caused by the removal of that employee's position, for one or several reasons not related to the employee. The removal of a position must be effective and have an actual serious cause.

The dismissal for reasons not pertaining to the employee's person may be *individual* or *collective.*

Collective dismissal is the dismissal, within thirty calendar days, ordered for one or more reasons not related to the employee, of:

- at least ten employees, if the employer that is dismissing them has more than twenty employees and less than 100 employees;
- at least 10% of the employees, if the employer that is dismissing them has at least 100 employees but less than 300 employees;
- at least thirty employees, if the employer that is dismissing them has at least 300 employees.

Upon the determination of the actual number of collectively dismissed employees, employees with individual labour contracts terminated at the employer's initiative,

4. Published in the Official Gazette, first part, no. 453 of 25 May 2006.
5. Published in the Official Gazette, first part, no. 303 of 29 June 1999.
6. Published in the Official Gazette, first part, no. 251 of 30 April 2013.
7. Published in the Official Monitor, first part, no. 466 of 25 June 2014.

for one or several reasons not related to the employee, are taken into account provided that there are at least five dismissals.

The solution pronounced by the European Court of Justice in Case C-449/93 *Rockfon A/S v. Specialarbejderforbundet i Danmark* (and, recently, in Case C-392/13 *Andrés Rabal Cañas v. Nexea Gestión Documental SA, Fondo de Garantía Salarial*) to define the term 'establishment'[8] has rarely been applied by the national courts. Usually, the Romanian Courts instead simply consider that the term 'establishment' refers to the employer as a whole.

The provisions regarding collective dismissal are not applied:

- to employees of public institutions and public authorities;
- in the case of individual labour contracts concluded for a definite period, except for the cases when these dismissals take place prior to the expiry date of these contracts.

§23.03 THE PROCEDURE

In the case that the employer intends to make collective dismissals, it is obliged to initiate, in due time and with a view to reaching an agreement, consultations with the trade union or, as applicable, the employees' representatives, on at least:

- the methods and means for avoiding collective dismissals or reducing the number of employees to be dismissed;
- mitigating the consequences of dismissals by resorting to social measures envisaging, *inter alia*, support for the professional re-qualification or re-conversion of the dismissed employees.

During the period of consultations, in order to allow the trade union or the employees' representatives to formulate proposals in due time, the employer is bound to supply them with all relevant information and to notify them in writing of the following:

- the total number and categories of employees;
- the reasons that determine the forecast dismissal;

8. 'The term "establishment" appearing in Article 1(1)(a) of Directive 75/129 on the approximation of the laws of the Member States relating to collective redundancies must be understood as meaning, depending on the circumstances, the unit to which the workers made redundant are assigned to carry out their duties. It is not essential, in order for there to be an establishment, for the unit in question to be endowed with a management which can independently effect collective redundancies. To make the definition of "establishment", which is a concept of Community law and cannot be defined by reference to the laws of the Member States, dependent on the existence of such a management within the unit would be incompatible with the aim of the directive since that would allow companies belonging to the same group to try to make it more difficult for the directive to apply to them by conferring on a separate decision-making body the power to take decisions concerning redundancies and by this means they would be able to escape the obligation to follow certain procedures for the protection of workers, such as their right to be informed and consulted.'

- the number and categories of employees that will be affected by the dismissal;
- the criteria applied, according to the law and/or collective labour contracts, in determining the priority order for dismissal;
- the measures applied for limiting the number of dismissals;
- the measures for mitigating the consequences of dismissals and the compensation to be granted to the dismissed employees, according to the legal provisions and/or the applicable collective labour contract;
- the date on which or the period during which the dismissals are bound to take place; and
- the time limit within which the trade union or, as the case may be, the representatives of the employees can make proposals to avoid or reduce the number of dismissals.

The criteria provided for in determining the priority order for dismissal are applied in order to categorize the employees after the evaluation of the achievement of performance objectives.

The obligation to consult the trade union or, as applicable, the employees' representatives is maintained irrespective of whether the decision that determined the collective dismissals is made by the employer or by an undertaking that controls the employer.

In the case that the decision that determines the collective dismissals is made by an undertaking that has control over the employer, the employer may not take advantage, in his failure to comply with the obligation to consult the trade union or, as applicable, the employees' representatives, of the fact that the undertaking did not supply the necessary information.

The employer is under the obligation to send a copy of the notification addressed to the trade union or, as applicable, the employees' representatives to the territorial labour inspectorate and the territorial employment agency on the same date that the notification is sent to the trade union or, as the case may be, to the employees' representatives.

The trade union or, as applicable, the employees' representatives may propose to the employer steps for avoiding the dismissals or diminishing the number of employees dismissed, within ten calendar days from the date of receipt of the notification.

The employer has the obligation to reply, in writing and stating good reasons, to the proposals forwarded by the trade union or, as applicable, the employees' representatives, within five calendar days of receipt.

In the case that, after the consultations with the trade union or the employees' representatives, the employer decides to apply the measure of collective dismissal, it is obliged to notify in writing the territorial labour inspectorate and the territorial employment agency, at least thirty calendar days before the date when the dismissal decisions are issued.

This second notification must include all relevant information with regard to the intention of collective dismissal, as well as the results of consultations with the trade union or the employees' representatives, particularly:

- the reasons for the dismissals;
- the total number of employees;
- the number of employees affected by the dismissal; and
- the date or the period when the dismissals begin to take place.

The employer has the obligation to send a copy of the notification addressed to the territorial labour inspectorate to the trade union or, as the case may be, to the employees' representatives, on the same date that the notification is sent to the territorial labour inspectorate and the territorial employment agency.

The trade union or the employees' representatives may forward their possible viewpoints to the territorial labour inspectorate.

Upon the reasoned request of either party, the territorial labour inspectorate, with the opinion of the territorial employment agency, may order the reduction of the period of thirty calendar days, without prejudice of the individual rights with regard to the notice period.

The territorial labour inspectorate has the obligation to inform within three working days the employer and the trade union or the employees' representatives, as applicable, on the reduction (or the extension) of the period of thirty calendar days, as well as of the reasons underlying this decision.

Within this thirty calendar day period, (or the period as reduced) the territorial employment agency must seek solutions to the problems raised by the planned collective dismissals and communicate them in due time to the employer and the trade union or, as the case may be, the employees' representatives.

Upon the motivated request of either party, the territorial labour inspectorate, after consultation with the territorial employment agency, may order the postponement of the date of issuing the dismissal decisions by ten calendar days, in the case that the issues related to the collective dismissal may not be solved by the date established in the collective dismissal notification as being the date of issuing the dismissal decisions.

The territorial labour inspectorate is obliged to inform in writing the employer and the trade union or the employee's representatives, as applicable, of the postponement of the date of issuing the dismissal decisions, as well as of the reasons underlying this decision, before the initial period provided in Article 72(1) expires.

In conclusion, the Romanian Labour Code does not require the approval of the collective redundancy by:

- the administration; or
- the employees' representatives or trade union.

The Courts have decided that the lack of any notification to the employees' form of representation or to the administration nullifies the entire collective dismissal procedure.

§23.04 THE SUPPORT MEASURES IN FAVOUR OF WORKERS

[A] Prohibitions

Article 59 of the Labour Code prohibits the employees' dismissal:

- based on criteria such as gender, sexual orientation, genetic characteristics, age, national origin, race, skin colour, ethnic origin, religion, political opinion, social origin, disability, family status or responsibility, trade union membership or activity;
- for the exercise, under the terms of the law, of their right to strike and trade union rights.

Employee dismissal may not be ordered:

- for the duration of one's temporary labour disability, as established in a medical certificate according to the law;
- for the duration of the suspension of the activity as a result of establishing a medical quarantine;
- for the duration an employed woman is pregnant, if the employer became acquainted with this fact before the issuance of the dismissal decision;
- for the duration of one's maternity leave;
- for the duration of one's leave for raising a child up to the age of 2, or, in the case of a disabled child, up to the age of 3;
- for the duration of one's leave for looking after a sick child up to the age of 7 or, in the case of a disabled child, for inter-current diseases, until he turns 18 years of age;
- for the duration of one's rest leave.

These temporary prohibitions are not applied in the case of dismissal for reasons due to the employer's judicial reorganization, bankruptcy or dissolution.

[B] Professional Evaluation

The last major change to the Romanian Labour Code, made in 2011, implied the introduction in the collective dismissal procedure of a professional evaluation of employees who are in a similar position. This gives the employer the possibility to maintain those employees who are – the most – professionally fit for their current position. The social protection reasons come in the second plan, and only for the employees who are on the same professional level.

When a company does not have an established professional evaluation criteria and procedure, it should adopt one before initiating a downsizing.

Because the creation, adoption and implementation of a professional evaluation procedure may be time consuming, companies that envisage a downsizing should act promptly and schedule the downsizing far enough into the future to allow the process to be created and fully applied.

[C] Compensation

According to Article 67 of the Labour Code, employees dismissed for reasons that do not pertain to their person benefit from active steps for unemployment control and may benefit from compensation under the terms stipulated by the law and the applicable collective labour contract.

Until 2011, the Collective Labour Contract at the National Level was in force, which produced effects for all the employees in all the units in the country. Under the National Collective Agreement for 2007-2010, employees were entitled to a payment equal to at least one month's salary upon dismissal for reasons not related to the employee.

Law no. 62/2011 on social dialogue eliminated this level of collective bargaining, so, currently, there is no minimum general level of compensation in the case of collective dismissal.

The Emergency Government Ordinance no. 98/1999 on social protection of persons subject to redundancy.

The notion of collective dismissal or redundancy was initially regulated by the Emergency Government Ordinance no. 98/1999 on social protection of persons subject to redundancy, as further amended. Since 1 March 2003, the provisions of the Labour Code on redundancy came into force, which differ from the previously instituted rules in certain respects as to the minimum number of dismissed persons, notification terms and security measures. Consequently, the provisions of Emergency Government Ordinance no. 98/1999 complete the provisions of the Labour Code and, if contrary to such provisions, are considered as repealed.

Employees with individual contracts of an unlimited duration, who are laid off through collective dismissals, during the company restructuring or reorganization processes, during partial or total closure of the activity or during the privatization or liquidation, may benefit from social protection measures regulated by Emergency Government Ordinance no. 98/1999.

The social protection measures afforded by Emergency Government Ordinance no. 98/1999 consist of compensatory payments, collective pre-dismissal services (counselling, informing, vocational orientation or placement) and active measures meant for limiting unemployment. Companies operating collective lay offs within restructuring programs may request and receive funding to support measures for economic revival.

The compensatory payments mainly aim at State-owned companies, nominated by Government decision. However, the State cannot afford to pay compensatory salaries in all cases.

The amounts granted as compensatory payments are established according to the law, depending on the employee's length of service. In order to receive compensatory payments, the employees should have worked for at least six months with the employer within the last twelve months before their dismissal.

The Emergency Government Ordinance no. 36/2013 is applicable between the years 2013 and 2018 and introduces social protection measures for employees laid-off as a result of collective dismissals.

According to this regulation, the Romanian government has taken account of the responsibilities assumed by Romania based on the memorandums of understanding signed with the International Monetary Fund and the European Union in 2009-2011.

The Romanian Government is obliged to remedy the shortcomings of public companies by implementing measures intended to lead to economic and financial restructuring, to curb losses and to ensure long-term efficient activity.

The principal goal of the ordinance is to diminish the negative effects of restructuring and reorganization of the employment.

The Ordinance introduces social protection measures for employees who are laid off as a result of collective dismissals in companies with a public equity majority or subordinated to local public administration.

Employees dismissed as a result of collective dismissals in such companies are entitled to the following rights:

- unemployment benefit;
- monthly compensatory income, which is basically the difference between the employee's former salary and the unemployment benefit. The amount is proportional to the number of years worked for a period between twelve and twenty-four months. Payment of the monthly compensatory income shall be terminated if the dismissed employee refuses to accept a job on the grounds that the salary is the same or lower than the compensatory income or if he/she refuses to participate in retraining programmes; and
- additional payments provided by economic operators derived from their revenue and expenditure budgets, in accordance with the applicable collective or individual labour contracts.

[D] The Right to Notice

Employees dismissed have the right to be given notice not less than twenty working days before.

There is an exception to this provision for employees who are on a trial period.

If, during the notice period, the individual labour contract is suspended, the notice period is suspended accordingly, except for the case of employees dismissed who are on a trial period.

The High Court of Cassation and Justice decided that the absence of mentioning the notice period in the dismissal decision does not imply the nullity of the decision if the employer could prove that the notice period was properly assured for the employee.

[E] Right to Re-employment

According to Article 74 of the Labour Code, within forty-five calendar days from dismissal, the employee dismissed by collective dismissal has the right to be re-employed with priority on the position re-established in the same activity, without examination, contest or trial period.

If during this period the same activity is resumed, the employer is obliged to send to the employee that has been dismissed from the position in which the activity is resumed on the same conditions of professional competence a written communication, by which the employee is offered the position of the activity resumed.

The employee has a maximum of five calendar days from the date of the employer's communication to accept in writing the position offered.

If the employee who is entitled to be re-employed does not accept the position in writing within the five calendar days, the employer may hire a new person for the vacant position.

The Courts have decided that the non-observance by the employer of the above obligation implies the nullity of the dismissal decision, in relation to the former employee who had the right to be re-employed.

§23.05 THE FORM OF THE DISMISSAL DECISION

The employer is obliged to issue an individual decision for each employee who is subject to redundancy.

Under the sanction of absolute nullity, the dismissal decision has to be communicated to the employee in writing and must contain:

- the legal and factual grounds of the dismissal;
- the duration of the termination notice period;
- the term in which the dismissal decision may be challenged and the court of law in front of which it shall be challenged; and
- the criteria for settling the priority order to dismissal.

§23.06 JUDICIAL CONTROL AND SANCTIONS

According to Article 78 of the Labour Code, a dismissal ordered in noncompliance with the procedure stipulated by the law is struck by absolute nullity.

In the event of a labour claim, an employer may not resort, before a court of law, to other de facto or de jure reasons than the ones stated in the dismissal decision.

If the dismissal was not based on good grounds or was unlawful, the court will order its cancellation and force the employer to pay the compensation equal to the indexed, increased and updated wages and the other rights the employee would have otherwise benefited from.

At the employee's request, the court, having ordered the cancellation of the dismissal, will restore the parties to the status existing before the issuance of the dismissal document.

If the employee does not request the reinstatement of the previous situation before the issuance of the dismissal document, the individual labour contract is rightfully terminated at the date when the judgment remains final and definitive.

§23.07 CONCLUSION

The current Romanian regulation of collective dismissal corresponds to the framework set by the Council Directive 98/59/EC of 20 July 1998 on the approximation of the laws of the Member States relating to collective redundancies into national legislation. However, as against the first form of the Labour Code, a decrease of the employee's protection measures was noted in recent years, to the minimum level of protection determined by the Directive.

Short Bibliography

Codul european al muncii si securitatii sociale [European Code of Labour and Social Security], Editura Wolters Kluwer Romania, Bucuresti, 2009.

Stefanescu, Ion Traian, *Tratat teoretic si practic de drept al muncii* [Theoretical and practical Treatise on Labour Law], Editura Universul Juridic, Bucuresti, 2014.

Ticlea, Alexandru, *Tratat de dreptul muncii* [Treatise on Labour Law], Editura Universul Juridic, Bucuresti, 2016.

CHAPTER 24
Collective Dismissal in the Slovak Republic

Pavol Kundrik[*]

§24.01 INTRODUCTION

Based on the current legal provisions stipulated by the Slovak Labour Code, the dismissal of a certain number of employees (above the statutory threshold) within a certain period of time leads to the application of the collective dismissal process under provision § 73 of the Labour Code.[1] The collective dismissal process has its own rules and specifics, which are aimed at the protection of employees during such dismissal.

§24.02 THE LAW

The law states that:

> ***Part II – Employment Relationship***
>
> *Termination of employment*
>
> *§ 73 of the Labour Code – Collective Dismissal*
>
> *(1) A Collective dismissal shall occur if an employer or a part of an employer terminates an employment relationship by notice for the reasons stipulated in § 63 section (1) letter a) and b)*[2] *, or if an employment relationship is*

---

* Head of Labour Law at PETERKA & PARTNERS.

1. Act No. 311/2011 Coll. The Labour Code as amended.
2. § 63 section (1):

   a) if an employer or part thereof 1) is winding up or 2) is relocating and an employee does not agree with the change in the agreed place of work,

   b) if an employee becomes redundant by written decision of an employer or competent body issuing a written resolution on change in duties, technical equipment or reduction in the number of employees with the aim of securing work efficiency, or on other organizational changes and an employer who is a temporary employment agency, even if an employee

terminated for another reason not related to the person of an employee, within 30 days
a) with at least 10 employees of an employer, who employs more than 20 and fewer than 100 employees,
b) with at least 10% of the total number of employees of an employer, who employs at least 100 and fewer than 300 employees,
c) with at least 30 employees of an employer, who employs at least 300 employees.

(2) With the aim of reaching an agreement, the employer is obliged, at least one month prior to commencement of the collective dismissal, to negotiate with the employees' representatives, and if there are no employees' representatives in the workplace, directly with the affected employees, the measures allowing the avoidance of the collective dismissal of the employees, or reduction thereof, mainly to negotiate the possibility of placing them in appropriate employment at the employer's other workplaces, also subsequent to preceding preparation, and measures for mitigating the adverse consequences of the collective dismissal of employees. To this end, the employer is obliged to provide the employees' representatives with all necessary information and to inform them in writing, in particular, as to:
a) the reasons for the collective dismissal,
b) the number and structure of dismissed employees,
c) the overall number and structure of employees employed by the employer,
d) the period during which the collective dismissal shall take place,
e) the selection criteria of the employees subject to termination of employment.

(3) The employer shall, at the same time, deliver a copy of the written information specified in section (2) together with the names, surnames and addresses of permanent residence of the employees whose employment relationship is to be terminated to the Office of Labour, Social Affairs and Family for the purposes of finding a solution to the problems associated with the collective dismissal pursuant to section (7).

(4) Following the negotiations on collective dismissal with the employees' representatives, the employer is obliged to deliver written information on the outcome of such negotiations to:
a) the Office of Labour, Social Affairs and Family,
b) the employees' representatives.

(5) The employees' representatives may submit comments relating to the collective dismissal to the Office of Labour, Social Affairs and Family.

(6) With regard to collective dismissals, the employer may give notice to employees for reasons as stipulated in § 63, section (1), letters a) and b), or propose termination of the employment relationship by agreement for the same reasons, at the earliest upon the expiry of one month from the day of delivery of the written information pursuant to section (4), letter a).

(7) The period as stipulated in section (6) shall be used by the Office of Labour, Social Affairs and Family to seek solutions to the problems raised by the planned collective dismissal. The Office of Labour, Social Affairs and Family may make a reasonable reduction in the period pursuant to section (6) on objective grounds; if so, it shall inform the employer immediately in writing of the reduction.

---

becomes redundant due to the termination of the temporary assignment under § 58 before the expiry of the period for which the fixed term employment was agreed.

(8) *If an employer violates the obligations stipulated in sections 2 to 4 and 6, an employee dismissed during the collective dismissal is entitled to salary compensation in the amount of at least two of his/her average monthly salaries under § 134.*

(9) *The provisions of sections (1) to (8) shall not apply to: a) termination of a fixed term employment relationship, upon the expiry of such term, b) crew members of vessels flying the flag of the Slovak Republic.*

(10) *The provisions of sections (6) and (7) shall not apply to an employer who was declared bankrupt by the court.*

(11) *If there are no employees' representatives at the workplace, the employer shall carry out the obligations indicated in sections 2 to 4 directly in relation to the affected employees.*

(12) *The employer must also comply with the obligations stipulated in sections 2 to 4 if the decision of collective dismissal is taken by a controlling undertaking as defined in § 241a section (3).*

(13) *For the purposes of a collective dismissal, an organizational unit of the employer that has the status of a branch/plant registered in the Commercial Register under applicable special regulation is deemed to be a part of the employer.*

§24.03 RATIONALE OF THE LAW

The provisions related to a collective dismissal as a special procedure, when dismissing a larger number of employees, were introduced to the previous Slovak Labour Code[3] by an amendment effective from 1 September 1996, based on the harmonization of the Slovak law with the European Directives 75/129/ECC and 92/56/ECC. The current Labour Code, which was adopted in 2001, took over the provisions related to the collective dismissal, and these were developed mostly under the influence of EU law and case law of the ECJ. The main points of the regulation of collective dismissals are: (1) information to and negotiation with employees' representatives (or directly with employees); (2) information to the local Office of Labour, Social Affairs and Family (hereinafter, the Labour Office); and (3) protection of employees prior to dismissal during the information period.

§24.04 COLLECTIVE DISMISSAL

[A] Definition and Threshold

As provided by the Labour Code,[4] a collective dismissal occurs if an employer (or its part) terminates an employment relationship either by: (1) notice (i.e., unilateral act of the employer) for organizational and redundancy reasons;[5] or (2) if the employment relationship is terminated for another reason not related to the person of an employee (i.e., by mutual agreement). Therefore, in order to trigger a collective dismissal, it is not

3. Act No. 65/1965 Coll. the Labour Code as amended; effective from 1 January 1966 until 31 March 2002.
4. § 73 section (1) of the Labour Code.
5. § 63 section (1) letter a) and b) of the Labour Code.

relevant whether the employment is terminated unilaterally or by agreement, as long as it is not related to the person of the employee.

The other two conditions, which trigger a collective dismissal, are:

(1) a period of thirty days during which the termination must take place; and
(2) the relevant number of employees which have to be dismissed, i.e.:
   - at least ten employees, when an employer employs more than twenty and fewer than 100 employees;
   - at least 10% from the total number of employees, when an employer employs at least 100 and fewer than 300 employees;
   - at least thirty employees, when an employer employs at least 300 employees.

The last criterion does not scale up after 300 employees, i.e., it applies equally, even if an employer employs 1,000 employees or more (assuming the other criteria of collective dismissal are met).

A collective dismissal does not apply in cases of termination of fixed-term employment contracts (due to the lapse of the agreed term), regardless of the number of dismissed employees. Generally, the collective dismissal process does not apply to state employees, at all.

[B] Information to and Negotiation with the Employees' Representatives

Under the provisions of the Labour Code, written information on collective dismissals must be prepared and delivered to the employees' representatives.[6] If no employees' representatives operate at the employer in question, the information must be delivered directly to the employees who will be affected by the collective dismissal. A copy of such written information must also be delivered to the local Labour Office (together with the names, surnames and addresses of residence of the affected employees).[7]

The written information must contain mainly:[8]

- the reasons for the collective dismissal;
- the number and structure of the employees whose employment will be terminated;
- the overall number and structure of employees employed by the employer;
- the period during which the collective dismissal shall take place;
- the criteria for selecting the employees whose employment will be terminated.

The written information on the collective dismissal must be delivered to the employees' representatives (or to the employees as indicated above) prior to the

6. Trade union, work council or work trustee.
7. § 73 section (3) of the Labour Code.
8. § 73 section (2) of the Labour Code.

negotiation meeting, and the employees' representatives should be given some time to study it – however, there is no period, established by law, which has to be observed between the delivery of the information and the negotiation.

The next step in the collective dismissal procedure is the negotiation (which in fact can only take place in the form of a discussion) on the collective dismissal with the employees' representatives. The subject of the negotiation should consist in: not only the measures avoiding or limiting the collective dismissal, but also the possibility of placement of the affected employees in other workplaces (even after additional necessary training) and the measures mitigating the adverse consequences of the collective dismissal. The Labour Code does not fix any deadline for employees' representatives to meet and discuss the collective dismissal.

The employer does not need any approval from the employees' representatives or the affected employees prior to commencing the collective dismissal. This means that any disapproval has no legal effect in relation to the intended dismissal.

[C] Information to the Labour Office

Once the negotiation with the employees' representatives is finished the employer must prepare written information on the results of such negotiation and send it to the local Labour Office, as well as to the employees' representatives – even though the representatives were present at the negotiation. The Labour Code does not state the period in which the written information on the results of the negotiation must be delivered to the Labour Office. The delivery to the Labour Office triggers the start of a one-month period,[9] after which the employer can actually start with the dismissal of employees.[10]

During this one-month period, the employer can be approached by the local Labour Office to discuss the collective dismissal,[11] the possibility of further employment of the employees or their employment with another employer. However, this does not influence the dismissal process, as the Labour Office cannot impede the collective dismissal even if no solution is found after such discussion. No consent or approval of the Labour Office is required.

[D] Dismissal of Employees

After the above-mentioned collective dismissal process is completed, the employer can start with the dismissal process itself, either by notice or by agreement. All statutory conditions related to the dismissal of employee and termination of the employment must still be observed, which are mainly:

9. The Labour Office can shorten the one-month period in exceptional cases. In such case, the Labour Office notifies the employer without delay.
10. § 73 section (6) of the Labour Code.
11. § 73 section (7) of the Labour Code.

- the offer duty, i.e., the obligation to offer an employee another free and suitable working position (if there is such a position), in the place which was agreed as the place of work;
- to respect the prohibition of notice, e.g., in cases of employees on sick-leave, maternity/parental leave, etc.
- negotiation duty with the employees' representatives about the notice of each affected employee;
- proper delivery of the notice;
- severance payment;
- severance period; and
- other formal requirements of the dismissal.

[E] Sanctions

Even though the Labour Code requires the employer to follow the collective dismissal rules, and prohibits the dismissal of employees during the above-mentioned one-month period,[12] a breach of these rules does not cause the invalidity of the dismissal of affected employees.

However, if the employer:

- does not inform/negotiate with the employees' representatives about the collective dismissal;
- does not inform the local Labour Office about the collective dismissal;
- does not provide the information about the results of the negotiation to the employees' representatives and/or Labour Office; or
- dismisses the employee(s) during the one-month period during which affected employees cannot be dismissed;

then the affected employee(s) is (are) entitled directly by the Labour Code to two of his/her average monthly salaries as compensation for a breach of the law by the employer.[13] Any other potential rights or entitlements of the employee related to the dismissal (severance payment, severance period, etc.) are not affected by the payment of this compensation.

The observance of Labour Law rules, including collective dismissal rules, is also protected by public law.[14] Therefore, if the employer breaches any rules/requirements regarding the collective dismissal under the Labour Code, the Labour Inspectorate may impose a financial penalty on such employer of up to EUR 100,000.[15] The Labour

12. § 73 section (6) of the Labour Code.
13. § 73 section (8) of the Labour Code.
14. Act No. 125/2006 Coll. on Labour Inspection and on amending and supplementing Act No. 82/2005 Coll. on Illegal Work and Illegal Employment and on amending and supplementing certain acts as amended.
15. § 19 section (1) letter a) of the Act on Labour Inspection.

Inspectorate can also impose a financial penalty on the managers and/or statutory bodies (of such employer) who caused the breach of obligations arising from the collective dismissal or gave instruction for such breach, consisting in up to four of their average monthly salaries.[16]

16. § 19 section (1) letter c) of the Act on Labour Inspection.

CHAPTER 25

Collective Dismissals in Slovenia

Miran Blaha

§25.01 INTRODUCTION

Until 1991, Slovenia had been one of the republics of the former Yugoslavia, a country with a different political and economic system characterized by social ownership, workers' self-management and full employment. Employment relationships were regulated according to this system. The employment of workers who became redundant due to organizational changes made by the employer, technological improvements or for economic reasons could not be terminated. For such a worker, the employer was obliged to provide an alternative job or employment with a different employer and, if necessary, additional training or re-training. The (national) employment service was also obliged to participate in this process.

In 1984, Yugoslavia ratified the Termination of Employment Convention (No. 158) of the International Labour Organization (ILO), and at the end of the 1980s, Yugoslavia's political and economic system began to change. Accordingly, the Basic Employment Rights Act and the Employment Relationship Act were adopted in 1989 and 1990, respectively, under which the employment of redundant workers could be terminated under certain conditions. In Slovenia, both Acts remained in force until 2003, and Slovenia assumed the obligations under ILO Convention 158 with the notification of succession in 1992. The provisions of the Employment Relationship Act regulating redundancies due to urgent operational reasons of the employer (technological, organizational, economic reasons) also included special provisions governing cases involving a larger number of redundant workers. These were cases where a larger number of workers – at least ten workers employed with an organization or employer employing up to 100 employees, at least 10% of workers employed with an organization employing 100-300 employees, or at least thirty workers employed with an organization employing more than 300 employees – was not needed for forty-five days in a row. In the event of individual and collective redundancies, it was mandatory to notify and cooperate with the relevant trade union, workers' representatives and, if redundancy involved a larger number of workers, the Employment Service.

On 1 January 2003, a new Employment Relationship Act entered into force in Slovenia. Although Slovenia was not yet a member of the EU (it became a member of the EU on 1 May 2004) at the time the Act was adopted, EU directives were taken into account in its drafting. In 2013, the Employment Relationship Act was amended such that a new Act was formally adopted, but there were no significant changes to the provisions on collective redundancies. Only the provision guaranteeing redundant workers a priority right to employment in the event of collective redundancies if the employer recruited new workers within one year was eliminated. The institution of the priority right to employment was eliminated on the grounds that guaranteeing this right only in the event of collective redundancies was contentious from the point of view of the equal treatment of workers, difficult to achieve, and not negatively sanctioned.

§25.02 LEGAL FRAMEWORK

[A] Constitution of the Republic of Slovenia

Constitution of the Republic of Slovenia (Ustava Republike Slovenije, Official Gazette of the Republic of Slovenia, no. 33/91-I, 42/97, 66/2000, 24/03 in 69/04) does not explicitly regulate termination of employment relationships. Article 49 of the Constitution states that 'freedom of work shall be guaranteed', that 'everyone shall choose his or her employment freely', that 'everyone shall have access under equal conditions to any position of employment' and that 'forced labour shall be prohibited'.

According to Article 66 of the Constitution 'the State shall create opportunities for employment and work, and shall ensure the protection of both by law'. This includes also the appropriate regulation of the termination of employment relationships. Only the legislature, not the parties to a collective agreement or employers themselves, may determine the reasons for the termination of an employment relationships.

[B] Employment Relationships Act

The fundamental law governing collective redundancies is the Employment Relationships Act (*Uradni list RS* (Official Gazette of the Republic of Slovenia), no. 21/2013, hereinafter: the ZDR-1).

The Act defines a business reason as the 'cessation of the need for the performance of certain work according to the conditions under the employment contract for economic, organizational, technological, structural or similar reasons on the employer's side'. An employer may terminate an employment contract only if there is a substantiated reason that prevents the continuation of work under the conditions set out in the employment contract. If an employment contract is terminated by the employer, the burden of proof rests on him.

An employer who establishes that due to business reasons the following number of workers will be redundant within a period of thirty days:

- at least ten workers employed with an employer employing more than twenty and fewer than 100 workers;
- at least 10% of workers employed with an employer employing at least 100 workers but fewer than 300 workers;
- at least thirty workers employed with an employer employing 300 workers or more;

is obliged to:

- draw up a dismissal programme for redundant workers (social plan);
- notify in writing the trade unions at the employer of the reasons for redundancies, the number and the categories of all employed workers, the foreseen categories of redundant workers, the foreseen term in which the work of workers will no longer be needed, and the proposed redundancy selection criteria. The employer must send a copy of the written notification to the Employment Service. With a view to reaching an agreement, the employer will previously have consulted the trade unions at the employer about the proposed redundancy selection criteria and, within the elaboration of the dismissal programme for redundant workers, about the possible ways of avoiding and limiting the number of dismissals and the possible measures for the prevention and mitigation of harmful consequences;
- notify the Employment Service in writing of the procedure for establishing the redundancies of a larger number of workers, the performed consultation with trade union, the reasons for the redundancies, the number and categories of all workers employed, the foreseen categories of redundant workers and the foreseen term in which the need for work will cease. The employer must send a copy of the written notification to the trade unions at the employer.

The employer may terminate employment contracts with redundant workers, taking into account the adopted dismissal programme for redundant workers, but not prior to the expiration of a thirty-day period from the day the written notification is sent to the Employment Service; this period can be extended to sixty days at the request of the Employment Service.

The dismissal programme for redundant workers must contain:

- the reasons for redundancies;
- measures for preventing or limiting to the greatest possible extent the termination of the workers' employment relationships, whereby the employer must check the possibilities of extending employment under changed conditions;
- the list of redundant workers;
- the measures and criteria for the selection of measures to mitigate the harmful consequences of the termination of the employment relationship, such as an offer for employment with another employer, providing financial assistance, assistance for starting an independent activity or the purchase of the pension qualifying period.

The dismissal programme for redundant workers must be evaluated financially.

The employer is obliged to consider and to take into account any proposals submitted by the Employment Service regarding possible measures for preventing or limiting to the greatest possible extent the termination of the employment relationships of workers and the measures for the mitigation of the harmful consequences of the termination of the employment relationships.

The employer must draw up a proposal for redundancy selection criteria. In agreement with the trade union at the employer, the employer may draw up its own redundancy selection criteria instead of using the criteria laid down in the collective agreement.

When defining redundancy selection criteria, the following in particular is taken into account:

- the worker's professional education and/or qualification for work and the necessary additional knowledge and skills;
- the worker's work experience;
- the worker's job performance;
- the worker's years of service;
- the worker's health condition;
- the worker's social status; and
- whether the worker is a parent of three or more minor children or the sole breadwinner in a family with minor children.

When determining workers who will become redundant, under the same criteria workers with a worse social status will be given priority as regards preserving their employment.

The temporary absence from work of a worker due to illness or injury, due to caring for a family member or for a severely disabled person, or due to parental leave or pregnancy may not be a redundancy selection criterion.

[C] Bankruptcy or Liquidation

In bankruptcy proceedings or in compulsory liquidation proceedings, the trustee in bankruptcy or liquidator, with a fifteen-day period of notice, may terminate employment contracts with employed workers who became redundant due to the initiation of the bankruptcy proceedings or compulsory liquidation of the employer.

Prior to terminating the employment contracts of a larger number of workers, the trustee in bankruptcy or liquidator must fulfil the obligation of notifying the trade unions at the employer and consult the trade unions about the possible ways of preventing and limiting the number of employment contract terminations and about the possible measures for preventing and mitigating harmful consequences, and must also fulfil the obligation of notifying the Employment Service.

In the event of a compulsory composition confirmed by a court decision, the employer, with a thirty-day period of notice, may terminate employment contracts with workers if these terminations of employment contracts are envisaged in the financial restructuring plan as one of the specific measures of financial restructuring.

Prior to the termination of employment contracts with a larger number of workers, the employer must fulfil all the obligations prescribed by law for the termination of employment contracts with a larger number of workers for business reasons.

[D] Workers' Representatives

Slovenia has a two-tier system of representation of workers' interests at employers, consisting of the trade union and elected workers' representatives. In practice, especially in the process of collective redundancies the decisive role is in trade unions. Trade unions have an important role in the process of election of the works council and many members of work councils are trade union's members or representatives.

[1] Trade Union

The trade union's status, powers and role in dismissing workers are laid down in the ZDR-1 and the Representativeness of Trade Unions Act (*Uradni list RS*, no. 13/93, hereinafter: the ZRSin). In the event of collective redundancies, the trade union at the employer participates in the collective redundancies procedure, irrespective of whether redundant workers are members of a trade union or which trade union they are members of.

In collective redundancies procedures, the trade union at the employer is deemed to be the representative trade union that has members employed with the employer and appoints or elects a trade union representative. If a trade union representative has not been appointed, the trade union will be represented by its president.

Representative trade unions at the employer are members of an association or confederation of trade unions, which is representative of the state territory. A trade union that is not a member of an association or confederation is also representative if at least 15% of the workers employed with the employer are members thereof.

Trade unions representative of the state territory, an industry, activity or profession are determined by a decision issued by the Minister of Labour on the basis of proof of compliance with the relevant conditions. A decision on the representativeness of the trade union at the employer is made by the employer.

[2] Elected Workers' Representatives

The Worker Participation in Management Act (*Uradni list RS*, no. 42/93, 56/2001 and 26/2007, hereinafter: the ZSDU) lays down the methods of and conditions for the participation of workers in the management of companies, irrespective of the type of ownership, employing at least fifty workers and cooperatives.

Rights relating to the participation of workers in management are exercised by workers individually or collectively through the works council or a worker representative, workers' assembly or workers' representatives in company management and supervisory bodies.

The employer must inform the works council of and request joint consultations on the status of the company and personnel issues before taking any decisions in this regard. The employer is obliged to arrange consultations between the works council and the employer to keep the works council informed of planned decisions concerning status and personnel issues, seek advice from the works council and make efforts to reconcile their views. A reduction in the number of workers is also considered to be a personnel issue.

If decisions regarding the company's status (a change in activity, a decline in economic activity, changes in the organization of production and technology-related changes) result in a reduction in the number of workers, which is considered to be a larger number of workers pursuant to the Employment Relationship Act, the employer must obtain consent from the works council within 8 days. The works council may refuse to give consent only if the proposal on reducing the number of workers does not include a proposed dismissal programme for redundant workers pursuant to the Employment Relationship Act or if the reasons for reducing the number of workers are not justified. The employer must not take any decisions if the works council refuses consent within eight days. If the works council refuses consent for other reasons, this refusal has no effect on the regularity and lawfulness of the employer's decision.

If the employer fails to inform the works council before taking a final decision or fails to request joint consultations on the status of the company and personnel issues, the works council has the right to stay the execution of individual decisions of the employer by way of a decision and initiate procedures for settling the dispute. The employer is not allowed to execute its decision until the final decision is made by the arbitration panel.

[E] Public Employees

The trade union also has a certain role in state bodies and bodies of local communities. Prior to adopting regulations affecting employment relationships or the status of public employees in state bodies and local community administrations, the Government, the competent minister or the head of the body must enable the representative sectoral and professional trade unions in state bodies and local community administrations to submit their opinions.

Representative trade unions in the body or representative sectoral and professional trade unions in state bodies and local community administrations are deemed to be representative trade unions operating within the body if they have a representative appointed in the body. A draft act or draft decision must be submitted to the representative trade union in the body, and a reasonable time limit for the formation of the opinion must be set. If the representative trade union in the body submits its opinion in the set time limit, the proposer must take such into account or invite the representative trade union to harmonize it. If the proposer fails to harmonize the draft act or the draft decision with the opinion of the representative trade unions in the body, a non-harmonized act or decision may be adopted. However, the reasons for not taking into consideration the opinion of the representative trade unions in the body must be explained in writing and submitted to the representative trade unions whose opinion was not taken into consideration.

In state bodies and local community bodies, instead of the provisions of the ZDR-1, the provisions of the Civil Servants Act (*Uradni list RS*, no. 56/2002 et seq., hereinafter: the ZJU) apply with regard to regular termination on the part of the employer for business reasons. The employment relationship of a public employee may be terminated or the public employee may be transferred to a post that does not correspond to his or her title due to a reduction in the scope of public tasks, the privatization of public tasks, for organizational, structural, fiscal or similar reasons.

The grounds for the termination of the employment relationship or the transfer for business reasons are determined on the basis of an amendment to the act or acts on internal organization and job classification (reorganization). The decision on reorganization may be adopted at the level of a body, whereas for state administration bodies, the decision on reorganization is adopted by the Government on the proposal of the body. Reorganization must include an explanation of the objectives of the reorganization and the reasons for it, an analysis of working tasks and procedures, the number and structure of posts and the number of public employees.

The head of the body must notify the representative trade unions in the body of the reorganization, with respect to which they may give their opinion on the analysis of working tasks and procedures, and coordinate the reorganization with them.

The dismissal programme (social plan) for redundant public employees is subject to the provisions of the Employment Relationships Act, whereby, as a rule, the number of public employees and redundant public employees is considered separately for each body to establish whether the reorganization affects a larger number of public employees.

[F] Collective Agreements

Many collective agreements comprise provisions on dismissals for economic reasons, especially on collective redundancies. Usually, they regulate more precisely the criteria for determining redundant employees, the procedure to be followed by the employer in this case, including the obligations in connection to informing the trade-unions, the content of a social plan in case of redundancy, severance payments, periods of notice and also a preferential right to employment and similar issues.

For example, the collective agreement for Slovenia's electrical energy industry specifies a time limit for the employer to notify the trade union in writing (at least two months prior to the implementation of measures to dismiss redundant workers) and provides that the dismissal programme for redundant workers must be submitted to the trade union no later than ten working days before it is considered by the employer. It also provides that the employer must inform workers of all activities related to redundancies and tackling the issue of redundancies and that workers must be informed in person of the possible ways to address their labour situation.

Some collective agreements provide for a special protection against dismissal for certain categories of workers additionally to the legislation (for example employees with small children, if both spouses are redundant at the same employer, etc.).

For example, the collective agreement for Slovenia's forestry sector lays down that the employment relationship of a worker whose spouse's employment has been terminated due to business reasons may be terminated only with his/her consent.

The general rule is that collective agreement may lay down rights which are more favourable for the workers than those laid down by law.

§25.03 THE PROCEDURE

Redundancies of a certain number of workers are usually a result of changes in the employer's operation due to different business reasons: economic, organizational, technological, structural or similar reasons. These changes, however, do not necessarily result in redundancies. In cases of a transfer of an undertaking or a part of an undertaking, workers are not dismissed but, by law, continue their work on the basis of the same employment contract at the new employer. In these cases, the rules on a change of employer apply that are defined by the ZDR-1 in accordance with Council Directive 2001/23/EC of 12 March 2001 on the approximation of the laws of the Member States relating to the safeguarding of employees' rights in the event of transfers of undertakings, businesses or parts of undertakings or businesses.

In the event of individual redundancies due to business reasons, the employer may explore possibilities to enable the worker to keep his job under changed conditions at the same employer or find a job with a different employer or pursue self-employed activity. However, by law, this is no longer an obligation of the employer. The employer is also obliged to inform the trade union of individual redundancies, but only if the worker requests that the trade union of which he is member is informed of the planned redundancy and the reason for it. If the worker is not a member of a trade union, upon the request of the worker, the employer must inform the works council and/or the worker representative.

[A] Business Reasons

Freedom to provide services – free economic initiative as guaranteed by the Constitution – entails the right of entrepreneurs-employers to freely decide on the legal form of their activity and the method and organization of the performance of this activity. If the employer decides to change its activity so that it results in redundancies, the court will not assess whether the stated reasons are reasonable, necessary or sensible or whether the changes in operations resulted in the anticipated, desired outcome. The court only decides whether the business reason is true or only fictional.

As a general rule, the scope of judicial review is limited when it comes to establishing whether the business reason exists. In the assessment of this reason, it is not essential whether the termination of a post was reasonable and whether it has really contributed or will contribute to the reduction of costs or the streamlining of operations. This is an autonomous decision of the employer, with which the court cannot interfere, although it is true that the business reason must not be fictional or conceal some other reason (*Judgment of the Supreme Court VIII Ips 205/2014 of 15 December 2014*).

The Supreme Court established that a decline in sales and failure to achieve the planned results were valid economic reasons for the termination of an employment contract. Whether the set objectives of the employer were realistic or not was not a decisive fact. The employer had the right to set objectives that economically justified the existing number of employees. Since these objectives were not achieved, the employer reduced the number of employees (*Judgment and Decision of the Supreme Court VIII Ips 92/2014 of 18 November 2014*).

A valid business reason for the termination of employment contracts with individual workers whose work is no longer needed by the employer to achieve its business objectives can be given in the face of negative economic trends which pose a threat of loss to the employer (thus in order to avoid a potential negative performance), rather than only after the employer has been making a loss for a longer period of time (*Judgment of the Supreme Court VIII Ips 72/2013 of 10 June 2013*).

Performance results and the extent of work have no effect on the lawfulness of the termination, since the employer may also decide to reorganize its business if the extent of work and performance results remain unchanged. The court does not examine the motives behind the reorganization (only exceptionally, for example, if reorganization was undertaken for discriminatory reasons) and these last motives cannot constitute a serious and valid reason for the termination of employment (*Judgment of the Supreme Court VIII Ips 231/2013 of 23 April 2014*).

Reorganization is undertaken when the employer decides that the tasks of a particular job will be divided among other employees, i.e. that the existing work will be performed by fewer employees. It is only when reorganization results in the termination of a job that this termination is assessed in terms of genuineness and justifiability. The court has no authority to assess whether reorganization – the termination of a job – was necessary or not, but it can only assess and decide whether the consequences of the termination of the job (the termination of the employment contract) were in accordance with the law. The job of the worker was terminated due to a different organization of work. The termination of the job was not fictional and the court did not find that it had been carried out on the basis of discriminatory treatment of the worker. At the employer, there was no longer a need for the worker's work for economic and organizational reasons, because the employer established that the work of one of the three employees employed in a particular job was no longer needed. Since it was easiest to divide the remaining work among other employees, the employer justifiably established that a business reason existed (*Judgment of the Supreme Court VIII Ips 231/2013 of 23 April 2014*).

It is within the competence of the employer to organize work and job roles in accordance with its needs and change this organization to reduce labour costs. That is why the court cannot assess whether the termination of a job as an independent organizational unit was necessary or not. The job was terminated by way of a decision of a competent body in a manner that took into account the statutory obligations with regard to the rights of workers who were employed in jobs that were terminated (*Judgment of the Supreme Court VIII Ips 261/13 of 28 January 2014*).

The employer did not have to substantiate the motives behind the termination of the job, as the employment contract was terminated for organizational reasons, whereby it was sufficient to prove that the job was terminated and the tasks of the job divided among other employees (*Judgment of the Supreme Court VIII Ips 185/13 of 27 January 2014*).

[B] Larger Number of Workers

Employers employing more than twenty workers are obliged to draw up a dismissal programme for redundant workers and provide information to and cooperate with the trade union, workers' representatives and the Employment Service. Although legislative provisions are sufficiently explicit, in practice, there are still some problems in establishing whether particular cases involve collective redundancies. In some cases, doubt can also arise as to whether there has been avoidance of the prescribed obligations.

[1] The Definition of the Employer

The question is whether the number of redundant workers is determined based on the number of all employees employed by the employer or on the number of employees employed in the part of the undertaking in which changes occurred, i.e. in the unit to which the workers made redundant are assigned to carry out their duties. The decision on how and to what extent changes that will result in redundancies are to be implemented lies with the employer.

Business and services within the employer are taken into account if they constitute a permanent and stable entity performing one or more (permanent) tasks with a particular number of workers, technical means and a particular organizational structure. It is essential to define in advance categories of redundant workers in a particular organizational unit, department, branch or similar unit defined at the level of the employer for which the same working conditions are required. Under the previous regulations, they included mutually replaceable workers employed by the employer. This definition, however, was too broad and caused too many problems in practice. The possibility of internal reassignment of workers does not only entail the possibility of reassigning a worker employed in a job that has been terminated to a different position, but also the possibility of reassigning other workers to a position that is being terminated.

In the case of associated companies (the parent company–subsidiary, a controlling company, a holding company or a group of companies), the basic rule is that in the event of the termination of the employment contracts of a larger number of workers due to business reasons, the employer's obligations must be fulfilled by the company that is the employer in the legal and formal sense. The same applies to cases where the business decision is made, for example, by the controlling company (*Judgment of the Higher Labour and Social Court Pdp 1171/2013 of 15 May 2014*).

However, to prevent possible abuses of rights, the worker's actual employer should also be taken into consideration. In particular case, the formal employer did not have its own production and its activity was entirely linked to the scope of business in other companies in the group. The employer had a contract with other companies in the group regarding the provision of particular services and, to that end, employed workers who actually worked in individual companies in the group. With reorganization, the work processes in the entire group were organized differently, including tasks performed centrally at the employer for other companies in the group. In such situations, an employer that adopts a dismissal programme for redundant workers must take into consideration possibilities at the level of the entire group when defining measures to prevent or limit the termination of the employment of workers; for example, the employer must check whether it is possible to continue employment under changed conditions with the actual employer (*Decision of the Supreme Court VIII Ips 145/2013 of 27 January 2014*).

[2] Time Frame

One of the possible ways to avoid obligations required by law in the event of collective redundancies is to dismiss redundant workers over a longer period of time so that, in any given period of thirty days, the number of such does not exceed the number that is considered a larger number by law. This entails 'rearranging' dismissals for the same or similar reasons several times in a row.

For example, seventy workers (over 10% of the employees) at the employer were redundant since 1 July 2009. These workers were temporarily laid off, and then, in November 2009, the employer terminated the employment contracts of only fourteen workers (less than 10% of all employees). The employer then continued this practice by terminating the employment contracts of other redundant workers in May 2010. If the need for work did not change significantly during the termination of the group of first employment contracts and during the preparations for the termination of the employment contracts of the remaining workers and if the remaining workers who were temporarily laid off were not in a special situation, the termination of the contracts without complying with the provisions of the ZDR-1 on the termination of a larger number of workers is unjustified (*Decision of the Supreme Court VIII Ips 90/2013 of 30 September 2013*).

On the other hand, the court examines whether a business reason existed at the time when the employment contracts were terminated. This is why, as a rule, it does not take into account any subsequent circumstances, for example, that the employer's performance improved and that the employer again employed workers, perhaps even in the same jobs which had previously been identified as redundant (*Judgment of the Supreme Court VIII Ips 36/2007 of 18 June 2007*). In such cases, the law no longer provides that dismissed workers have a priority right to employment.

The legislation in force until 2003 provided for temporary redundancies, i.e. workers whose work was not needed only temporarily. The employment relationship of these workers was not terminated; they 'were staying at home and waiting to resume work' and, during this period, received wage compensation. Temporary redundancy was deemed to be a redundancy situation in which the work of workers was no longer needed for a period of six months or less. The legislation in force from 2003 to 2013 did not provide for such a possibility. It only determined that a worker who did not work (was absent from work) for reasons on the part of the employer was entitled to wage compensation.

Pursuant to the Partial Reimbursement of Payment Compensation Act (the ZDPNP, *Uradni list RS*, no. 42/2009), which was in force from 6 June 2009 to 31 March 2011, employers could make a request for partial reimbursement of wage compensation for workers who temporarily could not be guaranteed work by the employer for business reasons. The temporarily redundant workers remained employed with the employer and their wage compensation was partly financed by the state. As regards workers who were temporarily laid off pursuant to this Act, it was deemed that, prior to and during the temporary lay-off, no grounds for the termination of their employment contract for business reasons occurred.

The ZDR-1-1, however, regulated the institution of temporary lay-offs anew. If the employer temporarily, but no longer than for six months in one calendar year, cannot guarantee work to the worker, the employer may, with the aim of preserving employment, temporarily lay the worker off by written notice. In the event of temporary lay-off, the worker is entitled to wage compensation in the amount of 80% of his average monthly salary for full-time work during the past three months or during the last three months prior to the start of the absence and is obliged to respond to the employer's invitation in a manner and under the conditions laid down in the lay-off notification. However, the Act does not provide that the employer should also consult and inform the trade unions about temporary redundancies, nor does it refer to the use of predetermined temporary redundancy selection criteria.

[3] Consideration of Workers Whose Employment Relationship was Terminated from Other Reasons

The law provides for the termination of the employment of a larger number of workers for business reasons, and the dismissal programme for redundant workers refers to reasons for such redundancies. This is why measures are envisaged to prevent or limit to the greatest extent possible the termination of employment relationships and to prevent and mitigate harmful consequences. Accordingly, the participation and role of the Employment Service are also defined, and the employer is bound by the adopted programme with regard to terminating employment contracts with redundant workers. Workers whose employment contract is terminated on a different basis (e.g., by way of the consensual termination of the employment contract; because they have reached retirement age) or who conclude a new contract with the employer without termination due to reorganization or continue their work in different units of the employer without any changes to their employment contract, are not included in the number of redundant workers for which a dismissal programme for redundant workers must be drawn up in accordance with the law (*Decision of the Supreme Court VIII Ips 70/2010 of 21 June 2011, Judgment of the Supreme Court VIII Ips 178/2012 of 4 March 2013 and Decision of the Supreme Court VIII Ips 192/2012 of 2 September 2013*).

Such practice allows for the avoidance of obligations by the employer in cases involving the termination of a larger number of workers. In view of the actual number of redundant workers, the employer and the affected workers agree in advance on the consensual termination of the employment relationship: due to retirement, also with the purchase of the pension qualifying period, employment with a different employer, reassignment to a different job at the same employer, etc. These are cases which the employer, taking into account the actual larger number of workers, would be obliged to take into consideration in the dismissal programme for redundant workers, whereby the employer would have to ensure cooperation with the trade union or workers' representatives and the Employment Service.

[4] Workers Employed under a Fixed-Term Contract and Employment Agency Workers

In accordance with the ZDR-1 an employer providing work (Temporary-work Agency) may not assign workers to work with an employer (user undertaking) and the user undertaking may not use the work of assigned workers in cases when the user undertaking has during the transitional period of the past twelve months cancelled employment contracts with a large number of workers employed with him.

The employer must prove how many and which workers employed for an indefinite period have become redundant. An approximate estimate of redundancies is not sufficient for the assessment of the lawfulness of the termination. This applies particularly to cases in which the employer employs fixed-term workers through an employment agency. Even if the need for the number of workers for regular production changes depending on the extent of orders, the fact remains that the employer obviously employed a particular number of workers for an indefinite period to do the tasks that were regularly needed. If the extent of orders changes (decreases), this means that fixed-term contract workers will be the first to become redundant. If the extent of orders (work) no longer allows for the employment of all permanent workers performing the same or similar work (jobs), these workers would be considered for redundancy. Terminating the employment of workers on permanent contracts, while concurrently recruiting fixed-term workers through employment agencies that provide workers to other employers to carry out the same or similar work undoubtedly constitutes abuse. An increased scope of work (for example, due to exceptional large-scale orders) may result in the need for the employment of additional workers, but it cannot be a reason for the 'replacement' of workers on permanent contracts by employment agency workers on fixed-term contracts (*Judgment of the Supreme Court VIII Ips 285/2008 of 16 November 2009*).

[C] Notification and Consultations

The provisions of the ZDR-1 are not fully identical to the provisions of the Directive 98/59/EC on the approximation of the laws of the Member States relating to collective redundancies since this is not the Directive's purpose; it does not affect the rights of Member States to apply or to adopt laws and regulations that are more favourable to workers.

Pursuant to the provisions of the ZDR-1, the employer must notify the Employment Service of the termination of employment contracts for business reasons with a larger number of workers by sending it a copy of the written notification informing the trade unions at the employer of the reasons for redundancies, the number and the categories of all employed workers, the foreseen categories of redundant workers, the foreseen term in which the work of workers will no longer be needed, and the proposed criteria for the determination of redundant workers. The next written notification to the Employment Service is a notice regarding the procedure for establishing the redundancies of a larger number of workers, the performed consultation with the trade unions, the reasons for the redundancies, the number and categories of all workers employed, the foreseen categories of redundant workers and the foreseen term in which the need for their work will cease. The employer must also send a copy of this notification to the trade unions. The first notification pursuant to the ZDR-1 is therefore a formal notice to the trade unions and not the Employment Service, but it also informs the Employment Service of everything it needs to be informed of since most of the data in both notifications are duplicated, except the data on the start of the consultations with the trade union. It is therefore also acceptable that the employer, when notifying the Employment Service, relies on the contents of the notification to the trade union which the Employment Service has already received, and communicates only the missing or modified data.

Furthermore, the Act determines that the employer may give notice of cancellation of employment contracts to redundant workers (by taking into account the adopted dismissal programme for redundant workers) only after the expiration of a thirty-day period from the day of the fulfilment of the obligation to notify the Employment Service, when the procedure for establishing the redundancies of a larger number of workers has already been started and the consultation with the trade unions has been concluded with a view to reaching an agreement with the trade unions regarding the proposed criteria for the determination of redundant workers and with a view to establishing a programme on the possible ways to avoid and limit the number of dismissals and the possible measures for the prevention and mitigation of the harmful consequences thereof.

It does not follow from the Directive and the ZDR-1 that the competent public authority (the Employment Service) should be notified of all consultations or only after the consultations between workers' representatives (trade unions) and the employers are concluded, because this notification refers to the projected collective redundancies and the consultations with workers' representatives and/or trade unions (the third paragraph of point 1 of Article 3 of the Directive). Thus the ZDR-1 and the Directive do not determine that such consultations should be concluded prior to the notification of the competent public authority, nor do they determine that during the consultations an agreement on the proposed criteria for the determination of redundant workers and the possible measures for the prevention and mitigation of the harmful consequences thereof should be reached. Also, such a conclusion does not follow from the Judgment of the Court of Justice of the European Union in Case C-188/03. An event constituting redundancy occurs with the declaration of the employer's intention to terminate the employment contract; the employer has the right to start collective redundancies after concluding the consultations referred to in Article 2 of the Directive and after the notification of the projected collective redundancies (*Judgment of the Supreme Court VIII Ips 62/2011 of 17 May 2012*).

Since the procedure for the termination of the employment contracts of a larger number of workers (notifications, consultations, the adoption of a programme, etc.) covers a prolonged period of time, the circumstances that led to establishing redundancies in the first place may change during the procedure. Therefore, the projected categories of redundancies (the trade unions and the Employment Service should be notified of the projected categories) do not necessarily remain the same until the programme is finally adopted. It is not essential for the lawfulness of the termination of an employment contract in which stage of the procedure the decision on the redundancy of a particular employee is adopted, but rather that the workplace and consequently the worker has been included in the adopted programme (*Judgment of the Supreme Court VIII Ips 216/2011 of 15 October 2012*).

The decisions for which the Worker Participation in Management Act (the ZSDU) requires the consent of the works council also include economic, organizational, technological, structural and similar business reasons on the part of the employer that may lead to collective redundancies under the ZDR-1. By assessing the justifiability of the reasons for such decisions, the workers' council in fact assesses the justifiability of the business reasons for the redundancies and as a consequence also the justifiability of the grounds for any subsequent terminations of employment contracts on such basis. The trade unions at the employer have no special power to assess the justifiability of the reasons for redundancies; the employer is only obliged to notify them in writing of these reasons. These are business decisions in which the works councils are entitled to participate on behalf of workers, but not trade unions.

The fact that the works' council did not give its explicit consent to the dismissal programme for redundant workers and/or to the changes in the employer's organization does not make the termination of the employment contracts illegal. The Employment Relationships Act only requires notification and consultation with the trade union, which the employer duly complied with in terms of both the trade union and the works council. The refusal of consent, although provided for by the ZSDU in such cases, has no effect on the regularity and lawfulness of the employer's decision if the proposal on reducing the workers includes a draft dismissal programme for redundant workers, or if the reasons for reducing the number of workers are not justified. Even if the works council did not participate in the decision-making process in terms of giving consent to organizational changes and the dismissal programme for redundant workers, this does not make the termination of workers' employment contracts illegal, provided the reasons for reducing the number of workers were not unjustified and provided the employer's proposal also contained the dismissal programme for redundant workers in compliance with the employment relationship regulations (*Judgment of the Supreme Court VIII Ips 106/2006 of 23 May 2006*).

The employer is obliged to consider and take into account any proposals submitted by the Employment Service regarding the possible measures for preventing or limiting to the greatest extent possible the termination of the employment relationships of workers and the measures for the mitigation of the harmful consequences of the termination of employment relationships.

The Employment Service is involved in seeking solutions to collective redundancies particularly in the context of active employment policy programmes pursuant to the Labour Market Regulation Act (Uradni list RS, No. 80/2010 et seq., hereinafter: the ZUTD): training and education, incentives for the employment of vulnerable groups of the unemployed, job creation, the promotion of self-employment, and the like. Redundant workers may participate in active employment policy measures even prior to the termination of their employment contract on the basis of a dismissal programme for redundant workers or notification of the trustee in bankruptcy.

Active employment policy also includes financing the programmes of foundations aimed at improving employment opportunities. The foundations may be set up by employers' associations, business chambers and trade unions to implement activities aimed at improving employment opportunities and to coordinate supply and demand in the labour market.

One of the active employment policy measures is also public work whose aim is to mobilize the unemployed, foster their social inclusion, preserve and develop their working abilities and promote the creation of new jobs. An employment contract for the provision of public work shall be concluded for a fixed period not exceeding one year, renewable for the same employer for up to one year. The payment for the work shall be determined as a percentage of the minimum wage according to the required level of education for the work carried out, with the right to reimbursement for meals during work and commuting to and from work.

[D] The Dismissal Programme (Social Plan)

Pursuant to the ZDR-1, the dismissal programme for redundant workers is a formal act with obligatory content, therefore the mere verification of other employment opportunities for workers and notifying the trade union of the projected redundancies and their reasons may not replace the aforementioned programme (*Judgment of the Supreme Court VIII Ips 17/2007 of 5 January 2008*). If the employer fails to adopt such a programme, the ordinary termination of an employment contract for business reasons is illegal (*Judgment of the Supreme Court VIII Ips 428/2006 of 27 March 2007*).

Prior to the final adoption of the programme and prior to the termination of employment contracts for business reasons, the employer notified and carried out consultations with the trade unions, as determined by the ZDR-1, but an agreement with the trade unions after consultations was not reached. The trade unions were informed that the redundancy selection criteria from the corporate collective agreement would be used, with the permanent redundancies and selection of workers carried out at the organizational unit level. The dismissal programme for redundant workers was lawfully adopted because establishing the criteria for the selection of a larger number of redundancies is the employer's responsibility, while reaching an agreement with the trade unions (after concluding consultations) is not a prerequisite for the implementation of a programme thus prepared (*Judgment of the Supreme Court VIII Ips 233/2010 of 3 October 2011*).

The requirement that the programme must be evaluated financially means that it must also include the financial implications of all its components: severance pay for redundant workers, the purchase of the pension qualifying period, retraining, financial assistance, and the like.

The employer has a lot of possibilities to find appropriate measures for continued employment of the redundant worker under changed conditions: redeployment to another adequate job with or without additional education and training or requalification, shorten full-time working hours, home and teleworking, transfer of the businesses, etc.

If there is no possibilities for continued employment under changed conditions, the employer is obliged to look for opportunities to mitigate the effects of termination of employment, as a rule, with the participation of the Employment service: the offer for employment with another employer, cash assistance, assistance for starting an independent activity, the purchase of pension insurance period, etc.

The purchase of the pension qualifying period is one of the possible measures for mitigating the harmful consequences of the termination of employment relationships. The insured person (worker) can purchase up to five years of the pension qualifying period in order to meet the conditions or to attain a more favourable pension assessment. The basis for the payment of the contribution for the inclusion of this period in the pension qualifying period is equal to the amount of the insured person's insurance base from the calendar year prior to the filing of the request, plus the percentage increase in pensions until the last day of the month in which the request for the inclusion of the specified periods in the pension qualifying period was filed; however, it may not be less than the amount of the average wage per employee in the Republic of Slovenia for the penultimate month preceding the month in which the request is made.

[E] Selection Criteria

In the ZDR-1, the redundancy selection criteria are listed only as an example. It merely serves as an orientation to negotiate on the selection of the relevant criteria for determining redundant workers and their evaluation, or to regulate such criteria in collective agreements and/or a special agreement with the trade union. When determining the redundancies, the employer is obliged to take into account the criteria defined in the binding collective agreement. Although the worker's job performance, which is the main criterion for keeping one's job under the collective agreement, is also considered as one of the selection criteria, it is not sufficient. According to the provisions of the collective agreement, it is also important how the job performance is taken into account. If job performance is determined as the main criterion for keeping a job in the collective agreement, and the method of determining or evaluating the job performance is also prescribed, the employer must determine or evaluate the job performance of comparable workers using the prescribed method (*Judgment of the Supreme Court VIII Ips 170/2010 of 17 October 2011*).

The criteria for determining the redundancies are designed to specify those workers whose work has become redundant, and not to create competition between the already specified redundant workers in the light of possible measures for preventing or limiting the harmful consequences of the termination of employment. An offer of employment at another workplace and/or an offer to continue working under changed conditions is one of the measures for preventing or limiting the termination of employment. The Act provides for the application of the criteria for determining workers whose work has become redundant for business reasons, but not for determining which workers will keep their job in the context of the application of those measures. Which redundant employees will keep their job and what measures will be used depends on the opportunities and needs identified by the employer. The employer is therefore not obliged to use any special criteria when deciding to offer a specific job to a particular worker among the redundant workers. If the employer has a vacancy that it may offer to any of the redundant workers, it may do so at its discretion and without being bound by any criteria. It must only ensure that its decision is not discriminatory (*Judgment of the Supreme Court VIII Ips 216/2011 of 15 October 2012*).

[F] Bankruptcy

In bankruptcy proceedings, the trustee in bankruptcy may terminate employment contracts with workers whose work became redundant due to the initiated bankruptcy proceedings with a fifteen-day notice period. Prior to terminating the employment contracts of a larger number of workers, the trustee in bankruptcy must fulfil the obligation of notifying the trade unions at the employer and the Employment Service, and consulting the trade unions with regard to possible methods for preventing and limiting the number of employment contract terminations and the possible measures for preventing and mitigating the harmful consequences thereof.

Thus the trustee in bankruptcy is obliged to notify in writing as soon as possible the trade unions at the employer and the Employment Service of the reasons for the redundancies, the number and the categories of all employed workers, the foreseen categories of redundant workers, the foreseen term in which the work of workers will no longer be needed, and the proposed redundancy selection criteria. Moreover, the trustee in bankruptcy has to consult with the trade unions on the methods for preventing and limiting the number of employment contract terminations and on the possible measures for preventing and mitigating the harmful consequences thereof.

If the trustee in bankruptcy fails to send the relevant data on the termination of employment contracts of a larger number of workers to the trade unions at the employer and to the Employment Service, and fails to consult with the trade unions regarding the possible methods of preventing and limiting the number of employment contract terminations and regarding the possible measures for preventing and mitigating the harmful consequences thereof, this entails that it failed to comply with the minimum obligations clearly and unambiguously determined by law. On the basis of such findings, the decision of the court that the contested termination of the employment contract is illegal is correct (*Judgment of the Supreme Court VIII Ips 90/2014 of 1 September 2014*).

§25.04 SUPPORT MEASURES

[A] Time Limits for a Dismissal

In the event of the termination of the employment contracts of a larger number of workers for business reasons, a specifically regulated and extensive selection process of redundant workers takes place, which includes the determination of specific notice periods. An employer may terminate the employment contract of redundant workers, taking into account the adopted programme for redundancies, but not before the expiration of the thirty-day period from the written notification sent to the Employment Service, and/or at the request of the Employment Service before the expiry of a sixty-day period. The notice periods refer to the programme for redundant workers, and in this context to the written notification sent to the Employment Service on establishing the redundancies of a larger number of workers, on the concluded consultations, the reasons for the redundancies, the number and categories of all workers employed, the foreseen categories of redundant workers, etc.

[B] Workers' Representatives

The employer may not cancel the employment contract of:

- a member of a works council, a worker representative, a member of a supervisory board representing workers, a workers' representative in the Employment Service's council; or of
- an appointed or elected trade union representative.

without the consent of the works council or the workers who elected him or without the consent of the trade union if this person acts in accordance with the law, the collective agreement and the employment contract, except if for a business reason he rejects the offered appropriate employment with the employer or in the event of the termination of the employment contract due to a procedure for the winding-up of the employer. The worker concerned is protected against dismissal for the entire term of his office plus one year after its expiry.

Trade unions must inform the employer of the appointment or election of a trade union representative. If the employer is not informed of the appointment of a trade union representative, and if there is no agreement between the trade union and the employer on the number of trade union representatives who enjoy protection against dismissal under the ZDR-1, the worker is not entitled to special legal protection against dismissal as a trade union representative. The freedom to determine the trade union representatives through whom the union members implement protection of their interests is an element of trade union freedom. The trade union has the right to freely determine and/or elect its trade union representatives. Determining the number of those trade union representatives from among the freely selected representatives who enjoy special legal protection against dismissal under the ZDR-1 is subject to the criteria agreed upon between the trade union and the employer (*Decision of the Supreme Court VIII Ips 453/2009 of 23 May 2011*).

The protection of a worker's representative is not absolute but may only be applied in the event of the termination of his or her employment contract on grounds of his or her trade union representative status or trade union activities. The protection may not be applied if the trade union representative, in the course of trade union activities, violates the law, the collective agreement or other prescribed or agreed upon obligations.

[C] Older Workers

The employer may not terminate for business reasons the employment contract of a worker who has reached the age of 58 or a worker who has only up to five years remaining to fulfil the pension qualifying period without the worker's written consent until the worker fulfils the conditions for acquiring the right to old-age retirement. This protection shall not apply

- if the worker is guaranteed the right to compensation covered by insurance against unemployment until he or she fulfils the conditions for old-age retirement;
- if the worker is offered new appropriate employment with the employer;
- in the event that the worker, upon the conclusion of the employment contract, has already fulfilled the conditions for protection against the termination of his or her employment contract as an older worker, unless an employment contract has been concluded in accordance with the preceding indent;
- in the event of the initiation of a procedure for the liquidation of the employer.

Whether a job offered by the new employment contract is appropriate is determined on the basis of job requirements as defined in the job classification act, and not on the basis of a comparison of the wages of the two jobs. Appropriate employment shall be deemed to be employment for which the required type and level of education are the same as were required for the performance of the work for which the worker concluded the previous employment contract, for working time as agreed upon under the previous employment contract, and where the location of work is no more than three hours' drive in any directions from the worker's place of residence by public transport or transport organized by the employer.

[D] Parents

An employer may not terminate the employment contract of a female worker during the period of her pregnancy or with a female worker who is breastfeeding a child of up to one year of age, nor may an employer terminate the employment contract of parents in the period when they are on parental leave uninterruptedly in the form of full absence from work and for one month after the end of such leave. At the time of such cases an employer may not undertake any action that would otherwise be required for the termination of the employment contract or the employment of a new worker. In this period, the employment relationship may not be terminated on grounds of termination by the employer, except if a procedure for the liquidation of the employer has been initiated after obtaining preliminary consent from the labour inspector.

If, when declaring termination and/or during the period of notice, the employer is not aware of the pregnancy of a worker, special legal protection against dismissal shall apply if the worker immediately or, in the event of obstacles which did not result from her fault, immediately after the elimination of these obstacles, but not after the expiry of the period of notice, informs the employer of her pregnancy, which shall be proved by submitting a medical certificate (*Decision of the Supreme Court VIII Ips 374/2007 of 24 February 2009*).

A worker who claims protection for breastfeeding a child shall notify her employer of the breastfeeding. An employer may (as in the case of pregnancy) accept the notice on breastfeeding (or pregnancy), but the fact that it agrees with the aforementioned protection based on mere notification (without the explicit medical certificate) must be expressed clearly. However, if the employer does not explicitly react to the notice of breastfeeding (without proof thereof) or if the employer also requires the submission of a medical certificate, it is the worker who must prove (by submitting a medical certificate) the fact of breastfeeding; the burden of proof lies with her and not with the employer (*Judgment and Decision of the Supreme Court VIII Ips 118/2013 of 25 November 2013*).

[E] Disabled Persons and Persons Absent from Work Due to Illness

The employer may terminate the employment contract of a person with a disability for his or her inability to carry out work under the conditions set out in the employment contract owing to disability and in the event of a business reason in cases and under the conditions laid down in the regulations governing pension and disability insurance or in the regulations governing employment rehabilitation and the employment of persons with a disability.

An employer can terminate an employment contract with a person with a disability whose rights are recognized by a final decision based on an established disability for an indefinite period without offering a new employment contract only when, on the grounds of an established disability or for business reasons, it is justifiably unable to observe the disabled person's right to be transferred to another workplace without or after the completed vocational rehabilitation or the right to reduced work time.

In cases where the employer employs at least five workers, the existence of these grounds for the termination of an employment contract (on grounds of disability or for business reasons) is established by a commission consisting of:

- a representative of the Pension and Disability Insurance Institute of the Republic of Slovenia;
- a representative of the Labour Inspectorate of the Republic of Slovenia;
- a representative of the Employment Service of Slovenia;
- a representative of the employer and a representative of the trade unions at the employer.

Even in the cases where the employer employs less than five workers, the existence of these grounds for the termination of the employment contract (on grounds of disability or for business reasons) may be established by such commission on the proposal of the Pension and Disability Insurance Institute, the Employment Service, the insured person or the employer.

However, the employer may terminate an employment contract if a disabled worker, without justifiable reasons,

- fails to sign a contract on vocational rehabilitation within the statutory period for such or does not start and/or complete the rehabilitation within the time specified in this contract;
- fails to meet the obligations specified in the contract on vocational rehabilitation;
- fails to start working in a different workplace; or
- fails to start working part-time.

The protection of disabled persons against dismissal shall not apply in cases of the initiation of a procedure for the liquidation of the employer.

The employment relationship of a worker whose employment contract has been terminated for a business reason and who is, upon the expiry of the period of notice, absent from work due to temporary incapacity to work due to illness or injury, shall be terminated on the day the worker returns to work or should return to work, but no later than upon the expiration of six months after the end of the period of notice.

[F] Notice Period

In the event of the ordinary termination of an employment contract by the employer for a business reason, the notice period shall be:

- fifteen days for up to one year of service with the employer;
- thirty days for a period from one year to two years of service with the employer.

After a two-year period of employment with the employer, the thirty-day notice period shall increase for each year of employment with the employer by two days, but shall not exceed sixty days. After a period of twenty-five years of service with the employer, the period of notice shall be eighty days unless a different notice period is specified by a branch collective agreement, but it shall not be less than sixty days.

The period of notice shall commence on the day following the service of the notice of termination or later, i.e. on the day determined by the employer in the notice of the employment contract termination in accordance with the dismissal programme for redundant workers.

[G] Severance Pay

An employer who terminate an employment contract for a business reason shall be obliged to pay severance pay to the worker. The basis for the calculation of severance pay is the average monthly wage that the worker received or which the worker would have received if he or she has worked during the last three months before termination.

The worker shall be entitled to severance pay amounting to:

- one-fifth of the wage basis referred to in the preceding paragraph for each year of employment with the employer if the worker has been employed with the employer for more than one and up to ten years;
- one-quarter of the wage basis referred to in the preceding paragraph for each year of employment with the employer if the worker has been employed with the employer for a period from ten to twenty years;
- one-third of the basis referred to in the preceding paragraph for each year of employment with the employer if the worker has been employed with the employer for a period exceeding twenty years.

The period of employment with the employer shall also include work for the employer's legal predecessors.

The amount of severance pay may not exceed tenfold the basis, unless otherwise stipulated by the collective agreement.

[H] Rights from Unemployment Insurance

A worker who has been insured for a period of at least nine months within the preceding twenty-four months shall be entitled to unemployment benefits.

An unemployed person can claim unemployment benefits amounting to:

- three months for an insurance period from nine months to five years;
- six months for an insurance period from five to fifteen years;
- nine months for an insurance period from fifteen to twenty-five years;
- twelve months for an insurance period over twenty-five years;
- nineteen months for insured persons older than fifty years, and for an insurance period of more than twenty-five years;

- twenty-five months for insured persons older than fifty-five years, and for an insurance period of more than twenty-five years.

The basis for the calculation of severance pay shall be the average monthly salary of the insured person received during the last eight months before termination.

The unemployment benefit for the first three months is paid in an amount of 80% of the basis and for a further nine months in an amount of 60% of the basis. After this period, the benefit is paid in an amount of 50% of the basis.

The minimum amount of the benefit shall not be less than EUR 350 and the highest amount shall not be higher than EUR 892.50.

The right to unemployment benefits may not be exercised by an insured person who has become unemployed due to his own fault or will. Such reasons shall also include the termination of an employment contract:

- based on a written agreement;
- due to the ordinary termination of an employment contract for business reasons or reasons of incapacity in cases where the employer offered a new employment contract for appropriate work and for an indefinite period, but the worker refused this offer;
- due to the employer's ordinary termination of employment in contradiction with the provisions of the law regulating employment relationships which provide special protection against the dismissal of a worker, but the worker failed to claim an arbitration award or judicial protection to protect his or her rights;
- if an older worker as defined by the act regulating employment relationships is not guaranteed the right to unemployment benefits until he or she fulfils the conditions for old-age retirement, however, he or she gave written consent to the termination of the employment contract for business reasons;
- if the worker during the notice period refuses new appropriate employment for an indefinite period offered by the employer or the Employment Service with another employer for unjustified reasons.

[I] Insolvency

In the event of the employer's insolvency and particularly in the case of bankruptcy, the protection of the workers' claims is provided for. The Financial Operations, Insolvency Proceedings and Compulsory Dissolution Act (Uradni list RS, No. 126/2007 et seq.; hereinafter: the ZFPPIPP) determines the pre-emptive right to repayment, so that certain workers' claims are settled in advance of the claims of other creditors:

- wages and benefits of workers whose work becomes redundant due to the initiation of bankruptcy proceedings for the period from the beginning of bankruptcy proceedings until the end of the notice period;

- severance pays for workers whose employment contracts were terminated by the trustee in bankruptcy because their work became redundant due to the initiation of bankruptcy proceedings or during bankruptcy proceedings;
- compensation for unused annual leave in the current calendar year.

The Guarantee Fund of the Republic of Slovenia Act (Uradni list RS, No. 25/97 et seq. – hereinafter: the ZJSRS) determines the rights of workers whose employment relationship was terminated due to the employer's insolvency. An employer is insolvent:

- if bankruptcy proceedings have been initiated against it;
- if a resolution on the confirmation of compulsory settlement with a financial reorganization plan became final;
- if in one of the other Member States of the European Union or of the European Economic Area in which the employer is established, insolvency proceedings are initiated pursuant to Council Regulation (EC) No. 1346/2000 of 29 June 2000 on insolvency proceedings (OJ L 160 of 30 June 2000, page 1) and Council Regulation (EC) No. 603/2005 of 12 April 2005 amending the lists of insolvency proceedings, winding-up proceedings and liquidators in Annexes A, B and C to Regulation (EC) No. 1346/2000 on insolvency proceedings (OJ L 100, 20 April 2005).

The condition for obtaining the rights is:

- in the case referred to in the first indent, that the worker registered his or her rights within the time periods set and in the manner specified in the ZFPPIPP;
- in the case referred to in the second indent, that the worker claimed the protection of his or her rights within the deadlines and in the manner laid down in the employment relationship regulations if his or her rights were not recognized in accordance with these regulations;
- in the case referred to in the third indent, that the worker, in compliance with the provisions of insolvency proceedings initiated in one of the other EU or EEA Member States, registered his or her claim.

The rights under the ZFPPIPP are rights to the payment of:

- outstanding wages for the last three months prior to the date of the termination of the employment contract;
- outstanding wage compensation for paid absence from work for three months prior to the date of the termination of the employment contract;
- wage compensation for unused annual leave to which a worker is entitled in the calendar year concerned;
- severance pay in the amount and under the conditions determined for redundant workers by the employment relationship regulations.

The payment shall be provided to the beneficiary:

- for the rights referred to in the first and second indents, in the amount of not more than three minimum wages, provided for by the law at the date of the decision issued, and decreased by taxes and contributions;
- for the right referred to in the third indent, in the amount of not more than half of the minimum wage, provided for by the law at the date of the decision issued, and decreased by taxes and contributions;
- for the right referred to in the fourth indent, in the amount of not more than one minimum wage, provided for by the law at the date of the decision issued, and decreased by taxes and contributions.

Claims against the beneficiary's employer and/or debtor in bankruptcy are transferred to the Fund up to the amount provided for under this Act on the enforcement date of the decision on the recognition of rights under this Act (subrogation).

With the transfer of the claim to the Fund, the Fund enters into a relationship vis-à-vis the employer and/or debtor in bankruptcy as a worker-creditor up to the amount of money paid on the basis of a decision on the recognition of rights under this Act.

§25.05 SANCTIONS AND JUDICIAL PROTECTION

[A] Penalties

The ZDR-1 prescribes fines for the violation of statutory obligations in the event of collective redundancies. The Labour Inspectorate supervises the implementation of such and also imposes fines.

A fine of between EUR 3,000 and EUR 20,000 shall be imposed on the employer and its responsible person if:

- it carries out the procedure for giving notice to a larger number of workers for business reasons contrary to the law (for example, it fails to adopt the dismissal programme for redundant workers, fails to inform the trade union and/or the workers' representative or the Employment Service);
- terminates the employment contract of a worker who enjoys special protection against dismissal in contradiction with the provisions of the ZDR-1 (workers' representatives, older workers, parents, persons with disabilities).

[B] Labour Disputes

If an employee believes that there is no valid reason for dismissal or that certain procedural requirement were not fulfilled properly by the employer, he or she may pursue a lawsuit claiming a dismissal to be illegal and invalid. An employee may bring an action before the competent Labour Court within thirty days from the day of the delivery of a dismissal. According to the Free Legal Aid Act, the state legal aid system is available for persons with low income.

The jurisdiction, organization and composition of Labour Courts as specialized courts within the ordinary courts and the special procedural rules by which these courts reach decisions in labour disputes regulates The Labour an Social Courts Act (Zakon o delovnih in socialnih sodiščih, Uradni lisr RS (Official Gazette of the Republic of Slovenia), no. 2/2004 in 10/2004, hereinafter: the ZDSS-1). Unless otherwise specified by the ZDSS-1 in a procedure in labour disputes, the provisions of the law governing civil procedure shall be used.

A Labour Court shall have jurisdiction for deciding in the individual labour disputes concerning concluding, the existence, duration and cessation of employment relations; and concerning rights, obligations and responsibilities under employment relations between workers and employer s and their legal successors.

A Labour Court shall have jurisdiction for deciding in the collective labour disputes concerning the validity of a collective agreement and its application between parties to the collective agreement or between parties to the collective agreement and other persons; concerning the concordance of collective agreements with the law, the mutual concordance of collective agreements and the concordance of general legal acts of the employer with the law and with collective agreements; concerning the participation of workers in management; concerning the competencies of trade unions in connection with employment relations and in connection with decisions on the representativeness of trade unions.

In labour disputes, a panel of the court of first instance is composed of a judge as president of the panel and two lay judges as members of the panel, of which one shall be elected from a list of candidates of workers, and the other from a list of candidates of employers. The High Labour and Social Court shall decide on appeals in a panel of three judges. The Supreme Court of the Republic of Slovenia shall decide on revision against decisions of the High Labour and Social Court in a panel of five judges.

[C] Parties in Labour Disputes

Trade unions and workers' representatives do not have the status of a party to proceedings in judicial proceedings on the lawfulness of the termination of employment contracts. In particular, they do not have legal standing in the event of collective dismissals. A trade union representative may only act as the authorized representative of a worker in an individual labour dispute. However, such an authorized representative in proceedings conducted before the first instance and the appellate courts must have passed the bar exam or he or she must be a lawyer hired by the trade union to represent its members. Representation by a lawyer is mandatory in the proceedings on points of law conducted before the Supreme Court (revision), except in labour disputes where a worker may also be represented by an authorized representative who is the trade union's representative. However, he or she must have passed the bar exam and be employed by a trade union to represent trade union members.

The trade union and workers' representatives are parties to the proceedings in collective labour disputes on the validity of the collective agreement and its implementation between the parties to the collective agreement or between the parties to the collective agreement and other persons; on the power to engage in collective bargaining; on the compliance of the collective agreement with the law, on the mutual consistency of collective agreements and the mutual compliance of the employer's general acts with the law and collective agreements; on the lawfulness of strikes and other industrial actions; on the participation of workers in management; on the powers of the trade union in the context of labour relations and in the context of determining the method of acquiring representative trade union status. In such disputes, the trade union or workers' representatives can be party to proceedings in disputes that have a common, collective importance not only for the trade union or workers' representatives, but also for redundant workers (for example, informing and consulting, determining and using the redundancy selection criteria, preparing the dismissal programme for redundant workers).

[D] The Consequences of Illegality: Reintegration or Judicial Termination

If a court decides that the termination of an employment contract is illegal, the employment contract remains valid. In practice this means that workers demand reintegration, i.e. to return to work with the employer, because the mere establishment of the illegality of the termination of an employment contract does not bring any immediate benefits to a worker. As a rule, the court establishes that the employment relationship still exists and that the employer is obliged to take the worker back to work at the same workplace under the terms of the employment contract that was illegally terminated. During the period when the worker did not work due to the illegal termination of the employment contract, all of his or her rights arising from the employment relationship are duly recognized, in particular the wage that he or she would have received if he or she had worked.

In assessing the legality of the termination of the employment contract, the court is bound by the declared reason for termination, relied on or explained by the employer in the notice of termination, and not by any other reasons. The burden of proof as to the existence of this reason lies with the employer. With its decision, the court does not interfere with the autonomy of the employer concerning its business decisions, and does not concern itself with assessing the facts and circumstances related to this decision. In the notice of termination, the employer must state and explain the actual reason for the termination of the employment contract, and the court, in assessing the legality of the termination of the employment contract, is bound by such a declaration. In the court proceedings, the employer may not expand the reasons or rely on reasons other than those stated in the notice of termination.

The employer's position may be difficult if, based on the final judgment, it must re-establish the employment relationship pursuant to the employment contract for a workplace that has been terminated and/or for a job which is no longer carried out. It could turn out, however, that due to the changed circumstances during the course of court proceedings, employment opportunities elsewhere have opened up for workers who have returned to the work. In such cases, the ZDR-1 provides for the possibility of judicial termination. If the court establishes that the employer's termination is illegal (for whatever reason), the court may, at the worker's or the employer's request, terminate the employment contract. The court shall take into account all circumstances and the interests of both contractual parties due to which the continuation of the employment relationship would not be possible.

Under the ZDR-1, the court may, on the proposal of the worker or the employer, note the duration of the employment relationship (whereas this period may only last until a decision is issued by the court of first instance), to recognize the worker's years of service and other rights under the employment relationship, and to grant the worker adequate compensation up to a maximum amount of eighteen monthly wages of the worker as paid in the three months prior to the termination of the employment contract. The statutory provision does not determine that a claim for judicial termination should always be lodged by the worker, because the motion for judicial termination may also be lodged by the employer, and the court could (noting that the termination of the employment contract is illegal, but considering the circumstances and the interests at issue, the continuation of employment would no longer be possible) decide for judicial termination and monetary compensation. If the employer indicates clearly enough the fact that the employment relationship and/or continuation of the employment relationship between the parties is no longer possible, among other reasons because there is no longer a work position available and there are no conditions for any continuation of the employment relationship, also by proposing the taking of evidence to this end, the court may terminate the employment contract for justified reasons.

Bibliography

ALJANČIČ FALEŽ, Vera. *Odpoved pogodbe o zaposlitvi iz poslovnega razloga večjemu številu delavcev*, Delavci in delodajalci, letnik VI, 1/2006 str. 23-63.

BEČAN, Irena, CVETKO, Aleksej, KLAMPFER, Marta, KONČAR, Polonca, KORPIČ-HORVAT, Etelka, KRESAL, Barbara, KRESAL ŠOLTES, Katarina, NOVAK, Janez, NOVAK, Mitja, PLEŠNIK, Tatjana, VODOVNIK, Zvone, SENČUR PEČEK, Darja, BELOPAVLOVIČ, Nataša, KALČIČ, Miran. *Zakon o delovnih razmerjih (ZDR) s komentarjem*, (Nova slovenska zakonodaja). 1. natis. Ljubljana: GV založba, 2008.

Employment Service of Slovenia: http://english.ess.gov.si/.

KONČAR, Polonca. *On Dual System of Workers' Representation in Slovenia, Worker's Representation in Central and Eastern Europe. Challenges and Opportunities for the Works Councils' System* Edited by: Roger Blanpain, Guest editor: Nikita Lyutov, Kluwer Law International, December 2013.

KRESAL, Barbara. Recent Developments in Slovenian Labour Law. *Europäische Zeitschrift für Arbeitsrecht*, 2013, bd. 6, št. 3, str. 388-394.

KRESAL, Barbara. Novejša sodna praksa Sodišča Evropske unije v zvezi s kolektivnimi odpusti. *Delavci in delodajalci*, ISSN 1580-6316, 2010, letn. 10, št. 2/3, str. 189-205.

KRESAL, Barbara. Primerjalnopravna ureditev odpovedi pogodbe o zaposlitvi iz poslovnih razlogov. *Delavci in delodajalci*, ISSN 1580-6316, 2009, letn. 9, št. 2/3, str. 431-446.

KRESAL, Barbara. 'Termination of Employment Relationship: The Legal Situation in Slovenia', available at http://ec.europa.eu/employment_social/labour_law/docs/report_slovenia_en.pdf (2006).

KRESAL, Barbara. *Termination of employment relationships: legal situation in the following Member States of the European Union: Bulgaria, Cyprus, the Czech Republic, Estonia, Hungary, Latvia, Lithuania, Malta, Poland, Romania, Slovakia and Slovenia.* Ljubljana: European Commission, Directorate General Employment, Social Affairs and Equal Opportunities, 2007.

KRESAL, Barbara. *Anticipating and Managing restructuring, Slovenia,* March 2010, ITC – ILO, National Background Paper.

Ministry of Labour, Family and Social Affairs: www.mddsz.gov.si/en/.

RAJGEL, B., ROJEC, M. 2007: *The employment-related legal and policy framework for company restructuring in Slovenia*, South-East Europe Review for Labour and Social Affairs, No. 3/2007, pp. 41-56 (www.ceeol.com).

CHAPTER 26
Collective Dismissals in Spain

Antonio Martín Valverde

§26.01 INTRODUCTION

Collective dismissals in the Spanish legal system have been the object of a very important reform comprised in Law 3/2012 and in concurrent or additional provisions. In order to present the law in force in this important legal institution, the points that I intend to address later on are: (a) an introductory overview of its sources and regulatory standards; (b) a presentation of the main innovation of Law 3/2012 on the matter, which is the abolition of the administrative approval in the procedure for adopting the agreement of collective dismissals; (c) a study of the difference, established by law and fixed by the judiciary, between the two forms of 'economic' dismissals or dismissals 'due to business reasons' – provided for in the Spanish legal system – which are the so-called objective dismissals of Article 52.*c* of the Workers' Statute (*Estatuto de los Trabajadores) [ET]* and the 'collective dismissals' of Article 51 ET; (d) the identification of good causes for economic layoffs or dismissals due to business reasons; (e) a presentation of the successive phases in the procedure for collective redundancies; (f) a description of the various legal remedies provided for in the law in force regulating the social jurisdiction (*Ley Reguladora de la Jurisdicción Social*) *[LRJS]* to appeal against or ratify the employer's decisions for collective redundancies; and (g) final considerations.

§26.02 OVERVIEW OF SOURCES AND REGULATORY STANDARDS

Besides the novelty in the normative content, the main feature deserving more attention in the law in force about collective redundancies is the plurality of sources and standards regulating them; this is a matter in which various national and international regulatory authorities have traditionally been involved; and this tradition continues today, as we shall see afterwards.

In the background, as a general framework of the scenario, we find international regulations and the general provisions of the Spanish law on the termination of the contract of employment. Among the international standards, ILO Convention No. 158 (1982) on the termination of employment relations and, above all, European Directive 98/59/EC on collective redundancies stand out. Most of the rules in the Spanish law concerning the matter, particularly those about the 'consultation period', are transcriptions of this EC regulation. The concept of collective dismissal itself in the Spanish legal system has followed very closely, though not in its entirety, the standard of the aforesaid directive. We will soon go back to this point.

In the Spanish law, the general list of grounds for the termination of the employment contract is gathered in Article 49 of the Workers' Statute, regulatory legal provision (since 1980) of the contractual relation of employment. This article identifies three major groups of causes of termination: causes linked to the unilateral will of either of the parties of the employment contract (employer or employee), causes linked to the joint will of the parties, and causes that have to do with events affecting one or the other party to the contract and materially or legally preventing continuity of the employment relation. With regard to the dismissal or termination of the employment contract by unilateral will of the employer, Article 49 ET provides for several assumptions, referred to with distinct expressions: '[disciplinary] dismissal of the worker' [Article 49.1.*k*], dismissal for 'objective reasons' [Article 49.1.*l*], 'collective dismissal' [Article 49.1.*i*], dismissal for 'force majeure' [Article 49.1.*h*], and 'termination of the state of juridical person of the contractor' [Article 49.1.*g*]. The regulation of these distinct grounds for dismissal is comprised in the following articles; as already noted, those dedicated to economic dismissal or collective dismissal due to business reasons are Article 51 ET (collective dismissal) and Article 52.*c* ET (objective dismissal for business reasons).

Article 51 ET is a very detailed provision; its present version includes eleven sections, some of which are very long, referring to the main regulatory and procedural aspects of the institute. As a matter of fact, it is an entire law compressed into a single article. One step behind the substantive and procedural regulation of Article 51 ET, as guarantee of the compliance of the substantive provisions, is Article 124 of the law regulating the social jurisdiction (*LRJS*) on the various legal remedies to enforce rights and duties of the actors or of the people affected by collective redundancies. This procedural law has also been object of recent approval, by Law 36/2011 of 10 October.

However, there are other characters on the legal stage. On the one side, with some risk of going unnoticed, we find ET's Twentieth Additional Provision, titled in a way that – despite all – expresses what directly deals with our subject of the research: 'Implementation of dismissal on economic, technical, organisational or productive grounds in the public sector.' On the other side, in the background of the scene, although in a slightly more visible spot, we find the commercial rules on insolvency proceedings (Articles 64 and 65 of the insolvency law, *Ley Concursal*), which include 'specialties' in terms of 'modification, suspension and termination of collective employment contracts', expressly invoked by way of Article 57.*b* ET.

Still to be described in this concert of regulatory powers are the supporting actors. An important supporting actor is the Government, holder of the regulatory power, which final provision 19.2 (*Disposición Final 19ª.2*) of Law 3/2012 has entrusted with the adoption of the regulations for collective dismissal procedures, termination of contracts and reduced working hours, 'with special attention' – among other aspects – 'to the consultation period', to 'the information to facilitate the workers' representatives in the same period' and to 'the actions of the labour authority to ensure their effectiveness'. This responsibility for regulation has been ruled by Royal Decree 1483/2012, of 29 October.

The other supporting actor in the plot of collective redundancies is the 'collective autonomy' or power of joint ruling of the workers' representatives and of the employer. Article 51.5 ET directly confers on the collective autonomy jurisdiction on a major policy issue in the matter, which is the choice of criteria to be taken into account for the selection of workers affected by layoffs, in case of collective layoffs that do not impact all the staff members of the company. In the wording of Article 51.5 ET itself, there are two types of petitions over which this specific power of regulation is assigned: generically, the 'collective agreement' (meaning the 'collective agreement of general scope' regulated in Title III of the Workers' Statute); and more specifically the 'agreement reached during the consultation period' under Article 51.2 ET itself. Of course, in this latter case, we are not talking about abstract rules or provisions but of acts or agreements for a particular collective dismissal.

Thus, the collective agreement is empowered to set – for a particular sector or industry – 'priorities of permanence in favour of other groups, such as workers with family responsibilities, older than a certain age or with disabilities'. In any case, labour law itself recognizes three priorities of permanence for collective redundancies; one in favour of the elected representatives of the workers in the company 'over other workers' [Article 68.b ET]; another, of similar origins and rank, given to trade union delegates in the company meeting certain requirements (Article 10.3 of the trade union freedom law, *Ley Orgánica de Libertad Sindical*); and a third one, in the public administration, in favour of 'permanent staff' engaged on merit, against employees with working arrangements that do not have such a condition (Twentieth Additional Provision ET, final paragraph).

In any case, the expressed authorization to the 'collective agreement' for fixing – respecting the legal priorities – other possible priorities of permanence within the company does not seem to have been enthusiastically received. The negotiating parties to collective agreements are not used to show much inclination to setting criteria of preference for permanence in the company, which are also – on the reverse – criteria of preference for the exit from it.

§26.03 THE ABOLITION OF THE ADMINISTRATIVE APPROVAL OF THE COLLECTIVE DISMISSAL SINCE THE LABOUR MARKET REFORM OF 2012

In short, the normative model of the collective dismissal existing until Law 3/2012 of 6 July could be described as 'layoff-proposal' by the entrepreneur, the validity of which depended on an act of administrative authorization. Since this legal reform, this system of layoff-proposal disappears to be replaced by a 'direct-layoff' by the employer, subject to strict rules of private or collective procedure. These rules of procedure are aimed at having a dismissal agreement which is the result of a decision taken in consultation and negotiation, for its effect and consequences, with the representation of workers.

The change of regulatory model meant a reallocation of the roles performed by the various subjects involved in the activity that leads to the final business decision of collective redundancies and also implied the corresponding terminations of the contracts of employment. In the past, the procedural activity or series of actions to which the collective dismissal was subject to revolve around two axes, which were the employer's proposal on the one hand and the administrative authorization on the other, while since Law 3/2012 the procedure revolves around a single axis: the entrepreneur's decision negotiated with the workers' representation to implement this type of downsizing.

In this model, recently set up in Spain although widespread in comparative law, the acknowledgement of the employer's role of protagonist in the decision of collective dismissal is meant to be balanced by two mechanisms of control. The function of the first of these mechanisms is to ensure that the business agreement of collective redundancies undergoes – before its adoption – a preventive check aimed at reaching a decision which is sufficiently informed and endorsed by the representation of the affected people. After the adoption, the decision of collective dismissal and the subsequent decisions of termination of the employment contracts are subjected to a rigorous check of legality by judges and courts, examining both the procedural aspects and the substance of the decisions.

The roles played in front of the labour authority and the other subjects involved in the procedure for collective redundancies have therefore experienced a remarkable mutation. The labour authority, which formerly looked over the correctness of the procedure and the soundness of the alleged causes from the inception, is now mainly confined to the first of these tasks and, secondarily, to mediating or making up disputes or conflicts arising between employers and employees. As a consequence, the legality check of the justification of the causes alleged by the employer has become the exclusive competence of judges and courts from the very first moment.

On their part, the collective subjects involved in the 'consultation period' have the opportunity to negotiate – in appropriate informed conditions – 'the chances of avoiding or reducing the collective redundancies and of mitigating their consequences' through 'social measures of accompaniment', among which we can mention 'outplacement' and 'activities for training or retraining to improve employability' (Article 51.2 ET). The 'consultation period' for collective redundancies can actually be found in Spanish law since 1994. But its effective function in the system of administrative authorization of collective dismissals before 2012 was not focused on the matters just described, but rather on the negotiation of compensation in favour of the dismissed people exceeding the minimum legal numbers. It was as such because, if an agreement had been reached in the consultation period, a green light would have virtually been given to administrative authorization.

As for the judicial control of collective redundancies, it is unquestionable that in the system before 2012 such a control already existed, with respect to the administrative authorization and its individual consequences. But it is not less true that the legality check now executed by the judge does not have the same significance in the two regulatory frameworks. In the previous system, it was essentially equal to the contentious-administrative order, which intervened after the labour authority had already issued an initial ruling on the legality of the dismissal in the act of authorization. In the current system, the 'direct' dismissal by the employer is immediately subjected to a just as 'direct' judicial scrutiny, which corresponds – since Law 36/2011 – to the judges and courts of the Social Jurisdiction, with the exception that we are going to see later on.

The list of subjects taking part in the collective redundancy procedure shall include, obviously, the employees affected by the dismissal. In actual fact, all forms of dismissal, including the collective dismissal of course, ultimately entail an essential and constitutive ingredient which is the termination of a person's relation of employment by unilateral decision of the employer. The collectivity of the dismissal is therefore referred to the causes, to the entrepreneurial decision of downsizing the company, and to the system of the proceeding but not, of course, to the final act of breach of the employment contract, which is – after all – the only thing deserving the name of dismissal.

The individual defence of the rights and interests of those workers made redundant through this mode of termination of the employment contract affects various aspects of the business action; from the application of preferences of permanence within the company to the determination of the factors (wage amount and length of service) of the compensation for dismissal, to the impact on the decision of ruling out possible allegations of discrimination, or to the repercussion on the agreement terminating the employment relation of possible shifts of suspension or unpaid leave of the terminated work contract. The organization of the legal remedies against acts of collective redundancy provided for in the new Article 124 LRJS has marked the boundaries of the territory of individual actions of the dismissed workers through the attribution of preference of execution and power of res judicata to other remedies and judicial decisions of collective scope over individual actions and their object. We will also go back to this topic later.

§26.04 THE 'NUMERICAL ELEMENT' OF THE CONCEPT OF COLLECTIVE REDUNDANCY: THE ECJ JUDGMENT OF 13 MAY 2015 AND THE JUDGMENT OF THE SUPREME COURT OF SPAIN OF 22 APRIL 2012

Another critical point in the legal system of the institute being considered is what is usually called 'numerical element' of the concept of collective redundancies. This note in the definition is made to differentiate the case of Article 51 ET (collective dismissal) from the case of Article 52.*c* ET (objective dismissal due to business reasons). The differentiation has an obvious practical significance, since, as resulting from the interpretation of Article 124.11 LRJS, a judgment of dismissal has to declare this latter's nullity when – among other assumptions – the basic requirements of the procedure of the aforementioned Article 51 ET have not been met; and such a failure to comply with the requirements may lead to a mistake or malice in calculating the numerical element in those cases where the mistaken or malicious counting leads to set up an objective dismissal for business reasons in place of something that was actually a termination of the employment contract exceeding the numbers established to qualify for collective redundancies.

The starting point of the analysis may be at this point the wording of the legal provision on the said numerical element, wording that has not undergone any changes in the latest legislative reform of the labour market expressed in Law 3/2012. In the current wording of Article 51.1 ET, the thresholds for collective dismissals of the preceding regulation of Law 11/1994 – inspired by European Directive 98/59/EC – are thus maintained. As you will remember, according to this provision we have to classify as collective dismissals 'those affecting at least': (a) '10 workers in those companies employing fewer than 100 workers'; (b) '10% of the number of workers in a company employing between one hundred and three hundred workers'; (c) 'thirty workers in companies employing more than three hundred workers'.

The establishment of numerical thresholds by the legislator aims at pursuing a purpose of normative clarity and consequential juridical security. The legislator's recourse to the numerical criterion is meant to facilitate the application of the law with a certain automatism, reducing or turning into unnecessary the judicial or administrative discretion in the corresponding applicative operations. However, the legal provision reproduced by Article 51.1 ET sets out a few problems of calculation that have complicated the operations of qualification of collective redundancies significantly more than one might think in light of the legislative technique being used.

First, Article 51 ET speaks of the 'company' as the counting unit for the calculation of the thresholds of collective redundancies, while Directive 98/59/EC refers to the 'establishment'. For years it has been interpreted that no conflict between the two standards existed in the administrative and judicial practice, because – it was argued – the provision of domestic law turned out to be more favourable to workers as it produced an effect of expansion of the notion of collective dismissals, towards a more protectionist system than the objective dismissal for business reasons. However the European jurisprudence, in a very recent decision, has not accepted this approach.

Indeed, ECJ judgment of 13 May 2015 (Case *Rabal Cañas*[1]) has specifically ruled out the said interpretative option, considering that the Spanish regulation is contrary to the mentioned directive. Therefore, in accordance with this jurisprudential line, the basis for calculating the numerical element of redundancies shall be the 'establishment', that is the technical unit of production, and not the 'company', that is the economic unit of production which can have multiple establishments. In the context of the said EC regulation, as well as in the Spanish law (Article 1.5 ET), the establishment is seen as a distinct subject with a certain degree of permanence and stability, which is assigned the performance of one or more given tasks and which has technical means and a sufficient organizational structure, regardless of having or not any legal, economic or financial autonomy (ECJ 15 February 2007 and 30 April 2015).

Another complication found in the delimitation of the two types of dismissals for business reasons comes from the arrangement of the chosen standard itself. As we can easily see, the mentioned articles of the Workers' Statute and of the EC regulation set the thresholds for collective redundancies not through a single number but through a relation or proportion between two terms, the concretion of which usually poses difficulties.

On the first term of the relation, which is the number of terminations of employment contracts, it should be noted – although we cannot go into more details here – that in accordance with Article 51.1 ET itself the assessable terminations of employment contracts are not only those that the employer formally agrees upon as economic layoffs or layoffs due to business reasons, but also 'any other brought about in the period of reference by the initiative of the employer' (Article 1 Royal Decree 1483/2012). The second term to be used in calculating collective dismissals is the census of workers, which can – and often does – vary over time. In accordance with the Spanish law we shall take into account the census existing on 'the day procedure starts' as reference date for calculation (Article 1 Royal Decree 1483/2012).

To the two above-mentioned factors – the number of assessable terminations of employment contracts and the census of the company – we shall still add a third factor constituent of the 'numerical element' of collective redundancies. This is the time period used as a term or deadline for calculating the terminations of employment contracts made in the company ('subsequent periods of ninety days' says Article 51.1 ET itself). Here we come across a rule preventing evasion of the law, as the legal provision itself records.

It seems unnecessary in this account to go into the details of all the problems regarding the outlined time calculations. It will suffice to note that the jurisprudence of the Social Chamber of the Supreme Court has already established a unified standard on this problematic aspect of the regulation. Within this legal line it is worth referring – quite carefully – to the resolution-guide, which is a judgment by the Supreme Court of 23 April 2012.

---

1. Case No. C-392/13, *Andrés Rabal Cañas v. Nexea Gestión Documental SA and Fondo de Garantía Salarial*, available at http://curia.europa.eu/juris/document/document.jsf?text=&docid=164259&pageIndex=0&doclang=EN&mode=req&dir=&occ=first&part=1&cid=176685 (last consulted 25 October 2015).

A first clarification provided by this Supreme Court decision concerns the accuracy of the initial days (*a quo*) and of the final days (*ad quem*) of the said term of ninety days. The answer to these questions flowed naturally from the very object of the dispute sent to trial, which was in the case (and will be, hypothetically, in other possible litigations) a termination of the employment contract found in the vicinity of the numerical boundary between the collective dismissal of Article 51 ET and the objective dismissal of Article 52.*c* ET. If the dismissal becomes collective owing to the exceedance of certain thresholds – the judgment states – the date of the individual dismissal being prosecuted plays the dual role of final date of calculation of the applicable threshold, which requires counting backwards up to ninety days prior the terminations of the employment contracts, and of viable initial day of calculation for possible later objective or collective dismissals.

This way of calculating 'subsequent periods of ninety days' derives from the following logical assumption: despite the object of discussion is the collective nature of the dismissal, in each individual's lawsuit for dismissal, the thing being judged in the end is the legal category of the termination of an individual employment relation. In this individual case the judge confines him/herself to assessing the categorization corresponding to the entrepreneurial decision, in light of the assessable terminations gathered in ninety days. Hence, the hypothetical violation of the law ('numerical element') in the dismissal being judged does not fall on previous layoffs or terminations, which in turn could and should be qualified following the same method of calculation.

But the mentioned judgment of the Supreme Court of 23 April 2012 contains an important clarification that introduces a new element of uncertainty in the already complicated regulation of the border line between collective and objective redundancies. As in the case under judgment in the said ruling, when the temporal proximity to the course of ninety days provided for in the law is immediate (it was two days in the case), and the employer has failed to provide sufficient proof of the occurrence of 'new grounds justifying such an action', we must normally apply Article 6.4 of the Civil Code on the rejection of the actions of individuals to evade the law.

The reasoning of the judgment, to which we cannot deny its resting on a consistent empirical basis, is summarized as follows: the short time frame that exists in the said case before the Court among the single terminations of employment contracts has the judge of the case suppose that the business decision to terminate the contract of employment was adopted in conjunction with the previous ones, roaming freely in time in order to avoid the procedure for collective redundancies. This way of proceeding – the ruling concludes – shall not prevent, in light of the mentioned provision of the Civil Code, the application of the legal standard that was meant to be eluded.

The notice to 'sailors' which was launched by the jurisprudence of STS[2] of 23 April 2012 is unequivocal: the border between objective dismissal and collective dismissal is a high risk area where circulation is very dangerous. It is actually a border

2. STS stands for *Sentencia del Tribunal Superior*, in English 'Judgment of the Supreme Court'.

line set as a numerical threshold. But, may I use the metaphor, the line is electrified, and can emanate high voltage current at the slightest carelessness, with the effect of producing the nullity of the dismissal. Therefore, better keep a safe distance from it.

§26.05 FAIR GROUNDS FOR ECONOMIC LAYOFFS (COLLECTIVE DISMISSALS AND OBJECTIVE DISMISSALS DUE TO BUSINESS REASONS): FROM THE DECISIONS OF THE SUPREME COURT TO THE WORDING OF THE LAW

Since the reform of the Workers' Statute by Law 11/1994 the legal wording of the causes of economic dismissals or dismissals due to business reasons conforms to a list of four terms: economic grounds, technical grounds, organizational grounds and productive grounds. In the aforementioned legal provision, the legislator confined himself to simply mentioning these sorts of grounds, without giving any further details on their scope, such as indicating the goal or objective to which the decision of economic dismissal should contribute. Under the terms of the law, the goal differed depending on the types of causes: overcoming the 'negative economic situation' for the strictly speaking economic reasons, and ensuring the 'future viability of the company and of employment in the company itself' for technical, organizational or productive reasons.

The wording of the four different areas of the company activity from which the causes or reasons justifying economic layoffs could come was clarified by the jurisprudence of the Social Chamber of the Supreme Court, especially in a judgment of 14 June 1996. The fulfilment – through economic dismissals – of objectives of contribution to overcoming a negative economic situation or the guarantee of future viability of the company and of employment was considered in this judgment as an additional requirement of legality to be assessed in every case. According to this, the assessment of said contribution had to adhere to standards or normal patterns of evolution of the running of the company that are used in the scientific and professional fields of the business management. This additional requirement was named in the STS of 14 June 1996 as 'connection of functionality' between the economic dismissal conceded and the goals, also economic, indicated in the regulation.

A subsequent legal provision regulating this matter, Law 63/1997, maintained the same policy framework of four the types of causes for economic layoffs besides the requirement of connection of functionality, although mitigating the rigour of the latter about the objective dismissal of Article 52.*c* ET. The goal of dismissing for economic reasons remained the one of overcoming negative economic situations. The goal of dismissing for technical, organizational or productive causes surely was, in the version of Law 63/1997, less demanding than the one in the previous legislation: instead of being that of ensuring the future viability of the company and employment, ever since that law entered into force and in order to justify the objective dismissal due to these causes, it was enough to appeal to the contribution to overcome 'difficulties' that had arisen in the respective areas of the business activity.

The regulation of 1997 on the causes of economic layoffs has remained in the Spanish labour regulations until Law 35/2010. This law introduced three important novelties in the regulation of the causes for economic layoffs. The first has been the adoption in the legal text of the definitions of the types of causes from the reviewed tetralogy, which was proposed by the mentioned judgment of the Labour Chamber of the Supreme Court of 14 June 1996. A second novelty has been the indication, through an exemplifying list, of typical cases of economic, technical, organizational or productive causes. The third innovation concerns, once again, the connection of functionality between economic redundancies and economic goals justifying them; in Law 35/2010, these goals do not imply a state of current crisis in the company, but they point to the ordinary business objectives of improving the 'competitive position in the market' or of 'better responding to the needs of the demand'. According to this approach, the collective dismissal would stop being a dismissal strictly due to business crises and could also be justified on a strategic decision of the employer based on the mere entrepreneurial interest.

The quick historical overview made earlier allows us to get an easier appreciation of the novelties of Law 3/2012, on the regulation of the issue we are interested in, incorporated in the current wording of Article 51.1 ET. These novelties are two of differing importance. First and foremost is the disappearance in the text of Article 51.1 ET of the requirement of 'connection of functionality'. The second and secondary one is the introduction of new qualifications of typical cases in the definition of strictly economic causes. We shall begin with the latter.

According to the wording of Law 35/2010, *stricto sensu* economic causes of economic layoffs occur 'in cases such as in the existence of present or envisaged losses, or [in cases of] a persistent decline in the level of income or sales'. However, Law 3/2012 added two clarifications on the range of the decrease in income or sales to the list above; one is to say that the mentioning of income refers to 'ordinary' income; and another one is to point out that the decline is defined as 'persistent' when, 'for three consecutive quarters', 'the level of ordinary income or sales in each quarter is lower than the one registered in the same quarter of the previous year'. In the exegesis of the current provision, it seems logical to think that the decline of levels must be a noticeable drop and not a mere arithmetic decline, which would turn out insignificant in practical terms. It also seems logical to think that the quarters mentioned in the law do not need to be calendar quarters, but any three-month periods which enable counting in three quarters of consecutive calendars (requirement of consecutiveness) the negative evolution of the running of the company.

As for the 'technical, organisational or productive' causes, the current wording of Article 51.1 ET contained in Law 3/2012 remains practically the previous wording of Law 35/2010. The key term of the respective definitions is 'change'. Let's check it out: 'It is understood that technical causes occur when there are *changes,* among others, in the field of the means or instruments of production.' On the other hand, the 'organisational reasons' occur 'when there are *changes,* among others, in the fields of the working systems and methods of the staff or in the way production is organised'. Finally, 'productive causes' can be seen 'when there are *changes*, among others, in the demand of products or services that the company intends to place on the market'. A first comment on the above legal definitions is to point out that the changes referred to for the technical and organizational causes are endogenous, as arising from the employer's decisions, while the changes of productive causes are exogenous, as originating in the environment outside the company: in the markets of goods or services.

The disappearance in the text of Article 51.1 ET of the citation of the connection of functionality has been interpreted differently in proposals by academics and commentators and in judicial decisions. For a part of the scientific interpretation and the judicial doctrine, what the legislator of 2012 wanted was that the assessment of the causes of economic layoffs was only an assessment of facts and not of goals or economic objectives; this is unequivocally uttered in the description of the grounds of Law 3/2012 itself: 'The Law now limits itself to defining the economic, technical, organisational or productive causes justifying these dismissals, and eliminates any other normative references that have been introducing elements of uncertainty ... It is now clear that the judicial control of dismissals should confine itself to the occurrence of facts: the causes.'

A Supreme Court decision of 20 September 2013 was inclined to this position. Between the acts or supporting facts allegedly indicated as the cause of collective redundancies and the corresponding business decisions there has to be – this ruling states – a mere relation of 'adequate' causality. Consequently, the judicial control of the alleged causes did not go beyond the verification of the reality of the facts or acts alleged by the employer, and the likelihood of connection of those with the adopted business decisions.

But according to another part of interpretations, which seems to have won the battle in the most recent jurisprudence, the judicial control of the connection of economic functionality between the cause and the act of dismissal is not limited to the verification of an adequate causality, but has to overcome other more demanding requirements, which have not found an entirely clear formulation yet. In some cases, the judicial control of the economic functionality of the decision for collective dismissal has emerged as a judgment of proportionality between the incidence of the alleged cause and the agreed number of redundancies (STS 29 January 2014). In other cases, the test of justification of the cause of collective dismissal seems to lean towards the need of an *ultima ratio* requirement: the redundancies would not be lawful if the employer could have implemented other measures – such as internal flexibility – which are less damaging to the worker's interests in the continuity of the employment relation.

Had this second interpretative line endured, the overcoming of the traditional thesis of dismissal for crisis would have faded away, as there would be no room for the collective redundancies arising from a strategic or anticipatory decision of the employer in the technical, organizational or productive fields. A proof of this is the STS of 18 February 2014, in which the justification for the dismissal remains 'an imbalance in the workforce caused by a negative economic situation, for which the court issues not only a judgment of legality but also one of reasonable adaptation between the alleged cause and the agreed measure'.

In conclusion, considering this interpretative line, the employer on whom the law places the burden of proof has to produce from the start a credible and convincing account of reasons for the economic dismissal, not only with respect to the company and staff in general but regarding the employment contracts of the specific workers affected by the measure restructuring the workforce. But it is not sufficient to have a consistent account of the existence and impact on the company of the alleged cause. Besides the appropriateness of the measure, additional requirements of necessity and proportionality, which are difficult to predict in practice, are required. A significant 'causal uncertainty' is still hovering about today in the Spanish practice of collective redundancies, despite the ongoing efforts of the legislator.

§26.06 THE (PRIVATE) PROCEDURE OF THE COLLECTIVE DISMISSAL

The issue of the Spanish regulation of collective redundancies that we are about to address is the matter of the procedure leading to their realization or implementation, directly inspired by Directive 98/59/EC. In the present study, it is not essential to elaborate on the many rules that make up this point, but it is very opportune to start off from an overview of the structure of this procedure, and of the subsequent phases that can be distinguished within it. These phases can be reduced to four: the consultation period, the 'final decision' of collective dismissal, the implementation of the subsequent single dismissals and the phase of complementary measures.

The consultation period with the employees' representatives in the company starts with a communication to these representatives and to the labour authorities about the decision of carrying out the collective redundancy, i.e., the joint dismissal of a group of workers based on the concurrence of economic, technical, organizational or productive causes. The communication shall be accompanied by extensive documentation which takes care of specifying the Rules of procedure for the collective redundancies. The points that must be recorded in said initial communication are: (a) causes of collective dismissal; (b) number and occupational classification of the affected workers; (c) number and occupational classification of the workers employed in the very last year; (d) period for the realization of the redundancies; (e) criteria taken into account for the designation of workers affected.

The presentation in proper conditions of the communication and of the documentation that must accompany it is vital for the good progress of the consultation period, and this is why the Law itself takes charge of pointing out that any absence or significant gaps in the contribution will cause the nullity of the decision of collective redundancies agreed upon (Article 124.11 LRJS). This provision has already been the subject of application in a judgment of the Social Chamber of the Supreme Court in which the existing legislation on collective redundancies is interpreted and applied (STS plenary session of 20 March 2013). The jurisprudential line marked in this ruling refers to the consideration of the documentary contribution as an essential procedural requirement (*ad sustantiam*), although not ritual or solemn (*ad solemnitatem*). The substantiality of the requirement has to be assessed, as expected, considering the intention of the legislator to establish the consultation period, which is none other than its development in appropriate conditions of information to the workers' representatives.

As already noted, the purpose of the consultation period, under which the requirement of documentary contribution has to be assessed, is twofold: on the one hand, sharing with the employees' representation data to get to know exactly the situation of the company supporting the communication of redundancy in the company's opinion, and on the other hand opening negotiations, limited to a short term and fixed in the consultation period, 'about the possibilities of avoiding or reducing the collective redundancies and of mitigating their consequences by means of social measures of accompaniment'. Again on this issue, the Rules of procedure of collective dismissal operate as an educational handbook on the two types of concrete measures – avoidance or reduction of layoffs, mitigation of their consequences – which are the subject of this first stage of the procedure (Article 8).

As one of the paragraphs of Article 51.2 ET makes sure of reminding, the negotiation of the decision to dismiss must be carried out '*bona fide*' (in good faith) and 'with a view to reaching an agreement'. Negotiating in good faith, in this context, implies the willingness to modify the distinct positions of 'the parties'; the use of the plural means that the negotiating attitude needs to be bilateral, thus including both the employer's and the workers' representatives. But negotiating in good faith does not force one or the other into dropping one's own position. The employer as well as the labour representation can stick to what suits their respective interests, provided that they behave in a minimally receptive way towards offers and counteroffers that may arise at the negotiating table. As the Supreme Court has said in the interpretation of this legal precept, 'negotiating in good faith implies a willingness to get persuaded and to try and persuade the other party of one's own reasons' (STS 27 May 2013).

In any case, we should not forget that the purpose of negotiating in the consultation period is a decision that ultimately belongs to the employer. Here lies the difference between the appraisal of good faith in the decision on collective redundancies (Article 51.2 ET) and the appraisal of good faith in negotiating collective bargaining agreements (Article 89.1 ET). In the latter case, unlike during the consultation period, the object of negotiation is fixing working conditions, the decision of which is not assigned to the managing power of the employer, but is collectively awarded to the parties to the employment contract and to the subjects setting up the collective bargaining agreements. It was not whimsically that the Community and the Spanish legislators have dubbed this stage of the procedure for collective redundancies as 'consultation period'; the party asking for consultation does so in order to adopt (or to share) a 'final decision' which is, after all, a concern of the party itself even if it is subjected to negotiation.

The notification of the 'final decision' of the entrepreneur, with or without an 'agreement' in the consultation period, is precisely the formality that initiates the second stage of the procedure for collective redundancies. It stands to reason that the 'extremes' concerning the affected workers, which are to be provisionally entered in the notice initiating the consultation period (Article 51.2 ET), have to be the ones entered – but now definitively – in the mentioned 'final decision of collective dismissal' as well (Article 51.2 ET last paragraph).

It also stands to reason that the content of the final decision referring to 'the workers' representatives and the labour authority' includes not only the number but also the names of the dismissed workers. In this way, the verification of compliance with the criteria taken into account for their selection will be facilitated, the payment of unemployment compensation to the dismissed workers will be arranged, and it will be possible to clear up uncertainties on possible additional measures of collective redundancies, which we will soon make reference to, depending largely on the individual circumstances of the affected workers.

Anyway, after this second phase of the procedure, once 'the decision [is] communicated to the workers' representatives', the notification of layoffs to those workers affected must be carried out 'individually' (Article 51.4 ET). The requirements for this individual notification are like those required by Article 53.1 ET for the objective dismissal due to business reasons of Article 52.*c*) ET. Another legal provision needs to be mentioned here, and it concerns the act of dismissal finalizing the procedure. By way of warning, 'at least thirty days shall pass between the date of communication of the opening of the consultation period to the labour authority and the date when the dismissal takes place'; note that the 'date when the dismissal takes place' does not have to coincide with the date of the final decision of collective dismissal, nor with the date of notification of the termination of the employment contracts of the workers affected.

Some additional measures are provided in the collective redundancy procedure. One is the obligation of communication of the 'sale of company assets' (not of 'those constituting the normal business trade') 'when termination affects more than the 50 percent of the workers' (Article 51.3 ET). Another one is 'the obligation to pay the amounts aimed to finance a special agreement' with the managing body, with respect to dismissed workers aged 'fifty-five or more' (Article 51.9 ET). A third one is the offer by the 'company that carries out collective redundancies affecting more than fifty employees' of 'an outplacement plan' (Article 51.10 ET). Finally, companies carrying out collective redundancies affecting 'workers aged fifty or more' 'shall make a financial contribution to the Treasury' (Article 51.11 ET).

§26.07 LEGAL REMEDIES FOR THE DECISION OF COLLECTIVE DISMISSAL AND OF THE AGREED-UPON LAYOFFS BASED ON IT

The legal remedies available once the collective dismissal procedure is over are four: (1) a collective impugnment of the final decision of collective dismissal through the workers' representatives; (2) an act by the tribunal against the final decision of collective dismissal conducted by the labour authority, if it is believed that fraud for misappropriation of unemployment benefits is incurring in it; (3) a legal action of the employer-plaintiff aimed at stating that 'the decision to terminate' (meaning its final decision of collective dismissal) was 'consistent with the law'; and (4) individual actions of the dismissed workers regarding some or other aspects of the dismissal affecting them.

In general, these legal remedies, now ruled by Article 124 LRJS (a rewording of Law 3/2012) are not parallel but one successive to the other. The order of their use is not inconsiderable either, but it is subject to a pre-set pattern of preferences. The purpose pursued by this combination of jurisdictional courses is to simplify the application of law in this complex matter by employing the typical procedural instruments in these situations, which Article 15 of the current Code of Civil Procedure calls 'protection of collective and common rights and interests'.

The impugnment of the decision of collective dismissal through the workers' representatives has to be filed within a period of expiration of twenty days (Article 124.6 LRJS), and has total right of way on the others. Its object can be both the possible lack of justification for the alleged causes of redundancies, and the possible failure to comply with the general steps of the procedure (Article 124.2 LRJS). The filing of this class action suspends, in turn, the expiration period of individual actions of dismissal (Article 124.6 LRJS) and of a possible court decision filed at a later stage (Article 124.7 LRJS).

The content of the collective judgment passed through this collective impugnment may be alternatively the categorization of the business decision as 'consistent with the law' (when the employer carrying out the procedure 'proves the concurrence of the legal reason provided'), as 'not consistent with the law' (when it 'has not proven' the occurrence of such 'legal reason'), or as 'null' ('when the employer has not gone through the consultation period or submitted the documents provided for', or when the dismissal 'has been executed in violation of fundamental rights and public freedoms') (Article 124.11 LRJS).

These specifications of collective redundancies are quite similar to the traditional ones in individual proceedings of dismissal, despite being referred to the final decision of collective dismissal or joint decision to terminate a certain number of employment contracts under certain criteria of preference in the order of layoffs. In any case, the qualification of nullity entails the declaration of the 'right of workers affected to reinstatement in their workplace' (Article 124.11 LRJS). Once established, the collective judgment 'shall take effect as res judicata (final decision) in the court decision where resolution is pending' (Article 124.7 LRJS) and 'in the individual proceedings' of dismissal carried out afterwards (Article 124.13.*b*) LRJS).

The preliminary suspension and the power of res judicata of the judgment that the current Law on Social Jurisdiction attributes to the proceedings of collective dismissals filed by workers' representatives allow us to cut through a litigious land which would, otherwise, be hardly practicable. In this way, the filing and resolution of the collective proceedings we are referring to, far from being a chance of dispute in the company to be avoided as much as possible, can paradoxically be a source of legal security and of peace of labour relations. Hence, the legislator has provided for a subsidiary mechanism for those times when workers' representatives have not used it.

When time came to set this subsidiary mechanism, the Law on Social Jurisdiction significantly discarded the path of public action by the tribunal, limiting it in this area to the defence of the general interest of preventing fraud in unemployment benefits; and it was inclined, on the other hand, to recognize the employer an action with the aim of declaring that it was consistent with the law for the collective dismissal agreed in the second stage of the procedure. We say 'significantly' because the discarding of the public action by the tribunal and the option of the employer's declaratory action well reveal the condition of the private procedure to be attributed, according to the majority of interpretations, to the current legislation on collective redundancies.

The subsidiary nature of the legal remedy set for the employer's declaratory action is shown in the different rules that shape its legal system: (a) it may be filed after the expiration in vain of the period of collective action; (b) the term for filing the employer's declaratory action is twenty days as well; (c) in this legal remedy, the workers' representatives stand in the symmetrical position of passive subjects in the juridical-procedural relation; (d) the issued judgment shall also take effect of '*res judicata* in the individual proceedings' that may be carried out afterwards (Article 124.3 LRJS).

The fourth legal remedy, which takes place once the previous ones are exhausted, is the individual action of the dismissed workers. The object of the action must be limited, as already noted, to the specific issues affecting the actors: the calculation of compensation, the existence of preferences of permanence that they could be accorded, the respect for the rule of non-discrimination, and so on.

The general conclusion to be drawn from the organization of the legal remedies we have just described is – even at the risk of repetition – the one already put forward a moment ago, which confirms the private nature of the procedure for collective redundancies. What is important in this way of proceeding are, above all, the employer's interest in the restructuring of the workforce and the interest of the affected workers that such restructuring operation is carried out under the best possible conditions from the professional and economic point of view. Hence, the preference for the collective impugnment, the creation of a subsidiary mechanism – usable by the employer that is dismissing – to obtain a single jurisdictional response on the qualification of the final decision, the limitation of the public action of the labour authority to the legal-public side effect of collective redundancies in the management of unemployment protection, and the opening of the jurisdictional course to dismissed workers after exhausting the previous ways.

§26.08 FINAL CONSIDERATIONS

The worker affected by collective redundancy, lawfully or for just cause, has right to a compensation of twenty days per year of service, with a maximum of twelve months. If the dismissal is declared unfair, compensation goes up to thirty three days per year of working with the firm with a maximum of twenty four months. If the dismissal is declared null, which occurs when there has been a violation of fundamental rights or a substantial omission of the requirements of the procedure (Article 124.11 LRJS), the employee is entitled to reinstatement in his/her job.

The replacement of the normative model of the administrative authorization by the model of 'consulted' and 'negotiated' direct dismissal has placed the Spanish system, after a long journey on its own, in the largest group within the compared systems. In particular, in the European Union, the authorization model seems to be existing only in countries of the extinct socialist bloc. This does not mean that the model adopted by Law 3/2012 responds to a uniform pattern. With the common denominator of direct dismissal, the differences in the legal regime of the economic layoffs or layoffs due to business reasons are quite significant in the distinct national laws. And perhaps, one of the most characteristic features of the Spanish law is the accumulation of quite demanding substantive requirements (causes) and procedural requirements (consultation period).

The good functioning of the judicial control over the entrepreneurial decision for collective redundancies is key to the Spanish law for the satisfactory fulfilment of the function assigned to the institute. It does not seem necessary to dwell more on the reasons for the statement above, in view of the account we are about to conclude.

This account has focused on certain points but, because of time and space, has left other likewise important issues behind, issues that perhaps we should list here, although without an exhaustive intention. One is the issue of the role of business groups in collective dismissals, as far as the obligations of communication and documentation are concerned. This issue has been considered in several Supreme Court rulings, most notably the one approved in the plenary or general assembly of 22 May 2013. Another interesting topic is that of dismissal for force majeure, regulated by Article 51.7 ET, last bastion of the requirement, if not of authorization, of the administrative 'ascertainment' of the situation of alleged force majeure. A third issue that we could not discuss here in detail is the subject of dismissal in the public sector, inevitably topical in view of the administrative restructuring process under way. Finally, among the 'specialties' of collective redundancy, in the event of bankruptcy and state of insolvency the attribution of jurisdiction to the judge of the proceedings stands out, although his/her decisions are appealable before the courts of 'supplication' (special appeal) of the social jurisdiction.

CHAPTER 27

Collective Redundancies in Sweden

Pia Nyblaeus

§27.01 INTRODUCTION

This chapter begins with a brief review of the Swedish labour market and a description of labour legislation and the institutions of the labour market. Then the basic regulations regarding collective redundancies are discussed: The Act (1976:580) regarding co-determination in employment (MBL), the Act (1982:80) regarding employee protection (LAS) and the Act (1974:13) regarding certain employment-promoting measures (Employment Promotion Act). Finally, there is a brief description of certain application rules for general and financial damages if the material rules are breached and of trial in court.

§27.02 THE LABOUR MARKET

The workforce in Sweden amounts to approximately 4.5 million people, 3.3 million of whom are employed in private companies and 1.3 million in the public sector, i.e. governmental and municipal. Approximately two thirds of the private employees are employed in service companies and one third in industry.

Like our neighbour Finland, Sweden is very much an exporting country. We are heavily dependent on developments in Europe, since this is where almost three quarters of our exports go. Of individual countries, Norway and Germany are our two largest export markets for goods. These are also the two countries from which we import most.

Before the vital importance of exports for our country's economy, the traditions of our major industrial groups, often located in quite small places, were of great significance for the development of the institutions of the labour market and the regulations of labour legislation. The so-called foundry spirit, built on collaboration between industrial owners and trade unions, has, for good or bad, put its mark on attitude and behaviour in the Swedish labour market.

Trade unions began to be built up in working areas around the turn of the last century and had their roots in the much earlier guilds for various crafts and trades, as well as role models in Denmark and Germany. The so-called industry federation principle was generally applied, meaning that employees in the same industry were organized in the same federation, regardless of their trade. The alternative principle of federations for specific trades was the exception.

Right from the beginning, the workers' federations were organized within a strong central organization, the Swedish Trade Union Confederation (LO), which was founded in 1898. Today, LO consists of fourteen federations with a total of 1.7 million members.

Salaried staff and professional employees only began to be organized in the 1940s and their central organization is the Swedish Confederation of Professional Employees (TCO), which currently has 1.2 million members and eighteen federations. Professional employees with an academic education are normally organized by the Swedish Confederation of Professional Associations (SACO) with twenty-three associations and 650,000 members. Certain federations for the privately employed within TCO and SACO also collaborate in the confederation PTK.

The employers were also quick to organize themselves, and their central organization, the Association of Swedish Employers (SAF), was formed in 1902. The organization is now called the Confederation of Swedish Enterprise (S) and has forty nine member federations with 65,000 member companies.

The public sector employers, i.e. the government and county and local authorities, have their own negotiating organizations, partly following the model of the private organizations. These are also counterparts to the federations within LO, TCO and SACO.

This universe of organizations saw its most important task as using negotiation and collective agreements to regulate employment conditions and pay on the labour market and to resolve disputes that arose. Legislation was limited to laws about collective agreements and labour courts, as well as some protective legislation on freedom of association, holidays, working hours and the working environment.

Pay, working conditions and dispute negotiation were regulated through central collective agreements.

Much of this changed during the 1970s, when legislators began to introduce new, more stringent laws on employment protection, co-determination, equal opportunity and discrimination and the right to various kinds of leave of absence. The consistent trend in these regulations was that they increased the influence of the trade unions over companies. In some respects, the position of the individual employee was also strengthened, but politically it was mainly the power of the trade unions that was in focus.

The new legislation was characterized by the regulation of detail combined with rules for damages aimed at employers. Some rules have now been modified and simplified, while the companies' routines have been adapted to the rules, which means that the number of disputes over application has been reduced. This presentation, however, will only consider the rules that apply to collective redundancies.

The rules on collective redundancies are almost entirely based on legislation and Council Directive 98/59/EC of 20 July 1998 on the approximation of the laws of the Member States relating to collective redundancies.

Employees' interests are to be taken care of by the local and central trade unions that have collective agreements with employees. Trade unions without collective agreements have certain rights of negotiation on behalf of their members, but without the power to enforce that trade unions with collective agreements have according to law. There are no rules in Sweden that require a trade union to have a certain degree of representation among employees or to be registered in order to have negotiating rights.

The individual company is covered by collective agreements either through membership of an employers' organization or by having itself concluded an agreement with a trade union in the form of a so-called local collective agreement. Collective agreements are generally concluded by federations at industry level and also determine the content of the local collective agreement.

Essentially, proceedings and decision processes in collective redundancies can be divided into two phases. The first phase is aimed at co-determined negotiations (referred to in Swedish as MBL negotiations) between the employer and the trade union that has a collective agreement in the workplace. The purpose of the negotiations is to clarify the scope of the redundancies, that is to say how many employees and which positions will remain and how many are to be made redundant. These questions are ultimately decided by the employer himself, but before making a decision he is bound to collaborate with the trade union in the manner stated in the MBL.

The second phase relates to which employees will be made redundant because of the lack of work. This is primarily regulated by rules in the LAS regarding order of priority, based on the employer's decision on which positions will remain.

§27.03 THE ACT REGARDING CO-DETERMINATION IN EMPLOYMENT (SFS 1976:580)

The MBL is divided into sections with the headings Freedom of Association, Right to Negotiation, Right to Information, Collective Agreements, Co-determination through Collective Agreements, Right of Determination in Disputes over Interpretation of Agreements, Union Right of Veto in Certain Cases, Labour Peace Guarantee, Mediation, Damages and Other Consequences and Dispute Negotiation and Legal Proceedings. With some exceptions, these sections are about the relationship between the employer and the trade union and their rights and obligations in respect of each other when there is a collective agreement between them. However, an employer also has certain obligations in connection with collective redundancies towards the trade unions that do not have a collective agreement with the employer, if they have members among the employees.

The section on Right to Negotiation in paragraphs 10-17 regulates the company's handling of collective redundancies and expresses the employer's obligations to the trade unions affected. Individual employees have no right to negotiation. Certain paragraphs are reproduced in their entirety in the appendix, while less significant rules are summarized in brief.

The section begins with a general negotiating rule (paragraph 10), which says that the union is entitled to negotiations with the employer in questions concerning the relationship between the employer and a member of the union who is or has been employed by the employer. The employer has a corresponding right to negotiate with the union. The parties' organizations also have such rights of negotiation with each other.

Note that the negotiating rule that is applied in connection with disputes and negotiations on collective agreements does not include any rule about postponement of decisions or action. One who fails to negotiate risks having to pay damages.

[A] Primary and Secondary Negotiation

The rules about primary and secondary negotiation apply between an employer and a union that are bound by a collective agreement with each other. These negotiations are usually called collaborative negotiations, because they are to be applied in connection with decisions and measures that the employer decides on itself.

The most important rule in connection with collective redundancies is the rule on so-called primary negotiation (paragraph 11); which is here repeated in full.

Before an employer decides on more important changes in his enterprise, he shall on his own initiative negotiate with the employee organization to which he is bound by collective agreement. The same action shall be taken before the employer decides on more important changes in the working or employment conditions of employees who belong to the organization.

If exceptional circumstances so require, the employer may make and implement decisions before he has complied with his obligation to negotiate according to the first sentence.

The primary negotiation obligation means that the employer must himself request negotiations with the unions affected before management decides on important changes in the company. As stated directly in the text of the act, the criterion 'more important changes' refers to two types of case: changes in the enterprise and changes in the working or employment conditions of individual employees.

Collective redundancies normally belong to the first type of case, but a redundancy because of lack of work (more about this term may be found below under the heading LAS) is an employer's decision that is a more important change for the employee.

Also, in implementing the directive the legislator expressly added that paragraphs 11 and 13 of the MBL cover most of the provisions on information and deliberation in connection with collective redundancies. However certain changes have occurred in paragraphs 4, 13, 15 and 28 of the MBL in order to fulfil the requirement in its entirety.

There is hardly cause to weigh down this presentation with further development of all the application problems that arise from the criterion 'more important change'. On the other hand, certain other application problems in connection with paragraph 11 will be discussed in more detail.

[B] When Must Negotiations be Requested

Since it is the employer who must request negotiations on his own initiative, the question arises of at what point during the decision-making process this request should occur. This must naturally be determined from case to case with the guidance of pronouncements in case law. But the principle is often stated that negotiations must be started in good enough time to be a natural and effective stage in the employer's decision-making process. The union's viewpoints shall thus be included in the basis for the company's decision in a meaningful way.

With more complicated decisions, negotiations should begin as early as the planning stage and then continue successively. The employer may not have already decided, but he may need to investigate certain questions in advance in order to assess what alternative courses of action may be on offer. Negotiation refers not only to meetings but also to other forms of contact between the parties. There is nothing to prevent a negotiation being structured into different aspects that are handled in parallel or individually in a decision process.

From a practical point of view, it is important that, before primary negotiation on comprehensive or complex downsizing processes, the employer attempts to plan the sequence of negotiation in its different stages right from the beginning. If possible, the parties should agree a schedule. However, even if this does not occur, the employer should on his own account prepare a schedule and keep to this, so that negotiations do not go astray from a time perspective. There is nothing to prevent the employer from setting up targets for decisions to be reached each time at future meetings.

[C] Two Phases

With collective redundancies, there is often a natural division into two phases, where the first part refers to the background and reason for the coming decision by the employer on the content of the downsizing of operations. This will clarify which positions are to remain or be changed and what financial, technical and organizational circumstances exist. It is natural for negotiations in this phase to proceed jointly with the unions involved, before the employer makes a decision.

The second phase affects who is to be made redundant and is discussed in more detail in the section on the rule for the order of priority in the LAS. Negotiations in this phase often occur separately with each of the unions involved whose members are affected. Any agreements on an order of priority list apply for each prioritized area.

[D] Groups of Companies

In groups, there are often specific problems in applying the rules on primary negotiation in connection with collective redundancies. For example, a parent company may give a subsidiary a directive to reduce its payroll costs or achieve certain key figures for these costs. This raises the question of whether primary negotiations are to occur in both parent company and subsidiary or only in one of the companies. The answer rests mainly on how precisely the instructions regarding the subsidiary's actions are formulated.

If the subsidiary has a great deal of room to manoeuvre in terms of what is to be done, then primary negotiations need only to be held there, but if the instructions expressly refer to collective redundancies, then some form of union influence is also required at parent company level.

It must be pointed out that case law is based on where in the group the actual decision on collective redundancies has taken place. The formal decision-making procedure, which is found in the Companies Act (2005:551) (ABL) has thus not been decisive.

According to Swedish law, the employer is responsible for ensuring that obligations according to, for example, the MBL are complied with, regardless of the fact that another company has actually taken the decision to change the enterprise. The fact that a company other than that legally defined as the employer has taken a binding decision does not free the employer from his liability to correctly perform statutory MBL negotiations.

Nowadays the larger Swedish groups usually have internal routines for how collaboration is to occur, in accordance with the law, between the group, the subsidiary and the union in questions of collective redundancies. Legal support for this may be found, among other places, in the Development Agreement (*see* below), which has regulations on common collaboration bodies for groups. Regardless of whether these routines take the form of a collective agreement or are purely an arrangement documented by personnel administration, the routines are normally respected. Foreign groups, which are not familiar with the strong influence of the unions in Sweden, are urged to show caution.

It should be underlined however that these negotiations refer to questions and decisions that the employer decides on himself. No form of settlement or common understanding with the union is required for collective redundancies to be implemented. If no agreement is reached, the employer decides independently which working tasks or positions are affected and how many employees are to be made redundant.

The employer's decision and reasons cannot be challenged in court or tried by any other authority. The law prohibits the employees and their unions from striking or taking any other offensive action for the purpose of changing the decision. Unlawful offensive action may cause both the union and the employees to be liable for damages. The main purpose of the MBL negotiations between employer and union is that such a collaboration on decisions regarding collective redundancies should give a well-considered basis for decision and a greater understanding on the part of the union.

[E] Postponement of Decision

As a general rule, the primary negotiation must be initiated, conducted and concluded before the employer has the right to decide on collective redundancies. In the case of a major downsizing, this negotiating procedure may take a long time, because of the need for investigations for example. The union may attempt to delay negotiations for the purpose of achieving better severance benefits, for example, or avoiding unpleasant decisions. If a union uses delaying tactics, the employer may rectify this in various ways, for example by creating its own schedule for the decision process. In spite of union protests, the employer may, during the course of negotiations, clarify some questions as being finalized and decide on them. Even if such questions may involve legal risks of liability, from the employer's point of view, a firm position is better than long-drawn-out proceedings that damage the company.

If there are exceptional reasons, the employer may make and implement decisions before the primary negotiation obligation has been fulfilled. In questions of collective redundancies, this relates to situations where large amounts are at stake if a decision cannot be made immediately. Negotiations must also take place in these cases, but afterwards. This rule must be applied with great caution and is a so-called safety valve and not always applicable if the employer has put himself under time pressure because of lack of planning.

[F] The Development Agreement and Other General Agreements

Collaboration and information between the company and the unions in the case of collective redundancies is also covered in several general collective agreements on the labour market. The basis is the so-called development agreement (UVA) between SN, LO and PTK, which among other things covers negotiations and information within groups of companies with the aid of common collaboration bodies and the union's right to engage so-called employee consultants in the event of downsizing.

The rules regarding employee consultants only apply to companies with more than fifty employees. However, if the parties are in agreement locally there is nothing to prevent such a consultant being appointed for companies with between twenty-five and fifty employees.

Before any changes in the company's finances and the employee's jobs, the union has the right under the UVA to engage, at the company's expense, a so-called employee consultant, to help them to analyse the 'basic facts that exist' so that they are better able to decide on the questions raised by the changes. However, the employee consultant has no mandate to negotiate.

The rules regarding an employee consultant describe how negotiations about requesting a consultant are to take place, how the consultant's task is to be specified and what cost is reasonable for the assignment. There are also rules about conflicts of interest, the consultant's competence and confidentiality questions.

It should be noted however that the UVA agreement does not include any rule regarding postponement that would mean that the employer would have to delay his decision during the time required by the employee consultant to complete the assignment.

[G] The Act Regarding Board Representation

The act regarding board representation, which applies to companies with more than twenty-five employees, may also come into play in connection with collective redundancies. However, one basis for this act is that information and decisions on the board do not release the employer from the obligation to also request primary negotiation. According to the preamble, neither do the rules on conflict of interest prevent the employees' representatives on the board from participating in discussion of decisions on collective redundancies or other collaborative negotiations. It may be added that the employees normally have representatives on the board other than those who negotiate.

[H] Collaborative Negotiations According to Paragraph 12

Negotiation (paragraph 12) also refers to actions and decisions that the employer decides himself but which do not involve a more important change. However, these provisions are generally irrelevant in the context of downsizing, with the possible exception of some associated problems.

In such cases it is up to the union to request negotiations. The employer must wait with making a decision unless there are special reasons. This refers only to the waiting time leading to inconvenience in practice.

[I] Right to Negotiation for Unions that Do Not Have a Collective Agreement with the Employer

According to the MBL, collaborative negotiations are primarily intended for those employers and unions that are bound by collective agreements between them. According to paragraph 13, other unions with members who are employed by the employer also have the right to negotiation in two situations: on the members' individual questions and with collective redundancies or questions of transfer of the business with companies not bound by collective agreement.

The first part of paragraph 13 refers not to collective decisions and changes but to questions that only have an individual significance for the employees who are members of unions without a collective agreement with the employer. In such cases, the employer must also negotiate in accordance with paragraph 11 or 12 with the outsider union.

Questions of collective redundancies in companies that are not bound by collective agreement are mainly regulated by the second point of paragraph 13.

This point states:

> If the employer is not bound at all by any collective agreement, the employer is obliged to negotiate in accordance with paragraph 11 with all affected employee

> organizations in questions of redundancy because of lack of work or such transfer of a company, an enterprise or part of an enterprise as is covered by 6 b in the Act (1982:80) on employment protection. This does not however apply if the employer is only temporarily not bound by any collective agreement.

Essentially, this provision means that employers who are not bound by a collective agreement must also request primary negotiation if collective redundancies will affect employees who are members of any union. Apart from this and the transfer of the enterprise, however, there is no primary negotiation obligation before any other important changes to the enterprise.

Both points assume that the employer asks employees in advance whether they are members of a union and if so which organization they are members of.

[J] Special Negotiation Rule in the MBL Paragraphs 14-17

Paragraph 14 states that an employer is obliged to negotiate in accordance with the collaboration rules with both local and central unions. Central negotiation must be requested from the union side. There is no specific deadline for a request for central negotiation in the MBL, but such rules are generally found in the collective agreement.

Note however that the essential obligation to await with decisions applies in principle until the central negotiations. However, this presupposes that the request for central negotiation must be made without delay, but that the union has the right to reasonable time for consultation. In practice however the delay involved in a central negotiation can be considerable, since a central negotiation can hardly be foreseen when the negotiations begin.

Paragraph 15 of the MBL includes a first point with certain general starting points for collaborative negotiations and a second and third point with specific information rules for negotiations on collective redundancies. In recent years, EU directives have been incorporated into the MBL, primarily Council Directive 98/59/EC and it must be interpreted with EU conformity. However, unlike the directive, the Swedish rules include no threshold value.

The obligation to negotiate in accordance with the first point means that the parties, themselves or through representatives, must attend the negotiation meeting and, if needed, present a proposal for solving the negotiation issues. There is nothing to prevent the parties choosing forms of negotiation other than a meeting, for example by communication by telephone or e-mail.

Note that the proposed solution need not be a compromise: a party may be content with stating its position and the reasons for it. It should be pointed out that in connection with collective redundancies, the employer has a certain obligation to explain the situation that has arisen and give financial reasons for cutting personnel. However, as stated previously, there is no possibility for the union to request that the employer's decision be tested in court or by any other authority.

The second point, which was included because of the EU directive, contains a description of the written information that the employer must provide to the unions involved in good time before a decision on collective redundancies. The last sentence on the calculation method for any compensation for redundancies over and above what follows from law or collective agreement is often not relevant in Sweden compared with other EU countries because severance pay in addition to that stated for collective insurance compensation is less common.

As described below in the section on the LAS, the term 'lack of work' is of a technical nature in law. The term refers not only to a concrete shortage of work tasks but also other reasons where the circumstances depend on conditions in the company, such as the company's finances, technical conditions or organization, and do not only refer to the employee personally.

The obligation to notify applies in respect of every union organization that is negotiating in the case, including those who exercise their right to negotiation according to paragraph 13 point two.

Unlike the EU directive, which has certain threshold values, information according to the second point must be generally sent with redundancies because of lack of work regardless how many employees are affected.

The third point, which also relates to the EU directive, refers to a Swedish act on employment-promoting measures (SFS 1974:13), (Employment Promotion Act). This point means that the employer must also give the unions involved a copy of the written notice that according to the law must be given to the Swedish Public Employment Service.

[K] The Employment Promotion Act

This act means that a company that intends to terminate the employment of at least five employees because of a lack of work must send a notice to the Swedish Public Employment Service at least two months in advance. The same applies if several such redundancies together amount to at least twenty employees over a ninety-day period.

If the number of redundancies is more than twenty-five but not more than 100, the notice period is four months. If more than 100 employees are to be made redundant, the notice period is six months.

The Employment Promotion Act divides the content of the notice into two parts.

The first part must contain all relevant information about the planned redundancies, with specific information about the reasons, the number of intended redundancies and what categories they belong to, the number of employees who are normally employed and what categories they belong to and when the downsizing is intended to be performed and when the redundancies can be expected to happen.

This first part of the notice to the Swedish Public Employment Service corresponds in part to the written notice to the unions affected that must be sent before the MBL negotiations.

The idea is that, with the aid of general information about the downsizing as early as possible, the Swedish Public Employment Service is able to assess what input might be required from them.

The second part can only be completed after the MBL negotiations and negotiations about order of priority are completed, so that a list can be drawn up of which employees are to be made redundant. The list is determined according to an agreement on order of priority with the affected unions or a unilateral employer's decision in accordance with the LAS.

When this has occurred, the employer must as soon as possible, and no later than one month before the downsizing, supplement the notice in writing with information about which employees are to be made redundant, relevant information about the MBL negotiations and a copy of the written notification according to paragraph 15 point two.

It must be underlined that the deadlines for notification in the Employment Promotion Act run parallel with the notice periods of termination of employment up until the point when the employee will leave the company according to the notice of termination. Against the background of the length of the notice period of termination, as well as the time taken for MBL negotiations and negotiations on the order of priority, the longer notice periods in paragraph 2a seldom mean any extension of the time period until the downsizing is performed.

Paragraphs 16 and 17 also give an indication of how the MBL negotiations are to be conducted and what applies in questions regarding deadline and other formal issues, such as on written minutes and how one party can unilaterally withdraw from negotiations. These regulations are often supplemented with central collective agreements and other agreements with the union.

It is important that the party that requests negotiations clarifies what questions the negotiations refer to. If the counterpart so requires, the request must be in writing with information about what the negotiations refer to.

Negotiations must proceed swiftly. If any party so requests, written minutes must be taken that are adjusted by both parties. By tradition, the employer normally takes the minutes. If another party has viewpoints about the content, he can attach an adjustment remark with his views to the minutes.

The parties usually agree on when the negotiations are concluded. However, in some collective agreements there are provisions that the negotiations are concluded when the minutes have been adjusted.

However, one party may unilaterally end negotiations by giving the counterpart written notification of withdrawal from negotiations.

One issue that used to be big problem was how employers could act if the union attempted to delay unpleasant decisions about collective redundancies, for example by requesting unnecessary investigations, refusing to act quickly or otherwise acting disloyally. There are many such cases in case law where the employer unilaterally ended negotiations if the union did not have good, objective reasons for its actions. This also applies if no negotiations ever took place. This question is discussed in more detail below.

A union that has a collective agreement with an employer is entitled to paid leave for its representatives for negotiations and other union activities that affect the workplace in question. Representatives of unions without a collective agreement are entitled to reasonable leave in order to participate in negotiations that affect their own members.

The MBL also has rules on an obligation of confidentiality for the union representatives who receive confidential information in connection with MBL negotiations. Regardless of the obligation of confidentiality however, the information may be passed on to the union's board, which is then subject to the same rules. For disputes regarding confidentiality there is a specific negotiating arrangement that has been designed for the purpose for the union by means of a reverse proceedings burden. As far as we know, this arrangement has not been tested to date in any legal dispute.

§27.04 THE ACT ON EMPLOYMENT PROTECTION (SFS 1982:80)

LAS is also divided into sections: Introductory Provisions, The Employment Contract, Termination by the Employer, Notice Period, Pay and Other Benefits During the Notice Period, Notice that Fixed-Term Employment Will Not Be Continued, Dismissal, Pay and Other Benefits During Lay-Off, Order of Priority for Termination, Preferential Right to Re-employment, Negotiations, Right to Remain in Employment Until the Age of 67, Disputes on the Validity of Termination and Dismissal, Damages, Limitation and Legal Proceedings.

However, in this presentation on collective redundancies, the only relevant sections are the rules for justifiable grounds for redundancy (paragraph 7), notice period (paragraph 11), rules during the notice period (paragraphs 12-14), rules for order of priority (paragraphs 22-23) and preferential right (paragraphs 25-27).

[A] Justifiable Grounds for Redundancy (Paragraph 7)

According to the text of the act, a redundancy must have justifiable grounds. It is the employer's responsibility to demonstrate the justifiable grounds. The reasons for termination and redundancy are normally divided into two groups: personal reasons and lack of work. Several rules in the LAS are only applicable to one or the other group.

Personal reasons refer to circumstances that relate to the employee personally such as breach of conditions, unlawful absence, collaboration problems or inability to cope with the work. Depending on the scope of the problem, the employer is sometimes required to attempt to remedy the situation before termination is carried out by means of milder actions such as warnings and orders or relocation to other duties. There is extensive case law in this respect, but this is outside the scope of this presentation.

The commonest case of lack of work is downsizing. Swedish law is based on the employer deciding the need for a workforce but there is a burden of explanation in connection with the MBL negotiations that must precede collective redundancies. As stated above, in these negotiations the employer must explain his reasons and the basis for the intended changes. Neither a court nor any other authority is empowered to question the financial commercial grounds for the decision.

The same applies if the decision does not depend on a shortage of incoming orders but on changes or movement of production or services for technical or financial reasons or if the employer wishes to reorganize his operation for other reasons in order to increase efficiency.

Against this background, the employee's security interest is satisfied instead of the rules for order of priority that follow from the law. Even though the employer decides which positions are to go and how many employees must leave, the selection from among the employees is determined by the rules for order of priority in the law or by the employer's agreement on order of priority with the union.

However, the order of priority only applies at the individual place of work or, if the union so requests, several places of work at the same location. If the employer has operations at several locations, the order of priority cannot be extended to other locations. On the other hand, the employer also has an obligation to investigate the possibility of relocating those who will be made redundant to operations in other locations. These relocation investigations only apply to vacancies at other locations.

To summarize, this means that the decision process for downsizing measures that involve collective redundancies has two phases in principle. The first phase consists of the MBL negotiations according to specific procedural rules, leading to a decision by the employer on how many employees must leave and what positions will be removed. The idea is that the employer's decision should preferably be based on agreement with the unions involved, but this does not prevent the decision from being unilateral. The decision cannot normally be legally challenged or overturned by a court.

The second phase means that those who are to be made redundant because of lack of work are selected with the guidance of the law's rules for order of priority or an agreement on order of priority with the union. The agreement may take the form of a priority list, but it might also consist of other or complementary criteria for the order of priority compared with the LAS.

One prerequisite for a valid priority list is that the employer is bound by a collective agreement either as a member of an employer organization or through a local collective agreement.

Employers without a collective agreement are only bound by the rules of the law.

A valid agreement on order of priority can only be legally challenged if it is discriminatory or infringes the employees' freedom of association.

[B] The Rules for the Order of Priority in the LAS

The most significant rules are found in paragraph 22. The basis is that employees with a longer combined period of employment take precedence in continued employment over employees with a shorter period. If the employee can only continue in employment by means of relocation, it is a condition of precedence that the employee has sufficient qualifications for the relocated work.

The combined period of employment also includes previous employment with the employer or with other companies within the group. All employment periods are counted whether full- or part-time and regardless of the form of employment. If more than one employee has the same period of employment, higher age gives precedence.

The term 'sufficient qualifications' refers to general professional qualifications that are necessary for the continued work. This is assessed on the basis of job descriptions and recruitment advertisements. It is not a prerequisite that the relocated employee is able to cope with the new tasks immediately, but only after a reasonable training period.

Case law indicates that it is essentially the employer who decides what qualification requirements apply for various positions and what governs the relocation possibilities that can be offered, provided that the requirement is not perceived to be unwarranted or excessive. It must be stressed however that better or worse individual suitability for a position carries no weight if several employees are in themselves suitably qualified.

As a rule, a priority arrangement is determined for each collective agreement area at the operating unit, provided that the area is affected by the downsizing. Unions involved can however request a joint priority arrangement for all operating units at the location, but this is unusual. On the other hand, it is not permitted to put together priority arrangements for several different collective agreement areas.

There is a special simplifying rule for small companies. An employer with no more than ten employees may exempt up to two employees who in the employer's judgment are of particular significance for the continuing operation. This judgment cannot normally be legally challenged.

Certain employees are outside the rules for order of priority. This applies to those who, according to paragraph 1, are not covered by the LAS, namely company managers, family members, household employees, certain employees with government employment support or other public employment support and apprentices at upper secondary level. These thus take precedence for continued employment regardless of the order of priority.

Employees aged 67 or older are also outside the priority arrangement, but take no precedence for continued employment.

[C] Practical Application Problems

The rules about order of priority belong, both politically and in practice, to the most controversial area in Swedish labour law. One of the reasons for this is that the unions see these rules as a cornerstone of their influence in the workplace. Employers object that the rules inhibit the company's development and efficiency. There is little space here however to describe this discussion, but only to point out certain practical application problems.

When it comes to downsizing, the procedure will differ depending on how extensive the redundancies are expected to be. The same applies to whether the downsizing affects the company as a whole or only certain departments. If the company (operating unit) is to be closed down completely, the rules about order of priority have no significance. On the other hand, the requirements of paragraph 7 regarding relocation of personnel are relevant if the company has other operating units at the location or elsewhere in the country. Such relocations are not covered by any rules for order of priority and only refer to vacancies. An assessment of what relocation possibilities can be offered is normally made together with the decision on redundancies.

If the company has more operating units at the same location, the union that has a collective agreement with the employer may request a joint priority arrangement, but this is by no means common. On the other hand, there is no possibility of having a joint priority arrangement for several different companies within the same group; the priority arrangement must be limited to one and the same legal entity.

As a rule, it is most appropriate for the employer to initially set up an organizational plan that clarifies which positions will remain and what qualifications will now apply for these. It is in the nature of the case that a tighter organization also affects the content of the remaining positions and thus also the qualifications that are required.

Usually a list is then drawn up of the personnel on the basis of period of employment and this is matched against the new organizational plan. This will already give an overview of what might represent problems in the forthcoming MBL negotiations. The organizational plan is also the basis for the employer's decisions in the first phase of a downsizing as to which positions will remain and how many employees are expected to be made redundant as a result of a lack of work.

From the employer's point of view, it may be appropriate to make the organizational plan as tight as possible right from the beginning. In terms of negotiation, it is easier to later accommodate the union in individual cases than to have to extend the downsizing because of deadlocks in the negotiations.

Determining which collective agreement areas are affected and which personnel belong to each area seldom causes any difficulty. Each area has its own order of priority circle. If the employer is not bound by collective agreement, the order of priority circles includes all personnel in the company regardless of which category is affected. These cases are more difficult to handle, since local agreements in order of priority are not valid.

Downsizing often involves a risk that employees will attempt to leave the company while the process is going on. This applies especially to qualified employees who are particularly important for the company's ability to cope with the reorganization that downsizing involves. Extended procedures can also lead to unnecessary costs and market disturbances.

The employer therefore has compelling reasons to push on the MBL negotiations and arrive at a decision quickly. It is in the ultimate interests of the union on the other hand to delay the decision for the purpose of reducing the number of redundancies and arriving at better terms for those who will be made redundant.

[D] Severance Payments

It must finally be added that compensation in addition to redundancy pay to those being made redundant as part of collective redundancies is regulated by certain central collective agreements and in cases where such compensation exists it is paid from funds that are financed from the employer's contributions. The employees who are covered by collective agreements are entitled to such compensation whether they are union members or not.

Unemployment compensation according to the legally regulated unemployment insurance (the so-called A-kassa) is more than 80% financed from taxes, but is administered by the labour organizations. Some unions also have additional insurance for their members. There is a special 'A-kassa' for non-union members.

This means that the question of special severance payments is generally not relevant when downsizing. Some larger groups and companies, which normally pay such remuneration in the event of downsizing abroad, have begun to make similar payments in Sweden too, at individual levels.

[E] Formal Rules on Redundancy

The formal rules on redundancy may be found in paragraphs 8-10 of the LAS. A notice of termination must be in writing and include an appeal reference stating what the employee must do if he or she wishes to have the termination declared invalid or claim damages. Declaring the termination invalid is normally only relevant with termination for personal reasons and not in the case of a lack of work, since any error in order of priority cannot lead to invalidity but only damages.

On the other hand, the notification of redundancies due to lack of work must include information on whether the person concerned has a preferential right to re-employment and how claims for preferential right must be notified.

The requirement for a written notification is a statutory regulation. Most employer organizations have devised forms for this purpose.

The notification does not have to state the employer's reasons for termination but generally states whether the termination is due to personal reasons or lack of work. However, if the employee so requests, the employer must give a written account of the circumstances.

The notification of termination is normally given to the employee personally but can also be posted as a registered letter. Termination is considered to have occurred when the employee receives the notice. If the employee cannot be found, termination is considered to have occurred ten days after the notification is sent.

Termination during a period when the employee is on holiday is considered to have occurred the day after the holiday finishes, at the earliest.

[F] Notice Periods, etc.

Notice periods are regulated by paragraph 11 of the LAS. The shortest notice period for both employer and employee is one month. After two years' total employment, the notice period is extended, for termination by the employer, in stages up to six months according to the text of the act. The LAS does not permit individual agreements on a shorter notice period from the employer.

During the notice period, certain special rules apply according to paragraphs 12-14 of the LAS. An employee serving notice is entitled to the same pay and employment benefits as before even if performing different duties or released from working during the notice period. However, if the employee has been partly or wholly released from working, the employer is entitled to deduct income that the employee has received or should have receive from other acceptable employment.

During the notice period, an employee serving notice may not be moved to work at another location if this makes it more difficult to seek new employment. The employee is also entitled to reasonable leave with maintained employment benefits in order to visit the Swedish Public Employment Service or to seek work in some other way.

[G] Preferential Right to Re-employment

An important provision that refers to redundancy due to lack of work is the preferential right to re-employment in paragraphs 25, 26 and 27 of the LAS. There is no corresponding provision in the directive and it is probably uncommon in the rest of the EU. This means that an employee who has been made redundant, who has been employed for at least twelve months during the previous three years, has a preferential right to re-employment in the company at which he or she was previously employed. The preferential right applies from the time of redundancy until nine months after employment ceased.

If the business is transferred to another employer, the same preferential right applies and the same applies after bankruptcy.

The preferential right applies to new appointments in the same collective agreement area and operating unit as the person was previously employed in.

If the person concerned received a written notification of termination with the correct appeal reference, it is a requirement that the preferential right is claimed in accordance with what appears in the notification. The preferential right cannot be claimed until this formal claim is made and this can occur at any time during the preferential right period.

A redundant employee who rejects a reasonable offer of re-employment loses the preferential right.

If several redundant employees have the preferential right to re-employment simultaneously, a priority list is drawn up based on the total period of employment and age, in manner corresponding to the order of priority for redundancy due to lack of work. The person with preferential right must also have sufficient qualifications for the new position.

According to paragraph 32 of the LAS, an employer who wishes to make a new appointment while there are former employees who were made redundant due to lack of work and who still have a preferential right to re-employment, must first hold MBL negotiations according to paragraphs 11-13. These negotiations correspond, as appropriate, to what is stated above regarding MBL negotiations when downsizing. When the preferential right period of nine months has expired, the obligation to hold negotiations ceases.

[H] Consequences and Disputes

Both MBL negotiations and LAS rules relating to handling collective redundancies are connected to sanctions in the form of damages. Damages are divided into two types: general damages and financial damages. General damages do not require financial damages but according to the legislator are a kind of compensation that is to be paid to the parties because of the infringement of their rights that the breach of the law involved. In Sweden the rules on general damages are mainly found in labour law and legislation on discrimination, but in recently years have also been extended to include intellectual property rights, among other things. Financial damages are determined according to the customary legal principles for damages.

An employer who is in breach of the rules for MBL negotiations may also be liable for damages to the union. Examples of such faults are that primary negotiation is not requested, that negotiations are requested too late or unilaterally terminated too early or that the rule regarding exceptional circumstances is invoked but is not applicable.

On the other hand, individual employees are not entitled to damages for breaches of the rules on MBL negotiations, since they have no independent right to negotiate.

The amount of damages can vary widely, depending on the nature and extent of the fault. The highest amount so far paid to a labour organization for a breach of the obligation to negotiate according to the MBL is EUR 30,000.

In the case of the LAS rules, it is normal that incorrect application will lead to both general and financial damages. The union can only receive general damages but the employee often claims both types of damages.

The rules on order of priority are the most difficult to apply. A breach of the priority arrangement normally leads to general damages of at least EUR 5,000 to the person who was made redundant. In addition, there are financial damages, which correspond to the redundant person's loss of pay and other employment benefits. This is set off against income that the employee has received or could receive however. According to a special maximum rule, the financial damages may not amount to more than sixteen months' pay with less than a five-year employment period, twenty-four months' pay with at least five but less than ten years' employment period and thirty two months' pay with an employment period of at least ten years.

If several redundant persons are passed over in the breach of the priority arrangement, all of them are entitled to general damages but only the one with the longest employment period is also entitled to financial damages.

If anyone considers themselves to have been passed over in connection with a valid priority arrangement agreement with the union, the agreement may only be challenged with reference to a claim of infringed freedom of association or discrimination.

Other faults in connection with the LAS rules on collective redundancies may lead to varying amounts of damages depending on the extent and nature of the fault, but the amounts are relatively modest in the cause of pure technical errors.

Neither the MBL negotiations nor the LAS rules allow for the imposition of fines in connection with collective redundancies. On the other hand, there are rules for this and certain other consequences in connection with the notification rules in the Employment Promotion Act.

[I] Legal Proceedings

According to the Act on legal proceedings in labour disputes (SFS 1934:371), labour disputes between parties who are bound by a collective agreement must be tried in the Labour Court as the first and only instance. The same applies to certain other labour disputes when the employee is represented by another union.

Other labour disputes, primarily where the employer is not bound by a collective agreement, are tried in the District Court as the First Instance. Appeals are heard in the Labour Court.

Before legal proceedings may be started in the Labour Court, the dispute must have been the subject of dispute negotiations according to the MBL and collective agreement.

Appendices: Paragraphs in Acts and Agreements

Employment Promotion Act paragraphs 1, 2 and 2a.
LAS paragraphs 7 points 1 and 2, 8-14, 22-25, 26-27, 38-39.
MBL paragraphs 10-17, 54-55.
UVA paragraph 12.

Employment (Co-Determination in the Workplace) Act (1976:580)

This is a translation and the Swedish version takes precedence.

10 §

An employees' organisation shall have the right to negotiate with an employer on any matter relating to the relationship between the employer and any member of the organisation who is, or has been, employed by that employer. An employer shall have an equivalent right to negotiate with an employees' organisation.
Employees' organisations shall also have the right to negotiate, in accordance with the first paragraph, in relation to any organisation of which the employer is a member, and similarly employers' organisations in relation to any organisation of which the employee is a member. SFS 1976:580

11 §

Before an employer takes any decision regarding significant changes in its activities, he shall, on its own initiative, enter into negotiations with the employees' organisation with which he is bound to negotiate under a collective bargaining agreement. The above-mentioned shall also apply prior to any decisions by an employer regarding significant changes in working or employment conditions for employees who belong to the organisation.
Where there is extraordinary cause, the employer may take and implement a decision before he has fulfilled his duty to negotiate under the first paragraph of this Section. SFS 1976:580

12 §

Should an employees' organisation as referred to in Section 11 so request, an employer shall also, in circumstances other than those mentioned therein, negotiate with that organisation before he takes or implements a decision that concerns a member of the organisation. Where there is special cause, however, the employer may take and implement the decision before he has fulfilled its duty to negotiate. SFS 1976:580

13 §

Where a matter specifically relates to the working or employment conditions of an employee who belongs to an employees' organisation in relation to which the employer is not bound by a collective bargaining agreement, the employer shall be obliged to negotiate with that organisation under Section 11 and Section 12.
Where an employer is not bound by a collective bargaining agreement, the employer shall be obliged to negotiate with all affected employees' organisations under Section

11 in all matters relating to termination of employment as a consequence of shortage of work or the transfer of an undertaking, a business or a part of a business subject to Section 6 b of the Employment Protection Act (1982:80). The above-mentioned provisions shall not apply, however, where the employer is only temporarily not bound by a collective bargaining agreement. SFS 1994:1686

14 §

Where there is a local employees' organisation, the obligation to negotiate under Sections 11 - 13 shall, in the first instance, be fulfilled through negotiations with that organisation.
If agreement is not reached during negotiations under the first paragraph of this Section, the employer shall, upon request, also negotiate with a central employees' organisation. SFS 1976:580

15 §

Any party who is under an obligation to negotiate shall, in person or through a representative, appear at negotiations meetings, and, where necessary, put forward a reasoned proposal for a solution of the matter to which the negotiations relate. The parties may jointly decide upon a form for negotiations other than through a meeting.
In conjunction with negotiations regarding a decision to terminate employment due to shortage of work, the employer shall in good time notify the other party in writing of the following matters:

- the reason for the planned termination;
- the number of employees who will be affected by the termination and the employment categories to which they belong;
- the number of employees who are normally employed and the employment categories to which they belong;
- the time period during which it is planned to carry out the termination; and
- the method of calculation of any compensation to be paid in conjunction with termination in addition to that which is required by to law or applicable collective bargaining agreements.

The employer shall also provide the other party with a copy of any notices that have been filed with the Employment Service (Arbetsförmedlingen) under the first and second paragraphs of Section 2a of the Act (1974:13) Concerning Certain Measures to Promote Employment. SFS 2007:402

16 §

Any party who wishes to negotiate shall serve a demand for negotiations upon the other party. If the other party so requests, the demand shall be in writing and shall state the matter about which negotiations are being requested.
In circumstances other than those referred to in Sections 11 - 13, negotiations meetings shall, unless otherwise agreed upon by the parties, be held within two weeks of receipt by the other party of a demand for negotiations, where the other party is an individual employer or a local employees' organisation, and otherwise within three weeks of receipt of such demand by the other party. In addition, the parties may agree in respect of a time and place for the negotiations.
Negotiations shall be conducted expeditiously. If a party so requests, minutes shall be kept, which shall be approved by both parties. Unless otherwise agreed to by the parties, negotiations shall be deemed to be concluded when a party who has fulfilled his duty to negotiate has given the other party notice in writing that he is withdrawing from the negotiations. SFS 1976:580

17 §

An employee who has been appointed to represent his organisation at negotiations may not be refused reasonable leave of absence in order to take part in those negotiations. SFS 1976:580

Damages and other sanctions

54 §

Unless otherwise provided below, an employer, an employee, or an organisation in breach of this Act or a collective bargaining agreement shall pay compensation for any loss that is incurred. SFS 1976:580

55 §

In assessing whether, and to what extent, a person has suffered loss, consideration shall also be given to such person's interest in compliance with statutory provisions or provisions in the collective bargaining agreement and to factors other than those of purely economic significance. SFS 1976:580

Employment Protection Act (1982:80)

This is a translation and the Swedish version takes precedence.

Notice of termination by the employer

7 §

Notice of termination by the employer must be based on objective grounds.
Objective grounds for notice of termination do not exist where it is reasonable to require the employer to provide other work in his service for the employee.
The transfer of an undertaking, a business or a part of a business under Section 6 b shall not, per se, constitute objective grounds for giving notice of termination of employment. This prohibition shall not, however, prevent an employer from giving notice of termination of employment as a consequence of economic, technical or organisational reasons that include changes to the workforce.
Notice of termination that is based on circumstances relating to the employee personally may not be based solely on circumstances that were known to the employer for more than two months before notice was given under Section 30 or, if no such notice was given, two months before the notice of termination. However, the employer may base the notice of termination entirely on circumstances known to him for more than two months if upon request by the employee or with the consent of the employee the employer has delayed in providing the information or giving notice of termination or where there are extraordinary reasons for invoking such circumstances. SFS 1994:1685

8 §

Notice of termination by the employer must be given in writing.
In the notice of termination, the employer must state the procedure to be followed by the employee in the event the employee wishes to claim that the notice of termination is invalid or to claim damages as a consequence of the termination. Such notice shall also state whether or not the employee has rights of priority concerning re-employment. Information shall also be included in the notice, where applicable, that notification is required in order for the employee to exercise such rights. SFS 1982:80

9 §

The employer is obligated, upon request by the employee, to state the circumstances on which the notice of termination is based. This statement must be in writing, where the employee so requests. SFS 1982:80

10 §

Notice of termination must be delivered to an employee personally. Where this cannot reasonably be required, notice may instead be posted by registered letter to the employee's last known address.
Notice of termination shall be deemed effective when received by the employee. Where the employee cannot be reached and notice of termination has been dispatched by letter according to the first paragraph, notice of termination shall be deemed effective 10 days after the letter was submitted to the post office for delivery. If the employee is on holiday, notice of termination shall be deemed effective not earlier than the day after the holiday ends. SFS 1982:80

Period of notice of termination

11 §

The minimum period of notice for both employer and employee shall be one month. The employee is entitled to notice of termination of employment of

- two months, if the aggregate length of the employment with the employer is at least two years but less than four years,
- three months, if the aggregate length of the employment with the employer is at least four years but less than six years,
- four months, if the aggregate length of the employment with the employer is at least six years but less than eight years,
- five months, if the aggregate length of the employment with the employer is at least eight years but less than ten years, and
- six months, if the aggregate length of the employment with the employer is at least ten years.

If an employee who is on parental leave under Section 4 or 5 of the Parental Leave Act (SFS 1995:584) is given notice of termination due to shortage of work, the period of notice shall start to run

- when the employee has completely or partially resumed work, or
- when the employee should have returned to work under the notice of parental leave that applies when the notice of termination is given.

SFS 2015:759

Pay and other benefits during the period following notice of termination

12 §

An employee who has been given notice is entitled to retain pay and other employment benefits during the period of notice, notwithstanding that the employee is not assigned any duties or is assigned duties different from those the employee previously performed. (SFS 1984:1008)SFS 1984:1008

13 §

Where the employer has stated that the employee need not be available for work following notice of termination or need only work for part of the period of notice any income earned by the employee from other employment during the same period may be deducted by the employer from benefits payable under Section 12, first paragraph. The employer is also entitled to deduct income that the employee obviously could have earned from other suitable employment during this period. SFS 1993:718

14 §

An employee who has been given notice of termination may not be transferred to another locality during the period of notice, if the employee's opportunities of seeking new employment are thereby impaired to an extent that is not insignificant.
An employee who has received notice of termination is also entitled, during the period of notice, to reasonable leave of absence from the employment with full employment benefits in order to visit an employment agency or otherwise seek work. SFS 1982:80

Order of priority in connection with termination of employment

22 §

In the event of notice of termination on the grounds of shortage of work, the employer shall observe the following rules on priority.
Before order of termination is determined, an employer with at most ten employees, irrespective of the number of in the group subject to order of priority rules, may exempt at most two employees who, in the opinion of the employer, are of particular importance for the future activities. When computing the number of employees at the employer, employees referred to in Section 1 are not included. The or those employees who are exempted have priority for continued employment.
Where the employer has several operational units, the order of termination shall be determined separately within each unit. The circumstance alone that one employee has his workplace at his home, does not mean that the workplace comprises a separate operational unit. If the employer is, or is usually, bound by a collective bargaining agreement, a special order of termination shall be established for each agreement

sector. Where, under circumstances as mentioned above, there are several production units in the same locality, a single order of termination shall be drawn up for all the units in the locality that fall within the agreement sector of an organisation of employees, provided the organisation makes a request to this effect not later than the time for negotiations under Section 29.
The order of termination for those employees who are not exempted is determined on the basis of each employee's total time of employment with the employer. Employees with longer employment times shall have priority over employees with shorter employment times. In the event of equal employment times, priority shall be given to the older employee. Where it is only possible to offer continued work to an employee with the employer following a re-location of the employee, priority shall be contingent on the employee possessing satisfactory qualifications for the continued work. (SFS 2000:763)SFS 2000:763

23 §

An employee who has reduced working capacity and who has, therefore, been given special duties by the employer shall be given priority for continued work, notwithstanding the rules on priority, where such can be accomplished without serious inconvenience to the employer. SFS 1982:80

24 §

repealed by *SFS 1984:1008*

Rights of priority for re-employment, etc.

25 §

Employees whose employment has been terminated as a consequence of shortage of work shall have rights of priority for re-employment in the business in which they were previously employed. These rights shall also apply with respect to employees who have been employed for a fixed term as provided in Section 5 and who have not been given continued employment due to a shortage of work. The right to priority, however, shall be contingent upon the employee having been employed by the employer for a total of more than twelve months during the last three years or, in the case of a former seasonal employee's right to priority for new seasonal employment, six months during the past two years, provided the employee possesses satisfactory qualifications for the new employment.
The right to priority shall apply from time of the notice of termination or when notice was given or should have been given under Section 15, first paragraph, and thereafter until nine months from the date that the employment ceased. With respect to seasonal employment, rights of priority shall instead apply from the time when notice was given or should have been given under Section 15, second paragraph, and thereafter until

nine months have elapsed from the commencement of the new season. Where during the above-mentioned periods of time the undertaking, the business or the part of the business in which the activities are conducted has been transferred to a new employer by such a transfer as is subject to Section 6 b, the right to priority shall apply with respect to the new employer. Rights of priority shall also apply in circumstances where the previous employer was put into bankruptcy.
Where the employer has several production units, or if the employer's business involves several collective bargaining agreement sectors, the rights of priority shall apply to employment within the unit and the collective bargaining agreement sector to which the employee belonged at the termination of the previous employment. Where, under such circumstances, there are several production units in the same locality, priority within the collective bargaining agreement sector of an organisation of employees shall apply to all of the employer's production units in the locality, provided such a request is made by the organisation not later than the time for negotiations as provided for in Section 32. SFS 2007:390

25 a §

Notwithstanding Section 25, a part-time employee who has notified his or her employer that he or she desires to have employment at a higher level of occupation, though at most full-time, has a priority right to such employment. This right is contingent upon the employer's need of labour being satisfied by the part-time employee being employed at a higher level of occupation and that the part-time employee possesses satisfactory qualifications for the new work tasks.
If an employer has several production units, the priority right applies to employment at the unit where the employee is engaged part-time.
The priority right does not apply as regards a person who is entitled to re-allocation of work under Section 7, second paragraph. SFS 2006:440

26 §

Where several employees are entitled to priority for re-employment under Section 25 or priority right to employment at a higher level of occupation under Section 25 a, the order in which they are inter se to be re-employed shall be determined on the basis of each employee's total period of employment with the employer. Employees who have longer periods of employment shall have priority over employees with shorter periods of employment. In the event of equal periods of employment, the employee who is senior in age shall be given priority. (SFS 1996:1424) SFS 1996:1424

27 §

Where notice regarding the right of priority to re-employment has been given under Section 8, second paragraph or Section 16, second paragraph, the right of priority may not be exercised by the employee prior to notice by the employee to the employer of his intention to exercise such right.

An employee who accepts an offer of re-employment shall not be obligated to commence the new employment until after a reasonable period of transition.

Where an employee declines an offer of re-employment that the employee should reasonably have accepted, any right to priority shall be forfeited. SFS 1982:80

Damages

38 §

An employer who violates this Act shall be liable for damages for loss suffered by the employee as well as pay and other employment benefits to which the employee may be entitled. An employee who fails to comply with the notice obligations mentioned in Section 11, first paragraph, shall be liable for damages to the employer.

Damages under the first paragraph may comprise both compensation for losses sustained and for violation of the Act. Compensation for losses in respect of the period following the cessation of employment may not, under any circumstances, exceed the amount mentioned in Section 39.

Where reasonable, damages may be reduced, in whole or in part. SFS 1982:80

39 §

Where an employer refuses to comply with a court order that notice of termination or a summary dismissal is invalid, or that a fixed-term employment shall be valid for an indefinite term, the employment relationship shall be deemed to have been dissolved. As a consequence of the employer's refusal to comply with the court order, the employer shall pay damages to the employee under the following provisions.

Damages are to be determined according to the employee's total period of employment with the employer at the time of dissolution of the employment relationship, and shall correspond to the following amounts:

- 16 months' pay for less than five years of employment;
- 24 months' pay for at least five years but less than ten years of employment;
- 32 months' pay for ten or more years of employment;

Damages may not be determined, however, in such a manner that such damages are calculated on the basis of a greater number of months than have actually been commenced with the employer. Where the employee has been employed by the employer for less than six months, the amount assessed shall correspond to six months' pay. SFS 2007:389

The Development Agreement

This is a translation and the Swedish version takes precedence.

§ 12 Employee consultant

Experience and competence

Under this agreement the employee representatives in the company are given the opportunity to partake in the appraisals of the company's economic situation and future. Such participation presumes a development of competence within these areas and responsibility to make your own judgements. The company contributes to education. In such situations as mentioned below special efforts may be needed to facilitate for the local unions to handle problems at hand.

Employee Consultant

The local unions are entitled to engage an employee consultant for a specific assignment before approaching changes with material importance for the company's economy and the employees' employment. The purpose is to give the unions an opportunity to analyse documentation and decide on the questions brought to life by the change. In this capacity, consultants may not be given negotiating assignments.
Employee consultant may be an outside expert (external consultant) or an employee (in-house consultant).
In other cases, not mentioned here an employee consultant may be appointed if the local parties are in agreement thereof. If an agreement is not reached, party may refer the question to the Council for development matters for an opinion.

Comment:

In the case when the unions partake in project work or in other ways mentioned in § 8, the experts hired by the company are assumed to provide supporting documents for a comprehensive illustration of the questions in connection with what has been expressed from all engaged in the project work.

Decision on Consultant

The company will guarantee reasonable costs for a consultant. Decision to appoint a consultant shall be preceded by negotiations with the employer. The scope of the assignment, contents and costs are to be specified and suggestions for vote based on personality shall be submitted. Agreement is to be the aim.

Competence

External consultant shall be a certified accountant or according to the unions have the necessary theoretical and practical competence.

Disqualification

Person with interests in breach of the company's commercial interests may not be appointed employee consultant. Person being employee consultant in another company may not be appointed without the approval of the employers' and the labour organisation. When the organisations assess the matter of disqualification, unnecessary hindrance may not be laid down.

Information from the management

Under the employment act and under this agreement the management is to provide the employee consultant assistance and information in the extent required for the assignment

Union representatives

The local unions appoint representatives among the employees to whom the consultant shall provide assistance and information.
The above mentioned representatives can with the management update information from the consultant to other local union representatives.
On request from the management the local union representatives shall inform the management on the consultants' work.

Confidentiality

The company or an individual may be harmed if the employee consultant passes on information acquired that should have been kept confidential.
Together, the local unions and the employer shall enter into an agreement with an external employee which is to include provisions on confidentiality and sanctions for violations of the confidentiality provision.

Comments

This provision aims at companies with at least 50 employees. If the local parties are in agreement, there is no bar to appointing an employee consultant in companies with 25 to 50 employees. In such case the rules in this provision applies.
The central parties shall draw up guidelines for confidentiality concerning employee consultants.

Employment Encouragement Act

This is a translation and the Swedish version takes precedence.

Notice of reduction in operations

1§ An employer aiming at executing a reduction in operations under §§ 2 or 3 shall within stipulated time give notice in writing to the Swedish Public Employment Service, if at least five employees are affected by the reduction. This also applies if the reduction during a period of 90 days may be assumed to lead to the number of terminations amounting to at least twenty in total.

2§ Notice of such reduction that may lead to termination is to be left

1. at least two months before the reduction, if the maximum number of employees affected by termination is 25,
2. at least four months before the reduction, if the number of employees affected by termination is more than 25 but less than 100,
3. at least six months before the reduction, if the number of employees affected by termination is more than 100.

2a A notice under 2 § above shall contain all relevant information on terminations planned and in particular contain information on

1. grounds for terminations planned
2. number of employees contemplated for termination and to what categories they belong
3. number of employees normally employed and to what categories they belong
4. time of the reduction to be executed and the period of time during which the terminations are to be executed. As soon as possible, however no later than one month before the reduction, the employer is to complement the notice in writing with

1. information on which employees being affected by the reduction,
2. relevant information on negotiations conducted before the terminations under 11 § Employment (Co-Determination in the Workplace) Act (1976:580) or under corresponding collective bargaining agreement, and
3. a copy of the written notice delivered to the opposite party under 11 § second paragraph of the Employment (Co-Determination in the Workplace) Act (1976:580)

The Swedish Public Employment Service may order the employer under penalty of a fine to fulfil his obligations.

CHAPTER 28

Collective Dismissals in the United Kingdom*

Alan C. Neal

§28.01 INTRODUCTION

Historically, the regulation of dismissals at the initiative of the employer in the United Kingdom was either left to the operation of normal civil contract rules or, in situations involving a 'public' component, might be subject to the rules of administrative law.

Thus, in the great majority of cases, where the relationship between employer and worker was subject to the normal civil law rules as they affected the contract of employment, the classic statement of the position under the Common Law could be summed up in the words of Lord Denning, in the 1969 case of *Richardson v. Koefod*, to the effect that, '...in the absence of express stipulation, the rule is that every contract of service is terminable by reasonable notice'.[1] Two points follow from this statement: (1) that it is possible to make express provision between the parties to the contract of service as regards the due notice required to terminate the relationship; and (2) that in all other cases the notice required by the Common Law will be 'reasonable notice'.

It therefore comes as no surprise to learn that, prior to intervention by the legislator in this area of employment relations, the notion of termination of employment at the initiative of the employer 'based on the operational requirements of the undertaking, establishment or service' had no place in the framework of regulation concerning termination of the employment relationship in the United Kingdom.[2] Thus,

* Manuscript completed on 30 November 2015 and last revised on 11 December 2015.
1. *Richardson v. Koefod*, [1969] 3 All ER 1264.
2. The terminology used in this area varies. Thus, the expression 'based on the operational requirements of the undertaking, establishment or service' is drawn from ILO Convention No. 158, Termination of Employment Convention 1982, Article 4, and was used in the earlier ILO Recommendation No. 119, Termination of Employment Recommendation 1963. A widely utilized

at a time when the ILO was preparing the ground for what eventually became the 1963 Recommendation (No. 119) concerning Termination of Employment at the Initiative of the Employer,[3] introducing the notion of termination 'based on the operational requirements of the undertaking, establishment or service' (Article 2(1)), such an approach to classification of employer initiated termination of employment constituted entirely novel ground for United Kingdom labour lawyers.

§28.02 THE REGIME INTRODUCED BY THE REDUNDANCY PAYMENTS ACT 1965

Indeed, only in 1965, in the wake of the adoption of ILO Recommendation No. 119, was any such concept introduced into United Kingdom labour law, in the shape of what has remained the modern notion in English Law of 'redundancy', by way of a statute enacted by the newly elected Labour government under Prime Minister Harold Wilson. That piece of legislation, in itself, reflected the beginning of what was to become a highly significant shift away from the previous approach of leaving regulation of the individual employment relationship to the normal Common Law rules of contract, in favour of the prescription of 'individual employment protection rights' through statute.[4]

The definition established for this new phenomenon of a 'redundancy dismissal' was set out in the Redundancy Payments Act 1965,[5] in terms that a dismissal was to be taken to be by reason of redundancy if the dismissal was:

---

term is that regularly found in United Kingdom law – 'redundancy' – found initially in the Redundancy Payments Act 1965, and now consolidated into section 98(2)(c) of the Employment Rights Act 1996. The expression 'termination of an employment contract at the initiative of the employer for reasons not related to the individual employee' is used by the report prepared for the European Commission, *Termination of Employment Relationships: Legal Situation in the Member States of the European Union* (updated version, Luxembourg 2006), although this is to be found under the general heading of 'Dismissal for economic reasons' (*see* at paragraph 3.3.4, p. 80). For recent explicit acknowledgement of the linguistic conundrum, *see* the Opinion of Advocate-General Wahl in joined Cases C-182/13, C-392/13 and C-80/14, at paragraph 37 (Note 16).

3. *Supra*.
4. The provisions introduced by the Redundancy Payments Act 1965 came into being shortly after the enactment of a Contracts of Employment Act 1963. However, with the enactment of the Industrial Relations Act 1971 a significant regulatory shift took place – heralding the modern era of pervasive legislative intervention into the field of individual employment relationships. What has, in the course of sixty years, developed into a formidable body of legislation was famously dubbed the 'floor of rights' for persons working in the United Kingdom labour market. *See* Lord Wedderburn, *The Worker and the Law* (3rd edition, Harmondsworth 1986), reflecting the same author's description of the Redundancy Payments Act 1965 as providing 'a valuable floor below which no worker (with two years' continuous service) may fall'. An early broad-brush presentation of the 'floor of rights' approach in comparative perspective was made by *S. Deakin*, 'The Floor of Rights in European Labour Law', (1990) 15 *New Zealand Journal of Industrial Relations* 219, while the notion remains in use and received express consideration in 2006 by the United Kingdom House of Lords Select Committee on Europe (Twenty-second Report), at paragraphs 108-111.
5. Contemporary evaluation of the 1965 Act can be found in *P. O'Higgins*, 'The Redundancy Payments Act, 1965', (1965) 23 *The Cambridge Law Journal* 222 and in *K. Wedderburn*, 'Trade Disputes Act 1965: Redundancy Payments Act 1965', (1966) 29 *Modern Law Review* 58, at 55ff.

attributable wholly or mainly to...the fact that the requirements of that business for employees to carry out work of a particular kind, or for employees to carry out work of a particular kind in the place where he was so employed, have ceased or diminished or are expected to cease or diminish.[6]

Thus, as summarized by the late Professor Wedderburn at the time:[7]

'A qualified worker is entitled to his redundancy payment (a) if dismissed by reason of redundancy or (b) laid off or kept on short time for the prescribed periods. He falls within (a) when his dismissal is '*attributable wholly or mainly*' to the fact either that his employer ceases temporarily or permanently, or intends so to cease, to carry on the business (either altogether or in the '*place*' of his employment), or that the requirements of that business for employees to carry out "*work of a particular kind*' have *ceased* or *diminished*, or are expected to do so.

The same commentator went on to observe that:

Plainly this definition – especially the words italicized – can provide a lawyers' field-day. The difficulties will undoubtedly be eased, however, by section 9, which provides that on any reference to a tribunal, an employee who is dismissed by his employer shall, unless the contrary be proved, be *presumed* to have been dismissed by reason of redundancy.

The modern definition of 'redundancy' for the purposes of individual dismissals is now to be found in section 139 of the Employment Rights Act 1996, which provides that:

For the purposes of this Act an employee who is dismissed shall be taken to be dismissed by reason of redundancy if the dismissal is wholly or mainly attributable to —

(a) the fact that his employer has ceased or intends to cease —
  (i) to carry on the business for the purposes of which the employee was employed by him, or
  (ii) to carry on that business in the place where the employee was so employed, or
(b) the fact that the requirements of that business —
  (i) for employees to carry out work of a particular kind, or
  (ii) for employees to carry out work of a particular kind in the place where the employee was employed by the employer, have ceased or diminished or are expected to cease or diminish.

Related provision is made so that, for the purposes of the section 1 definition, 'the business of the employer together with the business or businesses of his associated employers shall be treated as one (unless either of the conditions specified in paragraphs (a) and (b) of that subsection would be satisfied without so treating

6. Section 1(2)(b).
7. *Ibid*, at pp. 60-61.

them)',[8] while the expressions '*cease*' and '*diminish*' mean 'cease and diminish either permanently or temporarily and for whatever reason'.[9]

Case law developed since the coming into force of the Redundancy Payments Act 1965 clarified a number of issues arising in relation to those basic definitions within the framework of the new arrangements, and much of that case-law remains relevant and current today.[10] However, the 1965 regime related only to individual dismissals, and this individual approach continued after 1972 when new provisions on 'unfair dismissal' contained in the Industrial Relations Act 1971 were brought into force.

Mention of the 'unfair dismissal' regime is significant, given that 'redundancy' is included as one of the possible list of 'justifiable' reasons for termination within the framework of that particular protection.[11] It is also relevant because another category of 'potentially justifiable reasons' known as 'some other substantial reason of a kind such as to justify the dismissal of an employee holding the position which the employee held' (SOSR) has been developed to encompass individual 'economic dismissals' driven more by the interests of the enterprise than by matters touching the worker as an individual.[12]

§28.03 'COLLECTIVE DISMISSALS' IN THE WAKE OF DIRECTIVE 75/129/EEC[13]

It was only with the introduction of provisions reflecting obligations at the level of the EU - then the European Economic Community (EEC) - that any formal regulatory notion of 'collective dismissals' entered into the frame of reference of United Kingdom labour lawyers. Thus, as a member of the EEC since 1973,[14] the United Kingdom was

8. Section 139(2).
9. Section 139(6).
10. For a thoroughgoing treatment of the case-law developments in this context, *see inter alia* S. Deakin & G. Morris, *Labour Law* (6th edition, Oxford 2012), Chapter 5. The 'classic' treatment of these developments was provided by C. Grunfeld, *The Law of Redundancy* (2nd edition, London 1980).
11. *See* section 98(2)(c).
12. *See* section 98(1)(b) of the Employment Rights Act 1996, and the case-law developed out of that provision.
13. For detailed implementation reports on the United Kingdom position in relation to Directive 75/129/EEC and its successors, set in the context of implementation measures undertaken by other Member States, *see inter alia* Commission of the European Communities, *Report by the Commission on progress with regard to implementation of the Directive on the approximation of the laws of the Member States relating to collective redundancies (Council Directive 75/129/EEC of 17 February 1975)*, SEC (91) 1639 final (Brussels, 13 September 1991); and *Commission report on the implementation of Directive 92/56/EEC of 24 June 1992, amending Directive 75/129/EEC of 17 February 1975 on collective redundancies; consolidated by Council Directive 98/59/EC of 20 July 1998* (Luxembourg 1999).
14. The United Kingdom had entered into arrangements to join the founding EEC Member States, along with Denmark, the Republic of Ireland and Norway, by way of the Treaty concerning the Accession of the Kingdom of Denmark, Ireland, the Kingdom of Norway and the United Kingdom to the EEC and the EAEC, signed in Brussels on 22 January 1972. Following the decision of Norway not to proceed with its application for membership, the three new Member States joined with effect from 1 January 1973, and the terms of that Accession Treaty were adjusted accordingly. *See* Council Decision of the European Communities of 1 January 1973

party to the enactment of what eventually become Council Directive 75/129/EEC of 17 February 1975 on the approximation of the laws of the Member States relating to collective redundancies.[15] That measure emerged during a period when 'social policy' regulation at the European level developed on the basis of unanimous agreement between the then nine members of the EEC.[16] Specific legislative initiatives in that field were themselves elaborated within the framework of a series of 'Social Action Programmes' developed by the European Commission, the first of which – issued in 1974 – included the opening of a path towards an eventual instrument dealing with issues arising in the context of 'collective dismissals'.[17]

Following adoption of the 1975 Directive, a period of two years was provided for implementation by the Member State addressees,[18] and the United Kingdom responded to that obligation by introducing statutory arrangements under the heading of 'Procedure for Handling Redundancies'.[19] Those provisions introduced new duties in two key respects: (1) a duty in designated circumstances on 'an employer proposing to dismiss as redundant an employee of a description in respect of which an independent trade union is recognized by him' to 'consult representatives of that trade union about the

adjusting the instruments concerning the accession of new Member States to the European Communities (OJ 1973 No L 2/1, 1.1.73).

15. OJ 1975 L 48, p. 29.
16. *See* the legislative powers granted to this area through Article 100 of the Treaty of Rome, providing that: 'The Council, acting by means of a unanimous vote on a proposal of the Commission, shall issue directives for the approximation of such legislative and administrative provisions of the Member States as have a direct incidence on the establishment or functioning of the Common Market.' The eventual Council Directive 75/129/EEC additionally relied upon the provisions of Article 117 of the Treaty, declaring that: 'Member States hereby agree upon the necessity to promote improvement of the living and working conditions of labour so as to permit the equalisation of such conditions in an upward direction ... .They consider that such a development will result not only from the functioning of the Common Market which will favour the harmonisation of social systems, but also from the procedures provided for under this Treaty and from the approximation of legislative and administrative provisions.'
17. Thus, the Commission considered that '...a directive on collective dismissals (Action 1.7) should be adopted by the Council as a matter of urgent priority in order to reduce job insecurity, which is today a potent and evident cause of industrial unrest and suspicion'. The particular initiative was contained in the Social Action Programme 1974. *See* Council Resolution of 21 January 1974 concerning a social action programme (OJ C 13, 12.2.1974, p. 1), together with the Social Action Programme itself (*Bulletin of the European Commission*, Supplement 2/74). This constituted the first of a series of (normally five-yearly) policy 'pathway' documents evolved within the European Commission. Although this approach to setting out short/medium-term regulatory policy in the social field has not been entirely consistent and without 'hiccups', it has only been with the adoption of the so-called 'Europe 2020' strategy that the notionally five-yearly cycle has given way to more nebulous longer-term declarations of intent. *See* Communication from the Commission, *Europe 2020: A Strategy for Smart, Sustainable and Inclusive Growth*, (COM(2010) 2020 final (Brussels, 3.3.2010). A background to the policy debate leading to the 1974 Social Action Programme was provided in the European Commission's communication, *Preliminary guidelines for a Social Policy Program in the Community*, COM(71) 600 final (17 March 1971) – a document which, of course, was elaborated before the eventual accession of the United Kingdom to the EEC.
18. Article 6.
19. Contained in Part IV of the Employment Protection Act 1975, in sections 99-107. A thoughtful consideration of the context for that 1975 Act can be found in *K. Wedderburn*, 'The Employment Protection Act 1975. Collective Aspects', (1976) 39 *Modern Law Review* 169 and in *M. Freedland*, 'The Employment Protection Act 1975. Individual Aspects', (1976) 39 *Modern Law Review* 561.

dismissal…';[20] and (2) a duty to notify the Secretary of State (relevant government Minister) in writing where an employer was proposing to dismiss as redundant (a) 100 or more employees at one establishment within a period of ninety days or less; or (b) ten or more employees at one establishment within a period of thirty days or less'.[21]

[A] The Duty to Consult

The consultation requirements imposed by the original section 99 of the Employment Protection Act 1975 related only to an 'independent trade union' which was 'recognized' by the employer at the time of the proposed collective dismissal. Both the expressions 'independent' and 'recognized' as they applied to a trade union carried technical meanings under the legislative framework introduced into the United Kingdom in 1975.

Thus, in consequence of institutional arrangements introduced by that 1975 Act, an 'independent' trade union was declared to enjoy that status if it was in possession of a 'certificate of independence' issued by an officer known as the 'Certification Officer'.[22]

Meanwhile, by virtue of section 126(1) – the 'interpretation' section for the 1975 Act – 'recognition' was given a meaning by reference to provisions in section 11 of the statute.[23] Thus, the notion of trade union 'recognition' was declared to be 'the recognition of the union by an employer, or two or more associated employers, to any extent, for the purpose of collective bargaining'. In order to overcome the practical problem arising in a situation where the employer refused to 'recognize' a trade union, the 1975 Act established a procedure for obtaining an 'award' *in lieu* of recognition – which effectively consisted of a declaration of non-compliance against the recalcitrant employer coupled potentially with an imposition of terms and conditions of employment determined by a body known as the Central Arbitration Committee (CAC).[24]

This situation operated throughout the period in office of the minority Labour government which enacted the 1975 legislation and its successor which was returned to office with a parliamentary majority following elections in 1976. However, upon the

---

20. Section 99(1).
21. Section 100(1).
22. The procedure for seeking such a certificate of independence was set out in section 8 of the Act. Section 7 provided for the appointment of that officer. In relation to the role of the Certification Officer generally, *see D. Cockburn*, 'The Conciliation Officer', in L. Dickens & A. Neal (*eds*), *The Changing Institutional Face of British Employment Relations* (Alphen aan den Rijn 2006), pp. 91*ff*.
23. For consideration of the new post-1975 recognition arrangements, *see inter alia L. Dickens*, 'A.C.A.S. and the Union Recognition Procedure', (1976) 7 *Industrial Law Journal* 160.
24. *See* the arrangements set out in sections 11-16 of the Act. In relation to the activities of the Central Arbitration Committee, *see S. Gouldstone & G. Morris*, 'The Central Arbitration Committee', in L. Dickens & A. Neal (*eds*), *The Changing Institutional Face of British Employment Relations* (Alphen aan den Rijn 2006), pp. 79*ff*. For the principles developed through the early case-law on the provisions of the 1975 Act, *see A. Neal*, 'Trade Union Recognition for the purposes of the consultation requirements of Part IV of the Employment Protection Act 1975', (1979) 8 *Industrial Law Journal* 37.

election to office in 1979 of a Conservative government under Prime Minister Margaret Thatcher, this changed dramatically.

One of the first actions undertaken by the new government was to repeal the 'recognition' provisions of the 1975 Act, leaving nothing in their place.[25] In consequence, it became open for employers not only to refuse to extend recognized status to trade unions, but also to embark actively upon 'derecognition' of trade unions which hitherto had enjoyed recognized status. This state of affairs rapidly attracted attention and gave rise to concerns at a time when the tide of regulatory arrangements in the United Kingdom was widely perceived (in particular, on the parts of workers' organizations) as reflecting a 'one way street' in the direction of limiting the scope for collectivism and 'trade union power' in what had traditionally been characterized as a system developed in the space left by 'legal abstentionism' and a 'collective laissez-faire' approach to the autonomy of the collective actors.

In time, this led to action being taken by the European Commission against the United Kingdom government before the European Court of Justice – with the objection being raised that the repeal of the statutory recognition provisions to support trade unions faced with unwilling bargaining counterparty employers left such unions with no effective means to enforce the consultation obligations established by Directive 75/129/EEC in relation to proposed collective dismissals.[26] Thus, in Case C-383/92,[27] the Commission claimed that '...the United Kingdom has failed to fulfil its obligations under Articles 2 and 3 of the directive in not providing a mechanism for the designation of workers' representatives in an undertaking where the employer refuses to recognize such representatives'.[28]

The outcome of the Court's consideration in that litigation came as little surprise to the United Kingdom government, and represented a comprehensive rejection of the post-1980 arrangements for 'recognized trade unions' as constituting an adequate

25. Effected by section 19 of the Employment Act 1980.
26. This was particularly the case because there would therefore be no 'workers' representatives' as envisaged by Article 2 of the Directive. The same objection was raised in relation to the (broadly parallel) consultation provisions contained in Council Directive 77/187/EEC of 14 February 1977 on the approximation of the laws of the Member States relating to the safeguarding of employees' rights in the event of transfers of undertakings, businesses or parts of businesses – which makes reference to 'representatives of the employees' (*see* Article 6 in conjunction with Article 2).
27. Case C-383/92, *Commission of the European Communities v. United Kingdom of Great Britain and Northern Ireland*. The same issue concerning the absence of an appropriate channel for identifying and facilitating consultation with workers' representatives was also raised in relation to Directive 77/187/EEC (the 'transfers of undertakings' protection), and that matter, brought before the Court of Justice in Case C-382/92, was dealt with in parallel with Case C-383/92. Both judgments were delivered by the Court on 8 June 1994. It may also be mentioned that the United Kingdom government had formed a view that an identical issue arose in the context of the 'framework' Directive 89/391/EEC, on health and safety – although no infringement proceedings in relation to that Directive had been launched by the Commission.
28. *See* paragraph 13 of the judgment. The objections raised by the Commission in this case had been well rehearsed in the earlier implementation report: Commission of the European Communities, *Report by the Commission on progress with regard to implementation of the Directive on the approximation of the laws of the Member States relating to collective redundancies (Council Directive 75/129/EEC of 17 February 1975)*, SEC (91) 1639 final (Brussels, 13 September 1991).

means for compliance with the requirements of the Directive.[29] It also drew attention to a number of other areas in respect of which the United Kingdom provisions introduced by the Employment Protection Act 1975 were considered by the Court not adequately to give implementing effect to the requirements laid down in Directive 75/129/EEC.

Thus, in a second complaint, the Commission argued that the notion of 'redundancy' utilized by the Employment Protection Act 1975 was unacceptably narrower in scope than the Directive, since it was limited to 'cases where there is a cessation or reduction of the business of an undertaking or a decline in demand for work of a particular type'. It was pointed out that the Directive applied to 'collective redundancies' – 'that is to say, dismissals for one or more reasons not related to the individual workers concerned, which covers cases other than "redundancy"'.[30] Unsurprisingly, the United Kingdom government conceded the shortcoming on this point, thereby paving the way for the Court's condemnation on that issue as well.

Nor did the United Kingdom government resist the Commission's third complaint, to the effect that the purported implementation through the Employment Protection Act 1975 was deficient '...since it merely requires an employer to consult trade union representatives about proposed dismissals, to 'consider' representations made by such representatives and, if he rejects them, to "state his reasons"...', as compared with the requirement in Article 2(1) of the Directive that workers' representatives are to be consulted 'with a view to reaching an agreement' – with the added clarification in Article 2(2) that such consultations must 'at least, cover ways and means of avoiding collective redundancies or reducing the number of workers affected, and mitigating the consequences'.[31]

Finally, the Commission's fourth complaint – concerning the adequacy of the penalties provided by the Employment Protection Act 1975 for non-compliance on the part of an employer – was also upheld in the face of non-resistance by the United Kingdom government.[32]

---

29. The operative part of the judgment declared that: '...by failing to provide for the designation of workers' representatives where an employer does not agree to it, by laying down statutory provisions designed to implement Council Directive 75/129/EEC of 17 February 1975 on the approximation of the laws of the Member States relating to collective redundancies that are narrower in scope than the directive, by not requiring an employer contemplating collective redundancies to consult the workers' representatives with a view to reaching an agreement and in relation to the matters specified in the directive, and by failing to provide for effective sanctions in the event of failure to consult the workers' representatives as required by the directive, the United Kingdom has failed to fulfil its obligations under the directive and under Article 5 of the EEC Treaty'.
30. *See* paragraph 29.
31. *See* paragraph 34.
32. The Court of Justice (at paragraphs 41 and 42) made clear that '...it follows from section 102(3) of the EPA that a 'protective award' which an employer may, in an appropriate case, be ordered to make to a dismissed employee if he has failed to comply with the obligation to consult and inform the workers' representatives provided for in that statute may be set off against any amounts which he may otherwise be required to pay to that employee under the latter's contract of employment or in respect of breach of that contract, and, conversely, that any amounts so payable to the employee may be set off against a 'protective award' if the amount of that award is greater', and that 'By providing that a 'protective award' may be set off in full or in part against

In the wake of those conclusions by the Court of Justice in relation to implementation of Directive 75/129/EEC through the 1975 Act, amending legislation was introduced through The Collective Redundancies and Transfer of Undertakings (Protection of Employment) (Amendment) Regulations 1995.[33] By this time, the 1975 Act's provisions had been consolidated into the Trade Union and Labour Relations (Consolidation) Act 1992, which had absorbed sections 11-16 of the Employment Protection Act 1975 into new sections 188-198.[34]

Thus, the basic duty of consultation (now set out in section 188 of the 1992 Act) was completely recast, with an extension of the obligation to involve consultation with 'all the persons who are appropriate representatives of any of the employees who may be so dismissed',[35] and a stipulation in a new section 188(2) that:

> The consultation shall include consultation about ways of — (a) avoiding the dismissals, (b) reducing the numbers of employees to be dismissed, and (c) mitigating the consequences of the dismissals, and shall be undertaken by the employer with a view to reaching agreement with the appropriate representatives.

Furthermore, the duty to consult had already been amended to relate to a specific notion of 'redundancy' developed for the purposes of the collective dismissals procedure.[36] Thus - as is now to be found in the current definition contained in section 195(1) of the Trade Union and Labour Relations (Consolidation) Act 1992 - it is provided that:

> In this Chapter references to dismissal as redundant are references to dismissal for a reason not related to the individual concerned or for a number of reasons all of which are not so related.

That notion of 'dismissal as redundant' also attracts - as is the case for the definition of 'redundancy' found in section 139 of the Employment Rights Act 1996 for individual dismissals - a statutory presumption,[37] such that '...where an employee is or is proposed to be dismissed it shall be presumed, unless the contrary is proved, that he is or is proposed to be dismissed as redundant'.

Of particular significance for collective consultation arrangements in the United Kingdom system was the further provision that the notion of 'appropriate representatives of any employees' was henceforth to cover:

---

any amounts otherwise payable by an employer to an employee under the latter's contract of employment or in respect of breach of that contract, the United Kingdom legislation largely deprives that sanction of its practical effect and its deterrent value. Moreover, an employer will not be penalized even moderately or lightly by the sanction except and only to the extent to which the amount of the 'protective award' which he is ordered to make exceeds the sums which he is otherwise required to pay to the person concerned'.

33. S.I. 1995 No. 2587, which came into force on 26 October 1995.
34. The 1995 Regulations also made adjustments to the thresholds governing the scope of the duty to consult. *See* the reformulated section 188(1).
35. Contained in a new section 188(1).
36. By virtue of a substituted section 195, introduced by section 34(5) of the Trade Union Reform and Employment Rights Act 1993.
37. By virtue of section 195(2).

(a) employee representatives elected by them, or (b) if the employees are of a description in respect of which an independent trade union is recognised by the employer, representatives of the trade union, or (in the case of employees who both elect employee representatives and are of such a description) either employee representatives elected by them or representatives of the trade union, as the employer chooses.[38]

Arguably the most controversial aspect of this new arrangement was the introduction – both for the purposes of the collective dismissals procedure and in relation to consultation duties in the event of a proposed transfer of an undertaking – of a 'worker representation' channel additional to, and independent of, traditionally established trade union channels. This approach was deliberately adopted to thwart the widespread expectation amongst United Kingdom trade unions that the outcome of the litigation before the Court of Justice would result in broader statutory representative powers for established trade unions, and was underscored by the reclassification of the relevant representatives from 'trade union representatives' to 'appropriate representatives'. It also involved the introduction of a new (non-trade union) category of statutorily defined 'employee representatives'.[39] In consequence, it was provided that:

For the purposes of this Chapter persons are employee representatives if —

(a) they have been elected by employees for the specific purpose of being consulted by their employer about dismissals proposed by him, or
(b) having been elected by employees (whether before or after dismissals have been proposed by their employer) otherwise than for that specific purpose, it is appropriate (having regard to the purposes for which they were elected) for the employer to consult them about dismissals proposed by him, and (in either case) they are employed by the employer at the time when they are elected.

The technical position was additionally amended in 1999 by The Collective Redundancies and Transfer of Undertakings (Protection of Employment) (Amendment) Regulations of that year,[40] with section 188(1B) of the 1992 Act being substituted, while a newly inserted section 188A set out more detailed requirements in relation to the election of employee representatives.

Seen from a modern perspective, however, the issue of 'recognized' trade unions in the United Kingdom no longer plays such a significant role since the enactment of a statutory mechanism in 1999 for trade unions to seek an order through the courts obliging a recalcitrant employer to grant (full or partial) recognition for collective bargaining purposes. That regime, introduced by the 'New Labour' government of Prime Minister Tony Blair, involves the Central Arbitration Committee (CAC) in determining whether trade union applications for compulsory 'recognition' should be

38. By virtue of a new section 188(1B).
39. Section 196(1) of the 1992 Act, as substituted by Clause 6 of the 1995 Regulations. Those 'employee representatives' were also furnished with protection against detriment or dismissal by reason of either holding such a position or of having participated in an election for any such position.
40. S.I. 1999 No. 1925.

granted, and in monitoring compliance with any orders for recognition made through that process.[41]

Since the turn of the Millennium, further amendments have been made to the domestic United Kingdom provisions, with the most significant changes coming through The Trade Union and Labour Relations (Consolidation) Act 1992 (Amendment) Order 2013,[42] looking to improve implementation of the provisions at the European Union level – by now contained in the updated collective dismissals procedure set out in Council Directive 98/59/EC on the approximation of the laws of the Member States relating to collective redundancies.[43]

That instrument amended the consultation obligation in section 188 of the 1992 Act by reducing from ninety to forty-five the minimum number of days which must elapse before the first dismissal can take effect in cases where the employer is proposing to dismiss 100 or more employees as redundant within a period of ninety days or less. The opportunity was also taken to amend the scope of coverage in relation to fixed-term contracts, with a view to bringing the United Kingdom statutory provisions into line with the decision of the United Kingdom Supreme Court in the case of *University College Union v. University of Stirling.*[44]

---

41. *See* Trade Union and Labour Relations Act 1992, Schedule A1, introduced by the Employment Relations Act 1999. On the recognition arrangements introduced by that 1999 Act, *see*, for example, *B. McArthur*, 'The Efficacy of Statutory Recognition under New Labour: A Comparative Review (Part I)', (2004) 20 *International Journal of Comparative Labour law and Industrial Relations* 399; (Part II), 563.
42. S.I. 2013 No. 763, the provisions of which have applied to proposed collective dismissals made on or after 6 April 2013.
43. The original Council Directive 75/129/EEC was first amended by Council Directive 92/56/EEC of 24 June 1992 amending Directive 75/129/EEC on the approximation of the laws of the Member States relating to collective redundancies, and then repealed and replaced by Council Directive 98/59/EC of 20 July 1998 on the approximation of the laws of the Member States relating to collective redundancies. The most recent United Kingdom provisions purporting to implement provisions required by Directive 98/59/EC are to be found in The Collective Redundancies and Transfer of Undertakings (Protection of Employment) (Amendment) Regulations 2014 (S.I. 2014 No. 16). Effective from 31 January 2014, those provisions deal with the meeting-point between the Directive dealing with collective dismissals and the Directive regulating procedures in the event of transfers of undertakings, businesses or parts of undertakings or businesses (Council Directive 2001/23/EC), and insert new Sections 198A and 198B into the Trade Union and Labour Relations (Consolidation) Act 1992. The effect of those changes (contained in Regulation 3) is to make provision for a transferee to elect to consult, or start to consult, representatives of affected transferring individuals about the transferee's proposed dismissals before a transfer takes place. In what must rate as some of the most unfriendly language to challenge the notion of 'plain English', those provisions set out how sections 188 to 198 of the 1992 Act apply in cases where the transferee has made such an election.
44. *University College Union v. University of Stirling*, [2015] UKSC 26. The judgment of the Supreme Court departed from earlier decisions to the effect that collective consultation obligations did not extend to employees on fixed-term contracts who were dismissed on expiry of the fixed-term contract even where the reason for non-renewal was that the employer was making heavy losses or wanted to strengthen its economic position. *See*, for example, the approach adopted by the Scottish Court of Session in that case (reported at [2014] I.R.L.R. 284), as well as the approach taken by the President of the Employment Appeal Tribunal in the case of *Capital Energy Solutions v. Arnold*, [2015] I.C.R. 611. In consequence of the enactment of The Trade Union and Labour Relations (Consolidation) Act 1992 (Amendment) Order 2013 – which had already come into effect before delivery of the final judgment of the Supreme Court – it was intended that section 282 of the 1992 Act should be amended to exclude the expiry of fixed-term contracts from

A stimulus for some measure of reform in this area had already been provided by a United Kingdom government 'call for evidence' on the collective redundancy consultation rules, launched under the umbrella of the Coalition Government's broader 'Employment Law Review', initiated in May 2010.[45] The context for that government initiative was presented as a situation in which:

> The number of consultations over collective redundancies averages 4,700 notifications each year covering an average 2.8 million employees, 472,000 of whom are faced with redundancy. This has been increased by the recessionary impacts felt in 2009, when there was a spike of 6,609 notifications covering 3.6 million employees of whom 662,000 were facing redundancy. Without that spike, the average number of notifications each year would be 4,238.[46]

The eventual outcome of the government's consultation process paved the way to the statutory amendments which were eventually introduced in the 2013 Regulations, by way of a series of recommendations contained in the formal response published at the end of the consultation period.[47]

[B] The Duty to Notify

In addition to the duty of consultation with workers' representatives which is placed upon employers contemplating collective dismissals, the United Kingdom implementing provisions from the time of the enactment of the Employment Protection Act 1975 have also imposed criminally sanctioned duties for the employer to notify the Secretary of State and to confirm in writing that notification to the employee representatives entitled to be involved in the process.[48]

---

the provisions dealing with collective redundancies in the 1992 Act. The expiry of a fixed-term contract will not be excluded from the provisions dealing with collective redundancies if the employer is proposing to dismiss the employee as redundant and the dismissal will take effect before the point at which it was agreed in the contract that it would expire. It is suggested that this point could be on the expiry of a specific period of time. Alternatively, it could be on the completion of a particular task such as a research project or on the occurrence (or non-occurrence) of an event such as external funding for a particular role coming to an end. *See* the Explanatory Note to the Statutory Instrument.

45. Department for Business, Innovation and Skills, *Call for Evidence: Collective Redundancy Consultation Rules* (November 2011). That initiative proceeded on a very clear premise, expressed by the relevant Minister in terms that: 'We recognise that the existing rules are seen to present a barrier to employer flexibility in the labour market'.
46. The 'negative spin' given to the existing provisions was summed up in the introductory propositions setting out the perceived need for review of the position: 'Some employers have said during the Employment Law Review that the current 90 day minimum time period before the proposed dismissals can take effect slows their ability to restructure effectively and can put future business success at risk. They report that the difficulty in effecting redundancies has a negative impact on employers' confidence in hiring people, slows employees' re-engagement in the labour market and makes it harder for businesses to restructure to react effectively to changing market conditions. Ongoing uncertainty can also have a serious impact on workforce morale and productivity.'
47. *See* Department for Business, Innovation and Skills, *Collective Redundancies: Consultation on changes to the rules* (June 2012).
48. The Secretary of State is taken in the United Kingdom to be the 'competent public authority' as provided for in the Directive. *See* Article 3 of Directive 75/129/EEC – now Article 3 of Directive

The policy underlying these notification requirements emerges from the very earliest proposals for a Directive dealing with collective dismissals,[49] and involves ensuring the engagement of relevant (local and national level) agencies in the process of restructuring and job losses at a sufficiently early stage to enable assistance and advice to be provided through such mechanisms as public labour exchange agencies and the like.[50]

Thus, in addition to the obligation to consult with workers' representatives, employers are also obliged to notify the Secretary of State for Business, Innovation and Skills if they are proposing to dismiss as redundant twenty or more employees at one establishment within a ninety-day period.[51] The amount of notice required depends on the number of proposed dismissals: (1) for between twenty and ninety-nine redundancies in a ninety-day period, notice must be given at least thirty days before the first dismissal; while (2) for 100 or more redundancies in a ninety-day period, notice must be given at least forty-five days before the first dismissal.

In determining how many dismissals are being proposed for the purpose of these thresholds, dismissals already notified to the Secretary of State are discounted.[52] Thus, for example, if an employer notifies the Secretary of State of twenty proposed dismissals, and then proposes ten more, there is no obligation to notify afresh in relation to the additional ten. Furthermore, employees who work outside Great Britain

---

98/59/EC. Compare the United Kingdom and the European Union provisions with Article 14 of the ILO Convention No. 158, concerning Termination of Employment at the Initiative of the Employer (1982), which provides that: '(1) When the employer contemplates terminations for reasons of an economic, technological, structural or similar nature, he shall notify, in accordance with national law and practice, the competent authority thereof as early as possible, giving relevant information, including a written statement of the reasons for the terminations, the number and categories of workers likely to be affected and the period over which the terminations are intended to be carried out. (2) National laws or regulations may limit the applicability of paragraph 1 of this Article to cases in which the number of workers whose termination of employment is contemplated is at least a specified number or percentage of the workforce. (3) The employer shall notify the competent authority of the terminations referred to in paragraph 1 of this Article a minimum period of time before carrying out the terminations, such period to be specified by national laws or regulations.'

49. *See*, for the proposals already elaborated prior to the accession of the United Kingdom to the EEC, Commission of the European Communities, *Proposal for a Council Directive on the harmonization of the legislation of the Member States relating to redundancies*, COM(72) 1400 (Brussels, 8 November 1972). At that stage the treatment of collective dismissals was seen as 'only one special aspect of the laws on dismissal in their entirety' (*see* p. 2), and the significance and role to be played by 'the competent authority' was arguably somewhat greater than what eventually came to be provided for in the 1975 Directive.

50. The Directive provides for a two-stage notification: (1) The first stage requires notification in writing to the competent public authority. This must include all the relevant information concerning the proposed dismissals and the consultations held (other than the method used to calculate compensation). There is an exception for a situation of cessation of activity as the result of a judicial decision – in which case notification by the employer is only required if expressly requested by the competent authority. (2) The second stage involves the employer forwarding a copy of that notification to the workers' representatives. They, in turn, are able to send comments to the competent public authority.

51. Section 193 of the Trade Union and Labour Relations (Consolidation) Act 1992.

52. Section 193(3).

are not counted for the purposes of the threshold at which the employer is obliged to notify the Secretary of State.[53]

Where the duty to notify the Secretary of State arises, that is the entirety of the obligation placed upon the employer. There is no requirement in the United Kingdom for the employer to obtain any preliminary approval to dismiss – although there does remain the general statutory obligation not to 'unfairly dismiss' an employee.[54]

[C] Remedies and Sanctions

The statutory regime dealing with failures to comply with the consultation requirements of the collective dismissals procedure 'as set out in sections 188 and 188A of the Trade Union and Labour Relations (Consolidation) Act 1992' provides for complaints to be made to an Employment Tribunal in a variety of circumstances.[55]

Thus, where there is an alleged failure relating to the election of employee representatives, a complaint may be brought by any of the affected employees or by any of the employees who have been dismissed as redundant.[56] In the case of any other failure relating to employee representatives, the complaint may be brought by any of the employee representatives to whom the failure related.[57]

Where there is an allegation of failure relating to representatives of a trade union, a complaint may be brought by the trade union,[58] while in any other case a complaint may be made by any of the affected employees or by any of the employees who have been dismissed as redundant.[59]

It follows, therefore, that, if there is a recognized independent trade union, only the union will have legal standing to bring a complaint. Similarly, if there are elected representatives then one of them must bring the complaint. It will only be where there is no such union and no elected representatives that an individual employee can present a complaint to the Employment Tribunal.

The claim will be for a declaration that the complaint is well-founded, coupled with what the statute describes as a 'protective award' which may not exceed ninety days' pay.[60] Early domestic case-law appeared to have suggested that the starting point

53. Section 285 of the Trade Union and Labour Relations (Consolidation) Act 1992.
54. Under the provisions of Part X of the Employment Rights Act 1996, applicable to individual dismissals. In the context of individual dismissals where the reason or principal reason for the termination of the contract of employment is 'redundancy' (*i.e.*, that term as defined by section 139 of the 1996 Act), substantial case-law has been developed since the introduction of the protection in the Industrial Relations Act 1971. *See* the sources referred to *supra* footnote 10.
55. For the initial formal evaluation of the United Kingdom's compliance in this regard with the requirements of Directive 75/129/EEC, *see* Commission of the European Communities, *Report on the study of the system of sanctions applied when Member States transpose the provisions of Directives 75/129 and 92/65 on collective redundancies: Part I* (V/1451/98 – EN).
56. Section 189(1)(a).
57. Section 189(1)(b).
58. Section 189(1)(c).
59. Section 189(1)(d).
60. Section 189(2)-(4).

should be the maximum period (*i.e.*, ninety days),[61] but more recent cases have indicated a willingness to take into account the extent of the employer's default together with any mitigating factors.[62]

Where the complaint is brought by a union or elected representatives, the award will be made in respect of the class of employees affected. Otherwise, it can only be made in respect of any individual employee who brings a complaint.[63]

Once a protective award has been made, it is open to an individual to present a complaint to an Employment Tribunal on the ground that he is an employee of a description to which a protective award relates and that his employer has failed, wholly or in part, to pay him remuneration under the award.[64]

In relation to the employer's duty to notify the Secretary of State in accordance with section 193 of the 1992 Act, the sanctioning provision is to be found in section 194 of the Act. This provides that failure to provide the due notification to the Secretary of State constitutes a criminal offence, in respect of which the employer will be liable, on summary conviction, to a fine.[65]

§28.04 MISCELLANEOUS 'LOOSE ENDS'

Although, in general terms, it is arguably the case that the United Kingdom government has endeavoured to provide for employment protections in relation to collective dismissals which are in line with the arrangements set out in what is now Directive 98/59/EC, there nevertheless remain a number of 'loose ends' which have given rise to continuing controversy in this area.

[A] The Issue of When the Article 2 Duty is Triggered

One of the longest-running, and still unresolved, issues has related to the exact point at which the employer duty to consult is triggered. This arises because the United

61. *See*, for example, the decision and observations of the Court of Appeal in *Susie Radin v. GMB*, [2004] IRLR 400.
62. As, for example, in the Employment Appeal Tribunal case of *AEI Cables v. GMB*, [2013] EAT/0375/12, (a case involving consultation failures arising in the context of a liquidation), and the discussion of the authorities contained in that judgment.
63. *See* the decision of the Employment Appeal Tribunal in the case of *Independent Insurance Co Ltd v. Aspinall*, [2011] IRLR 716, holding that, where an individual claimant seeks a protective award under sections 188-189, the Employment Tribunal only has jurisdiction to make an award in his favour and cannot make an award that benefits other redundant employees.
64. Section 192.
65. Section 194. The statutory provision was drafted in terms that: 'An employer who fails to give notice to the Secretary of State in accordance with section 193 commits an offence and is liable on summary conviction to a fine not exceeding level 5 on the standard scale'. The 'standard scale' was provided for in section 37(2) of the Criminal Justice Act 1982 for offences committed prior to 12 March 2015. During that period a maximum figure of £5,000 had been set by the Criminal Justice Act 1991. Since then, for offences committed on or after 12 March 2015, the position has been changed by section 85 of the Legal Aid, Sentencing and Punishment of Offenders Act 2012, so that an offence which would have been punishable on summary conviction (in the Magistrates' Court) by a fine of GBP 5,000 or more is now punishable by an unlimited fine.

Kingdom legislator's implementation of the Article 2(1) requirement to provide for such consultation 'Where an employer is contemplating collective redundancies…' has been made in terms that cause the duty to arise 'Where an employer is proposing to dismiss as redundant…'. It has been regularly pointed out that 'contemplating… redundancies' is different from 'proposing to dismiss', and that the former (the formulation used in the Directive) is likely to arise at a point in time before the employer reaches a position of 'proposing to dismiss'.[66]

This apparent shortcoming in the United Kingdom's implementation of the collective dismissal provisions was raised directly in Case C-583/10, *United States of America v. Nolan,* where the Court of Appeal referred to the Court of Justice of the European Union the question: 'Does the employer's obligation to consult about collective redundancies, pursuant to Directive 98/59, arise (i) when the employer is proposing, but has not yet made, a strategic business or operational decision that will foreseeably or inevitably lead to collective redundancies; or (ii) only when that decision has actually been made and he is then proposing consequential redundancies?'.[67] The dispute had arisen in the context of a claim made by a member of staff employed at an American army base located in the United Kingdom.

However, in the event, the Luxembourg Court declined to deal with the question, since, 'by virtue of the exclusion laid down by Article 1(2)(b) of Directive 98/59, the dismissal of staff of a military base does not, in any event, fall within the scope of that directive'.[68] That technical evaluation thus led to the conclusion of the Court that they did not have jurisdiction to reply to the question posed by the United Kingdom Court of Appeal.

It has been a matter of some interest subsequently to observe the United Kingdom's Supreme Court grappling with a variety of legislative *vires* issues, as well as specific matters relating to Directive 98/59/EC and its inter-relationship with the regime established by the Trade Union and Labour Relations (Consolidation) Act 1992 to regulate the area of collective dismissals.[69] One reason for this problem receiving such detailed attention has been that the underlying question concerning the compatibility of the wording in section 188 of the Trade Union and Labour Relations

66. *See*, in particular, the observations of the Court of Appeal (*per* Glidewell, L.J.) in the case of *R v. British Coal and Secretary of State for Trade and Industry, ex parte Vardy*, [1993] ICR 750, and the discussion of issues arising out of those observations in the judgment of Elias P., in the Employment Appeal Tribunal case of *UK Coal Mining Ltd v. (1) National Union of Mineworkers (Northumberland Area), (2) The British Association of Colliery Management*, [2007] UKEAT/0397/06 and [2007] UKEAT/0141/07 (at paragraph 37 of the judgment – and in the following paragraphs dealing with the subsequently altered position given statutory amendments since the judgment in *Vardy*).
67. *See* at paragraph 19 of the judgment.
68. The Court went on to observe that this was the case '…irrespective of whether or not it is a military base belonging to a non-member State. In those circumstances, it is not necessary specifically to take into account the fact that, in this case, it was a military base belonging to a non-member State, that question having implications in international law (in the context of the employment of staff of an embassy of a non-member country, *see* Case C-154/11 *Mahamdia* [2012] ECR, paragraphs 54-56).
69. *The United States of America v. Nolan*, [2015] UKSC 63. The decision of the Supreme Court was handed down on 21 October 2015.

(Consolidation) Act 1992 with the wording found in Article 2 of Directive 98/59/EC had been raised in an earlier case,[70] where the Employment Appeal Tribunal had noted the observations of the Court of Appeal in a previous decision to the effect that:

> It is to be noted that the obligation to consult under the statute arises only once there is a proposal to dismiss. This does not reflect the language of the Directive which requires consultation when dismissals are 'contemplated'. The courts have held that notwithstanding the obligation to seek to interpret domestic law consistently with EU law, it is not possible to construe 'proposed' as the equivalent of 'contemplated'... .[71]

At the end of the day, however, the conclusion of the Supreme Court in relation to the specific (still unanswered) question has been that 'the questions raised by *UK Coal/Fujitsu* and the Court of Appeal's reference will in the present case have to be resolved, if ever necessary, domestically without further assistance from the Court of Justice'.[72] That being acknowledged, it was then observed that 'Whether it will be necessary to resolve them in this case appears doubtful'.[73]

70. The Employment Appeal Tribunal case of *UK Coal Mining Ltd v. (1) National Union of Mineworkers (Northumberland Area), (2) The British Association of Colliery Management*, [2007] UKEAT/0397/06 and [2007] UKEAT/0141/07.
71. The EAT drew specific attention to '...the observations of Glidewell LJ in *R v. British Coal and Secretary of State for Trade and Industry, ex parte Vardy*, [1993] ICR 750, followed by Lindsay P, giving the judgment of the EAT in *MSF v. Refuge Assurance plc*, [2002] IRLR 324, paragraph 42; and to similar effect the judgment of the EAT (Lord Johnstone presiding) in *Scotch Premier Meat Ltd v. Burns*, [2000] IRLR 369. As Lindsay P said in the *MSF* case, the obligation to consult when redundancies are contemplated means when they are envisaged as a possibility; it is a more amorphous and earlier state than the point in time when they are proposed; the proposed redundancies occur at a later stage when the state of mind is more certain. His Lordship cited a definition of 'to propose' from the Oxford English Dictionary, namely 'to lay before another or others as something which one offers to do or wishes to be done.'
72. The Supreme Court was specifically concerned with the closely related issue raised by a reference of the Finnish Supreme Court to the CJEU of the first of four questions in Case C-44/08, *Akavan Erityisalojen Keskusliitto (AEK) ry v. Fujitsu Siemens Computers Oy*: 'Is Article 2(1) of Directive 98/59/EC to be interpreted as meaning that the obligation under that provision to embark on consultations when 'contemplating collective redundancies' of employees and 'in good time' requires consultations to be started when it is established from strategic decisions or changes that have been made relating to the activity that a need for collective redundancies of employees follows? Or is the provision in question to be interpreted as meaning that the obligation to start consultations already arises on the basis of the employer contemplating measures or changes affecting the activity, such as a change in production capacity or a concentration of production, as a consequence of which a need for collective redundancies is to be expected?'. The CJEU in that case held that: '1. Article 2(1) of Council Directive 98/59/EC of 20 July 1998 on the approximation of the laws of the Member States relating to collective redundancies must be interpreted to mean that the adoption, within a group of undertakings, of strategic decisions or of changes in activities which compel the employer to contemplate or to plan for collective redundancies gives rise to an obligation on that employer to hold consultations with workers' representatives; 2. Whether the obligation has arisen for the employer to start consultations on the collective redundancies contemplated does not depend on whether the employer is already able to supply to the workers' representatives all the information required in Article 2(3)(b) of Directive 98/59; 3. Article 2(1) of Directive 98/59, read in conjunction with the first subparagraph of Article 2(4) of that directive, must be interpreted to mean that, in the case of a group of undertakings consisting of a parent company and one or more subsidiaries, the obligation to hold consultations with the workers' representatives falls on the subsidiary which has the status of employer only once that subsidiary, within which collective redundancies may

[B] The Scope of the Notion of 'Establishment' in Directive 98/59/EC?

A particularly high-profile reference to the CJEU concerning collective dismissals consultation duties in the context of retail chain-store insolvencies raised the question of how the notion of the 'establishment' should be approached for the purposes of the definitions contained in Article 1 – and, hence, for the 'threshold' of twenty workers which triggers the Directive's duties.[74]

The issue considered concerned whether those workers who had been employed in shops within the employer's retail chain which consisted of less than twenty employees were within the qualifying threshold to trigger a consultation duty. In simplistic terms, was the individual unit to be considered on its own for the purpose of computing the number of employees, or was the overall retail chain's workforce to be aggregated for that purpose.[75]

In a judgment handed down on 30 April 2015, the CJEU clarified that, for the purposes of triggering the consultation duty in Directive 98/59/EC, the notion of 'establishment' in Article 1 of that Directive 'must be interpreted as not precluding national legislation that lays down an obligation to inform and consult workers in the event of the dismissal, within a period of 90 days, of at least 20 workers from a particular establishment of an undertaking, and not where the aggregate number of dismissals across all of the establishments or across some of the establishments of an undertaking over the same period reaches or exceeds the threshold of 20 workers'.[76]

---

be made, has been identified; and 4. Article 2(1) of Directive 98/59, read in conjunction with Article 2(4) of that directive, must be interpreted to mean that, in the case of a group of undertakings, the consultation procedure must be concluded by the subsidiary affected by the collective redundancies before that subsidiary, on the direct instructions of its parent company or otherwise, terminates the contracts of employees who are to be affected by those redundancies.'

73. *See* at paragraphs 10 and 11 of the Supreme Court's decision (*per* Lord Mance, giving the reasons adopted by the majority of the Court).
74. Case C-80/14, *Union of Shop, Distributive and Allied Workers (USDAW), B. Wilson v. WW Realisation 1 Ltd, in liquidation, Ethel Austin Ltd, Secretary of State for Business, Innovation and Skills*.
75. The United Kingdom reference by the Court of Appeal in Case C-80/14 was dealt with by the CJEU at around the same time as a case referred from an Industrial Tribunal in Ireland (C-182/13, *Lyttle and others v. Bluebird UK Bidco 2 Ltd*). Mention may also be made of a third case, referred from Spain, (C-392/13, *Cañas v. Nexea Gestión Documental and another*), in which the judgment was handed down around the same time – although that case was concerned with the problem in the context of an 'undertaking', which had been the Spanish legislator's choice of expression, rather than the term 'establishment' used in the United Kingdom and Irish provisions.
76. By its first question, the United Kingdom Court of Appeal had asked the Luxembourg Court: '(a) In Article 1(1)(a)(ii) of Directive 98/59, does the phrase 'at least 20' refer to the number of dismissals across all of the employer's establishments in which dismissals are effected within a 90 day period, or does it refer to the number of dismissals in each individual establishment?'; and '(b) If Article 1(1)(a)(ii) of that directive refers to the number of dismissals in each individual establishment, what is the meaning of 'establishment'? In particular, should 'establishment' be construed to mean the whole of the relevant retail business, being a single economic business unit, or such part of that business as is contemplating making redundancies, rather than a unit to which a worker is assigned their duties, such as each individual store?'.

Subsequent to the decision of the Luxembourg Court it had been anticipated that the case would have returned to the United Kingdom Court of Appeal, where further clarification would be forthcoming as to the practical significance of the outcome for those concerned with the duty to consult in relation to collective dismissals. However, it has been reported that, eventually, no hearing has taken place before the Court of Appeal, with the case being determined on the basis of consent given by both sides. The episode has therefore closed without any further judicial assistance in relation to the application of Article 1 of the Directive, with the words of the CJEU remaining the current source of inspiration for elucidation of the notion of 'establishment' in this context.

[C] Enforcing the Duty to Notify

Finally, in the aftermath of some notorious cases involving closures of enterprises at very short notice, the attention of the United Kingdom government has been firmly focused upon the effectiveness of the enforcement provisions associated with the duty to notify the Secretary of State in the event of pending collective dismissals.[77] It may be noted that this was also one of the areas of concern highlighted by the government in their formal response published at the end of the period of consultation over the collective dismissals arrangements, undertaken as part of the broader 'Employment Law Review'.[78]

Thus, there has been a consultation undertaken by the government's Insolvency Service, seeking views on: (a) existing understanding of the current requirements of consultation in an insolvency situation; (b) factors that facilitate and inhibit effective consultation in an insolvency context; (c) the role of directors and insolvency practitioners in consulting within an insolvency context; and (d) how timely notification is achieved in an insolvency context. The consultation period closed in June 2015, and the government has published a summary of responses received.[79]

At the time of writing, the eventual 'next steps' in response to this exercise are unknown. Nevertheless, it is becoming increasingly clear that the government regards 'effective enforcement' (including full utilization of the criminal law penalties associated with the collective dismissals regime) as a matter for further promotion.[80]

---

77. *See*, for example, the highly critical comments in House of Commons, Committees on Impact of the closure of City Link on Employment, *Impact of the closure of City Link on Employment*, First Joint Report of the Business, Innovation and Skills and Scottish Affairs Committees of Session 2014-15, Twelfth Report of the Business, Innovation and Skills Committee of Session 2014-15 (HC 928), Fifth Report of the Scottish Affairs Committee of Session 2014-15, published on 23 March 2015.
78. *See* Department for Business, Innovation and Skills, *Collective Redundancies: Consultation on changes to the rules* (June 2012), *supra* footnote 45.
79. *See* The Insolvency Service, Responses to Call for Evidence on Collective Redundancy Consultation for Employers facing Insolvency (November 2015).
80. Indeed, in the City Link situation mentioned above (*supra* footnote 77) prosecutions were commenced against three former directors of the company, by reference to their alleged failure to comply with the notification duty contained in section 193 of the Trade Union and Labour Relations (Consolidation) Act 1992. The criminal proceedings resulted in the acquittal of all

§28.05 SUMMARY

Following the consolidation of the collective dismissals provisions into the Trade Union and Labour Relations (Consolidation) Act 1992, and subsequent legislative amendments introduced in response to the modified content of the latest Directive 98/59/EC and subsequent case-law developments, the modern position in the United Kingdom may thus be summarized as follows.

A general regime of protection for employees against 'unfair dismissal' operates in the United Kingdom under provisions contained in Part X of the Employment Rights Act 1996. That arrangement is enjoyed by individual employees, and requires an employer to act 'reasonably' in deciding to terminate the contract of employment of a qualifying employee for a reason included in a group of statutorily recognized 'reasons for dismissal'. The reasons set out in the 1996 Act include dismissal by reason of 'redundancy' – a statutory term of art which is defined in section 139 of the 1996 Act. The reasons also include a category of 'some other substantial reason of a kind such as to justify the dismissal of an employee holding the position which the employee held' – something which has been developed to cover so-called business reorganizations where associated job losses (whether within or outside the definition of 'redundancy' in section 139) may or may not be involved.

Redundant employees also enjoy an entitlement to payment of a 'redundancy payment', under a scheme originally introduced in 1965 by the Redundancy Payments Act of that year.

In relation to 'collective dismissals', duties of consultation and notification have been placed upon United Kingdom employers in line with the provisions now to be found in Directive 98/59/EC. Those duties arise in the context of a notion of 'redundancy' defined in section 195(1) of the Trade Union and Labour Relations (Consolidation) Act 1992, which extends more widely than the individual protections under the Employment Rights Act 1996.

The obligation for an employer to consult 'appropriate representatives' arises if the employer is proposing to dismiss as redundant twenty or more employees at one establishment within a period of ninety days or less. This obligation extends not just to 'redundancy' in the sense in which that term was developed in the wake of the Redundancy Payments Act 1965, but also to broader situations involving restructuring of an enterprise. The statutory consultation must be for at least thirty days in every case. However, where the employer is proposing to dismiss more than 100 employees in such circumstances, the consultation must be for forty-five days.

In cases where an employer proposes to take action comprising the non-renewal of fixed-term contracts, in combination with declaring redundancies for some other

---

three accused. However, the Deputy District Judge who delivered the verdict was at pains to stress that the outcome was dependent upon the particular facts of the case before him, commenting that: "I would add only that no employer should take that finding to be a precedent that an employer can avoid its responsibility under section 193 simply by going into administration. My finding in this case that no proposal had been made is based on the evidence in this case, not on a general principle in relation to administration generally.'

members of the permanent (non-fixed-term) staff, the former do not count towards the '20 employees' threshold required to trigger the collective consultation obligations.

The obligation is to consult any 'independent trade union' which is recognized by the employer. If there is no such recognized independent trade union, the employer is expected either: (1) to consult with employee representatives authorized or elected to consult on proposed redundancies; and/or (2) to arrange elections of such representatives for that purpose.

The specific information which should be disclosed as part of the consultation process is indicated in detailed statutory provisions, and reflects the information requirements set out in Directive 98/59/EC.

Failure by an employer to comply with the duty of consultation may be met with the award of a 'protective award', payable to the affected workers.

Failure by the employer to comply with the statutory duty to notify the Secretary of State as required may result in criminal prosecution, with the possibility, on conviction, for the imposition of a fine in an unlimited amount.

ANNEX

United Kingdom statutory provisions (as amended)

[Updated as of amendments effective from 31 January 2014]

TRADE UNION AND LABOUR RELATIONS (CONSOLIDATION) ACT 1993

CHAPTER II

PROCEDURE FOR HANDLING REDUNDANCIES

Duty of employer to consult representatives

188 DUTY OF EMPLOYER TO CONSULT REPRESENTATIVES.

(1) Where an employer is proposing to dismiss as redundant 20 or more employees at one establishment within a period of 90 days or less, the employer shall consult about the dismissals all the persons who are appropriate representatives of any of the employees who may be affected by the proposed dismissals or may be affected by measures taken in connection with those dismissals.

(1A) The consultation shall begin in good time and in any event —

- (a) where the employer is proposing to dismiss 100 or more employees as mentioned in subsection (1), at least 45 days, and
- (b) otherwise, at least 30 days,

before the first of the dismissals takes effect.

(1B) For the purposes of this section the appropriate representatives of any affected employees are –

- (a) if the employees are of a description in respect of which an independent trade union is recognised by their employer, representatives of the trade union, or
- (b) in any other case, whichever of the following employee representatives the employer chooses: –
  - (i) employee representatives appointed or elected by the affected employees otherwise than for the purposes of this section, who (having regard to the purposes for and the method by which they were appointed or elected) have authority from those employees to receive information and to be consulted about the proposed dismissals on their behalf;
  - (ii) employee representatives elected by the affected employees, for the purposes of this section, in an election satisfying the requirements of section 188A(1).

(2) The consultation shall include consultation about ways of —
   (a) avoiding the dismissals,
   (b) reducing the numbers of employees to be dismissed, and
   (c) mitigating the consequences of the dismissals,

   and shall be undertaken by the employer with a view to reaching agreement with the appropriate representatives.

(3) In determining how many employees an employer is proposing to dismiss as redundant no account shall be taken of employees in respect of whose proposed dismissals consultation has already begun.

(4) For the purposes of the consultation the employer shall disclose in writing to the appropriate representatives —
   (a) the reasons for his proposals,
   (b) the numbers and descriptions of employees whom it is proposed to dismiss as redundant,
   (c) the total number of employees of any such description employed by the employer at the establishment in question,
   (d) the proposed method of selecting the employees who may be dismissed,
   (e) the proposed method of carrying out the dismissals, with due regard to any agreed procedure, including the period over which the dismissals are to take effect,
   (f) the proposed method of calculating the amount of any redundancy payments to be made (otherwise than in compliance with an obligation imposed by or by virtue of any enactment) to employees who may be dismissed,
   (g) the number of agency workers working temporarily for and under the supervision and direction of the employer,
   (h) the parts of the employer's undertaking in which those agency workers are working, and
   (i) the type of work those agency workers are carrying out.

(5) That information shall be given to each of the appropriate representatives by being delivered to them, or sent by post to an address notified by them to the employer, or (in the case of representatives of a trade union) sent by post to the union at the address of its head or main office.

(5A) The employer shall allow the appropriate representatives access to the affected employees and shall afford to those representatives such accommodation and other facilities as may be appropriate.

(6) ...

(7) If in any case there are special circumstances which render it not reasonably practicable for the employer to comply with a requirement of subsection (1A), (2) or (4), the employer shall take all such steps towards compliance with that requirement as are reasonably practicable in those circumstances. Where the decision leading to the proposed dismissals is that of a person controlling the employer (directly or indirectly), a failure on the part of that person to provide information to the employer shall not constitute special

circumstances rendering it not reasonably practicable for the employer to comply with such a requirement.

(7A) Where —

(a) the employer has invited any of the affected employees to elect employee representatives, and

(b) the invitation was issued long enough before the time when the consultation is required by subsection (1A)(a) or (b) to begin to allow them to elect representatives by that time,

the employer shall be treated as complying with the requirements of this section in relation to those employees if he complies with those requirements as soon as is reasonably practicable after the election of the representatives.

(7B) If, after the employer has invited affected employees to elect representatives, the affected employees fail to do so within a reasonable time, he shall give to each affected employee the information set out in subsection (4).

(8) This section does not confer any rights on a trade union, a representative or an employee except as provided by sections 189 to 192 below.

188A

(1) The requirements for the election of employee representatives under section 188(1B)(b)(ii) are that –

(a) the employer shall make such arrangements as are reasonably practical to ensure that the election is fair;

(b) the employer shall determine the number of representatives to be elected so that there are sufficient representatives to represent the interests of all the affected employees having regard to the number and classes of those employees;

(c) the employer shall determine whether the affected employees should be represented either by representatives of all the affected employees or by representatives of particular classes of those employees;

(d) before the election the employer shall determine the term of office as employee representatives so that it is of sufficient length to enable information to be given and consultations under section 188 to be completed;

(e) the candidates for election as employee representatives are affected employees on the date of the election;

(f) no affected employee is unreasonably excluded from standing for election;

(g) all affected employees on the date of the election are entitled to vote for employee representatives;

(h) the employees entitled to vote may vote for as many candidates as there are representatives to be elected to represent them or, if there are to be representatives for particular classes of employees, may vote for as many candidates as there are representatives to be elected to represent their particular class of employee;

(i) the election is conducted so as to secure that –

(i) so far as is reasonably practicable, those voting do so in secret, and

(ii) the votes given at the election are accurately counted.

(2) Where, after an election of employee representatives satisfying the requirements of subsection (1) has been held, one of those elected ceases to act as an employee representative and any of those employees are no longer represented, they shall elect another representative by an election satisfying the requirements of subsection (1)(a), (e), (f) and (i).

189 COMPLAINT AND PROTECTIVE AWARD.

(1) Where an employer has failed to comply with a requirement of section 188 or section 188A, a complaint may be presented to an employment tribunal on that ground –

(a) in the case of a failure relating to the election of employee representatives, by any of the affected employees or by any of the employees who have been dismissed as redundant;

(b) in the case of any other failure relating to employee representatives, by any of the employee representatives to whom the failure related,

(c) in the case of failure relating to representatives of a trade union, by the trade union, and

(d) in any other case, by any of the affected employees or by any of the employees who have been dismissed as redundant.

(1A) If on a complaint under subsection (1) a question arises as to whether or not any employee representative was an appropriate representative for the purposes of section 188, it shall be for the employer to show that the employee representative had the authority to represent the affected employees.

(1B) On a complaint under subsection (1)(a) it shall be for the employer to show that the requirements in section 188A have been satisfied.

(2) If the tribunal finds the complaint well-founded it shall make a declaration to that effect and may also make a protective award.

(3) A protective award is an award in respect of one or more descriptions of employees —

(a) who have been dismissed as redundant, or whom it is proposed to dismiss as redundant, and

(b) in respect of whose dismissal or proposed dismissal the employer has failed to comply with a requirement of section 188,

ordering the employer to pay remuneration for the protected period.

(4) The protected period —

(a) begins with the date on which the first of the dismissals to which the complaint relates takes effect, or the date of the award, whichever is the earlier, and

(b) is of such length as the tribunal determines to be just and equitable in all the circumstances having regard to the seriousness of the employer's default in complying with any requirement of section 188;

but shall not exceed 90 days.

(5) An employment tribunal shall not consider a complaint under this section unless it is presented to the tribunal —

(a) before the date on which the last of the dismissals to which the complaint relates takes effect, or

(b) during the period of three months beginning with that date, or

(c) where the tribunal is satisfied that it was not reasonably practicable for the complaint to be presented during the period of three months, within such further period as it considers reasonable.

(5A) Where the complaint concerns a failure to comply with a requirement of section 188 or 188A, section 292A (extension of time limits to facilitate conciliation before institution of proceedings) applies for the purposes of subsection (5)(b).

(6) If on a complaint under this section a question arises —

(a) whether there were special circumstances which rendered it not reasonably practicable for the employer to comply with any requirement of section 188, or

(b) whether he took all such steps towards compliance with that requirement as were reasonably practicable in those circumstances,

it is for the employer to show that there were and that he did.

190 Entitlement under protective award.

(1) Where an employment tribunal has made a protective award, every employee of a description to which the award relates is entitled, subject to the following provisions and to section 191, to be paid remuneration by his employer for the protected period.

(2) The rate of remuneration payable is a week's pay for each week of the period; and remuneration in respect of a period less than one week shall be calculated by reducing proportionately the amount of a week's pay.

(3) ...

(4) An employee is not entitled to remuneration under a protective award in respect of a period during which he is employed by the employer unless he would be entitled to be paid by the employer in respect of that period —

(a) by virtue of his contract of employment, or

(b) by virtue of sections 87 to 91 of the Employment Rights Act 1996 (rights of employee in period of notice),

if that period fell within the period of notice required to be given by section 86(1) of that Act.

(5) Chapter II of Part XIV of the Employment Rights Act 1996 applies with respect to the calculation of a week's pay for the purposes of this section.

The calculation date for the purposes of that Chapter is the date on which the protective award was made or, in the case of an employee who was dismissed before the date on which the protective award was made, the date which by virtue of section 226(5) is the calculation date for the purpose of computing the amount of a redundancy payment in relation to that dismissal (whether or not the employee concerned is entitled to any such payment).

(6) If an employee of a description to which a protective award relates dies during the protected period, the award has effect in his case as if the protected period ended on his death.

191 TERMINATION OF EMPLOYMENT DURING PROTECTED PERIOD.

(1) Where the employee is employed by the employer during the protected period and —
 (a) he is fairly dismissed by his employer otherwise than as redundant, or
 (b) he unreasonably terminates the contract of employment,
 then, subject to the following provisions, he is not entitled to remuneration under the protective award in respect of any period during which but for that dismissal or termination he would have been employed.

(2) If an employer makes an employee an offer (whether in writing or not and whether before or after the ending of his employment under the previous contract) to renew his contract of employment, or to re-engage him under a new contract, so that the renewal or re-engagement would take effect before or during the protected period, and either —
 (a) the provisions of the contract as renewed, or of the new contract, as to the capacity and place in which he would be employed, and as to the other terms and conditions of his employment, would not differ from the corresponding provisions of the previous contract, or
 (b) the offer constitutes an offer of suitable employment in relation to the employee,
 the following subsections have effect.

(3) If the employee unreasonably refuses the offer, he is not entitled to remuneration under the protective award in respect of a period during which but for that refusal he would have been employed.

(4) If the employee's contract of employment is renewed, or he is re-engaged under a new contract of employment, in pursuance of such an offer as is referred to in subsection (2)(b), there shall be a trial period in relation to the contract as renewed, or the new contract (whether or not there has been a previous trial period under this section).

(5) The trial period begins with the ending of his employment under the previous contract and ends with the expiration of the period of four weeks beginning with the date on which the he starts work under the contract as renewed, or the new contract, or such longer period as may be agreed in

accordance with subsection (6) for the purpose of retraining the employee for employment under that contract.

(6) Any such agreement —

(a) shall be made between the employer and the employee or his representative before the employee starts work under the contract as renewed or, as the case may be, the new contract,

(b) shall be in writing,

(c) shall specify the date of the end of the trial period, and

(d) shall specify the terms and conditions of employment which will apply in the employee's case after the end of that period.

(7) If during the trial period —

(a) the employee, for whatever reason, terminates the contract, or gives notice to terminate it and the contract is thereafter, in consequence, terminated, or

(b) the employer, for a reason connected with or arising out of the change to the renewed, or new, employment, terminates the contract, or gives notice to terminate it and the contract is thereafter, in consequence, terminated,

the employee remains entitled under the protective award unless, in a case falling within paragraph (a), he acted unreasonably in terminating or giving notice to terminate the contract.

192 Complaint by employee to employment tribunal.

(1) An employee may present a complaint to an employment tribunal on the ground that he is an employee of a description to which a protective award relates and that his employer has failed, wholly or in part, to pay him remuneration under the award.

(2) An employment tribunal shall not entertain a complaint under this section unless it is presented to the tribunal —

(a) before the end of the period of three months beginning with the day (or, if the complaint relates to more than one day, the last of the days) in respect of which the complaint is made of failure to pay remuneration, or

(b) where the tribunal is satisfied that it was not reasonably practicable for the complaint to be presented within the period of three months, within such further period as it may consider reasonable.

(2A) Section 292A (extension of time limits to facilitate conciliation before institution of proceedings) applies for the purposes of subsection (2)(a).

(3) Where the tribunal finds a complaint under this section well-founded it shall order the employer to pay the complainant the amount of remuneration which it finds is due to him.

(4) The remedy of an employee for infringement of his right to remuneration under a protective award is by way of complaint under this section, and not otherwise.

Duty of employer to notify Secretary of State

193 Duty of employer to notify Secretary of State of certain redundancies.

(1) An employer proposing to dismiss as redundant 100 or more employees at one establishment within a period of 90 days or less shall notify the Secretary of State, in writing, of his proposal
(a) before giving notice to terminate an employee's contract of employment in respect of any of those dismissals, and
(b) at least 45 days before the first of those dismissals takes effect.

(2) An employer proposing to dismiss as redundant 20 or more employees at one establishment within such a period shall notify the Secretary of State, in writing, of his proposal
(a) before giving notice to terminate an employee's contract of employment in respect of any of those dismissals, and
(b) at least 30 days before the first of those dismissals takes effect.

(3) In determining how many employees an employer is proposing to dismiss as redundant within the period mentioned in subsection (1) or (2), no account shall be taken of employees in respect of whose proposed dismissal notice has already been given to the Secretary of State.

(4) A notice under this section shall —
(a) be given to the Secretary of State by delivery to him or by sending it by post to him, at such address as the Secretary of State may direct in relation to the establishment where the employees proposed to be dismissed are employed,
(b) where there are representatives to be consulted under section 188, identify them and state the date when consultation with them under that section began,
(c) be in such form and contain such particulars, in addition to those required by paragraph (b), as the Secretary of State may direct.

(5) After receiving a notice under this section from an employer the Secretary of State may by written notice require the employer to give him such further information as may be specified in the notice.

(6) Where there are representatives to be consulted under section 188 the employer shall give to each of them a copy of any notice given under subsection (1) or (2).
The copy shall be delivered to them or sent by post to an address notified by them to the employer, or (in the case of representatives of a trade union) sent by post to the union at the address of its head or main office.

(7) If in any case there are special circumstances rendering it not reasonably practicable for the employer to comply with any of the requirements of subsections (1) to (6), he shall take all such steps towards compliance with that requirement as are reasonably practicable in the circumstances.
Where the decision leading to the proposed dismissals is that of a person controlling the employer (directly or indirectly), a failure on the part of that

person to provide information to the employer shall not constitute special circumstances rendering it not reasonably practicable for the employer to comply with any of those requirements.

194 Offence of failure to notify.

(1) An employer who fails to give notice to the Secretary of State in accordance with section 193 commits an offence and is liable on summary conviction to a fine not exceeding level 5 on the standard scale.

(2) Proceedings in England or Wales for such an offence shall be instituted only by or with the consent of the Secretary of State or by an officer authorised for that purpose by special or general directions of the Secretary of State. An officer so authorised may prosecute or conduct proceedings for such an offence before a magistrates' court.

(3) Where an offence under this section committed by a body corporate is proved to have been committed with the consent or connivance of, or to be attributable to neglect on the part of, any director, manager, secretary or other similar officer of the body corporate, or any person purporting to act in any such capacity, he as well as the body corporate is guilty of the offence and liable to be proceeded against and punished accordingly.

(4) Where the affairs of a body corporate are managed by its members, subsection (3) applies in relation to the acts and defaults of a member in connection with his functions of management as if he were a director of the body corporate.

Supplementary provisions

195 Construction of references to dismissal as redundant etc.

(1) In this Chapter references to dismissal as redundant are references to dismissal for a reason not related to the individual concerned or for a number of reasons all of which are not so related.

(2) For the purposes of any proceedings under this Chapter, where an employee is or is proposed to be dismissed it shall be presumed, unless the contrary is proved, that he is or is proposed to be dismissed as redundant.

196 Construction of references to representatives.

(1) For the purposes of this Chapter persons are employee representatives if —

(a) they have been elected by employees for the specific purpose of being consulted by their employer about dismissals proposed by him, or

(b) having been elected or appointed by employees (whether before or after dismissals have been proposed by their employer) otherwise than for that specific purpose, it is appropriate (having regard to the purposes for which they were elected) for the employer to consult them about dismissals proposed by him,

and (in either case) they are employed by the employer at the time when they are elected or appointed.

(2) References in this Chapter to representatives of a trade union, in relation to an employer, are to officials or other persons authorised by the trade union to carry on collective bargaining with the employer.

(3) References in this Chapter to affected employees are to employees who may be affected by the proposed dismissals or who may be affected by measures taken in connection with such dismissals.

197 Power to vary provisions.

(1) The Secretary of State may by order made by statutory instrument vary —

(a) the provisions of sections 188(2) and 193(1) (requirements as to consultation and notification), and

(b) the periods referred to at the end of section 189(4) (maximum protected period);

but no such order shall be made which has the effect of reducing to less than 30 days the periods referred to in sections 188(2) and 193(1) as the periods which must elapse before the first of the dismissals takes effect.

(2) No such order shall be made unless a draft of the order has been laid before Parliament and approved by a resolution of each House of Parliament.

198 Power to adapt provisions in case of collective agreement.

(1) This section applies where there is in force a collective agreement which establishes —

(a) arrangements for providing alternative employment for employees to whom the agreement relates if they are dismissed as redundant by an employer to whom it relates, or

(b) arrangements for handling the dismissal of employees as redundant.

(2) On the application of all the parties to the agreement the Secretary of State may, if he is satisfied having regard to the provisions of the agreement that the arrangements are on the whole at least as favourable to those employees as the foregoing provisions of this Chapter, by order made by statutory instrument adapt, modify or exclude any of those provisions both in their application to all or any of those employees and in their application to any other employees of any such employer.

(3) The Secretary of State shall not make such an order unless the agreement —

(a) provides for procedures to be followed (whether by arbitration or otherwise) in cases where an employee to whom the agreement relates claims that any employer or other person to whom it relates has not complied with the provisions of the agreement, and

(b) provides that those procedures include a right to arbitration or adjudication by an independent referee or body in cases where (by reason of an equality of votes or otherwise) a decision cannot otherwise be reached,

or indicates that any such employee may present a complaint to an employment tribunal that any such employer or other person has not complied with those provisions.

(4) An order under this section may confer on an industrial tribunal to whom a complaint is presented as mentioned in subsection (3) such powers and duties as the Secretary of State considers appropriate.

(5) An order under this section may be varied or revoked by a subsequent order thereunder either in pursuance of an application made by all or any of the parties to the agreement in question or without any such application.

Employees being transferred to the employer from another undertaking

198A.

(1) This section applies where the following conditions are met —

(a) there is to be, or is likely to be, a relevant transfer,

(b) the transferee is proposing to dismiss as redundant 20 or more employees at one establishment within a period of 90 days or less, and

(c) the individuals who work for the transferor and who are to be (or are likely to be) transferred to the transferee's employment under the transfer ("transferring individuals") include one or more individuals who may be affected by the proposed dismissals or by measures taken in connection with the proposed dismissals.

(2) Where this section applies, the transferee may elect to consult, or to start to consult, representatives of affected transferring individuals about the proposed dismissals before the transfer takes place ("pre-transfer consultation").

(3) Any such election —

(a) may be made only if the transferor agrees to it, and

(b) must be made by way of written notice to the transferor.

(4) If the transferee elects to carry out pre-transfer consultation —

(a) sections 188 to 198 apply from the time of the election (and continue to apply after the transfer) as if the transferee were already the transferring individuals' employer and as if any transferring individuals who may be affected by the proposed dismissals were already employed at the establishment mentioned in subsection (1)(b) (but this is subject to section 198B), and

(b) the transferor may provide information or other assistance to the transferee to help the transferee meet the requirements of this Chapter.

(5) A transferee who elects to carry out pre-transfer consultation may cancel that election at any time by written notice to the transferor.

(6) If the transferee cancels an election to carry out pre-transfer consultation —
(a) sections 188 to 198 no longer apply as mentioned in subsection (4)(a),
(b) anything done under those sections has no effect so far as it was done in reliance on the election,
(c) if the transferee notified an appropriate representative, a transferring individual or the Secretary of State of the election or the proposed dismissals, the transferee must notify him or her of the cancellation as soon as reasonably practicable, and
(d) the transferee may not make another election under subsection (2) in relation to the proposed dismissals.

(7) For the purposes of this section and section 198B —
"affected transferring individual" means a transferring individual who may be affected by the proposed dismissals or who may be affected by measures taken in connection with the proposed dismissals;
"pre-transfer consultation" has the meaning given in subsection (2);
"relevant transfer" means —
(a) a relevant transfer under the Transfer of Undertakings (Protection of Employment) Regulations 2006,
(b) anything else regarded, by virtue of an enactment, as a relevant transfer for the purposes of those Regulations, or
(c) where an enactment provides a power to make provision which is the same as or similar to those Regulations, any other novation of a contract of employment effected in the exercise of that power,
and "transferor" and "transferee" are to be construed accordingly;
"transferring individual" has the meaning given in subsection (1)(c).

Section 198A: supplementary

198B.

(1) Where section 198A applies and the transferee elects to carry out pre-transfer consultation (and has not cancelled the election), the application under section 198A(4)(a) of sections 188 to 198 is (both before and after the transfer) subject to the following modifications —
(a) for section 188(1B)(a) substitute —
"(a) for transferring individuals of a description in respect of which an independent trade union is recognised by the transferor, representatives of that trade union,
(aa) for employees, other than transferring individuals, of a description in respect of which an independent trade union is recognised by the transferee, representatives of that trade union, or";
(b) in section 188(5), for "the employer" substitute "the transferor or transferee";

(c) in section 188(5A), for "shall allow the appropriate representatives access to the affected employees and shall afford to those representatives such accommodation and other facilities as may be appropriate" substitute "shall ensure that the appropriate representatives are allowed access to the affected transferring individuals and that such accommodation and other facilities as may be appropriate are afforded to those representatives";

(d) in section 188(7), at the end insert —

"A failure on the part of the transferor to provide information or other assistance to the transferee does not constitute special circumstances rendering it not reasonably practicable for the transferee to comply with such a requirement.";

(e) where an employment tribunal makes a protective award under section 189 ordering the transferee to pay remuneration for a protected period in respect of a transferring individual, then, so far as the protected period falls before the relevant transfer, the individual's employer before the transfer is to be treated as the employer for the purpose of determining under sections 190(2) to (6) and 191 the period (if any) in respect of which, and the rate at which, the individual is entitled to be paid remuneration by the transferee under section 190(1);

(f) in section 189, at the end insert —

"(7) If on a complaint under this section a question arises whether the transferor agreed to an election or the transferee gave notice of an election as required under section 198A(3), it is for the transferee to show that the agreement or notice was given as required.";

(g) in section 192, at the end insert —

"(5) If on a complaint under this section a question arises whether the transferor agreed to an election or the transferee gave notice of an election as required under section 198A(3), it is for the transferee to show that the agreement or notice was given as required.";

(h) in section 193(6), for "the employer" the second time it appears substitute "the transferor or transferee";

(i) in section 193(7), at the end insert —

"A failure on the part of the transferor to provide information or other assistance to the transferee does not constitute special circumstances rendering it not reasonably practicable for the transferee to comply with any of those requirements.";

(j) in section 196(1), in the closing words, for "employed by the employer" substitute "employed by the transferor or transferee";

(k) for section 196(2) substitute —

"(2) References in this Chapter to representatives of a trade union are to officials or other persons authorised by the trade union to carry on collective bargaining with the transferee.".

(2) Where section 198A applies and the transferee elects to carry out pre-transfer consultation (and has not cancelled the election), both before and

after the transfer section 168(1)(c) applies as follows in relation to an official of an independent trade union who, as such an official, is an affected transferring individual's appropriate representative under section 188(1B)(a) —

(a) in relation to the official's duties as such a representative, the reference in the opening words of section 168(1) to an independent trade union being recognised by the employer is to be read as a reference to an independent trade union being recognised by the transferor;

(b) the references in section 168(1)(c) to the employer in relation to section 188 are to be read as references to the transferee.".

CHAPTER 29

Regulation of Collective Redundancies: European Union Countries at the Mirror of Global Standards and Trends

Angelika Muller[*]

Job losses cannot be prevented by the labour market regulation. However, one of the main functions of the labour law is to guarantee the fairness of processes in order to mitigate negative impact of collective redundancies on workers, enterprises and societies.

Restructuring and redundancies continue to figure among worrying news worldwide. This is particularly visible in Europe where consequences of the global economic crisis continue to nurture controversy in the policy and academic debate over the optimum level of employment protection legislation (EPL). The rules on collective dismissals for economic reasons are an important aspect of EPL whose objective is to balance the requirement of flexibility for employers with the need of security for workers.

The objective of the paper is to review the regulation of European Union (EU)'s countries on collective dismissals for economic reasons in light of international and regional standards, comparative indicators and global trends. In the globalized economy, for policy discussion on countries' competitiveness, the assessment of national labour market regulations in a comparative perspective may be of particular relevance. In this paper, the main references used for EU countries are relevant conventions and recommendations of the International Labour Organisation (ILO) and

* This chapter is based on updated abstracts from previous publications (Muller, 2011 and 2012) Responsibility for opinions expressed in signed articles rests solely with their authors and publication does not constitute an endorsement by the ILO.

EU directives. The comparative benchmarks developed by the Organisation for Economic Co-operation and Development (OECD) and the World Bank are also mentioned, as they have been influencing labour law reforms in Europe. The data from comparative labour law is used to compare the EU group with other regions. Policy makers worldwide are increasingly interested in global and regional trends, even if there are some evident limitations for copying any foreign experience. Examples of recent reforms in EU countries are provided to illustrate main trends in the region, without, however, pretending to provide the comprehensive list of the reforms.

In this paper, the comparative overview of regulation on collective dismissals are focused on the following aspects: definition of collective redundancies, procedures of consultation with workers' representatives and of notification to public authorities, authorization of redundancies by third parties, selection criteria for workers to be dismissed, employer's obligation to consider other options before terminating workers' employment, and priority right for re-employment. The comparison of EU countries with other regions will allow some conclusions on policy choices for national reforms of EPL and further comparative research.

§29.01 INTERNATIONAL STANDARDS AND INDICATORS FOR NATIONAL LABOUR LAWS

In the comparative literature, collective dismissals for economic reasons may also be called by different terms: mass redundancies, retrenchment, downsizing, or layoffs. In this paper, despite slightly different meanings in various legislations, these expressions are used interchangeably. The only exception is 'lay-offs', whose use is avoided, as in some countries this term means the termination of employment, while most frequently its significance is a temporary suspension of contracts of employment.

[A] International Labour Standards

The International Labour Conference adopted in 1950 a resolution in which the tripartite delegates noted the absence of international labour standards on termination of employment issues.

In 1963, the ILO was the pioneer of international regulation in this field with its Termination of Employment Recommendation No. 119. Two decades later, in 1982, Convention No. 158 and Recommendation No. 166 on Termination of Employment were adopted to become the main ILO standards on the topic of dismissals at the initiative of the employer.

In 2015, thirty-five ratifications of Convention No. 158 were registered (*see* Table 28.1). Sweden was the first country to ratify this instrument in 1983. In total, ten EU countries ratified Convention No. 158: Cyprus, Finland, France, Latvia, Luxembourg, Portugal, Slovakia, Slovenia, Spain, and Sweden. In comparison to other regions, the group gathering together EU and non-EU countries, counts the most important number of ratifications.

Table 28.1 Ratification of the ILO Convention on Termination of Employment (No. 158) of 1982

Countries Which Have Ratified ILO Convention No. 158 (Year of Ratification)	
Africa	Cameroon (1988), Central African Republic (2006), Democratic Republic of Congo (1987), Ethiopia (1991), Gabon (1988), Lesotho (2001), Malawi (1986), Morocco (1993), Namibia (1996), Niger (1985), Uganda (1990), Zambia (1990)
Americas and the Caribbean	Antigua-and-Barbuda (2002), Saint-Lucia (2000), Venezuela (1985)
Asia and the Pacific	Australia (1993), Papua-New-Guinea (2000)
European Union	Cyprus (1985), Finland (1992), France (1989), Latvia (1994), Luxembourg (2001), Portugal (1995), Slovakia (2010), Slovenia (1992), Spain (1985), Sweden (1983)
Europe (non-EU) and Caucasus	Bosnia-Herzegovina (1993), Macedonia (former Yugoslav Republic (FYR) of) (1991), Moldova (1997), Montenegro (2006), Serbia (2000), Turkey (1995), Ukraine (1994)
Middle-East	Yemen (1989)

Note: Brazil ratified Convention No. 158 in January 1995 and denounced it in November 1996.
Source: NORMLEX, ILO, 2015.

The legitimacy of Convention No. 158 and Recommendation No. 166 is rooted in the international tripartite consensus at their adoption in 1982. Nevertheless, the controversy on EPL worldwide is reflected in the continued debate in the ILO Governing Body over the status of Convention No. 158 and Recommendation No. 166. The group of workers' representatives insists on promoting these instruments, while the group of employers proposes to revise them. Critics of Convention No. 158 often mention the low level of ratification. However, the level of ratification is comparable to that of other ILO standards, especially at that period of transition in the 1990s when most socialist countries turned to the market economy. Moreover, the influence of Convention No. 158 and Recommendation No. 166 is also confirmed by the fact that most national labour laws around the world have been inspired, to a different extent, by several provisions of these ILO standards. Convention No. 158 has also proven its usefulness for lawyers and judges in domestic courts litigation, even in countries which have not ratified it (ILO, 2011).

More recently, as a reply to the global financial and economic crisis, the delegates to the International Labour Conference in 2009 unanimously adopted the Global Jobs Pact, by which the ILO standards on termination of employment were recognized relevant and of particular importance in times of crisis.

The ILO Committee of Experts on the Application of Conventions and Recommendations (CEACR), in its general observation on Convention No. 158 in 2009, affirmed that the principles underlying the Convention constituted a carefully constructed balance between the interests of the employer and the workers, in particular as evidenced by its provisions concerning dismissals for economic (technological, structural, operational) reasons of enterprises.

[B] Directives of the European Union

For members of the European Union, the binding references are contained in EU directives. For the purpose of our study, the most relevant is the European Council Directive 98/59/EC of 20 July 1998 on the approximation of the laws of the Member States relating to collective redundancies. The Directive, which contains several requirements similar to the provisions of Convention No. 158 and Recommendation No. 166, has been transposed into national legislation of twenty-eight countries.

[C] OECD Indicator of Employment Protection Strictness

The methodology which has been developed by the OECD to measure the strictness of EPL is one of the most referred to in comparative research. The sources of regulation used are labour laws, although practice of enforcement and collective bargaining are taken into account where possible (Venn, 2009). The summary indicator of employment protection for each country is calculated through twenty-one items. The collected information is classified into three main areas: individual dismissals of workers with regular contracts, regulation of temporary employment, and specific requirements for collective dismissals (OECD, 2013).[1]

The main concern raised by labour lawyers concerning the OECD methodology is that it suggests that any additional procedures for termination of employment contribute to a higher score of EPL strictness (*see* Table 28.2). For such purely economic approach which does not take into account other social and legal aspects, the OECD methodology of indicators to measure the strictness of employment protection has been contested by several researchers (Bertola et al., 2000). Nevertheless, national policy makers, including in Europe, frequently refer to these scores to justify national reforms aimed at reducing the rigidity of labour law.

With specific focus on collective redundancies, the OECD methodology on EPL contradicts the OECD Guidelines for Multinational Enterprises, which were revised in 2011. Among recommendations for responsible business conduct in a global context, the OECD encourages employers to engage in meaningful cooperation with workers' representatives and governmental authorities in considering changes in their operations which would have major employment effects upon the workforce, in particular in case of collective dismissals, so as to mitigate to the maximum extent practicable adverse effects. This document recognizes that this important principle of cooperation is widely reflected in the law and practices of adhering countries, although the approaches of ensuring such opportunity for meaningful co-operation are not identical in all OECD countries.

1. The detailed methodology of the OECD Employment Protection Indicators may be found at: http://www.oecd.org/els/emp/All.pdf.

Table 28.2 OECD's Indicator on Individual and Collective Dismissals

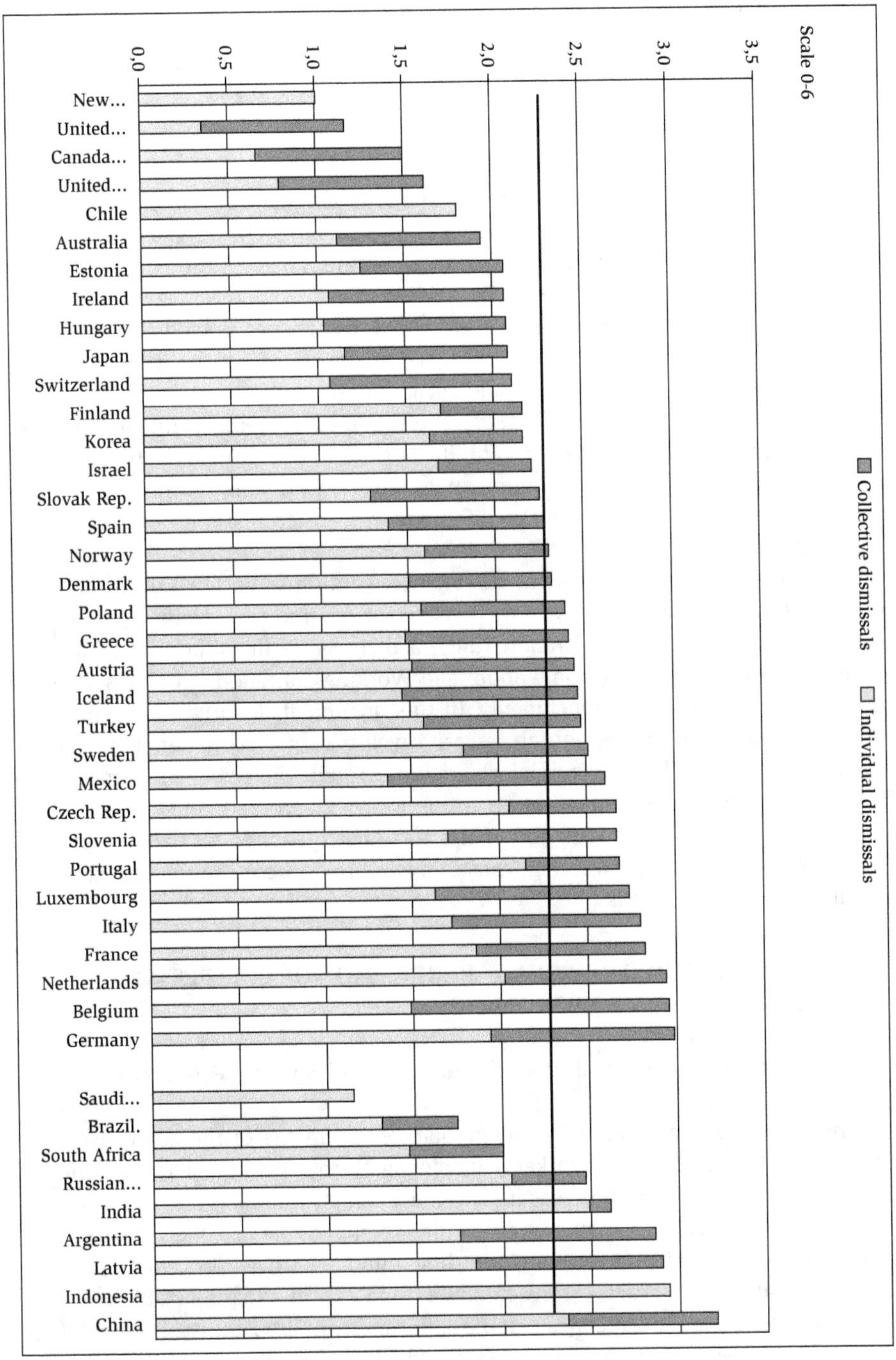

Source: OECD, 2013.

[D] 'Employing Workers' Indicators in the World Bank's 'Doing Business'

The annual report *Doing Business* published by the World Bank since 2003 is another benchmark for international comparison. The employment protection index measures the rigidity of hiring and firing rules. The difficulty of redundancy index is relevant to the topic of the paper.

Further to critics expressed by the ILO and international trade unions, as well as the controversy provoked in academic circles (Lee et al., 2008), the Employing Workers Indicator (EWI) was removed from the ranking to the annex of the *Doing Business* report in 2010. The World Bank publicly declared that it would no longer refer to the EWI as a basis for policy advice. However, in many countries, including in Europe, governments continue to plead for reforming national labour legislations, in particular to improve the business environment and attract investors.

Since the 2011 report *Doing Business*, the World Bank reaffirms that its methodology is 'fully consistent' with relevant ILO Conventions. However, the detailed analysis shows that several indicators on redundancy are promoting approaches opposite to the spirit and letter of the ILO standards on termination of employment (Muller, 2012).

In this regard, it is to note some dissonance within the World Bank Group. The rationale behind the methodology of the EWI seems contradictory to the approach of the International Finance Corporation (IFC), a member of the World Bank Group, whose Performance Standard 2 on 'Labour and Working Conditions' contains a 'Good Practice Note: Managing Retrenchment'. In this document, for investment projects involving a significant number of job losses, a well-managed redundancy process is defined as achieving the commercial objectives through the respect of procedures aimed at mitigating the negative impact of job losses on workers and communities. Interestingly, the vocabulary and procedures have been inspired by Convention No. 158 and Recommendation No. 166 whose texts were entirely reproduced in these guidelines of the World Bank.

§29.02 COMPARATIVE REVIEW OF REGULATION OF COLLECTIVE DISMISSALS FOR ECONOMIC REASONS

[A] Definition of Collective Redundancies and Specific Procedures

Convention No. 158 recognizes the operational requirements of the enterprise as a valid reason for terminating worker's employment relationship. The operational requirements are understood as reasons of an economic, technological, structural or similar nature. Dismissals for such reasons may be individual or collective. Usually, collective dismissals, which meet some threshold numbers, trigger procedural requirements to consult with workers' representatives and to notify the public authorities.

Convention No. 158 stipulates that the applicability of procedures of consultation and notification may be limited to cases in which the number of workers whose termination of employment is contemplated is at least a specified number or percentage of the workforce. Convention No. 158 does not contain, however, any quantitative criterion or thresholds to determine collective dismissals.

The European Union Directive 98/59/CE of 1998 on the approximation of the laws of the Member States relating to collective redundancies contains more detailed provisions of the quantitative definition of collective dismissals for economic reasons. For the purposes of this Directive, 'collective redundancies' means dismissals effected by an employer for one or more reasons not related to the individual workers concerned where, according to the choice of the Member States, the number of redundancies is:

(i) either, over a period of thirty days:
  - at least ten in establishments normally employing more than twenty and less than 100 workers;
  - at least 10% of the number of workers in establishments normally employing at least 100 but less than 300 workers;
  - at least thirty in establishments normally employing 300 workers or more,

(ii) or, over a period of ninety days:
  - at least twenty, whatever the number of workers normally employed in the establishments in question.

In case of collective dismissals for economic reasons, both Convention No. 158 and EU Directive similarly foresee two main procedures.

First, an employer contemplating terminations of employment for reasons of an economic, technological, structural or similar nature, should provide the workers' representatives concerned in good time with relevant information, including reasons for the terminations contemplated, the number and categories of workers likely to be affected and the period over which the terminations are intended to be carried out. In respect of Convention No. 158, consultations are to be held with the workers' representatives concerned, as early as possible, on measures to be taken to avert or to minimize the terminations and measures to mitigate the adverse effects of any terminations on the workers concerned, such as finding alternative employment.

Second, Convention No. 158 requires an employer contemplating terminations of employment for reasons of an economic, technological, structural or similar nature, to notify the competent public authority as early as possible, with relevant information, including a written statement of the reasons for the terminations contemplated, the number and categories of workers likely to be affected and the period over which the terminations are intended to be carried out. Recommendation No. 166 details the role that the public authority may play to mitigate the impact of collective dismissals for economic reasons. For instance, it refers to the promotion of the placement of the workers affected in suitable alternative employment, or income protection during training and retraining.

The analysis of labour laws of 126 countries (Table 28.3) shows that the majority (53%) have a statutory definition of collective dismissals with prescribed specific procedures. In a third of the reviewed countries (30%), the law specifies the specific procedures in case of collective redundancies, without giving any quantitative definition of mass dismissals. Less than one-fifth of the countries reviewed (17%) do not have any provisions related to collective dismissals for economic reasons.

Table 28.3 Statutory Definition of Collective Dismissals for Economic Reasons with Specific Procedures (126 Countries)

The Law Defines Collective Dismissals for Economic Reasonsand Prescribes Specific Procedures	
Africa	Angola, Burkina Faso, Democratic Republic of Congo, Côte d'Ivoire, Ethiopia, Gabon, Morocco, Mozambique, Niger, Senegal, South Africa, Uganda, Zimbabwe
Americas and the Caribbean	Argentina, Canada, Colombia, Peru, United States, Venezuela
Asia and the Pacific	Australia, China, Japan, Republic of Korea, Kyrgyzstan, Pakistan
European Union	Austria, Belgium, Bulgaria, Cyprus, Czech Republic, Denmark, Estonia, Finland, France, Germany, Greece, Hungary, Ireland, Italy, Latvia, Lithuania, Luxembourg, Netherlands, Poland, Portugal, Romania, Slovakia, Slovenia, Spain, Sweden, United Kingdom
Europe (non-EU) and Caucasus	Albania, Armenia, Belarus, Bosnia and Herzegovina, Croatia, Georgia, Iceland, Macedonia (FYR), Montenegro, Norway, Russian Federation, Serbia, Switzerland, Turkey
Middle-East	-
The Law Does Not Define Collective Dismissals for Economic Reasons, but Prescribes Specific Procedures	
Africa	Algeria, Cameroon, Central African Republic, Comoros, Egypt, Ghana, Madagascar, Mauritius, Namibia, Nigeria, Rwanda, Seychelles, Tanzania, Tunisia, Zambia
Americas and the Caribbean	Honduras, Mexico, Panama, Paraguay
Asia and the Pacific	Afghanistan, Bangladesh, Cambodia, India, Iran, Kazakhstan, Mongolia, New Zealand, Philippines, Sri Lanka, Thailand, Turkmenistan, Viet Nam
European Union	-
Europe (non-EU) and Caucasus	Azerbaijan, Moldova, Ukraine
Middle-East	Jordan, Syrian Arab Republic, Yemen

The Law Does Not Define Collective Dismissals for Economic Reasons and Does Not Prescribe Specific Procedures	
Africa	Lesotho, Libya, Malawi
Americas and the Caribbean	Antigua and Barbuda, Brazil, Chile, Costa Rica, Cuba, El Salvador, Guatemala, Jamaica, Nicaragua, Saint Lucia, Uruguay
Asia and the Pacific	Indonesia, Israel, Malaysia, Maldives, Singapore
European Union	-
Europe (non-EU) and Caucasus	-
Middle-East	Kuwait, Saudi Arabia, United Arab Emirates

Source: NORMLEX, ILO, 2015; Doing Business, World Bank, 2015.

The global comparative analysis of countries under review shows that at the European continent, the labour law of most countries contains the requirements of both consultation and notification. This comparison puts in evidence that the group of EU countries is the most homogeneous: all countries have defined in their labour laws the collective dismissals and prescribed specific procedures of consultation with workers representatives and notification to public authorities.

Among recent reforms on this topic, in 2010 Greece increased the thresholds of collective dismissals. The reform of the labour law in Spain in 2010 provided a detailed definition of 'negative economic situation'.

Another trend has been observed in Europe concerning the reduction of the time for consultations. The question is whether such shortened periods of consultations with workers' representatives would allow elaborating genuine alternatives. In Spain, the reform of 2010 limited the time of consultation to thirty days (and fifteen days in enterprises with less than fifty employees), while before the time framework was of thirty days minimum. At the same time in the United Kingdom, the statutory period was reduced from ninety to thirty days for consultation on redundancies affecting 100 and more employees.

[B] Authorization of Collective Redundancies by Third Parties

The ILO, the OECD and the World Bank have similar positions on the interference of third parties to approve the termination of employment decided by the employer. However, the ILO, in respect of national legal traditions, promotes the position that it is through tripartite social dialogue that countries should decide on the regime applicable to terminations of employment.

Convention No. 158 does not limit the managerial power of the employer to dismiss workers, nor requires any authorization to obtain from public authorities or workers' representatives. In this paper, we do not examine specific cases of the termination of employment of some protected categories of workers (trade union officials, pregnant women), which usually require to be authorized by the competent public authorities (e.g. labour inspection).

The global overview shows that the employer has to obtain an authorization from the public authorities to proceed with collective redundancies in a limited number of countries. These thirty-five countries out of 187 represent the group of 19% (Table 28.4).

Table 28.4 Authorization of Collective Dismissals for Economic Reasons by Third Parties (187 Countries and Territories)

Collective Dismissals for Economic Reasons Must be Authorized by Third Parties (35 Countries – 19%)	
Africa	Angola, Cabo Verde, Central African Republic, Chad, Congo, Democratic Republic of Congo, Egypt, Eritrea, Equatorial Guinea, Gabon, Guinea-Bissau, Morocco, Mauritania, Sao Tomé-et-Principe, Seychelles, Sudan, South Sudan, Zimbabwe
Americas and the Caribbean	Honduras, Mexico, Panama, Paraguay
Asia and the Pacific	Afghanistan, India, Iran, Kiribati, Lao, Nepal, Sri Lanka, Viet Nam
European Union	Greece, Netherlands
Europe (non-EU) and Caucasus	San-Marino
Middle-East	Jordan, Syria

Source: EPLex, NORMLEX, ILO, 2015; Doing Business, World Bank, 2015.

The legislation of most EU countries does not require anymore any authorization for collective dismissals for economic reasons. In Estonia, the new labour law of 2009 suppressed the authorization by the labour inspection of collective dismissals. In 2012, Spain abolished the authorization of collective redundancies by the public authorities.

In the Netherlands, further to recent intense social dialogue on labour law amendments, the government and social partners confirmed in 2014 that economic redundancies would remain subject to the approval by the public employment service. In case of refusal, the employer can go through the labour court to terminate employment relationship with his or her workers.

In Greece, the on-going discussion with the European Commission and International Monetary Fund (IMF) still focuses on the proposal of the government and social partners to give a tripartite commission the right to examine, and thus authorize or prohibit, cases of collective redundancies.

Some interesting examples are provided by collective agreements. For instance, in 2010 in Germany, the company Siemens by its collective agreement on restructuring committed to avoid dismissals by the use of such measures as internal mobility and work sharing. The management of the enterprise agreed to go beyond legal requirements and obtain an approval by the trade union of any dismissals for economic reasons.

[C] Employer's Obligation to Consider Other Options Before Dismissals

Recommendation No. 166 provides guidance on examples of measures which could be adopted to avert or minimize dismissals for economic, technological or structural reasons, such as, among others, restriction of hiring, spreading the workforce reduction over a certain period of time to permit natural reduction of the workforce, internal transfers, training and retraining, voluntary early retirement with appropriate income protection, restriction of overtime and reduction of normal hours of work.

The review of 194 countries and territories (Table 28.5) shows that in less than half of the countries (41%), the employer has a legal obligation to consider other options before proceeding with dismissals.

All EU countries, with the exception of Malta, have legal provisions on the employer's obligation to consider other options before dismissals. In some countries (e.g., Sweden), this issue is mainly dealt with through collective bargaining.

Table 28.5 Statutory Obligation for Employers to Use Dismissals as the Last Resort (194 Countries and Territories)

	The Employer is Legally Obliged to Consider Other Options Before Dismissals
Africa	Algeria, Angola, Burkina Faso, Cabo Verde, Cameroun, Ethiopia, Gabon, Ghana, Morocco, Mozambique, Namibia, Niger, Sao Tomé-and-Principe, Senegal, Sierra Leone, South Africa, Tanzania, Tunisia, Zambia, Zimbabwe
Americas and the Caribbean	Antigua-and-Barbuda, Canada, Peru, Venezuela
Asia and the Pacific	Afghanistan, Australia, Cambodia, China, Republic of Korea, Indonesia, Japan, Kazakhstan, Kirghizstan, New Zealand, Pakistan, Taiwan (China), Tajikistan, Turkmenistan, Uzbekistan, Viet Nam
European Union	Austria, Belgium, Bulgaria, Cyprus, Croatia, Czech Republic, Denmark, Estonia, Finland, France, Germany, Greece, Hungary, Ireland, Italy, Latvia, Lithuania, Luxembourg, Netherlands, Poland, Portugal, Romania, Slovakia, Slovenia, Spain, Sweden, United Kingdom
Europe (non-EU) and Caucasus	Armenia, Belarus, Bosnia-Herzegovina, Iceland, Kosovo, FYR of Macedonia, Moldova, Montenegro, Norway, Russian Federation, Serbia, Turkey, Ukraine
Middle-East	-

The Employer Is Not Legally Obliged to Consider Other Options Before Dismissals	
Africa	Benin, Botswana, Burundi, Central African Republic, Chad, Comoros, Congo, Democratic Republic of Congo, Côte d'Ivoire, Djibouti, Egypt, Eritrea, Gambia, Guinea, Guinea-Bissau, Equatorial Guinea, Kenya, Lesotho, Liberia, Libya, Madagascar, Malawi, Mali, Mauritania, Maurice, Nigeria, Rwanda, Sao Tomé-and-Principe, Seychelles, Somalia, Sudan, South Sudan, Swaziland, Togo, Uganda
Americas and the Caribbean	Argentina, Bahamas, Barbados, Belize, Bolivia, Brazil, Chile, Colombia, Costa Rica, Cuba, Dominican Republic, Dominique, El Salvador, Equateur, Grenada, Guatemala, Guyana, Haiti, Honduras, Jamaica, Mexico, Nicaragua, Panama, Paraguay, Peru, Puerto Rico (United States), Saint-Lucia, Saint-Kitts-and-Nevis, Saint-Vincent-and-the-Grenadines, Suriname, Trinidad-and-Tobago, United States, Uruguay
Asia and the Pacific	Bangladesh, Bhutan, Brunei Darussalam, Fiji, Hong Kong (China), India, Iran, Israel, Kiribati, Lao, Malaysia, Maldives, Marshall Islands, Micronesia, Mongolia, Myanmar, Nepal, Palau, Papua-New-Guinea, Philippines, Salomon Islands, Samoa, Singapore, Sri Lanka, Thailand, Timor-Leste, Tonga, Vanuatu
European Union	Malta
Europe (non-EU) and Caucasus	Albania, Azerbaijan, Georgia, San Marino, Switzerland
Middle-East	Bahrain, United Arab Emirates, Iraq, Jordan, Kuwait, Lebanon, occupied Palestinian territories, Oman, Qatar, Saudi Arabia, Syria, Yemen

Source: EPLex, NORMLEX, ILO, 2015; Doing Business, World Bank, 2015.

In 2010, France amended its labour code to precise that the offer of alternative employment abroad should be at the equivalent level of wages. This law was adopted in reaction to some collective dismissals when workers were offered employment in other countries with salaries several times inferior to the level of wages in France.

Voluntary departures, as one of possible alternatives, should be dealt with care. On the one side, some enterprises may face risks of disorganization and loss of competencies as a consequence of restructuring. On the other side, the legal regulation of voluntary departures should be taken into account. For instance, the reform of 2010 in France allowed the termination of an employment relationship by common agreement between the employer and the worker. However, the French Cour de Cassation decided in 2011 that such voluntary redundancies for economic reasons should be counted in the number of dismissals whose number would require the establishment of a social plan.

[D] Selection Criteria for Workers to be Redundant

Pursuant to Recommendation No. 166, in case of redundancy due to economic or similar reasons, the employer should select the workers to be dismissed according to criteria, established wherever possible in advance, which give due weight both to the interests of the enterprise and to the interests of the workers.

The global review shows that the law specifies criteria for selection of workers in case of redundancy in around 44% out of 193 countries. In some countries, such criteria are defined by collective agreements or codes of good practices. The analysis by regions (Table 28.6) puts in evidence that the majority of developed countries, as well as in Africa and Central and Eastern Europe, the law provides indications on the criteria to take into account. Such legal criteria are less frequently found in Asia and the Pacific, Latin America and the Caribbean, and the Middle East.

As regards the EU group, seventeen out of twenty-eight countries have the statutory provisions on the selection criteria for workers to be redundant.

Table 28.6 Legal Provisions on Selection Criteria for Workers to be Redundant (193 Countries and Territories)

	The Law Provides Criteria for Selection of Workers in Case of Redundancy
Africa	Algeria, Angola, Benin, Botswana, Burkina Faso, Burundi, Cameroun, Cabo Verde, Central African Republic, Chad, Comoros, Congo, Democratic Republic of Congo, Egypt, Ethiopia, Gabon, Gambia, Guinea-Bissau, Equatorial Guinea, Kenya, Liberia, Madagascar, Mali, Morocco, Mauritania, Mauritius, Niger, Nigeria, Rwanda, Senegal, Sierra Leone, Swaziland, Togo, Tunisia
Americas and the Caribbean	Antigua-and-Barbuda, Argentina, Cuba, Dominique, Honduras, Mexico, Panama, Puerto Rico (United States), Trinidad-and-Tobago
Asia and the Pacific	Bangladesh, Cambodia, China, India, Kirghizstan, Malaysia, Nepal, Pakistan, Philippines, Sri Lanka, Tajikistan, Uzbekistan, Viet Nam
European Union	Austria, Croatia, Estonia, France, Germany, Greece, Italy, Latvia, Lithuania, Malta, Netherlands, Poland, Portugal, Romania, Slovenia, Spain, Sweden
Europe (non-EU) and Caucasus	Azerbaijan, Belarus, Kosovo, Moldova, Montenegro, Norway, Russian Federation, San Marino, Ukraine
Middle-East	Lebanon, Syria

The Law Does Not Mention Any Criteria for Selection of Workers in Case of Redundancy	
Africa	Côte d'Ivoire, Djibouti, Eritrea, Ghana, Guinea, Lesotho, Libya, Malawi, Mozambique, Namibia, Seychelles, Somalia, South Africa, Sudan, South Sudan, Tanzania, Uganda, Zambia, Zimbabwe
Americas and the Caribbean	Bahamas, Barbados, Belize, Bolivia, Brazil, Canada, Chile, Colombia, Costa Rica, Dominican Republic, El Salvador, Equateur, Grenade, Guatemala, Guyana, Haiti, Jamaica, Nicaragua, Paraguay, Peru, Saint-Lucia, Saint-Kitts-and-Nevis, Saint-Vincent-and-the-Grenadines, Sao Tomé-and-Principe, Suriname, United States, Uruguay, Venezuela
Asia and the Pacific	Afghanistan, Australia, Bhutan, Brunei Darussalam, Fiji, Hong Kong (Chine), Indonesia, Iran, Israel, Japan, Kazakhstan, Kiribati, Republic of Korea, Lao, Maldives, Marshall Islands, Micronesia, Mongolia, Myanmar, New Zealand, Palau, Papua-New-Guinea, Salomon Islands, Samoa, Singapore, Taiwan (China), Thailand, Timor-Leste, Turkmenistan, Tonga, Vanuatu, Viet Nam
European Union	Belgium, Bulgaria, Cyprus, Czech Republic, Denmark, Finland, Hungary, Ireland, Luxembourg, Slovakia, United Kingdom
Europe (non-EU) and Caucasus	Albania, Armenia, Bosnia-Herzegovina, Georgia, Iceland, FYR of Macedonia, Serbia, Switzerland, Turkey
Middle-East	Bahrain, Iraq, Jordan, Kuwait, occupied Palestinian territories, Oman, Qatar, Saudi Arabia, United Arab Emirates, Yemen

Source: EPLex, NORMLEX, ILO, 2015; Doing Business, World Bank, 2015.

Concerning the selection of employees for redundancy, the legal practice in many countries pleads for clear, although flexible, regulation of this issue. After consultation with workers' representatives, the employer should ensure that objective selection criteria be applied fairly and consistently. Criteria should be measurable, such as qualification, performance and disciplinary records. During the assessment exercise, each manager should also be cautious in using the absence records, as the inclusion of disability or maternity related absences could result in a disability or sex discrimination claim respectively.

In Estonia, the new labour law in 2009 replaced the detailed list of criteria of selection by the general principle of non-discrimination. In Romania, the reform in 2011 added a new provision that any criteria of selection should be applied after assessment of worker's performance.

Interestingly, in several countries, including EU members (Netherlands, Sweden), the criterion 'Last In, First Out' is still used as a method of selection for redundancy. It means that the employer must retrench the worker who is the last person employed in that category. The rationale is to reward loyalty and maintain stable and most experienced workforce. However, entitlements varying with length of service may be challenged as indirect age discrimination, unless the scheme is justified. Progressively, such a criterion is abandoned, as it puts younger workers at a particular disadvantage.

In Sweden, the only possible exemption from the seniority principle applies to companies with fewer than ten employees, where the employer has his or her discretion to decide upon two employees to be exempted from this principle.

In the jurisprudence of the United Kingdom, the use of length of service is admitted as one of the criteria in a redundancy selection matrix. The case law has given more details on the conditions of validity of 'Last In – First Out', which has to be embodied in a collective agreement and under the express condition that it is not the unique criterion employed in the selection process. Otherwise, this criterion may be considered in case law as indirect discrimination on the grounds of age. Even if loyalty should be rewarded, young workers are particularly prejudiced by this rule. Moreover, the criterion of absences, particularly those relating to illness or childbirth, should be used with circumspection, in that it may constitute discrimination based on the grounds of sex, health or maternity.

[E] Priority Right for Re-employment

Recommendation No. 166 stipulates that workers dismissed for economic reasons should be given a certain priority of re-employment, if the employer re-hires workers with comparable qualifications. This may be subject to some conditions, such as an explicit worker's desire to be rehired which should be expressed within a given period of time.

The review of the laws of 192 countries (Table 28.7) demonstrates that 38% of countries have legally defined priority rules for re-employment. Thirteen EU countries have foreseen in their labour laws the possibility for workers to be given a priority in case the employer re-hires workers.

Table 28.7 Priority Rules for Re-employment (192 Countries)

	The Law Provides Priority Rules for Re-employment
Africa	Angola, Benin, Botswana, Burkina Faso, Burundi, Cameroun, Central African Republic, Chad, Comoros, Congo, Democratic Republic of Congo, Côte d'Ivoire, Djibouti, Gabon, Gambia, Guinea-Bissau, Equatorial Guinea, Lesotho, Liberia, Madagascar, Mali, Morocco, Mauritania, Niger, Sao Tomé-and-Principe, Senegal, Sierra Leone, Tanzania, Togo, Tunisia
Americas and the Caribbean	Barbados, Dominique, Mexico, Paraguay, Peru, Puerto Rico (United States), Saint-Kitts-et-Nevis, Saint-Vincent-and-the-Grenadines
Asia and the Pacific	Afghanistan, Bangladesh, Cambodia, China, Republic of Korea, India, Nepal, Pakistan, Papua-New-Guinea, Sri Lanka, Taiwan (China)
European Union	Austria, Croatia, Cyprus, Finland, France, Italy, Luxembourg, Malta, Netherlands, Poland, Portugal, Romania, Sweden

Europe (non-EU) and Caucasus	Albania, Bosnia-Herzegovina, Kosovo, Norway, San Marino, Serbia, Turkey, Ukraine
Middle-East	Jordan, Lebanon, Yemen
The Law Does Not Provide Priority Rules for Re-employment	
Africa	Algeria, Cabo Verde, Egypt, Eritrea, Ethiopia, Ghana, Guinea, Kenya, Libya, Malawi, Maurice, Mozambique, Namibia, Nigeria, Rwanda, Seychelles, Somalia, South Africa, Sudan, South Sudan, Swaziland, Uganda, Zambia, Zimbabwe
Americas and the Caribbean	Antigua-and-Barbuda, Argentina, Bahamas, Belize, Bolivia, Brazil, Canada, Chile, Colombia, Costa Rica, Cuba, Dominican Republic, Ecuador, El Salvador, Grenada, Guatemala, Guyana, Haiti, Honduras, Jamaica, Nicaragua, Panama, Saint-Lucia, Surinam, Trinity-and-Tobago, United States, Uruguay, Venezuela
Asia and the Pacific	Australia, Bhutan, Brunei Darussalam, Fiji, Hong Kong (Chine), Indonesia, Israel, Iran, Japan, Kazakhstan, Kiribati, Kirghizstan, Lao, Malaysia, Maldives, Marshall Islands, Micronesia, Mongolia, Myanmar, New Zealand, Palau, Philippines, Solomon Islands, Samoa, Singapore, Thailand, Tajikistan, Timor-Leste, Tonga, Turkmenistan, Uzbekistan, Vanuatu, Viet Nam
European Union	Belgium, Bulgaria, Denmark, Czech Republic, Estonia, Germany, Greece, Hungary, Ireland, Latvia, Lithuania, Slovakia, Slovenia, Spain, United Kingdom
Europe (non-EU) and Caucasus	Armenia, Azerbaijan, Belarus, Georgia, Iceland, FYR of Macedonia, Moldova, Montenegro, Russian Federation, Switzerland
Middle-East	Bahrain, Iraq, Kuwait, occupied Palestinian territories, Oman, Qatar, Saudi Arabia, Syria, United Arab Emirates

Source: EPLex, NORMLEX, ILO, 2015; Doing Business, World Bank, 2015.

Table 28.8 shows the difference of duration of the period of priority for re-employment.

Table 28.8 The Time During Which the Priority Rules for Re-employment Apply

Time Period for the Priority Rules for Re-employment	*Countries*
1.5 month	Romania
6 months	China, Netherlands, Serbia, Turkey
8 months	Cyprus
9 months	Finland, Sweden
1 year	Bangladesh, Democratic Republic of Congo, France, Gabon, Italy, Jordan, Luxembourg, Morocco, Pakistan, Peru, Tunisia, Ukraine
2 years	Burkina Faso, Cambodia, Cameroon, Comoros, Niger, Senegal

Time Period for the Priority Rules for Re-employment	*Countries*
3 years	Republic of Korea
No time limits	Afghanistan, Sri Lanka, Mexico, Yemen
Explicit reference in law to collective agreements	Côte d'Ivoire, Madagascar
Mentions in the Code of good practices	Lesotho, Malaysia, Tanzania

Source: EPLex, NORMLEX, ILO, 2015.

In 2009, Estonia suppressed the priority of re-hiring of six months. In 2011, Romania reduced it from nine months to forty-five calendar days, which amounted in practice to delete this provision, as it would be naive to expect that the economic situation of an enterprise might be improved in one month and a half. In 2013, Slovenia abolished the priority of re-employment of one year.

§29.03 CONCLUSIONS

The global review of laws regulating collective dismissals for economic reasons shows that provisions on collective redundancies exist in around two thirds of the countries. In opposition to developing countries whose regulation is incomplete on many aspects, the majority of labour market economies, including EU countries, have the detailed regulation of collective redundancies.

Without doubt, the EU region appears as most homogenous group with the comprehensive legal regime on this topic. Although there is a great diversity of details, the main principles are common. Most provisions are in line with ILO standards. The influence of EU directives appears decisive in the process of harmonization of national labour laws of the EU Member States.

The comparative overview of recent reforms allows to perceive some worrying movement towards the deregulation of labour legislations in the EU countries. Some observers are of the opinion that recent labour law reforms in Europe show a loosening of EPL in respect of the protection of workers in case of collective dismissals (Schömann, 2014). Even if it is necessary to simplify some procedural requirements, it is vitally important not to destroy the set of legal rules on these issues developed by EU countries.

The deregulation agenda has been encouraged, namely for the issue of collective dismissals, by the main international benchmarks for EPL: the OECD's index of strictness of EPL and the indicator 'Employing workers' of the World Bank's 'Doing Business'. Despite some recent methodological changes, most requirements for collective dismissals are still considered by both organizations as additional costs and procedural inconvenience which increase the rigidity of EPL. On that basis, countries willing to make their EPL less rigid should suppress most procedures for collective dismissals. Obviously, such approach does not take into account positive consequences of having transparent and fair process concerning redundancies. This appears in contradiction with ILO's standards, as well as policy documents of these institutions, such as the OECD Guidelines for Multinational Enterprises and the IFC (World Bank) Guidelines on managing retrenchment. Such lack of coherence in policy advice from international institutions is confusing for countries and damageable for the institutions of the multilateral system.

Social dialogue appears as the core procedural response in the search for measures to avoid or minimize the social and economic impact of collective dismissals. Enterprises, which protect their workers at times of crisis and restructuring, would be better prepared to meet market opportunities at the recovery. A strong correlation exists between redundancies and disengagement of the workforce. Fair procedures, in which workers are given a voice, are paramount to avoid de-motivation and reduced morale among the staff. Policy makers cannot leave this matter for deregulation, as negative consequences affect the whole societies causing economic problems and psychological inter-generational trauma (Uchitelle, 2006).

Labour law has proven its primary role in encouraging the socially responsible human resources management for redundancies which includes adequate consultation, objective selection criteria and consideration of alternatives to dismissals. Supiot (2010) points out that a freedom to choose the most convenient (cheapest) legal system ('law shopping') is incompatible with the rule of law and potentially dangerous in the globalized market where national labour laws are subject to the global competition.

Controversial arguments are advanced in discussions on the optimum extent of EPL in its potential impact on labour markets. However, in various circles, there is a growing understanding that economic growth could not be sustainable if not accompanied by social progress, and that flexibility for employers should go hand in hand with job security for workers.

References

Bertola, Giuseppe; Boeri, Tito; Cazes, Sandrine. 2000: 'Employment Protection in Industrialised Countries: The Case for New Indicators', in *International Labour Review*, Vol. 139, No. 4.

ILO. 2011: 'Termination of Employment Instruments', Background Paper for the Tripartite Meeting of Experts on Convention 158 and Recommendation 166, Geneva.

Lee, Sangheon; McCann, Deirdre; Torm, Nina. 2008: 'The World Bank's 'Employing Workers' Index: Findings and Critics', in International Labour Review, Vol. 147, No. 4.

OECD. 2011: 'Guidelines for Multinational Enterprises', OECD Ministerial Meeting, Paris.

OECD. 2013. « Protéger l'emploi, renforcer la flexibilité: un nouveau regard sur la législation sur la protection de l'emploi », dans Perspectives de l'emploi de l'OCDE 2013, Editions OCDE.

Muller, Angelika. 2011: 'Employment Protection Legislation Tested by the Economic Crisis: A Global Review of the Regulation of Collective Dismissals for Economic Reasons', DIALOGUE in Brief No. 3, ILO, Geneva.

Muller, Angelika. 2012: 'Labour Law Reforms at the Crossroads of ILO Standards and OECD and World Bank's Indexes: A Global Review of Regulation on Collective Redundancies', Paper prepared for the World Congress of the ILERA, Philadelphia, USA.

Schömann, Isabelle. 2014: 'Labour Law Reforms in Europe: Adjusting Employment Protection for the Worse?', Working Paper 2014/02, European Trade Union Institute (Bruxelles, ETUI).

Supiot, Alain. 2010: 'L'esprit de Philadelphie. La justice sociale face au marché total'. Paris, Seuil.

Uchitelle, Louis. 2006: 'The Disposable American: Layoffs and Their Consequences', Knopf.

Venn, Danielle. 2009: 'Legislation, Collective Bargaining and Enforcement: Updating the OECD Employment Protection Indicators', OECD Social, Employment and Migration Working Paper 89, Paris.

World Bank. 2014: Doing Business 2015 (Washington, DC).

Index

www.ingramcontent.com/pod-product-compliance
Lightning Source LLC
LaVergne TN
LVHW020003031026
849161LV00023B/861
9789041158307